CAREER DEVELOPMENT AND COUNSELING OF WOMEN

CAREER DEVELOPMENT AND COUNSELING OF WOMEN

Edited by

L. SUNNY HANSEN, Ph.D.
Professor, Psychoeducational Studies
College of Education
University of Minnesota
Minneapolis, Minnesota

and

RITA S. RAPOZA, Ph.D.
Instructor and Research Associate
Wilson Learning Corporation
Eden Prairie, Minnesota

CHARLES C THOMAS · PUBLISHER
Springfield · Illinois · U.S.A.

Published and Distributed Throughout the World by

CHARLES C THOMAS • PUBLISHER

BANNERSTONE HOUSE

301-327 East Lawrence Avenue, Springfield, Illinois, U.S.A.

ISBN 0-398-03669-1

Library of Congress Catalog Card Number: 77-4755

With THOMAS BOOKS *careful attention is given to all details of manufacturing and design. It is the Publisher's desire to present books that are satisfactory as to their physical qualities and artistic possibilities and appropriate for their particular use.* THOMAS BOOKS *will be true to those laws of quality that assure a good name and good will.*

Printed in the United States of America

N-1

Library of Congress Cataloging in Publication Data

Main entry under title:

Career development and counseling of women.

Bibliography: p.

Includes index.

1. Vocational guidance for women—Addresses, essays, lectures. 2. Women—Employment—Addresses, essays, lectures. 3. Counseling—Addresses, essays, lectures, I. Hansen, Lorraine Sunny. II. Rapoza, Rita S.

HD6058.C225 331.7'02'024042 77-4755

ISBN 0-398-03669-1

To Tor – who is a liberated and liberating human being.

To Sonja and Torrey – whose career development I hope will be enhanced by the new career patterns and options available to them.

L.S.H.

To Don

R.R.B.

CONTRIBUTORS

Thelma G. Alper, Ph.D.
Psychologist
Judge Baker Guidance Center
Boston, Massachusetts

Helen S. Astin
Professor of Higher Education
University of California at Los Angeles
Los Angeles, California

Jeanne K. Barnett
Social Science Advisor
Office of the Assistant Secretary for Policy, Evaluation and Research
U.S. Department of Labor
Washington, D.C.

Stephen E. Bemis
Project Director
The Edgar D. Mitchell Corporation
Washington, D.C.

Donald H. Blocher, Ph.D.
Professor of Education
State University of
New York at Albany
Albany, New York

Nancy S. Cole
Associate Professor of Education
University of Pittsburgh
Pittsburgh, Pennsylvania

Patricia Auer Engelhard
Counselor
Edina Public Schools
Edina, Minnesota

Helen S. Farmer, Ph.D.
Assistant Professor
University of Illinois at Urbana
Urbana, Illinois

Jane Goodman
Counselor and Trainer
Continuum Center for Adult Counseling and Leadership Training
Oakland University
Oakland, California

L. Sunny Hansen, Ph.D.
Professor and Program Coordinator
Counseling and Student Personnel Psychology
University of Minnesota
Minneapolis, Minnesota

Gary R. Hanson
Assistant Director
Development Research
The American College Testing Program
Iowa City, Iowa

Lenore W. Harmon, Ph.D.
Professor of Educational Psychology
University of Wisconsin-Milwaukee
Milwaukee, Wisconsin

Peggy J. Hawley, Ph.D.
Professor of Education
Coordinator of Graduate Programs and Research
San Diego State University
San Diego, California

Janice Neipert Hedges
Senior Economist
Bureau of Labor Statistics
U.S. Department of Labor
Washington, D.C.

Lynda Lytle Holmstrom, Ph.D.
Associate Professor of Sociology
Boston College
Boston, Massachusetts

Harriet Holter, Ph.D.
Professor, Social Psychology
University of Oslo
Oslo, Norway

Kathryn Otto Jones
Language Arts Teacher
Edina Public Schools
Edina, Minnesota

Mary Bach Kievit, Ph.D.
Associate Dean
Graduate School of Education
Rutgers — The State University
New Brunswick, New Jersey

Lee Knefelkamp, Ph. D.
Assistant Professor
Counseling and Student
Personnel Services
University of Maryland

Harold J. Leavitt
Professor
Graduate School of Business
Stanford University
Stanford, California

Mary M. Leonard, Ph.D.
Counselor
University of Maryland Counseling Center
Assistant Professor
College of Education
University of Maryland

Jean Lipman-Blumen
Director
Research on Women
National Institute of Education
Washington, D.C.

Rosalind K. Loring
Dean
College of Continuing Education
University of Southern California
Los Angeles, California

Marjorie Fiske Lowenthal
Human Development Program
University of California
San Francisco, California

Anna Louise Miller
Counselor
DeKalb High School
DeKalb, Illinois

Megan K. Monroe
Antioch College
Yellow Springs, Ohio

Thelma Myint
Bureau of Social Science Research
Washington, D.C.

Bernice L. Neugarten, Ph.D.
Professor
Department of Behavioral Sciences
University of Chicago
Chicago, Illinois

John J. Pietrofesa
Professor and Coordinator, Counseling and Guidance
Wayne State University
Detroit, Michigan

Dale J. Prediger
Director, Developmental Research Department
The American College Testing Program
Iowa City, Iowa

Lenore Sawyer Radloff
Center for Epidemiologic Studies
National Institute of Mental Health
Bethesda, Maryland

Lorraine M. Rand
Ohio University
Athens, Ohio

Edna E. Raphael, Ph.D.
Associate Professor of Labor Studies and Sociology
Pennsylvania State University
University Park, Pennsylvania

Rhona Rapoport
Co-director, Institute of Family Environmental Research
London, England

Robert N. Rapoport
Co-director, Institute of Family Environmental Research
London, England

Rita S. Rapoza, Ph.D.
Instructor and Research Associate
Wilson Learning Corporation
Eden Prairie, Minnesota

Bernice Sandler
Director
Project on the Status and Education of Women
Association of American Colleges
Washington, D.C.

Nancy K. Schlossberg
Professor
College of Education
University of Maryland
College Park, Maryland

Eleanor Bernert Sheldon, Ph.D.
President
Social Science Research Council
New York, New York

Anne Steinmann, Ph.D.
President
Maferr Foundation, Inc.
An Affiliation of the Research Department, Postgraduate Center for Mental Health
New York, New York

Richard J. Stiggins, Ph.D.
Director of Test Development
The American College Testing Program
Iowa City, Iowa

Donald Super, Ph.D.
Professor Emeritus
Teachers College, Columbia University
New York, New York

Roxann A. Van Dusen
Consultant, Agency for International Development
U.S. Department of State
Washington, D.C.

Louise Vetter, Ph.D.
Research Specialist
The Center for Vocational Education
The Ohio State University
Columbus, Ohio

Lawrence Weiss
Human Development Program
University of California
San Francisco, California

Theodora Wells, M.B.A.
Consultant
Wells Associates
Beverly Hills, California

PREFACE

FOUR YEARS AGO, when the idea for this book of readings was first conceived, there was relatively little in the literature specifically on the topic of "Career Development of Women" and what counselors and other human service workers could do to facilitate it. During the time in which work on this volume has progressed, there has been a virtual explosion of articles, books, monographs, and special journal issues directly or indirectly related to the content included here. The fact that there has been such a mushrooming, not only of research studies, conceptualizations, and essays, also, but of women's programs, courses, and other interventions, attests not only to the vitality of the topic but to the dedication of those committed to providing opportunities for more positive growth and development of women.

In spite of the improved state of the art of the psychology and counseling of women today, this volume should fill a special need for those working in education and industry who want to examine female options in education, work, and family from a career development perspective. The unique life span focus on not only the economic or paid work role but also on the multiple role options available to women and men in a changing society should provide a useful framework for designing individual and institutional programs to facilitate female development. The concomitant concern about male socialization and about barriers which limit male development and roles is fully recognized and acknowledged but is not the major focus of this collection.

Authors included in the volume, many of them female, represent a variety of work backgrounds but are especially from the disciplines of psychology, sociology, and economics and from the applied fields of counseling, teaching, and personnel work. A deliberate effort was made to select from among the work of those who, in the editors' opinion, are making significant contributions to the counseling psychology and career development literature. While four of the chapters are original contributions to this book of readings, most of the chapters have appeared in other journals and monographs and are reprinted with permission. We are grateful to the many authors, editors, organizations, and publishers who granted the use of their articles in this volume.

Career Development and Counseling of Women has indeed been a shared effort of the editors. Communication with many outstanding women has been one of the real benefits of undertaking a project such as this. We have worked together over long distances in selecting, organizing, and commenting on what we regard as a useful theoretical-pragmatic collection of studies and essays on the career development of women.

L.S.H.
R.S.R.

INTRODUCTION

THE NEED for this book on career development and counseling of women has existed for a long time and has been punctuated by the national and international interest in the psychology and development of women from many sectors, especially education and work. The special interest of the editors in creating a book of this kind has stemmed from Professor Hansen's experience in searching for appropriate material to use in a course she has taught on this topic over the past four years and from Dr. Rapoza's research on "Academic Self-Concepts of Adolescent Females" for her Ph.D. dissertation. The career development of women—and what we do to facilitate it through counseling, curriculum, and the human services—has become a critical contemporary issue in academia, in the public schools, in business and industry, and in the community at large. A book of readings on this topic should be of interest not only to those teaching courses related to women but to all persons concerned about women's development, especially those with an interest in career and the relationship of work roles to other roles in changing work and family structures.

The purpose of this book is to draw together for both practitioners and theoreticians some of the significant literature relating to the psychological development of women as it relates to their careers and their ways of making decisions about and integrating roles in work, family, community, and leisure. The term *career development* is deliberately defined in the broad sense to include much more than occupation, and the term *career* is used, as it is in some of the current theorizing on this topic, in the sense of "a time-extended working out of a purposeful life pattern through work, paid and unpaid, undertaken by an individual." While the departure point is work, as one significant way in which the individual interacts with environment, there is no intent to glorify or romanticize that part of life; instead it provides a framework for self-exploration and for the experiences, choices, and events which determine the kinds of roles one takes on at different stages of one's life.

While the psychological literature has dwelt much on the differences between women and men in attitudes toward career, much of it focused on traditional roles of women and used those as a baseline. Thus, there is considerable literature on such topics as sex-role socialization, home-career conflict, sex differences in vocational interests, and influences on vocational choice. Although all of these are important in examining female career development, the emphasis in this volume is on a developmental concept of career as a continuous, lifelong process of learning to manage the developmental tasks of various life stages, on integrating the work role with other roles, and on gaining a sense of agency and self-direction in one's life. Changing roles of women and men are viewed in the contemporary context, in which the career motif has been revitalized and broadened and has captured the imagination and concern of many counseling psychologists and human service workers, as well as women themselves. Despite an abundance of studies and articles on sex-role differences, little attempt previously has been made to view female development from a conceptual framework of career development. Many of the career development theories as well as current career education concepts have been written from a male perspective, with a focus on males and traditional male ways of viewing work. Hence, the need for a book on the career development of women. That framework, along with strategies for promoting positive growth of women through counseling and curriculum, provides the context of this book.

The emphasis on *career* combined with *development* and on changing patterns of female *career development* over the life span is what makes this volume unique. While the contribution of the women's movement to our awareness is fully acknowledged, the focus is not on issues raised by the women's movement alone but on (1) what the psychological-sociological literature, both theory and research, tells us about career-related variables in female development; (2) the current status of women and work, mostly in America but also from an international perspective; (3) the changing patterns of women's lives through choices of a variety of career patterns, e.g. the single life, dual career families, shared positions, and other alternatives; (4) impact of female career decisions on males and vice versa; and (5) ways in which psychologists, counselors, teachers, social workers, and others can intervene at all levels of development to facilitate positive female growth.

It was not possible to deal with all aspects of women's roles and development in a volume of this nature. A conscious effort was made to identify female researchers and practitioners who are doing significant work in the field. The collection was carefully selected and organized to provide a sampling of research, thought, and action relating to certain important variables which affect female career development. Some of the articles are intended to stimulate thought and discussion on the current status of women in their changing roles; others are designed to promote action in making a variety of career patterns and multiple options possible for women in American society.

An implicit assumption is that women's roles are affected by those of men and that increasing attention must be given to male socialization as well as to that of women. The editorial comments at the beginning of each section are attempts to provide a critical perspective on some of the issues raised and to help readers see how the themes of the volume fit together.

The editors are aware that in the wide range of material included in this volume some of the language employed may not reflect the most desirable phrasing in terms of modern "nonsexist" usages. Because the primary purpose of the book is to report significant content, no attempt has been made to revise or reedit articles to insure that nonsexist styles of expression are always used.

There are several areas which the editors would have liked to include in this collection: views of women and work in the early years of the country's history; fuller coverage of the differences in attitudes toward women's roles in diverse ethnic cultures; the place of voluntarism and its effects on the status of women; the extensive literature on the employed mother and the effects of maternal employment on preschool children, preadolescents, and adolescents; the area of men's socialization and its impact on women's expectations and aspirations, as well as on those of males; the attitudes of other women about what women do and can do; the emerging work on psychological androgyny; and others. For a variety of reasons, including the unavailability of specific articles and space limitations, these topics were not dealt with as fully or as directly as we would have liked.

Section I presents a series of articles in which psychologists and sociologists have begun to describe patterns of women's careers over the life span. While many of these attempts at theory-building regarding women's patterns began with the assumption that the modal role of women is homemaker, current thinking has moved considerably beyond that kind of normative framework. The importance of these theories is not that they provide the last word on female career development—indeed, most of them are inadequate and partial—but that they open the door and provide stimulus to thinking about women in other than traditional roles. These theories also point up the fact that while there are many within-sex differences in female career patterns, there also are differences between the career patterns of women and men. A comprehensive, fully developed and tested theory of female career development is yet to be formulated.

Section II presents articles on variables related to female career decision making, aspirations, achievement motivation, and self-concepts, as well as barriers which inhibit positive development of women in these areas. While much of the early work in achievement motivation almost ignored or gave only token attention to females, a number of research studies in the sixties and seventies have contributed to our knowledge in this area. From a discussion of vicarious and direct achievement to a study of female attitudes toward planning, the section sheds light on some of the attitudes, motivations, fears, and vocational self-concepts of women.

Section III deals with the ways in which children and youth are socialized through such influences as sex-role prescriptions, occupational stereotyping, and sex stereotyping in educational institutions. These influencers of female (and male) development through an occupational socialization process are discussed as they impact the lives of the elementary school child, adult women, and business and industry personnel. The learned helplessness related to depression in adult women has important messages for career development approaches designed to increase women's sense of power and control in their lives. The articles are intended to stimulate awareness of developmental differences and similarities in the various levels and institutions as well as to create awareness of multiethnic differences in perceptions of self and career.

Recognizing the importance of the economic aspects of women's lives, Section IV focuses primarily on the current status of women in the world of paid work in American society. Articles present many facts about what is happening to women both in professions and skilled trades, their distribution in the work force, and myths and facts about their participation in the work force. Articles discussing special problems of women in vocational education and in labor unions highlight the commonalities of women as they seek opportunities in various sectors of the labor force.

Section V presents a series of articles which illustrate the changing life roles, career patterns, and life-style options engaged in or available to American women and men. The influence of males on female career development, as well as the influence of women's changing roles on male roles, *is* noted. The fact that work roles affect other roles and vice versa is also emphasized. Importance of this section rests on the notion of multiple options for women and men and the changing work and family patterns which make these multiple options possible. The need to negotiate and plan for these roles is suggested.

Section VI, building upon the preceding one, presents articles which reflect a variety of single person or two-person life patterns—the equal partnership marriage, the dual career family, the divorced person, the welfare person, the professional woman, the widow, and the single woman. Variables discussed include the impact of socioeconomic status, marital status, and the impact of children in the particular life-style. While the full range of alternatives is not covered, the articles point up some of the stresses and conflicts women face as they learn to not only cope with but manage the various tasks and phases of the life cycle.

Section VII introduces direct suggestions as to what we can do to facilitate female growth and development, especially from the perspective of counseling and counseling psychology. Articles include reviews of literature along with practical recommendations for what counselors can do, especially through counseling and through curriculum, to change systems and their own behavior in ways which will facilitate rather than impede female growth and career decision making. Among strategies suggested besides counseling are curricular experiences, continuing education programs, systems change, career education, assertive training, career centers, and career planning courses, groups, and seminars.

Vocational assessment both for women and men has come under fire in recent years, and many prominent educators are among the critics of tests and test users. Bias in vocational interest inventories, use of test results for channeling, and inappropriateness of tests for prediction (instead of for exploration) all have been challenged. Section VIII briefly discusses a few measurement variables related to female educational-vocational planning along with some of the issues involved in vocational interest measurement. It also presents a proposed set of guidelines for the assessment of sex bias and sex fairness in interest inventories developed through the National Institute of Education.

Section IX looks at female career development from a cross-cultural international perspective. If this section were to be complete, it would include articles on multiethnic differences not only *across* cultures but *within* the American culture, including sex-role perspectives of Black, Chicano, and other ethnic minority women. Recognizing that sex roles have an even larger cultural context, however, the articles present views of women in the work world in selected developed and developing countries. As one of the Scandinavian countries reputedly advanced in women's status, Norway provides a special laboratory for examination of women's work and family roles. The universality of women's career development problems is dramatically illustrated in a report on equal pay for equal work written especially for International Women's Year.

In Section X, a selected annotated bibliography of bibliographies provides useful references and special resources to help those involved in facilitating the career development of women.

Because anyone working with women needs to be aware of federal laws and regulations, the widely disseminated chart produced by the Association of American Colleges is reproduced in Appendix 1. Finally, in Appendix 2, a guide from the Labor Department provides suggestions for increasing women's options, particularly in the often neglected trade and technical areas.

ACKNOWLEDGMENTS

WE WISH to acknowledge the contributions of several people in completing this book. The editors are especially indebted to research assistants Jill Stebbins and Cynthia Marsh, the latter of whom provided eleventh hour assistance in helpful commentary and criticisms of the collection; to graduate students Elizabeth Gama, Maureen Gevirtz, and Courtenay Sickles, who in taking one of the pilot courses in which this book was used made insightful comments and gave helpful feedback; and to secretaries Jim Scharfer, Kate Mackay, and Linda Howse, who assisted in typing the manuscript and other critical detail work. A special word of thanks to Virginia Bernabe Tellas for her attention and concern while facilitating correspondence between the editors and the various authors, publishers, and organizations. Thanks also to Sheila Herbert, teaching assistant, for invaluable research assistance.

While the significance of this book of readings in the long run will be determined by its users, it has been a stimulating experience for the editors to delve into and integrate this rich collection of ideas on such an important topic. The task has been demanding but will be well rewarded if readers find their thinking expanded and their practices modified by the ideas and suggestions contained herein.

Finally, the editors extend a deep note of thanks to their spouses and families who have a real appreciation of what multiple roles of women and men mean.

L. SUNNY HANSEN
RITA S. RAPOZA

CONTENTS

CAREER DEVELOPMENT AND COUNSELING OF WOMEN

Section I

PATTERNS OF FEMALE CAREER DEVELOPMENT

One of the major questions confronting counselors and others concerned with the career development of women is the degree to which existing theoretical formulations based largely upon the study of career patterns of men are really applicable to the problems and experiences of women. As Vetter points out, the "occupational behavior of women has not been treated comprehensively in the counseling literature, largely because women as workers have been perceived as individually transient and collectively insignificant due to the type and level of jobs available to them in our society." Although far from comprehensive, several theories do acknowledge differences between male and female patterns and provide a framework for looking at the career development of women.

In the first chapter in this section, Vetter examines several approaches that focus particularly on the concerns and experiences of women. These formulations suggest means to classify and describe alternative career patterns for women. Inherent in some approaches is the assumption that homemaker is the modal and/or optimal role, and other patterns are deviants from this choice. One theorist postulates that vocational and homemaker roles are largely mutually exclusive, while other approaches describe patterns in which homemaking and paid employment are combined. These theories at least provide a starting point for exploration of nontraditional roles and of emerging life career patterns for women.

Two approaches, interdisciplinary in nature, emphasize that both the social experiences which influence personality development of workers and the conditions of occupational opportunity which influence implementation of choices must be considered in a theory of occupational choice. This sociological perspective seems essential to the development of a theory accounting for the occupational behavior of women.

Vetter also describes several factors that may modify career choices of women; these variables probably affect male and female behavior quite differently. Included among these factors are occupational sex stereotyping, choice between home and vocation, fear of negative effect on children due to maternal employment, and male attitudes about the vocational role of women.

In the second chapter, Astin and Myint report the results of a large scale study of more than five thousand young women and their patterns of career development in the five years after high school. They conclude that there is great need for career counseling services for females both in the period immediately prior to graduation from high school and in the relatively turbulent years that follow.

Next in this section is one of the classical contributions to the field of career development. In this chapter, first published in 1957, Donald Super outlines his developmental schema and relates career development to life stages. This formulation probably has had more influence in giving shape and structure to our present view of career development than any other single source. Although much of Super's work has been directed toward the career development of men, his emphasis on the developmental nature of career development as a "continuous lifelong process of developing and implementing a self-concept" seems particularly important in formulating a comprehensive theory of career development in women. Super acknowledges that there are differences between the career patterns of women and men and suggests a classification scheme for female career patterns. He closes with a challenging set of questions which must be answered in order to advance our present state of knowledge and theory about career development. In fact, he has begun to answer some of these questions and to expand his theory in a way more inclusive of women in recent writings. He sees the many roles of one's career as those of child, student, worker, spouse, parent, homemaker, citizen, "leisurite," annuitant, and patient. The theaters in which the roles are played include home, community, school, work place, and retirement community or home.

The last chapter by Van Dusen and Sheldon is a recent summary of the status of American women viewed from a life cycle perspective. The individual's life is seen as a variety of statuses and roles which may occur in sequence, combination, and/or juxtaposition. While roles associated with family are certainly central to many women, sequences of student, career, and community roles are also significant. This analysis provides a particularly exciting framework from which to view career development of women.

Van Dusen and Sheldon point out that until recently the family life cycle has been equated with the female life cycle. This assumption has resulted in the myth that there were two kinds of women: those who got married and those in paid occupations. The authors present facts to show that such a clear separation of work and marriage never existed and is even less likely to occur in the future. They trace the changes in traditional family life over the last twenty-five years and emphasize the growing interrelatedness of work and family life for women. Several changes in society which have had a direct impact on this trend are discussed. First, in the area of education, young women have greater opportunities to gain access for training for career mobility. Also, educational channels are increasingly available to married women, women with children, and women over twenty-five years of age. Secondly, women are marrying later, having fewer children, and therefore spdeing less time in the traditional childbearing phase of life. A third factor in causing change in women's roles is the growth of the number of female heads of households; this is viewed as a transitional status which an increased proportion of women will enter and leave at some point in their lives. Finally, due to a number of factors, the makeup of the female labor force has changed significantly over the last fifty years.

The theoretical formulations described in Section I, while far from the final word, provide a stimulus for thinking about new career patterns for women. As Vetter's literature review reveals, these approaches are far from complete. Van Dusen and Sheldon point out that past assumptions about career patterns of women have not always fit the facts. Their analysis of sequential roles in the life cycle is an integrative one; looking at career development from the perspective of multiple roles occurring within developmental life stages may be most congruent with today's complex society.

The issues raised by the chapters in this section have special significance for counselors working with women. Vetter states that we as counselors must do a better job in helping women look at life-style options; too often women still view their alternatives in terms of an either/or choice in relation to marriage and paid work. Women need to be aware of the variety of patterns that exist, both traditional and nontraditional, such as the two career family or dual career pattern described by Van Dusen and Sheldon. Women also need to be aware of the concepts of life stages, developmental tasks, and multiple roles and to be adequately prepared to deal with these changes.

Chapter 1

CAREER COUNSELING FOR WOMEN*

LOUISE VETTER

THE OCCUPATIONAL BEHAVIOR of women has not been treated comprehensively in the counseling literature, largely because women as workers have been perceived as individually transient and collectively insignificant due to the type and level of jobs available to them in our society. Oppenheimer (1968) documented the sex-labelling of jobs. She found that "female jobs" are those which depend on skilled but cheap labor, those where most of the training is acquired before employment, and those where career continuity is not essential. Female jobs are jobs which exist all over the country, hence mobility or the lack of it is not usually a serious handicap. In view of these facts, it is necessary to document the need for career counseling with women before discussing the application of career development theories to women and before discussing factors which affect vocational behavior in women.

NEED FOR CAREER COUNSELING

If we define "career" as the sequence of occupations in the life of an individual, then we need to look at the following facts (Women's Bureau, 1972b): "About 32 million women are currently employed. These women constitute about 38 percent of the labor force. Ninety percent of women will be employed at some time in their lives. The median wage paid to women is less than 60 percent of that paid to men and the differential is increasing."

The following evidence suggests that women *do* take their jobs seriously (Women's Bureau, 1972a). Of the 32 million women in the labor force in March, 1971, nearly half were working because of pressing economic need. They were either single, widowed, divorced, or separated or had husbands whose incomes were less than $3,000 a year. Another 5.4 million had husbands with incomes between $3,000 and $7,000. When absentee rates due to illness and injury are examined

**From The Counseling Psychologist, 1973, 4 (1), 54-67.*

little difference between men and women is found; they average 5.2 days a year for women and 5.1 days a year for men. Studies on labor turnover indicate that net differences for men and women are generally small. In manufacturing industries, the 1968 rates of accessions per 100 employees were 4.4 for men and 5.3 for women; the respective separation rates were 4.4 and 5.2.

Recent federal legislation, executive orders, and the pending twenty-seventh amendment to the Constitution (the Equal Rights Amendment) will undoubtedly have major impact on women's career patterning. For example, Executive Order 11246, as amended, requires that most federal contractors (producing both goods and services) have an affirmative action plan for hiring and promoting women in jobs where they are currently under-utilized.

The foregoing information is typically not included in the educational programs for preparing counselors. However, if vocational counseling should occupy a central place in counseling psychology, as suggested by Samler (1964) at the Greyston Conference, these facts, as well as the following theoretical and empirical findings, deserve coverage in pre-service and in-service counseling programs.

THEORIES OF CAREER DEVELOPMENT

Although Osipow (1968) indicated that "few special explanations or concepts have been devised to deal with the special problems of the career development of women" and that "most of the masculine-based tests and theories fail to really provide a useful vehicle for the understanding of the career development of women (p. 247)," four theoretical approaches which have relevance to women will be considered, along with two tentative sets of postulates proposed specifically for looking at women's careers. The interested reader is referred to reviews of career development by Tennyson (1968) and by Holland and Whitney (1969); Kievit's (1972) review and synthesis of the literature on women in the world of work; Astin, Suniewick and Dweck's (1971) annotated bibliography on women's education and careers; and to extended critiques of the theories of career development by Osipow (1968) and Crites (1969). The four general approaches to be considered are those of Super, Roe, Holland, and Blau, Gustad, Jessor, Parnes, and Wilcox. Psathas (1968) and Zytowski (1969) have presented approaches based exclusively on women's experience.

Super's Developmental Self-Concept Theory

Super suggested that persons strive to implement their self-concepts by choosing to enter the occupation they see as most likely to permit them self-expression. He further suggested that the particular behaviors people engage in to implement their self-concepts vocationally are a function of the individual's stage of life development. Vocational behaviors can be better understood by viewing them within the context of the changing demands of the life cycle.

According to Super (1963a), self-concept formation requires people to recognize themselves as distinctive individuals, yet at the same time be aware of the similarities between themselves and others. A person's self concept is continually developing. Vocational maturity (Super, 1963b), defined in terms of the congruence between an individual's vocational behavior and the expected vocational behavior at that age, allows the observer to assess the rate and level of an individual's development with respect to career matters.

Super (1957) identified four types of career patterns which men follow: stable, conventional, unstable, and multiple-trial. He also provided a possible classification of women's career patterns. These are: stable homemaking (no significant work experience), conventional (work after education but not after marriage), stable working (single women who work continuously), double-track (married women who work continuously), interrupted (married women who work, then are fulltime homemakers, then return to work), unstable (in and out of the labor force at irregular intervals), and multiple-trial (a succession of unrelated jobs).

Research

Crites (1965) reported that his research indicated only a few differences between boys and girls in their self-reports of vocational attitudes, thus leading him to conclude that sex may not be an important factor in the maturation of vocational attitudes. However, a later study by Smith and Herr (1972), using Crites' Vocational Development Inventory-Attitude Scale with 534 girls and 489 boys in the eighth grade and 495 girls and 502 boys in the tenth grade, found "females possessed more maturity in terms of their attitudes toward work and career planning than did males in the eighth and tenth grades (p. 181)." Putnam and Hansen (1972), in a study of 375 eleventh grade girls, found that self-concept and own feminine role concept were useful in predicting vocational maturity (measured by Crites' scale). They found that the more the girl viewed her role as being liberal, or contemporary, the higher was her level of vocational maturity.

Mulvey (1963) studied the career patterns of 475 women who had graduated twenty to twenty-seven years previously from the public high school of Providence, Rhode Island. She found that one-third of her sample accepted homemaking and child-rearing exclusively as a career, but suggested that the work role is more central to woman's existence and more internalized than many writers would contend. Level of education and level of aspiration were the most important determinants of career pattern. The career patterns were closely related to the life developmental cycle.

In a recent study (Vetter, in process), a national cross-sectional sample of 4,807 women was categorized into career patterns. Of the total group, 22 percent fell into the stable homemaking group, 27 percent conventional, 3 percent stable working, 14 percent double track, 16 percent interrupted, and 18 percent unstable. The multiple-trial category was not used because of overlap with other categories. Marital and family status, educational and attitudinal variables are being studied in relationship to the career patterns.

Roe's Personality Theory of Career Choice

Roe was concerned with the effects of early childhood experiences on the development of personality. In particular, she contended that early experiences influence people's orientation to the interpersonal world around them in a way that leads them to move toward or away from people. She also developed an occupational classification system which allows predictions about the nature of the occupations that people would prefer if they were person oriented, as opposed to those they would approach if they were not oriented toward people (Roe, 1957).

Research

Osipow (1972) indicates that, while a considerable body of research exists testing Roe's theory, most of it has yielded data that do not support the theory in its general outline. He feels that if the theory were redefined and the links between early childhood experiences and personality were more clearly delineated it might be shown to have greater validity than is at first apparent.

Kriger (1972) has proposed one such redefinition of Roe's original scheme to account for women's career development. She used this formulation to study the careers of sixty-six women (twenty-two homemakers, twenty-two career women in female-dominated occupations, and twenty-two career women in male-dominated occupations) who were married, living with their husbands, the mother of at least one child, middle-class, and graduates from college. She interpreted her results as supporting the contention that the primary vocational decision for women is the decision between "working" and "not working," with the choice of a specific occupational area a secondary choice. The decision to have a career was seen as a function of the child-rearing mode of the parents, whereas the particular field of occupation and the level within it that a woman chooses to pursue was seen as a function of her level of achievement motivation.

Holland's Career Typology Theory

Holland (1966) postulated six types of individuals and six corresponding work environments. The six types are the following:

Realistic: aggressive, physically oriented, "masculine" person who prefers the concrete rather than the abstract.

Intellectual (later called Investigative): the person who is primarily concerned with thinking rather than acting and who tends to avoid close, interpersonal contact.

Social: the person who seeks close, interpersonal relations through such vocational activities as are found in teaching or therapy.

Conventional: the person who exhibits great concern for order, rules, regulations and self-control.

Enterprising: the person who uses verbal skills to manipulate and dominate other people.

Artistic: the person who seeks self-expression through artistic means.

Holland (1966) states that "in our culture, most persons can be categorized as one of six types (p. 9)" but then goes on to say:

> Unfortunately most of our empirical knowledge about personality and vocational behavior has been obtained in studies of men. Consequently, it is difficult to construct a theory of personality that applies equally to men and women. The present theory is no exception: it is based chiefly on studies of men and is probably less useful for understanding the behavior of women. A special but closely related theory for women is desirable, but at this point I have none to offer. (p. 13)

However, he did develop a classification for female student vocational choices, which included seven categories: Intellectual, Social-Intellectual, Social-Conventional, Social-Enterprising, Social-Artistic, Conventional and Artistic (Holland and Whitney, 1968).

Research

Holland and Whitney (1968) used the classification scheme cited above to study the stability of vocational choices of 1571 college women freshmen over a period of eight or twelve months. They found that about 60 percent of the women selected the same occupation on both occasions, 14 percent selected an occupation in the same subgroup, 5 percent selected an occupation in a closely related subgroup, and 5 percent selected a remotely related occupation in the same major class; thus 84 percent of the women's successive occupational choices were in the same major occupational class. Another 9 percent selected "closely related" or "related" occupations in a related major group. Only 1 percent indicated clearly unrelated second choices, with an additional 5 percent of the responses unclassifiable or undecided.

A group of 1576 college men were studied at the same time, with 69 percent of the successive occupational choices being in the same major class. Ten percent were in a "closely related" or "related" subgroup in a related major class, with 11 percent making an unrelated second choice, and 10 percent unclassifiable or undecided.

A possible interpretation of these results is that women are more vocationally mature at the college freshman level. Another possible interpretation is that the women perceive fewer options open to them and so make fewer changes among the limited number of choices available.

Harvey (1972) found correlational evidence which supported the validity of Holland's Vocational Preference Inventory for adult women. However, the *Social* scale and the *Artistic* scale of the VPI remained in doubt.

A Conceptual Framework for Occupational Choice—Blau, Gustad, Jessor, Parnes, and Wilcock

Blau et al. (1956) presented a conceptual scheme for use in systematic research which could be the basis for a theory of occupational choice. The interdisciplinary collaborators (from sociology, psychology and economics) identified two analytically distinct aspects within the social structure which affect occupational choice: (1) the matrix of social experiences which channel the personality development of potential workers and (2) the conditions of occupational opportunity which limit the realization of their choices. Occupational choice was conceived as a continually modified compromise between preferences for and expectations of being able to enter various occupations.

In addition, Blau and his colleagues stated that it is an oversimplification to conceive of occupational choice and selection as occurring at one point in time, even if this is defined as a limited time interval rather than as an instant, and even if the effects of earlier developments are taken into consideration. They suggest that a series of successive choice periods must be systematically analyzed to show how earlier decisions limit or extend the range of future choices.

Parnes, one of the collaborators, appears to be partially implementing the conceptual scheme in a longitudinal study of women aged thirty to forty-four (Shea, Spitz, and Zeller, 1970).

Toward a Theory of Occupational Choice for Women—Psathas

Building on the approach of Blau et al. (1956), Psathas (1968) described a number of factors which appear to operate in special ways for women on their way to occupational choices. He indicated that an understanding of the factors which influence entry of women into occupational roles must begin with the relationship between sex role and occupational role. He cited as first order relationships the intention to marry, time of marriage, reasons for marriage, and husband's economic situation and attitude toward his wife's working.

Additional factors to be considered include family finances, social class, education and occupation of parents, and values. He reiterates the idea that the setting in which occupational choices are made must be considered, along with the developmental process by which they are made.

Apparently this approach has not generated any research.

Toward a Theory of Career Development for Women—Zytowski

Zytowski (1969), working independently of Blau *et al.* and of Psathas, presented nine postulates in an attempt to characterize the distinctive differences in the work life of men and women, the developmental stages unique to women, their patterns of vocational participation, and the determinants of the patterns. The postulates follow:

1. The modal life role for women is described as that of the homemaker.
2. The nature of the women's role is not static; it will ultimately bear no distinction from that of men.
3. The life role of women is orderly and developmental and may be divided into sequences according to the preeminent task in each.
4. Vocational and homemaker participation is largely mutually exclusive. Vocational participation constitutes departure from the homemaker role.
5. Three aspects of vocational participation are sufficient to distinguish patterns of vocational participation: age or ages of entry, span of participation, degree of participation.
6. The degree of vocational participation represented by a given occupation is defined as the proportion of men to the total workers employed in the performance of that job.
7. Women's vocational patterns may be distinguished in terms of three levels, derived from the combination of entry age(s), span and degree of participation, forming an ordinal scale.
8. Women's preference for a pattern of vocational participation is an internal event and is accounted for by motivational factors.
9. The pattern of vocational participation is determined jointly by preference (representing motivation) and by external (such as situational and environmental) and internal (such as ability) factors.

Research

Wolfson (1972) studied postulate seven and postulate nine by defining five career patterns and studying the relationships between the patterns and twenty-nine motivational, external, and internal factors. She used the three patterns defined by Zytowski (mild—very early or late entry, a brief span, and a low degree of participation; moderate—early entry, a lengthy span, and a low degree of participation; and unusual—early entry, a lengthy or uninterrupted span, and a high degree of participation) and two additional groups: a group which had never worked since leaving college and a High Moderate group, composed of women from the Moderate group who had worked eighteen years or more.

The sample consisted of 306 women who had participated in a twenty-five year follow-up study of counseled versus non-counseled students. Career patterns were not predictable from information known about a student when she was a college freshman but were predictable from data collected five years later. Variables related to education and marriage were the most powerful predictors of vocational patterns. The number of years spent in college and the percentage of graduates increased progressively from the "Never Worked" group to the "Unusual" group, with the implication that career commitment is closely correlated with the amount of education obtained. Marital status was a highly discriminating factor. Husband's income, number of children, age of youngest child, and satisfaction with marriage also discriminated among vocational pattern groups. The findings were interpreted as suggesting that the High Moderate and Unusual groups probably represent a vocationally-oriented population and the other three a homemaking-oriented population.

Postulate four is refuted on the basis of evidence from the Women's Bureau (1971) insofar as 40 percent of women who are married and living with their husbands are employed. In addition, unless by definition a man must be present to constitute a home, a high percentage of widows and divorced women are employed in addition to maintaining households and many single women workers are responsible for maintaining their own homes.

FACTORS AFFECTING CAREER CHOICES AMONG WOMEN

Occupational sex stereotyping occurs early in the socialization of children. Schlossberg and Goodman (1972) studied children's sex stereotyping of occupations. They found that kindergarteners and sixth graders felt that a woman's place was clearly *not* fixing cars or television sets or designing buildings. The children did say that a woman could work as a waitress, nurse, or librarian. In contrast, they did not feel that men had to be similarly limited.

Meyer (1970) studied the views of 132 boys and girls in grades three, seven, and eleven toward the sex-linking of occupations. She found that boys and girls have strong stereotypic ways of behaving toward traditionally sex-linked occupations.

Harmon (1971) found that college women had considered a very restricted range of occupations during adolescence. This may have resulted from the kind of stereotyping noted above.

Horner (1969) has documented a motive to avoid success in college women. Anticipation of success over a male can provoke anxieties in women such as fear or loss of femininity and self-esteem. Thus, fear of success can inhibit positive achievement and directed motivation and behavior.

Goldberg (1968) reported that 140 college women evaluated a professional article more negatively if they thought it was authored by a woman, even in traditionally female professions. When the author was presented as a man, the women consistently rated the article as more valuable and the author as more competent.

Gray-Shellberg, Villareal, and Stone (1972) studied the resolution of career conflicts by fifty-seven male and fifty-seven female college students and seventy-two male and sixty-three female noncollege adults. A significant number of women in the two samples studied were motivated to subordinate their interests to those of a fiancé or husband and the men, too, perceived this as the accepted state of affairs. The stereotypes revealed in the subjects' responses reflected strong societal expectations that a woman shall be supportive of a man and not seek self-expression through a career. The authors indicated that the removal of economic, political, and legal barriers to women's achievement, while important, will probably not significantly affect the occupational status of women unless it is accompanied by a fundamental change in both external and internalized expectations of the "proper" female role.

Women have been led to believe that maternal employment is related to potential juvenile delinquency in their children. Actually, studies show that whether or not a mother is employed does not appear to be a determining factor in causing juvenile delinquency. It is the quality of a mother's care rather than the time consumed in such care which is of major significance (Women's Bureau, 1972b).

The implication that married women take jobs away from men has probably deterred some women from seeking employment. In fact, there were 18.5 million married women (husband present) in the labor force in March 1971, while the number of unemployed men was 3 million. If all the married women stayed home and unemployed men were placed in their jobs, there would be 15.5 million unfilled jobs. Moreover, most unemployed men do not have the education or the skill to qualify for many of the jobs held by women, such as secretaries, teachers, and nurses (Women's Bureau, 1972b.).

Home—Career Dimension

Watley and Kaplan (1971) did a follow-up study in 1965 of 883 women who had won National Merit Scholarships during the years 1956-60. They found that 85 percent of the women said that they definitely planned on having a career. Those seeking an immediate career scored higher on scholastic ability tests than those who either planned no career or who planned to delay entering them. Many more women, regardless of their plans, expressed problems relating to their gender than expressed problems that interfered with making and implementing their plans. The problem of discrimination was cited most frequently.

Harmon (1970) studied the career commitment of 169 women ten to fourteen years after college entrance. Differences between the "career committed" and "noncommitted" groups were found but none of them offered a basis for predicting career commitment before women begin programs of higher education. These results are consistent with those of Astin and Myint (1971). They found that post-high school experiences were the best determinants of career outcomes. Educational attainment and marital-family status best predicted whether women would choose to pursue careers in the sciences, professions, and teaching, or to be housewives and office workers.

Tangri (1970) studied the occupational choices of 200 college women. She found that Role-Innovators (those whose choices are of occupations now dominated by men) aspire to a higher level of accomplishment in their field than Traditional choosers. They also expressed greater commitment to their vocations. She found that Traditionals tend more than Role-Innovators to displace their achievement concerns onto the future husband, whereas Role-Innovators are more likely to generalize from their own generally high level of expectations for self to expectations for future husbands. Role-Innovators reported as many romantic relationships and significantly more non-romantic friendships with the opposite sex than did Traditionals.

Almquist (1969) studied the occupational choices and career salience of one class in a woman's college of a medium-sized university over the four years of their college experience. Career salience was defined as the extent to which the women planned to be employed in addition to being married and having a family. "Atypical choosers" were those women who want to enter jobs in which over 70 percent of the workers are now male. She found no support for the hypothesis of deviance which would suggest rejection of the traditional obligations of the female role; rather there was support for an enrichment hypothesis, with broader learning experiences which lead to a less stereotyped version of the female role in which work in a high level career is a significant part. Career salient atypical choosers had more work experience and more varied work experience related to their ultimate career choices than did noncareer salient, typical choosers. Their mothers more often had a consistent history of working and they had been influenced by college professors and people in the occupation who influenced and persuaded them to pursue an important career themselves.

Levine (1969) studied the marital and occupational plans of single women in four professional schools. Almost all women in Law and Medicine did not plan any withdrawal from the labor force, while the majority of those in Nursing and Teaching planned to withdraw from the labor force when they have young children to care for. Descriptions of experiences in graduate professional schools suggested that women in Law and Medicine were learning that they could maintain feminine identity and sex-role without leaving the profession. In addition, they were treated as members of a high status professional school. In contrast, the women in Nursing and Teaching were discovering that there is a separation between important aspects of sex-role and work-role. Moreover, women in Nursing and Teaching tended to feel that they are treated as members of low status groups within the university and reacted by planning to devote time and energy in the future to the marital position.

Turner (1972) studied socialization and career orientation among black (N=28) and white (N=45) college freshmen women. She found that blacks were far likelier than whites to expect full-time paid employment. Fifty-four percent of blacks, but only 16 percent of whites, expected full-time paid employment, while 53 percent of whites and 21 percent of blacks expected to be homemakers, working for pay, if at all, only before children were born or after they were grown. Socioeconomic status did not lead to differentiation of these expectations. There was no overlap of demographic, developmental, and attitudinal variables that differentiate high and low career expectation among blacks and whites. High career expectation among whites was related to: parental behavior which stressed competitiveness as opposed to obedient and "good" behavior; equalitarian, self-striving attitudes toward women's roles; less paternal disappointment should the student drop out of college, as well as a tendency toward lower parental aspirations for the student's highest academic degree. Among blacks, full-time career expectation was related to perceptions of the preferences and expectations of significant others regarding their career involvement, as well as to appreciation of parental strictness. They also stressed the importance of holding a good job in order to find a high-status husband.

Since blacks expect so much more career involvement than whites and since black mothers were far more likely to have worked, and worked earlier during the students' childhoods, it might seem plausible that the students' career expectations would be related to maternal work history among both races. Instead, the extent of maternal employment during the students' childhoods in the study did not differentiate high and low career expectations among either race. The findings suggested that these young black women may be especially responsive to the expectations of significant others that they carry the responsibility implied by full-time employment. They expect to work full-time while preferring less work involvement and reporting negative attitudes toward their mothers' employment. For black women, fulltime career expectation may imply a deep sense of responsibility more than an anticipation of personal fulfillment.

Tucker (1971) studied the self and inter-group perceptions of homemakers, elementary teachers, and research scientists as related to feminine sex-role and occupational choice. Homemakers saw themselves as having feminine characteristics and viewed teachers and scientists as masculine, but they saw teachers as feminine when compared to scientists. Teachers attributed to scientists the same masculine traits that homemakers did, but they saw homemakers as similar to themselves. Scientists attributed some feminine characteristics to themselves and some masculine traits to the other two groups. Homemakers were not work oriented nor did they overtly express dissatisfaction with their concept of themselves in the culturally-accepted feminine sex-role. Homemakers and teachers viewed scientists as having masculine characteristics and excellent social skills and as being independent, creative problem solvers, characteristics which the scientists did not perceive themselves as having.

This attribution to scientists of characteristics incongruent with the scientist's self-concepts might well be a discouraging factor in the choice of science as an occupation by many women, even if they have the initial interests and aptitudes necessary for successful pursuit of this field.

Nagely (1971) studied forty college-educated working mothers, twenty employed in traditional female occupations and twenty who had careers in male-dominated occupations. Pioneers were found to be more career-committed than Traditionals and to have more successfully integrated the roles of homemaker and worker. Pioneers' fathers were more highly educated and their husbands were employed at higher occupational levels. Pioneers more frequently reported that their fathers approved of women working outside the home. Pioneers were also more likely to refuse to give up their careers if requested by their husbands, more reluctant to move to another city for their husband's professional advancement, and feel that their professional activities were as important as their husbands. They also indicated that they had a greater voice in determining how the family income was spent, took more responsibility for disciplining their children, and were more likely to feel that their husbands should help with household tasks. They were also more likely to report that being a woman was a disadvantage in their fields. The woman who makes the strongest recommendation for combining career, marriage, and family is the one who reports that her career allows her to make full use of her talents.

Rossi (1965) reported that, of 3,500 women college graduates of the class of 1961, one-fifth had no career goals other than homemaking; not quite half reported long-range career goals in traditional fields in which women predominate; only 7 percent were Pioneers with long-range career goals in predominantly masculine fields.

Astin (1969) studied 1,657 women who earned their doctorates in the United States during 1957 and 1958 (86% of the total group). She found that 91 percent of them were in the labor force and 81 percent were working full time. Women who interrupted their careers did so because of child bearing and child rearing; the median length of time for such interruptions was fourteen months. Over half the women had been or were still married at the time of the survey; the married women had smaller families than women in general. Astin's findings suggested needed changes: encouragement of young women to achieve advanced training and establishment of scholarships in career fields that women usually do not enter. She also suggested that opportunities for part-time study and employment need to be increased, that day-care centers are needed, that tax laws should be changed to permit deductions for household workers, and that discriminatory practices against women in higher education roles and the world of work need to be eliminated.

Farmer and Bohn (1970) studied the level of career interest in women and the relationship to home-career conflict reduction. They designated six scales of the Strong Vocational Interest Blank for women as Career scales and eight as Home scales. They found that scores on Career scales were increased and scores on Home scales were decreased when fifty working women (25 married, 25 single) were instructed to respond as though men liked intelligent women, men and women are promoted equally in business and the professions, and raising a family well is very possible for a career woman. Whether the responding woman was married or single did not affect the responses. The authors concluded that the level of vocational interest in women, irrespective of their marital status, would be raised if home-career conflict were reduced.

As pointed out by Kievit (1972), it is evident that college students, college graduates, and women in the professions have been the subjects of much of the research effort to date. She says: "If indeed the concern with women workers is based on the valuing of work as a source of life satisfaction for all citizens, as well as manpower resources to meet requirements of a changing technology and economy, surely more intensive study of clerical, skilled, semi-skilled, and less prestigious service occupations is needed. (p. 67)"

All too often in career counseling with men, the only role considered is that of the occupational role. Bailyn (1969) points out that the husband's approach to integrating family and work in his life is as important to marital satisfaction as his wife's attempt to integrate career and family. In this study, marriages tended to be happier when the husband found satisfaction in both career and family than when the husband was either just career– or family-oriented.

Male Attitudes

Male attitudes about the vocational roles which adult women should pursue are an important factor in determining what adult women will do (or will be permitted to do).

Entwistle and Greenberger (1970) studied the responses of 270 boys and 305 girls, ninth graders in seven schools of various socioeconomic and ethnic composition in Baltimore, to questions on women's role. Girls expressed more liberal views than boys on whether women should work, hold the same jobs as men, and derive satisfaction from problem solving. However, both groups responded negatively when questioned about women holding men's jobs. The greatest disparity existed on the question of whether women should work at all, with girls responding positively and boys negatively. Among the boys, blacks were more liberal than whites and middle-class whites were more liberal than blue-collar whites. A greater discrepancy was found between middle-class girls and boys than between blue-collar girls and boys, with the middle-class sex difference especially marked among the high IQ group. This suggests that girls with greatest work potential will face strong opposition from their future mates.

Nelson and Goldman (1969), in studying the attitudes of high school students and young adults toward the gainful employment of married women, found general acceptance by men of the dual role for women except in the case of their own wives.

McMillan (1972) studied the attitudes of college men (1085 unmarried male dormitory residents on a midwestern university) toward career involvement of married women. The attitudes of the total sample regarding career involvement for their future wives were categorized as follows:

12.0% — no further work career after marriage.

37.8% — work in profession after marriage until the time of children, and then no further work unless absolutely necessary.

39.6% — work in profession after marriage until the time of children, devoting full time to family during the children's early years, and then returning to the profession as the children grow older.

3.8% — work in the profession rather continuously after marriage, taking off only short periods of time as required for family matters.

6.8% — none of the above options since I do not plan to get married.

Thus, nearly half of this sample did not consider the possibility of a lifetime career for their spouses, even with an interruption for child-raising. Among the different majors being pursued by the male students, the most notable differences seemed to be that business majors and science and mathematics majors preferred less career involvement for their future wives than did education majors and humanities and social science majors.

Meier's (1972) study of college youth's attitudes toward social equality for women found female undergraduates (N=99) scoring higher on feminine social equality than male undergraduates (N=120). She also found that where the mother predominates in the attitudinal socialization of the child and when the mother exhibits involvement in occupational roles outside the home that the males were more positive about female social equality. If this finding is generalizable, then as more women are taking their place in the occupational world, the attitudes of their children will become more accepting of her right to be there.

Kaley (1971), in studying the attitudes toward the dual role of the married professional woman, found that married professional women have positive attitudes toward their dual role of career and marriage while married professional men have negative attitudes toward the dual role. She indicated that a review of research on the attitudes of professionally employed men and women toward women's dual role supports the hypothesis that negative attitudes held by both men and women inhibit qualified women from seeking higher education and professional careers.

Simpson (1969), in studying employing agents from six fields of humanities and social sciences in six institutions of higher education, found that employing agents discriminate against academic women when they choose between equally qualified candidates for faculty posts. However, they select a statistically significant number of superior women in preference to less well qualified men. Simpson found no significant difference among deans, departmental chairmen, or faculty in their discriminatory behavior toward equally qualified male and female candidates or in their selection of superior candidates over less qualified males. He also found that, generally, those who discriminate against academic women also exhibit negative attitudes toward women in general.

The myth that men do not like to work for women supervisors probably discourages women from considering administrative careers. Actually most men who complain about women supervisors have never worked for a woman. In one study where at least three-fourths of both the male and female respondents (all executives) had worked with women managers, their evaluation of women in management was favorable. On the other hand, the study showed a traditional/cultural bias among those who reacted unfavorably to women as managers (Women's Bureau, 1972b).

CONCLUSIONS FOR COUNSELORS

Suniewick (1971) pointed up a conflict which is reflected in the data currently available. On one hand, statistics show that women are discriminated against in their pursuit of education and in their attempts to find careers. On the other hand, conflicts they face as they attempt to enter worlds formerly the province of men and as they endeavor to change their image and status are pointed out. She asserted that obvious implications of research findings are seldom mentioned: implications that changes need to occur in the institutions that educate women, in the world of work, and in women themselves as they deal with the conflict between career and marriage. She stated that "the obvious finding is that women are not being helped to resolve the conflict; rather they are being asked to accept their roles as wives and mothers and to make their career goals secondary to the other 'natural' functions of women in society (p. 21)." She asked how it is possible for a woman to endeavor to live as an individual as she sees fit when underutilization of woman-power, sex-labeling of jobs, woman's responsibility for children and family, prejudice against women in the world of work, and other cultural limitations continue to hinder woman's equal access to work. She sees little evidence of change occurring in educational institutions to assist women in gaining access to fields of study normally open only to men, although the need for the professions and vocations to accept qualified women on an equal basis with men has been clearly shown.

If "women" are "people," it will naturally be assumed that, as adults, they will combine a number of roles, such as worker, parent, household member, community participant. The counselor will work with these people to enable them to maximize their individual development.

However, we have not yet reached this stage in American culture. In many instances, women are viewed as a separate class, rather than as individuals with individual abilities, interests, and aspirations. Administrators, employers, teachers, and counselors make decisions about women's education and women's employment on the basis of their sex, rather than on their individual interests, abilities, and capacities.

Counselors must not continue to perpetuate such a situation. (Neither should anyone else, but this chapter is intended for an audience of counseling psychologists.) It seems time for counseling psychology to pick up the challenge, rather hesitantly offered by Samler (1964), to become involved in social action, to make it a definite part of our professional task to set out to affect the status quo.

A number of sources are available to the counselor who is working in career counseling with girls and women. These include publications of the Women's Bureau (1966, 1970), Berry, Kern, Meleney, and Vetter (1966), Westervelt (1966), Bruemmer (1969, 1970), Mathews (1969), Murphy (1969), Eyde (1970), and the National Vocational Guidance Association's monograph (1972) on counseling girls and women over the life span.

REFERENCES

Almquist, E.M. Occupational choice and career salience among college women. (Doctoral dissertation, University of Kansas) Ann Arbor, Michigan: University Microfilms, 1969. No. 69-21, 484.

Astin, H.S. *The woman doctorate in America.* New York: Russell Sage Foundation, 1969.

Astin, H.S. and Myint, T. Career development of young women during the post-high school years. *Journal of Counseling Psychology,* 1971, *18,* 369-393.

Astin, H.S., Suniewick, N., & Dweck, S. *Women: A bibliography on their education and careers.* Washington, D.C.: Human Service Press, 1971.

Berry, J., Kern, K.K., Meleney, E., & Vetter, L. *Counseling girls and women—awareness, analysis, action.* Kansas City, Missouri: University of Missouri and Missouri Department of Labor and Industrial Relations, March, 1966.

Blau, P.M., Gustad, J.W., Jessor, R., Parnes, H.S., & Wilcock, R.C. Occupational choice: A conceptual framework. *Industrial and Labor Relations Review,* 1956, *9,* 531-543.

Bruemmer, L. The condition of women in society today: A review—Part I. *Journal of the National Association of Women Deans and Counselors,* 1969, *33,* 19-22.

Bruemmer, L. The condition of women in society today: An annotated bibliography—Part 2. *Journal of the National Association of Women Deans and Counselors,* 1970, *33,* 89-95.

Crites, J.O. *Vocational psychology.* New York: McGraw-Hill, 1969.
Crites, J.O. Measurement of vocational maturity in adolescence. *Psychological Monographs,* American Psychological Association, 1965.
Entwistle, D.R. & Greenberger, E. *A survey of cognitive styles in Maryland ninth graders: IV: Views of women's roles.* Baltimore: Center for the Study of Social Organization of Schools, Johns Hopkins University, November, 1970.
Eyde, L.D. Eliminating barriers to career development of women. *Personnel and Guidance Journal,* 1970, *49,* 24-27.
Farmer, H.S. & Bohn, M.J., Jr. Home-career conflict reduction and the level of career interest in women. *Journal of Counseling Psychology,* 1970, *17,* 228-232.
Goldberg, P. Are women prejudiced against women? *Trans-Action,* 1968, April, 28-30.
Gray-Shellberg, L., Villareal, S., & Stone, S. Resolution of career conflicts: The double standard in action. Paper presented at 80th Annual Convention of the American Psychological Association, Honolulu, Hawaii, September, 1972 (mimeo).
Harmon, L.W. The childhood and adolescent career plans of college women. *Journal of Vocational Behavior,* 1971, *1,* 45-46.
Harmon, L.W. Anatomy of career commitment in women. *Journal of Counseling Psychology,* 1970, *17,* 77-80.
Harvey, D.W.H. The validity of Holland's Vocational Preference Inventory for adult women. ((Doctoral dissertation, The University of Connecticut) Ann Arbor, Michigan: University Microfilms, 1972. No. 72-14, 234.
Holland, J.L. *The psychology of vocational choice.* Waltham, Mass.: Blaisdell Publishing Company, 1966.
Holland, J.L. & Whitney, D.R. *Changes in the vocational plans of college students: Orderly or random?* Iowa City: Research and Development Division, American College Testing Program, April, 1968. (ACT Research Report No. 25)
Holland, J.L. & Whitney, D.R. Career development. *Review of Educational Research,* 1969, *39,* 227-235.
Horner, M.S. Fail: Bright women. *Psychology Today,* 1969, *3*(6), 36-41.
Kaley, M.M. Attitudes toward the dual role of the married professional woman. *American Psychologist,* 1971, *26,* 301-306.
Kievit, M.B. *Review and synthesis of research on women in the world of work.* Columbus, Ohio: ERIC Clearinghouse on Vocational and Technical Education, The Center for Vocational and Technical Education, The Ohio State University, March, 1972. (Information Series No. 56)
Kriger, S.F. Need achievement and perceived parental child-rearing attitudes of career women and homemakers. *Journal of Vocational Behavior,* 1972, *2,* 419-432.
Levine, A.G. Marital and occupational plans of women in professional schools: Law, medicine, nursing, teaching. (Doctoral dissertation, Yale University) Ann Arbor, Michigan, University Microfilms, 1969. No. 69-13, 353.
McMillan, M.R. Attitudes of college men toward career involvement of married women. *Vocational Guidance Quarterly,* 1972, *21,* 8-11.
Matthews, E.E. The counselor and the adult woman. *Journal of the National Association of Women Deans and Counselors,* 1969, *32,* 115-122.
Meier, H.C. Mother-centeredness and college youths' attitudes toward social equality for women: Some empirical findings. *Journal of Marriage and the Family,* 1972, *34,* 115-121.
Meyer, M.M. Patterns of perceptions and attitudes toward traditionally masculine and feminine occupations through childhood and adolescence. (Doctoral dissertation, Michigan State University) Ann Arbor, Michigan: University Micro-

films, 1970. No. 70-15, 084.

Mulvey, M.C. Psychological and sociological factors in prediction of career patterns of women. *Genetic Psychology Monographs,* 1963, *68,* 309-386.

Murphy, G. *New approaches to counseling girls in the 1960s.* Washington, D.C.: Women's Bureau, U.S. Department of Labor, 1966.

Nagely, D.L. Traditional and pioneer working mothers. *Journal of Vocational Behavior,* 1971, *1,* 331-341.

National Vocational Guidance Association. *Counseling girls and women over the life span.* Washington, D.C.: National Vocational Guidance Association, Division of the American Personnel and Guidance Association, 1972.

Nelson, H.Y. & Goldman, P.R. Attitudes of high school students and young adults toward the gainful employment of married women. *The Family Coordinator,* 1969, *18,* 251-255.

Oppenheimer, V.K. The sex-labeling of jobs. *Industrial Relations,* 1968, *7,* 219-234.

Osipow, S.H. Implications for career education of research and theory on career development. Paper presented at National Conference on Career Education for Deans of Colleges of Education, Columbus, Ohio, April, 1972.

Osipow, S.H. *Theories of career development.* New York: Appleton-Century-Crofts, 1968.

Psathas, G. Toward a theory of occupational choice for women. *Sociology and Social Research,* 1968, *52,* 253-268.

Putnam, B.A. & Hansen, J.C. Relationship of self-concept and feminine role concept to vocational maturity in young women. *Journal of Counseling Psychology,* 1972, *19,* 436-440.

Roe, A. Early determinants of vocational choice. *Journal of Counseling Psychology,* 1957, *4,* 212-217.

Rossi, A.S. Who wants women scientists? In Mattfeld, J.A. and Van Aken, C.G. (Eds.) *Women and the scientific professions.* Cambridge, Mass.: The M.I.T. Press, 1965.

Samler, J. Where do counseling psychologists work? What do they do? What should they do? In Thompson, A.S. and Super, D.E. *The professional preparation of counseling psychologists: Report of the 1964 Greyston Conference.* New York: Bureau of Publications, Teachers College, Columbia University, 1964, 43-68.

Schlossberg, N.K. and Goodman, J. A woman's place: Children's sex stereotyping of occupations. *Vocational Guidance Quarterly,* 1972, *20,* 266-270.

Shea, J.R., Spitz, R.S., & Zeller, F.A. *Dual careers: A longitudinal study of labor market experience of women.* Columbus, Ohio: Center for Human Resource Research, The Ohio State University, May, 1970. (Volume I)

Simpson, L.A. A study of employing agents' attitudes toward academic women in higher education. (Doctoral dissertation, Pennsylvania State University) Ann Arbor, Michigan: University Microfilms, 1969. No. 69-9810.

Smith, E.D. & Herr, E.L. Sex differences in the maturation of vocational attitudes among adolescents. *Vocational Guidance Quarterly,* 1972, *20,* 177-182.

Suniewick, N. Beyond the findings: Some interpretations and implications for the future. In Astin, H.S., Suniewick, N. and Dweck, S. *Women: A bibliography on their education and careers.* Washington, D.C.: Human Service Press, 1971, 11-26.

Super, D.E. Self-concepts in vocational development. In Super, D.E., et al. *Career development: self concept theory.* New York: CEEB Research Monograph No. 4, 1963(a).

Super, D.E. Vocational development in adolescence and early adulthood: tasks and behaviors. In Super, D.E. et al. *Career development: self-concept theory.*

New York: CEEB Research Monograph No. 4, 1963(b).

Super, D.E. *The psychology of careers.* New York: Harper and Row, 1957.

Tangri, S.F.S. Role-innovation in occupational choice among college women. (Doctoral Dissertation, The Univesrity of Michigan) Ann Arbor, Michigan: University Microfilms, 1970. No. 70-4207.

Tennyson, W.W. Career development. *Review of Educational Research,* 1968, *38,* 346-361.

Tucker, B.Z. Feminine sex-role and occupational choice: A study of self and intergroup perceptions of three groups of women. (Doctoral dissertation, Temple University) Ann Arbor, Michigan: University Microfilms, 1971. No. 71-10, 837.

Turner, B.F. Socialization and career orientation among black and white college women. Paper presented at 80th Annual Convention of the American Psychological Association, Honolulu, Hawaii, September, 1972.

Vetter, L. *Career patterns of a national sample of women.* Columbus, Ohio: The Center for Vocational and Technical Education, The Ohio State University, in process.

Watley, D.J. & Kaplan, R. Career or marriage?: Aspirations and achievements of able young women. *Journal of Vocational Behavior,* 1971, *1,* 29-43.

Westervelt, E.M. Woman as a compleat human being. *Journal of the National Association of Women Deans and Counselors,* 1966, *29,* 150-156.

Wolfson, K.T.P. Career development of college women. (Doctoral dissertation, University of Minnesota) Ann Arbor, Michigan: University Microfilms, 1972. No. 72-20, 160.

Women's Bureau, U.S. Department of Labor. *Counseling Girls Toward New Perspectives.* Washington, D.C.: Women's Bureau, 1966.

Women's Bureau, U.S. Department of Labor. *Expanding opportunities for girls: Their special counseling needs.* Washington, D.C.: Women's Bureau, 1970.

Women's Bureau, U.S. Department of Labor. *Women workers today.* Washington, D.C.: Women's Bureau, 1971.

Women's Bureau, U.S. Department of Labor. *The myth and the reality.* Washington, D.C.: Women's Bureau, March, 1972(a).

Women's Bureau, U.S. Department of Labor. *Twenty facts on women workers.* Washington, D.C.: Women's Bureau, 1972(b).

Zytowski, D.G. Toward a theory of career development for women. *Personnel and Guidance Journal,* 1969, *47,* 660-664.

Chapter 2

CAREER DEVELOPMENT OF YOUNG WOMEN DURING THE POST-HIGH SCHOOL YEARS*

HELEN S. ASTIN AND THELMA MYINT

This study, utilizing the Project TALENT Data Bank, was designed to study the career development of 5,387 women during the five-year period after high school. Multiple-discriminant analysis was the primary method of analysis utilized in this study. From the predictor variables employed, the post-high school experiences were the best determinants of career outcomes. Educational attainment and marital-familial status best predicted whether women would choose to pursue careers in the sciences, professions, and teaching or to be housewives and office workers. Of the personal variables, scholastic aptitudes—in particular those related to mathematics—and socioeconomic status, as well as early career choices, were the best predictors. With respect to the patterns of stability and change in career plans over time, brighter women either maintained or raised their vocational aspirations whereas the less academically capable women planned on less demanding careers.

THIS STUDY explores the career development of women during the five-year period after high school. It was initiated by queries such as (a) What personal characteristic and post-high school experiences affect young women's career choices? (b) How stable is career choice between these two points in time? (c) How well can career patterns five years after high school graduation be predicted from measures of selected personal characteristics and post-high school experiences? (d) Which of the personal and post-high school variables utilized are the better predictors?

To give the reader a greater understanding of the problem of vocational choice and development, a brief review of some of the theoretical positions and the relevant empirical data follows.

---

*The research reported herein was performed pursuant to a grant with the Office of Education, United States Department of Health, Education, and Welfare, Grant No. OEG-3-9-090027-0017(010).

From Journal of Counseling Psychology, Monograph, July 1971, 18 (4), 369-393.

THEORETICAL ORIENTATIONS AND CONCEPTUAL FRAMEWORKS

Super (1951, 1953, 1957), Roe (1956), Ginzberg, Ginsburg, Axelrad, and Herma (1951), and Holland (1959) regard vocational behavior as a developmental process whereby a person makes vocational decisions that are congruent with his or her self-concept or personal orientation. Tiedeman (Tiedeman, O'Hara, & Baruch, 1963; Tiedeman, O'Hara, & Matthews, 1958), on the other hand, takes a psychosocial approach and emphasizes more the person's social environment and the influence that it exerts upon his vocational development. He also stresses the decision-making process that underlies vocational behavior. With respect to this process, Hilton (1962) suggests that the primary motive in decision making is to maintain a low level of cognitive dissonance. Whereas Strong (1943) sees interests as primary factors in decision making, Rosenberg (1957) reports that values are the primary influences. Holland (1962) agrees with this view but he adds that a person searches for a work environment that is congruent with his personal orientation. Blau, Gustad, Jessor, Parnes, and Wilcock (1956), on the other hand, perceive the decision-making process as being strongly governed by expectations of future outcomes.

Besides attempting to construct a theory of vocational development, scientists have formulated concepts geared to operational definitions and measurement. Thus, empirical research has attempted to conceptualize and measure variables that account for occupational behavior. On the one hand, personal variables can be defined in terms of a person's sex, abilities, aptitudes, interests, values, needs, and motives, and, on the other hand, environmental experiences are reflected by one's socioeconomic status, parents' attitudes, peers, and experiences with school and other institutions.

EMPIRICAL RESEARCH

Many studies have investigated the stability of occupational choices over periods of time (Astin, 1963; Campbell, 1965; Clark, 1961; Davis, 1962; Holland & Nichols, 1964; Rosenberg, 1957). A wealth of studies also concerns the prediction of career choices. Roe (1953), using the life history approach and test data, compared male psychologists and anthropologists to biologists and physicists. She found that anthropologists and psychologists earn about the same scores on verbal tests; however, psychologists do significantly better than anthropologists on measures of mathematical ability and spatial relations. On the other hand, differences between the natural scientists and social scientists in spatial relations aptitude are not significant. Cultural background and sex were also differentiating variables in career choice. For example, women choose teaching more often, whereas men prefer engineering. Ten years later Astin (1963), studying the career expectations of graduating college seniors, reported that later career choices could be predicted from major field choices as freshmen.

Among students aspiring to a certain career, those who are least like the majority are the ones who are most likely to change to a different choice. For example, "masculine" occupations (those initially chosen more often by men than by women) lose more women than men over time, just as occupations that are initially preferred by women lose fewer women over time. Thus, women who at first choose masculine occupations (such as engineering) tend to change to more feminine occupations (such as teaching) later on. Similarly, occupations that initially attract the more academically able students tend to lose relatively more of their less able students later on (Davis, 1965; Nichols, 1964; Werts, 1966). In explanation, Astin (1967) reported that career changes occur as a result of personal development and of educational experiences that enable students to define their vocational goals more realistically.

Efforts to measure vocational maturity have been reported by some investigators. Super (1960), in a longitudinal study of 105 boys in the ninth grade, measured vocational maturity at different developmental stages. Similarly, Gribbons and Lohnes (1969) initiated a longitudinal study designed to measure and describe career patterns from early adolescence into early adulthood. One of their goals was to develop a scale of vocational maturity that could predict career patterns. They reported that (a) vocational maturity was predictive of subsequent vocational aspirations and plans and (b) the educational and occupational goals of young people become more realistic over time.

Cooley (1963) in his study *Career Development of Scientists* and Cooley and Lohnes (1968) in their monograph *Predicting Development of Young Adults* attempted to predict career outcomes and to differentiate career groups on the basis of antecedent personal characteristics. They reported that differences among individuals which result in different choice behaviors can be described adequately by locating individuals as points in a multidimensional behavior space. Employing the group multiple-discriminant analysis technique, they illustrated the separation of career groups and, from the loadings of the predictor variables, defined the different dimensions.

Little research or few attempts at constructing a theory have been directed toward the career development of women, however.

Tyler (1964) conducted a longitudinal study of interests, abilities, and personal and social characteristics at different developmental levels in order to identify the antecedents of scientific interests in boys and of career interests in girls. She reported that science interests, as measured by the Strong Vocational Interest Blank (SVIB), in most cases crystallize before the age of fourteen and that they tend to persist. The male subjects with scientific interests and the female subjects with career interests were differentiated from those without such interests primarily by their having masculine-oriented activities and interests. Although abilities and achievements did not differentiate the boys with science interests from those with nonscience interests, the career-oriented girls exhibited greater abilities and achievements at all developmental levels than did the noncareer-oriented girls.

In 1964, Roe, after giving considerable thought to the meaning of "career" for American women, stated that "studies of occupational histories for men and women may require different concepts." Some studies have focused on the behavioral and personal characteristics of career-oriented versus noncareer-oriented women (Elton & Rose, 1967; Gysbers, Johnston, & Gust, 1968; Harmon, 1967; Rand, 1968). Astin, (1968a, 1968b) using Project TALENT data, studied the career development of girls during the high school years. The present study may be considered an adjunct to those studies, since it replicated the design, but the time focus shifted from the high school years to five years after high school.

OBJECTIVES OF STUDY

The study reported here sought insights into the psychosocial aspects of career development in young women. Hopefully these insights will help young women make more appropriate educational plans and vocational decisions.

The war years saw a shortage of male labor; this resulted in an influx of women into the labor force. Although immediately after the war the proportion of working women decreased somewhat, still the overall proportion has been increasing steadily. One may describe the post-war years as a time of revolution in women's employment. The 1940 Census indicated that the proportion of females (14 years and over) in the labor force was 27 percent and by 1965 this proportion had risen to 37 percent. In actual numbers, the increase is even more phenomenal: from 14 million to 26 million (United States Department of Commerce, 1967). More recently, such organizations as NOW (National Organization for Women), Radical Women, and other women's liberation groups have given added impetus to the cause of women's actualization and participation in the world of work, and we may expect to see continuous and large increases of women in the labor force. Thus an understanding of the influences on the career development of women becomes of great importance.

This study has two goals: (a) to isolate antecedent factors (measures obtained during the senior year in high school) that predict later career choices (five years after high school) and (b) to determine the factors that relate to career change and career stability during the five post-high school years. The specific questions it tries to answer are as follows:

1. What personal characteristics of twelfth-grade girls predict their vocational choices five years after high school?

2. What college and other post-high school experiences affect the career plans of women?

3. What are the personal and intellectual traits of women who persist in a career as opposed to the traits of those who change their career plans?

METHOD

Sample

The study utilized longitudinal data on a national sample of women from the Project TALENT Data Bank. The sample consisted of female subjects who had been tested in 1960 when they were seniors in high school. They were followed up in the fall of 1961 (one year after high school) and again in January 1966 (approximately five years after high school). Project TALENT was initiated by the American Institutes for Research and the University of Pittsburgh with support from the United States Office of Education. In 1960, approximately 100,000 twelfth-grade students in more than 1,300 secondary schools were selected for a random stratified sample. The stratifying variables were (a) school category—public, parochial, and private; (b) location—geographic region and city size; (c) size of senior class. The 1960 sample members were tested for two days with a battery of tests and questionnaires that yielded about 2,000 items of information about each student, including aptitude and achievement test scores and information on activities, preferences, aspirations, and family background (Flanagan, Dailey, Shaycoft, Gorham, Orr, & Goldberg, 1962).

In 1965, follow-up data were obtained from about one-third of the original respondents. The 1965 follow-up was a mailed questionnaire which contained items of information on employment, education, and marital history since 1960.

Because of this study's special focus and the method of analysis, the sample for most of the analyses was a subsample of the original Project TALENT group. The inclusion of a subject in the subsample depended on whether she had provided data in the 1960 survey as well as in the 1965 followup. Thus the study sample comprised 17,009 cases. In order to equalize the *ns* in the ten career groups somewhat, the authors resampled within each career category (see Table

2-I). The resultant sample of 7,002 cases was further reduced to 5,387 because some data were incomplete.

TABLE 2-I
Distribution of Subjects in the 10 Career Groups before and after Sampling

Career groups	*ns* in 1960	Resampling ratio	*ns* after resampling
Natural Sciences	454	All	454
Professions	355	All	355
Teaching	3,694	1/3	1,231
Health Fields	2,144	1/3	715
Business	501	All	501
Arts	555	All	555
Social Service/ Social Sciences	661	1/2	330
Office Work	4,539	1/3	1,513
Housewife	1,463	1/3	487
Miscellaneous	2,643	1/3	881
Total	17,009	—	7,022

This sample was used for the multivariate analyses. However, all 17,009 cases were used to examine patterns of stability and change in career choices. The large shrinkage in sample size yielded a non-representative sample which does not permit accurate estimates of population parameters. However, having a representative sample was not crucial since the primary interest was in the relationship and interaction of the variables and in their influence on career choices.

Instruments

The measures used, i.e. the predictor variables and the criterion variables, were developed from information furnished by the students in the sample during the 1960 and 1965 assessments. The selection of variables was based on an a priori judgment of measures that could be meaningful and useful as predictors of career choice.

Personal Characteristics

The thirty-six personal variables were test scores and other information obtained while the students were in the twelfth grade: five information test scores, six aptitude and achievement test scores, three temperament scales, four interest scores, ten measures of career plans, counseling experiences regarding college plans or future occupations, status of physical health, father's encouragement of going to college, socioeconomic index, grades in high school, and life goals.

The information test scores assessed the student's knowledge in many areas. In selecting the five areas, the authors tried to include some that would reflect masculine as well as feminine interests. The scores included were from subtests in Literature, Art, Mathematics, Mechanics, and Total Information (a composite of all the information subtest scores). The aptitude and achievement tests were selected to measure abstract thinking, verbal skills, and mathematical aptitudes. They included the following test scores: Total English, Reading Comprehension, Total Mathematics, Mechanical Reasoning, Creativity, and Abstract Reasoning. Although both Reading Comprehension and Abstract Reasoning are tests of reasoning, Reading Comprehension is primarily a measure of verbal ability. The Creativity Test was primarily a measure of ingenuity.

The Project TALENT Interest Inventory consisted of seventeen interest scales, from which four that represent divergent patterns of interest were selected: Physical Science, Literary/Linguistic, Social Service, Business/Managerial. The three temperament scales were Sociability, Impulsivity, and Mature Personality.

The socioeconomic index was derived from nine items in the Student Information Blank; these included such things as parents' education, parents' occupation, modern conveniences in the home, and number of books in the home.

Life goals comprised two dichotomous variables (plans for a college degree and plans for an advanced degree). Health status and grades in high school were continuous variables.

Scores on the measures of twelfth-grade career plans were based on the ten career groups which constituted the ten criterion variables. Each career choice was classified into the appropriate group; this classification is discussed in the section below entitled Criterion Variables.

Post-High School Experiences

The thirteen post-high school variables were measures obtained from the five-year follow-up. They covered experiences since high school, such as educational status, i.e. whether the person has attended one or more colleges, whether she is or has been to graduate school, whether she has received a degree, and if so, what. Marital status, number of children, and number of jobs the subject held since high school were also included in this category.

Criterion Variables

In any study of career development, the question of occupational classification is difficult. What are the most meaningful and appropriate categories into which to sort occupations? Scientists have used various criteria to classify occupations. Some classifications have been made on the basis of activities performed, others on the personal characteristics of those in the occupations. The degree of skill required in an occupation also has served as a basis of classification. This study employs an a priori classification of occupations that represents a compromise of the following considerations: research-based schemes, the limits imposed by the categories originally used in the Project TALENT study, and the numbers of subjects in each category. To illustrate a problem encountered in developing the ten-group classification, it should be pointed out that the authors were forced to classify together Biological and Physical Sciences because of the small number of women choosing physical sciences. The same was true with the Social Service/Social Science groups which were combined because of the limits imposed by the small number of women who choose the social sciences. Moreover, the category of Housewife is a troublesome one as it represents in some sense a transcendent category and is not a career group similar to the others. This is especially bothersome with the Project TALENT data since the subjects were forced to indicate a choice of either housewife or another career plan. The occupational information used for the development of criterion measures came from an open-ended question in the five-year follow-up survey. The responses to this open-ended question were coded into thirty-one careers by the Project TALENT staff and these were used to develop the ten-group classification. These same thirty-one career choices also were listed in the Student Inventory Blank, a questionnaire the students completed while in the twelfth grade. The classification used in the present study was as follows:

1. Natural Sciences
   (Mathematician, physical scientist, biological scientist, engineer)
2. Professions
   (Physician, dentist, lawyer, pharmacist, clergyman)
3. Teaching
   (Teacher, librarian)
4. Health Fields
   (Nurse, medical or dental technician)
5. Business
   (Businessman, accountant)
6. Arts
   (Artist, entertainer, writer)
7. Social Service/Social Sciences
   (Social worker, social scientist)
8. Office Work
   (Secretary, office clerk, typist)
9. Housewife
10. Miscellaneous

(All other choices: Sales; armed forces; protective, skilled structural service; farmer; and unclassified).

Statistical Analysis

The study utilized two methods of analysis. The first, multiple-discriminant analysis, dealt with the prediction of occupational choices five years after high school. The second used univariate statistics. In order to study occupational stability and change, *t* ratios were employed to evaluate mean differences between groups maintaining the same career plans and those changing plans over the five-year span. The groups were compared on selected aptitude and interest measures.[1]

To assess the degree to which the personal characteristics of twelfth-grade girls and their later experiences predict vocational choices five years after high school, a multivariate statistical procedure, multiple-discriminant analysis, was most appropriate. The multiple-discriminant analysis procedures summarize the predictive value of the antecedent variables by reducing them to a few discriminant functions. The discriminant functions separate the criterion groups on the basis of their centroids (group mean vectors) and dispersions (group variances). The composition of each function is reflected in the differential predictive value of each of the antecedent variables.

The discriminant analysis procedure also produces "centour" scores which reflect the extent to which a subject resembles the members in each of the ten career groups. The centour score is a converted discriminant score interpreted as a centile score. Therefore, the probability of a person's membership in a particular group depends on the similarity of his profile to the group's mean profile.

Three discriminant analyses were used to examine the predictive value of each battery of tests, i.e. personal versus post-high school measures; one included the thirty-six personal variables obtained when the subjects were twelfth graders; the second included the thirteen post-high school variables; and the third both sets of variables (personal and post-high school experiences).

The second set of analyses dealt with the question of stability and change in career plans. For this purpose, each subject was classified as a "persister," a "defector," or a "recruit" on the basis of her career choice in the twelfth grade and her career choice five years later. For instance, if she chose one of the natural sciences in the twelfth grade and the same career five years later, she was classified as a persister. If, on the other hand, she shifted to another choice, she was categor-

---

[1]The multivariate discriminant analyses utilized the sample of 5,387 cases, whereas the univariate analyses were done with the sample of 17,009 cases. The distribution of career choices and shifts over time were based on a weighted sample of 7,901,372 subjects.

ized as (a) a natural science defector and (b) as a recruit to the career she chose in the five-year follow-up survey. Consequently, the 17,009 subjects were classified in thirty subgroups:

1. Natural Sciences: Persisters ($n = 58$), defectors ($n = 317$), recruits ($n = 30$)
2. Professions: Persisters ($n = 38$), defectors ($n = 237$), recruits ($n = 48$)
3. Teaching: Persisters ($n = 599$), defectors ($n = 392$), recruits ($n = 636$)
4. Health Fields: Persisters ($n = 232$), defectors ($n = 307$), recruits ($n = 144$)
5. Business: Persisters ($n = 32$), defectors ($n = 341$), recruits ($n = 106$)
6. Arts: Persisters ($n = 82$), defectors ($n = 368$), recruits ($n = 72$)
7. Social Service/Social Sciences: Persisters ($n = 203$), defectors ($n = 45$), recruits ($n = 117$)
8. Office Work: Persisters ($n = 369$), defectors ($n = 818$), recruits ($n = 394$)
9. Housewife: Persisters ($n = 201$), defectors ($n = 169$), recruits ($n = 1{,}454$)
10. Miscellaneous: Persisters ($n = 149$), defectors ($n = 430$), recruits ($n = 1{,}454$).

The persisters, defectors, and recruits were compared on the following measures from the Project TALENT Battery: (a) *aptitude and achievement measures*—Grand Total Information, English Total, Reading Comprehension, Creativity, Mechanical Reasoning, Abstract Reasoning, and Mathematics Total and (b) *interest measures*—Physical Science, Literary/Linguistic, Social Service, and Business/Managerial. The subjects also were compared on high school grades and socioeconomic status.

The statistical significance of mean differences on these measures between persisters and defectors, persisters and recruits, and defectors and recruits within each career group was evaluated by means of t ratios. In addition, the means and standard deviation on six achievement and interest measures for the total initial (twelfth grade) and total final (five years after high school) groups choosing each of the ten career fields were computed in order to ascertain the extent of differentiation among the groups over time. The results and discussion of the career stability and change patterns follow the presentation of the findings utilizing the multivariate analyses.

RESULTS AND DISCUSSION

Three separate discriminant analyses were performed using different sets of predictor variables in order to ascertain the predictive value of early personal measures as compared with later experiences, to evaluate the interaction of personal variables with post-high school experiences, and to ascertain what effect post-high school experiences have on career outcomes after accounting for the effect of personal characteristics.

The results of the three discriminant analyses are presented below.

First Discriminant Analysis

The first discriminant analysis in the prediction of career plans five years after high school utilized the thirty-six personal measures as predictor variables, including eighteen test scores, fifteen items from the Student Information Blank (ten of which comprised the students' career choices in the twelfth grade), cumulative grade point average in high school, information on whether the girls had counseling about college or career, health status, and the degree to which the girls were encouraged by their fathers to go to a college. Added to these were a socioeconomic index and the student's goals with respect to higher education.

The criterion variables were the ten career groups. Each subject was classified into one of these groups on the basis of her career choice at the time of the five-year follow-up.

The discriminant analysis yielded five functions with significant canonical correlations. A canonical correlation represents the product-moment correlation between linear functions of the two sets of variables, i.e. between the predictor variables and the ten career groups scored as dummy variables. The discriminating information accounted for by each of the five functions was 37.70, 25.10, 12.80, 8.45, and 5.86 percent, respectively.

Table 2-II presents the centroids of the groups in reduced space for each of the five discriminant functions. They are listed in rank order. Table 2-III reports the significant weights of the variables for each of the five discriminant functions.

The first discriminant function separates the natural sciences, social service/social sciences, the professions, and teaching groups, (the last three having rather similar centroids of .890, .865, and .812) from the housewife and office work groups. The predictor variables with the highest weights on this function are Mathematics Information, Mathematics Total, Information Total, Literature Information, Reading Comprehension, aspirations for an advanced degree, and aspirations for a college degree. The predictor variable of twelfth-

TABLE 2-II

Centroids of Groups in Reduced Space: 36 Personal Variables

Rank order	First discriminant function	Second discriminant function	Third discriminant function	Fourth discriminant function	Fifth discriminant function
1	1.108 Sciences	.386 Arts	2.108 Sciences	1.520 Arts	.838 Sciences
2	.890 Social Service	.344 Teaching	.703 Professions	.195 Business	.324 Arts
3	.865 Professions	.168 Business	.639 Social Service	.099 Professions	.093 Health Fields
4	.812 Teaching	.132 Office Work	.235 Business	.099 Miscellaneous	.079 Miscellaneous
5	.540 Arts	.074 Housewife	.187 Arts	.083 Social Service	.052 Teaching
6	.379 Health Fields	.048 Social Service	.182 Miscellaneous	.021 Health Fields	.014 Business
7	.005 Business	— .003 Sciences	—.008 Housewife	—.015 Housewife	.000 Office Work
8	—.274 Miscellaneous	— .078 Miscellaneous	—.050 Office Work	—.135 Office Work	— .039 Housewife
9	—.504 Housewife	— .285 Professions	—.231 Health Fields	—.138 Teaching	— .621 Social Service
10	—.670 Office Work	—1.745 Health Fields	—.328 Teaching	—.740 Sciences	—1.368 Professions
Canonical *R*	.614	.501	.358	.291	.242

Note. Sciences stands for Natural Sciences, and Social Service includes Social Service/Social Sciences.

grade career choice of office work and business carried negative weights. Judging from the weights of the aptitude, and achievement variables, the underlying dimension of this function may be interpreted as overall scholastic aptitude. Girls who made higher aptitude scores while in high school were more likely to aspire to careers in the natural sciences, social services or the social sciences, the professions, and teaching five years later, whereas those with lower academic ability tended to plan careers in office work or to be housewives. One may also interpret the separation of the career groups as indicative of a career commitment dimension. That is, at one end of the continuum are careers requiring greater preparation and commitment, whereas at the other end are careers a woman can enter without much academic preparation. The high weights that tests of mathematical aptitude and achievement carry in the prediction of career outcomes five years after high school are of special interest. A similar finding was reported by Astin (1968) in predicting career choices of girls during the high school years. Girls from higher socioeconomic backgrounds were more likely to choose careers in the sciences (natural and social), the professions, and teaching, and this likelihood was even greater if they perceived their fathers as encouraging them to pursue higher education.

The second function separates the health fields as a career choice from the arts and teaching distinctly with a negative centroid of 1.745 for the health fields as compared with a centroid of .386 for the arts and of .344 for teaching. The predictor variable with the greatest weight in this function is twelfth-grade career choice in the health fields (—.92); on the other hand, early choices in the arts and teaching carried positive weights (.18 and .37, respectively). The dimension that emerges from this function is "early occupational commitment." Because of the early and specific training required in the health fields, such as nursing, one would expect girls going into that field to decide early and to hold to this choice over time, since the greatest predictor of this career outcome was a similar choice five years earlier.

The third discriminant function separates the natural sciences (centroid of 2.108), the professions (centroid of .703), and the social service/social sciences (centroid of .639) from teaching (centroid of —.328) and health fields (centroid of —.231). This dimension reflects a masculine–feminine orientation. According to this dimension, girls who in the twelfth grade chose a natural science career aspired to an advanced degree, had a strong interest in physical science, and were likely, five years later, to plan careers in the natural sciences, the professions, or the social sciences rather than in teaching, the health fields, or office work. The aptitudes that carried positive significant weights on this function were Mathematics Total, Mathematics Information,

TABLE 2-III

Scaled Discriminant Vectors: 36 Personal Variables

First discriminant function		Second discriminant function		Third discriminant function		Fourth discriminant function		Fifth discriminant function	
Variable	Weight	Variable	Weight	Variable	Weight	Variable	Weight	Variable	Weight
Mathematics Information	.75	"Teaching"	.37	"Natural Sciences"	.66	"Arts"	.87	"Natural Sciences"	.51
Mathematics Total	.67	"Arts"	.18	Advanced degree plans	.40	Grades	—.20	"Arts"	.22
Information Total	.65	"Office Work"	.14	Physical Science Interest	.36	Physical Science Interest	—.21	"Health Fields"	.19
Literature Information	.61	College degree plans	.11	"Professions"	.32	"Office Work"	—.22	College degree plans	.18
Reading Comprehension	.55	"Professions"	—.16	Mathematics Total	.29	"Natural Sciences"	—.29	Mechanical Reasoning	.15
Advanced degree plans	.53	Physical Science Interest	—.18	Mathematics Information	.24	Social Service Interest	—.29	Mature Personality	—.14
College degree plans	.51	"Health Fields"	—.92	Information Total	.21	"Teaching"	—.35	Advanced degree plans	—.19
"Teaching"	.50			Mechanical Reasoning	.21			"Social Service"	—.42
Literary/Linguistic Interest	.49			"Health Fields"	—.21			"Professions"	—.64
English Total	.47			College degree Plans	—.27				
Socioeconomic status	.46			Social Service Interest	—.37				
Physical Science Interest	.44			"Teaching"	—.56				
Art Information	.43								
Grades	.39								

Variable	Weight
Counseling about college	.37
Creativity	.34
Mechanical Reasoning	.32
Father's encouragement	.30
Mature Personality	.29
Social Service Interest	.26
Mechanical Information	.24
"Natural Sciences"	.21
"Business"	—.21
"Office Work"	—.61

Note: Words in quotes represent the twelfth-grade career choice variable. Only the largest negative and positive weights are shown.

and Mechanical Reasoning.

The fourth discriminant function can best be interpreted as an artistic dimension. It separates the arts criterion group from the natural science group. The largest weight is carried by the twelfth-grade choice of a career in the arts.

The last function that significantly separated the groups placed the natural science group at one end with a centroid of .838 and the professions at the other end with a centroid of −1.368. The social service/social sciences group also was separated from the natural sciences with a centroid of −.621. The significant predictors were twelfth-grade career choices, with positive weights for the natural sciences and the arts and negative weights for the professions and social service/social sciences. Generally, the dimension here is a "people versus things" orientation.

In summary, the first function in this analysis reflects an academic orientation; the second is early occupational commitment or early commitment to the health fields; the third is a masculine–feminine dimension; the fourth is an artistic versus scientific orientation; and the fifth is a people versus things orientation. The most interesting fact to emerge from this analysis is that scholastic aptitudes, especially in mathematics, and high educational aspirations are the best predictors of a career orientation among young women. Moreover, early career choices (such as during the twelfth grade) are predictive of similar career choices five years later.

A hits-and-misses classification to the career groups on the basis of the thirty-six personal predictors was performed. The subjects were sorted into the ten occupational groups on the basis of their discriminant scores, which in turn were converted into centour scores. Table 2-IV reports the results. Of the 5,387 predictions, 2,981 were hits, or correct placements. The overall hit rate was estimated at 41.79%. The criterion groups of teaching and the health fields had the highest hit rates (35.3 and 36.0 percentage points better than chance, respectively). On the other hand, the predictions made about subjects with plans to enter the professions and the arts were the poorest.

Second Discriminant Analysis

The second analysis employed the thirteen variables reflected in experiences of the subjects during the five years after high school with respect to jobs, further education, and marital status. The first three significant discriminant functions accounted for 50.84, 12.53, and 2.59 percent, respectively, of the discriminating information in the thirteen predictor variables.

Table 2-V reports the centroids of the groups and Table 2-VI the positive and negative weights of the predictor variables. The first dis-

TABLE 2-IV

Hits and Misses Classification: 36 Personal Variables

Career groups	1	2	3	4	5	6	7	8	9	10	*n*
Natural Sciences (1)	*58*	11	10	4	0	2	1	0	2	0	88
Professions (2)	5	*38*	16	5	0	6	5	2	7	2	86
Teaching (3)	96	45	*655*	70	17	126	64	13	128	21	1235
Health Fields (4)	16	35	24	*232*	0	9	15	3	31	11	376
Business (5)	10	10	23	5	*15*	14	4	9	42	6	138
Arts (6)	11	9	20	4	2	*81*	7	0	14	6	154
Social Service/ Sciences (7)	20	18	33	11	3	14	*45*	0	17	1	162
Office Work (8)	21	15	72	33	6	33	14	*124*	413	32	763
Housewife (9)	55	47	192	101	20	105	35	107	*923*	70	1655
Miscellaneous (10)	50	36	81	74	7	54	26	45	277	*80*	730
Number of predictions made	342	264	1126	539	70	444	216	303	1854	229	5387
% Correct	16.9	14.4	58.2	43.0	21.4	18.2	20.8	40.9	49.8	34.9	
Expected by chance (%)	1.6	1.6	22.9	7.0	2.6	2.9	3.0	14.2	30.7	13.6	
Better than chance (%)	15.3	12.8	35.3	36.0	18.8	15.3	17.8	26.7	19.1	21.3	

Note: 41.79% hit rate.

TABLE 2-V

Centroids of Groups in Reduced Space: 13 Post-High School Variables

Rank order	First discriminant function	Second discriminant function	Third discriminant function
1	1.35 Sciences	.60 Professions	.82 Sciences
2	1.12 Social Service	.53 Business	.41 Professions
3	1.04 Teaching	.52 Office Work	.15 Social Service
4	.68 Professions	.30 Health Fields	.05 Office Work
5	.39 Arts	.26 Arts	.10 Miscellaneous
6	.14 Business	.23 Miscellaneous	.01 Housewife
7	—.09 Health Fields	.20 Social Service	—.07 Teaching
8	—.28 Miscellaneous	—.11 Sciences	—.20 Business
9	—.61 Housewife	—.15 Teaching	—.26 Arts
10	—.62 Office Work	—.41 Housewife	—.29 Health Fields
Canonical *R*	.713	.354	.161

Note: Sciences stands for Natural Sciences, and Social Service includes Social Service/Social Sciences.

criminant function separates the natural sciences, social service/social sciences, and teaching from office work and housewife. Important predictors included having a BA degree, having attended more than one college[2] as an undergraduate, and having been to graduate school or attending it at the time of the follow-up. Having an AA degree carried a large negative weight. Being married and having children were also negative predictors for careers in sciences and teaching as opposed to being a housewife or doing office work. College and graduate school attendance differentiated girls with different career commitments and plans.

TABLE 2-VI

Scaled Discriminant Vectors: 13 Post-High School Variables

First discriminant function		Second discriminant function		Third discriminant function	
Variable	Weight	Variable	Weight	Variable	Weight
BA degree	.89	Single	.78	Graduate school attendance	.62
Transferred colleges	.78	Looking for job	.20	Single	.19
Attended college	.77	Has worked full time	.18	High school graduate	—.10
Graduate school attendance	.61	Graduate school attendance	—.10	Has advanced degree	—.19
Single	.37	BA degree	—.14	Married	—.20
Has advanced degree	.14	Children	—.57	Has worked full time	—.31
Has worked full time	—.10	Married	—.84	Transferred colleges	—.34
Married	—.35			Attended college	—.37
Has children	—.45				
AA degree	—.89				

Note: Only the largest positive and negative weights are shown.

The second discriminant function separates the criterion groups on a marital status dimension. The only high positive predictor was being single, while the high negative predictors were the variables of being married and having children. The career groups with high centroids on the second discriminant function were professions, business, and office work as opposed to housewife. Single girls approximately twenty-three years old, independent of their educational status, are more likely to plan careers in the professions, business, and office

[2]The variable "transferred colleges" indicates more that a person has continued college, rather than dropping out after a short stay or never going to college.

work than are married women, who often see their present and future career as housewife.

The third discriminant function separates the natural sciences from the health fields. The most important predictor variable is graduate school experience. Women who continue their education to graduate school were more likely to be planning careers in the natural sciences.

The second discriminant analysis indicates that educational experiences and marital status since high school are predictive of women's career choices five years after high school. College graduates and those who indicated that they have been transfer students, rather than having dropped out of or never been to college, were more likely to plan careers in natural sciences, social service/social sciences, teaching, and the professions. Furthermore, graduate school attendance is a significant predictor of career plans in the natural sciences. Finally, single women compared to married women were more likely to plan careers in the professions, in business, and in office work.

An assignment to the ten career groups on the basis of the thirteen post-high school variables yielded a hit rate of 49.91 percent. Table 2-VII reports the results of this sorting of subjects. The highest hit rate was for the teaching group (a 56.7 percent correct rate or 33.8 percentage points better than chance). The second most easily predicted group was the housewife category (a 53% hit rate or 22.3 percentage points better than chance). The predictor variables employed in this analysis were poor measures for predicting the health fields and social service/social sciences careers, whereas, being married and having children were helpful in predicting outcomes such as being or planning to become a housewife.

Third Discriminant Analysis

The third discriminant analysis utilized forty-nine predictor variables, thirty-six personal variables, and thirteen post-high school variables. This analysis resulted in five significant discriminant functions accounting for 53.4, 27.1, 15.6, 12.1, and 9.6 percent, respectively, of the discriminating information in the forty-nine predictor variables. (Since these functions are nonadditive, their sum is not limited to 100%.)

The first function discriminates the criterion groups of natural sciences, social service/social sciences, teaching, and the professions from the office work and housewife groups. This distinction is similar to the one observed in the first and second analyses.

Table 2-IX presents the weights of the variables in each of the discriminant functions. The positive significant weights in the discrimination of the career groups (sciences, social service, teaching, and

TABLE 2-VII

Hits and Misses Classification: 13 Post–High School Variables

Career groups	1	2	3	4	5	6	7	8	9	10	*n*
Natural Sciences (1)	*9*	0	70	0	0	0	0	4	4	1	88
Professions (2)	6	*5*	39	0	1	0	0	18	14	3	86
Teaching (3)	16	13	*932*	0	6	6	0	52	179	31	1235
Health Fields (4)	0	5	95	*0*	1	0	0	86	172	17	376
Business (5)	0	1	43	0	*2*	0	0	39	42	11	138
Arts (6)	0	2	66	0	1	*3*	0	21	52	9	154
Social Service/ Sciences (7)	4	2	120	0	2	1	*0*	7	16	10	162
Office Work (8)	0	0	18	0	6	4	0	*305*	401	29	763
Housewife (9)	0	0	128	0	2	2	0	111	*1396*	16	1655
Miscellaneous (10)	4	3	132	0	4	1	0	191	358	*37*	730
Number of predictions made	39	31	1643	0	25	17	0	834	2634	164	5387
% correct	23.1	16.1	56.7	0	8.0	17.6	0	36.6	53.0	22.6	
Expected by chance (%)	1.6	1.6	22.9	7.0	2.6	2.9	3.0	14.2	30.7	13.6	
Better than chance (%)	21.5	14.5	33.8	—7.0	5.4	14.7	—3.0	22.4	22.3	9.0	

Note: 49.91% hit rate.

TABLE 2-VIII

Centroids of Groups in Reduced Space: 49 Personal and Post–High School Variables

Rank order	First discriminant function	Second discriminant function	Third discriminant function	Fourth discriminant function	Fifth discriminant function
1	1.214 Sciences	.273 Teaching	1.741 Sciences	.516 Office Work	1.549 Arts
2	1.110 Social Service	.244 Housewife	1.053 Professions	.489 Business	.216 Professions
3	1.079 Teaching	.170 Arts	.689 Social Service	.449 Arts	.114 Social Service
4	.682 Professions	.087 Office Work	.512 Business	.081 Teaching	.072 Housewife
5	.422 Arts	.008 Business	.333 Arts	.072 Miscellaneous	.067 Miscellaneous
6	.050 Business	— .082 Miscellaneous	.278 Office Work	— .030 Health Fields	.066 Business
7	.011Health Fields	— .142 Social Service	.239 Miscellaneous	— .087 Professions	— .005 Health Fields
8	— .287 Miscellaneous	— .202 Sciences	— .198 Housewife	— .095 Social Service	— .120 Teaching
9	— .628 Housewife	— .678 Professions	— .308 Teaching	— .310 Housewife	— .377 Office Work
10	— .661 Office Work	—1.794 Health Fields	— .413 Health Fields	—1.546 Sciences	— .517 Sciences
Canonical *R*	.731	.521	.395	.348	.310

Note: Sciences stands for Natural Sciences, and Social Service includes Social Service/Social Sciences.

TABLE 2-IX

Scaled Discriminant Vectors: 49 Personal and Post–High School Variables

First discriminant function		Second discriminant function		Third discriminant function		Fourth discriminant function		Fifth discriminant function	
Variable	Weight	Variable	Weight	Variable	Weight	Variable	Weight	Variable	Weight
BA degree	.86	"Teaching"	.28	"Natural Sciences"	.47	Single	.52	"Arts"	.80
Transferred colleges	.76	"Office Work"	.24	Single	.47	Has worked full time	.22	Socioeconomic status	.23
Attended college	.75	Children	.21	Advanced degree plans	.32	"Arts"	.21	Children	.22
Mathematics Information	.60	Married	.20	"Professions"	.29	Mechanical Reasoning	—.21	Art Information	.21
Graduate school attendance	.59	Mathematics Information	—.21	Physical Science Interest	.27	Total Information	—.22	Literature Information	.13
Mathematics Total	.55	"Professions"	—.22	Children	—.24	Physical Science Interest	—.24	Graduate school attendance	—.15
Information Total	.52	Physical Science Interest	—.27	Social Service Interest	—.32	Advanced degree plans	—.25	"Natural Sciences"	—.16
Literature Information	.49	"Health Fields"	—.87	"Health Fields"	—.35	Mathematics Information	—.25	Business/Managerial Interest	—.17
"Teaching"	.47			"Teaching"	—.42	Mathematics Total	—.29	Social Service Interest	—.25
Reading Comprehension	.44			Married	—.49	Children	—.40	"Teaching"	—.26
College degree plans	.43					"Natural Sciences"	—.46	"Office Work"	—.34
Advanced degree plans	.43					Married	—.57		
Literary/Linguistic Interest	.41								
English Total	.38								

Socioeconomic status	.38
Single	.35
Art Information	.35
Physical Science Interest	.34
Grades	.33
Counseling about college	.30
Abstract Reasoning	.29
Creativity	.27
Father's encouragement	.25
Mature Personality	.24
Social Service Interest	.22
Married	—.33
Children	—.42
"Office Work"	—.48
AA degree	—.86

Note: Only high positive and negative weights are listed. Words in quotes represent twelfth-grade career choices.

the professions) from the noncareer orientation groups (office work and housewife) were carried by selected aptitude variables and by college and graduate school attendance. On the other hand, being married and having children as well as holding an Associate of Arts degree were negative predictors of high career aspirations among young women.

A high socioeconomic status and the father's encouraging the girl to go to college continued to be important predictors of her career orientation five years after high school.

The dimension operating here is one of high aptitude and high educational aspirations. However, pursuing higher education and graduate training were better predictors than were the aptitude test scores, although both sets of variables were important. Nevertheless, the best predictor was completing college.

In the second function, the health fields (centroid = −1.79) and the professions (centroid = −.68) were separated from teaching and housewife. The predictor variable of choosing a career in the health fields while in high school carried the greatest weight (−.87). As was discussed earlier, the dimension is one of early occupational commitment since an early career choice in one of the health fields was the best predictor of the same career choice five years later.

On the basis of its predictors, the third function may be called a masculine–feminine orientation which separates careers in the natural sciences, the professions, and social service/social sciences from those such as nurses, medical or dental technicians, teachers, and housewives. The best predictor variables were choosing a natural science career while in high school, being single five years after high school, and having aspirations for an advanced degree while in the twelfth grade. In other words, girls with these attributes were more likely to be planning careers in the natural sciences or the professions five years after high school. On the other hand, girls who in the twelfth grade chose careers in the health professions or teaching and were married at the time of the follow-up were likely to be planning at that time on careers in the health fields, in teaching, or exclusively as housewives.

The fourth discriminant function separated the choices in office work and business from choices in the natural sciences. Being employed full time after high school and being single were the best predictors of office work and business careers five years after high school. On the other hand, high aptitude scores and high educational aspirations were negative predictors of such career outcomes.

The fifth significant discriminant function can be best described as an artistic orientation. It separates the arts group from all other career groups and, in particular, from the natural sciences and office work groups. The largest weight was carried by the predictor variable of a career choice in the arts while in high school. Coming from a high socioeconomic background and making high scores on the Art Information Test while in high school also were significant predictors. In addition, having children carried a significant weight. This indicates that women with children can and do pursue careers in the arts.

The results that emerged from the third discriminant analysis indicate that graduation from college is the best predictor of career choices in the natural sciences, social service/social sciences, teaching, and the professions, whereas nongraduation predicts doing office work and being a housewife. An early commitment, that is, a twelfth-grade career choice in the health fields, the natural sciences, or the arts, was predictive of similar career choices later on. Moreover, high aptitudes, especially in mathematics, high socioeconomic status, and an encouraging father remain important predictors of a career orientation.

The hits-and-misses classification utilizing the forty-nine predictor variables is presented in Table 2-X. Of the classifications 2,714 were correct, or 50.38 percent. The teaching career group had the highest rate of correct placements, 45.8 percentage points better than chance. Next came the office work and the health fields, with 36.8 percentage points and 36.2 percentage points, respectively, better than chance. Predictions were incorrect most often for the professions and the arts, only 15.6 percentage points and 16.7 percentage points, respectively, better than chance.

Using the forty-nine variables the authors examined the similarities and differences among the career groups. The Mahalanobis distance matrix summarizes the discriminant analysis results on the basis of similarities and differences in the profiles of the groups. The numerical values indicate the similarity between the groups; the smaller the number, the greater is the resemblance between that pair.

Table 2-XI indicates that women with career choices in the natural sciences, the professions, and social service/social sciences are different from women with plans to be housewives, to do office work, or to be in business. Moreover, the women with choices in the natural sciences differ more from women aspiring to the professions such as medicine and law than from women with choices in the social sciences. The interests, aptitudes, and life experiences of women in teaching and the professions are more similar to one another than they are to those of women in the natural sciences.

Summary of the Results of Discriminant Analyses

A brief comparison of the findings that resulted from the three discriminant analyses follows; it is intended to highlight the value of the different sets of variables in predicting career outcomes over time.

TABLE 2-X

Hits and Misses Classification: 49 Personal and Post–High School Variables

Career groups	1	2	3	4	5	6	7	8	9	10	*n*
Natural Sciences (1)	*56*	11	13	4	1	1	2	0	0	0	88
Professions (2)	5	*38*	17	5	0	6	4	4	4	3	86
Teaching (3)	85	39	*755*	67	10	101	58	22	78	20	1285
Health Fields (4)	12	30	21	*231*	0	8	12	14	39	9	376
Business (5)	7	7	21	5	*18*	14	4	22	29	11	138
Arts (6)	8	8	28	4	2	*72*	4	2	22	4	154
Social Service/ Sciences (7)	19	17	44	11	1	13	*45*	1	7	4	162
Office Work (8)	6	14	31	33	13	27	9	*264*	313	53	763
Housewife (9)	27	25	105	101	8	80	17	106	*1141*	45	1655
Miscellaneous (10)	40	32	64	74	11	46	20	83	266	*94*	730
Number of predictions made	265	221	1099	535	64	368	175	518	1899	243	5387
% correct	21.1	17.2	68.7	43.2	28.1	19.6	25.7	51.0	60.1	38.7	
Expected by chance (%)	1.6	1.6	22.9	7.0	2.6	2.9	3.0	14.2	30.7	13.6	
Better than chance (%)	19.5	15.6	45.8	36.2	25.5	16.7	22.7	36.8	29.4	25.1	

Note: 50.38% hit rate.

TABLE 2-XI

Mahalanobis Distance Matrix: 49 Predictor Variables

Career groups	1	2	3	4	5	6	7	8	9	10
Natural Sciences (1)	.00	10.89	9.36	15.69	11.66	13.37	7.71	15.81	15.17	12.13
Professions (2)	10.89	.00	7.12	8.89	7.00	8.57	5.80	9.52	9.83	7.23
Teaching (3)	9.36	7.12	.00	8.37	4.38	4.94	2.94	7.27	6.51	4.81
Health Fields (4)	15.69	8.89	8.37	.00	6.71	9.43	9.12	6.87	6.75	5.07
Business (5)	11.66	7.00	4.38	6.71	.00	4.30	5.14	2.54	3.30	1.90
Arts (6)	13.37	8.57	4.94	9.43	4.30	.00	6.08	6.62	6.13	4.52
Social Service/ Sciences (7)	7.71	5.80	2.94	9.12	5.14	6.08	.00	9.02	8.84	6.17
Office Work (8)	15.81	9.52	7.27	6.87	2.54	6.62	9.02	.00	1.32	1.21
Housewife (9)	15.17	9.83	6.51	6.75	3.30	6.13	8.84	1.32	.00	1.13
Miscellaneous (10)	12.13	7.23	4.81	5.07	1.90	4.52	6.17	1.21	1.13	.00

The four dimensions that emerged as orientations to career outcomes were (a) an aspiration for higher education or an intellectual dimension; (b) a marital status or home commitment dimension; (c) an early career commitment dimension, and (d) a masculinity–femininity dimension.

The first orientation, aspiration for higher education or intellectuality, was the most important predictive dimension of career choices of women. This dimension was reflected in the first discriminant function which accounted for most of the variance in the criterion groups. Moreover, it was equally important in all three separate analyses. Among the post-high school variables, having a bachelor's degree and attending graduate school were the best predictors of careers in the natural sciences, social service/social sciences, and teaching. Lack of these conditions tended to predict more often choices in office work and as a housewife.

The analysis with only the personal variables as predictors suggests that high scores in mathematics as well as other aptitudes (such as English or reading comprehension) predict career choices in the natural sciences, social service/social sciences, teaching, and the professions, whereas women who named Housewife or Office Work as their choices tend to score lower on aptitude and achievement tests. However, the aptitude variables accounted for less of the variance in differentiating the career groups than did the educational measures reflected in college attendance and completion. That is, the personal variables explained 37.3 percent of the variance, compared with 53.8 percent which was explained using the thirteen post-high school variables only.

The third analysis included both sets of predictor variables—personal and post-high school. When both aptitude test scores obtained in high school and post-high school educational variables are introduced, the latter again emerge with higher weights in the prediction of career outcomes among women. The predictor variables—college graduation, mathematical aptitude, general wealth of information, and specific information on literature—were predictive of career choices in the natural sciences, social service/social sciences, and teaching.

The single best predictor was attainment of a BA degree. Marital status or home commitment, the second dimension, appeared in the analysis employing only the thirteen post-high school variables. That is, being married and having children emerged as important predictor variables in separating the occupational groups after the educational status variables had been controlled. However, when the personal variables were also included in the third analysis, marital status carried weights only in the third and fourth discriminant functions of that analysis.

Career commitment, as measured by early career plans, emerged in the second discriminant function of both the first and third discriminant analyses separating the health group from all other career groups and, more specifically, from the arts and teaching groups. The predictive variables with high weights were twelfth-grade career choices in these groups.

The dimension termed masculinity–femininity separated the natural sciences, the professions, and social service/social sciences choices from careers in office work, the health fields, and teaching. This dimension was reflected in the variables that separated the groups in the third discriminant function.

STABILITY AND CHANGE IN THE CAREER PLANS OF YOUNG WOMEN

Thus far, the authors have attempted to examine the personal characteristics of twelfth-grade girls that predict their vocational choices five years after high school. The work, educational, and family experiences after high school that influence these career choices were also examined. In this section, stability and change in career plans of young women following high school is examined. The primary aim is to identify the personal and intellectual characteristics of women who persist in a career choice, as opposed to those who change their plans.

The career expectations of 17,009 (or 7,901,372 weighted sample *N*) young women were examined during the twelfth grade and again five years after high school. Tables 2-XII and 2-XIII present the distribution of career choices and the shifts that occurred during the five-year period after high school. In the twelfth grade, the three most favored choices were teaching, the health fields, and office work. The fewest career choices among high school girls were those in the natural sciences and in the professions. Moreover, these two unpopular choices become even less popular over time and five years after high school, they had lost more than half of their former recruits. The health fields and office work suffered similar losses. The popularity of teaching remained about the same and the choice of housewife almost quadrupled. The stability rate is highest for occupational groups considered feminine in that they usually attract more women than men. That is, more women that earlier chose teaching, the health fields, office work, the arts, and housewife tended to indicate similar preferences five years later, whereas women initially choosing the professions or business careers tended to change those choices. Table 2-XIII indicates that most persons who changed from their initial field tended to move into teaching careers, office work, or the housewife category. Changes into natural sciences or professions oc-

TABLE 2-XII

Career Choice Distribution of Women in the Twelfth-Grade (1960) and 5 Years after High School (1965)

(in Percentages)

Career groups	1960	1965	Stability rate
Natural Sciences	1.8	.6	14.6
Professions	2.1	.8	5.1
Teaching	17.6	15.3	46.9
Health Fields	12.5	6.2	33.5
Business	3.1	2.0	5.2
Arts	3.1	2.0	25.0
Social Service/ Science	3.4	2.3	19.1
Office Work	27.7	15.9	27.9
Housewife	10.7	38.4	60.2
Miscellaneous	18.1	16.5	26.3

Note: The percentages in this table represent population estimates. They are based on a weighted *N* of 7,901,372 cases.

curred less frequently. Thus, shifts take place toward choices that are considered feminine or more appropriate for women. This finding is similar to those reported in earlier studies (Astin, 1968; Davis, 1965; Werts, 1966). People usually change their career plans to occupational groups whose members are similar to themselves with respect to abilities, interests, and other personal characteristics. This increasing homogeneity within groups may result from what the self and others consider appropriate behaviors for women. However, changes may also occur as a result of growing awareness of the skills and aptitudes necessary and appropriate as well as of the length of time and commitment required to complete training in and pursue certain occupations successfully. To discover how much awareness may influence choice, the similarities and differences among persons planning the same careers over time and those shifting their choices were examined.

Since earlier studies (Astin 1967, 1968b) suggested that career changes occur as a result of personal development and educational experiences that enable students to define goals more realistically, three main hypotheses were tested with the data reported here. First, girls who change from an initial career choice in the fields of natural science, teaching, or the professions tend to obtain lower scores on measures of aptitude and achievement than girls who maintain their initial choices in these fields. Similarly, girls who initially aspire to

TABLE 2-XIII

Proportions Shifting from each Career Choice between the Twelfth Grade and 5 Years after High School
(in Percentages)

1960	1965 career groups									
Career groups	1	2	3	4	5	6	7	8	9	10
Natural Sciences (1)	*14.6*	.9	26.3	4.6	2.0	1.4	8.0	8.3	12.9	21.1
Professions (2)	1.3	*5.1*	12.0	12.2	1.1	1.3	5.2	6.2	33.0	22.6
Teaching (3)	.3	1.4	*46.9*	1.6	2.5	3.0	3.6	8.4	23.2	9.2
Health Fields (4)	1.3	.8	8.3	*33.5*	.6	.2	1.1	8.4	29.3	16.6
Business (5)	—	2.1	10.5	.5	*5.2*	.2	.7	26.4	41.3	13.1
Arts (6)	.2	2.4	11.9	2.1	5.1	*25.0*	3.4	7.9	28.8	13.2
Social Service/ Sciences (7)	—	2.9	22.8	4.7	1.6	.7	*19.1*	5.4	27.3	15.3
Office Work (8)	—	.1	2.7	.8	2.5	1.2	.4	*27.9*	49.4	14.9
Housewife (9)	.1	.2	5.0	3.5	.5	.5	.3	13.7	*60.2*	16.1
Miscellaneous (10)	.2	.3	14.1	3.0	2.0	1.4	1.8	14.6	36.4	*26.3*

Note: The career shifts presented in this table are based on a weighted N of 7,901,372 cases.

careers as either housewives or office workers will be more likely to change their plans if they make relatively high scores on measures of aptitude and achievement. Second, girls who change their early career plans, compared with those who persist with their plans, will score lower on measures of interests most characteristic of girls choosing that particular career field. Finally, as a result of the patterns in career shifts over time, the career groups will become more differentiated from one another in terms of the personal characteristics of the individuals in the group.

On the basis of the first hypothesis, it was predicted that the defectors from each one of the career-oriented occupational groups (natural sciences, teaching, the professions, and social service/social sciences) would score significantly lower on the ability measures employed than would the persisters in these groups.* In addition, it follows that the defectors from the housewife and office work groups would score significantly higher than the persisters in these two groups. Table 2-XIV presents the means and standard deviations of the subgroups as well as the mean differences among the three subgroups, persisters, defectors, and recruits, on eight aptitude and achievement measures.

The eight measures chosen were Information Total, English Total, Mathematics Total, Reading Comprehension, Abstract Reasoning, Creativity, Mechanical Reasoning, and grades.

Table 2-XIV indicates that the defectors from the four career-oriented groups—natural sciences, the professions, teaching, and social service/social sciences—scored significantly lower than did the persisters on the aptitude and achievement measures. Moreover, women in the health fields also were likely to shift their initial choice if they achieved lower aptitude scores than did the other women in the group. On the other hand the brighter women who initially planned careers as office workers and housewives were more likely than the less able women to change their plans five years later. Thus, with some exceptions the findings support the first hypothesis. The notable exceptions are in business and the arts; in these fields, although the means of the defector subgroups were lower than those of the persisters, the differences are not statistically significant.

With respect to choices in the arts and business, factors other than academic aptitude are important in decisions to pursue careers in these fields. Perhaps an interest in business and artistic ability are more important in these career choices than are scholastic aptitudes.

*A persister was a person who had the same career plans in the twelfth grade and five years later. A defector was a person who had different plans at the time of the five year follow-up from the plans she expressed in the twelfth grade. A person was classified as a recruit to an occupational group five years after high school if she had different career plans in the twelfth grade.

TABLE 2-XIV

Mean Differences of Persisters, Defectors, and Recruits within Career Groups on Eight Aptitude and Achievement Measures

Career groups	Total Information			English Total			Mathematics Total			Reading Comprehension		
	M	*SD*	*t*	*M*	*SD*	*t*	*M*	*SD*	*t*	*M*	*SD*	*t*
Natural Sciences												
Persisters	295.9	31.1	4.50**	102.2	5.6	4.71**	43.0	6.4	4.00**	45.0	2.8	3.66**
Defectors	268.8	44.9	1.35	97.2	7.7	2.22*	37.6	10.0	1.65	41.6	7.2	2.42*
Recruits	285.8	35.8	—2.09*	99.3	6.2	—1.42	40.3	8.9	—1.42	42.8	5.7	— .93
Professions												
Persisters	264.7	35.6	2.09*	98.8	7.0	2.74*	35.6	10.0	2.95**	43.1	3.2	3.34**
Defectors	246.1	52.7	— .22	93.5	11.6	.60	29.9	11.2	.80	38.4	8.6	.87
Recruits	266.7	42.8	—2.52*	97.9	7.3	—2.51*	33.9	9.8	—2.28*	42.1	6.5	—2.82**
Teaching												
Persisters	249.4	36.9	5.41**	96.9	8.7	4.75**	31.2	9.1	5.30**	40.7	5.8	5.77**
Defectors	235.2	44.9	— .88	94.2	8.9	1.76	28.0	10.0	.92	38.1	8.5	.97
Recruits	251.4	43.1	—5.74**	96.0	8.9	—3.19**	30.7	9.9	—4.31**	40.4	7.0	—4.63**
Health Fields												
Persisters	250.1	36.0	5.49**	95.3	7.1	4.54**	29.6	7.9	4.44**	39.9	5.6	5.36**
Defectors	230.1	45.8	3.68**	90.9	13.4	3.17**	26.1	10.1	2.59**	36.3	9.0	2.82**
Recruits	234.3	46.3	— .91	92.5	10.2	—1.25	27.3	9.4	—1.23	37.9	8.2	—1.79
Business												
Persisters	217.6	38.7	1.14	91.4	8.2	1.63	29.1	8.8	3.79**	34.8	10.9	.64
Defectors	208.5	43.3	—2.46*	88.5	9.9	— .67	23.0	8.6	.31	33.7	9.0	—1.80
Recruits	240.6	47.9	—6.47**	92.8	10.2	—3.84**	28.4	11.3	—5.18**	38.1	8.3	—4.43**
Arts												
Persisters	247.1	44.3	1.11	94.8	10.4	.27	26.9	10.0	.78	39.6	8.4	.25
Defectors	241.2	43.7	— .67	94.5	10.0	—1.04	26.0	8.9	—1.60	39.4	7.6	—1.40
Recruits	251.7	37.8	—1.90	96.4	7.4	—1.50	29.5	9.8	—2.93**	41.2	5.1	—1.97
Social Service/ Sciences												
Persisters	260.2	34.0	2.85**	99.5	6.5	4.18**	34.7	8.2	4.91**	43.1	3.8	3.40**
Defectors	239.1	46.8	.28	93.4	9.2	1.88	26.8	10.1	.79	38.8	8.1	1.83
Recruits	257.9	48.2	—3.42**	96.9	8.2	—3.38**	33.3	9.9	—5.66**	41.0	7.1	—2.40*
Office Work												
Persisters	202.0	37.9	.11	90.6	8.9	1.01	20.2	6.8	— .81	33.1	8.6	— .84
Defectors	201.7	37.8	—3.90**	90.0	9.7	.76	20.5	6.7	—4.67**	33.6	8.2	—2.63**
Recruits	214.1	45.1	—4.98**	90.0	11.9	— .02	23.0	9.4	—5.20**	34.8	9.0	—2.39*
Housewife												
Persisters	208.0	45.4	—3.30**	88.3	12.7	—2.20*	21.3	8.0	—4.20**	33.5	9.3	—2.21*
Defectors	224.7	51.3	—2.21*	91.2	12.3	—3.43**	25.3	10.2	—3.05**	35.7	9.6	—2.61**
Recruits	215.3	42.9	2.64**	90.9	9.7	.33	23.3	8.8	2.75**	35.2	8.6	.68
Miscellaneous												
Persisters	199.4	47.1	—5.43**	86.1	12.4	—4.86**	20.2	9.3	—4.78**	31.9	9.2	—5.11**
Defectors	224.0	47.7	—4.16**	91.1	10.4	—3.18**	24.4	9.4	—4.19**	36.3	8.9	—3.05**
Recruits	219.9	55.2	1.23	89.7	12.3	1.99*	24.2	10.8	.31	34.7	10.0	2.65**

TABLE 2-XIV *(Continued)*

Career groups	Abstract Reasoning			Creativity			Mechanical Reasoning			Grades		
	M	*SD*	*t*	*M*	*SD*	*t*	*M*	*SD*	*t*	*M*	*SD*	*t*
Natural Sciences												
Persisters	12.1	1.9	2.03*	13.4	3.2	2.19*	14.0	3.2	2.76	4.9	.8	3.44**
Defectors	11.4	2.5	.28	12.2	3.8	.93	12.4	4.1	.60	4.4	.9	2.46
Recruits	11.9	1.7	—1.25	12.7	3.4	— .68	13.6	2.8	—1.50	4.4	.9	.04
Professions												
Persisters	11.4	2.3	2.09*	11.4	3.3	.94	12.2	3.5	2.41	4.4	.9	2.02
Defectors	10.4	2.8	.79	10.8	4.0	—1.22	10.6	3.7	1.45	4.0	1.0	.61
Recruits	11.1	1.9	—1.53	12.3	3.5	—2.49*	11.1	3.4	— .80	4.3	1.0	—1.46
Teaching												
Persisters	10.9	2.1	3.84**	11.3	3.6	3.00**	10.4	3.6	1.86	4.1	.9	4.65**
Defectors	10.3	2.7	— .05	10.6	3.8	.17	10.0	3.8	—2.02*	3.9	.9	— .04
Recruits	10.9	2.3	—3.78**	11.3	3.6	—2.88**	10.9	3.8	—3.55**	4.1	.9	—4.67**
Health Fields												
Persisters	10.7	2.2	3.89**	11.1	3.2	2.62*	11.0	3.3	2.71**	3.8	.9	2.25*
Defectors	9.9	2.6	1.21	10.3	3.8	1.14	10.1	3.8	2.66**	3.7	.9	.19
Recruits	10.4	2.3	—2.10*	10.7	3.6	—1.06	10.0	3.7	.35	3.8	1.0	—1.68
Business												
Persisters	10.1	2.8	.90	8.7	3.9	— .82	9.4	3.9	.26	4.1	1.0	2.07*
Defectors	9.6	3.0	— .53	9.3	3.8	—2.60*	9.3	3.8	—1.05	3.7	1.0	1.77
Recruits	10.4	2.6	—2.43*	10.8	4.0	—3.47**	10.3	4.1	—2.45*	3.7	1.0	— .12
Arts												
Persisters	11.1	2.7	1.08	11.2	3.8	.54	10.6	3.7	— .38	3.8	.9	— .37
Defectors	10.8	2.4	.51	10.9	3.6	— .06	10.7	3.7	—1.71	3.8	.9	—1.07
Recruits	10.9	2.2	— .39	11.2	4.0	— .59	11.6	3.7	—1.81	3.9	1.0	—1.00
Social Service/ Sciences												
Persisters	11.5	2.1	3.04**	11.6	3.5	1.83	10.1	3.6	.41	4.2	.8	2.73**
Defectors	10.3	2.5	1.22	10.6	3.6	.86	9.8	3.7	— .82	3.8	1.0	.08
Recruits	11.0	2.2	—2.74**	11.0	4.1	—1.09	10.6	3.9	—1.83	4.2	1.1	—3.49**
Office Work												
Persisters	9.4	2.6	— .60	9.1	3.8	—1.53	8.5	3.3	—1.73	3.7	.9	1.29
Defectors	9.5	2.5	—1.77	9.5	3.6	—2.26*	8.8	3.4	—4.53**	3.6	.9	.62
Recruits	9.8	2.9	—1.62	9.7	3.8	—1.21	9.6	3.9	—3.69**	3.6	.9	— .57
Housewife												
Persisters	9.6	2.7	—1.20	9.9	3.4	—1.22	9.4	3.5	—1.37	3.5	1.0	—1.78
Defectors	9.9	3.0	—1.59	10.3	4.0	— .09	9.9	3.8	— .37	3.7	1.0	—2.43*
Recruits	9.9	2.6	.20	9.9	3.8	1.43	9.5	3.6	1.44	3.7	.9	.23
Miscellaneous												
Persisters	8.8	3.1	—4.93**	8.5	3.8	—4.28**	9.0	3.8	—1.88	3.4	1.0	—2.58*
Defectors	10.1	2.7	—2.77**	10.1	3.8	—3.82**	9.6	3.5	—1.77	3.7	1.0	—2.78**
Recruits	9.6	3.1	2.72**	9.9	3.9	.75	9.6	4.0	— .04	3.7	1.0	— .25

Note: For each career group, the *t* ratios were performed first between persisters and defectors, next between persisters and recruits, and last between recruits and defectors.

*$p < .05$.

**$p < .01$.

However, the Mathematics Total score and high school grades differentiated the defectors from the persisters in the business group.

Of all eight aptitude and achievement measures, only two—Mechanical Reasoning and Creativity—did not differentiate as adequately among the subgroups as did the scholastic aptitude measures. Mechanical reasoning measures an aptitude for mechanical matters and creativity usually reflects a person's ingenuity.

The second hypothesis implied that persisters in the natural sciences will manifest more interest in physical science than will the defectors from this field. Similarly, persisters in teaching and in social service/social sciences will show a stronger interest in social service and in literature/linguistics than will the defectors from these groups. Finally, the business persisters will score higher on business interest than will the defectors. Table 2-XV presents the results, utilizing the four interest measures. Persisters in the natural sciences, health fields, and business groups scored significantly higher on the Physical Science Interest measure than did the defectors. However, the mean differences on Physical Science Interest scale between defectors and persisters were not significant for the teaching and professions career groups. Thus, an interest in physical science differentiates among subjects in the natural sciences but not in the other career-oriented groups (the professions and teaching). Regarding the Literary/Linguistic Interest scale, the persisters in the teaching group scored significantly higher than did the defectors. The same, however, was not true with respect to the Social Service Interest scale.

Of the four interest measures employed, an interest in physical science differentiated the persisters from the defectors in natural science, the health fields, and business; an interest in literature and linguistics differentiated the defectors from the persisters in the teaching groups; and scores on the Business/Managerial Interest scale differentiated the two subgroups in the business career category.

In order to test the third hypothesis that occupational groups become more homogeneous over time, the means and standard deviations on four ability measures (Information Total, English Total, Reading Comprehension, and Mathematics Total) were computed for the groups as they were constituted in the twelfth grade and as they were constituted five years later.

These results, presented in Table 2-XVI, suggest that the general tendency for all groups is to become more homogeneous over time, as is indicated by the smaller standard deviations for the final composition of the groups. Moreover, gains in the overall ability level of the women in most of the final career groups are reflected in the mean score increases. Over time, the greatest mean increases in aptitude occurred in the natural sciences, the professions, the health fields,

TABLE 2-XV
Mean Differences of Persisters, Defectors, and Recruits within Career Groups on Four Interest Measures

Career groups	Physical Science			Literary/ Linguistic			Social Service			Business/ Managerial		
	M	*SD*	*t*	*M*	*SD*	*t*	*M*	*SD*	*t*	*M*	*SD*	*t*
Natural Sciences												
Persisters	29.4	5.7	3.84**	26.8	7.6	1.83	22.1	7.7	— .52	17.5	8.8	1.29
Defectors	25.1	8.1	.35**	24.7	7.8	— .28	22.7	7.4	— .21	16.2	7.2	1.57
Recruits	24.1	8.7	.62	27.3	8.0	—1.69	22.5	8.2	.12	14.5	7.8	1.17
Professions												
Persisters	20.2	8.4	.93	25.9	7.7	.29	25.5	6.1	.44	15.9	6.7	—1.91
Defectors	18.7	9.3	1.06	25.4	8.6	— .52	24.9	7.8	— .63	18.3	7.1	.68
Recruits	18.2	8.7	.35	26.8	7.7	— .98	26.5	8.4	—1.29	14.8	8.1	3.00**
Teaching												
Persisters	14.8	8.0	.12	27.4	7.6	2.54*	30.0	5.5	1.82	18.5	7.1	— .59
Defectors	14.7	8.3	—4.48**	26.1	8.3	.79	29.3	5.7	12.69**	18.8	7.5	1.73
Recruits	17.0	9.1	—3.88**	27.1	7.7	—1.88	25.2	7.4	9.30**	17.8	7.5	2.07*
Health Fields												
Persisters	18.3	7.3	2.50*	23.4	8.1	1.82	27.3	6.5	1.64	15.6	7.4	.56
Defectors	16.7	7.7	1.44	22.2	7.9	—1.85	26.4	6.8	.52	15.2	7.6	—3.35**
Recruits	17.1	9.4	— .47	25.1	8.9	—3.51**	27.0	6.8	— .86	18.1	7.1	—3.92**
Business												
Persisters	16.5	7.9	2.49*	21.5	9.7	1.21	23.3	8.7	.05	21.6	7.9	2.09*
Defectors	12.9	7.8	.86	19.5	8.8	—1.49	23.2	7.7	.14	18.6	7.7	1.90
Recruits	15.1	8.2	—2.49*	24.3	9.2	—4.86**	23.1	7.8	.18	18.8	7.2	— .14
Arts												
Persisters	12.0	7.1	— .21	27.1	8.2	.04	19.8	8.1	—1.76	14.7	7.7	— .70
Defectors	12.2	7.4	—3.27**	27.1	8.4	— .02	21.4	7.7	—3.50**	15.4	7.8	—2.64*
Recruits	16.5	9.7	—4.28**	27.1	8.3	— .06	24.3	7.9	—2.84**	18.2	8.5	—2.73**
Social Service/ Sciences												
Persisters	15.7	6.8	1.93	29.3	5.7	1.81	26.3	5.5	—1.17	18.9	6.9	— .37
Defectors	13.3	7.9	—2.46*	27.0	8.1	1.19	27.7	7.1	1.12	19.4	7.4	.55
Recruits	19.4	9.2	—6.34**	27.8	7.6	— .90	25.0	7.4	3.22**	18.2	7.4	1.34
Office Work												
Persisters	10.8	7.2	1.70	20.5	8.1	1.65	26.3	7.1	— .61	18.2	7.4	.83
Defectors	10.1	6.8	—4.67**	19.7	8.6	—3.37**	23.9	7.0	—2.36*	17.8	7.7	— .06
Recruits	13.4	7.7	—7.52**	22.6	8.5	—5.53**	24.9	7.6	—2.24*	18.2	7.7	— .91
Housewife												
Persisters	10.2	7.5	—2.46*	19.1	8.6	—4.43**	23.7	7.2	— .74	14.5	7.3	—2.14*
Defectors	12.1	7.4	—3.17**	23.0	8.5	—3.22**	24.3	6.8	— .61	16.2	7.9	—4.38**
Recruits	12.1	8.0	.02	21.2	8.9	2.48*	24.1	7.3	.35	17.0	7.6	—1.31
Miscellaneous												
Persisters	11.3	8.3	—2.11*	20.0	9.4	—4.57**	22.0	7.0	—1.52	15.8	7.5	—1.43
Defectors	13.0	8.5	—2.97**	23.9	8.8	—2.42*	23.1	7.4	—2.70**	16.8	7.6	— .84
Recruits	13.7	8.9	—1.29	22.0	8.5	3.52**	23.9	7.7	—1.69	16.4	7.9	.87

Note: For each career group, the *t* ratios were performed first between persisters and defectors, next between persisters and recruits, and last between recruits and defectors.

* $p < .05$.

** $p < .01$.

teaching, and business. The mean aptitudes of the housewife and miscellaneous groups were lower five years after high school.

On the basis of the findings reported with respect to the patterns of change and stability in career plans, greater differentiation among groups indeed occurs over time. The brighter women either raise

TABLE 2-XVI

Means and Standard Deviations of the Initial and Final Composition of the Career Groups on Four Ability Measures

Career groups		Ability measures							
		Total Information		English Total		Reading Comprehension		Mathematics Total	
	n	*M*	*SD*	*M*	*SD*	*M*	*SD*	*M*	*SD*
Natural Sciences									
Initial	375	272.46	44.22	98.01	7.60	42.09	6.78	38.43	9.72
Final	88	292.49	33.16	101.23	5.95	44.27	4.19	42.09	7.50
Professions									
Initial	275	248.70	51.09	94.23	11.24	39.03	8.23	30.72	11.20
Final	86	265.80	39.77	94.29	7.15	42.53	5.36	34.66	9.91
Teaching									
Initial	991	243.79	40.83	95.82	8.87	39.68	7.13	29.93	9.58
Final	1235	250.42	40.21	96.44	8.80	40.54	6.49	30.96	9.53
Health Fields									
Initial	539	238.67	42.99	92.79	11.36	37.86	7.90	27.61	9.41
Final	336	244.04	40.96	94.21	8.52	39.14	6.79	28.74	8.59
Business									
Initial	373	209.29	43.03	88.73	9.83	33.79	9.19	23.51	8.81
Final	138	234.24	46.91	92.45	9.76	37.30	9.05	28.54	10.80
Arts									
Initial	450	242.26	43.89	94.55	10.11	39.40	7.78	26.19	9.15
Final	154	249.26	41.46	95.54	9.16	40.35	7.11	28.10	10.01
Social Service/ Sciences									
Initial	248	242.94	45.45	94.50	9.07	39.59	7.73	28.19	10.21
Final	162	258.56	44.71	97.60	7.86	41.57	6.46	33.71	9.47
Office Work									
Initial	1187	201.82	37.85	90.18	9.47	33.45	8.34	20.42	6.73
Final	763	208.23	42.17	90.29	10.60	34.02	8.85	21.62	8.36
Housewife									
Initial	370	215.64	48.87	89.63	12.58	34.51	9.52	23.16	9.30
Final	1655	214.39	43.25	90.60	10.13	35.01	8.69	23.09	8.70
Miscellaneous									
Initial	579	217.64	48.77	89.84	11.15	35.17	9.14	23.32	9.52
Final	730	215.69	54.31	88.95	12.38	34.13	9.86	23.39	10.63

Note: Initial represents the 1960 survey, and Final the 1965 follow-up survey.

their aspirations or maintain their earlier high aspirations. On the other hand, less academically able women plan careers that are less demanding with respect to abilities and required training.

SUMMARY AND IMPLICATIONS

The study reported here utilized longitudinal data collected by and maintained in the data bank of Project TALENT. The sample consisted of high school senior girls who were surveyed in 1960 and followed up in 1965. The study was designed to explore the career development of women during the five-year period after high school. The primary interest was in isolating predictor variables—in this case, personal characteristics as high school seniors and experiences during the period that followed—of career outcomes five years after high school. The study addressed itself to three specific questions:

1. What are the personal characteristics of twelfth-grade girls that predict their vocational choices five years after high school?

2. What are the educational and other experiences since high school that affect women's career plans during these years?

3. What are the personal and intellectual traits of women who persist in a career as opposed to those who change their career plans?

Since the research was primarily interested in differentiating career choices on the basis of antecedent variables, the method of multiple-discriminant analysis was used.

The authors were able to predict the career choices of women five years after high school with varying degrees of accuracy. Some of the antecedent variables were better predictors than others and some choices could be predicted with greater accuracy than others.

Invariably, the post-high school behaviors with respect to education and marital status were the best environmental predictors of career outcomes. For example, going to college and receiving a BA degree were predictive of plans to pursue careers in the natural sciences, the professions, and teaching. On the other hand, being married and having children were predictive of plans to be a housewife. In addition to the post-high school behaviors, certain personal characteristics at the time of the senior year in high school were predictive of career outcomes five years later. In particular, aptitudes and expressed interests differentiated among the girls with different career choices. For instance, high overall scholastic aptitude differentiated girls with aspirations in natural sciences, teaching, and the professions. Early interest and initial career choice of one of the health fields or the arts predicted similar choices later on. Moreover, variables that would be termed masculine, that is, an interest in mechanical matters and in physical science as well as high aptitude in mathematics, differentiated girls with an orientation in fields more often favored by men than by women, for instance, the natural sciences and the professions, as opposed to teaching and the health fields.

In summary, girls who in high school score high on scholastic aptitudes, especially on mathematical ability, and who plan to pursue higher education and aspire to an advanced degree usually choose fields that require greater career commitment—the natural and social sciences, the professions, and teaching. Plans to do office work or to be a housewife usually are made by girls with less aptitude and fewer academic interests. If these girls get married, they will more likely plan to be housewives, but if they remain single, they tend to pursue office work. Girls who have an interest in social service and the health fields but little interest in pursuing advanced education usually continue to choose those careers. Full-time employment after high school graduation, an early interest in business and management, a BA degree, and unmarried status proved to be the best predictors of plans to pursue a business career.

Plans to be an artist are best predicted by similar plans at an earlier age and by artistic interests and aptitudes.

Despite the great instability of the career plans between the high school senior year and five years later (close to one-half of the twelfth-grade female population changed their career plans during this period), early patterns and interests predict later career outcomes. Since, at the time of high school graduation, many women must decide whether to continue their education or to go to work, counselors and educators should assume the responsibility for guiding these young women and helping them make the educational and vocational plans most appropriate for them and most responsive to the needs of society. This help is most necessary for women planning to pursue careers that require specialized training.

Appropriate guidance becomes even more crucial for girls who have low aspirations in high school and who later learn that doing office work or being a housewife is not commensurate with their interests or abilities. If they recognized and appreciated their skills at an earlier age, they might have been better able to make wise decisions at that time.

Looking at patterns of stability and change in career choices, we find that the less scholastically capable girls defect more often from careers that require high aptitudes and long, rigorous training. Conversely, brighter girls are likely to change initial plans of being housewives and office workers. These observations can be interpreted in a number of ways. Since the brighter students who as seniors name the natural sciences, the professions, and teaching as their favored occupations usually maintain their plans over time, perhaps the more capable students are more perceptive about their own interests and aptitudes at an earlier age and thus are able to choose careers that are more realistic and more appropriate to their personal qualities. The intellectually less capable, on the other hand, tend to make relatively unrealistic career plans which they must change later on. Another interpretation is that as students mature, their educational and vocational goals become more realistic and more consistent with the aptitudes and skills required for successful educational and vocational experiences. Thus the whole process may be inevitably and totally dependent on maturation.

One of the interesting results of these shifts in and out of different occupational groups is that within-group homogeneity with respect to measured aptitudes increases and that talent becomes more evenly distributed across the different occupational categories. Both outcomes can be viewed in positive ways. That intellectual talent becomes better distributed as a result of the shifts has favorable implications for the overall development and utilization of our human resources. However, that the shifts entail the greatest defection from the sciences and the professions and into more feminine occupations is distressing. Having interests and skills that are like those of the rest of the group members may be psychologically comforting and less anxiety producing, but homogeneity may have negative effects in the long run—first, because it perpetuates sexual inequalities and second, because it allows the maintenance of possibly out-moded entrance requirements as well as of standards about what constitutes acceptable performance in a field. Thus, as long as women are overchoosing teaching and men the physical sciences, it remains difficult for a man to become an elementary school teacher and a woman a physicist, whatever their own desires and interests and the benefits to society that such "unconventional" choices would produce. Moreover, the practice of law, the workings of the courts, the planning of cities, and other such areas where women might make a contribution will remain static as long as men are the predominant figures in these fields.

REFERENCES

Astin, A.W. Undergraduate institutions and the production of scientists. *Science,* 1963, *141,* 334-338.

Astin, H.S. Patterns of career choices over time. *Personnel and Guidance Journal,* 1967, *45,* 541-546.

Astin, H.S. Career development of girls during the high school years. *Journal of Counseling Psychology,* 1968, *15,* 536-540. (a)

Astin, H.S. Stability and change in the career plans of ninth grade girls. *Personnel and Guidance Journal,* 1968, *46,* 961-966. (b)

Blau, P.M., Gustad, J.W., Jessor, R., Parnes, H.S., & Wilcock, R.C. Occupational choice: A conceptual framework. *Industrial Labor Relations Review,* 1956, *9,* 531-543.

Campbell, D.P. The stability of vocational interests within occupations over long time spans. Unpublished manuscript, University of Minnesota, Center for Interest Measurement Research, 1965.

Clark, K.E. *Vocational interests of nonprofessional men.* Minneapolis: University of Minnesota Press, 1961.

Cooley, W.W. *Career development of scientists: An overlapping longitudinal study.* Cambridge, Mass.: Harvard Graduate School of Education, 1963.

Cooley, W.W., & Lohnes, P.R. *Predicting development of young adults.* Palo Alto, Calif.: American Institutes for Research, Project TALENT, 1968.

Davis, J.A. *The role of higher education in career allocation.* Paper presented at the meeting of the American Sociological Association, Washington, D.C., August 1962.

Davis, J.A. *Undergraduate career decisions.* Chicago: Aldine, 1965.

Elton, C.F., & Rose, H.A. Significance of personality in the vocational choice of college women. *Journal of Counseling Psychology,* 1967, *14,* 293-298.

Flanagan, J.C., Daily, J.T., Shaycoft, M.F., Gorham, W.A., Orr, D.B., & Goldberg, F. *Design for a study of American youth.* Boston: Houghton Mifflin, 1962.

Ginzberg, E., Ginsburg, S.W., Axelrad, S., & Herma, J.L. *Occupational choice: An approach to a general theory.* New York: Columbia University Press, 1951.

Gribbons, W.D., & Lohnes, P.R. *Career development from age 13 to age 25.* (Final Report to the United States Office of Education, Project No. 6-2151, Grant No. OEG-1-7-062151-0471) Washington, D.C.: Department of Health, Education, and Welfare, 1969.

Gysbers, N.C., Johnston, J.A., & Gust, T. Characteristics of homemaker- and career-oriented women. *Journal of Counseling Psychology,* 1968, *15,* 541-546.

Harmon, L.W. Women's working patterns related to their SVIB housewife and "own" occupational scores. *Journal of Counseling Psychology,* 1967, *14,* 299-301.

Hilton, T.L. Career decision-making. *Journal of Counseling Psychology,* 1962, *9,* 291-298.

Holland, J.L. A theory of vocational choice. *Journal of Counseling Psychology,* 1959, *6,* 35-45.

Holland, J.L. Some exploration of a theory of vocational choice: I. One- and two-year longitudinal studies. *Psychological Monographs, 1962, 76*(26, Whole No. 545).

Holland, J.L. *The psychology of vocational choice.* Waltham, Mass.: Blaisdell, 1966.

Holland, J.L., & Nichols, R.C. Explorations of a theory of vocational choice: III. A longitudinal study of change in major field of study. *Personnel and Guidance Journal,* 1964, *43,* 235-242.

Nichols, R.C. Career decisions of very able students. *Science,* 1964, *144,* 1315-1319.

Rand, L. Masculinity or femininity? Differentiating career-oriented and homemaking-oriented college freshmen women. *Journal of Counseling Psychology,* 1958, *15,* 444-450.

Roe, A. A psychological study of eminent psychologists and anthropologists, and a comparison with biological and physical scientists. *Psychological Monographs: General and Applied,* 1953, *67*(2, Whole No. 352).

Roe, A. *The psychology of occupations.* New York: Wiley, 1956.

Roe, A. Personality structure and occupational behavior. In H. Borow (Ed.), *Man in a world at work.* Boston, Mass.: Houghton Mifflin, 1964.

Rosenberg, M. *Occupations and values.* Glencoe, Ill.: Free Press, 1957.

Strong, E.K., Jr. *Vocational interests of men and women.* Stanford, Calif.: Stanford University Press, 1943.

Super, D.E. Vocational adjustment: Implementing a self-concept. *Occupations,* 1951, *30,* 88-92.

Super, D.E. A theory of vocational development. *American Psychologist,* 1953, *8,* 185-190.

Super, D.E. *The psychology of careers.* New York: Harper, 1957.

Super, D.E., & Overstreet, P.L. *The vocational maturity of ninth grade boys.* New York: Columbia University, Teachers College Bureau of Publications, 1960.

Tiedeman, D.V., O'Hara, R.P., & Baruch, R.W. *Career development: Choice and adjustment.* Princeton, N.J.: College Entrance Examination Board, 1963.

Tiedeman, D.V., O'Hara, R.P., & Matthews, E. *Position choices and careers: Elements of a theory.* (Harvard Studies in Career Development No. 8) Cambridge, Mass.: Harvard Graduate School of Education, 1958.

Tyler, L.E. The antecedents of two varieties of vocational interests. *Genetic Psychology Monographs,* 1964, *70,* 177-227.

United States Department of Commerce. *Statistical abstracts of the United States.* (Table No. 324, p. 229) Washington, D.C.: United States Government Printing Office, Bureau of the Census, 1967.

Werts, C.E. Career changes in college. *National Merit Scholarship Corporation Research Reports,* 1966, 2(7).

Chapter 3

CAREER PATTERNS AND LIFE STAGES*

DONALD E. SUPER

THE TERM *career pattern* originated in the field of sociology, in the study of social mobility by means of occupational mobility (3, 4, 7, 11). It closely parallels, both in meaning and in time, the psychological concept of *life stages* (2). The sociological term refers to the sequence of occupations in the life of an individual or of a group of individuals. This sequence may be analyzed in order to ascertain the major work periods which constitute a career. The psychological term is derived from the analysis of life histories in which the major events and concerns group themselves and vary from one stage of life to another, justifying the classification of life into a sequence of characteristic stages.

The first research in career patterns was carried out by Davidson and Anderson (3) in the city of San Jose, California, and published in 1937, although many of its concepts were derived from Sorokin's work on social mobility (11) a decade earlier. Job sequences of men from various socioeconomic groups were traced and patterns of careers characteristic of each group were established. Further work along the same lines by Miller and Form (4) in 1949 added substantially to theory and fact in this field.

The basic life stages of infancy, childhood, adolescence, adulthood, and old age have of course been known and widely used since time immemorial. Important work in psychological life stages was done by Buehler (2) in 1933 and was utilized by some writers of texts in developmental psychology in subsequent years (9). But the concept of life stages has not been used as much as it might have been in the formulation of research problems or in organizing the data of vocational psychology.

*From Donald E. Super. *The Psychology of Careers.* New York: Harper & Row, Publishers, Inc., 1957.

LIFE STAGES

The psychological life stages defined by Buehler as a result of the analysis of life histories were five in number. The Growth Stage extends from conception to about the age of fourteen. It is followed by the Exploratory Stage, which includes the period from about age fifteen to about twenty-five. The Establishment Stage comes next, including the years from twenty-five to about forty-five. Then comes the Maintenance Stage, which ends at about sixty-five. The final stage is that of Decline, beginning at about sixty-five.

The age limits are considered by Buehler to be approximations, which vary considerably from one person to another. Some people keep on exploring, that is, attempting to find their places in life and to develop and implement adequate self-concepts, for some years after they enter their thirties; some have already "found themselves" vocationally, socially, and personally by the time they are in their twenties, and are well on the way to establishment before they are twenty-five. Goethe, for example, was famous at twenty-five, Pascal was a celebrity at a younger age. Some people, to take the other extreme, keep on being professionally active long after they are sixty-five. Gladstone and Winston Churchill are two outstanding examples, as was also Goethe (Pascal died in middle age).

The processes of exploration, establishment, maintenance, and decline are not simply vocational, but involve all aspects of life and living. They operate in the lives of women as well as of men, as Buehler showed. Adolescent *exploration* includes developing an understanding of the self, trying out the role of budding adult, finding a mate, finding an occupation, finding one's place in the community. *Establishment* similarly includes establishing a family, a home, and a role in the community as well as making a place for one's self in the world of work by establishing a practice, building a business, or developing a work history which makes one easily classifiable as an assembly line worker or as a buyer of ladies' garments. *Maintenance* is the process of holding one's own in the family, keeping the home intact, keeping up appearances in the community, and seeing that the business continues to flourish or that the textbooks get revised periodically and keep on selling. *Decline* manifests itself not only physically in decreased energy and stamina, and vocationally in the need to taper off in the volume of sales handled, in the number of students seen, or in the need to transfer from work as a longshoreman to work as a night watchman, but also in decline in other respects, as in the lessening of family responsibilities and restriction of roles in the community. The older person becomes less active in the community as he enters the stage of decline, restricting the number and complexity of his activities; he also becomes less active in the home, leaving more of the maintenance and repair work to others, taking less responsibility for the direction of family life and family affairs, and in due course even taking less responsibility for himself.

The *sociological classification of life stages* by Miller and Form is work centered, although they were concerned also with security (4, 7). They distinguish first the *Preparatory Work Period,* in which the child begins to develop an orientation to the world of work through home, neighborhood, and school activities. Then comes the *Initial Work Period,* beginning with the first part-time or summer work experience at about the age of fourteen, in which the adolescent is introduced directly to the world of work as a part-time or marginal participant. The *Trial Work Period* follows, beginning with entry into the regular labor market some time between sixteen and twenty-five and continuing until a stable work position is located, usually after considerable changing of jobs, until a type of work is found in which the young adult can hold his own, at about the age of thirty-five. The *Stable Work Period* begins at about age thirty-five and continues until age sixty; it corresponds to the latter part of Buehler's Establishment and to most of her Maintenance Stages. Finally, the *Retirement Period* begins at sixty or sixty-five.

Career Patterns: Men

The basis of Miller and Form's classification of work periods was the work histories of a small but selected sample of men in the state of Ohio. Having established that their job sequences could be classified into these five stages, they then proceeded to see if the sequences of these work periods were patterned in different ways in different occupational or socioeconomic groups. This was as Davidson and Anderson had done fifteen years earlier, with this important innovation: they utilized the concept of life stages or work periods, thus making the description of job sequences easier and more meaningful. Four types of career patterns were found in this sample of men, simplifying Miller and Form's sixfold classification (7) to eliminate duplication, which may be described as follows:

1. THE STABLE CAREER PATTERN. In this category are found most professional careers, many managers, some skilled workers, and to a lesser extent semi-skilled and clerical workers. These are persons who have gone directly from school or college into a type of work which they have consistently followed: in other words, they have essentially skipped the trial work period.

2. THE CONVENTIONAL CAREER PATTERN. In this pattern the sequence of jobs follows the typical progression from initial through trial to stable employment. This pattern is most typical of manage-

rial, skilled, and clerical workers, but characterizes some professional and domestic workers.

3. The Unstable Career Pattern. Here the sequence is trial-stable-trial: the worker does not succeed in establishing himself permanently in what might have been a lifetime job or occupation, but instead gives up his potential career in one field and goes off in a different direction in which he may or may not establish himself. This sequence is seen most often in semi-skilled, clerical, and domestic workers.

4. The Multiple-trial Career Pattern. This is the pattern of frequent change of employment, with no one type sufficiently prolonged or dominant to justify calling the person established in a career. This type of sequence is observed most often in domestic, clerical, and semi-skilled workers, who not infrequently shift from one type of work to another and accumulate the most disconnected of work histories.

When the incidence of these career patterns was analyzed according to occupational groups, it was found that *professional* workers typically have varied initial work experiences and tend to proceed immediately from college to stable professional employment. *Managerial* workers typically have varied initial work experience, varied trial jobs, and then stabilize as managers. *Clerical and sales* workers normally have a variety of low-level initial experiences, somewhat varied trial jobs, and their careers stabilize rather late. *Skilled* workers have patterns rather like those of clerical and sales workers. *Semi-skilled* workers have somewhat varied initial and trial jobs, stabilize late. *Unskilled* and *domestic* workers are vertically immobile during their initial and trial periods and tend not to stabilize in any one field but rather have a succession of varied low-level occupations. The higher the level of the occupation of the father, the greater the likelihood that the son will have a stable career pattern.

Miller and Form found that 73 percent of the white collar workers had secure types of career patterns; of these, the professionals were the most secure, 88 percent of them having had stable work histories. Only 46 percent of the blue denim workers were so fortunate, among whom the unskilled were worst off with only 24 percent having stable histories.

Miller and Form, as well as Davidson and Anderson in their earlier study, have brought out clearly the relationship between father's education and father's occupation, father's occupation and son's education, and son's education and son's occupation. The "apprenticeship" years of the managerial and skilled workers are clearly shown by these studies, and direct relationship between trial and stable employment is brought out for the other occupational groups.

What these figures do not bring out is the variations from these patterns in each occupational group. Knowledge of the career pattern which characterizes most sons and daughters of semi-skilled workers is helpful in vocational guidance, but equally important is knowledge of the nature, frequency, and causes of variations. It is important to know why some sons and daughters of assembly line workers enter professional occupations, why some sons of physicians become office clerks and longshoremen. The determinants of career patterns have virtually not been studied, except singly and in quite different contexts, as in the analysis of the relationship between intelligence and occupational level (14).

Career Patterns: Women

Despite the numerous and valuable studies of women's occupations and careers conducted by the Women's Bureau of the United States Department of Labor (15) and various interested groups and individuals (e.g., 5), women's careers have not been studied in the way in which Miller and Form studied men's careers. The emphasis in this chapter is therefore inevitably on men's careers. With a steadily increasing percentage of women in the work force, and larger numbers of married women continuing to work after marriage, or returning to work after their children are old enough for this to be possible, this discrimination in favor of men—who, incidentally, have no "Men's Bureau," die sooner, must live longer to receive Federal Old Age Benefits, and leave the bulk of the wealth in the control of women—is regrettable. As Mueller points out in her delightful but erudite treatise on *Educating Women for a Changing World* (8), there are "many differences in the life patterns and social roles of men and women."

The sex roles of men and women are socially as well as biologically determined, as anthropological studies and the changing roles of women during the past century make clear. But women's careers, career orientations, and career motivations differ from those of men and are likely to continue to differ in important respects. An adequate discussion of these differences becomes especially important as larger numbers of women participate in the work force. Since adequate data on the career patterns of women are lacking, an attempt is made below to organize into a logical scheme what data there are, together with some observations made in observing women's careers. In doing this, it is important to point out that woman's role as childbearer makes her the keystone of the home, and therefore gives homemaking a central place in her career.

This biological fact explains the findings of studies of the interests of women reviewed briefly by Mueller (8) and in more detail by this writer (12). Mueller concludes her summary of interest research by stating:

> This is a quantitative and erudite manner of saying that girls will be girls, or at least 90 percent of them will be girls, and the other 10 percent may find themselves in Who's Who! [She continues:] The significant thing is the far more uniform and standardized pattern of feminine interests than of masculine. John may want to be a lawyer, physician, engineer, farmer, statistician, radio announcer, but Mary, nine times out of ten, can see no further than her marriage. She wants a little job that will put her immediately into the company of men.

What the interest research shows is a dominant interest in "male association," which, as Mueller points out, needs to be taken into account along with the facts on the increasing percentage of working women.

It seems likely that the career patterns of women may be classifiable in the system outlined below.

1. THE STABLE HOMEMAKING CAREER PATTERN. This category includes all women who marry while in or very shortly after leaving school or college, having expected to do so and having had no significant work experience.

2. THE CONVENTIONAL CAREER PATTERN. In this pattern of working followed by homemaking, the young woman leaving school or college goes to work for a period of several months or several years, in an occupation which is open to her without training beyond that which she obtained in her general education, in brief professional education substituted for general education, or in some relatively brief post-high school or postcollegiate education. Clerical work, teaching, nursing, occupational therapy, and secretarial work illustrate these types of occupations. They are generally viewed as stopgaps, but may first be thought of as life careers, with subsequent change of aspirations. They are often valuable as an opportunity for developing independence and a sense of being a person in one's own right. Marrying after this relatively brief work experience, the young woman becomes a full-time homemaker.

3. THE STABLE WORKING CAREER PATTERN. The sequence in this type of career pattern is one of entering the work force on leaving school, college, or professional school and embarking upon a career which becomes the woman's life work. She may perceive it as a life career from the start: a small percentage of young women do have strong career (as contrasted with homemaking) motivation and interest. Or she may at first view her working career as a preliminary to marriage, whether as a stopgap job, a working career to continue with marriage, or a working career to resume after a period of full-time homemaking. This perception of working as a preliminary to

marriage not infrequently changes to a perception of working as the life career, especially in parts of the country and in times in which women are more numerous than men. The change of orientation is, in these instances, often a difficult one to make.

4. THE DOUBLE-TRACK CAREER PATTERN. This is the pattern of the woman who goes to work after completing her education, marries, and continues with a double career of working and homemaking. She may take occasional time out for childbearing. The pattern is most common near the upper and lower ends of the occupational scale, among women physicians and scientists, and among women domestics, presumably because the challenge of the work, or the income it produces, is important to the woman in question. The double role is in neither case easy, for the married working woman usually has two jobs, one with and one without pay.

5. THE INTERRUPTED CAREER PATTERN. Here the sequence is one of working, homemaking, and working while or instead of homemaking. The young woman works for some time, then marries, and then, when her children are old enough for her to leave them, when financial needs—including those resulting from being widowed or divorced—or interest in working become dominant, she returns to work. If she has children, the age at which she decides they can be left depends upon her socioeconomic status: the higher the level of the family, the older and more independent the children must be before the mother believes she may leave the home for work. The work to which the married woman returns may be that of her original working career, or it may be different: which it is depends upon what she has done with her training and experience during the full-time homemaking period, her interest in and ability to obtain refresher training, new interests developed while a homemaker, retraining possibilities, and local manpower needs and requirements. Thus many former teachers return to teaching, but relatively few former secretaries return to secretarial work.

6. THE UNSTABLE CAREER PATTERN. In women this type of career pattern consists of working, homemaking, working again, returning to full-time homemaking, etc. It results most often from irregular economic pressures which make extra earnings necessary despite homemaking preferences or needs, or from poor health necessitating giving up employment, or from a combination of these. This pattern is observed most often at the lower socioeconomic levels.

7. THE MULTIPLE-TRIAL CAREER PATTERN. This pattern is the same in women as the similarly named pattern in men: it consists of a succession of unrelated jobs, with stability in none, resulting in the individual having no genuine life work.

Some Important Questions

The present state of knowledge and thinking concerning career patterns indicates that four kinds of questions may be asked concerning them. Most of these have not been answered at all adequately, and only one of them has been the subject of specific study.

1. What is the nature and content of the sequence of events in the life history, specifically schooling, job seeking, and job holding? This is the question of the shape of the career pattern and of its parts; it includes the question of the differences in the career patterns of various occupational groups. It has been studied by several sociologists, but the data are as yet very limited in nature and are derived from small and possibly inadequate samples.

2. What traits and factors determine the sequence of jobs in the career pattern, and how do they account for the frequent deviations from the normal pattern for a given socioeconomic group? This is the question of the role of intelligence, special aptitudes, interests, and personality traits. It has been studied in other connections by many psychologists, but rarely as a multivariate problem and never in relation to career pattern theory, only in relation to questions of vocational choice and success.

3. What is the nature of the changes in the individual's thinking about work and about himself in relation to work? There has been little study of this question, although one study by a team representing several social sciences has been published (6). It is odd that the process of occupational choice has been so completely neglected: the Social Science Research Council's Seminar (1), Roe's treatise (10), and the long-term Career Pattern Study (13, 14) are rare exceptions.

4. How can the study of job sequences, of the interaction of traits and factors, and of perceptions of self and of occupations, be brought to bear simultaneously to provide a better understanding of the nature and determinants of career patterns?

5. What are the important differences in the career patterns of women, as compared with those of men? And what are their causes?

6. What are the factors associated with these differences?

REFERENCES

1. Blau, P.M., Gustad, J.W., Jessor, R., Parnes, H.S., and Wilcock, R.C. Occupational choice: a conceptual framework. *Industrial Labor Relations Review,* 1956, *9,* 531-543.
2. Buehler, Charlotte. *Der menschliche Lebenslauf als psychologisches Problem.* Leipzig: Hirzel, 1933.
3. Davidson, P.E., and Anderson, H.D. *Occupational mobility in an American community.* Stanford: Stanford University Press, 1937.
4. Form, W.H., and Miller, D.C. Occupational career pattern as a sociological instrument. *American Journal of Sociology,* 1949, *54,* 317-329.

5. Foster, R.G., and Wilson, Pauline P. *Women after college.* New York: Columbia University Press, 1942.
6. Ginzberg, E., Ginsburg, S.W., Axelrad, S., and Herma, J.L. *Occupational choice.* New York: Columbia University Press, 1951.
7. Miller, D.C., and Form, W.H. *Industrial sociology.* New York: Harper, 1951.
8. Mueller, Kate H. *Educating women for a changing world.* Minneapolis: University of Minnesota Press, 1954.
9. Pressey, S.L., Janney, J.E., and Kuhlen, R.G. *Life: a psychological survey.* New York: Harper, 1939.
10. Roe, Anne. *The psychology of occupations.* New York: Wiley, 1956.
11. Sorokin, P.A. *Social mobility.* New York: Harper, 1927.
12. Super, D.E. *Appraising vocational fitness by means of psychological tests.* New York: Harper, 1949.
13. ———. Career patterns as a basis for vocational counseling. *Journal of Counseling Psychology,* 1954, *1,* 12-20.
14. ———, Crites, J.O., Hummel, R.C., Moser, Helen P., Overstreet, Phoebe L., and Warnath, C.F. *Vocational development: A framework for research.* New York: Teachers College Bureau of Publications, (1957).
15. United States Department of Labor. *Handbook of facts on women workers.* Washington: Government Printing Office, 1950.

Chapter 4

THE CHANGING STATUS OF AMERICAN WOMEN: A LIFE CYCLE PERSPECTIVE*

ROXANN A. VAN DUSEN AND ELEANOR BERNERT SHELDON

THE "LIFE CYCLE," a familiar concept to the public and to the media, has recently been receiving substantial attention from social scientists (Riley, Johnson, & Foner, 1972). The life cycle (or "life course") is a way of conceptualizing the aging process: a sequence of statuses and roles, expectations and relationships, constituting, in the broadest meaning of the word, an individual's "career." While the life cycle is universal, it is also infinitely varied. It is shaped by the variety of roles and opportunities available to an individual, as well as by the resources that individual can marshal at various stages of his or her "career."

In the past decade or so, sociologists and other social scientists have borrowed from demographers the concepts and techniques of cohort analysis for studying the process of social change. To state it simply: Social change has been viewed as the succession of cohorts through various stages of the life cycle. This cohort-analytic perspective highlights three important components of social change: (a) change associated with the aging process; (b) change associated with changes in the "external" environment; and (c) change associated with the replacement of one group of people (usually the succession of age groups) by the next.

Consider, first, the aging process: An individual's life is patterned by a variety of role sequences, probably the most important of which is the family life cycle, but also including sequences of student, career, and community roles. The combination and juxtaposition of various

*This article was the APA Invited Address presented by Eleanor Bernert Sheldon at the meeting of the American Psychological Association, Chicago, August 1975. *From American Psychologist, 1976, 31, 106-116. Copyright 1976 by the American Psychological Association. Reprinted by permission.*

role sequences provide texture to an individual life cycle. Certain roles are traditionally associated with certain ages: student roles with the young; parental roles with the middle years; life alone (whether as a result of divorce, widowhood, or lifelong singleness) with the middle aged and elderly.

Second, the historical times during which an individual matures also affect expectations and behavior: the 1930s Depression, World War II, the Vietnam War—all have an impact on patterns of marriage, fertility, and employment.

Finally, each birth cohort has a unique pattern of experiences as it progresses through the life cycle, experiences that may be seen as the interaction of the aging process and the period during which it occurs. The cohort that grew up and reached maturity during the 1930s bears the mark of the Depression. The baby-boom cohort faces (and will continue to face) sharp competition for education, for jobs, and for a variety of social services—the consequences of belonging to a group that is larger than both the group it follows and the one that will follow it.

The combination of the notion of the life cycle (and subcycles within it) and the notion of cohort succession provides a powerful tool for characterizing and understanding some of the recent changes in the roles and status of American women. Some of these changes have resulted from changes in the perception of appropriate role sequences for women; some are the result of the interaction of social, political, and economic events of the 1960s and 1970s; and some of the changes (and certainly the speed of the changes) may be attributed to the fact that the cohort that reached maturity in the past few years is not an ordinary cohort but rather the baby-boom generation.

Let us examine, briefly, some of these changes. It was noted at the outset that the *family* life cycle constitutes perhaps the most important subcurrent of an individual's life cycle. It is certainly the most important subcycle if that individual happens to be a woman. In fact, the tendency until recently has been to equate the family life cycle with the female life cycle. After all, most women marry at some point in their life, and most married women have children. In 1974, for instance, 95 percent of all women 35 and older had been married at least once, and all but about 10% of them had had at least one child (U.S. Department of Commerce, 1974d, 1975a). Most women's lives have been regulated by the family life cycle, their "career" choices to one extent or another circumscribed by the responsibilities attending their family roles—the bearing and rearing of children.

From this presumed identity of female and family life cycles, there developed well-defined notions of what activities and roles are appropriate for women of different ages, corresponding to different stages of the family life cycle. These expectations were, to some extent, suspended for women who did not fit the mold: the 5% or 10% who never married and the ever-increasing number of divorced, separated, and widowed women. Thus there developed the notion that there are two categories of women: those who are married and those with careers.

In fact, of course, such a dichotomy never existed. In 1950, one quarter of all married women who were living with their husbands were in the labor force; more than one quarter of all women in intact marriages who had school-age children were employed; more than 10% of married women with husband present and preschool children were in the labor force. The number of women who combine career and family roles has risen steadily since then. Nevertheless, it has only been in the last decade or so that notions about what activities and roles are appropriate for women at each stage of the family/female life cycle have become somewhat less rigid. Slowly, social definitions of women's roles are catching up with reality.

Many have seen this trend as the increasing overlap and similarity of men's and women's life cycles. An alternative is to view this trend as the decreasing salience of marriage and the family in the life choices of women. Presser (1973) examined some of the consequences for women and for the family of perfect fertility control. Many of the changes she envisioned are becoming evident in the trends to be highlighted in this chapter: continuing education for women, an orientation toward lifelong careers, smaller families, and child-free marriages. This is not to suggest that all of these changes may be directly attributed to greater contraceptive efficiency. But what it does suggest is that the distinction (in terms of roles and expectations) between child-free women and those with children (whether by choice or through contraceptive failure) is gradually disappearing. Or, to phrase it differently, the family life cycle is becoming but one of a number of subcurrents in the lives of American women.

In documenting some of the facets of this general trend, it is important not only to examine changes in several key aspects of women's (and men's) lives—education, marriage and the establishment of a separate household, childbearing, and labor force participation—but also to examine these changes with a view to the variable effects on different age groups at different stages in the life cycle.

EDUCATION

It is appropriate to begin the discussion of changes in the status of American women with some information on changes in their educational attainment. Education has traditionally been regarded as an early stage of the life cycle—a stage that is completed before a career (be it job, marriage, family, or whatever) is launched. Furthermore, the educational system plays a major role in influencing the goals and expectations of individuals; it also is a major source of the contacts and training that will enable the individual to pursue those goals. Thus, the education system plays both a formal and an informal role in channeling individuals into certain lifework and life-styles.

That there has been a steady rise in the educational attainment of the U.S. population over the past 35 years is well known: the proportion of Americans between the ages of 25 and 34 with at least 4 years of high school has risen from 35% in 1940 to 80% in 1974. The percentage of female high school graduates 20 and 21 years old who have completed at least some college has risen from 24% in 1940 to 46% in 1974; the comparable figures for men are 30% in 1940 and 49% in 1974 (U.S. Department of Commerce, 1974a).

Yet important differences exist between men and women both in the level of educational attainment of each group and in the types of educational training each pursues. For instance, though women are somewhat more likely to finish high school than are men, women are less likely to continue on to college. And if they do go on to college, women are less likely to complete all 4 years. In 1974, 47% of all white women between 25 and 34 years old had completed high school but had no college training, and an additional 33% had completed some college. The comparable figures for white males are 38% with only a high school degree, and 44% with at least some college (U.S. Department of Commerce, 1974a).

There are several stereotypic explanations for these sex differences in educational attainment. First, it is argued, a family is more likely to invest in a son's education than in a daughter's, in the belief that the son *must* be able to find a job, but the daughter may not have to. Second, even if the daughter intends to work, most jobs open to her do not require a college degree: skills necessary for secretarial, clerical, and operative positions can be learned on the job. And third, so the argument goes, the daughter will undoubtedly get married and have children, and will in any case stop her education at that point.

Indeed, marriage and childbearing have traditionally been considered sufficient reasons for women to terminate their schooling, though the parallel roles for men (husband and father) did not, in general, preclude a man from continuing to be a student as well. In discussing the results of a recent national survey, Campbell, Converse, and Rodgers (1975) state the following:

> The proportion of unmarried young women who report attending school of some kind (61 percent) is twice as high as that of their married age cohort

> [18-29] (29 percent), but the proportion of unmarried men of this age [who report attending school] (47 percent) is virtually identical to that of married men (48 percent). When asked why they had terminated their formal education when they had, almost half of the married women referred to their marriage; this response was far less common among young married men.

These explanations for sex differences in educational attainment have taken a rather severe beating in the past decade. First, the argument that women need not support themselves: Increasing numbers of women are the sole wage earners for their families or are economically independent. In March 1973, 42% of all women in the labor force were single, widowed, divorced, or separated, and thus (to a greater or lesser extent) economically on their own; another 19% of the female labor force were married to men with less than $7,000 annual income (U.S. Department of Labor, 1975). Increasingly, women must face the likelihood that at some point in their lifetime they will have to support themselves or contribute to the family income.

Second, the argument that women's work does not require extensive training or educational degrees fails on two counts: (a) women are bringing more education to their traditional jobs and thus making that training a requirement of the position (most secretaries, for instance, are now expected to have some college training); and (b) women are beginning to challenge the rigidity with which "women's work" has been defined, and in seeking entrance to "male jobs," they have had to acquire the prerequisite educational background.

And third, the argument that women will give up their schooling for marriage and family: Increasing numbers of women, in examining their prospects for entering or reentering the labor force, are not abandoning their educational careers upon marriage and the advent of children. The composition of the student population of the United States—in terms of both age and sex—is rapidly changing. Between 1970 and 1974, the number of women in college increased by 30%, while the number of men only increased by 12%. Furthermore, although overall graduate school enrollment has dropped 9% since 1969, the proportion of women in graduate school continues to rise. In 1971, women earned 42% of all BAs and 40% of all MAs. Although women constituted only 14% of all PhDs awarded in 1971, that number is likely to rise quickly in the next few years, for the pool of candidates from which they are drawn is growing rapidly (both in actual numbers and compared with men) (U.S. Department of Labor, 1975).

Not only is the proportion of women seeking education beyond the high school diploma fast approaching that of men, women are also beginning to compete with men to gain entry to the high-prestige occupations that were traditionally closed to them. The proportion of women enrolled in professional schools for such fields as law, medicine, architecture, and engineering, although still low, has risen steadily since 1960. For instance, of the total enrollment in law schools, women accounted for 4% in 1960, 12% in 1972, and 19% in 1974. The same trend may be seen in total enrollments in medical schools, in which women represented 6% of the total in 1960, 13% in 1972, and 18% in 1974. The increasing proportion of women in the first-year class of these programs suggests that these trends will continue (McCarthy & Wolfle, 1975; Parrish, 1974).

Finally, evidence exists that fewer women are abandoning their educational plans upon marriage and childbearing, or they are setting aside these plans only temporarily. This trend may be seen in the number of women 25 years and older who are in school. Between 1970 and 1974, for instance, the college enrollment of women between the ages of 25 and 34 rose from 409,000 to 831,000—an increase of 102%. The comparable increase for men between 25 and 34 was 46%: from 940,000 to 1,371,000 in 1974. Of women in college between the ages of 16 and 34, those 25 years and older rose from 14% in 1970 to 21% in 1974 (U.S. Department of Commerce, 1975c).

During the period 1970–1974, part-time enrollment in college increased 50%, compared with a 10% increase in the number of full-time students. The role that the older college students play in this trend toward part-time continuing education is evident: 63% of the 25–34-year-olds were enrolled on a part-time basis in 1974, compared with only 17% of those in the traditional college cohort (18–24-year-olds) (U.S. Department of Commerce, 1975c).

These changes have had two important effects on the lives of American women. First, the young women in the age cohort that traditionally constituted the student population (those under age 25) are facing much less resistance—social and institutional—in their efforts to gain access to the training that is a prerequisite for career mobility. Second, and perhaps more important, those women *not* in the traditional student cohort—those who are older, who are married, or who have children—are no longer deemed to have "missed the boat" by having taken on family roles before completing their schooling. "Student" is no longer synonymous with "pre-adult."

In the following sections, some of the push and pull factors associated with the return of older women to school will be discussed: changes in the marital and childbearing patterns that have made continuing education more easy to arrange and changes in the labor market that have made that education more desirable to acquire—at least for women.

MARRIAGE AND CHILDBEARING

Three of the most remarkable trends in the past two decades have all had a direct effect on the phasing of what was traditionally considered the main portion of a woman's life cycle—namely, marriage and childbearing. Specifically, women are postponing marriage, postponing childbearing within marriage, and reducing their family size expectations.

Take marital patterns, for instance. The median age at first marriage for women has risen from 20.3 in 1950 to 21.1 in 1974. Furthermore, in the age group in which most men and women traditionally marry (20–24), the percentage of women remaining single has risen from 28% in 1960 to 39% in 1974—an increase of one third. In general, while the percentage remaining single is up sharply for persons under 35, it continues to decline for persons 35 and over (U.S. Department of Commerce, 1974d). The long-term effect of the trend among the 20–24 cohort to remain single may be a later marriage age, or it may be a growing commitment to lifelong singleness; it is too early to say.

There are many explanations for this dramatic change in marriage patterns in the last 25 years. First, the expansion of educational opportunities for women has provided them with alternatives to their traditional life choices, and they are postponing (sometimes indefinitely) parental roles in favor of occupational careers. Second, there is increasing acceptance of nontraditional living arrangements; couples who might have bowed to social pressure to marry no longer feel compelled to do so. Third, the 1960s saw a dramatic rise in the number of young marriage-age men inducted into the armed forces, and thus made relatively inaccessible to the marriage market. But, in addition to these and other explanations for delayed marriage, demographers have given us one other: *the marriage squeeze.* Since women tend to marry men two or three years older than themselves, the women of the baby boom reached marriage age before the comparably large male marriage cohort. Or, to put it another way, there were not enough men in the appropriate age groups for the marriage-age women. For some women, then, the postponement of marriage may have been involuntary—the demographic fallout of the baby boom (Glick & Parke, 1965; Parke & Glick, 1967).

In part as a consequence of postponed marriage, in part for other reasons, women are postponing childbearing. For instance, 70% of white women married between 1955 and 1959 had their first child in the first 24 months of marriage; ten years later, i.e. among women married between 1965 and 1969, only 60% had had their first child within two years of marriage. The same trend is seen for later-order births as well. It should be noted, however, that in the same ten-year comparison for black women, the trend is reversed (U.S. Department of Commerce, 1974c).

Not only are women having their children later, they are also having, and planning to have, fewer children. This phenomenon has given us another term in the popular lexicon on the changing life cycle: *the birth dearth.* Between 1960 and 1974, the percentage of ever-married women between the ages of 15 and 19 who were child-free increased by 25% (from 44% to 56%); for ever-married women 20–24, those child-free rose by two thirds (from 24% to 41%); and for ever-married women 25–29, the rise was close to 60% (from 13% to 20%) (U.S. Department of Commerce, 1975a). It is interesting to note that this drop in births since 1960 will produce a reverse marriage squeeze in the next five years or so: young men will be locating mates from a *smaller* cohort of women.

In 1974, the birth rate in the United States reached a point lower even than the level reached during the 1930s Depression: 14.8 per 1,000 population. Not only the birth rate but the fertility expectations of women have dropped dramatically and quickly. In 1955, 38% of women aged 18–24 expected to have four or more children (U.S. Department of Labor, 1973); between 1967 and 1974, the proportion of women in this age group who expected to have four or more children dropped by more than two-thirds: from 26% in 1967 to 8% in 1974. At the same time, the number of women anticipating two children rose dramatically: from 37% of the women 18–24 in 1967 to 56% in 1974—an increase of 50%. For women in the 25–29 age range, the increase in the number expecting only two children was even more dramatic: from 29% in 1967 to 52% in 1974 (U.S. Department of Commerce, 1975a).

At the same time that family size expectations are decreasing, there is an increasing proportion of childless women who expect to *remain* childless: in 1974, 11% of childless married women 14–24 and 27% of childless married women 25–29 did not expect to have any children. These figures represent an increase of 23% in just three years in wives under 30 who do not plan to have children (U.S. Department of Commerce, 1975a).

In short, then, women have been entering the traditional family cycle more slowly, and because of their smaller families, they have been spending less time in that phase of their life.

FEMALE HEADS OF HOUSEHOLDS[1]

One way to examine some of the changes that have taken place in family living arrangements in the past two decades is to look at changes in female-headed households. Between 1954 and 1969, the number of female heads of families increased by about 40%; this number grew another 22% between 1970 and 1974, so that by 1974 female-headed households represented 10% of all households in the United States, and approximately 15% of all families with children. Much of this change reflects the increase in the number of black female family heads. Since 1960 there has been a 10% increase in the number of white female family heads, and a 35% increase in the number of black female family heads. In 1973, black women represented 28% of all female family heads (U.S. Department of Commerce, 1975b).

Female heads of households are younger (on average) than previously and more apt to be divorced, separated, or single, rather than widowed. Between 1960 and 1973, the median age of women who headed families declined by about 5 years, from 50.5 in 1960 to 45.1 in 1973, with black female family heads about 9 years younger than their white counterparts (U.S. Department of Commerce, 1974b). The shift toward younger, divorced or separated female family heads (from older, widowed family heads) will no doubt continue as a result of the continuing and rising rate of divorces and separations. In 1973, 37% of female family heads were widowed, 13% unmarried, and 50% divorced or separated. This is in contrast with 1960, when 50% of them were widowed and 36% divorced or separated (U.S. Department of Commerce, 1974b).

There are two fundamental reasons for interest in and concern for increases in the number of households headed by women. First, as a group, these households are particularly disadvantaged. Two thirds of all female household heads have less than a high school education. In 1972, more than half of them had incomes below the poverty threshold ($4,254), compared with less than 10% of male heads of households. In 1973, a higher proportion of children under 18 years of age lived in fatherless families than ever before: about 10% of white children and 38% of black children. Nearly one half of all female family heads between the ages of 25 and 44 have three or more children. In short, increasing numbers of children are experiencing the economic disadvantages which attend households headed by

[1]Any woman 14 years old or older may head a family if she is not married and living with her husband. She may or may not live alone, and if she lives with others, they may or may not be related to her. If she lives alone or with nonrelatives, she is called a primary individual. If she lives with others who are related to her by blood, marriage, or adoption, she is the head of a primary family. For a detailed discussion of households headed by women, see Ross and MacIntosh (1973).

women (U.S. Department of Commerce, 1974b; U.S. Department of Labor, 1975; Waldman & Whitmore, 1974).

The second major reason for interest in the growth of female-headed households is that increasing numbers of women have experienced or will experience this status at some point in their lives. The shift toward later marriage age, when combined with the ability and inclination of young single women to leave their parents' homes and set up their own households, has been a major element in the increase in households of "primary individuals" who are female. The rise in the number of children born to unmarried women, coupled with the tendency for these women to set up their own household rather than move in with relatives, has also contributed to the trend.

But the major factor in the rise in the number of households headed by women is the increasing likelihood that a marriage will end in divorce or separation. The number and rate of divorces increased in 1974 for the twelfth straight year. The ratio of divorced people to those in intact marriages has risen from a level of 35 per 1,000 in 1960 to 63 per 1,000 in 1974, with approximately 50% more divorced women than divorced men in 1974—an indication of the greater likelihood that divorced men will remarry. Perhaps the most important element in this trend has been the shift in the age patterns of divorce in recent years. In 1974, the ratio of divorced persons to persons in intact marriages was higher for those under 45 years old (66 per 1,000) than for those 45 years and over (59 per 1,000), representing a reversal of the situation a decade earlier (U.S. Department of Commerce, 1974d).

It has been argued that the rise in the number of families headed by women represents not a preference for single-parent families but rather a transitional status which increasing proportions of women will enter (and leave) at some point in their lives (Ross & MacIntosh, 1973). The vast majority of the individuals who are postponing marriage today are likely to marry at some point; a growing proportion of them will experience separation and divorce; and an increasing proportion of those divorced will experience remarriage. Between 1960 and 1969, the rate of remarriage of divorced women rose by almost 11% (from 122.1 per 1,000 divorced women to 135.4). In contrast, the remarriage rate for widows has remained fairly constant: 36.1 per 1,000 widows in 1960 to 39.3 per 1,000 in 1969. Thus, the major group of women who are likely to remain in female-headed households are widows. But, as noted earlier, widows represent a shrinking proportion of the total female household heads (NCHS, 1973).

If, in fact, there has been a decrease in the importance of marital status in predicting or determining the sorts of activities and roles a woman adopts, part of the reason is that marriage is not eternal. More and more women are spending more and more time in roles that lie outside the traditional family life cycle. The length of time after childhood and before marriage is growing, as is the number of women spending time between marriages.

It is not really surprising that the social perception of appropriate female roles is catching up with the reality of post-World-War-II America. It is rather more surprising that it has taken so long to recognize that the "career woman" and the mother may be one and the same person. But then, as Keller (1972) has noted, the working woman is "one of America's best kept secrets."

LABOR FORCE PARTICIPATION[2]

The contrast between the female labor force of 1920 and that of the 1970s is striking. In 1920, the typical working woman was single, under 30 years old, and from the "working class." Today, most working women are married; over two thirds of them have child-rearing responsibilities in addition to their jobs; they represent the entire socio-economic spectrum; and more than half of them are 40 or over.

Between 1950 and 1973, overall labor force participation of women rose by one third. Although women who have never married have been and continue to be much more likely to work, the distinction between never married and other categories of women in terms of their labor market activity is rapidly disappearing. While the labor force participation of never-married women rose 13% between 1950 and 1974 (from 50.5% to 57.2%), it rose over 80% for married women who were living with their husbands (from 23.8% to 43.0%).

Since the mid-1960s, the greatest increase in labor force participation of women has been among those in the 25–34 age range—the ages during which women are most intensively involved in child-rearing, and the ages at which female labor force participation has traditionally been lowest. Among women 25–34, the proportion in the labor force has risen from 36% in 1960 to 50% in 1973—an increase of close to 40% in thirteen years (U.S. Department of Labor, 1975).

Several reasons can be given for the changing composition of the female labor force over the past several decades, some of which have already been highlighted. The rise in the educational attainment of young women in the past several decades has given women access to jobs that were previously inaccessible to them because they lacked the requisite training. Demographic trends have also played a role in encouraging increasing numbers of women to enter the labor force and

[2]For a discussion of trends in female labor force participation in the United States in the twentieth century, see Oppenheimer (1970). For additional information, see the annual publication of the U.S. Department of Labor, *Manpower Report of the President.*

to stay there. Because young women have been postponing marriage, and postponing childbearing within marriage, they experience a relatively long period of time after completing high school or college during which they may advance in their careers. And increasingly, women are finding it difficult to give up the economic independence, as well as the challenge, recognition, and satisfaction they derive from their jobs. Over a third of married women with preschool children were in the labor force in 1974, as contrasted with only 12% in 1950.

In a study of female labor market activity using data from the 1960 U.S. Census, Sweet (1973) found that women with more education were more likely to be in the labor force while their children were preschoolers than were those women with less than a high school education. Sweet suggests two reasons for these findings: differences in child-spacing patterns and differences in previous labor market experience. If women with less education are likely to have the second child relatively quickly, they will be pregnant again while the first child is still a preschooler, and thus less interested in returning to the job. And with good reason: The jobs less educated women perform tend to be more hazardous than the jobs open to women with a college education.

Well-educated women are more likely to have worked both before marriage and before childbearing, and for a longer period of time. This fact has two consequences: (a) the family's consumption patterns have become adapted to two incomes, a level of living difficult to abandon; and (b) these women, with their relatively recent work experience, have greater contact with the labor market and knowledge of job opportunities and are more likely to find employment when they want it.

In addition to affecting the number of women in the labor force, demographic trends have also affected the composition of the female labor force, more particularly the shift from a young, unmarried female labor force to a middle-aged, married one. This shift has been explained, in part, by the concept of a *life cycle squeeze* (Gove, Grimm, Motz, & Thompson, 1973; Oppenheimer, 1974). Expenses are particularly high two times during the typical family life cycle: the first occurs soon after the couple is married, when the acquisition of home and other accoutrements of married life usually takes place; the second occurs when children reach adolescence. Both are times when the husband's income alone is not likely to be sufficient to cover these expenses: the first because he is at the beginning of his career at the time that he is beginning his marriage; the second because the time when the costs of maintaining the family are highest (adolescence of children) may not coincide with the time when his income reaches its peak. Oppenheimer (1974) finds that men in occupations where the peak median earnings in 1959 were $7,000 or more were much more likely to have their incomes rise roughly in proportion to increases in the cost of maintaining their families. However, men in occupations with peak median incomes under $7,000 in 1959 were likely to experience peak child-care costs at a time when they were not earning much more, and sometimes less on average, than were younger men with younger and therefore less expensive children. These situations create strong economic pressures for an additional income, and are undoubtedly one reason why young brides continue to work after marriage and why women in their forties and fifties have entered or reentered the labor market in record numbers in recent years.[3]

Changes in the U.S. economy in the twentieth century have also encouraged women to enter and remain in the labor force. The industries and occupations that have expanded most rapidly (particularly during the period after 1940) are those that were the major employers of women. This trend has been characterized as a shift from the goods-producing economy prior to World War II to the service-producing economy of the 1970s (Waldman & Whitmore, 1974). The post-World-War-II baby boom created the need for an expansion of a wide variety of services—educational, medical, governmental, and recreational among them—services in which most women workers were concentrated.

But while the demand for female labor was rising, the women who traditionally filled these jobs—the young and the single—constituted a stable or declining population, at least until the late 1960s. The dramatic expansion and changing composition of the female labor force in post-World-War-II America, then, are seen in part as the response of older married women to the growing demand for female labor (Oppenheimer, 1970).

Let us consider for a moment the notion of a demand for female labor and the question of the sex labeling of jobs and professions. It is well known that women are highly concentrated in a few occupations in which they constitute an overwhelming majority of all workers. For instance, in 1960, elementary school teachers and registered nurses accounted for almost 54% of all female professional employment; in 1970, they were still just over 46% of all female professionals (Fuchs, 1975). Oppenheimer (1970) has argued that the U.S. labor market is actually two markets—male and female—and that men and women in most cases do not really compete for the same jobs. The expansion of "women's" occupations after World War II led not to a

[3]Comments by A. J. Jaffe and Murray Gendell on Oppenhemier's article appear in *Demography* (1975, *12*, 331-336). Gendell notes that it may be the financial squeeze that propels middle-age women into the labor force (as Oppenheimer suggests), or it may be the decreased child-care responsibilities associated with adolescent children which *enables* women to seek outside employment.

demand for additional labor but to a demand for additional *female* labor.

The principal employer of women today, as it was in 1940, is the service industries and, more particularly, professional services (medical and health, education, and legal) (Waldman & McEaddy, 1974). As Oppenheimer (1970) has suggested, a number of reasons can be given for the persistence of sex labels on certain jobs:

1. Such "women's jobs" as teaching, nursing, and secretarial work depend on skilled but cheap labor in fairly large quantities—and women who are entering the labor force for the first time, or reentering after a long absence, are willing to accept pay that is not commensurate with their skills or training.
2. Most of the training for these occupations is acquired *before* employment. Thus the employer does not bear the risk of investing time and money training women, with the attendant possibility that they will soon leave.[4]
3. These "women's jobs" do not require a long-term commitment, or extensive sacrifice of time, and thus women, who have traditionally been seen as secondary earners who lack high career aspirations, are attracted to them.[5]
4. These jobs exist all over the country, and thus women are not usually handicapped by their mobility (if their husbands must move frequently in their jobs) *or* their immobility (if their husbands must stay in one place).
5. Finally, these jobs have traditionally been held by women. The jobs are thought to call on skills that are innately female (the greater manual dexterity often attributed to women) or on skills that are acquired in the home (the patience to work with children!). Furthermore, these traditional female jobs rarely put women in a supervisory position over men—a situation that is thought to create rebellion among male underlings.

Considerable debate continues as to whether there has been any change in the sex labeling or sex segregation of occupations in recent years (Fuchs, 1975; Gross, 1968; Hedges & Bemis, 1974; Knudsen, 1969). Gross (1968) has argued, for instance, that what small decrease there may be in occupational segregation is due not to the entrance of women into traditionally male occupations but the reverse: a "decreased resistance by female occupations to the entry of

---

[4]A recent study examines patterns of quitting for men and women, and finds that quitting to exit the labor force is larger for women, and quitting to move to another job is larger for men. Barnes and Jones (1974) also find that total female quitting is usually greater than male quitting, but male quitting is more variable from year to year.

[5]For a discussion of the assumptions about female career aspirations, see Crowley, Levitin, and Quinn (1973).

males" (p. 198). Fuchs (1975) has argued that the trend is much more complex. A drop in an index of occupational segregation could occur either as a result of a change in the average amount of segregation within occupations or as a result of differential rates of growth of occupations. Using a simple index of sex segregation, which may be interpreted as the proportion of people who would have to shift to occupations dominated by the opposite sex in order to eliminate sex segregation, Fuchs finds a drop of 7 percentage points between 1960 (66.2%) and 1970 (59.2%). Fuchs notes that between 1960 and 1970 some occupations became less segregated: the greatest changes were among elementary school teachers and registered nurses (in female-dominated professions) and among engineers, accountants, and science technicians (in male-dominated professions). At the same time, the less sex-segregated occupations (e.g. college and secondary school teachers, computer specialists, health technologists) were growing more rapidly.

If there is today less resistance to female employment in traditionally male-dominated occupations, it has not been without its adverse consequences. In the 1976 recession, women workers accounted for significantly larger proportions of the unemployed—a fact that underscores their recent entry and consequent low status in a range of occupations (U.S. Department of Labor, 1975). And among women who have been able to keep their jobs, there seems to be no decrease in the income differentials between men and women. The grim news in the 1975 *Manpower Report of the President* was that "nearly two-thirds of all full-time, year-round female workers earned *less* than $7,000 in 1972" while "over three-quarters of full-time, year-round male workers earned *over* $7,000." Even when earnings are adjusted for hours worked and level of education of the worker, the large differentials in earnings between male and female workers persist. For instance, Suter and Miller (1973) found, in working with income data from 1966, that "if women had the same occupational status as men, had worked all their lives, had the same education and year-round full-time employment in 1966, their income would be . . . 62 percent of that received by men (p. 962)."

The sex labeling of jobs, the occupational segregation of women, and the consequent income differentials between men and women have been remarkably persistent in the face of dramatic demographic and socioeconomic changes. But it is precisely these changes that will inevitably restructure the career experiences and labor market activity of women in the next several decades. The present female occupational distribution, as is noted in the 1975 *Manpower Report,* is the result of myriad influences, some in early childhood: "Role differentiation in early life later affects educational and occupational choices, hours and location of work, and other factors which relegate women to lower level positions in the lower paying industries" (U.S. Department of Labor, 1975).

The change that is coming can already be seen in the choices young women have been making in their educational and their family "careers." Because marriage is no longer an end in itself, because so many women spend time outside of marriage or in between marriages, because family/parental roles occupy a relatively short portion of a woman's total life in today's two-child society, because women are receiving the education and training (and with it the career aspirations) to cause them to plan for and expect employment opportunities parallel to those of men, and, finally, because all of these conditions represent changes from the recent past, to note that the pattern of female labor force participation is likely to change is anticlimactic.

However, despite all these changes, nowhere is it suggested that the pattern of female occupational choices, earnings, or job mobility will approximate that of men, and certainly not in the near future. The reasons have nothing to do with women's skills or aspirations, and surprisingly little to do with the prospects for economic recovery in the United States in the next few years. The reasons have everything to do with the life cycle concerns discussed above. Although marital status and parental responsibilities are likely to become less salient in women's career choices, women will continue to bear the major responsibility for children, and it is their careers that will continue to be marked by the need to accommodate both parental and occupational roles.

Whether female labor force participation will approximate that of males, or even whether it should—given that the distribution of mothers, and most of the responsibilities that accompany that role, is 100% female—is not a particularly fruitful line of inquiry. More productive of insight will be some close attention to the social and economic lags created by these recent social and demographic trends. Two examples come readily to mind: the "two-career family" and the "dual career" woman.

The two-career family is one in which both the husband and the wife are employed; it characterizes a growing portion of all U.S. families. Traditionally, career mobility has involved some geographic mobility. A family with school-age children and headed by one wage earner is not particularly mobile; the two-career family is even less so. What will be the effects on the labor market of the increased reluctance or inability of talented young people to move to further their careers? Or, alternatively, what will be the effect on marriage and divorce patterns on the continued importance of a certain amount of geographic mobility in furthering one's career?

Second, "dual careers": Dual careers refer to the combination and juxtaposition of parental and occupational responsibilities which confront increasing numbers of women. As more and more women with family responsibilities enter the labor force, certain institutional changes may be necessary—among them, the improvement of child-care facilities, increased flexibility of work schedules, and better provisions for job training. At what cost will these changes to accommodate the dual career woman be made? Or, alternatively, what will be the costs (social and otherwise) of *not* making the necessary institutional changes?

CONCLUSION

At the outset it was suggested that one way of summarizing these various trends was in terms of the declining importance of the family life cycle in the woman's total life cycle—the diminishing social importance of the distinction between married women and those who are unmarried (never married, no longer married, not yet married). In examining this general proposition, recent changes in a number of areas which have a direct impact on a woman's life choices were highlighted: education, marriage, childbearing, and employment.

The essential message has been: The traditional family life cycle for women has been slowly disappearing for the past quarter century; the rapid-paced changes of the past decade have released the secret, and another sacred myth is being dispelled. With the death of the myth, little doubt now exists that during the last decades of the century these trends will exert a profound effect on family, economy, social values—and, of course, the changing bases of self-identification and of sex roles.

REFERENCES

Barnes, W.F., & Jones, E.B. Differences in male and female quitting. *Journal of Human Resources,* 1974, *9,* 439-451.

Campbell, A., Converse, P.E., & Rodgers, W. *The perceived quality of life.* Ann Arbor: University of Michigan, 1975. (Prepublication draft)

Crowley, J.E., Levitin, T.E., & Quinn, R.P. *Facts and fictions about the American working woman.* Ann Arbor: University of Michigan, Institute for Social Research, January 1973. (Mimeo)

Fuchs, V.R. A note on sex segregation in professional occupations. *Explorations in Economic Research,* 1975, *2,* 105-111.

Gendell, M. Further comment on V.K. Oppenheimer's "The life-cycle squeeze: The interaction of men's occupational and family life cycles." *Demography,* 1975, *12,* 333-336.

Glick, P.C., & Parke, R., Jr. New approaches in studying the life cycle of the family. *Demography,* 1965, *2,* 187-202.

Gove, W.R., Grimm, J.W., Motz, S.C., & Thompson, J.D. The family life cycle: Internal dynamics and social consequences. *Sociology and Social Research,* 1973, *57,* 182-195.

Gross, E. Plus ça change . . . ? The sexual structure of occupations over time. *Social Problems,* 1968, *16,* 198-208.

Hedges, J.N., & Bemis, S.E. Sex stereotyping: Its decline in skilled trades. *Monthly Labor Review,* 1974, *97,* (May), 14-22.

Jaffe, A.J. Comment on V.K. Oppenheimer's "The life-cycle squeeze: The interaction of men's occupational and family life cycles." *Demography,* 1975, *12,* 331-332.

Keller, S. The future status of women in America. In C.F. Westoff & R. Parke, Jr. (Eds.), *Demographic and social aspects of population growth* (Research Reports of the Commission on Population Growth and the American Future, Vol. 1). Washington, D.C.: U.S. Government Printing Office, 1972.

Knudsen, D.D. The declining status of women: Popular myths and the failure of functionalist thought. *Social Forces,* 1969, *48,* 183-193.

McCarthy, J.L., & Wolfle, D. Doctorates granted to women and minority group members. *Science,* 1975, *189,* 856-859.

National Center for Health Statistics. *Remarriages, United States* (Series 21, No. 25, Vital and Health Statistics). Rockville, Md.: Author, December 1973.

Oppenheimer, V.K. *The female labor force in the United States: Demographic and economic factors governing its growth and changing composition* (Population Monograph Series, No. 5). Berkeley: University of California, 1970.

Oppenheimer, V.K. The life-cycle squeeze: The interaction of men's occupational and family life cycles. *Demography,* 1974, *11,* 227-245.

Parke, R., Jr., & Glick, P.C. Prospective changes in marriage and the family. *Journal of Marriage and the Family,* 1967, *29,* 249-256.

Parrish, J.B. Women in professional training. *Monthly Labor Review,* 1974, *97* (May), 40-43.

Presser, H. Perfect fertility control: Consequences for women and the family. In C.F. Westoff et al. (Eds.), *Toward the end of growth.* Englewood Cliffs, N.J., Prentice-Hall, 1973.

Riley, M.W., Johnson, M., & Foner, A. (Eds.). *Aging and society.* New York: Russell Sage Foundation, 1972.

Ross, H.L., & MacIntosh, A. *The emergence of households headed by women.* Washington, D.C.: Urban Institute, June 1973. (Unpublished paper)

Suter, L.E., & Miller, H.P. Components of differences between the incomes of men and career women. *American Journal of Sociology,* 1973, *79,* 962-974.

Sweet, J.A. *Women in the labor force.* New York: Seminar Press, 1973.

U.S. Department of Commerce, Bureau of the Census. Educational attainment in the United States: March 1973 and 1974 (P-20, No. 274). *Current Population Reports.* Washington, D.C.: Author, December 1974. (a)

U.S. Department of Commerce, Bureau of the Census. Female family heads (P-23, No. 50). *Current Population Reports.* Washington, D.C.: Author, July 1974. (b)

U.S. Department of Commerce, Bureau of the Census. Fertility histories and birth expectations of American women: June 1971 (P-20, No. 263). *Current Population Reports.* Washington, D.C.: Author, April 1974. (c)

U.S. Department of Commerce, Bureau of the Census. Marital status and living arrangements: March 1974 (P-20, No. 271). *Current Population Reports.* Washington, D.C.: Author, October 1974. (d)

U.S. Department of Commerce, Bureau of the Census. Fertility expectations of American women: June 1974 (P-20, No. 277). *Current Population Reports.* Washington, D.C.: Author, February 1975. (a)

U.S. Department of Commerce, Bureau of the Census. Population profile of the United States: 1974 (P-20, No. 279). *Current Population Reports.* Washington, D.C.: Author, March 1975. (b)

U.S. Department of Commerce, Bureau of the Census. School enrollment—Social and economic characteristics of students: October 1974 (P-20, No. 278). *Current Population Reports.* Washington, D.C.: Author, February 1975. (c)

U.S. Department of Labor. *Manpower report of the President.* Washington, D.C.: U.S. Government Printing Office, annual.

Waldman, E., & McEaddy, B.J. Where women work—An analysis by industry and occupation. *Monthly Labor Review, 1974, 97*(May), 3-13.

Waldman, E., & Whitmore, R. Children of working mothers. *Monthly Labor Review,* 1974, *97*(May), 50-58.

Section II

FEMALE ASPIRATIONS, MOTIVATION, AND CAREER DECISION MAKING

It is evident that women do not achieve or contribute as much as men in the fields of science, technology, business, the humanities, or the arts, and that many women choose occupations that demand less than their full potential. It is less apparent why this is so. It seems clear that the attitudes and motivations that underlie the career aspirations, plans, and decisions of women are the inevitable products of social norms and socialization processes that put women into powerful psychological conflict as they are forced to cope with vocational choices. The chapters in this section highlight some of the factors related to female aspirations, motivation, and career decision making, but by no means represent an exhaustive review of the literature in this area.

The original work on achievement motivation (McClelland et. al., 1953) was based on male subjects; when women's response data did not fit the theory, they were ignored. It was assumed that for women the achievement motive is less central than the affiliative motive, while the reverse is true for men. The publication of Matina Horner's (1969, 1970) work provided a new look at female achievement (or lack of it); her study posited that women were motivated to avoid success. Horner's work was followed by a flurry of research on the "fear of success;" subsequent findings were often inconsistent and frequently have been challenged.

In the first chapter in this section Alper looks at the methodological problems involved in studying women's achievement motivation. She concludes that the "Now-you-see-it-now-you-don't phenomenon" in the female achievement motivation literature appears to be a function of wide methodological differences from study to study but that sweeping generalizations about the fear of success variable may be unfounded. One important point is that most of the investigations in this area have studied achievement motivation with projective techniques; the crucial question raised by Alper is whether or not individuals high and low in the motive to avoid success actually do differ in real life achievement situations. Finally, Alper suggests that as shifts in social role expectations now occurring are felt, women's willingness to express achievement needs may sharply increase.

In an original contribution for this book, Farmer identifies and reexamines some of the variables that inhibit achievement and career motivation for women, such as home-career conflict, work discrimination beliefs, reduction in academic self-confidence, fear of success, and vicarious achievement motivation. Farmer also suggests that career guidance for the seventies must emphasize coping skills for the world of tomorrow, including planning for multiple roles and adjusting to changing career opportunities. She defines and discusses the concept of androgyny or sex-free roles.

The third article in this part describes in an intriguing way how some women have dealt with the socially-induced conflict between need for achievement and the social disapproval directed toward women who dare to strive or compete directly. Lipman-Blumen and Leavitt examine what they term vicarious versus direct achievement orientations. They describe three types of vicarious and three types of direct routes to achievement arranged along a continuum. Many women meet achievement needs indirectly through the accomplishments of significant others such as husbands, fathers, or children. Social norms typically imply that marital and maternal roles, largely vicarious in nature, are the most desirable and appropriate roles for women. In contrast, men typically achieve directly through their own successes. The authors examine the differential socialization processes that contribute to the differing achievement orientations of males and females. The authors suggest that increased flexibility in both occupational and family roles for both women and men is desirable; perhaps different achievement orientations are suitable to females and males at different stages in the life cycle. Individual preferences for sequential roles versus concurrent roles need to be explored. Roles within organizations and social institutions also require redefinition to take advantage of the full range of achievement orientations.

In a cross-sectional study of the future plans of junior and senior high school girls and college women, Rand and Miller concluded that a new cultural imperative of marriage and occupational career is emerging for American women. Although most of the women chose the typical and stereotyped feminine occupations, the majority opted for plans that involved combining a vocation, marriage, and motherhood. Rand and Miller point out that family and occupational career roles can no longer be viewed as mutually exclusive choices and that sophisticated attempts either to understand the aspirations of women or to help women realize those aspirations must involve the interaction of these two major life roles. This is the same phenomenon that Van Dusen and Sheldon (see Chapter 4) declared to be the basis for a new life cycle pattern for women. While the results of the Rand and Miller study are encouraging, their findings are inconsistent with other studies in terms of both the consistency in choice found across ages and the proportion of women choosing a marriage/occupational career combination. It may be possible that a social desirability phenomenon is operating; it is currently socially appropriate for women to choose both marriage and an occupation. These young women may have answered the questionnaire in the socially appropriate direction without really thinking through their future plans and aspirations. It would be enlightening to know what kinds of life pattern choices these young women eventually make.

In the final chapter in this section, Rapoza and Blocher report a study of the plans and aspirations of high school females. They report the familiar findings that female educational aspirations tend to decline as high school graduation approaches. Their most surprising finding, however, is the basic difficulty that many high school girls find in reporting *any* kind of educational or vocational plan at all. This is consistent with some earlier studies which found a lack of planfulness and information-seeking behavior in adolescent females.

Although somewhat fragmented and inconsistent, the current research in achievement motivation has made several important contributions to the development of female psychology of achievement. It has caused us to reexamine the male model of achievement and become aware of male biases in the literature. The construct of achievement motivation may need to be expanded to account for differing modes and processes of achievement in women. It seems likely that an explanation of female achievement motivation will need to integrate a number of interacting variables; any formulation based on one factor such as motive to avoid success is too simplistic. Other factors found to be related to female achievement include locus of control, expectancies, reinforcement history, risk taking behavior, fear of loss of affiliation, and socialization. It also seems important to identify mechanisms used by women to integrate and cope with conflicting needs.

The process of career decision making may also represent differing processes for males and females. Several variables unique to women must be accounted for in an explanation of female occupational choice. The psychological, sociological, and economic influences on career decision making need to be examined from a female perspective if we are to obtain an adequate knowledge base about how women's career decisions are made over the life span.

The implications for intervention at all ages are clear. The data presented by Rand and Miller and Rapoza and Blocher suggest that young women still require more education in relation to nontraditional occupations for women and assistance with planning and decision making. However, it is essential that women not simply be presented with information about new options but also be aided in coping with conflicts that arise due to conflict-producing factors such as fear of loss of affiliation. Lipman-Blumen and Leavitt suggest that women need to be assisted in making transitions from one kind of achievement orientation to another at different life stages. While the studies presented in this section are provocative and shed considerable light on aspects of female career motivation and aspirations, there is still much to be investigated about those factors which inhibit and those which facilitate female career decision making and development. Related issues are discussed in more detail in Sections V and VI.

As stated previously, the chapters in this section provide only a sampling of the literature in this area. Some of the following references may help the reader gain a broader perspective on the topics introduced.

BIBLIOGRAPHY

Horner, M.S. Fail: bright woman. *Psychology Today,* 1969, *3*(6), 36-38, 62.

Horner, M.S. Femininity and successful achievement: a basic inconsistency. In J. M. Horner & D. Gutman (Eds.), *Feminine Personality and Conflict.* Belmont, Ca: Brooks/Cole, 1970.

Horner, M.S. The motive to avoid success and changing aspirations of women. In J.M. Bardwick (Ed.), *Readings on the Psychology of Women.* New York: Harper & Row, 1972.

Maccoby, E.E., and Jacklin, C. N. Achievement motivation and self-concept. In E.E. Maccoby and C.N. Jacklin (Eds.), *The Psychology of Sex Differences.* Stanford, Ca.: Stanford University Press, 1974, 134-163.

McClelland, D.C., Atkinson, J.W., Clark, R.A., & Lowell, E.L. *The Achievement Motive.* New York: Appleton-Century Crofts, 1953.

Mednick, M.T.S., Tangri, S.S., & Hoffman, L.W. *Women and Achievement: Social and Motivational Analyses.* New York: John Wiley & Sons, 1975.

Unger, R.K. and Denmark, F.L. (Eds.). *Woman: Dependent or Independent Variable?* New York: Psychological Dimensions, Inc., 1975.

Chapter 5

ACHIEVEMENT MOTIVATION IN COLLEGE WOMEN: A Now-You-See-It—Now-You-Don't Phenomenon*

THELMA G. ALPER

BEGINNING with the earliest studies by McClelland, Atkinson, Clark, and Lowell (1953), achievement motivation research based on male subjects typically has yielded significant and readily replicable findings. Until recently, however, this has not been the case when female subjects were used. An example of this discrepancy is that for males, achievement-oriented instructions (emphasis on leadership capacity and intelligence) increase the McClelland et al. (1953) need for achievement score, while task-oriented, neutral, or relaxed instructions depress it. Comparable shifts have rarely been reported for females. Instead, both achievement and neutral instructional sets evoke equally high need for achievement scores in women, e.g. see Alper & Greenberger (1967); Veroff, Wilcox, & Atkinson (1953). Similar discrepancies arise when other hypotheses are tested: Veroff, Feld, and Crockett (1966), for example, hypothesized that picture cues closely related to the storyteller's own occupation would be less effective evokers of achievement imagery than unrelated cues. This hypothesis held for male subjects, but not for female subjects. To cite one more example, in the French and Lesser (1964) study, despite some positive support for the major hypothesis, the thrust of their main argument concerning achievement motivation in women was weakened in the end by a wholly unanticipated, statistically significant, *contrary* finding.

In addition to the inconsistency of the findings across sexes, what is also striking is the relative paucity of studies based on females. A survey of the specialized texts in this area reveals just how minimal

*This article was presented originally as the presidential address at the meeting of the New England Psychological Association, New Haven, Connecticut, November 1971. It has been updated to include additional studies. *From American Psychologist, 1974, 29, 194-203. Copyright 1974 by the American Psychological Association. Reprinted by permission.*

the research on women has been. The first such text, *The Achievement Motive* (McClelland et al., 1953), devoted 8 of its nearly 400 pages to studies of women. By 1958, interest in the achievement and related motives had grown so rapidly that the record book *Motives in Fantasy, Action and Society* (Atkinson, 1958) required 873 pages to cover the literature, but the research on female achievement motivation was relegated to a single footnote (p. 77). Nine years later, Heckhausen (1967) in *The Anatomy of Achievement Motivation,* concentrating on the more recent American and foreign literature in this field, added only a handful of new studies based on female subjects. Of the 215 pages in this book, 9 dealt with sex differences.

Clearly, between 1953 and 1967, researchers seem to have been considerably less interested in female than in male achievement motivation. Why should this have been the case? Do equivocal and/or contradictory findings discourage continued research? Perhaps so. But a more fundamental question is, Why sex differences in the first place? Up to this point, most researchers seem to have assumed that male and female achievement motivation is governed by essentially the *same* laws, despite the theoretical implications of Field's (1951) early findings.

According to Field, achievement motivation in women, but not in men, is linked to the need for social acceptability, that is, the need to be liked. Prior manipulation of this need, it developed, could raise the McClelland et al. (1953) need for achievement score of women but had no effect on the scores of men. McClelland et al. (1953) interpreted these findings to mean that for women the achievement motive is less central than the affiliative motive, while the reverse is true for men. If this is so, it follows that if one wishes to study achievement motivation in its pure form, one *should* use male subjects, and as Sarason and Smith (1971) decried, this is exactly what most researchers have continued to do. But why, then, was Field's affiliation lead not more fully pursued? Unfortunately, affiliation arousal, at least within Field's framework, also turned out to be undependable for arousing need for achievement in women (see Atkinson's [1958] report of Vogel's [1954] findings).

Throughout the 1950s and 1960s a few investigators continued to use the original McClelland et al. (1953) approach for arousing achievement motivation, encouraged, perhaps, by Angelini's (1955) findings that an achievement-oriented instructional set could significantly increase the achievement motivation scores of women as well as of men. Though Angelini's results turned out to be no more readily replicable than those of Field, a number of seemingly relevant variables did begin to emerge. Among these were sex of the stimulus figures (Alper, 1957; Lesser, Krawitz, & Packard, 1963; Veroff, Wilcox,

& Atkinson, 1953), the effect of the sex and position of the stimulus figures relative to each other (Alper & Greenberger, 1967), differences in value orientation (French & Lesser, 1964; Lesser et al., 1963), and age and family situation of the storyteller (Baruch, 1967).

With the publication of Matina Horner's (1969, 1970) work, a more substantive answer to the question as to why the past research on women had not been more fruitful came into prominence: Women, according to Horner, do not really want to be achievers, they want to be liked. Field's (1951) data had, of course, already pointed in this direction. But now the evidence was more compelling. Given the stimulus "After first term finals, Anne finds herself at the top of her medical school class," over 65% of Horner's University of Michigan coeds told avoidance of success stories, while to the "John" form of the stimulus, over 90% of the male subjects told success stories. Both the intrasex and intersex differences were statistically significant. Because the avoidance themata in the Anne stories focused mainly on Anne's fear (a) that no one would like her now that she was so achieving or (b) that because she was so achieving perhaps she was not really very feminine, Horner's findings would seem to indicate that even in these days of women's liberation, on the projective level at least, women still perceive female achievement to be incompatible with the values of our culture. How else can one explain the vehement denial of Anne's achievement? Horner was told "the computer made a mistake" or "it was just a fluke" or "she won't be able to keep it up."

The 65% avoidance reported by Horner in 1968, 1969, and 1970 was based on the sample of 88 females she tested in 1964. Would more recent testing yield as high a percentage of avoidance stories? Using the same stimulus with a sample of "very high ability juniors at an outstanding coed university where the emphasis on achievement is very high," Horner (1972) reported that 85% of these later subjects told avoidance stories. Our own data, based on Wellesley College undergraduates tested in the academic year 1970–1971, are of this same order. Given the Anne stimulus, almost 89% told avoidance stories. The sample here, though limited to 26 students, can be regarded as reasonably representative of the college population.

To get a measure of how females would react to the John form of the stimulus, we used a second group of comparable size. Now the percentage of avoidance stories plummeted to 50, a significant shift from the 89% told to the Anne stimulus, though still higher than the less than 10% Horner (1968) originally reported for her male subjects. In other words, not only do these very bright women seemingly not want (expect) to be achievers themselves, but they may also expect (want) men to be less achievement motivated than men really are. Data obtained on a comparable sample of 40 Dartmouth College males in response to the Anne stimulus did not support a similar pattern in men's expectations of women. Quite to the contrary, only 62.5% of the men told avoidance stories (Marcuse & McMonagle, 1971), as compared with the 89% noted above in the Wellesley College data. This difference is statistically significant. Can it be that the nontraditional concept of the achieving woman is now more acceptable to men than to women? Two stories taken from the Dartmouth College sample convey the flavor of many of the protocols: The male storyteller recognizes Anne's fear of success and tries to allay her anxiety.

Anne: "Christ! I don't believe it."
John: "Anne, that's great. I mean it's fantastic!"
Anne: "I don't know John, I mean, I never expected anything like this. I mean, God, I'm going to have to think about this."
John: "What's to think about, you made it, you're on top!"

* * * * *

Anne did all the work assigned to her during the term and occasionally extra but she certainly did not expect to be at the top of her class at the end of finals. When she realized this she was very pleased but subconsciously worried about the reactions her fellow students would have. Would they think her above them and avoid her? This bothered her to such an extent that she tried to keep it to herself but one day soon after a good friend approached her and said, "Congratulations, Anne, I hear you're at the top of your class. I'm really proud of you." And Anne was too.

Lois W. Hoffman's (personal communication, February 1973) recent replication of Horner's (1968) original design suggests that the traditional concept of the achieving man may also be becoming less acceptable to men. Tested in the early 1970s, 79% of Hoffman's University of Michigan male subjects told avoidance of success stories to the John stimulus. This is a striking change from the less than 10% avoidance Horner obtained approximately eight years earlier. Hoffman's female subjects, however, did not show a comparable shift over time. Instead, avoidance of success continued to be the major female response to the Anne stimulus.

But can we really conclude from the studies to date that American women do not want to be achievers? Variations in the percentages of avoidance stories from study to study are fairly large, suggesting that sampling differences, as well as the wide range in years of testing, may be affecting the results. In addition, Anne's achievement is in a traditionally female-inappropriate field, that is, medicine. Is this what makes Anne's success so dangerous? To answer this question, in one set of studies we dropped the medical school reference leaving only "After first term finals, Anne finds herself at the top of her class." As predicted, in repeated samplings at Wellesley College, the reworded stimulus evoked significantly *fewer* avoidance stories than the original wording; the percentage typically approached 50. Similar results have been obtained with female subjects tested in other noncoeducational settings. For example, in a study done in two southern colleges, one for black women, the other for white women, the new wording evoked 36% avoidance of success stories for the black sample and exactly 50% for the white sample (Grainger, B., Kostick, B., & Staley, Y., 1970).

If the cultural stereotype has been the real villain here, then changing the stimulus to read "After first term finals, Anne [John] finds herself [himself] at the top of her [his] nursing school class" should result in a significant *increase* in the percentage of success stories in female subjects and a significant decrease of such stories in male subjects. To date we have tested only the first half of this proposition. In this study, the subjects were enrolled in two different noncoeducational colleges. One group consisted of 30 junior college women, all of whom were preparing to be nurses; the other of 37 women in a small, four-year liberal arts college. Within each group, half were given the "Anne medical school" stimulus, and half the "Anne nursing school" stimulus. The hypothesis was upheld only for the first group: those who were preparing to be nurses. For these subjects, the medical school form evoked 20% success stories; the nursing school form, 86% success stories. This difference was statistically significant ($\chi^2 = 7.23$, $p < .01$). In the liberal arts sample, however, the two forms evoked success and avoidance stories about equally often. The striking finding with this latter group was the valuing of a liberal arts education and the devaluing of nursing as a career for women. Whether the "nursing school" stimulus would yield similar results in a sample drawn from a more prestigious four-year liberal arts college remains to be seen. Similarly, should we expect professionally oriented but not nursing-oriented females to respond as the nurses do, that is, with success stories?

In short, the now-you-see-it–now-you-don't phenomenon in female achievement motivation research may be attributable to wide differences in how the motive has been measured. Yet, if we are to account for the sizable group of coeds who *do* tell success stories (35% in Horner's original sample; 50% at Wellesley College when the medical school reference was omitted), the search must go beyond sampling and stimulus variables.

As early as the 1950s, evidence was beginning to accumulate which demonstrated that personality factors could affect the achievement motivation scores of women. Field, it will be remembered, had proposed as early as 1951 that being liked was more important to women than to men. Morrison's (1954) finding that the need for achievement scores of females elected by their peers to positions of leadership were significantly higher than those of nonoffice holders is consistent with Field's proposal, if one assumes, as Morrison did, that females who seek office *are* more concerned with peer acceptance, i.e. popularity with peers, than females who do not. Three years later, Alper (1957) reported similar results, but only when the stimulus figure was male. Yet, the connection between concern for peer acceptability and associating achievement as more appropriate for males than for females had not yet become explicit.

The first step in this direction was taken by Lesser et al. (1963) when an unexpected, statistically significant interaction emerged in their data: Bright, high-achieving high school girls scored higher on need for achievement only when responding to *female* picture stimuli under an achievement-oriented, as compared to a more neutral, instructional set, while equally bright underachievers showed the increase only to the *male* pictures. The authors had anticipated that both groups would show the increase to both sets of pictures. Using Mead's (1949) sex role stereotype argument, Lesser et al. (1963) argued that unlike the underachievers, the high achievers *do not* accept the cultural stereotype that achievement is female inappropriate. A follow-up study by French and Lesser (1964) supported this interpretation only in part. Using a specially designed role-orientation value measure, they found that woman's-role-oriented college women did indeed score higher on need for achievement, as measured by French's Insight Test, when responding to statements about women engaged in domestic and social activities, while intellectually oriented college women scored higher when the activities involved intellectual pursuits. But clearly this was not the whole story because, regardless of individual role orientation, achievement scores were always higher under the intellectual set when the stimulus involved males. Apparently, the values of the culture can transcend personal values. The extent to which the particular format of the value-orientation measure (as used in this study, "answer as you think *most girls* would answer") may favor this type of transcendence is worth considering. This should not, however, negate the seeming importance of the role-orientation variable. And this is where our work at Wellesley College began.

Our basic hypothesis has been that traditionally role-oriented women, as in Mead's (1949) framework, are less likely to be achievement oriented, e.g. career oriented, than women whose role orientation is nontraditional. In testing this hypothesis, three considerations have dominated our research: (a) the need for, and construction of, a viable role-orientation measure; (b) the selection of stimulus cues for evoking achievement motivation; and (c) the development of methods for scoring the resulting protocols. Since the rationale of the procedures we used for meeting each of these objectives is described elsewhere (Alper, 1973), only a brief report is included here.

After trying out a number of standardized femininity–masculinity scales, we finally decided to design our own. The end product, known now as the Wellesley Role-Orientation Scale (WROS), is a twenty-four-item pencil-and-paper self-rating scale consisting of three seven-item subscales and three filler items. The three areas tapped by the subscales are (a) traits college girls generally regard as "feminine" rather than as "masculine"; (b) role activities they find acceptable for themselves as women; and (c) career and/or career-oriented activities they consider more appropriate for men than for women.

In our current work, the WROS has imbedded in it the thirty-eight-item Levinson and Huffman (1955) Traditional Family Ideology Scale (TFI). Presented as a "questionnaire designed to sample opinions and attitudes toward problems facing college girls," the subject was originally required to indicate merely agreement or disagreement with each item. We are now using a seven-point scale (from strongly disagree to strongly agree). Unlike French and Lesser (1964), we ask the subject to answer in terms of how she herself feels about each statement. In repeated samplings, the correlations between the TFI and the WROS continue to be positive and highly significant, i.e. high-WROS scorers favor a traditionally oriented family pattern while low-WROS scorers do not. On the other hand, the WROS seems to correlate only weakly with the sex-stereotype measure of Rosenkrantz, Vogel, Bee, Broverman, and Broverman (1968) and not at all with the Crowne-Marlowe (1964) Social Desirability Scale.

The first extensive use of the WROS with Wellesley College undergraduates was begun in the academic year 1964–1965. At that time, the typical range of scores for unselected samples, using the agree–disagree format, was 5–19, the total possible range being 0–21. Through 1967, the average score remained at 8.5. By 1969, the typical range was more constricted, 4–14, and the average had dropped to just under 8. In current samplings at Wellesley College and other comparable noncoeducational eastern schools, 14 remains the top score for unselected samples, but at the lower end there is an occasional 2 and an even more occasional 1 (Grainger, 1971). The average now approaches 7 rather than 8. As expected, moreover, the range for a small "consciousness-raising" group, a highly selected Wellesley College sample, is very constricted, 1–8. Yet even for constricted samples, the scores continue to have validity. Dividing the distributions into thirds, highs and lows within these constricted distributions differ from each other in the same ways as do highs and lows from wider distributions. What are these differences, and how have we tested for them?

Having suspected that the now-you-see-it–now-you-don't aspect of previous findings in this area might in part be attributable to differences in the strength of the achievement cues, we chose for our initial study the two pictures which Veroff, Atkinson, Feld, and Gurin (1960) had found particularly effective for arousing achievement imagery in adult subjects, namely, their "chem lab" and "machine shop" pictures. The chem lab shows two women in a laboratory setting; in the machine shop the two figures are men. In both, one person is watching, while the other is actively working at a task.

Using the McClelland et al. (1953) creative imagination instructions, but omitting all references to leadership capacity and intelligence, we found that both pictures did indeed pull strong achievement imagery as measured by their discrete variable scoring approach. But the need for achievement scores so derived did not differentiate between subjects who scored at different points along the WROS continuum, nor did the total score distinguish between successful and unsuccessful achievement striving. A more clinically oriented scoring scheme was needed. Since even a cursory review of the stories revealed a number of different themata, we decided to try a thema analysis. We subsequently learned that Horner (1968) had also abandoned the McClelland et al. (1953) scoring system in favor of a thema analysis and that only then did the striking sex differences in her data emerge.

For reasons detailed elsewhere (Alper, 1973), blind thema analysis works well for the chem lab stimulus and less well for the machine shop. For the chem lab, four major thema categories emerge: *successful achievement; dangers of achieving; task completion* devoid of achievement striving; and *themas unrelated* either to achievement or task completion. Within Horner's framework, the four would reduce to two categories: *success* and *avoidance of success.*

With rare exceptions, thema category and role orientation, as measured by the WROS, have been found to be clearly related: Success stories are significantly more often told by low-WROS scorers (subjects who score in the lower third of the WROS distribution) than by high-WROS scorers (subjects who score in the upper third). In Wellesley College parlance, the first group is referred to as the "low fems," or "lows," the second group as the "high fems," or "highs." Some highs also tell success stories, but as is shown below, their stories differ markedly from lows' success stories. "Danger" stories appear at both ends of the WROS continuum with about equal frequency, while task completion and unrelated themata are more typical of highs than of lows.

Lows' success stories include four subthemata: hard work pays off;

support by an achieving model; achievement through cooperative effort; and achievement facilitated by competition or rivalry. Here is an example of the hard work pays off subthema, as told by a low:

> This lady scientist, like Madame Curie, is about to make an amazing discovery. She has been trying for months to find a cure for cancer and in spite of almost giving up because of repeated failures, she and her assistant know that this is the moment. If she drops the right amount of solution into the tube, it will neutralize and that will be the answer to her years of effort. She will do it.

The next story, also told by a low, illustrates the support subthema:

> The instructor is showing her student how to do a step in a complicated experimental procedure. The student has been working on the experiment for some time and is nearly at the end of her work. She is observing carefully what the other woman does, and, when she returns to her own work, will repeat the procedure with care and precision and will be able to finish her project and achieve significant results. The instructor would like the student to become an able scientist and is pleased with her work.

Highs' success stories are characterized by very different subthemata. These include instrumental success (the achievement is instrumental to the gratification of a need other than achievement qua achievement, usually affiliation); woman as man's helper; and to achieve, women have to work harder than men. An example of each, as told by highs, follows:

> [Instrumental success] Two unmarried Wellesley College chemistry professors are titrating a solution. They expect to find a new theory of nuclear activity involved in the solution process that will be critical to the instant coffee concerns. They hope to make a lot of money so they can go on a cruise and meet some eligible bachelors. They both fall in love with MIT professors and live satisfiedly ever after.
>
> [Woman as man's helper] These two ladies are PhD holders in chemistry who are working for the hospital in a surgeon's research laboratory. They are married but wanted to do something for a career with research work filling the bill. They don't want fame but rather to help mankind in their small way to find a cure for hepatitis. They will be of great assistance to the doctor and will perform a valuable function in doing the tasks that the doctor doesn't have time to do.

Note that the first story is present oriented (finding husbands), while the second appears to be future oriented (after marriage). Stories in this latter category often explicitly state that the women no longer have young children to tend to.

The next story illustrates a high's version of the hard work pays off thema, with the special twist that to succeed, a woman would have to work *harder* than a man:

> It is a time when women scientists are not common. They are in the minority and are often looked down upon by men. Therefore, they have to work extra hard to prove themselves. These two female technologists are working on a biochemistry experiment. The one standing is trying to train the younger woman whom she feels has much potential. Through their hard work and dedication

> to their project they will succeed. They will not only make a name for themselves . . . .

Since the *project* is successful, the protocol qualifies as successful achievement. But whether the achievement finally wins them acceptance by men is less certain. The story remains unfinished. Moreover, a downgrading of the status of the women (here to technologists) occurs to this stimulus only in the stories told by highs.

Combining the dangers of success, task completion, and unrelated imagery themata into a single category, avoidance of success, it is clear that it is the highs, not the lows, who tell such stories.[1] The difference between the two groups is statistically significant. As noted above, both highs and lows tell stories involving dangers of success. But there is a striking between-group difference in the nature of the projected danger: For highs, the danger is either to the *person* of the achiever or to her interpersonal relationships; for lows, the danger is that the *project* will fail. Thus, it is the highs' avoidance pattern, rather than the lows', which is the better fit for Horner's (1968, 1969, 1970) category of avoidance of success as a way of coping with the fear of being disliked.

Here is an example of a danger of success story, as told by a high:

> The lady with the test tube is a movie star who has sunk to doing TV commercials. The other is an admiring nobody [who] pities her . . . . They both fade into oblivion. No one will like them or pay attention to them . . . . The star commits suicide and the other marries a florist and gets fat.

The story, though perhaps tongue in cheek, seems to have a moral: A career, even a glamorous one, can only lead to "oblivion"; better to settle for the more conventional, if somewhat unshapely, role of the married woman.

The downgrading of the status of women in the chem lab situation turns out to be more characteristic of highs than of lows only when *both* stimulus figures are female. It does not hold when the stimulus involves a man and a woman (Alper et al., 1972). Using specially posed picture stimuli,[2] we had expected that highs would perceive the male as having the higher status regardless of his role, worker or watcher, while lows would assign the figures equal status roles. But the chi-square analysis of the data failed to support this simplistic prediction. On the other hand, the overall results are consistent with the role theory framework of the research as a whole. Though both pictures now tend to evoke more success stories from highs than from

[1]In the McClelland et al. (1953) scoring system, "danger" stories would qualify as achievement imagery (AI), whereas task completion stories and stories unrelated to achievement would be scored as TI and UI, respectively.

[2]The seeming age differences between the two figures in the original chem lab picture, their relative positions and postures, as well as the laboratory equipment, were reproduced as closely as possible in the new stimuli.

lows ($.10 < p > .05$), unlike lows, highs typically attribute the success to the man: When the man is the worker, he achieves his goal, he solves the problem at hand; when the woman is the worker, the man instructs her, that is, tells her how to perform the task, and if the project is successful, it is the man who is credited with the achievement, the woman serving merely as his assistant. In lows' success stories, the success is the result either of the joint efforts of the two people or of the woman in the role of the worker. In other words, highs continue to perceive achievement as female inappropriate; lows do not.

But life for the achievement motivation researcher is never simple when the subjects are females. The results just reported were based on data obtained at Wellesley College in September 1971 on the opening day of classes. The subjects were 24 upperclassmen, all members of a limited-enrollment upper level course entitled "The Psychological Implications of Being Female." Because students accepted in the course are required to meet several departmental prerequisites, the sample, though captive, could be regarded as a self-selected, special interest group. Would a less psychologically sophisticated sample of underclassmen respond in the same way? To answer this question, we tested the 113 women in our beginning psychology course, dividing them at random into two groups. The woman-watching–man-working picture was shown to one group; the man-watching–woman-working picture, to the other. Differences in the WROS scores of the two groups were well within the limits of chance.

A chi-square analysis of the data failed to confirm the findings for the older group because now both pictures tended to evoke more avoidance of success than success themata. In the group given the woman-watching stimulus, 80% of the lows and 82% of the highs told avoidance stories ($p < .01$ within each group). To the man-watching stimulus, 69% of the lows and 80% of the highs told avoidance stories. The difference for lows was not significant but that for highs approached significance ($.10 < p > .05$). Incidentally, both pictures evoked significantly more avoidance than success themata in middle-WROS scorers.

On the surface, then, the data for these younger, less psychologically sophisticated college women are seemingly more consistent with Horner's (1968) basic Anne stimulus findings than with either our original chem lab data or the new data for the older group. It is only when the individual WROS scores for all 113 subjects (highs, middles, and lows) are subjected to an analysis of variance for unequal *N*s that role orientation again emerges as an important variable. Picture cue, thema, and perceived status of the man and woman, as separate factors, turn out not to be related to WROS scores. Status $\times$ Picture

Cue is related, however: Regardless of thema (success or avoidance), the mean WROS score of subjects who tell unequal status stories is lower for the man-watching picture; for the woman-watching picture, the mean WROS score is lower for subjects who tell equal status stories ($p = .05$). It is the woman-watching situation, then, which, regardless of the fate of the project, more readily permits the egalitarianism of lows to emerge.

From the beginning of our research with the role-orientation variable, we suspected that neither the highs nor the lows necessarily represent dynamically homogeneous groupings. Returning to our original data using, for example, the Veroff et al. (1960) chem lab stimulus, though most highs told avoidance of success stories, a few told instrumental success stories. Within the lows, most told straightforward success stories; a few expected the project to fail. The differences in these themata call to mind four of the patterns that Douvan and Adelson (1966) described as characteristic of adolescent girls: the unambivalent high feminine, the ambivalent high feminine, the unambivalent low feminine, and the ambivalent low feminine. Douvan and Adelson are of the opinion that both ambivalent groups are in conflict about their femininity even though they admit that they have no direct evidence to support this. Our projective approach would seem to offer a viable vehicle for accumulating relevant evidence. What seem to be needed here, however, are stimuli which, unlike the laboratory setting of the chem lab, readily lend themselves to opting for alternative roles: domestic, nondomestic, or some combination of the two. To this end, we used a new picture stimulus, the "kitchen scene." A youngish woman is seen in the foreground, and a small child, seated in a high chair, is to her right. The woman is painting the child's portrait. In the left background, something (a cake, pie, roast?) can be seen through the glass panel of the oven door.

The subjects for this study were 78 Wellesley College undergraduates, all members of the author's child psychology course. The testing was done during the first meeting of the class before any instructor bias could have influenced either the WROS scores or the thematic content of the stories. Thema differences between high- and low-WROS scorers were in the predicted direction and clearly significant (the chi-square, corrected for continuity, was significant beyond the .001 level).

The themata most frequently found in the highs' data were as follows: (a) Motherhood is put ahead of a career; the woman puts the painting aside in order to attend either to the baby's needs or to her own need just to enjoy or play with the child. (b) Motherhood and achievement are casually combined; painting is described as a hobby, and the end product is destined to be given either to doting grandparents or to an equally appreciative husband. (c) Motherhood and a career *cannot* be combined. One may wish to combine them, but in the end, achievement wishes must be put aside for they get one into trouble—one cannot be both a professional and a mother. When one tries to combine roles, the cake burns, the child gets restless, or the husband disapproves—he wants his dinner ready when he gets home. Logically, Themata *a* and *b* would be appropriate to the high who is unambivalent in her acceptance of the role the culture traditionally assigns to women, while Thema *c* suggests some discomfiture with the demands of the traditional role, yet a need somehow to stay with it.

The themata most frequently found in the lows' data were as follows: (a) A career is placed ahead of the wife and mother role; the woman is a professional artist who has been called in to do the portrait. (b) Career, marriage, and motherhood can be successfully combined; the woman is an accomplished artist and is continuing to use her talents now that she is married. (c) Marriage and career cannot be combined; marriage is fraught with disappointments for one has to give up too much; therefore, it is better to walk out on the marriage and to pursue the career. All too frequently the career also fails, not because the woman is inadequate, but because society is. Again, logically, Themata *a* and *b* would be consistent with the value pattern of the unambivalent low, while Thema *c*, with its introduction of the danger theme, would be more characteristic of an ambivalent low.[3]

Having identified ambivalence–unambivalence by a fantasy measure, the next question is, Can these patterns be predicted from the WROS alone? While we do not yet have a definitive answer to this question, the two procedures we have worked out to test it seem promising. One procedure is based on decision-time theory, the expectation being that highs who are role ambivalent, as measured by thema category, will take longer to agree with the WROS items than highs who are role unambivalent, while lows who are role ambivalent will take longer to disagree with the items than lows who are role unambivalent (Grainger, 1971). The other procedure uses the standard deviation of the subject's WROS score. The expectation here is that a role-ambivalent subject, again as measured by thema category, will have a larger variance around her own scale mean than a role-unambivalent subject. The first procedure could be used with either of the WROS formats: agree–disagree or strongly disagree–strongly agree. The second procedure would be suitable only for the latter format, strongly agree–strongly disagree.

Our search for the antecedents of differing achievement motivation

---

[3]The intensity of the anger expressed by many of these girls suggests Shils's (1954) pattern of "far left authoritarianism" rather than genuine egalitarianism. See Bardwick and Douvan (1972) and Rossi (1972) for further discussions of sex role ambivalence.

patterns has just begun and has included so far both projective approaches and life-history data. The life-history materials are still too incomplete to report, but we do have some new projective data derived from a large sample of Wellesley College undergraduates, mainly freshmen and sophomores. The stimuli used here were two parent–child pictures. One, a mother figure and little girl, is an altered form of Murray's (1943) Thematic Apperception Test Card 7GF. The other, a father figure and little girl, is Card 10G from the Michigan Picture Test (Andrew, Hartwell, Hutt, & Walton, 1953). In both pictures, the figures are facing each other.[4] In addition to the modified creative imagination instructions described earlier, half of the subjects in this study were told that the grown-up in the picture was "upset about something," the other half that the "child was upset about something."

Our analysis of the data has centered around two questions: (a) Do highs and lows react differently to these two instructions? (b) Does sex of parent figure make a difference? We found that the themata for high- and low-WROS scorers *do* differ significantly; sex of parent makes some difference within each group, but the person who is upset, parent or child, does not. Regardless of sex of the parent figure, and regardless of which figure is said to be upset, highs significantly more often than lows attribute the upsettedness to the child's poor academic achievement ($p = .01$); in lows' stories, more often than in highs', the cause of the upsettedness is behavior unacceptable to the adult ($p = .01$). The most common complaints here are defiance of parental authority and clumsiness. Only occasionally do lows mention poor achievement. But when they do, lows see the parent figure under these circumstances as supportive and nurturant, while highs see the parent figure as derogating and punitive. There is also a between-group difference in the outcome of such stories. In lows' stories, the child typically ends up as an achiever; in highs' stories, performance is typically not improved. While these differences occur in response to both pictures, they reach significance for the father–daughter picture ($p = .05$) and approach significance for the mother–daughter picture ($.10 < p > .05$).

The crucial question, of course, is, Are lows, in fact, better achievers than highs? There is some evidence that they are. For the subjects who served in the original WROS study (Alper, 1973), both weighted Scholastic Aptitude Test scores and college grades were available. The Scholastic Aptitude Test scores of highs and lows did not differ, but the college grades of the lows tended to be higher ($p = .10$). Lows, then, not only fantasize achievement, they actually do achieve. Judging from these data, it now seems likely that the high-achieving high school girls in the Lesser et al. (1963) study, the highly competi-

[4]For a more detailed description of these stimuli, see Alper and Greenberger (1967).

tive, high-achieving coeds in Angelini's (1955) Brazilian study, and Horner's (1970) University of Michigan coeds who not only told success stories in response to the Anne stimulus but also performed better in competitive situations would all have at least one factor in common: Namely, they would presumably all score as lows on the WROS. Perhaps these girls also have in common a history of positive parental support and encouragement to be achievers, a pattern some investigators associate with high need for achievement in latency-aged boys (e.g. see Rosen & D'Andrade, 1959; Smith, 1969). As for our high-WROS scorers, if in fact they *have* been exposed to a more authoritarian child-rearing climate than our low scorers, as the high-positive correlation between the WROS and the TFI suggests, then the recurrent thema of the dangers of success which runs through their fantasy material, as well as the perception of parental figures as derogating and punitive, are also consistent. In such a climate, female achievement presumably would be regarded as sex inappropriate and would not be positively reinforced.

In conclusion, the now-you-see-it–now-you-don't phenomenon in the female achievement motivation literature appears to be a function more of wide methodological differences from study to study than of basic instability of the motive. Among the more important variables to be considered here are (a) personality factors, specifically differences in the sex role orientation of the subjects; (b) sampling differences (e.g. age, psychological sophistication, degree of ego involvement in the task, and perhaps even intrinsic differences in the demand quality of the settings from which samples are drawn—the more social, affiliative, emphasis of coeducational institutions versus the more academically competitive emphasis of the noncoeducational); (c) form and contextual differences in stimulus cues ranging from unspecified area and level of achievement to very specifically sex-inappropriate areas; and (d) differences in the procedures used in scoring the resulting protocols. The effect of experimentally manipulating such factors has been demonstrated in the new research reported here and in references to studies by other investigators.

One other shortcoming of some of the previous work in this area should be mentioned: a too rigid adherence, especially in the early studies, to the male model of achievement motivation. In our culture, men are not only expected to achieve, they are also expected to want to achieve. Women, on the other hand, have neither been expected to achieve nor to want to do so. It now appears that both generalizations may be too broad, that indeed a reversal of attitudes may be taking place, with men now less interested in being achievers (Hoffman, personal communication, February 1973), and women more willing to recognize that achievement may be female appropriate as well as male appropriate.

REFERENCES

Alper, T.G. Predicting the direction of selective recall: Its relation to ego strength and *n* achievement. *Journal of Abnormal and Social Psychology,* 1957, *55,* 149-165.

Alper, T.G. The relationship between role-orientation and achievement motivation in college women. *Journal of Personality,* 1973, *41,* 9-31.

Alper, T.G., & Greenberger, E. Relationship of picture structure to achievement motivation in college women. *Journal of Personality and Social Psychology,* 1967, *7,* 362-371.

Alper, T.G., Leet, H., Bragg, E., & Eister, D.Z. The Effect of the Sex of the Stimulus-Cue Figures on the Achievement Fantasies of College Women. Unpublished paper, 1972.

Andrew, G., Hartwell, S.W., Hutt, M.L., & Walton, R.E. *Michigan Picture Test.* Chicago: Science Research Associates, 1953.

Angelini, A.L. Um novo métado para avaliar a motivacão humano. [A new method of evaluating human motivation.] *Boletin Faculdade de Filosofia Ciences San Paulo,* 1955, No. 207.

Atkinson, J.W. (Ed.) *Motives in fantasy, action and society.* Princeton, N.J.: Van Nostrand, 1958.

Bardwick, J.M., & Douvan, E. Ambivalence: The socialization of women. In J.M. Bardwick (Ed.), *Readings on the psychology of women.* New York: Harper & Row, 1972.

Baruch, R. The achievement motive in women: Implications for career development. *Journal of Personality and Social Psychology,* 1967, *5,* 260-267.

Crowne, D.P., & Marlowe, D. *The approval motive: Studies in evaluative dependence.* New York: Wiley, 1964.

Douvan, E., & Adelson, J. *The adolescent experience.* New York: Wiley, 1966.

Field, W.F. The effects of thematic apperception of certain experimentally aroused needs. Unpublished doctoral dissertation, University of Maryland, 1951.

French, E., & Lesser, G.S. Some characteristics of the achievement motive in women. *Journal of Abnormal and Social Psychology,* 1964, *68,* 119-128.

Grainger, B. The Motive to Avoid Success and Its Relationship to Sex-Role Orientation in College Women. Unpublished honors thesis, Wellesley College, 1971.

Grainger, B., Kostick, B., & Staley, Y. A Study of Achievement Motivation of Females in Two Southern, Noncoeducational Segregated Colleges. Unpublished paper, 1970.

Heckhausen, H. *The anatomy of achievement motivation.* New York: Academic Press, 1967.

Horner, M.S. Sex differences in achievement motivation and performance in competitive and non-competitive situations. Unpublished doctoral dissertation, University of Michigan, 1968.

Horner, M.S. Fail: Bright woman. *Psychology Today,* 1969, *3*(6), 36-38, 62.

Horner, M.S. Femininity and successful achievement: A basic inconsistency. In J.M. Bardwick, E. Douvan, M.S. Horner, & D. Gutmann (Eds.), *Feminine personality and conflict.* Belmont, Calif.: Brooks/Cole, 1970.

Horner, M.S. The motive to avoid success and changing aspirations of women. In J.M. Bardwick (Ed.), *Readings on the psychology of women.* New York: Harper & Row, 1972.

Lesser, G.S., Krawitz, R.N., & Packard, R. Experimental arousal of achievement motivation in adolescent girls. *Journal of Abnormal and Social Psychology,* 1963, *66,* 59-66.

Levinson, D., & Huffman, P.E. Traditional family ideology and its relation to

personality. *Journal of Personality,* 1955, *23,* 251-273.
Marcuse, N., & McMonagle, E. Achievement Motivation in College Males. Unpublished paper, 1971.
McClelland, D.C., Atkinson, J.W., Clark, R.A., & Lowell, E.L. *The achievement motive.* New York: Appleton-Century-Crofts, 1953.
Mead, M. *Male and female.* New York: Morrow, 1949.
Morrison, H.W. Validity and behavioral correlates of female need for achievement. Unpublished master's thesis, Wesleyan University, 1954.
Murray, H.A. *Thematic Apperception Test.* Cambridge: Harvard University Press, 1943.
Rosen, B., & D'Andrade, R. The psychosocial origins of achievement motivation. *Sociometry,* 1959, *22,* 185-218.
Rosenkrantz, P., Vogel, S., Bee, H., Broverman, I., & Broverman, D.M. Sex role stereotypes and self-concepts in college students. *Journal of Consulting and Clinical Psychology,* 1968, *32,* 287-295.
Rossi, A.S. The roots of ambivalence in American women. In J.M. Bardwick (Ed.), *Readings on the psychology of women.* New York: Harper & Row, 1972.
Sarason, I.G., & Smith, R.E. Personality. *Annual Review of Psychology,* 1971, *21,* 393-446.
Shils, E.A. Authoritarianism: "Right" and "left." In R.E. Christie & M. Jahoda (Eds.), *The authoritarian personality.* Glencoe, Ill.: Free Press, 1954.
Smith, C.P. (Ed.) *Achievement related motives in children.* New York: Russell Sage Foundation, 1969.
Veroff, J., Atkinson, J.W., Feld, S.C., & Gurin, G. The use of thematic apperception to assess motivation in a nationwide interview study. *Psychological Monographs,* 1960, *74*(12, Whole No. 499).
Veroff, J., Feld, S.C., & Crockett, H.J. Explorations into the effects of picture-cues on thematic apperceptive expression of achievement motivation. *Journal of Personality and Social Psychology,* 1966, *3,* 171-181.
Veroff, J., Wilcox, S., & Atkinson, J.W. The achievement motive in high school and college age women. *Journal of Abnormal and Social Psychology,* 1953, *48,* 108-119.
Vogel, M.D. An investigation of the affiliation motive in college age women using low cue strength pictures. Unpublished honors thesis, University of Michigan, 1954.

Chapter 6

WHY WOMEN CHOOSE CAREERS BELOW THEIR POTENTIAL

HELEN S. FARMER

Abstract

Women have not caught up with the opportunities available to them to contribute to society through their careers. Not only do women not contribute as much as men to the humanities, arts, and sciences, they do not contribute commensurate with their talents and potential. It is assumed that women's lesser contribution through their careers is related to their motivation. Several factors related to inhibited career and achievement motivation in women are examined, based on evidence in the research literature. A related study in progress is described. A humanistic goal for both sexes is proposed, based on sex-free roles.

IT HAS LONG been known that women do not achieve or contribute as much as men in the fields of science, the humanities, and the arts (Astin, 1973; Maccoby and Jacklin, 1974; Rossi and Calderwood, 1973; Commission on the Status of Women, 1970) in spite of the fact that they represent over 40% of the professional labor force today (Blitz, 1974) and have represented at least 30% of the professionals since 1890. Fewer women proportionately rise to the top of their chosen profession, business, or trade. Although women represented 40% of the professional and technical workers in 1974, they represented less than 20% of the managers and administrators that year (see Chapter 19) and a majority of these women were elementary school teachers.

Many attitudes are thought to hinder women from developing their full potential as persons. Attitudes of husbands, parents, teachers, counselors, and employers, to name a few, may also hinder development. "A woman's place is in the home," "Babies need their mothers when they are young," "Women were not intended to compete in a man's world," "Find a husband and he'll take care of you," and "A woman can experience success through her husband" are a few of the attitudes that may inhibit the full work-related development of many girls and women.

The dilemma confronted is that women, found to be equally as intelligent as men (Maccoby and Jacklin, 1974), do not contribute to society through their work in proportion to their participation. Why do women scientists, artists, writers, educators, and social scientists not contribute as much as men? What inhibits their achievement motivation and productivity? Two illustrations follow, suggesting part of an answer.

Paula is a woman who grew up focusing her energies and daydreams on preparing for a career. She invested little, if any, time in dreaming about the role of wife and mother or in practicing for these roles. Paula met a man at graduate school preparing to enter the same career as herself, and she fell in love and married him. Implicit in her thinking was the belief that they would *both* continue their careers and that if a family came along, they would *both* share in the childrearing responsibilities equally. She had not bothered to check this assumption with her husband, and it turned out that he had no intention of giving time to childrearing—that, in fact, his career was the single priority of his life. Paula's career went by the boards for a time, ten years to be exact, while she raised three children, did volunteer work in the community, and some part-time work related to her professional training. When she came to see me for counseling, Paula was carrying an accumulation of disappointment, frustration, and anger born out of false expectations and belief in equality of the sexes, i.e. equal opportunity and equal responsibility.

Paula's case is a reversal of the counseling needs of many women. A majority of women are socialized in the home and school to expect to grow up to be wives and mothers (Tyler, 1964) and their problems develop out of lack of satisfaction in these roles (Friedan, 1963) at which point they begin to look for satisfaction in other roles, i.e. working wife, volunteer worker, etc. Other women are faced with the necessity of work when their husbands die or abandon them. Ann, described next, is such a woman.

Ann is a bright woman who ranked in the top three percent in her high school physics class. However, she was not interested in pursuing a career commensurate with her scientific ability. Instead, she planned to marry and raise a family. She married before finishing college and settled down to the serious business of being the best mother and wife in her neighborhood. Her husband found a younger woman more attractive than Ann and left her at the age of forty-two. With the new divorce laws in some states (Ann lives in California), a woman cannot expect to be supported indefinitely by her estranged husband, if she is at all able to work. Usually a reasonable time is allowed by the courts for a woman to obtain some training (two years is typical) before she is responsible for her own economic support. At this point in her life, Ann arrived in my counseling office confused and hurt. Her early promise in the natural sciences held little appeal for Ann now and any training she could obtain in two years could only prepare her for a technician role in the sciences at best.

It can be seen in the case of both Paula and Ann, both high ability women, why their contribution to society through their careers was less than that for men of comparable ability. For both women their most productive years were spent raising a family rather than furthering their career competencies. It is unlikely that this situation will change much, until men (husbands and fathers) begin to share equally the responsibility for home and family with their wives.

A review of more than forty research studies published since 1970 (Farmer & Backer, 1975) on division of household and childrearing activities between husband and wife indicated that women still accept the major responsibility for these tasks. More men are beginning to share homemaking responsibilities for marketing, cooking, home repairs, and child care (Hedges & Barnett, 1972), but the number of husbands sharing responsibility equally for these tasks is insignificant.

Does the Working Mother Hurt her Children?

A common belief among men and women alike is that the working woman *by definition* neglects her children, especially if she works when they are very young (Kievit, 1972; Darling, 1973). An even more pervasive belief among women and men of all cultures is that woman's primary responsibility is in the home (Darling, 1973; Mead, 1974). These two beliefs are related. The thinking goes as follows: If a woman's primary responsibility is to see that the new generation of children grow up strong and healthy, physically and psychologically, she cannot do that and work outside the home eight hours a day.

There is some research supporting the relationship between working mothers and juvenile delinquency (White, 1972). However, the evidence is stronger for a causal relationship between rejecting, permissive mothers and delinquency (White, 1972).

Studies on the mother's attitude toward working and the effect of her attitude on her children indicate that mothers who feel anxious or unhappy about working tend to have angry, hostile children (Hoffman, 1963). In contrast, children of mothers who like their work are more outgoing and confident. Rapoport (Chapter 25) noted that an increasing emphasis on partnership in dual-career families had a positive effect on children's attitudes toward their mother's working. Cultural acceptance of the working mother can reduce guilt feelings of working women and, in turn, reduce the negative effect on children

(Rabin, 1965; Wallston, 1973).

In summary, whether or not the children of working women are affected negatively appears to depend on at least two factors. The first is the attitude of the mother (and of society) about women working. A more accepting attitude has been found to have a positive effect on children of working mothers (Wallston, 1973). The second factor is availability of adequate substitute care for young children. This factor is not approaching resolution in the U.S. or elsewhere and is one that should command the attention of government and community agencies (Darling, 1973).

With improved technology and automation, homemaking is no longer a full time activity for most women (Huber, 1973). This, combined with the lower birth rate, relieves many mothers to return to work earlier than previously or to continue working while raising their families (see Chapter 19). Women can expect to have working lives of at least twenty-five years today if they interrupt their careers to raise a family, and forty years (equivalent to a man's) if they raise a family without interrupting their careers (see Chapter 19).

The U.S. Women's Bureau (Chapter 19) published statistics indicating that 90 percent of all women work at some time in their lives, and that over 60 percent of the women who work do so because they have to (i.e. they are heads of households, or their husbands earn less than a minimum wage).

The growth of the feminist movement in the 1960s and its continuing expansion in the 1970s has led to a variety of interventionist strategies aimed at accelerating equal opportunity for all women (Farmer and Backer, 1975). Some of the strategies include legislation, assertiveness training, consciousness raising, multiple role planning, women's studies program, and encouragement to women to enter and train in the non-traditional professions (engineering, physics, law, and medicine). These interventionist strategies are typically provided in a "shotgun" fashion rather than based on careful diagnosis of the factors contributing to women's unequal status and the relation of this status to the narrower question of why women contribute less to society through their careers (Farmer and Backer, 1975).

A brief review of research on achievement motivation and career motivation in women follows, closing with an identification of some of the factors suggested by the research inhibiting such motivation in women.

Achievement Motivation

Maccoby and Jacklin's (1974) review of 58 studies on achievement motivation in women reported a series of studies indicating that women have lower levels of academic self-confidence and are less competitive compared with men. They noted that this difference between the sexes in self-confidence does not appear in elementary or high school students but appears first in college in a substantial number of studies. It might be speculated that this difference appears in college as women approach marriage and career decisions and that marriage-career conflict (Matthews and Tiedeman, 1964) may contribute to the lowered self-confidence and achievement motivation noted in college women by Drew and Patterson (1974).

Astin (1973) found that girls perform as well as boys in math, science, and tests of spatial relationship up to about age ten, thereafter their performance becomes increasingly poorer. Astin has suggested that this effect is due, at least in part, to differential reinforcement on the part of parents and teachers.

The model of achievement motivation developed by Atkinson (1974) and McClelland (1971) identified the following factors as critical for high achievement motivation: an internal standard of excellence, independence, persistence, preference for tasks of intermediate difficulty, high academic performance, and clearly defined goals. Bardwick (1971) suggested that this is a male model of achievement motivation, based on her review of the evidence on achievement motivation when it was examined separately for boys and girls. Alper (1974) has called achievement motivation in women the "now-you-see-it–now-you-don't" phenomenon, based on her more recent review and her own research for more than a decade on achievement motivation in college women. Maccoby and Jacklin's (1974) conclusions that differences between the sexes do not become significant until women reach college is not supported by Alper's review. However, rather than clear-cut differences in the elementary and high school years in achievement motivation between the sexes, Alper points to the illusive quality of female achievement motivation. Bardwick (1971) refers to the differences as one of "ambivalence" for women, created by their pull toward both achievement and affiliation-with-the-opposite-sex and their "fear" that success in one rules out success in the other.

Maehr (1974) recently proposed that situational variables may play a critical role in achievement motivation as it manifests itself within different racial and cultural groups. Katz (1973) for example found that women have less "fear of success" when responding to cues which presented women in socially sanctioned achievement situations (i.e. Anne, a medical student in a medical class that is half female) than when women were presented in nontraditional roles (i.e. Anne, the only female in her medical class). Providing a contextual change in the stimulus cue had a dramatic effect on these women's fear of success. Monohan, Kuhn, and Shaver (1974) found another contextual variable (coed versus noncoed school setting) with a significant effect of the level of fear of success in high school girls.

Thelma Alper (1974) has been studying the relationship of sex-role orientation to achievement motivation in women for more than a decade. She has found that women with traditional female orientations, attitudes, and beliefs score lower on achievement motivation measures than women with nontraditional female orientations. The Wellesley Role Orientation Scale (WROS) has been developed by Alper for her research, and its predictive ability has stood up over a series of replicated studies. Entwisle and Greenberger (1972) found that high IQ girls generally held more liberal views than average and low IQ girls, and that high IQ girls from blue collar homes were the most liberal about women's roles.

Career Motivation in Women

There are developmental and situational differences in the vocational choice process for girls compared with boys. Following the Terman and Miles classic study, Tyler (1964) studied the development of sex differences in play and school. Tyler suggested that although girls appear to be precocious in social development they tend to lag behind boys in career development, especially at the college level. Similarly, other researchers (Campbell, 1974; Harmon, 1972) have suggested that women's vocational interests may crystallize somewhat later than men's and be organized in a different way. Strong's (1955) earlier studies support the view that men and women in the same professions have significantly different career interests.

Strong (1955) has always encouraged the use of the women's form of his Vocational Interest Blank (SVIB-W) for use with women in career counseling unless they score below 30 standard score points on the Femininity/Masculinity scale (50 points being the mean). The widespread use of only the men's form of the SVIB with women is not supported by its author or by developmental research on the nature of women's career interests (Harmon, 1972; Tyler, 1964).

The current 1974 revision of the Strong-Campbell Interest Inventory (SCII) replaces the Strong Vocational Interest Blanks for men and women, has one form for both sexes, and represents a promising new way to measure career motivation in women.

Ginzberg (1966) documented another important difference in the career choice process for women. He noted that girls cannot realistically plan on a career until they know what kind of man they will marry (provided that they plan to marry). Their financial status and freedom to continue their education will be partially determined by their husband's careers and their attitudes toward educated and working women. In addition, the number of children that a woman plans for, or has, will affect the pattern of her career life. She may elect an interrupted career pattern or a parallel track system as suggested by Super (1957). Ginzberg postulated that this greater uncertainty in planning is probably the major difference between the sexes in their career development.

An interesting finding by Astin (1973), studying over 5,000 women five years out of high school, was that girls who have high career motivation and pursue graduate level professional study often show an exceptional aptitude for mathematics early in their education. In fact, mathematics aptitude was found to be the best predictor of career motivation for this sample of women.

In other research Astin (1969) found that women doctorates ($N = 1547$) were as highly motivated to work as men and that over 90 percent of the women graduating with Ph.D.s in 1957 were still in the labor force eight years later. Such findings suggest that women who seek graduate level degrees are not intellectual dilettantes but serious professionals.

Women may still choose a stable homemaking career, however. At the present time, about 50 percent of all women choose not to work (see Chapter 19). Early exposure to multiple role planning early in their education for those girls and women who will choose not to work may contribute to their freedom to choose freely, having been informed of all the options.

Achievement-Motivation and "Fear of Success" for Women

Horner (1968) has researched avoidance of achievement in women which she calls "fear of success" for more than a decade and documented the changing strength of this "fear" when competitive factors are changed. For most women, Horner found that they had less fear of success when competing against themselves than when they were competing with other students. The opposite was true for most males. Tomlinson-Keasey (1974) found that married women students with children had significantly lower "fear of success" than unmarried coeds. We might infer that these women had less fear of academic success since they had found a husband who accepted their academic aspiration. The married women were also a more select group and highly motivated to return to study.

Katz (1973) adapted Horner's research on achievement motivation in women by providing additional prompting cues to her subjects. Katz required two groups of subjects to respond to the same cues with the following addition (undergraduates in a small Western college):

1. All Anne's classmates in medical school are men. "After first term finals, Anne finds herself at the top of her class" (quotes

indicate Horner's cues).

2. Half of Anne's classmates in medical school are women. "After first term finals, Anne finds herself at the top of her class."

Respondents to the second condition, both men and women, had significantly less measured fear of success themes than those in the first condition. Katz concluded that the second cue provided the necessary social sanction for women to be comfortable with Anne's success in medical school.

Lipman-Blumen (1972) has proposed an operational definition of the lower aspiration level of women in her description of a vicarious achievement "ethic" or value whereby many women choose indirect achievement satisfaction, conditioned from birth to experience pleasure through the successes of important other male persons in their lives (father, brother, boyfriend, husband, boss) rather than directly through their own successes. An example might be a girl who said she did not want to be the President (or Director, etc.) but just wanted to work with him. The vicarious achievement motive suits well the woman who wants to avoid primary responsibility on the job but at the same time benefit from the successes of the boss through reflected glory. Another example is the woman who views her primary responsibility as that of home and family, wants to work, but does not want to bring her work home with her on weekends.

Lipman-Blumen (1972) found only 12 percent of a sample of married college females ($N = 643$) free of the vicarious achievement motive. Twelve percent of this group were pursuing a PhD whereas none of those measuring high on vicarious achievement motivation were pursuing PhD's. Bettelheim (1969) has suggested that education is an enhancement for boys, whereas for girls it is a form of insurance in case they do not make it in marriage. Therefore, he assumed that women who enter "direct achievement" occupations such as law or medicine experience a loss in femininity. Similarly, men who enter "vicarious achievement roles" such as nurse, elementary school teacher, or librarian experience a loss of masculinity.

Harmon (1972) found it harder to predict the stability of career choice for college coeds compared to men. She found that women who aspired to high level careers in their freshman year often changed their choices to less demanding careers by the time they were college seniors. Harmon hypothesized that lack of reinforcement in the environment for their high aspirations indirectly reinforced lower career aspiration level for these women. In support of Harmon's finding, Hawley (1972) found that college women were influenced to raise or lower their aspiration level depending on whether or not the attitudes of men toward working women were positive or negative.

Tomlinson-Keasey's (1974) findings that married (older) coeds had higher levels of achievement motivation compared to unmarried coeds as well as lower "fear of success," also lends support to this thesis. Research on the contribution of marriage plans to achievement motivation is being conducted by Drew and Patterson (1974) under contract to H.E.W.: N.I.E. in Washington D.C.

Work Discrimination

That women have been discriminated against in the labor force has been conclusively documented in the past few years (see Chapter 19; Sweet, 1973). Discrimination takes a variety of forms, from practices at the point of obtaining training (Astin, 1973) to practices in hiring, promoting, and providing on-the-job training, and salary increases (Fuchs, 1974; Parrish, 1974; Blitz, 1974). Attitudes of employers (Stimson, 1973; Taylor, 1973), employees (Crowley, Levitin and Quinn, 1973), and women themselves (Hawley, 1972; Medvene and Collins, 1974) toward women working indicate widespread belief in "myths" about women which are not verified by the facts of their behavior. Eleven of these myths with the related facts have been gathered together by the Women's Bureau (Chapter 19). These myths form the basis for a measure of work discrimination attitudes developed by Janice Birk at the University of Maryland (Birk, Cooper, and Tanney, 1973).

The relation of work discrimination to career motivation in women has not been clearly demonstrated. In the research of Farmer and Bohn (1970) for example, career motivation was increased for a group of employed women, when they were given role set (Sarbin, 1954) instructions to reduce attitudes about work discrimination. However, the role set also included instructions to reduce home-career conflict and fear of success (Horner, 1973), leaving the evidence on the effect of work discrimination inconclusive. In continuing research on career and achievement motivation in women, the author is currently examining the relationship of seven factors to such motivation, to try and tease out the contribution of each.

Achievement and career motivation in girls differs from that of boys as a result of as yet several poorly defined factors. Some of these factors have been identified in the research literature. (a) *Reduction in academic self-confidence* for girls in college (Tomlinson-Keasey, 1974); (b) *Fear of success* in college and high school women, found in varying degrees depending on the perceived social sanction given to women's careers (Horner, 1973; Katz, 1973; Monahan et al, 1974); (c) *Vicarious achievement motivation* found to contribute to women's contentment with traditional career roles such as secretary, elementary school teacher, and nurse (Lipman-Blumen, 1972); (d) *Home-career conflict* found in both college women and working women to inhibit career motivation (Morgan, 1962; Farmer & Bohn, 1970); (e) *Work discrimination* beliefs have been found to inhibit career motivation (Birk et al., 1973); (f) Studies of academic motivation have found *risk taking behavior* lower in girls than in boys (see review by Maccoby & Jacklin, 1974); and (g) A seventh factor, *sex role orientation,* was also found to affect achievement motivation (Alper, 1974; Entwisle, 1972).

Previous studies have typically looked at the effect of one of these variables, and have not controlled for the possible effect of the others on motivation. Other research has examined the effect of these variables on academic motivation, still other research the effect on career motivation, rather than both.

The author's present study is examining the potency of the above seven variables to predict (a) achievement motivation and (b) career motivation in samples of high school students, college undergraduates, and women returning to higher education after an absence of at least five years.

At least two benefits of this line of research should be the following:

(1) The research should, at the very least, shed more light on the causes of lower achievement or career motivation in women and the related lower interest in preparing for and entering the professions. A more differentiated picture of achievement motivation in women as compared to men should emerge.

(2) This research will lead to the development of a measure capable of identifying why a particular high ability girl or woman is low in achievement or career motivation and would permit early diagnosis of inhibiting attitudes. This diagnostic measure would enable counselors and teachers to prescribe change strategies more precisely than is now possible and reduce the likelihood that the wrong treatment would be given, i.e. that a highly assertive girl be given assertiveness training, etc.

Sex Free Roles: A Humanistic Goal

A number of writers recently have suggested that we should begin to teach our children more flexible attitudes toward sex roles; attitudes making it comfortable for boys to cook and take care of children, for example, and for girls to wield a hacksaw or drive a tractor. Psychological androgyny is the term several of these writers have used to describe this goal (Bardwick, 1974; Bem, 1974; Calderone, 1972; Lewis, 1973; Maccoby, 1974; Mead, 1974; Saario, 1973). The Greek word "andros" means man and "gyne" means woman, so "androgynous" literally means man-woman or "both male and female in one," according to Webster.

The word is used now to refer to "sex-free" roles, not bisexuality as in the past. Thus, we have Maccoby and Jacklin (1974) speaking of increasing sex-free-ego-space; Lee and Gropper (1974) speaking of a bi-cultural curriculum in the schools; and Calderone (1972) speaking of reciprocal sex roles replacing complementary ones: "The attitude that we are human beings first and then male and female, and that the things that we do and enjoy are not what distinguish the sexes, should begin to permeate not only the attitudes with which we bring up our children but their toys and their children's literature." Bardwick (1974) warns against trusting legislation alone to bring about the necessary changes to make equality for the sexes in work and the economy a reality. She suggests instead a long-range view which has goals for *both* sexes. A shortrange view is one which would have women achieve all that men have achieved and to inherit their disenchantment with success. The long view, on the other hand, emphasizes *multiple options* for both men and women, rather than stereotyped roles for either sex.

Kagan (1972) and Kohlberg (1966) found that highly sex-typed individuals invested a lot of psychological energy in maintaining their sex-typed image. In contrast, the more androgynous individual can shift roles with the changing situation's demands without threat. The androgynous person is comfortable being assertive, self-confident, independent, dependent, nurturant, and tender, when appropriate.

A bicultural curriculum for the schools is proposed by Lee and Gropper (1974) to promote the development of sex-free people. Basically, they suggest that boys and girls should have equal access to educational and cultural experiences, resources, and training. Their proposal is less expensive than changing all the textbooks, although that may be desirable as well. Lee and Gropper illustrate how a classroom teacher might facilitate biculturalism in the classroom with the following incident:

> The boy takes some playdough in a pot to the stove. He announces that he is cooking. The mother (another pupil) says "Daddies don't cook." The 'dog' (another pupil) says the same thing. The boy moves back from the stove—he says in a quiet voice, "My poppy cooks. . ." He stands off at a distance looking at the stove. He looks uncertain about what to do next. The teacher was watching the interaction, and she tells the two girls that daddies sometimes do cook. The boy immediately returns to the stove and starts to cook.

The notion of "androgyny" may be termed the philosophy toward which forward-thinking counselors can strive for both men and women.

Career guidance for the seventies should have as its primary goal preparing young persons, both women and men, for survival in the world of the future, not the present, and certainly not the past. The coping skills needed for survival in the world of tomorrow will require more critical thinking and imagination than ever before. As super-technology and automation take over more and more of the routine jobs, the role of men and women in the world of work will become increasingly similar, focused on brain power and problem solving. Critical skills for a future oriented career guidance curriculum should thus include teaching persons how to predict future events, make critical judgments and decisions, make "tentative career choices," cope with novel environments, plan for multiple roles, and adjust to changing career opportunities.

REFERENCES

Alper, T. Achievement motivation in college women: A now-you-see-it—now-you-don't phenomenon. *American Psychologist,* 1974, *29,* 194-203.

Astin, H. *The woman doctorate in America.* New York: The Russell Sage Foundation, 1969.

Astin, H.S. *Preparing women for careers in science and technology.* Paper presented at the Massachusetts Institute of Technology Workshop on Women in Science and Technology, Boston, May, 1973.

Atkinson, J.W. & Raynor, J.O. *Motivation and achievement.* Washington, D.C.: V.W. Winston & Sons, 1974.

Bardwick, J.M. Androgyny and humanistic goals, or goodbye cardboard people. In M.L. McBee & K.A. Blake (Eds.), *The American woman: Who will she be?* New York: Macmillan, 1974.

Bardwick, J. *Psychology of women.* New York: Harper and Row, 1971.

Bem, S. The measurement of psychological androgyny. *Journal of Consulting and Clinical Psychology,* 1974, *42* (2), 155-162.

Bettelheim, B. *The children of the dream.* London: Macmillan, 1969.

Birk, J., Cooper, J., & Tanney, M. *Racial and sex role stereotyping in career information illustration.* Paper presented at the meeting of the American Psychological Association, Montreal, August, 1973.

Blitz, R. Women in the professions, 1870-1970. *Monthly Labor Review,* 1974, *97,* 34-39.

Calderone, M.S. New roles for women. *The University of Chicago School Review,* 1972, *80,* 275-280.

Campbell, D.P. *SVIB—SVII manual.* Stanford, Ca.: Stanford University Press, 1974.

Commission on the Status of Women. *Participation of women in the economic and social development of their countries.* New York: United Nations, 1970.

Crowley, J., Levitin, T., & Quinn, R. *Facts and fictions about American working women.* Ann Arbor, Michigan: University of Michigan Institute for Social Research, Survey Research Center, January, 1973.

Darling, M. The role of women in the economy: Meeting of experts. Washington, D.C. Unpublished manuscript, 1973.

Drew, D. & Patterson, M. Noah's ark in the frog pond: The educational aspirations of males and female undergraduates. Unpublished manuscript, 1974. (Available from the authors, National Research Council, Washington, D.C.).

Entwisle, D. & Greenberger, E. Adolescents' views of women's work role. *American Journal of Orthopsychiatry,* 1972, *42,* 648-656.

Farmer, H. Helping women to resolve the home-career conflict. *Personnel and*

Guidance Journal, 1971, *49,* 795-801.

Farmer, H. & Bohn, M. Home-career conflict reduction and the level of career interest in women. *Journal of Counseling Psychology,* 1970, *17,* 228-232.

Farmer, H. & Backer, T. *Women at work: A counselor's sourcebook.* (in press, 1975, available in draft form from HEW;NIE, Washington, D.C.).

Friedan, B. *The feminine mystique.* New York: W.W. Norton, 1963.

Fuchs, V. Women's earnings: Recent trends and long-run prospects. *Monthly Labor Review,* 1974, *97,* 23-25.

Ginzberg, E. & Associates. *Life styles of educated women.* New York: Columbia University Press, 1966.

Harmon, L. Variables related to women's persistence in educational plans. *Journal of Vocational Behavior,* 1972, *2,* 143-153.

Harmon, L. Career counseling for women. In D. Carter and E. Rawlings (eds.), *Psychotherapy for women: Treatment toward equality.* Springfield: Thomas, 1975.

Hawley, P. Perceptions of male models of femininity related to career choice. *Journal of Counseling Psychology,* 1972, *19,* 308-313.

Hedges, J. and Barnett, J. Working women and the division of household tasks. *Monthly Labor Review,* 1972, 97, 4-22.

Hoffman, L.W. Effects on children: Summary and discussion. In F.I. Nye and L.W. Hoffman (eds.), *The employed mother in America.* Chicago: Rand McNally and Co., 1963, 190-212.

Horner, M. Sex differences in achievement motivation and performance in competitive and non-competitive situations. Unpublished doctoral dissertation, University of Michigan, Ann Arbor, 1968, No. 69-112, 135.

Horner, M., Tresemer, D., Berens, A., & Watson, R., Jr. Scoring manual for an empirically derived scoring system for motive to avoid success. Unpublished monograph, Harvard University, 1973.

Huber, J. (Ed.) *Changing women in a changing society.* Chicago: The University of Chicago Press, 1973.

Kagan, J. The emergence of sex differences. *School Review,* 1972, *80,* 217-227.

Katz, M. *Female motive to avoid success: A psychological barrier or a response to deviancy?* Princeton, N.J.: Educational Testing Service, 1973.

Kievit, M. *Review and synthesis of research on women in the world of work.* Washington, D.C.: U.S. Government Printing Office, 1972.

Kohlberg, L. A cognitive-developmental analysis of children's sex-role concepts and attitudes. In E.E. Maccoby (Ed.), *The development of sex differences.* Stanford, Ca: Stanford University Press, 1966.

Komarovsky, M. Cultural contradictions and sex roles. *American Journal of Sociology,* 1946, *52,* 184-189.

Koontz, E. *Plans for widening women's educational opportunities.* Washington, D.C.: U.S. Government Printing Office, 1972.

Lee, P.C., & Gropper, N.B. Sex-role culture and educational practice. *Harvard Educational Review,* 1974, *44,* 369-410.

Lewis, F. When I grow up I want to be androgynous. *Phi Delta Kappa,* 1973,*55,* 140.

Lipman-Blumen, J. How ideology shapes women's lives. *Scientific American,* 1972, *226,* 34-42.

Maccoby, E. & Jacklin, C. *The psychology of sex differences.* Stanford, Ca: Stanford University Press, 1974.

Maehr, M. *Sociocultural origins of achievement.* Monterey, Ca: Brooks-Cole, 1974.

Maehr, M. Culture and achievement motivation. *American Psychologist,* 1974,

29, 887-896.
Matthews, E. & Tiedeman, D. Attitudes toward career and marriage and the development of life style in young women. *Journal of Counseling Psychology,* 1964, *11,* 375-384.
McClelland, D. *Assessing human motivation.* New York: General Learning Press, 1971.
Mead, M. Foreword. In M.L. McBee and K.A. Blake (eds.), *The American woman: Who will she be?* New York: MacMillan, 1974.
Medvene, A., & Collins, A. Occupational prestige and its relationship to traditional and nontraditional views of women's roles. *Journal of Counseling Psychology,* 1974, *21* (2), 139-143.
Monohan, L., Kuhn, D., & Shaver, P. Intrapsychic versus cultural explanations of the "fear of success" motive. *Journal of Personality and Social Psychology,* 1974, *29,* 60-64.
Morgan, D. Perceptions of role conflicts and self-concepts among career and non-career college educated women. Unpublished doctoral dissertation. Teachers College, Columbia University, New York, 1962.
Parrish, J. Women in professional training. *Monthly Labor Review,* 1974, *97,* 41-43.
Psathas, G. Toward a theory of occupational choice for women. *Sociology and Social Research,* 1968, *52,* 253-268.
Rabin, A.I. *Growing up in the kibbutz.* New York: Speinter, 1965.
Rossi, A. & Calderwood, A. (Eds.). *Academic women on the move.* New York: Russell Sage Foundation, 1973.
Saario, T.N., Jacklin, C.N., and Tittle, C.K. Sexrole stereotyping in the public schools. *Harvard Educational Review,* 1973 (Aug.), *43(3),* 386-416.
Sarbin, T. Role theory. In G. Lindzey (Ed.), *Handbook of social psychology* (Vol. 1). Cambridge, Massachusetts: Addison-Wesley, 1954.
Stimson, C. (Ed.). *Discrimination against women: Congressional hearing on equal rights in education and employment.* New York: R.R. Bowker Co., 1973.
Strong, E. *Vocational interests 18 years after college.* Minneapolis: University of Minnesota Press, 1955.
Super, D. Theory of vocational choice. *The Counseling Psychologist,* 1969, *1,* 2-10.
Sweet, J. *Women in the labor force.* New York: Harcourt Brace, 1973.
Taylor, S. Education leadership: A male domain? *Phi Delta Kappan,* 1973, *55,* 124-128.
Thomas, H. Underlying constructs of locus of control of reinforcement. Paper presented at the annual meeting of the American Educational Research Association, Washington, April, 1975.
Tomlinson-Keasey, C. Role variables: Their influence on female motivational constructs. *Journal of Counseling Psychology,* 1974, *21,* 232-237.
Tyler, L. The antecedents of two varieties of interest patterns. *Genetic Psychological Monograph,* 1964, *70,* 177-227.
Wallston, B. The effects of maternal employment on children. *Journal of Child Psychology and Psychiatry,* 1973, *14,* 81-95.
White, R. *The enterprise of living.* New York: Holt, Rinehart, and Winston, 1972.

Chapter 7

VICARIOUS AND DIRECT ACHIEVEMENT PATTERNS IN ADULTHOOD*

JEAN LIPMAN-BLUMEN AND HAROLD J. LEAVITT

Abstract

This chapter presents a typology of direct and vicarious achievement orientations relevant to adult problems. Direct and vicarious achievement patterns are related to sex role socialization and sex-linked occupational choice. An achievement-sexuality scoring system is described for channeling adults into traditional sex-linked occupations. Recommendations are developed for re-evaluating and redesigning adult occupational and interpersonal roles which would take into account vicarious and direct achievement orientations.

VICARIOUS AND DIRECT ACHIEVEMENT PATTERNS IN ADULTHOOD

As current restrictive definitions of adult roles become more fluid, there is need to reconsider the validity of achievement patterns as they traditionally have been taught. Such a reconceptualization is a relevant task, because socialized achievement patterns are important precursors of adult occupational and sex roles.

Orientations toward achievement are one way in which adults differ markedly from one another. Some adults achieve their goals by confronting their environment directly. Others seek achievements through manipulation of interpersonal relationships. Still others take a more indirect approach, experiencing pleasure through the accomplishments of others. This chapter presents a typology of achievement orientations among adults, along with an effort to provide some theoretical linkages to early socialization and adult occupational and sex roles.

---

*The authors are indebted to Denise Abrams, Jessie Bernard, Reuben Harris, Gail Parks, Susan Schaefer and Ann Tickamyer for helping them to clarify their ideas in numerous conversations.
*From *The Counseling Psychologist, 1976, 6, 26-32.*

These orientations presumably are developed early in life; however, there is no reason to believe in their immutability. While one particular achievement orientation may assume salience for an individual, other less developed styles may remain accessible, ready to be evoked under changing circumstances.

It is not surprising, nonetheless, that individuals accustomed to using one primary achievement style may experience difficulty making these transitions. Counselors may begin to encounter such difficulty more commonly among their clients in response to accelerating shifts in occupational and sex role expectations.

Vicarious Achievement Patterns

The enigma of achievement patterns has captivated the imaginations of social scientists for many years (McClelland, Atkinson, & Lowell, 1953). Different correlates and different methodologies have been explored to plumb the depths of achievement motivation; however, systematic understanding of the problem remains elusive. Sex differences in achievement motivation have been particularly difficult to map because of the erratic and seemingly uninterpretable nature of the data on female subjects (Angelini, 1955; Baruch, R., 1967; French & Lesser, 1958; Lesser, Krawitz & Packard, 1963; McClelland et al., 1953; Veroff, Wilcox, & Atkinson, 1953).

More recent work by Horner (1968, 1969, 1972) has led to a plethora of studies focused upon one possible resolution of the inconsistent findings on female achievement patterns: fear of success (Alper, 1973, 1974; Baruch, G., 1973; Curtis, Zanna, & Campbell, 1973; Hoffman, 1972, 1974; Katz, 1972; Levine & Crumrine, 1975; Romer, 1975; Tresemer, 1974). The methodological storm that has arisen regarding the burgeoning fear-of-success literature has obscured the importance of investigating other achievement patterns in both women and men. One such pattern which has won only scant attention (Blumen, 1970; Lipman-Blumen, 1972, 1973; Papanek, 1973; Tresemer & Pleck, 1972) is vicarious achievement.

In a general way, a vicarious achievement orientation involves finding personal fulfillment through a relationship with another, through the activities and qualities of another individual with whom the vicarious achiever, to some degree, identifies. Conceptually, we can consider a continuum of vicarious to direct achievement orientations. At least three points along the *vicarious* portion may be labelled: altruistic, contributory, and instrumental.

By *altruistic vicariousness* we mean the tendency to take satisfaction and pleasure from someone else's activities, qualities, and/or accomplishments as if they were one's own. This vicarious achiever basks in the reflected glory of the individual with whom s/he identifies.

Being associated with the direct achiever is enough. The altruistically vicarious achiever can derive pleasure simply from having a relationship with a direct achiever. The relationship is primary. It is an end in itself. One example is the stereotypical self-effacing wife of the "great man," whose role is simply to be there to nurture him.

The *contributing vicarious achiever* is characterized by enabling or facilitating behavior and attitudes toward the direct achiever. The contributing individual, like the altruistic one, takes pleasure in the characteristics and successes of the other individual as if they were his/her own. But in the case of the contributing person, the pleasure is derived primarily from the belief that s/he has contributed in some measure to the success of the direct achiever, if only by maintaining the relationship.

Oftentimes, the contributing person can accept the other individual's success as his/her own, because s/he, indeed, has had a hand in it. The contributing vicarious achiever may make her/himself indispensable to the direct achiever, thereby meeting her/his own needs both to help and be helped.

To the contributing vicarious achiever, the relationship is important both intrinsically, for its own sake, and also extrinsically, as the medium through which the contributing person achieves. A recent statement from a political wife summed up this orientation when she remarked that if she lost her husband, she also would be losing her best friend and her career (McCarthy, 1974).

Papanek's (1973) treatment of the two-person career, and Coser and Rokoff's (1971) and Coser & Coser's (1974) work on "greedy institutions" focus on contributing vicarious achievement roles for women. The political wife who campaigns for her husband and the graduate student's wife who types his papers are examples of contributing vicarious achievers.

Parents who encourage their children to attempt roles which they regret not having entered themselves may be considered within the camp of contributing vicarious achievers. Hollywood mothers who push their offspring to become child stars are examples of this form of vicarious achievement.

An *instrumental vicarious achiever* is more likely to perceive relationships as means to other things. It is the avenue to security, status, love, money, achievement, and even other relationships. The instrumentally vicarious person may manipulate the relationship in order to achieve other ends, including success of various sorts which the vicarious individual may feel unsuited to attempt on his/her own. The relationship is used as the means to meet other needs. The man who marries the boss's daughter exemplifies this type.

For heuristic purposes, we can begin to imagine a continuum

where altruistic vicariousness is one polar position, with contributory vicariousness placed somewhere beyond it, and instrumental vicariousness still somewhere farther along the continuum. The opposite pole of the continuum is the direct achievement end, with several forms of direct achievement (which we shall describe below) spanning the positions at this end.

Identification

Basic to this conceptualization of vicarious achievement is the concept of identification with another individual, usually a "significant other." By identification, we do not necessarily mean a perceived similarity of personality characteristics or character structure. Rather, identification here means accepting as one's own the interests, goals, and sometimes values of another individual.

The degree of identification that the vicarious achiever experiences with another individual may vary from very intense to very attenuated. One possible result of intense identification, where the vicarious individual can barely distinguish him/herself from the other individual, is shared responsibility for the results of the direct achiever's actions or qualities. This responsibility sharing may involve both the negative and positive aspects of achievement. We expect that this type of identification is more likely to occur when the relationship between two individuals is direct, intimate, reciprocal, involved and significant, such as in relationships between family members.

This type of shared responsibility probably is always characteristic of altruistic vicariousness, typically true of contributory vicariousness, and sometimes true of instrumental vicariousness, where the identification process may be much more attenuated. For example, the altruistic parent whose child is a valedictorian may experience both strong identification and shared responsibility; conversely, the parent whose child suffers an emotional breakdown may suffer also through intense identification and sense of guilt.

The contributing father, who feels that his intense coaching has contributed to his son's athletic prowess, probably will feel responsible for the child's failure. But one also can imagine a more instrumentally vicarious parent who uses his son's performance as a surrogate for his own. Such a vicarious parent possibly may reject responsibility for his protégé's inadequacy.

In the case of instrumental vicariousness, too, we should expect a range of degrees of identification. For example, the stage mother may identify very strongly, albeit selfishly, with her child's successes and failures. However, an instrumentally vicarious courtesan or campaign worker might be disappointed at the failure of the other individual, but then might readily abandon the relationship in favor of an attachment to a more promising individual.

Identification does not necessarily imply emotional symmetry between the individuals involved. Although this type of emotional symmetry may increase the level of identification on the part of the primary identifier, it is not a necessary component of identification. The sense of identification may be primarily unilateral or reciprocal. For example, film stars often are the objects of identification for their devoted followers, without reciprocal involvement with their fans.

The important point is simply that one individual takes as his or her own the goals, values and interests of another individual. Some degree of identification appears to be a necessary condition for the development of active or specific (versus latent or generalized) vicarious achievement orientation.

The tendency toward a vicarious achievement orientation can exist without a specific object of identification. We suggest that it is a generalized orientation that subsumes a readiness to identify with others, while the actual individual with whom the vicarious achiever identifies may vary over time (and for women, particularly, may covary with stages in the life cycle). In addition, the absence of a specific individual at any given point in time will not vitiate the vicarious achievement orientation, although it probably will convert it to its latent form. Thus, the vicarious achievement orientation develops as an abstract and latent mode in which to cast behavior, and may, in fact, be activated by the process of identification with a particular "significant other."

It is possible that the vicarious achievement orientation, once established, may drive its possessor to seek appropriate individuals with whom to identify for need fulfillment. And once the underlying pattern of vicarious achievement orientation is established, with its built-in predisposition to seek an object of identification, the actual identification of a specific individual may trigger the whole dynamic, casting it in its specific or active (rather than its generalized or latent) mode.

Direct Achievement

As suggested earlier, the other end of the continuum is the direct achievement pole. Again, it is possible to distinguish several "types" of direct achievers: intrinsic, competitive, and instrumental.

The *intrinsic direct achievement* orientation is characterized by the intrinsic pleasures of accomplishment. Individuals with this primary orientation are more attuned to individual accomplishment, the task at hand, than to other people or things (Deci, 1975). This type of individual is more involved with him/herself (as compared with the "other" orientation of altruistic vicarious types) and uses the self as a means to achieve goals. Confronting the environment, exercising one's autonomy, wresting accomplishments from the milieu by one's own efforts, experiencing the thrill of success are all trademarks of the intrinsic direct achiever.

The intrinsic direct achiever pits him/herself against a standard of excellence, an abstract expected level of performance, rather than against other individuals. The accomplishment is an end in itself; it is its own reward. This individual has some of the characteristics of McClelland et al.'s (1953) high N achievement person and Maslow's (1954) "self-actualizer." We would expect that this type of individual, more involved in her/his own self, is more comfortable working alone, rather than in the distracting context of a team—unless individual performance feedback is available within the team context.

The *competitive direct achievement* orientation is distinguished by the need to outdo a competitor. The excitement of achievement is specifically enhanced by the fact that the success is accomplished within a competitive setting, proving that the individual is not only succeeding, but succeeding more than anyone else in the competition.

Like the intrinsic direct achiever, the competitive individual uses the self to accomplish the goal. The competitive direct orientation, however, involves others. The self is used as a mechanism to prove the individual's superiority to other contenders. To the competitive achiever, relationships are secondary to the achievement. In fact, the often attenuated relationship to other competitors provides the means for the desired end: the demonstration of the competitive direct achiever's greater self-worth. The process of winning against competitors is the basic challenge. In some respects, the competitive direct person may be likened to Christie's high Machiavellian individual (Christie & Geis, 1970) who is motivated by the game itself, who delights in the bargaining process, and who often wins because s/he persists in the game long after the other players have wearied and lost their motivation to engage in the fray. The dedicated linebacker whose joy comes in the competition, as well as the individual whose pleasure is spoiled by comparable successes of others, are examples of the competitive direct achiever.

The third type of direct achiever is the *instrumental direct.* S/he uses his/her own achievements as a generalized means for achieving other goals, particularly relational goals, such as nurturance and affiliation, as well as more traditional goals, including power, status and more success. The instrumental direct achiever uses whatever talents and success s/he has to meet her/his other needs. In a sense, this individual uses her/his direct achievement skills as a medium through which s/he can acquire relationships to people.

Increased status, as well as control and power over other individuals, are not inconsequential concerns to the instrumental direct achiever. Concern with status, control, and power in no way detracts from the seriousness and skill with which the instrumental direct achiever performs a task. Performing well is a necessary first order of business, first to satisfy the individual's own egoistic needs, and next to legitimate claims to other secondary gains of success. High standards of performance create the links that bind others to her/him in awe, in fear, in love, in greed, in ambition, and in genuine respect. Not only sustained ability to perform, as in Weber's (1940) charismatic leader, but also exploitation of the vicarious needs of others, sustains the control that the instrumental direct achiever has over her/his following. The political figure who delights in the role of social lion, but must continually succeed politically to maintain both professional and social coteries, fits this mold. The successful businessperson whose campaign contributions lead to an ambassadorial appointment is another example of the instrumental direct achiever. The powerful male who uses (indeed seeks) his power to entice or coerce women into sexual relationships is still another.

It is perhaps unnecessary to caution that the described typology is meant primarily as an heuristic device.[1] It is clear that only rarely, outside the pages of a novel, are we likely to find clear cut "ideal typical" cases in the Weberian sense. For example, one individual could encompass both competitive and instrumental direct achievement characteristics. And we are more likely to find such "hybrid" individuals than either "pure" type.

We further would argue that any one of these orientations may have *primary* salience for an individual, while simultaneously being linked to a secondary achievement orientation. Thus, it is entirely conceivable to think of an individual whose primary achievement mode is one of the direct orientations, and whose secondary mode is a vicarious one, or vice versa. Other factors, such as context, specificity of relationship, time, centrality of the situation to one's value hierarchy, stage in the life and/or work cycle and even hormonal level, may mitigate the actual achievement response of a given individual in a specific instance. Thus, the same individual may be primarily a competitive direct achiever in the context of work life, but a contributing vicarious achiever within the parental role.

Underlying Factors[2]

There are important psychological and sociological dimensions to the achievement problem. The psychological model underlying this

[1]For a description of an empirical test of this model see Leavitt, H.L., Lipman-Blumen, J., Schaefer, S., & Harris, R. *Patterns of achievement behavior in men and womens Preliminary findings*. Unpublished manuscript, 1975. (Available from J. Lipman-Blumen, National Institute of Education, Washington, D.C. 20208.)

[2]For a more particular explication of the underlying model see Jean Lipman-Blumen & Harold J. Leavitt, *Toward a Theory of Direct and Vicarious Achievement,* submitted for publication.

typology is a now fairly conventional one (Freud, 1938; Maslow, 1954; Murray, 1938) of both the learning of needs and the learning of instrumental means for trying to satisfy those needs. We categorize needs into three major types: *physical* needs, assumed to be largely innate and largely operant from birth; and two classes of needs which we shall call *social* and *egoistic*. Our model assumes that social and egoistic needs are primarily learned. The key initial learning stems from differential degrees of reinforcement in the satisfaction of physical needs. The important learning mechanism is assumed to be the dependency of the infant on the behavior of parents and other forces in his/her environment.

The line of argument runs as follows: Infants are caught from the outset in dependency relationships. Different individuals experience different degrees of difficulty in satisfying their physical needs. Some children can satisfy most of their physical needs with relatively little effort most of the time in this dependent setting. Others, for various reasons, find that their available repertoire of behaviors yields only long delays, irregularities, and frustration.

Infants whose early experiences are mostly satisfying are presumed, in this model, to generalize two related, but conceptually separable, perspectives. First, they will learn to value highly these satisfying relationships as ends in themselves. That is, they will develop relatively strong social orientations. Second, they also will learn a generalized achievement orientation—in this case vicarious (relational)—as the preferred means for need satisfaction of all kinds. That is, they will prefer tools they know how to use successfully—in this case, behavioral tools for manipulating relationships with others.

At the other extreme, children who, during this period of infantile dependency, encounter difficulty in satisfying their physical needs will learn quite different patterns of needs and will have to search for new behavioral means. They will develop stronger needs for independence, autonomy, and achievement—the egoistic needs. They also will develop a generalized *independent* and *direct* orientation for achievements of all kinds. That is, they will prefer acting *directly* on the world to acting *indirectly* on it through relationships with other people.

The Socialization of the Sexes and Differential Achievement Orientations

We turn now to the issue of differential learning of achievement orientations of females and males. There is a general social science hypothesis that American male children characteristically have been more positively reinforced earlier in life for direct, independent behavior, and female children have been reinforced more for indirect (vicarious), dependent, relational behavior (Maccoby & Jacklin, 1974).

Cross-cultural studies of sex role socialization (Block, 1972) suggest that this belief extends far beyond the boundaries of American culture.

One important distinction between the socialization practices focused upon boys and girls appears to be consistent across many cultures. The distinction revolves around the contrasting qualities of directness, agency, initiation, and activity for boys versus vicariousness, communion, implementation, and passivity for girls (Bakan, 1966; Bandura & Walters, 1963; Gough, 1966). This basic discrimination between males and females is strongly developed by adolescence.

Individuals who adopt a vicarious achievement mode most likely, according to our model, also would have strong affiliation needs. Hoffman's (1974) review of the affiliation literature focuses on the relationship between females' affiliation needs and achievement motives. She concludes that girls' (compared to boys') less frequent engagement in independent exploration of their environments is related to early parental conditioning. Girls receive greater protection and support from parents (particularly mothers), less encouragement to establish a separate identity from mothers, and less mother-child conflict associated with establishing an individual identity.

This pattern tends to support the formation of dependency in girls, to socialize girls to expect help from others, including help in the mastery of their environments. Thus, affiliation is a means of achieving mastery for girls. More often, they are socialized to seek help from others in mastering their environments, compared to boys who are more likely to be pressured into individualistic effectance and competence (White, 1963) through direct mastery of the environment. In this way, the link between affiliation and achievement may be strengthened in girls. Therefore, it should come as no great surprise if we find that women project the fulfillment of their own achievement needs onto the accomplishments of an individual with whom they have established strong affiliative bonds.

If women are not socialized to direct mastery of their environments, i.e. effectance, and are encouraged to seek help from others in accomplishing tasks, it would not be extraordinary to discover that some women may eschew direct confrontation with their adult environments beyond the confines of the home and are comfortable having someone else (husband or child) act for them. The vicarious achievement syndrome, when it exists among women, is a natural outgrowth of this set of conditions.

This has been the long and, until recently, the unremitting history of sex role socialization in the United States and many other countries. It has conditioned the expectations of females and males alike for their own and each other's behavior. Thus, despite the fact that the Women's Movement has wrought surprisingly swift and sharp changes in female behavior in some quarters, the stereotypes of the "dependent," vicarious achieving female and the direct, competitive male persist.

In an investigation of sex differences in achievement patterns (Leavitt, Lipman-Blumen, Schaefer & Harris, 1975), some preliminary findings suggest that while female college students see women as direct achievers, unfettered by dependency longings, their male colleagues tend to perceive females in standard societal stereotypes—as vicarious achievers. Conversely, while male college students think that males can enjoy vicarious achievement patterns, their female colleagues persist in interpreting male behavior within the traditional sex stereotypes of direct, competitive patterns.

Generalized stereotypes about sex-linked behavior have their impact on every aspect of social life. They have a particularly negative effect on females' educational and occupational aspirations. In a recent study (Blumen, 1970; Lipman-Blumen, 1972) of correlates of educational aspiration of married women, the vicarious achievement ethic was linked directly both to traditional sex role stereotypes and low educational aspirations. In a subsample of married female college graduates, 40% of the women who held vicarious achievement orientations also reported no expectation of continuing their formal education. Among women who reported strong direct achievement orientations, only 12% gave this response. In addition, 60% of the women who described themselves as vicarious achievers also reported they subscribed to the standard sex stereotypes, compared to 24% of the direct achievers.

The vicarious achievement ethic, when applied to women, implies that marital and maternal roles—largely vicarious in nature—are *the* most desirable and appropriate roles for women. Within marriage, women vicariously may achieve family status, rank, power, and money. Occupational roles for females often are treated as temporary waiting stations for the unmarried, until they can be rescued by marriage and maternity, or as emergency measures in times of family financial difficulty, for the married. These notions persist despite the rapid increase of women (including married women and mothers of young children) in the labor force. Even when women do enter the labor force, they are channeled into roles that closely mirror their nurturant, enabling roles within the family: teacher, nurse, secretary, waitress, stewardess. Similarly, males are channeled into direct achievement roles, which are consonant with the male stereotype.

Sexuality-Achievement Scores

The remarkably persistent segregation of both women and men into sex-typed occupations is facilitated by a special mechanism: a sexuality-and-achievement score. It is a two-dimensional scoring system in which points are awarded or deducted for the sexuality (or glamour) and achievement potentials of various jobs when occupied by a female or a male. Underlying this system is the assumption that direct achievement roles are more highly valued by society than vicarious ones.

When vicarious jobs are filled by women, they receive a "plus" for sexuality or glamour and a "minus" for achievement potential. The aura of sexuality that surrounds traditional male and female jobs, when occupied by the "appropriate sex" person, is a social mechanism for attracting and retaining the "correct gender" worker. Oftentimes, this aura is more imagined than real and may serve to obscure the more menial aspects of the role. For example, the glamour and excitement that surround the image of the airline stewardess go far to minimize and conceal the drudgery of serving meals and responding to passengers' needs within very tight space and time constraints.

Conversely, sexuality decrements for entering the "wrong" role for one's sex steer individuals away from these roles. For example, the nursing role offers positive sexuality points for female entrants, but produces negative sexuality points for male nurses. The very old and the very young, perceived as devoid of sexuality in American culture, are reasonably protected from this occupational allocation mechanism. Thus, in the relatively small number of cases where the very old and the very young are employed, they are allowed to enter cross-sex roles without noticeable censure. The young (or very old) male babysitter provides such a case.

Males who enter "appropriate," i.e. direct achievement, roles receive the highest scores: plus for sexuality and plus for achievement. Females who enter traditional feminine, i.e. vicarious, occupations receive a plus for sexuality and a minus for achievement. When women intrude on traditional male, i.e. direct achievement, occupational roles, they also receive a mixed rating, but this time the plus is for achievement and the minus is for sexuality. Males who trespass on traditional female roles receive the most damaging scores of all: minus for sexuality and minus for achievement.

It is clear that entering "sex-inappropriate" roles is dangerous for both women and men, but it is more dangerous for men who become "contaminated" by "women's work." For instance, the male secretary is maligned for the low level role he occupies and his lack of masculinity. Slightly better off is the female mathematician or surgeon who is seen as an accomplished, but unfeminine, creature. One structural way of diluting the double onus of the male in a vicarious role is to promote him as swiftly as possible to an administrative or managerial role, which is characterized by a greater degree of direct achievement. As a result, it is not surprising that, although most of the elementary school teachers are women, the majority of elementary school principals are men. Similar examples exist within the fields of library science, nursing, and social work where males more often hold the higher status administrative roles.

In childhood, females with strong egoistic needs are allowed their expression. Boys, on the other hand, who express affiliative needs are more likely to encounter parental constraint (Maccoby & Jacklin, 1974). And from the few available studies (Maccoby & Jacklin, 1974), it appears that fathers, more than mothers, are the ones who reward daughters for traditionally feminine behavior and punish boys for stepping over the sex role boundaries. The sexuality-achievement scoring mechanism described above is the adult world continuation of this same phenomenon.

Flexibility in Adulthood

Dissatisfaction with sex roles, work roles, generational and racial roles has spawned considerable rethinking about traditional ways of allocating adult roles. Until recently, lower status individuals—women, the elderly, the very young, the poor, and other minorities—have been channeled into vicarious roles and then criticized for their "choices." Higher status individuals in sex, age, and cultural groups were tracked into direct achievement roles. But new research and new political demands have opened the door to a broader view of role choice.

As a result, we have begun to think about moving males into roles which can meet their stifled social needs and women into roles in which they can express more directly their egoistic needs. Perhaps it is not untenable to begin to talk in terms of different achievement orientations being suitable to males and females at different stages in the life cycle. This, in turn, leads us to consider different occupations or careers—perhaps a set of minicareers—for individuals, rather than one life-long choice in which changing levels of egoistic and social needs are only poorly handled. We also might consider the possibility of more role freedom, based upon looser role definitions.

Taking vicarious and direct achievement modes into account, perhaps it is time for us to begin designing mathematics and science courses to meet the special needs of vicarious achievers, and language and literature courses for direct achievers. Recent work on cognitive style and the hemispheres of the brain (Levine, 1966), as well as research on bicognition and cultural differences (Ramirez & Castaneda, 1975), offer important insights into ways of developing and meeting both social and egoistic needs, vicarious and direct orientations, emotional and analytic styles. The work of Baltes (1973) and Baltes and Labouvie (1973) suggests that learning is possible into late adulthood;

and this should imply that retraining individuals to use both vicarious and direct modes, depending upon the situation, can be accomplished with mature adults.

Crisis is a condition under which all roles change with surprising ease (Lipman-Blumen, 1973, 1974, 1975a, 1975b). All social systems, from the two-person relationship, to families, to organizations, to large-scale societies, witness role change in the face of crisis when reallocation of resources becomes paramount. Further studies of defused crisis should permit us to develop strategies for introducing role change at different points throughout adulthood. Transitional points in the life cycle are obvious candidates—almost natural experiments—for crisis-engendered treatment, times when individuals can learn most easily how to move across the barriers that separate vicarious and direct achievement modes.

Many occupational roles, which consume a great part of adult lives, would benefit from redesign. Various roles which are archetypes of direct achievement would gain from an infusion of vicarious attributes, and vice versa. If, for example, the surgeon's role called for more nurturant behavior, and the nurse's role allowed more direct decision-making and initiative, most likely both these professionals and their patients would reap a harvest of improved relations and better health (Lipman-Blumen, 1975c).

Increasingly, we see the questioning of the analytical role of the manager (Leavitt, 1975); more intuitive, "feminine" qualities are being urged for this role. Indeed one can argue that the role of the manager is being steadily redefined from an entirely direct achievement role (in the tradition of the military commander) to a more mixed role involving morale building, counseling, and other vicarious types of behavior. The very nature of contemporary models of problem-solving which emphasize analytic, i.e. masculine, skills to the exclusion of intuitive, i.e. feminine, strengths, currently is being reconsidered (Leavitt, 1975).

New organizational structures which allow for the expression of both egoistic and social needs, as well as direct and vicarious achievement orientations are being recommended. Such changes in structure should open new opportunities to both males and females, from different cultural traditions, to test the individual balance of vicarious and direct achievement styles most compatible with their needs.

Further research on the demands of institutions in terms of achievement orientations would provide valuable information regarding adult development and change. Institutions which reward intrinsic, asocial, apolitical, and iconoclastic behavior are increasingly rare. Some institutions permit such behavior only as the reward for outstanding achievement. Most American work organizations reward primarily direct achievement behavior, preferably competitive or instrumental. Instrumental vicarious behavior and contributing vicarious behavior usually characterize lower level jobs within institutions; and it is not merely coincidental that these positions are most often occupied by women, other minorities and the youngest members of an organization. How achievement orientations change in adulthood to respond to the demands of the organization is an important area for additional investigation.

Adult interpersonal roles, particularly family roles, are equally likely candidates for reevaluation. The instrumental-expressive dichotomy (Parsons & Bales, 1955) has come under direct assault as a meaningful paradigm for family roles. The future of marriage has been described (Bernard, 1972a, 1972b, 1975) in ways that offer new insights and possibilities. The emerging psychology and sociology of women are hopeful omens. But much remains to be done to loosen the constraints that hold males in the bonds of direct achievement and females in the grip of vicariousness.

Adult sexuality is another domain where traditional concerns of directness and vicariousness have played havoc. Medical technology and the Feminist Movement have made great inroads into stereotyped sexual behavior profiles of adult men and women. The new learning associated with sexual behavior–including searching behavior, experimentation, new awareness, and new satisfaction–might serve as a model for delineating the changeovers that are necessary in other aspects of adult life.

Sex stereotypes, linked to achievement stereotypes, require more clinical investigation. Sex stereotypes seem more internally consistent than the actual behavior of females and males. If we considered individuals within the context of their own life space and age cohorts, we probably would discover a wide range of individual, rather than sex-related patterns.

In any case, we propose that it may be time to try to change sex stereotyped achievement orientations to utilize the potential of vicarious and direct patterns, regardless of sex. It also may be time to redefine roles in organizations and other social institutions to take advantage of the full range of achievement orientations.

REFERENCES

Alper, T.G. The relationship between role-orientation and achievement motivation in college women. *Journal of Personality,* 1973, *11,* 9-31.

Alper, T.G. Achievement motivation in college women: A now-you-see-it–now-you-don't phenomenon. *American Psychologist,* 1974, *29,* 194-203.

Angelini, A.L. (A new method for evaluating human motivation.) *Boletin Faculdade de Filosefia Ciences, Sao Paulo,* 1955, No. 207.

Bakan, D. *The duality of human existence.* Chicago, Ill.: Rand McNally, 1966.

Baltes, P.B. Prototypical paradigms and questions in life-span research on development and aging. *Gerontologist,* Winter 1973, pp. 458-467.

Baltes, P.B., & Labouvie, G.V. Adult development of intellectual preference: Description, explanation, and modification. In C. Eisdorfer & M.P. Lauton (Eds.), *Psychology of adult development and aging.* Washington, D.C.: American Psychological Association, 1973.

Bandura, A., & Walters, R.H. *Social learning and personality development.* New York: Holt, Rinehart & Winston, 1963.

Baruch, G.K. *The motive to avoid success and career aspirations of 5th and 10th grade girls.* Paper presented at the meeting of the American Psychological Association, Montreal, Canada, 1973.

Baruch, R. The achievement-motive in women: Implications for career development. *Journal of Personality and Social Psychology,* 1967, *5*(3), 260-267.

Bernard, J. *The sex game.* New York: Atheneum, 1972a. (Originally published, 1968).

Bernard, J. *The future of marriage.* New York: Bantam, 1972b.

Bernard, J. Sex role transcendence and sex role transcenders. In *Women, wives, mothers: Values and options.* Chicago, Ill.: Aldine, 1975.

Block, J.H. *Conceptions of sex role: Some cross-cultural and longitudinal perspectives.* (Mimeographed paper.) Bernard Moses Memorial Lecture, University of California, 1972.

Blumen, J.L. *Selected dimensions of self-concept and educational aspirations of married women college graduates.* Unpublished doctoral dissertation, Harvard University, 1970.

Christie, R., & Geis, F.R. *Studies in machiavellianism.* New York: Academic Press, 1970.

Coser, R.L., & Coser, L.A. The housewife and the greedy family. In L.A. Coser, *Greedy institutions.* New York: The Free Press, 1974.

Coser, R.L., & Rokoff, G. Women in the occupational world: Social disruption and conflict. *Social Problems,* Spring 1971, pp. 535-554.

Curtis, R., Zanna, M., & Campbell, W. *Fear of success, sex, and perceptions and performance of law school students.* Paper presented at the meeting of the Eastern Psychological Association, Washington, D.C., 1973.

Deci, E.L. *Intrinsic motivation.* New York: Plenum, 1975.

French, E., & Lesser, G.S. Some characteristics of the achievement motive in women. *Journal of Abnormal and Social Psychology,* 1958, *68,* 45-48.

Freud, S. *The basic writings of Sigmund Freud.* (A.A. Brill, Ed. and trans.). New York: Random House (Modern Library), 1938.

Gough, H.G. A cross-cultural analysis of the CPI femininity scale. *Journal of Consulting Psychology,* 1966, *30,* 136-41.

Hoffman, L.W. Early childhood experiences and women's achievement motives. *Journal of Social Issues,* 1972, *28*(2), 129-155.

Hoffman, L.W. Fear of success in males and females: 1965 and 1972. *Journal of Consulting and Clinical Psychology,* 1974, *42*(3), 353-358.

Horner, M.S. *Sex differences in achievement motivation and performance in competitive and non-competitive situations.* Unpublished doctoral dissertation, University of Michigan, 1968.

Horner, M.S. Fail: Bright woman. *Psychology Today,* November, 1969, *62,* 36-38.

Horner, M.S. Femininity and successful achievement: A basic inconsistency. In J.M. Bardwick, E. Douvan, M.S. Horner, & D. Gutman (Eds.), *Feminine personality and conflict.* Belmont, Calif.: Brooks/Cole, 1970.

Horner, M.S. The motive to avoid success and changing aspirations of women.

In J.M. Bardwick (Ed.), *Readings on the psychology of women.* New York: Harper & Row, 1972.

Katz, M.L. *Female motive to avoid success: A psychological barrier or a response to deviancy?* (Unpublished manuscript, Stanford University, School of Education, 1972). Published under Lockheed, M.E., *Sex Roles,* March 1975, pp. 41-50.

Leavitt, H.J. *Managerial psychology* (3rd ed.). Chicago: The University of Chicago Press, 1972.

Leavitt, H.J. Beyond the analytic manager. *California Management Review,* Spring 1975, pp. 5-12; Summer 1975, pp. 11-21.

Leavitt, H.J., Lipman-Blumen, J., Schaefer, S., & Harris, R. Patterns of achievement behavior in men and women: Preliminary findings. Unpublished manuscript, 1975. (Available from J. Lipman-Blumen, National Institute of Education, Washington, D.C. 20208.)

Lesser, G.S. Achievement motivation in women. In D.C. McClelland & R.S. Steele (Eds.), *Human motivation.* Morristown, N.J.: General Learning Press, 1973.

Lesser, G.S., Krawitz, R.N., & Packard, R. Experimental arousal of achievement motive in adolescent girls. *Journal of Abnormal and Social Psychology,* 1963, *66,* 59-66.

Levine, A., & Crumrine, J. Women and the fear of success: A problem in replication. *American Journal of Sociology,* 1975, *80,* 964-974.

Levine, S. Sex differences in the brain. *Scientific American,* 1966, *214*(4), 84-90.

Lipman-Blumen, J. How ideology shapes women's lives. *Scientific American,* 1972, *226*(1), 34-42.

Lipman-Blumen, J. Role de-differentiation as a system response to crisis: Occupational and political roles of women. *Sociological Inquiry, 1973, 43*(2), 105-129.

Lipman-Blumen, J. *The vicarious achievement ethic and nontraditional roles for women.* Paper presented at the meeting of the Eastern Sociological Society, New York, 1973.

Lipman-Blumen, J. *The relationship between social structure, ideology and crisis.* Paper presented at the meeting of the American Sociological Association, Montreal, Canada, 1974.

Lipman-Blumen, J. A crisis framework applied to macrosociological family changes: Marriage, divorce and occupational trends associated with World War II. *Journal of Marriage and the Family,* November, 1975a.

Lipman-Blumen, J. Vicarious achievement roles for women: A serious challenge for women. *Personnel and Guidance Journal,* 1975b, *53*(9), 650.

Lipman-Blumen, J. *A sociological perspective on emerging health care roles: A paradigm for new social roles.* Paper presented at the annual meeting of the American Association for the Advancement of Science, New York, January, 1975c.

Maccoby, E.M., & Jacklin, C.N. *The psychology of sex differences.* Stanford, Calif.: Stanford University Press, 1974.

Maslow, A. *Motivation and personality.* New York: Harper, 1954.

McCarthy, A. Political wives. *The Potomac/Washington Post,* March 17, 1974, pp. 10-12; 21-26; 32.

McClelland, D.C., Atkinson, R.A., & Lowell, E.L. *The achievement motive.* New York: Appleton-Century Crofts, 1953.

McClelland, D.C., & Steele, R.S. (Eds.) *Human motivation.* Morristown, N.J.: General Learning Press, 1973.

Murray, R.A. *Explorations in personality.* New York & London: Oxford University Press, 1938.

Papanek, H. Men, women and work: Reflections on the two-person career. *American Journal of Sociology,* 1973, *78,* 852-70.

Parsons, T., & Bales, R.F. *Family socialization and interaction process.* Glencoe, Ill.: The Free Press, 1955.

Ramirez III, M., & Casteneda, A. *Cultural democracy, bicognitive development, and education.* New York: Academic Press, 1975.

Romer, N. *Sex differences in the development of the motive to avoid success, sex role identity and performance in competitive and non-competitive conditions.* Paper presented at the meeting of the American Educational Research Association, Washington, D.C., 1975.

Tresemer, D. Fear of success: Popular but unproven. *Psychology Today,* 1974, *7*(10), 82-85.

Tresemer, D., & Pleck, J.H. Maintaining and changing sex-role boundaries in men (and women). Paper presented at the Radcliffe Institute Conference, *Women: Resources for a Changing World.* Cambridge, Mass., 1972.

Veroff, J., Wilcox, S., & Atkinson, J. The achievement motive in high school and college-age women. *Journal of Abnormal and Social Psychology,* 1953, *48,* 103-119.

Weber, M. (The sociology of charismatic authority). From *(Max Weber: Essays in Sociology).* (H.H. Gerth & C.W. Mills, Eds. and trans.). New York: Oxford University, 1946.

White, R.W. Ego and reality in psychoanalytic theory. *Psychological Issues,* 1963, *3*(3). (Monograph II).

Chapter 8

A DEVELOPMENTAL CROSS-SECTIONING OF WOMEN'S CAREERS AND MARRIAGE ATTITUDES AND LIFE PLANS*

LORRAINE M. RAND AND ANNA LOUISE MILLER

A new cultural imperative, "marriage and a career," is probably emerging. This conclusion is based on study of a random sample of 180 women (60 each) in junior high, high school, and college. Amazing consistency appeared in this cross-sectioning of women's attitudes toward Education, Occupation, Marriage, and Life Plans. The cultural imperative "to marry" was present at age 12, but by adulthood, the biological surge for early marriage had been passed and/or fulfilled, and career emerged as part of a life pattern. As young women develop, they become more liberal in their attitudes and desires about work, which can now be fulfilled because of the relaxing cultural interdiction against married women working.

THE CULTURAL imperative of marriage is about to give way to the duality of marriage-career, due to changes in the economy, education, male-female attitudes, and conveniences, both household and otherwise. Therefore, it is important to understand where women fit facts about career and marriage into their lives at a time when this combination seems to be gaining support from over 40% of the women in this culture (U.S. Department of Commerce, 1970).

Empey (1958) did a study using data obtained from a probability sample of (1) all seniors in the public high schools in the state of Washington, 1004 of whom were women and (2) 403 undergraduate students at the State College of Washington, 190 of whom were women. His findings indicated that approximately 80% of the young women sampled preferred marriage over a career. Matthews and Tiedeman (1964), in a study of 432 junior high girls, 282 senior high girls, and 523 young adult women, found that young women were

**From Journal of Vocational Behavior, 1972, 2, 317-331. Courtesy of Academic Press, Inc.*

experiencing conflict between career and marriage. Zytowski (1968) in a theoretical presentation suggested that vocational and homemaking participation were mutually exclusive. Thus, in view of rapid cultural advances, the questions about those three time-extended views become (1) are young women's preferences for marriage over career uniform and high or if not (2) do young women experience conflict of career with marriage, or (3) do they see the combination of career and marriage as mutually exclusive or compatible?

In this study, these questions were approached more specifically: namely, do girls in junior high, high school, and college differ in attitudes and plans about education, marriage, occupation, and life plans? This study thereby exposes that part of the general phenomenon of the present career and marriage dynamic shown by a cross-sectional view of young women seen at three levels of development. However, the data's developmental story also interestingly illumines the cultural change implied in our theory.

METHOD

A questionnaire was constructed to assess differences, attitudes, and future plans of junior high and high school girls from Huntington, West Virginia, and college women from Athens, Ohio. The questionnaire was pretested in September 1969 on a sample of young women from each of these populations, refined, and revised. The revised questionnaire was then administered in December 1969, to a random sample of 60 girls each in junior high and high school, using grade level as the sampling unit, and to 60 women college residents at a dormitory who were representative of each of the four college classes. A cross-section of socioeconomic class and scholastic ability appeared in each of the samples.

Results

Education

The first part of the questionnaire assessed girls' attitudes toward education: (1) their interest in college, (2) their actual plans for college, (3) their reasons for wanting a college education, and (4) the reasons they thought their parents had for encouraging them to attend college.

Table 8-I shows that over 95% of the junior high school girls are both interested in and plan to go to college. Senior high school girls show only that level of interest in college until the eleventh grade, and their actual plans for college start to decline in proportion a grade earlier and diminish to 60% by the twelfth grade. This 60% level for college plans in twelfth grade fits quite well with the 43% figure for women who actually do attend college five years out of high school as reported in Project TALENT's national longitudinal study of career development (Flanagan, Shaycoft, Richards, & Claudy, 1971). Economic reality, the marriage imperative, or outright disinterest seems to cut into college aspirations early in high school.

TABLE 8-I
Percentage of Girls in Junior High and High School Interested in and Planning to Go to College

Grade	*N*	Interested in going to college	Planning to go to college
7	20	95	95
8	20	100	100
9	20	95	100
10	20	95	80
11	20	95	75
12	20	75	60

The next question on education ascertained women's reasons for attending college. They were asked to choose from the options listed in Table 8-II.

TABLE 8-II
Most Important Reason for Going to College

Reason	Percentage		
	Junior high *N*=60	High school *N*=60	College *N*=60
Parents want them to go	2	—	—
Friends going to college	3	—	3
Enjoy learning	12	10	3
Prepare for specific occupation	32	45	52
Finding suitable mate	—	—	2
Avoid usual activities	—	—	8
Get scholarship	7	—	—
Increase knowledge	20	17	18
Develop social skills	3	2	—
Financial independence	18	13	11
Other	3	11	3
No response	—	2	—

The most important reason chosen at each level was "to prepare for a specific occupation" and this reason increases in importance as young women progress through their education. This choice indicates the assimilation by girls of current educational practice—that of choosing a major or being specific early in life. Since the percentage of women going to college to "increase knowledge" remains developmentally constant, it thereby becomes increasingly subordinate in the minds of the young women to "preparation for a specific career."

Note also that 2% of the women in only the college group chose the reason: "finding suitable mate." Younger women may not think of love and marriage consciously as a reason for attending college, merely knowing it is a natural phenomenon whenever they are interacting with males. Therefore, they may not perceive "finding a mate" as a reason for going to college which they express openly.

Women's perceptions of why their parents wanted them to attend college were different from their own reasons. Table 8-III lists options

TABLE 8-III
Most Important Reason Girls Thought Their Parents Had For Wanting Them to Go to College

Reason	Percentage		
	Junior high $N=60$	High school $N=60$	College $N=60$
They went to college	—	2	—
Prepare for specific occupation	13	13	15
Increase chances of good career	47	37	40
Increase chances of finding suitable mate	—	—	1
Develop social skills	2	2	2
Become financially independent	17	8	13
Increase knowledge	8	10	13
Become independent	5	5	13
Other	4	17	3
No response	4	6	—

available for choice. Junior high, high school, and college girls thought their parents' main reason for wanting them to go to college was to "increase chances of good career." This choice showed no developmental trend. The girls were again given the option "prepare for specific occupation" to compare with "increase chances of good career" and they chose the latter, indicating that although they may think more specifically themselves, they perceive their parents' wishes in more general terms. It is interesting that they did not perceive their parents as wanting them to attend college to "increase knowledge." This may suggest that girls, in stating their own perceptions of parental reasons for going to college, see knowledge as worthless unless it is negotiable in a career framework.

Occupation

This section in the questionnaire assessed women's attitudes about work after graduation from high school. They were asked if they planned to work, to list both fantasy and actual occupations they were considering, reasons for choosing each of these kinds of occupations, and kinds of work activities and conditions they would prefer.

A strong desire to work was indicated by the junior high, high school, and college women, with 95% of them planning on work after completion of their education. Thus, no developmental trend was noted, which is an interesting finding, along with the fact that in 1960, Project TALENT data indicated that 90% of the senior high school girls expressed an interest in a particular career whereas only 10% were interested in being housewives (Flanagan, Shaycroft, Richards, & Claudy, 1971). The writers thought that college women would all express a desire for work and a less universal response was expected from the younger women, particularly those in high school (Matthews & Tiedeman, 1964). But the data suggest that Women's Lib has influenced young Appalachian women.

An open-ended fantasy-type question was included, assessing that type of work girls would like to do regardless of cost, training, entrance requirements, and the like. The findings indicated that fantasy and actual choices were almost identical for young women in junior high, high school, and college.

In regard to the occupations they were planning to enter, teaching was the most popular choice at each level and increased from junior high through college (See Table 8-IV). Also women in college were more specific in their choice of occupation. This may be because (1) college women have more knowledge of what kinds of jobs are available within specific fields and (2) most college women must choose a particular major within a department.

It is interesting to note that even though the majority of young women in this study, at each educational level, have broken the cultural barrier concerning work, with 95% planning to work, they are still struggling with the old cultural imperative that there are male jobs and female jobs. Evidently girls in this study are still feeling the press of sex-stereotyped occupations, i.e. teacher, secretary, and the like, for women. However, a comparison of the more often selected occupations in this study with the Project TALENT 1960 data concerning girls' similar occupational choices indicates an escalation from the stereotyped lower-level occupations to professional type occupations (See Table 8-V).

Girls' reasons for choosing a particular occupation were centered around their interests and abilities with 43% in junior high, 49% in high school, and 45% in college indicating this reason for their occupational choice. Table 8-VI shows that the other reasons for choosing a particular occupation are less prominent as motivators. No developmental trends appear with the possible exception that length and difficulty of training decreases developmentally as a reason for choosing an occupation.

TABLE 8-IV
Occupations Chosen

	Percentage		
Occupation	Junior high N=60	High school N=60	College N=60
Teacher	36	43	55
Speech therapy	—	—	4
Airline stewardess	—	—	3
Social worker	2	10	6
Interior decorator	2	—	2
Fashion designer	—	—	2
Politician	—	—	2
Counselor	—	—	2
Systems analyst	—	—	2
Creative writer	—	—	2
Marketing	—	—	2
Dental hygiene	—	—	2
Special education	—	—	2
Actress	3	—	2
Research in foods	—	—	2
Home economist	—	—	2
Fashion merchandiser	—	—	2
Journalist	—	—	2
Photographer	—	—	2
Interpreter	—	—	2
Bank teller	2	—	—
Secretary	22	7	—
Model	3	3	—
Salesman	2	—	—
Doctor	5	10	—
Artist	8	4	—
Veterinarian	3	—	—
Lawyer	2	—	—
Nurse	8	8	—
Scientist	2	—	—
Speech	—	2	—
Dancer	—	2	—
Computer science	—	3	—
Clerk	—	4	—
Housewife	—	2	—
Engineer	—	2	—

TABLE 8-V
Comparison of Selected Occupational Choices Expressed by High School Women

	Percent[a]	
Occupational choice	Project TALENT 1960 N=41483	This study 1969 N=60
Housewife	10.2	2
Secretary, clerical	30.2	11
Nurse	10.1	8
Teacher	12.8	43
Engineer	0.0	2
Doctor	0.4	10

[a]Sets selected from a larger group of choices.

TABLE 8-VI
Reasons for Choosing Particular Occupations

	Percentage		
Reasons	Junior high N=60	High school N=60	College N=60
Ability and interests	43	49	45
Length and difficulty of training	13	9	1
Place of training (i.e., college)	7	3	2
High salary	8	20	15
Security	8	10	15
Parents and friends approve	13	6	8
Stereotyped "feminine" occupations	8	3	12
Other	—	—	2

In the last question of the occupation section, the women were asked to select the top three of seven job factors most important to them. The findings (See Table 8-VII) indicated that "personal satisfaction and enjoyment of the work" was ranked number one by girls in junior high, high school, and college. The importance of this choice increased steadily from junior high to college.

In addition, the hierarchical position of the job factors, ranked second and third in importance by girls at all three levels of development, showed developmental variation. "Rate of pay" figured in the hierarchies at all three developmental levels; "hours in relationship to my family schedule" in two; and "opportunities for advancement" in only one. Developmentally, junior high school women make family obligations dominant over work in their career and life planning,

TABLE 8-VII
Most Important of Seven Job Factors in Employment

	Junior high N=60 Percent of choices			High school N=60 Percent of choices			College N=60 Percent of choices		
	1st	2nd	3rd	1st	2nd	3rd	1st	2nd	3rd
Personal satisfaction and enjoyment of the work	65	—	—	70	—	—	75	—	—
Rate of pay	—	—	25	—	27	—	—	27	—
Hours in relationship to my family schedule	—	28	—	—	—	18	—	—	—
Opportunities for advancement	—	—	—	—	—	—	—	—	25

whereas high school and college women do not. However, young adult women are pretty straightforwardly vocationally dominated. The high school women show the transitional percentages of such a shift—"rate of pay" moved up in importance and "work interference with family obligations" moved down (Table 8-VII).

In summary, all three levels ranked "personal satisfaction and enjoyment of the work" as number one and this choice increased in importance from junior high to college. High school and college women ranked "rate of pay" as number two. There was no agreement between the levels on the third most important employment factor. However, it appears that family considerations in work hours are secondarily important in junior high and not very important to the college level women in this study.

Data on the type of work activities young women preferred showed that over one half of the women in junior high, high school, and college chose long-term projects as opposed to short-term projects, along with some preference for a job requiring maximum training as opposed to minimum training. These attitudes showed an increasing developmental trend. About 75% and more of the girls at three levels indicated that they would be interested in work which required intelligence, judgment, and responsibility, and approximately 80% preferred work with people. However, there were no marked developmental trends in these attitudes (Table 8-VIII).

Marriage

The first question about attitudes toward marriage was concerned with two issues: (1) whether girls wanted to get married or not and (2) whether they expected to marry or not. Almost all the girls in junior high, high school, and college, 95%, not only would like to get

TABLE 8-VIII
Attitudes Toward Types of Work

	Percentage		
	Junior high N=60	High school N=60	College N=60
Long-term projects	54	68	68
Short-term projects	46	32	32
Maximum training	52	57	65
Minimum training	48	43	35
Work requiring intelligence, judgment and responsibility	80	73	95
Work that is routine and not demanding	20	27	5
Work with people	83	85	78
Work alone	17	15	22

married, they expected to marry. In addition, there is a perfect relationship between their desires and expectations for marriage.

When girls were asked at what age they expected to marry, they were given the options listed in Table 8-IX. The most popular age range to marry was 20 to 24 years. While this is true in all developmental periods, some interesting differences in regard to marriageable age appeared among the junior high, high school, and college groups. Two trends appear, the one expected and the other not. First, as expected, the average age desired for marriage is a little higher in the older college women than in the younger junior high school girls. Second, a rather high proportion of high school women unexpectedly express desire for marriage before age 20, which isn't very far away from their age while answering the question. Thus, the biological or social surge seems to dominate in high school and college. Only the junior high girls "put off" marriage from their immediate present thoughts to any marked degree.

TABLE 8-IX
Comparison of Girls in Regard to Expected Age of Marriage

		Percentage		
	N	Marry at age 19 or before	Marry at ages 20-24	Marry at ages 25-30
Junior high	60	10	83	7
High school	60	32	63	5
College	60	2	81	17

Life Plans

Life plans were largely defined in terms of the degree of work involvement young women anticipated in their lives, especially within marriage. They were asked to choose the life plan they expected to follow in the future, as well as the one they would have chosen at age 12. The life plans, portrayed in Table 8-X, reflect many combinations of involvement and work, marriage, and motherhood. Findings indicate that women in junior high, high school, and college anticipate very similar life plans. The most popular life plan chosen was "to work most of the time combining a career, marriage, and motherhood," with 25 to 35% of each group making this choice. This plan was slightly more popular among college women than among women at other levels and was accompanied by an interest in returning to work after children are in school. Work, marriage, and children seem capable of simultaneous management to many modern young women. Further very few students–only 2 to 3%–chose extreme plans: Plan A "to never work" or Plan D "to work most of the time and remain single." This finding supports a previous one in this study, namely that 95% of the girls plan to work sometime in their lives and that 97% of the girls expect to marry. It is also consistent with the 1960 Project TALENT findings that 90% of the girls had definite career interests (Flanagan, Shaycroft, Richards, & Claudy, 1971).

TABLE 8-X
Future Life Plans

	Percentage		
Life plans	Junior high N=60	High school N=60	College N=60
A To never work	2	2	3
B To work until marriage and never work again	7	10	10
C To work until the birth of children and never work again	18	11	17
D To work most of the time and remain single	2	—	2
E To work most of the time combining a career, marriage, and motherhood	28	25	35
F To return to work after children are in school	20	22	20
G To return to work after children are grown	15	21	8
H Other	8	8	5

Students were asked to recall the plan they might have chosen at age 12. These data, presented in Table 9-XI, must be interpreted cautiously since one cannot assume high reliabilities for retrospective data. Also, the length of recall is different for girls at different levels;

that is, error of recall is probably greatest for college girls since recall time is longer.

TABLE 8-XI
Life Plan Perceptions at Age 12

Life plans	Percentage		
	Junior high N=60	High school N=60	College N=60
A To never work	18	23	25
B To work until marriage and never work again	15	18	23
C To work until the birth of children and never work again	11	20	21
D To work most of the time and remain single	10	20	20
E To work most of the time combining a career, marriage, and motherhood	22	3	2
F To return to work after children are in school	8	8	8
G To return to work after children are grown	7	—	—
H Other	7	7	7

Large differences exist in life plans attributed to age 12 and those life plans now chosen. The most obvious difference is the choice "not to work" at age 12 whereas their present plans include a combination of career and marriage or return to work after children are in school or grown. These data suggest that cultural imperatives about marriage and child rearing hold in young adolescence but change in favor of work and marriage by young adulthood.

The last question in this section dealt with attitudes about working wives. About three of four girls at each level did not think that managing a home was too much with a career. High school and college girls did give slightly more "yes" responses than did junior high school girls, suggesting a developmental shift. Over one half of the students at each level agree that working while fulfilling the role of mother is bad and over one half agree that working mothers are admired by others. This apparent discrepancy suggests some conflict for women about the ability to manage homemaking, children, and work in their lives, even though they expect to manage just that as they mature (Table 8-XII).

DISCUSSION

Recapitulating findings beginning with life plans, data indicate that girls opted for the plans that involve work, the majority of them choosing "work most of the time combining a career, marriage, and motherhood." The percentage choosing work options alone is small;

TABLE 8-XII
Attitudes Toward Working Wives

	Percentage marking "yes"		
	Junior high N=60	High school N=60	College N=60
Managing a home considered too much with a career	18	28	30
Working mothers considered bad for children	58	72	68
Working wives are admired by others	62	55	60

the majority of decisions are within plans that involve work either a good portion of life or part of life. However, when the younger women were asked to state what they thought their life plans were at age 12, they expressed a desire to work until children were born and then never work again. Also, a small percentage at age 12 said they expected to work most of the time and remain single. Thus younger women's attitudes about work change as they become a part of what is going on in their generation rather than what is being advocated by the former generation.

Going on to occupational attitudes, most of the girls chose the typical and stereotyped feminine occupations. This is consistent with the culture as male and female jobs still exist, even though such stereotypes are currently being challenged, with women moving into jobs such as contractor, roofer, horse jockey, plumber, and the like. The move toward a job regardless of its male-female suitability is revealed in stated reasons for choosing a particular occupation, i.e. "ability and interest." These reports showed no developmental trend but consistently high agreement. The thread of being oneself at work moves into the area of most important job factors in employment as well. Women at all three educational levels rank "personal satisfaction and enjoyment of the work" first, and a developmental difference then appeared. High school and college girls marked "rate of pay" as number two in importance but show no agreement on the third most important job factors in employment. The fact that opportunity for advancement was rated third by the college girls may be an indication that satisfaction of job and maintenance of self is more important than advancement at this level. Personal satisfaction and enjoyment of one's work is perhaps more important to this generation of students than it has heretofore been to students (Flanagan & Jung, 1971), particularly in view of the fact that some of the students are questioning the work ethic, with greater numbers defining work outside the traditional work structure. Weaving into this thought pattern is the finding that over 78% of the students at all three levels want to work with people and want work that involves intelligence, judgment, and responsibility.

Education comes into the picture as preparation for the occupational choices the girls have been expressing. The majority of the girls in junior high and high school were interested in going to college, but this interest dropped in the twelfth grade. Conversely, the percentage planning to go to college remained high until the tenth grade when it began to decrease and markedly diminished by the twelfth grade, perhaps due to more experience and maturity with resulting increase of realism in planning. Girls give primarily vocational reasons for planning to go to college. They emphasize "preparation for a career" first and "increase knowledge" second. Perceptions of parental reasons for wanting them to attend college were also vocational. At this point of development, young women experience the biological surge and indicate that they are thinking seriously about marriage. This study found the majority of young women at all levels wanted to marry and expected to marry. The most popular choice of time to marry was from 20 to 24 but older adolescent (high school) women wanted to marry before 20. In regard to their attitude about working wives, about one half felt that working mothers were bad for children but also felt working wives were admired by others. However, despite this residual feeling about working mothers, there was a strong agreement at all three developmental levels that managing a home was not too much with a career.

In summary, the cross-sectioning of women's attitudes toward career, marriage, and life planning revealed amazing consistency. The cultural imperative to marry is reported to have been present at age 12, but by adulthood, the biological surge for early marriage, expected in late adolescence and early adulthood, has been passed and/or fulfilled, and career emerges as a manageable and desirable part of a life pattern. There is some residual concern about the fate of children in a marriage in which career and marriage are pursued in cooperative fashion, but in general, attitudes toward vocationalism and self-definition through work have emerged and are in a somewhat dominant position in determining a woman's life patterns. What does the seeming change in the status of the marriage imperative mean for women's development? What appears to be happening is that today's young women express a desire for a career and marriage. This contradicts Empey's (1958) findings that approximately 80% preferred marriage over a career. In addition, today's young women seem to be indicating less frustration about the combination of career-marriage in contrast to the Matthews and Tiedeman (1964) finding that young women do experience conflict between career and marital duties. Therefore, what may now be occurring is that, as young women develop, they are caught up in the cultural imperative for marriage without vocational participation, and at this moment marriage and career may be mutually exclusive, as Zytowski (1968) suggests. However, with further development, they seem to become more liberal in their attitudes and desires about work, which can now be fulfilled because of the relaxing cultural interdiction against married women working. Thus, vocational hierarchial restructuring (Miller and Tiedeman, 1971) can occur within socially accepted bounds, as young women begin to see vocational and homemaking participation as mutually compatible. Therefore, the marriage-career combination emerges as a new way of life. Statistics indicate that over 40% of the women in the United States are combining marriage and career and even more women will, in the future, be involved in this combination (U.S. Department of Commerce, 1970).

Some of the findings in this somewhat regional study are quite consistent with the national Project TALENT data. This consistency leads us to believe that, although we investigated in an area purported to be isolated from the cultural norm (Weller, 1966), young urban Appalachian women are no different in their aspirations and attitudes concerning work than are young urban women nationally. The Project TALENT Data Bank, therefore, might well be used to determine if young women's aspirations and attitudes about work differ more by population density, as we now suspect, than by geography, as many still hold.

REFERENCES

Empey, L.T. Role expectations of women regarding marriage and a career. *Marriage and Family Living,* 1958, *20,* 152-155.

Flanagan, J.C., & Jung, S.M. *Progress in education, 1960-1970: A sample survey.* Palo Alto, California: American Institutes for Research, 1971.

Flanagan, J.C., Shaycoft, M.F., Richards, J.M., Jr., & Claudy, J.G. *Project TALENT: Five years after high school.* Palo Alto, Calif.: American Institutes for Research and the University of Pittsburgh, 1971.

Matthews, E. & Tiedeman, D.V. Attitudes toward career and marriage and development of life style in young women. *Journal of Counseling Psychology,* 1964, *11,* 375-384.

Miller, A.L., & Tiedeman, D.V. Hierarchical restructuring and career education. *Career Development as a Lifelong Process.* Massachusetts Personnel and Guidance Association Workshop, October 29, 1971.

U.S. Department of Commerce. *Statistical Abstract of the United States 1970.* Washington, D.C.: Bureau of Census, 1970.

Weller, J.E. *Yesterday's people.* Lexington, Kentucky: University of Kentucky Press, 1966.

Zytowski, D.G. Toward a theory of career development for women. *Personnel and Guidance Journal,* 1969, *47,* 660-664.

Chapter 9

A COMPARATIVE STUDY OF ACADEMIC SELF-ESTIMATES, ACADEMIC VALUES, AND ACADEMIC ASPIRATIONS OF ADOLESCENT MALES AND FEMALES*

RITA S. RAPOZA AND DONALD H. BLOCHER

A cross-sectional sample of 1577 adolescents, representing a 10 percent random sample of the public secondary school population of a major Midwestern city, was studied to investigate the relationships of academic self-estimates, academic values, and educational-vocational aspirations to sex and grade level. Data were analyzed using a two-way analysis of variance. Findings suggested that girls' self-estimates of scholastic ability are as high as the self-estimates of boys, and that girls place significantly more importance on school grades and achievement than boys. There was a trend among girls for reported educational-vocational plans to stabilize in the later high school years in the direction of lower educational aspirations than those reported by boys.

DESPITE the tremendous surge of interest in the psychology of women that has accompanied the movement for women's rights, there is still a considerable imbalance between what is known about the psychological development of men and women. Research on achievement motivation in women is limited in that attempts to understand the impact of the motivations, satisfactions, aspirations, and achievements involved in a woman's work life must still be largely extrapolated from findings based on males (McClelland et al., 1953; McClelland, 1961; Atkinson, 1958). Although general findings from the classical studies on achievement motivation in men do have considerable relevance for understanding similar factors in women (Atkin-

*The data in this study are taken from a doctoral dissertation by R. S. Rapoza in partial fulfillment of the requirements of the Doctor of Philosophy degree at the University of Minnesota.

son and Litwin, 1960; Brody, 1966; French, 1956; Mahone, 1966; O'Connor et al., 1966), two major differences between men and women are suggested in the research. First, a dynamic of "fear of success" may operate more strongly in women than in men to inhibit achievement motivation. Perceived negative consequences for success, including loss of eligibility in heterosexual relationships (Horner, 1970; Coleman, 1961), loss of perceived femininity (Mead, 1949), and the emergence of intrapersonal conflict (Kagan and Moss, 1962; Maccoby, 1966) may affect women's level of aspiration. Second, research also provides limited support for the position that achievement motivation in girls may be aroused more by needs for external social and emotional support than by a need for confirmation of internal standards of excellence as the basis for self-esteem (Horner, 1970; Gordon, 1971; Bardwick and Douvan, 1972; Bardwick, 1971).

Observed differences between men and women in aspiration and achievement have led to extensive theorizing and to some empirical research comparing self-concepts of boys and girls. There has been considerable research that links scholastic achievement and level of academic aspirations with positive self-concept and self-esteem (Ford and Muse, 1972; Hummel and Sprinthall, 1965; Silverman, 1964).

Generally, empirical studies of women's self concepts as compared with their concepts of males indicate some devaluing of female characteristics (Connell and Johnson, 1970; McKee and Sherriffs, 1959; Rosenkrantz et al., 1968; Gove and Tudor, 1973). Research also indicates that women are very sensitive to values and attitudes that they attribute to men in regard to sex appropriate behavior, and that they generally perceive and conform to a rather passive-submissive set of role expectations on the part of significant males (Hawley, 1971; Steinmann, et al., 1964).

Due to a lack of sophistication in much of the research on career aspirations in women, which treat career and family as mutually exclusive choices, it is difficult to accurately evaluate past studies. The most discerning studies indicate that many women seek to combine career and family oriented goals (Rand and Miller, 1972; Zissis, 1964; Slocum and Bowles, 1967). Studies generally show that women have lower academic and occupational aspirations than men (Hauser, 1971; Rand and Miller, 1972) and that levels of response to competition and risk-taking situations are typically lower on the part of girls than boys (Morgan and Mausner, 1972; Houts and Entwisle, 1968; Crandall and Rabson, 1960). Research on intellectual development of men and women indicates that qualitative rather than quantitative sex differences in various aspects of intellectual functioning exist (Maccoby, 1966; Tyler, 1968). Some developmental studies suggest that intellectual development in women slows or ceases earlier than in men (Terman and Oden, 1947; Bradway and Thompson, 1968; Bayley and Oden, 1955; Haan, 1963).

PURPOSE OF THE STUDY

The research summarized above indicates several areas in which knowledge gaps exist in the literature relating to motivations and aspirations of adolescent girls and women. This study was addressed to investigating questions which might lead to a better understanding of the motivational and intellectual development of girls.

Hypotheses

The following specific null hypotheses were investigated:

1. There are no differences between sexes irrespective of grade level on a measure of Academic Self-Estimate.
2. There are no differences between grade levels irrespective of sex on a measure of Academic Self-Estimate.
3. There are no differences between sexes irrespective of grade level on a measure of Academic Values.
4. There are no differences between grade levels irrespective of sex on a measure of Academic Values.
5. There is no interaction between grade level and sex on a measure of Academic Self-Estimate.
6. There is no interaction between grade level and sex on a measure of Academic Values.

METHOD

Sample

The primary student data obtained in the study were collected from a 10 percent random sample of secondary school students in a major Midwestern city. A field worker visited each of eighteen secondary schools and administered the Student Questionnaire to the sample in classroom size groups. In addition to the questionnaire data, the field workers also did personal interviews with small subsamples of students within each school to determine attitudes toward the data collection process. A total of 1577 usable student questionnaires was obtained.

The students in the sample came from eighteen secondary schools, six senior high schools, and twelve junior high schools. They were selected within each school by taking every tenth name from the alphabetized enrollment roster in the school.

Instrument

The Student Questionnaire was designed as part of a larger study of student personnel services. The section of the instrument used in the present report was entitled "Academic Self-Estimate" and consisted of sixteen items designed to measure three aspects of the students' self-concepts.

Items 1 through 8 dealt with a student's confidence in his or her ability to achieve in school and were scaled on a five point basis from low to high. These items are listed below.

1. How do you rate yourself in school ability compared with your close friends?
   ____1. I am the poorest
   ____2. I am below average
   ____3. I am average
   ____4. I am above average
   ____5. I am among the best

2. How do you rate yourself in school ability compared with those in your class at school?
   ____1. I am among the poorest
   ____2. I am below average
   ____3. I am average
   ____4. I am above average
   ____5. I am among the best

3. Where do you think you will rank in your high school graduating class?
   ____1. Among the poorest
   ____2. Below average
   ____3. Average
   ____4. Above average
   ____5. Among the best

4. Do you think you have the ability to complete college?
   ____1. No
   ____2. Probably not
   ____3. Not sure either way
   ____4. Yes, probably
   ____5. Yes, definitely

5. Where do you think you would rank in your class in college?
   ____1. Among the poorest
   ____2. Below average
   ____3. Average
   ____4. Above average
   ____5. Among the best

6. In order to become a doctor, lawyer, or university professor, work beyond four years of college is necessary. How likely do you think it is that you could complete such advanced work?
   ____1. Most unlikely
   ____2. Unlikely
   ____3. Not sure either way
   ____4. Somewhat likely
   ____5. Very likely

7. Forget for a moment how others grade your work. In your own opinion, how good do you think your work is?
   ____1. Much below average
   ____2. Below average
   ____3. Average
   ____4. Good
   ____5. Excellent

8. What kind of grades do you think you are capable of getting?
   ____1. Mostly As
   ____2. Mostly Bs
   ____3. Mostly Cs
   ____4. Mostly Ds
   ____5. Mostly Fs

Items 9 through 15 below dealt with the importance the student attached to success in school and were scaled on a four point basis.

9. How important to you are the grades you get in school?
   ____1. Grades do not matter to me at all
   ____2. Not particularly important
   ____3. Important
   ____4. Very important

10. How important is it to you to be high in your class in grades?
    ____1. Does not matter to me at all
    ____2. Not particularly important
    ____3. Important
    ____4. Very important

11. How do you feel if you do not do as well in school as you know you can?
    ____1. Does not bother me at all
    ____2. Do not feel particularly badly
    ____3. Feel badly
    ____4. Feel very badly

12. How important is it to you to do better than others in school?
    ____1. Does not matter to me at all
    ____2. Not particularly important
    ____3. Important
    ____4. Very important

13. Which statement best describes you?
    ____1. I do not care about any particular grades
    ____2. I like to get about the same grades as everyone else
    ____3. I like to get better grades than almost everyone else
    ____4. I like to get better grades than everyone else

14. In your schoolwork, do you try to do better than others?
    ____1. Never
    ____2. Occasionally
    ____3. Most of the time
    ____4. All of the time

15. How important to you are good grades compared with other aspects of school?
    ____1. Good grades do not matter to me at all
    ____2. Some other things in school are more important

____3. Good grades are among the important things in school
____4. Good grades are the most important thing in school

Item 16 measured academic aspiration level and required the respondent to indicate further educational-vocational plans.

16. Would you please indicate your plans by checking the line below that best describes what you plan to do. Thank you for your help.
____1. I plan to go to college
____2. I plan to go to a trade or vocational school (including such schools as business, secretarial, skilled trades, drafting, barbering, beauty school, etc.) Please name the school if you know. ____________
____3. I plan to get a job
____4. I plan to enter military service
____5. I have other plans: (Please indicate briefly) ____________

Analysis

The first stage of the analysis of data involved the computation of a matrix of intercorrelations showing inter-item correlations for the 16 items of the Academic Self-Estimate Questionnaire. The inspection of the content of the 16 items suggested the existence of three content clusters. As indicated above, items 1 through 8 dealt with the self-perception of ability to achieve in school. Items 9 through 15 dealt with the perceived value or importance of academic successes and item 16 with educational aspirations.

The hypotheses developed for the study involved these logical content dimensions. The matrix of intercorrelations was computed to determine whether or not the items did indeed relate to each other in a way that supported the existence of these three relatively independent variables.

Inspection of the matrix showed that the items clustered the way predicted from the content analysis. (See Table 9-I) As a result of the examination of this matrix of intercorrelations it was deemed appropriate to proceed with hypothesis testing using the two scales (items 1-8 and 9-15) separately and summing within them to obtain two overall scale scores labelled "Academic Self-Estimate" and "Academic Values." A two way analysis of variance approach was chosen for hypothesis testing. It was also decided to handle item 16 separately as a measure of "Educational Aspirations."

RESULTS

The analysis of variance results for Academic Self Estimate Scores (items 1-8) did not show significant differences for null hypotheses 1, 2, and 5 (see Table 9-II). There were no differences between the

Table 9-I
Inter-item Correlations for Individual Items of Academic Self Estimate and Academic Value Scales

Item	1	2	3	4	5	6	7	8*	9	10	11	12	13	14	15
1	1	.55	.51	.42	.45	.30	.42	—.44	.12	.15	.11	.10	.29	.19	.06
2		1	.58	.45	.49	.30	.44	—.49	.15	.20	.14	.13	.30	.22	.08
3			1	.52	.60	.36	.43	—.51	.15	.23	.15	.17	.33	.24	.07
4				1	.70	.48	.39	—.48	.19	.18	.15	.12	.30	.21	.11
5					1	.46	.40	—.44	.19	.24	.17	.17	.33	.24	.13
6						1	.26	—.27	.19	.24	.19	.18	.29	.23	.15
7							1	—.39	.19	.21	.12	.16	.28	.27	.10
8								1	—.08	—.13	—.12	—.07	—.29	—.21	—.05
9									1	.59	.45	.40	.41	.36	.47
10										1	.44	.56	.46	.40	.41
11											1	.40	.33	.32	.37
12												1	.49	.44	.38
13													1	.49	.36
14														1	.35
15															1

*The scaling in item 8 is reversed thus revealing negative correlations

sexes irrespective of grade level on the measure of Academic Self-Estimate. There were no differences between grade levels irrespective of sex on the measure of Academic Self-Estimate. There was no significant interaction between grade level and sex on the measure of Academic Self-Estimate. (See Table 9-III for means and standard deviations.)

Table 9-II
Analysis of Variance of Academic Self-Estimate Scores By Sex and Grade Level

Sources of Variance	Degrees of Freedom	Mean Square	F	P
Grade Level	5	30.76	1.40	<.2230
Sex	1	8.20	.37	<.5421
Grade × Sex	5	5.67	.26	<.9362
Error	1308	22.04		
TOTAL	1319	66.67		

The analysis of variance results on the Academic Value Scores (items 9-15) were mixed. Null hypotheses 3 and 4 were rejected at the level .0001 (see Table 9-IV). Results showed that the Academic Value Scores of boys irrespective of grade level were significantly lower

Table 9-III
Descriptive Statistics for Academic Self-Estimate Scores by Sex and Grade Level

Grade		Male			Female	
Level	N	Mean	S.D.	N	Mean	S.D.
7	107	21.70	5.10	112	22.10	3.94
8	126	21.43	5.06	94	21.89	4.36
9	128	21.81	4.23	116	22.03	4.03
10	134	20.92	4.45	114	21.22	4.95
11	102	21.63	5.07	101	21.31	4.40
12	87	22.16	5.39	99	21.93	5.16

than those of girls. Results also showed that the Academic Value Scores between grade levels irrespective of sex were significantly lower as grade level increased. Null hypothesis 6 could not be rejected. There was no interaction between grade level and sex on the measure of Academic Values. (See Table 9-V for means and standard deviations.)

Calculation of percentages of males and females who responded to item 16 gave the following results (see Table 9-VI). In general, results on this item showed considerable variability from grade level to

Table 9-IV
Analysis of Variance of Academic Value Scores by Sex and Grade Level

Sources of Variance	Degrees of Fredom	Mean Square	F	P
Grade Level	5	349.38	26.98	<.0001
Sex	1	326.14	25.19	<.0001
Grade × Sex	5	16.07	1.24	<.2874
Error	1425	12.95		
TOTAL	1436	704.54		

Table 9-V
Descriptive Statistics for Academic Value Scores by Sex and Grade Level

Grade		Male			Female	
Level	N	Mean	S.D.	N	Mean	S.D.
7	126	21.27	3.41	131	31.93	3.19
8	139	21.19	3.40	110	21.29	3.31
9	135	19.17	3.92	128	20.48	3.51
10	139	19.12	3.84	118	20.09	3.38
11	105	18.19	4.29	112	19.56	3.57
12	93	17.83	3.77	101	19.30	3.54

TABLE 9-VI
PERCENTS AND NUMBERS OF MALES AND FEMALES RESPONDING TO EACH PLAN CATEGORY FOR GRADES 7, 9 AND 12

RESPONSE CATEGORY	GRADE LEVEL											
	7				9				12			
	Male		*Female*		*Male*		*Female*		*Male*		*Female*	
	%	*(N)*	%	*(N)*	%	*(N)*	%	*(N)*	%	*(N)*	%	*(N)*
College	36	(50)	51	(72)	46	(66)	51	(73)	59	(57)	46	(51)
Trade or Vocational School	11	(16)	6	(8)	12	(18)	10	(14)	14	(14)	13	(14)
Job	13	(18)	18	(25)	8	(12)	11	(16)	9	(9)	19	(21)
Military	8	(11)	0	(0)	9	(13)	1	(1)	6	(6)	0	(0)
Other Plans	2	(3)	6	(8)	6	(8)	10	(14)	3	(3)	8	(9)
Did not Respond	30	(42)	20	(29)	19	(28)	17	(24)	8	(8)	14	(16)
TOTALS	100	(140)	101*	(142)	100	(145)	100	(142)	99*	(97)	100	(111)

*Did not add to 100% because of rounding errors.

grade level in the junior high school years for both boys and girls. In the senior high school years a noticeable trend suggested that girls' responses stabilized in the direction of plans reflecting lower educational aspirations at twelfth grade as indicated by lower percentages for girls in the college plans category. Similarly, higher percentages were observed for girls in the job, other, and non-response categories. The latter finding seems to suggest that girls have greater uncertainty at twelfth grade than do boys.

Overall then, a smaller proportion of twelfth grade girls reported college plans than did their male classmates or their female counterparts in ninth grade. Similarly a greater proportion of girls in twelfth grade either reported intentions to enter the labor market directly or failed to respond at all to this item.

DISCUSSION

One of the major implications of this study concerns the need for longitudinal research into the development of basic motivational and attitudinal structures of female adolescents. The findings of this study lend considerable support to the position taken by Bardwick and others concerning the motivations and aspirations of young women. Basically, the female subject in this study reported academic values and academic self-concepts that were as positive or more positive than those reported by males. These values and attitudes were not, however, translated into the same kinds of plans and aspirations as those reported by boys. Apparently positive academic self-concepts and educational values do not yield the same plans and aspirations for education that are fostered in boys by these factors. Other considerations, possibly in the form of role expectations, apparently intervene to lower aspirations.

The position taken by Bardwick and others has been that values and attitudes in girls are more heavily shaped by needs to conform to expectations articulated in family and school than is true for boys. One interpretation of the results of this study is that female students follow the norms of school and family in regard to academic values and self-perceptions rather than acting upon more deeply internalized beliefs in the importance of their own educational development.

For this possibility to be fully explored, considerable basic longitudinal research will need to be accomplished. Studies focused on the socialization of boys and girls, particularly in the areas of independence training, tolerance for social isolation and disapproval, and openness to risk-taking, are badly needed. Cross-sectional research cannot supply needed answers in many of these areas.

Before effective interventions can be designed more knowledge of the socialization processes already at work in the lives of developing women is needed. If an over-conforming, other-directedness is a basis for the motivational malnourishment of young women, high pressured, propagandistic interventions are only likely to aggravate the problem.

Even after basic information regarding the socialization process is made available, there is a need for girls to develop decision-making skills and to examine occupational and educational options that are feasible and desirable for them rather than merely conforming to perceived societal expectations. Perhaps for a young girl, the development of a strong inner standard of excellence would be the most valuable cognitive framework in helping her to understand and to choose appropriately from among a variety of life styles and patterns.

REFERENCES

Atkinson, J.W. (Ed.). *Motives in fantasy, action and society.* Princeton, N.J.: Van Nostrand, 1958.

Atkinson, J.W. and Litwin, G.H. Achievement motive and test anxiety conceived as motive to approach success and motive to avoid failure. *Journal of Abnormal and Social Psychology,* 1960, *60,* 52-63.

Bardwick, Judith M. *Psychology of women: a study of bio-cultural conflicts.* New York: Harper and Row, 1972.

Bardwick, Judith M. and Douvan, Elizabeth. Ambivalence: the socialization of women. In Judith M. Bardwick (Ed.), *Readings on the Psychology of Women.* New York: Harper and Row, 1971.

Bayley, Nancy and Oden, Melita H. The maintenance of intellectual ability in gifted adults. *Journal of Gerontology,* 1955, *10,* 91-107.

Bradway, Katherine P., and Thompson, Clare W. Intelligence at adulthood: a twenty-five year follow-up. In Don E. Hamachek (Ed.), *Human Dynamics in Psychology and Education.* Boston: Allyn and Bacon, 1968.

Brody, N. Achievement motive, test anxiety, and subjective probability of success in risk-taking behavior. In John W. Atkinson and Norman T. Feather (Eds.), *A Theory of Achievement Motivation.* New York: Wiley, 1966.

Crandall, V.J., and Rabson, A. Children's repetition choices in an intellectual achievement situation, following success and failure. *Journal of Genetic Psychology,* 1960, *97,* 161-168.

Coleman, J.S. *The adolescent society.* Glencoe, Ill.: The Free Press, 1961.

Connell, D.M., and Johnson, J.E. Relationship between sex-role identification and self-esteem in early adolescents. *Developmental Psychology,* 1970, *3,* 268.

Ford, W.S., and Muse, D. *Self-concept and students' future educational plans.* Tallahassee, Fla.: Institute for Social Research, 1972.

French, E.G. Motivation as a variable in work partner selection. *Journal of Abnormal and Social Psychology,* 1956, *53,* 96-99.

Gordon, C. Social characteristics of early adolescence. *Daedalus,* 1971, *100,* 931-960.

Gove, W.R. and Tudor, Jeannette F. Adult sex roles and mental illness. *American Journal of Sociology,* 1973, *78,* 812-835.

Haan, Norma. Proposed model of ego functioning: coping and defense mechanisms in relationship to IQ change. *Psychological Monographs,* 1963, *77,* No. 571.

Hauser, R.M. *Socioeconomic background and educational performance.* The

Arnold M. and Caroline Rose Monograph Series. Washington, D.C.: American Sociological Association, 1971.

Hawley, Peggy. What women think men think: does it affect their career choice? *Journal of Counseling Psychology*, 1971, *18*, 193-199.

Horner, Matina S. Femininity and successful achievement: A basic inconsistency. In E.L. Walker (Ed.), *Feminine Personality and Conflict*, Belmont, Calif.: Brooks/Cole Publishing, 1970.

Houts, P. and Entwisle, Doris R. Academic achievement effort among females: achievement attitudes and sex role orientation. *Journal of Counseling Psychology*, 1968, *15*, 284-286.

Hummel, R. and Sprinthall, N. Underachievement related to interests, attitudes, and values. *Personnel and Guidance Journal*, 1965, *44*, 388-395.

Kagan, J. and Moss, H.A. *Birth to maturity.* New York: Wiley, 1962.

Maccoby, Eleanor E. Sex differences in intellectual functioning. In Eleanor E. Maccoby (Ed.), *The Development of Sex Differences.* Stanford, Calif.: Stanford University Press, 1966.

Mahone, C. Fear of failure and unrealistic vocational aspirations. In John W. Atkinson and Norman T. Feather (Eds.), *A Theory of Achievement Motivation.* New York: Wiley, 1966.

McClelland, D.C. *The achieving society.* Princeton, N.J.: Van Nostrand, 1961.

McClelland, D.C., Atkinson, J.W., Clark, R.A., and Lowell, E.L. *The achievement motive.* New York: Appleton, 1953.

McKee, J.P. and Sherriffs, A.C. Men's and women's beliefs, ideas, and self-concepts. *American Journal of Sociology*, 1959, *64*, 356-363.

Mead, Margaret. *Male and female.* New York: Morrow, 1949.

Morgan, Sherry W. and Mausner, B. *Behavioral and fantasized indicators of avoidance of success in men and women.* Paper presented at the Eastern Psychological Association, April 27-29, 1972, Boston, Massachusetts.

O'Conner, Patricia, Atkinson, J.W., and Horner, Matina. Motivational implications of ability groupings in schools. In John W. Atkinson and Norman T. Feather (Eds.), *A Theory of Achievement Motivation.* New York: Wiley, 1966.

Rand, Lorraine M. and Miller, Anna Louise. A developmental cross-sectioning of women's careers and marriage attitudes and life plans. *Journal of Vocational Behavior*, 1972, *2*, 317-331.

Rosenkrantz, P., Vogel, Susan, Bee, Helen, Broverman, Inge, and Broverman, D.M. Sex-role stereotypes and self-concepts in college students. *Journal of Consulting and Clinical Psychology*, 1968, *32*, 287-295.

Silverman, I. Self-esteem and differential responsiveness to success and failure. *Journal of Abnormal and Social Psychology*, 1964, *69*, 115-119.

Slocum, W.L. and Bowles, R.T. *Educational and occupational aspirations and expectations of high school juniors in the State of Washington.* Report No. 1. Pullman: Washington State University, Vocational-Technical Research and Development Project, 1967.

Steinmann, Anne, Levi, J., and Fox, D.J. Self-concept of college women compared with their concept of ideal woman and men's ideal woman. *Journal of Counseling Psychology*, 1964, *11*, 370-374.

Terman, L.M. and Oden, Melita H. *The gifted child grows up.* Stanford: Stanford University Press, 1947.

Tyler, Leona E. Individual differences: sex differences. In David L. Sills (Ed.), *International Encyclopedia of the Social Sciences.* New York: Crowell, Collier and Macmillan, 1968.

Zissis, C. A study of the life planning of 550 freshman women at Purdue University. *Journal of the National Association of Women, Deans and Counselors*, 1964, *18*, 153-159.

Section III

OCCUPATIONAL SOCIALIZATION AND SEX-ROLE STEREOTYPING

PERHAPS the greatest barrier inhibiting women from developing their full potential and choosing from among the full range of occupational and life-style alternatives is the prevalence of social and occupational stereotypes that reflect underlying sexist myths and attitudes. These stereotypes are the products of socialization processes beginning in infancy that subtly shape the perceptions and attitudes of both women and men in our culture. Section III deals with the ways in which children, youth, and adults are socialized through such influences as sex-role training and prescriptions, occupational stereotyping, and sex stereotyping in counseling, therapy, and education.

Occupational sex biases are formed early in the socialization of children. In the first chapter, Schlossberg and Goodman discuss the results of an investigation which revealed that elementary school children hold stereotypes about occupations based on sex. The children excluded women from "male" jobs more than they excluded men from "female" jobs. They also tended to choose occupations for themselves that fell into traditional masculine or feminine categories. The authors discuss these findings in relation to the impact of sex stereotypic thinking on the aspirations and expectations of girls and conclude that early educational experiences must be changed if real equality of opportunity for women and men is to be achieved.

Women in high administrative positions in both education and business and industry have many barriers to hurdle. Myths about working for a female boss and women's attitude toward women are among them. Loring and Wells examine the ways in which stereotypic thinking affects women who aspire to managerial positions. Such myths as the belief that women lack aggressiveness or are too emotional for the business world may inhibit opportunities for advancement for women.

Radloff and Monroe discuss the relationship between the sense of helplessness experienced by many women and depression. The incidence of depression consistently has been found to be higher in women than in men. The authors identify elements of the traditional female role which may contribute to depression, such as (a) feminine stereotypes which include characteristics related to helplessness, (b) female training in which helplessness, passivity, and dependency are reinforced and adaptive responses are punished, and (c) the general low status and lack of power experienced by women. Radloff and Monroe recommend special training programs to help women learn to take direct and effective action toward solving problems and coping with the environment. They caution, however, that intervention programs will face an uphill battle as long as society itself punishes success in women and rewards helplessness.

In the next chapter the findings of a task force established by the American Psychological Association to examine the extent and manner of sex bias and sex-role stereotyping in psychotherapeutic practice are reported. Sexism can occur in relation to values in psychotherapy, the therapists' knowledge of psychological processes in women, and in the theory, scientific research, and psychological assumptions on which the practice of psychotherapy is based. A survey of women psychologists presumed to have had experience as consumers and practitioners of psychotherapy revealed four general areas of perceived sex bias and sex-role stereotyping: (a) fostering traditional sex roles; (b) bias in expectations and devaluations of women; (c) sexist use of psychoanalytic concepts; and (d) responding to women as sex objects, including seduction of female clients. Biased treatment may also occur differently for special groups of women, such as ethnic minorities, gay women, and women from lower socioeconomic levels, although little data are available. Recommendations are made by the task force in relation to needs for increasing sensitivity of therapists and development of guidelines for nonsexist psychotherapeutic practice.

Schlossberg and Pietrofesa review the evidence on sex bias in the attitudes of vocational counselors and conclude that bias operates among both female and male counselors. For example, in a study conducted by the authors, counselors displayed more bias against females entering a traditionally masculine occupation than against females entering a so-called feminine occupation. They also discuss sex bias in guidance materials used in vocational counseling; see Section VIII for a more complete discussion. Schlossberg and Pietrofesa conclude with recommendations for counselor training.

Finally, Engelhard, Jones, and Stiggins report some progress toward the reduction of sex bias among counselors. They report that counselors gave less biased responses to an instrument designed to measure counselor attitudes towards women in 1975 than those obtained six years earlier.

It seems clear that sex stereotyping, reinforced through the socialization process, is a serious limiting factor to the full career development of women. Many aspects of career development are restricted, including level of achievement, development of abilities, expression of interests, occupational aspiration and choice, and life-style choice. Furthermore, traditional views about what constitutes femininity conflict with maximum realization of women's potential in relation to both psychological health and vocational development. If women, through the socialization process, are taught to view themselves as passive, dependent, and helpless, they will not be able to see themselves as competent individuals capable of taking leadership roles. Much of our thinking in psychology has rested on the assumption that masculinity and femininity represent the extremes of a unidimensional, bipolar trait; achievement, independence, and competence belong at the masculine end while passivity, dependence, and nurturance fall on the feminine end of the continuum. (See Constantinople [1973] for a detailed discussion of this issue.) This dualistic way of thinking makes it difficult for women to see themselves as both competent and feminine.

It is our belief that broad institutional change moving toward a more androgynous view of human beings is necessary to facilitate the optimal career development of each woman and man. We agree with Bem (1975) that femininity and masculinity "represent complementary domains of positive traits and behaviors and that it is possible for an individual to be both feminine and masculine, caring and competent, and oriented toward affiliation and achievement, depending on the context of the situation. Only when the artificial constraints of gender are eliminated is one free to be one's own unique blend of temperament and behavior."

The chapters in this section highlight some of the important issues in relation to sex role and occupational stereotyping and the socialization process but by no means present an exhaustive treatment of the literature. Differences in socialization related to ethnic and socioeconomic background were not explored. The following references may be helpful in gaining a broader understanding of this area.

BIBLIOGRAPHY

Bem, S.L. Beyond androgyny: Some prescriptions for a liberated sexual identity. Keynote address for APA-NIMH Conference on the Research Needs of Women, Madison, Wisconsin, May 31, 1975. In J. Sherman & F. Denmark (Eds.), *Psychology of Women: Future Directions of Research.* Psychological Dimensions, in press.

Bem, S.L. & Bem, D.J. Case study of a nonconscious idealogy: Training the woman to know her place. In D.J. Bem (Ed.), *Beliefs, Attitudes and Human*

Affairs. Belmont, Ca.: Brooks/Cole, 1970.

Birk, J.M., Cooper, J. & Tanney, M.F. *Racial and sex role stereotyping in career information illustration.* Paper presented at the American Psychological Association, Montreal, August, 1973.

Broverman, I.K., Broverman, D.M., and Clarkson, F.E. Sex role stereotypes and clinical judgments of mental health. *Journal of Consulting and Clinical Psychology,* 1970, *34,* 1-7.

Broverman, I.K., Vogel, S.R., Broverman, D.M., Carlson, F.E., & Rosenkrantz, P.S. Sex-role stereotypes: a current appraisal. *Journal of Social Issues,* 1972, *28*(2), 59-78.

Constantinople, A. Masculinity-femininity: An exception to a famous dictum. *Psychological Bulletin,* 1973, *80*(5), 389-407.

Maccoby, E.E., & Jacklin, C.N. *The Psychology of Sex Differences.* Stanford, Ca.: Stanford University Press, 1974.

Mednick, M.T.S., Tangri, S.S., & Hoffman, L.W. (Eds.). *Women and Achievement: Social and Motivational Analyses.* New York: John Wiley and Sons, 1975.

Unger, R.K. & Denmark, F.L. (Eds.). *Woman: Dependent or Independent Variable?* New York: Psychological Dimensions, Inc., 1975.

Witt, S.H. Native women today; sexism and the Indian woman. *Civil Rights Digest,* Spring 1974, 29-35.

Chapter 10

A WOMAN'S PLACE: CHILDREN'S SEX STEREOTYPING OF OCCUPATIONS*

NANCY K. SCHLOSSBERG AND JANE GOODMAN

FROM birth, males and females are viewed differently, often in a way suggesting inferiority for women. The handling in infancy, the number and kinds of toys in toddlerhood (7), and the encouragement of dependence or independence during preschool years all reinforce the conclusion one little five-year-old made to her mother, "Boys have more chances than girls." Toys for very young children seem to be designed to reinforce these role limitations and stereotypes. Girls get miniature mothering or household work items or nurse's kits; boys get cars and trucks and doctor kits.

Several studies of five-year-olds demonstrate the degree to which contemporary society differentially socializes boys and girls. One, reported in Maccoby's book (1), shows that when five-year-olds were exposed to a series of paired pictures depicting sex-appropriate activities, both sexes knew what little boys and little girls were expected to do. Mothers cook and clean; fathers work.

This stereotyping at age five is continued in adolescence. In studying the occupational fantasy life of adolescents, Douvan and Adelson (2) found that "the bulk of girls' choices (95 percent) fall into the following four categories: personal aide, social aide, white collar traditional, and glamor fashion."

Adolescents who enter college maintain the notion of differential achievement for boys and girls. A recent experiment with two groups of college students illustrates this. The experimenter asked one group to complete a story based on the clue, "After first term finals, John finds himself at the top of his medical school class." The other group

*From *Vocational Guidance Quarterly*, 1972, 20, 266-270.

had the same assignment, but "Anne" was substituted for "John." The group story about John was very positive. In dealing with Anne the students were less enthusiastic. Typical comments were: "Anne is an acne-faced bookworm . . . her fellow classmates are so disgusted with her behavior that they jump on her in a body and beat her. . . . Anne doesn't want to be No. 1 in her class . . . . she drops down to ninth in the class and then marries the boy who graduates No. 1" (3).

This early socialization of women partially explains why women are employed, for the most part, in jobs that are extensions of the work they do at home. "Over half the women workers are employed in only 21 of the 250 distinct occupations listed in the Bureau of Census. One-fourth of all employed women were in five occupations —secretary-stenographer, household worker, bookkeeper, elementary school teacher, and waitress" (4). It is obvious that the job openings do not, in themselves, make it easy for women, or for those who counsel them, to abandon traditional occupations for untried areas of endeavor. As the present study demonstrates, girls, as well as boys, believe that a woman's opportunities in the world of work are more limited than a man's.

PROCEDURE

This study was designed to discover the degree to which elementary school children hold stereotypes about occupations based on sex. The differences between kindergarteners and sixth graders, between boys and girls, and between two elementary schools—one predominantly middle and upper-middle class, the other a model cities project school —were studied. All the children in the kindergarten and the sixth grade of the two schools were asked to respond to twelve drawings, representing work settings of six occupations traditionally considered feminine and six occupations traditionally considered masculine. The occupations were classified as "feminine" or "masculine" according to the major sex represented in the occupation. Of the feminine occupations, the ones chosen for this study were those employing over a fourth of all employed women—secretary-bookkeeper, household worker, elementary school teacher, waitress, and nurse. The masculine jobs are prominent among those identified (4) as fields in which there will be a need for more personnel in the 1970s—a need that cannot be filled by men alone. The masculine fields included in this study were doctor, dentist, architect-draftsman, television-radio repairman, mechanic, and laboratory scientist.

To discover the degree to which children stereotype occupations, the children were helped to identify the picture by the interviewer, who said, for example: "This is where a person works who fixes televisions and radios. Could a man work here? Could a woman work here?" The order of these questions, as well as the order of the pictures, was random. The wording "could" rather than "does" or "should" was used to enable the children to free themselves from their perceptions of present occupational segregation and from their feelings about sex-appropriate occupations. In addition, each child was asked, "What do you want to be when you grow up?"

RESULTS

A child's response was considered to be stereotyped when the child said, "No, a man could not work here" about one of the feminine occupations, or "No, a woman could not work here" about one of the masculine occupations. The data were analyzed in terms of number of stereotyped responses. The results from the model cities kindergarten are not included, for the children did not seem to relate to the study in a meaningful way, possibly because the interviewer was white or possibly because the interviewer was middle class.

The data indicate: (a) no appreciable increase in stereotyping from kindergarten to sixth grade; (b) the sixth graders at the model cities school held more stereotypes than those at the middle income school; (c) the children were more ready to exclude women from men's jobs than to exclude men from women's jobs; (d) with few exceptions, the children chose jobs for themselves that fall within the usual stereotypes, e.g. most children felt either men or women could be doctors or nurses, but the boys all chose to be doctors and the girls, nurses; (e) there was some disparity between the amount of stereotyping of one occupation and another.

KINDERGARTEN AND SIXTH GRADE STEREOTYPING. There was no significant difference between the role stereotypes held by the middle class sixth graders and those held by the middle class kindergarteners. Although it might be expected that the sixth graders, with their greater experience of the world, would be more aware of the real sexual division of labor, it was apparent that they also were more responsive to the difference between the interviewer's "could" and their perception of reality as it "is." They frequently expressed this in comments such as, "Sure, a woman *could* fix cars, but she wouldn't like it much," or "She *could,* if she got some overalls."

MODEL CITIES AND MIDDLE INCOME SIXTH GRADERS. The middle income sixth graders were consistently less stereotyped than the model cities sixth graders. The middle income elementary school is in a community where many of the mothers work at professional jobs, and this perhaps enables the children to view women as having more capabilities than do the model-cities project school children, whose community includes women working almost exclusively at low-level, women's jobs.

FEMININE AND MASCULINE OCCUPATIONS. The boys and girls interviewed excluded women from men's jobs more than they excluded men from women's jobs. There were 78 responses indicating that only a woman could do one of the women's jobs. There were 156—or twice as many—responses indicating that only a man could do one or another of the men's jobs. To state it another way, women were considered unable to do men's work twice as often as men were considered unable to do women's work.

A tentative explanation for this phenomenon is that the children believe that while a "man can do anything," a woman's powers are more limited. Evidence for this is found in many of the children's informal comments. Even when the children's responses did not exclude a woman from a man's occupation (and therefore do not show up as stereotyped responses in the data), they often added qualifying comments. For example, when shown the picture depicting an architect-draftsman and asked if a man could do that, all the children said "yes." When asked if a woman could do that, many of those who said "yes" added, "if she had special training," or "if she went to a special school," or some similar statement. Somehow, a man was assumed to have all the expertise necessary. Not a single child specified special training or any other qualifications for a man for either the masculine or feminine occupations. In several cases where a child said a woman *could* work in an occupation, it was clear that he felt she *should not*. For example, one boy, when asked if a woman could be an auto mechanic, said, "Sure, she could, if she were one of these 'woman's lib' types."

STEREOTYPING OF CHILDREN'S OWN CAREER PLANS. Eighty-three percent of the girls and 97 percent of the boys who chose any occupation chose an occupation traditionally reserved for their sex. Although approximately 75 percent of the children felt men could be nurses, no boy chose this occupation. (Ten of the girls said they wished to be nurses when they grew up.) Although approximately 89 percent of the children felt women could be doctors, none of the girls chose this occupation. (Seven of the boys wanted to be doctors when they grew up.)

RELATIVE STEREOTYPING OF DIFFERENT OCCUPATIONS. A striking aspect of the data is the disparity between the amount of stereotyping of one occupation and another. One hundred percent of the model cities project sixth graders, boys and girls, said a woman could not fix televisions and radios or cars. Only 10 percent said she could not be a doctor. Seventy-six percent said a man could not be a housekeeper; only 5 percent excluded him from the teaching profession.

In the middle class sixth grade, 48 percent of the children felt a woman could not be an auto mechanic, only 5 percent that she could not be a doctor. Thirty-eight percent said a man could not be a housekeeper; none said he should be excluded from waiting on tables, or teaching.

Similar disparities were demonstrated in the middle class kindergarten. Fifty-nine percent of the children excluded women from fixing cars, only 11 percent from fixing teeth. Nineteen percent said a man could not be a housekeeper; none excluded him from secretarial work.

CONCLUSION

According to the children we interviewed, a woman's place was clearly *not* fixing autos or television sets or designing buildings. The children, however, said she could work as a waitress, nurse, or librarian. Clearly the issue was not that they felt a woman's place was in the home, but rather that it was in certain specified occupations. By contrast, they did not feel that men had to be similarly limited. A man could fix automobiles or teach children or even be a nurse. A woman was not granted this freedom. And often when women were not actually excluded, they were thought to need special training that men did not need. Although the children were asked, "*Could* a woman do that?" and "*Could* a man do that?" they evidently responded in terms of *do* men or women do these things.

The sex typing of occupations "reflects—and perpetuates—the differential status of male and female" (6). Thus, children's early notions of differential achievement for men and women need to be changed. It is much easier for elementary school personnel to keep options open than it is to convince a forty-year-old woman that it is appropriate for her to achieve. This study looked at one small dimension of a complex problem, but the dimension studied can be rectified. If children are to develop the flexibility required to deal with tomorrow's world, they must learn to make the transition between "do," "could," and "will"—and educators can influence this learning.

REFERENCES

1. Dornbush, S.M. Afterword. In E.E. Maccoby (Ed.), *The development of sex differences.* Stanford: Stanford University Press, 1968.
2. Douvan, E., & Adelson, J. *The adolescent experience.* New York: Wiley, 1966.
3. Horner, M.S. Woman's will to fail. *Psychology Today,* November 1969, *3,* 36-38, 62.
4. Hedges, J.N. Woman at work, woman workers and manpower demands in the 1970s. *Monthly Labor Review,* 1970, *93,* (6) 19-34.
5. Maccoby, E.E. (Ed.) *The development of sex differences.* Stanford: Stanford University Press, 1966.
6. Moore, L. *Allocation of rewards and minority member recipients.* Wayne State University, 1971. (Mimeo)
7. Polk, B. *Socialization of little girls.* Speech given at Wayne State University Teach-In on Women, Detroit, October 1970.

Chapter 11

OUR SEX-ROLE CULTURE*

THEODORA WELLS AND ROSALIND K. LORING

"IT IS INDEED a pleasure to meet a capable, well-educated career woman who has managed to retain her femininity." Quoted from a letter following an interview for a managerial position with a large real estate firm, this was written by a personnel man to a woman applicant.[1] Obviously it was intended as a compliment. Equally obviously, he had expected that a capable, well-educated career woman would not be "feminine."

LANGUAGE REFLECTS SOCIETY'S VALUE OF MAN OVER WOMAN

"She thinks like a man" is an old compliment given to women who are so exceptional that they can only be complimented in male terms. Underneath, it carries the implication that to be like a man is good; to be like a woman is not. The same implicit approval would hardly be conveyed in, "She thinks like a woman!" Our language is permeated with these sex-linked connotations that place higher value on men. Many of these reverse compliments reflect the widely-held expectations for men and women. It becomes apparent how prejudicial sex-labeling is when we consider that the real question should be, "Does this woman think like a *manager?*" Language and the social value attached to certain words have a subtle, powerful effect in forming attitudes and behaviors.

TRADITIONAL EXPECTATIONS FOR WOMEN DEFINE THEIR "PLACE"

A look at the characteristic attitudes that management men and women express about women in management reveals the traditional expectations held for women and their "place."[2]

"The requirements for a manager—toughness and concern only for the dollar—do not and will not ever mix with the cultural idea

*From R. K. Loring and T. Wells. *Breakthrough: Women into Management.* New York: Van Nostrand Reinhold Company, 1972.*

ascribed to (but not necessarily found in) females. Someone has to stand for the things spiritual, kindness, and tolerance. So, as a culture, all of us look to women to personify this." *Chief engineer, extractive industry (Man)*

"It's still a fact that most people want a home and family. There is no necessity for more than one person in the family to have a career. It is only logical and sensible that the man be that person simply because of woman's biological role. She's needed at home." *Treasurer, financial institution (Man)*[3]

"More women should be at home to instill our moral values in growing children. It's an investment in the future of our country that is badly needed." *Dean, Graduate School, State University (Man)*

"There are very few who can stand the stress and strain of present-day business without it affecting their family relationships. A woman enjoys an outlet from routine household chores, but very few choose to go higher when it affects their homes and families." *President, consumer goods manufacturer (Woman)*

"When a woman tries to come across as smarter than all the men around, she makes it harder for all of us." *Director, Social Welfare Agency (Woman)*[4]

"I think competing with men dishonors a woman's natural abilities. She tries to meet men's challenges because she feels that what she, as a woman, can do isn't worth much." *Owner-director, advertising agency (Woman)*

These statements, and the assumptions and implications behind the words, betray traditional values based on sex-role expectations:

- women are best suited to home and family
- women should leave home only by necessity; men belong outside the home
- the nuclear family has no acceptable alternatives
- women are spiritual and men are not
- women being at home with children insures that moral values are transmitted
- women contribute vitally to our moral values if they stay home (by implication, they make no such contribution if they do not stay home)
- kindness and tolerance have no place in business, only toughness and concern for the dollar; only women have the former and only men the latter
- women *personify* valuable qualities; men *do* the important work
- if *some* women try to demonstrate superiority over men, it hurts *all* women

- even when one particular woman is more able than an individual man, she should not let this be known
- competition is for men and cooperation is for women
- women dishonor themselves and their own "natural abilities" if they attempt to meet "men's" challenges
- challenges belong to men because challenges must be met with aggressiveness
- aggressiveness belongs to men and is not in the repertoire of woman's "natural abilities"

It is striking to note three themes running through these assumptions. Whether the speaker is man or woman, most traditional attitudes define women in terms of, and in relation to, men. The standard is male; women are compared against that standard. The mood is established that women are valued for those qualities of kindness and tolerance, spirituality or humanness which are not a part of the expectations of what a "real" man is. Perhaps this is why ministers and counselors, mostly male, carry an onus of being ineffectual—not "real" men.

The implication is that softer qualities are nice, in fact essential, to the continuation of the race but are not important in management. Because of the biological fact that women give birth, an innate desire to nurture is attributed to them forever after.

Men are supposed to be tough, concerned for the dollar, practical, and objective enough to face the facts and act accordingly. Even if someone has to get hurt in the process, a man is supposed to be strong enough to do what has to be done. Such strength, toughness, and total responsibility, even occasional, necessary violence, are attributed to men as "natural." To do anything else is considered as weakness, a "feminine" quality. This must be avoided at all costs if a man is to be a man—a doer and a leader.

Second, these assumptions are held to be true for *all* men and *all* women. Any noticeable variance from the standard description of what a "real" man or a "real" woman is like can make that person vulnerable because he or she is different. Certainly many men have conflicts within themselves about their leadership ability when they are not tough and do not want to be. And many women have inner conflicts between nurturance and tough-mindedness.

Most importantly, there is a silent, pervasive assumption that men and women are *totally* different, that there is no commonality in the characteristics attributed to each sex. A dichotomy is set up, not recognizing the great overlap in the distributions of the human characteristics of the two sexes. For example, Harry Levinson finds that the exceptional executive needs to have "ministrative" qualities.[5]

These are stereotypically attributed to women, yet are becoming valued in contemporary managers (men). On the other hand, some women managers are quite capable of risk-taking and have decision-making abilities usually attributed to men. All of these qualities describe self-confident *people* and are not confined to one sex or the other. Culturally prescribed behaviors are deeply rooted in the backgrounds of most of us. They underlie our legal and economic systems and pervade birth, marriage, death, and inheritance patterns. Most of us are weaned on them, beginning with whether we are placed on pink or blue receiving blankets, and are reinforced through every phase of our lives by all major institutions: marriage, family, education, church, military, corporations, social agencies, government, media. The total society functions through social definitions that have become part of the conventional wisdom—what Everybody Knows.

Even when a review of these silent assumptions reveals a basic incongruity with personal experience, change is not automatic. This change is particularly uncomfortable. The status quo, even if it is incongruous, is known. Resistance to change, shared by most people, has caused the formation of stereotypes as well as their perpetuation long after their social usefulness has passed. To stereotype people is to cast them in molds constructed from the groupings in which it is convenient to classify them—race, religion, sex, national origin, and age. But such categorizations ignore the wide variations that exist within each category and the dangers of shortcuts in dealing with masses of data and crowds of people who touch our daily lives.

The serious mistake is in believing that all individuals within each category are essentially alike. The danger is the potential loss of those capabilities not assumed to be present. Since most male managers and administrators have learned to stereotype women employees as possessing low capabilities, such mold-casting has resulted in tremendous underutilization of the capabilities of many women.

WOMAN DEFINED AS SEDUCTRESS, WITCH, MADONNA AND . . . STUPID

One archetypal image of woman as seductress is reinforced with unremitting repetition in an endless avalanche of ads: automobile, motorcycle, and computer equipment ads heavily loaded with sprawled, straddled women with challenging, luring eyes; commercial key-clubs sell status on the strength of "don't-touch" sex; reclining double-lounge chairs with intense female in black, filmy negligee, eyes drawing you close; woman in predatory crawl on someone's carpet; women in black lace foundation being unzipped, instructing women how they too can be seductive if they buy; titillation and sex.

Closely associated is the theme of the feminine evil—the dangerous sex—permeating the subliminal bombardment. Strange powers of women—over which men have no control. Sex and seduction with sin stirred in is the basic brew for witchery—the ultimate evil power of woman to destroy men. Through seduction, Lorelei devastated the sailors of the Teutonic world. Through seduction, Circe corraled men to become pigs. Wicked witches still thread through the stories read to our children: Hansel and Gretel, Snow White and the Seven Dwarfs; Hallowe'en tales paint her astride her broom, silhouetted across the moon. Endlessly, women have been portrayed as dangerous, seductive, destructive, unpredictable—like hurricanes. Eroticism and evil are essential qualities of women, according to ancient myths and current beliefs. Today advertisers sell billions of dollars of merchandise and services by exploiting this archetypal image.

At the other extreme of ancient imagery is the madonna—the sweet, soft, delicate, tender mother/child (often undistinguishable pictorially —both feature innocence). This image sells toilet paper, deodorants, lingerie, and perfume. One classic ad promoting trading stamps as a sales incentive featured a home snapshot of the sweet, eternally feminine wife. The caption: "The most powerful incentive ever invented by man—woman." In one brilliant stroke, this ad succinctly summarized the male invention of the innocent, dependent, consumer wife who looks to her husband to provide all things and for which all men strive.

How simplistic this modern-day version of the ancient division of labor based on reproductive biology. How weary the consumer, worker, or manager who attempts to keep people and functions in neat, tidy little boxes. Accumulating evidence demonstrates that women are no longer succumbing to stereotyped advertising. And so it is with work.

Today, most jobs are "in between" jobs. Survival depends on recognizing a quite different range of values, sometimes including opposing values. Early agrarian patterns have no relevance for a modern, industrialized society. Yet the myth of dependency, supportiveness, nurturance, and maintenance as the nature and purpose of woman lingers on. The soft image of innocent motherhood is enshrined in the media's religion of consumerism long after major changes in marriage and family patterns; long after major changes in employment and education resources; long after technology has vastly increased the range of work that can be performed by either men or women.

The media reflect a third dominant theme: Women are presented as not very bright, certainly not logical. In some instances, they appear downright stupid, especially when it involves handling money or demonstrating reasoning ability. For example, a computer equipment company ran a double-spread of red lips invitingly parted, captioned: "We taught our data entry system to speak a new language: Dumb Blond."

Of course, men are not exempt from the blandishments of advertising. One computer systems ad shows four mildly seductive women simperingly vying for attention. The caption cozily suggests that, "Time sharing can be a problem . . . if you are trying to support too much expensive equipment." It carries the happy implication, of course, that the reader (probably a married male) can easily cope with the sexual joys of four lovely ladies. But there are few practical matters a man must concern himself with—time, for instance. So, to have his cake and eat it too, it appears he will have to time share.

The requirement to have manly equipment is rather openly referred to in a motor oil ad that carried the jingle: "The only difference between men and boys is the size and cost of their toys." The question is: Do these portrayals still sell merchandise? Are the admen's predictions accurate that men buy the sexual aura with the product? Ah, the power of sexual fantasies!

THE MODEL OF THE MANAGER IS MASCULINE

"The model of the successful manager in our culture is a masculine one. The good manager is aggressive, competitive, firm, just. He is not feminine; he is not soft or yielding or dependent or intuitive in the womanly sense. The very expression of emotion is widely viewed as a feminine weakness that would interfere with effective business processes. *Yet the fact is that all these emotions are part of the human nature of men and women alike.* (Emphasis ours.) Cultural forces have shaped not their existence but their acceptability; they are repressed, *but this does not render them inactive.* (Emphasis his.) They continue to influence attitudes, opinions, and decisions." This is the professional manager as defined by Douglas McGregor.[6]

A successful manager is assumed to be objective, unemotional, logical—a hard-nosed decision-maker dealing only with facts. He is expected to repress those aspects of himself that are associated with the feminine in our culture—softness, yielding, dependence, and intuitiveness. To express emotion is seen as "feminine weakness."

THE MASCULINE MODEL SETS UP DOUBLE BINDS FOR MEN

Faced with accepting women as managers, a male manager may well feel he is expected to accept in them those very qualities he has had to reject in himself to become a manager. Hence, this double-bind: **If he accepts women as managers, he has to accept as permissible-for-a-manager the emotions he had repressed in himself; if he accepts the prescribed unemotional manager's role, he cannot accept women (the feminine) as managers.**

Not just the model of a manager, but the very value of masculinity can seem to be threatened by women moving into management. It shakes up the traditional role of men in relation to women. Richard W. Smith, in "Why Men Need to Put Women Down," spells out the role-relationship: "A male, in order to be a socially accepted "regular fellow" must be first, a warrior (or at least warrior-like); second, a highly-active procreator; and third, an economic provider. Females, in turn, must be married, economically and emotionally dependent, and mothers."[7] When a woman steps out of her traditional role she upsets the balance of both roles. She can easily be seen as threatening the worth and masculine identity that a man finds in the "conquering" of work. It raises the question: "If a woman can do a man's job as well as he, how can a man maintain that it takes that extra measure of ability (virility) to qualify for such work?"[8]

Many men may well wonder how to relate to this unexpected change—"What do you do with them?" To be aggressive and competitive is to be that way *with other men.* The male role requires that women be taken care of, not fought. Second, the symbol of a highly active procreator is the man who chases and beds women. Clearly this is not appropriate in relating to women managers as professional colleagues. Third, as an economic provider a man is subjected to legal and social pressures that say, "A man who can't support a family isn't much of a man," and conversely, "A good supporter is a high-status *he*-man."[9] A woman manager may adhere to the feminine role by being married and a mother, but she definitely is *not* economically and emotionally dependent.

So, many men feel locked into another double-bind: **If he is a man as prescribed, he cannot relate to a woman on an equal (male) basis; if he is his own person, relating equally to women, he risks being seen by other men as "not much of a man"—or manager either.**

While many managers can appreciate a woman's competence, they often find it difficult to simply accept it as just that. Somehow, competence and feminine sexuality don't seem to go together. The idea that a man "controls his women" is widespread. When a woman becomes a manager functioning as his colleague or superior, control over her is no longer available nor appropriate for the man. Again, conflict between male-role and work-role.

Education, some tough choices and compromises in his career, and expectations from families may constitute a large personal investment in a man's masculine identity and feelings of being valuable as a person. With women as managerial competitors, this investment may feel devalued.

The unequal concept has been with us a long time, deeply rooted in the Protestant ethic and our marriage system. We come from American beginnings that did not include women as citizens under the Constitution. Under laws of coverture, married women were "dead in the law" and found divorce virtually unavailable, while unmarried women were legally treated as minors. In spite of progress through new legislation, equal rights and equal protection under constitutional law remain ambiguous today.[10] Yet to be accomplished are the States' ratification of the Equal Rights Amendment and the courts' interpretations of Revised Order 4 and other work-related decisions.

SOCIAL ROLES FOR WORK, SEX, AND MARRIAGE ARE INTERTWINED

Inextricably intertwined are at least three major role patterns that affect the relationships between men and women and create difficulties for women in the process of becoming managers. To talk about one is to talk about all three. First are *sex-roles* which underlie the pattern of male "superiority" and female "inferiority." Second are *marital-roles* of husband and wife where power, intelligence, and responsibility traditionally rest with the husband while the wife is perceived as a helpmate "living through" her husband and children. Third are *work-roles* where men are in the leadership and decision-making roles and women are in the housekeeping and nurturing tasks of industry, government, education, and services.

These three culturally entrenched patterns have contributed to the ubiquitous nonconscious attitudes of dominance and subordinancy. Roles by virtue of one's physical sex impinge on the work situation. Robert Townsend, for example, contending that many men "spend most of (their) waking hours in sex-fantasy day-dreams," advises women, "This kind of competition is a real pushover."[11] We disagree about the weakness of the competition since it seems evident that men have not only sex-fantasies but also *sex-role fantasies* firmly rooted in historical male supremacy. It has long been fact as well as fantasy that men have power over women.

Social sex-role power is further enhanced by marital roles whereby wives of managers, and sometimes husbands of managers, feel proprietary rights on their spouses, making demands on their time and energies that impact the work situation. The jealousy and possessiveness which so often characterize marriages can increase the pressures under which managers operate. As more women enter management, there is increasing speculation about the influence of marital status. Single women are often discussed as to the degree of their sexual frustration and, thus, their potential sexual availability. On the other hand, married women may or may not be considered "off-limits" for sexual involvements. In some industries, such as the entertainment field, being married is usually not a barrier. Divorced women are often considered to be more flexible in their sexual standards and thus easier to approach. Whatever the marital status, there are many factors—age, appearance, "vibrations"—that determine whether speculations evolve into action.

Marital status also affects selection and promotion policies. Ranging from traditional anti-nepotism rulings to whether or not a married woman should hold a responsible job, there are concerns about whether she *or her husband* actually makes her employment decisions. Administrators have been juggling concerns such as

- Deciding that husbands and wives can work in the same department provided that . . . neither is involved in making employment decisions about the other. (a new ruling at Stanford University)
- Does the woman have serious commitment to the organization, or does she treat her work as a time-filler depending on her husband's activities?
- Expecting women to prove the need for the position as opposed to assuming that a man has the need in his traditional breadwinner role.
- Assuming that motivation is based on economic need. Mark the assumptions . . . . if a woman is married, her husband works and supports her . . . . economic need is the only need that really motivates people . . . . the requirement to support is the only fair basis for employment.

Some management men perpetuate these assumptions by recognizing their own interest in making no change. One advertising agency executive appeals to the "nurturing nature" of women when he put it this way: "Higher education has wised you (women) up . . . all of this makes men a little uneasy. And a little wistful. Men don't want things to change. They haven't changed and they don't want women to change . . ."[12]

Clearly, men on the average are different from women on the average because of differential opportunities for development. Comparable opportunity for developing the capabilities and potentials of both men and women must be available before we can know whether or not there is any shred of intrinsic difference between the sexes in handling the managerial role. Separating the biological and social conditioning facets in the personality development of both women and men is virtually impossible. "It is clear that until social expectations for men and women are equal, until we provide equal respect for both men and women, our answers . . . will simply reflect our prejudices."[13] There is no valid basis now available for understanding what meaning, if any, biological differences have for any specific function. The authority that tells women and men who they are and what they are supposed to do is too deeply imbedded into the social context to make that possible.

It is hardly remarkable, then, that men find it difficult to see women in the work-role of manager. Patterns in leadership and management are deeply entrenched. Psychiatrist Robert Seidenberg described it this way: "We must recognize that our society is overwhelmingly dominated by male 'homosexuality' in religion, politics, higher education, law, big business, the armed forces, and practically all other important institutions . . . the reality that men in general prefer to spend most of their time in each others' company, compete, make contracts, plan and make decisions together, and in their leisure time, play together. Very little time is spent with women; their opinions are generally held in low esteem; they are never present in the higher echelons of decision-making, and are not brought into games of leisure. They are sexual partners, but this takes only a few minutes a week, just enough time to establish that the male is a heterosexual, which he obviously is not, based on his apparent preferences as found in time-spent studies . . . For most men, women are good to sleep with—not to stay awake with."[14]

Labeling this pattern as homosexuality is rather strong. We feel more inclined to describe it as monosexuality—a one-sex scene with heterosexual interludes. In this all-male climate, the reality of women as peers is bound to be disturbing. The real shock is the reality of the difference between recognizing the principle of equal opportunity and having to live with its consequences personally.

WHAT ARE THE TRAITS VALUED IN MEN; IN WOMEN?

Whether biology or socialization is the rationale for stereotyping, certain traits are ascribed to each sex. When these traits are displayed by the designated appropriate sex, then they are socially valued. For example, aggressiveness is ascribed to men. Socially valued when shown by men, it is denigrated when demonstrated by women. So strongly supported are the attitudes about this difference that both men and women easily define a woman "unfeminine" if she displays certain "aggressive" behavior.

In an effort to understand attitudes about the aggressiveness of women's career choices, an opinion survey sampled men and women under 30 and women over 30. Occupations for women frequently rated "aggressive" by men were public relations, engineer, and city planner. Other behaviors rated for aggressiveness included:

- tries to get elected to public office
- becomes a supervisor of men
- manages the family budget

Comparisons between the responding groups reveal that age, above and below the generation watershed of 30 years, is less a factor than is sex. Women over 30 (45 percent) and under 30 (50 percent) are closer in their agreement on the aggressiveness of occupational choices for women than are males (60 percent) and females (50 percent) both under 30. (Interestingly, male veterans gave 20 to 40 percent lower ratings of aggressiveness than non-veteran college men did, in all cases. Presumably veterans' experiences make the difference.) [15]

One widely-quoted study of college students of both sexes reflects a range of stereotypes of the larger society from which today's professional management is drawn. Both men and women students agreed on the following:

Valued Traits, When Displayed by Men:

Aggressive
Independent
Unemotional
Hides emotions
Objective
Easily influenced
Dominant
Likes math and science
Not excitable in a minor crisis
Active
Competitive
Logical
Worldly
Skilled in business
Knows the way of the world
Feelings not easily hurt
Adventurous
Makes decisions easily
Never cries
Acts as a leader
Self-confident
Not uncomfortable about being aggressive
Ambitious
Able to separate feelings from ideas
Not dependent
Not conceited about appearance
Thinks men are superior to women
Talks freely about sex with men
Direct

Valued Traits, When Displayed by Women:

Does not use harsh language
Talkative
Tactful
Gentle
Aware of feelings of others
Religious
Interested in own appearance
Neat in habits
Quiet
Strong need for security
Appreciates art and literature
Expresses tender feelings

Both men and women agreed that masculine traits are more socially desirable than feminine traits. Thus, "women also hold negative values of their worth relative to men." Since these researchers were working with outstanding college achievers, they concluded that the impact of negative stereotypes on the self-concepts of women were "enormously powerful."[16]

LESSER SOCIAL VALUE OF WOMEN PRODUCES "MINORITY STATUS"

Recent legislation and the feelings many women have about themselves refer to "minority status" as defined by sociologists. Many Americans react negatively to this definition since women are statistically 51 percent of the population. Nonetheless, an accurate accounting of the potential for individual control of one's life style, one's destiny, reveals the lack of female power to do so. Helen Hacker, in 1951, compared the attributes which most people believed to be true about a minority group and about women. In view of the strong press of ethnic minorities in recent years to change the stereotypic attitudes, the concern and pressure from women to do likewise may well be understood through her comparison.

With both blacks and women, roles are in flux resulting in a conflict between achieved status and ascribed status.[17]

BLACKS	WOMEN
Ascribed Attributes	
Inferior intelligence, smaller brain, scarcity of geniuses.	Inferior intelligence, smaller brain, scarcity of geniuses
More free in instinctual gratifications. More emotional, "primitive," and childlike. Imagined sexual prowess envied.	Irresponsible, inconsistent, emotionally unstable. Lack of strong superego. Women as temptresses.
Common stereotype, "inferior"	Common stereotype, "weaker"
Rationalizations of Status	
Thought all right in his place. Myth of contented black.	Woman's place is in the home. Myth of contented woman—"feminine" woman is happy in subordinate role.

Accommodation Attitudes

Supplicatory whining intonation of voice	Rising inflection, smiles, laughs, downward glances
Deferential manner	Flattering manner
Concealment of real feelings	"Feminine wiles"
Outwit "white folks"	Outwit "men-folk"
Careful study of points at which dominant group is susceptible to influence	Careful study of points at which dominant group is susceptible to influence
Fake appeals for directives: show of ignorance	Appearance of helplessness

Discriminations

Limitations on education–should fit "place" in society	Limitations on education–should fit "place" in society
Confined to traditional jobs–barred from supervisory positions. Their competition feared. No family precedents for new aspirations.	Confined to traditional jobs–barred from supervisory positions. Their competition feared. No family precedents for new aspirations.
Deprived of political importance	Deprived of political importance
Social and professional segregation	Social and professional segregation

TRAITS AND ATTITUDES TAUGHT TO WOMEN PRODUCE A DOUBLE STANDARD OF MENTAL HEALTH

These attributes, learned because of being female, have become part of the standards of mental health held by practicing psychiatrists, psychologists, and psychiatric social workers, both men and women. In a 1970 study, a group of this composition was asked to describe a healthy adult, (sex unspecified), a healthy male, and a healthy female, using the sex-role stereotypes described above. These "people-helpers" were found to hold *a double standard of mental health.* They perceived the healthy adult, sex unspecified, to be closely similar to the healthy male, but significantly different from the healthy female. Both men and women clinicians agreed that the so-called healthy mature woman, compared to men, is

more submissive	less independent
less adventurous	more easily influenced
less aggressive	less competitive
more excitable in minor crisis	more easily hurt (feelings)
more conceited about appearance	less objective
	less inclined to math and science

Practicing clinicians perceived these traits as healthy in women, not healthy in men.[18] This might be how your psychiatrist views your daughter. Certainly, these traits parallel the sex-role stereotypes on which girl-children are weaned.

The researchers put it this way: "This constellation seems a most unusual way of describing any mature, healthy individual . . . It places women in the conflictual position of having to decide whether to exhibit those positive characteristics considered desirable for men and adults, and thus have their "femininity" questioned . . . or to behave in the prescribed feminine manner, accept second-class adult status, and possibly live a lie to boot."[19] They observed that even in a climate of equality of opportunity and freedom of choice, social pressures to conform to sex-roles restrict career choices open to women and, to a lesser extent, to men. But women no longer are so accepting of the behavior prescribed for them. One of the authors, commenting on militant women's views, said; "A special kind of hatred is reserved by liberationists for psychoanalysts and psychiatrists who in their treatment of women have encouraged them to adjust, to accept their status . . ."[20]

For managers, much of life is lived in the realms of ideas, decisions, conceptualizations. It is experience we need in order to undo the damage of thinking and defining in the narrow terms of established culture. Legislators, scholars, psychiatrists, managers, men and women alike, all have been exposed to the history of separate roles for the sexes. For many people these role expectations may be very comfortable. For others, such ascribed attributes have proved to be both self limiting and societally limiting. Our conviction is that the highest productiveness and achievement are possible when we maintain a minimum of sex-related roles, and provide a maximum of possible choices for individual style and directions of growth.

Ask Yourself

- How do I define femininity—by behavior? appearance? language? occupation? a style, a manner?
- Similarly, how do I define masculinity?
- In order for me to be comfortable with a woman as a manager, how would I rate these traits? What are my priorities?

REFERENCES

1. Private communication to Theodora Wells.
2. The following quotes, except as footnoted, are from Bowman, Garda W., N.B. Worthy, and S.A. Greyser, "Are Women Executives People?" *Harvard Business Review,* July-August, 1965.
3. Private communication.
4. *Ibid.*

5. Levinson, Harry, *The Exceptional Executive, A Psychological Conception,* New York, The Mentor Executive Library, 1968, pp. 175-203.
6. McGregor, Douglas, *The Professional Manager,* (Edited by Caroline McGregor and Warren G. Bennis), New York, McGraw-Hill Book Co., 1967, p. 23.
7. Smith, Richard Warren, "Why Men Need to Put Women Down," paper delivered to the California State Psychological Association, Monterey, California, January, 1970, p. 4.
8. *Ibid.,* p. 11.
9. *Ibid.,* p. 9.
10. For a carefully documented study of the legal status of women today, see Kanowitz, Leo, *Women and the Law, The Unfinished Revolution,* Albuquerque, New Mexico, 1969. It should be noted that in this book, Professor Kanowitz takes a stance against the Equal Rights Amendment which he has subsequently reversed in testimony before Congress.
11. Townsend, Robert, *Up the Organization* (with new chapters added). Greenwich, Conn., Fawcett Publications, Inc., 1970, p. 210.
12. Hobbs, Whit, Senior Vice President of Benton & Bowles, quoted in "Place for Women in Management." *Los Angeles Times,* November 8, 1967, p. 16.
13. Weisstein, Naomi, "Woman as Nigger," *Psychology Today,* October 1969, p. 20 ff. Condensed from "Kinder, Kuche, Kirche as Scientific Law: Psychology Constructs the Female," *Motive,* March-April 1969, p. 84.
14. Seidenberg, Robert, *Marriage in Life and Literature,* New York, Philosophical Library, Inc., 1970, pp. 13-14.
15. Loring, Rosalind K., "Aggressiveness in Women Opinion Survey," administered in various UCLA Extension courses through the Department of Daytime Programs and Special Projects, January, 1971; and at San Fernando State College, February, 1971.
16. Rosenkrantz, P., S. Vogel, H. Bee, I. Broverman, and D. Broverman, "Sex-Role Stereotypes and Self-Concepts in College Students," *Journal of Consulting and Clinical Psychology,* 32, No. 3, June, 1968, pp. 287-295.
17. Hacker, Helen Mayer, "Women as a Minority Group," *Social Forces,* 30, October, 1951, pp. 60-69. This comparison is slightly edited from the original.
18. Broverman, I., D. Broverman, F. Clarkson, P. Rosenkrantz, and S. Vogel, "Sex-role Stereotypes and Clinical Judgments of Mental Health," *Journal of Consulting and Clinical Psychology,* 34, No. 1, February, 1970, pp. 1-7.
19. *Ibid.,* p. 6.
20. Loring, Rosalind K., "Love and Women's Liberation," Chapter in Otto, Herbert (editor), *Love Today—A New Exploration,* New York, Association Press, 1972, p. 83.

Chapter 12

SEX DIFFERENCES IN HELPLESSNESS—WITH IMPLICATIONS FOR DEPRESSION

LENORE SAWYER RADLOFF AND MEGAN K. MONROE

THERE is more depression among women than men. In an interpretive review of research studies, Weissman & Klerman (in press) examine many proposed explanations for this observed epidemiologic fact. They conclude that there is convincing evidence "that social role plays an important role in the vulnerability of women to depression." They further suggest that "elements of the traditional female role, *either through learned or real helplessness,* may contribute to depression" (italics added). In discussing depression in the context of powerlessness, Bart (1975) also suggests that the learned helplessness model of depression (Seligman, 1975) is useful in understanding the "depressenogenic" features of the traditional female role.

It should be noted that these authors acknowledge the complexities of depression and the possible biological bases for some depression. However, biology cannot explain the fact that further studies have found a consistent sex difference in depression among married people but not among the widowed and the never-married (Radloff, 1975). Differential levels of helplessness related to sex/marital status roles may mediate this pattern of findings.

Seligman defines helplessness as follows: "a person or animal is helpless with respect to some outcome when the outcome occurs independently of all voluntary responses" (1975, p. 17). It is helplessness by this definition (noncontingency of response and reinforcement; nothing you do matters) which Seligman has shown to be related to depression. This model is compatible with clinical descriptions of symptoms of depression (helplessness, hopelessness, reduced activity, passivity, retarded ability to learn adaptive responses, discouragement, sadness). It is also compatible with other current theories of depression, including Lewinsohn's reinforcement model (1974) and

Beck's cognitive model (1974). In reinforcement terms, helplessness training trials are also extinction trials. If the subject tries many responses and *none* have any effect on the outcome, then the probabilities of these responses recurring in that situation are reduced. If the subject experiences helplessness in many different situations, generalization may occur, and the subject may stop responding altogether even in new situations. It would not be surprising if the subject began to show signs of emotional distress and depression.

For the purposes of the present chapter, evidence of training in helplessness will be inferred from evidence of experiences of nonreinforcement of responses *and* from evidence of punishment of responses which are generally considered adaptive in our culture (an obvious approach-avoidance conflict). The literature of many fields will be sampled, including studies of sex role stereotypes, childrearing practices, "fear-of-success," "causal attribution," small group influence processes, ascribed status, and power in the family. Studies will be discussed in terms of their relevance to reinforcement contingencies, in both past history and current situations.

In summary, the argument is that if women in our society have more helplessness than men, and if helplessness contributes to depression, then a sex difference in helplessness could explain the excess depression in women as compared to men. The major premise, that women have more helplessness, has often been asserted. The purpose of this chapter is to present research evidence to test its plausibility.

WHAT DO WE EXPECT OF FEMALES?

What are some of the influences in a woman's life which may lead to helplessness? First, there is the feminine stereotype, which has been studied intensively. It does include characteristics which seem related to helplessness. Women are described or portrayed as not active, not independent, not competent, not successful, not able to take care of themselves, and in need of help and protection by

- parents (Rubin et al., 1974; Maccoby and Jacklin, 1974; Tuddenham et al., 1974),
- teachers (Juhasz, 1974),
- children (Hartley and Klein, 1959; Bernhagen, 1974; Tavris, 1975),
- TV programs (Sternglanz & Serbin, 1974),
- TV cartoons (Miller, 1974),
- TV commercials (McArthur & Resko, 1975),
- children's literature (Hillman, 1974),
- textbooks (Child et al., 1946; Shirreffs, 1975),

- advertising (Stemple and Tyler, 1974; Mosher, 1976; Smith, 1974) and even
- psychotherapists (Broverman et al., 1970).

In one study of first-born, new-born babies, girls were described by parents as smaller, weaker, and more in need of nurturance than boys, even though, in fact, they were equally big and healthy (Rubin et al., 1974). In another study (Sternglanz and Serbin, 1974), children's television programs were found to have many more male than female characters. The male characters were more aggressive, constructive, and got more *rewards* for *actions*. The female characters most often got *no consequences* at all. The psychotherapists studied by Broverman saw the healthy adult *female* as different from the healthy *adult*. They described the female as less independent, more easily influenced and more "excitable in a minor crisis." From a psychoanalytic view, traits which the culture calls "feminine" include submissiveness, being a follower rather than initiator, fear of self-assertion, and helplessness. One writer suggests that these traits result from a woman's accepting the "dependent solution." Trying to do things for yourself may produce anxiety. Girls are encouraged to give up trying and depend on others to do things for them. Boys are urged to tolerate the anxiety and keep trying, so that they may eventually succeed (Symonds, 1973, p. 42-44).

The stereotype of how a female should behave is widespread in our culture. It does include the expectation that she is less able than a male to get what she wants directly, by her own actions. But do the stereotypes really have any effect? Apparently they do for various reasons. Simple imitation, especially of models seen as "appropriate" probably does play some part (Feshbach, 1971; Maccoby and Jacklin, 1974). Presumably, a girl would imitate female models, who are likely to behave in "feminine" ways. Studies have also shown that simply labelling a person (or having expectations of her) may affect her behavior. The study called "Pygmalion in the classroom" (Rosenthal and Jacobson, 1971) is a dramatic example. Teachers were told that certain children would suddenly improve in their school work and indeed they did improve. But how could this happen? What is the mechanism? The authors suggest that the teachers may have noticed achievements of these children and rewarded them more quickly than previously. Therefore, the children learned to achieve more. In other words, the effects of "labelling" are not magical but may be simply the result of expectations which lead to reinforcement and therefore learning of the expected behavior.

This is very similar to the mechanism called "shaping" in the child development literature. It simply means shaping a child's behavior by learning theory principles: reward desired behavior, ignore or punish undesired behavior. Social psychology describes how groups enforce conformity to norms and expectations (Festinger, 1953; Schachter, 1953). Intense communication to persuade a person to conform may be followed by social rejection and isolation of anyone who deviates too far. Stereotypes define what behavior is expected of a female and, therefore, how she will be treated. Inappropriate behavior will usually be ignored, sometimes punished. The feminine stereotype seems to define any active goal-oriented behavior as inappropriate for a female, i.e. she should not be active, skillful, competent, successful, competitive, assertive. If all such behavior is ignored or punished, she is being treated with direct helplessness training (by Seligman's definition): her actions cannot bring rewards.

How Do We Behave Toward Female Children?

Stereotypes aside, are females *treated* differently from males? Maccoby and Jacklin (1974) found very few consistent differences in the way boys and girls are treated. However, one difference they did find was that the actions of boys more often have consequences (rewards or punishments) than do those of girls. For example, one study found that nursery school teachers respond more to boys than to girls for the same actions (Serbin et al., 1973). The actions of the girls were often simply ignored. In another study (Jackson and Lahaderne, 1971), sixth grade teachers were found to interact more with boys than girls, especially on matters not related to instruction.

Studies have not identified consistent differences in treatment of sons and daughters by mothers (Moss, 1967; Clarke-Stewart, 1973). However, fathers apparently do treat them differently, being more task-oriented with sons and socially-oriented with daughters (Block, 1973). Bronfenbrenner (1961) found that each parent was most likely to be active and firm with the child of the same sex, more lenient and indulgent with the opposite-sex child. However, the father's "indulgence" toward his daughter was likely to be combined with anxious overprotectiveness. (See also Block, 1975; Gurwitz and Dodge, 1975). When fathers were more actively involved with their daughters (presumably being "indulgent" but overprotective and restrictive), the daughters scored lower on measures of responsibility and leadership.

Studies show that people see females as in need of being helped and protected (Block, 1975) and that they actually do help them more (Latane and Dabbs, 1975; Unger, 1975). Therefore, females may learn to depend on others and not learn to help themselves, as the "feminine" stereotype suggests. Bronfenbrenner has described the early training of boys and girls as follows: "With sons, socialization seems to focus primarily on directing and constraining the boy's impact on the environment. With daughters, the aim is rather to protect the girl from the impact of environment. The boy is being prepared to mold his world, the girl to be molded by it" (Bronfenbrenner, 1961, p. 260).

Studies show that in many cultures girls are kept close to home, helping with babies and food preparation from a very early age. Boys start responsible behavior later, but when they do, they range farther from home, with very little adult supervision. Girls are more with their mothers; boys are more with peers. There is evidence that this encourages the development of more dependency on people in girls, more self-reliance in boys (Whiting and Whiting, 1975; Barry et al., 1957; Mischel, 1970; Maccoby and Masters, 1970; Hoffman, 1972).

It may also lead to the male advantage in mathematical and spatial ability, which apparently develops during early adolescence (Bing, 1963; Berry, 1966; Maccoby and Jacklin, 1974). This is about the time when girls are expected to stop being "tomboys" and start being "feminine." It is also about the same time that children stop stereotyping school achievement as "feminine" and start stereotyping it as "masculine" (Kagan, 1964; Juhasz, 1974). At the individual level, children who sex-type mathematics as masculine and reading as feminine perform accordingly, even when matched on IQ and liking of the subject (Dwyer, 1974). It has also been found that girls who would prefer to be boys were as high in spatial ability as boys who prefer to be boys. The girls who preferred to be girls (perhaps those who were more accepting of the "feminine" stereotype) were low on spatial ability (Nash, 1975). It is possible that the kinds of childhood experiences most typical for boys (freedom of movement, exploration, experiencing the natural rewards and punishments of the environment) encourage the development of both "self-reliance" and "spatial ability" (Arbuthnot, 1975).

Such childhood experiences may also influence girls to become career women. Career women are likely to have had working mothers, to be autonomous, and to have high mathematical and spatial ability (Astin, 1975). Astin suggested that daughters of working mothers may benefit from "benign neglect." They may be allowed more independence and freedom of movement than daughters of full-time housewives. There is some evidence that they have higher need-achievement (Powell, 1963) and self-reliance (Douvan, 1963). There is no consistent evidence that maternal employment has bad effects on daughters, when the data are controlled for socioeconomic factors and the mothers' reasons for working (Hoffman, 1963a; Burchinal, 1963; Nye et al., 1963; Siegel et al., 1963; Baruch, 1973).

In summary, there is some direct evidence of a sex difference in helplessness training, i.e. that the actions of girls are less likely to have consequences than are the actions of boys. There is also evidence of related concepts. Boys are treated in ways which are likely to lead to competence, self-reliance, and the ability to cope effectively with the world. Girls are more likely to depend on other people and fail to develop important skills.

How Do We Behave Toward Female Adults?

As girls grow up, competence of a certain kind continues to be discouraged. In "fear of success" studies, the subjects are given a short statement describing an incident of success or failure for an imaginary person (most studies have used task-oriented definitions of "success"). The subjects then tell a story about what will happen to the person next. When the imaginary person is female, both male and female subjects predict unpleasant consequences (especially social rejection) following success (Horner, 1968; Winchel et al., 1974; Feather and Raphelson, 1974). When the imaginary person is male, success has mainly good consequences. A study of British girls of high school age (Feather and Simon, 1975) found that unsuccessful females and successful males were rated (by many measures) as much more acceptable people than successful females and unsuccessful males. In another study (Costrich et al., 1975) assertive females and non-assertive males were rated less likeable and more in need of therapy than non-assertive females and assertive males. These studies may demonstrate fear of success or fear of female success or simply the rejection of deviates (Tresemer, 1974, Zanna and Pack, 1975).

Another line of thinking sees female gender as an ascribed low status (Thompson, 1971; Janeway, 1974). The literature on status and its effects can then be applied to sex roles. Unger (1975) has done a thorough analysis of this application, citing evidence of the low status of women. The resultant lack of power is in some ways similar to helplessness. Women talk less than men in group discussions (Alkire et al., 1968); they demand and are given less personal space; and patterns of eye contact and touching reflect their low status (Unger, 1975). Women have less influence in problem solving groups (Wahrman and Pugh, 1974). Even when given the "right answer" by the experimenter, women could not get it accepted by the group. The men still talked more and were more often chosen as leaders (Altemeyer and Jones, 1974). Any attempt to "use power," i.e. influence the group, was seen as "pushy" and did not increase ratings of their competence for women as it did for men (Johnson, 1974). In groups with only one woman, the contributions of women were ignored or punished. Women were not allowed to compete freely for status. They tended to give up their efforts after a while, *becoming depressed instead* (Wolman and Frank, 1975). Women can't even gain status by becoming more competent. Achievement brings punishment along with whatever rewards it may bring.

There is also evidence that the reward value of success is weaker for women than men. In causal attribution studies, subjects are asked to explain the causes of success or failure, either of an imaginary person or of their own performance on a task. These studies as reviewed by Frieze (1975) find that success of females is likely to be attributed to luck or effort, failure to lack of ability (Feather and Simon, 1975). This means that success for a woman is seen as not her personal responsibility, not stable, and not likely to be repeated in the future. Failure is more likely to be seen as personal, stable, and likely to be repeated. Success of men, on the other hand, is more often attributed to ability, failure to bad luck or lack of effort. If men fail, they expect to do better in the future and therefore will keep trying. In other studies (Goldberg, 1968; Lavach and Lanier, 1975), the products and achievements of women were rated as less significant and less valued than those of men, i.e. less reinforcement for the women who produced them. When it comes to actual behavior, women who score high on "fear of success" measures do poorly in competitive tasks (Horner, 1968). In another study, high ability women underachieved in competition with men, regardless of fear of success scores (Morgan and Mausner, 1973).

Women are also faced with less power in their everyday lives. Enough has been written about the low power of women in the political, economic, and occupational sphere so that it does not need to be repeated here. (See for example, Polk, 1974; Terry, 1974; Knudsen, 1969; Astin, 1975; Frymier et al., 1975; Chubin, 1974; Williams et al., 1974; Centra, 1974; HEW National Council for Educational Statistics, 1974; Levitin et al., 1971; Kiesler, 1975; Komisar, 1974; Epstein, 1970; Rosen and Jerdee, 1975; Safilios-Rothschild, 1971; Brandwein et al., 1974; Dion and Earn, 1975; Glass and Singer, 1972; Pendergrass et al., 1976.)

Women have less power in "a man's world," but there is also evidence that they have little power at home, in the "woman's place." In a particularly interesting analysis, Gillespie (1971) suggests that the enormous male advantage in status in society at large makes it very unlikely that women could have equal power in the family (see also Unger, 1975). Research supports this position. Note that the usual criterion of power in the family is influence in decision making, which is likely to be related to control over one's reinforcements.

In any individual marriage, the husband is likely to have higher status than the wife, due to the tradition that a woman should marry a man "she can look up to" (Bernard, 1973). A male advantage in various outside sources of power increases his power in the family. Lack of educational, occupational, and economic opportunities in the outside world makes the wife economically dependent on her husband (Gillespie, 1971; Epstein, 1974) especially if she has children (Bernard, 1975; Gavron, 1966; Heer, 1963; Hoffman, 1963b; Blood and Wolfe, 1960). If the wife is employed, her power is somewhat greater, especially in blue collar families (Blood, 1963; Heer, 1963). As the status of the husband goes up, the power of the wife in the family goes down (Gillespie, 1971; Heer, 1963; Goode, 1963).

Suburbanization, lack of contact with family and friends, and lack of participation in community and social organizations keep a wife isolated and *emotionally* dependent on her husband. Having preschool children increases the isolation (Gavron, 1966; Gillespie, 1971). Early socialization toward dependency on people and "needing love" increases the dependency (Epstein, 1974). It has been shown (Thibaut and Kelley, 1959; Wolfe, 1959) that the person who needs a relationship more has less power in that relationship. Other, more direct sources of power for the husband include the likelihood that both husband and wife have *been socialized to believe* that she is inferior, the legal backing of the patriarchal rights in the marriage contract, and physical violence which is more commonly used or threatened than we like to admit (Gillespie, 1971; Crawford, 1976). Unpleasant life circumstances (such as bad housing, low income, lack of help with housework, lack of safe places for children to play) are particularly hard for an isolated mother to cope with (Gavron, 1966).

In summary, competence in women is seen as a deviation from the behavior expected of them according to their low status and the social norms of the feminine stereotype. Women are not expected to achieve and they sometimes deliberately fail. This may be partly because in the past they have received fewer rewards and more punishments for achievements. If they do try to succeed or exercise power, their accomplishments may be undervalued by themselves and others. Their success is attributed to good luck, so that repeated success is not expected. Social rejection, isolation, and being ignored are often the fruits of a woman's efforts.

WHAT ARE THE MENTAL HEALTH IMPLICATIONS?

There is evidence that females are more likely to learn "helplessness" (by lack of reinforcement of instrumental actions) than males. To the extent that helplessness contributes to depression, it can be seen as a potential mediator of the excess depression experienced by women. It should be noted that there may be more than one kind of depression and helplessness is probably only one factor (among many) which may influence helplessness. Certainly poverty, lack of education, race, and age are likely to affect helplessness in both sexes (Seligman, 1975).

To further test the value of the helplessness hypothesis, it should be possible to predict different levels of depression in different subgroups (of men and women) according to their relative helplessness. Actual measures of helplessness have not yet been applied to this task. However, it is plausible to suggest that certain groups of women are less likely to have internalized the "helplessness" aspects of "femininity"; for example, women who attain advanced education, high status careers, high income, and women who do not marry. These are groups who have relatively low levels of depression (Radloff, 1975). In other words, groups presumed to be low on helplessnesss have been found to be low on depression.

There is some indirect evidence of a link between "helplessness training," "femininity," and mental health at the individual level. Unpredictability in the environment, i.e. "helplessness," has been shown to interfere with healthy child development (Piuck, 1975; Murray, 1975; Murphy, 1972; Caldwell, 1970; Clarke-Stewart, 1973; Bell and Ainsworth, 1972). The feminine pattern of attributing success to luck and failure to lack of ability is related to low self-esteem (which is related to depression) (Frieze, 1975). People who score as "external" on the Rotter scale, i.e. who do *not* see themselves as responsible for their outcomes, are more depressed (Abramowitz, 1969). High scores on "femininity" relate to low self-esteem (Baruch, 1973). Lack of open communication in the family (which may relate to helplessness) is related to depression (Weissman and Paykel, 1974; Warren, 1975; Brown, 1975). There is also preliminary evidence that before adolescence, boys may have more depression (Albert and Beck, in press) and lower self-esteem (Bohan, 1973) than girls, but that the reverse holds after adolescence. The age shift in these mental health measures occurs in the junior high years, as do the age shifts in mathematical and spatial ability and active acceptance of sex roles.

There is some preliminary evidence that the sex difference in depression is a manifestation of an increased *susceptibility* to react with depression, given life problems. In groups with no problems, there may be no sex difference (Brown, 1975; Kedward and Sylph, 1974; Horowitz et al., 1973; Dohrenwend, 1973). However, Beck and Greenberg (1974) suggest that the problems which typically "trigger" depression may be "sex typed." They are related to lack of power to control one's own life and are more likely to be experienced by women. In other words, women may experience more problems *and* be more likely to respond to problems with depression. More research is needed which directly studies why some people react to some life problems with depression and other people react in other ways. Of particular interest would be research which tests the effects of past training in helplessness (as defined behaviorally) on susceptibility to depression, and the role of current helplessness (lack of power to control one's own life) in precipitating episodes of depression.

Finally, what are the implications for treatment and (even more important) for prevention of depression? Analyses of education, child-rearing practices, and the media should take special note of "helplessness training"; remedial programs should encourage contingent reinforcement of instrumental responses. The effects of changes should be evaluated. Beck and Greenberg (1974) said, "a young woman would do well to concentrate on preventing future depression by cultivating habits of self-respect and self-reliance and by leading a balanced life." Can we actually treat and prevent depression by treating and preventing helplessness? Training strategies especially for women are being developed and tested. A woman can learn to be aware of what she wants, to take direct action to get it, and to take credit for her successes. But to avoid helplessness, her environment must cooperate. People must stop punishing her for successful action. They must stop protecting her and doing things for her and start allowing her own actions to have their natural consequences in a natural environment. Treatment and prevention programs should take this into account.

ANNOTATED BIBLIOGRAPHY

Abramowitz, S.I. Locus of control and self-reported depression among college students. *Psychological Reports,* 1969, *25,* 149-150.

A significant correlation was found between depression and Rotter's internal-external scale. Those who do not see themselves as responsible for their outcomes are more depressed.

Alkire, A.A., Collum, M., Kaswan, J., and Love, L. Information exchange and accuracy of verbal communication under social power conditions. *Journal of Personality and Social Psychology,* 1968, *9,* 301-308.

Females talked less than males in both mixed and single-sex discussion groups.

Albert, N. and Beck, A. Incidence of depression in early adolescence: A preliminary study. *Journal of Youth and Adolescence* (in press).

Small samples of seventh and eighth grade boys and girls were tested on the Beck Depression Inventory. Boys were more depressed than girls in seventh grade; boys were less depressed than girls in eighth grade.

Altemeyer, R. and Jones, K. Sexual identity, physical attractiveness and seating position as determinants of influence in discussion groups. *Canadian Journal of Behavior,* 1974, *6,* 357-375.

In a small group problem-solving situation, women had more difficulty in getting a solution accepted by the group regardless of the subject of the problem. Males talked more and were chosen as leaders more often, especially by the women in the group.

Arbuthnot, J. Sex, sex-role identity, and cognitive style. *Perceptual and Motor Skills,* 1975, *41,* 435-440.

Reviews studies of sex differences in "field independence." Discusses whether field independence is related to "masculinity" per se or to rigid sex typing.

Astin, H.S. Women and work. Presented at conference *New Directions for Research on Women,* Madison, Wisconsin, 1975.
Studies find that career women are more autonomous, have more mathematical ability, and are more likely to have had employed mothers. Suggests that working mothers rear their children to be more self-reliant. Perhaps girls who are allowed to explore the environment become autonomous and develop mathematical/spatial ability which increases career options. High ability, low SES males are more likely to go to college than comparable females.

Barry, H., Bacon, M.K., and Child, I.L. A cross-cultural survey of some sex differences in socialization. *Journal of Abnormal and Social Psychology,* 1957, *55,* 327-332.
In many cultures, females are socialized towards nurturance, obedience, and responsibility for household tasks, while males are socialized toward self-reliance and achievement.

Bart, P.B. Unalienating abortion, demystifying depression and restoring rape victims. Presented at American Psychiatric Association, Anaheim, 1975.
Discusses abortion, depression, and rape from a feminist perspective, with emphasis on the role of powerlessness. Suggests that the traditional female role is "depressenogenic" and that Seligman's helplessness model helps to explain the relationship between powerlessness and depression.

Baruch, G.K. Feminine self-esteem, self-ratings of competence, and maternal career commitment. *Journal of Counseling Psychology,* 1973, *20,* 487-488.
Reviews studies which find high "femininity" scores correlated with low self-esteem. Daughters of working mothers have lower self-ratings of competence, but this effect was attributable to those whose mothers worked but preferred not to work.

Beck, A.T. The development of depression: A cognitive model. In R.J. Friedman and M.M. Katz (Eds.), *The psychology of depression: Contemporary theory and research.* Washington, D.C.: V.H. Winston, 1974, pp. 3-27.
Depression is seen as the result of a negative, pessimistic view of the self, the world, and the future. Success experiences improved the self-image and mood of depressed patients.

Beck, A. and Greenberg, R. Cognitive therapy with depressed women. In V. Franks and V. Burtle (Eds.), *Women in therapy.* New York: Brunner/Mazel, 1974, pp. 113-131.
Life events that typically trigger depression tend to be sex-typed. Women might avoid depression by gaining more control over their lives.

Bell, S. and Ainsworth, M. Infant crying and maternal responsiveness. *Child Development,* 1972, *43,* 1171-1190.
If a baby's crying brings immediate response from a caretaker, the baby cries less and develops more "secure attachment patterns" and better communication skills.

Bernard, J. *The future of marriage.* New York: Bantam, 1973.
Reviews studies which show that marriage is better for men than for women. Custom of women "marrying up" means the best women and worst men stay unmarried. Women are trained to be dependent, but get little emotional support from husbands.

Bernard, J. *The future of motherhood.* Baltimore: Penguin, 1975.
Reviews studies of mental health effects of motherhood on mothers.

Bernhagen, L.F. Sexuality, personality and stereotyping. *School Health Review,* 1974, *5,* 23-26.
Project with eighth grade boys and girls revealed their stereotypes of their own sex and the opposite sex.

Berry, J.W. Temne and Eskimo perceptual skills. *International Journal of Psychology,* 1966, *1,* 207-229.
Field dependence is higher in cultures which stress conformity. In cultures with greater sex-role differentiation, females are more field dependent than males.

Bing, E. Effects of child rearing practices on development of differential cognitive abilities. *Child Development,* 1963, *34,* 631-643.
Suggests relationship between verbal ability, help-seeking, and dependence.

Block, J.H. Conceptions of sex role: Some cross-cultural and longitudinal perspectives. *American Psychologist,* 1973, *28,* 512-526.
Sex-role socialization studies show that boys are pressured to behave as agents, doing things and competing. Girls are encouraged to behave in communion with others, talking and being reflective.

Block, J.H. Another look at sex differentiation in the socialization behaviors of mothers and fathers. Presented at conference *New Directions for Research on Women,* Madison, Wisconsin, 1975.
Reviews and reevaluates some studies reviewed in Maccoby and Jacklin. Fathers are more likely than mothers to treat sons and daughters differently.

Blood, R.O. The husband-wife relationship. In F.I. Nye and L.W. Hoffman (Eds.), *The employed mother in America.* Chicago: Rand McNally, 1963, pp. 282-305.
Studies find that the working wife has more power in economic decisions, less in everyday household decisions, than the housewife does.

Blood, R.O. and Wolfe, D.M. *Husbands and wives: The dynamics of married living.* New York: Free Press, 1960.
The wife's power in the family goes down as the number of children goes up and is especially low if there are preschool children.

Bohan, J.S. Age and sex differences in self-concept. *Adolescence,* 1973, *8,* 379-384.
Self-esteem of girls goes down with age; boys fluctuate. By grade ten, boys' self-esteem is significantly higher than girls' self-esteem.

Brandwein, R., Brown, C. and Fox, E. Women and children last: The social situation of divorced mothers and their families. *Journal of Marriage and the Family,* 1974, *36,* 498-514.
A review and analysis of four family functions (economy, authority, housework/child care, and emotional support) which are disrupted by separation/divorce.

Bronfenbrenner, U. Some familial antecedents of responsibility and leadership in adolescents. In L. Petrullo and B. Brass (Eds.), *Leadership and interpersonal behavior.* New York: Holt, Rinehart and Winston, Inc., 1961, pp. 239-271.
In this study of sex differences in socialization, parents were found to be more firm, active and demanding with a child of the same sex as the parent. Responsibility and leadership were highest in boys but lowest in girls with high involvement with the father.

Broverman, I.K., Broverman, D.M. and Clarkson, F.E. Sex role stereotypes and clinical judgments of mental health. *Journal of Consulting and Clinical Psychology,* 1970, *34,* 1-7.

Psychotherapists judged the "healthy adult female" to be more submissive, less independent, less adventurous, more easily influenced, less aggressive, more "excitable in a minor crisis," feelings more easily hurt, more emotional, more conceited about appearance, less objective, more dislike of math and science than the healthy adult and the healthy adult male. To be a healthy adult, a woman must deviate from the stereotype of a healthy female.

Brown, G., Bhrolchain, M.N. and Harris, T. Social class and psychiatric disturbance among women in an urban population. *Sociology,* 1975, *9,* 225-254.

Psychiatric patients have more life events losses and long-term life problems than a sample of "normals." Working class women, especially with preschool children, had more depression *if they had life problems* than middle class women or women without children. A close "confidante" relationship with husband or boyfriend seemed to "protect" from depression, even in the face of life problems. Results are discussed in terms of susceptibility and precipitating factors.

Burchinal, L.G. Personality characteristics of children. In F.I. Nye and L.W. Hoffman (Eds.), *The employed mother in America.* Chicago: Rand McNally, 1963, pp. 106-121.

A variety of measures of personality and adjustment of children showed no relationship to maternal employment, after adjusting for socioeconomic status.

Caldwell, B. The effects of psychosocial deprivation on human development in infancy. *Merrill-Palmer Quarterly,* 1970, *16,* 260-277.

A lack of predictability and stimulation was found in the environment of low socioeconomic children.

Centra, J.A. *Women, men and the doctorate.* Princeton, New Jersey: Educational Testing Service, 1974.

Women with doctorates receive lower income than men, even when matched on qualifications and experience. The pay differential increases with length of experience.

Child, I.L., Potter, E.H., and Levine, E.M. Children's textbooks and personality development. *Psychological Monographs,* 1946, *60,* (Whole No. 279).

Children's readers portray male and female characters in stereotyped ways.

Chubin, D. Sociological manpower and womanpower: Sex differences in career patterns of two cohorts of American doctorate sociologists. *The American Sociologist,* 1974, *9,* 83-92.

Female Ph.D. sociologists are under-represented on faculties of Ph.D. granting schools, even when matched with men for number of publications.

Clarke-Stewart, A. Interactions between mothers and their young children: Characteristics and consequences. *Monographs of the Society for Research in Child Development,* 1973, *38,* 6-7.

No differences were found in maternal behavior due to sex of infant. Contingent response of mother to infant distress signals correlates with other "optimal maternal care" measures and with measures of "competence" of the infant.

Costrich, N., Feinstein, J., Kidder, L., Marecek, J., and Pascale, L. When stereotypes hurt: Three studies of penalties for sex-role reversals. *Journal of Experimental Social Psychology,* 1975, *11,* 520-530.

Three studies found that an aggressive female and a passive male were rated as less liked and more "in need of therapy" than an aggressive male and a passive female. Results are interpreted in terms of social penalties for sex-role deviance.

Crawford, C. Reported in: Women as victims of crime. *Behavior Today,* 1976, *7,* pp. 4-5.
Estimates that wife-beating occurs in 50 percent of marriages.

Dion, K.L. & Earn, B.M. The phenomenology of being a target of prejudice. *Journal of Personality and Social Psychology,* 1975, *32,* 944-950.
Attributing failure to being the target of prejudice led to more negative affect (sadness, anxiety) and stress than did attributing it to other causes.

Dohrenwend, B.S. Social status and stressful life events. *Journal of Personality and Social Psychology,* 1973, *28,* 225-235.
Life events classified as more or less controllable by the person were related to symptoms of psychological distress. For women, uncontrollable events were more closely related to symptoms. For men, both kinds of events were equally related.

Douvan, E. Employment and the adolescent. In F.I. Nye and L.W. Hoffman (Eds.), *The employed mother in America.* Chicago: Rand McNally, 1963, pp. 142-164.
Full or part-time working mothers in the middle-class home and part-time working mothers in the working class home were associated with higher family interaction and child-rearing towards autonomy and self-reliance. The effect was stronger on daughters than sons.

Dwyer, C.A. Influence of children's sex role standards on reading and arithmetic achievement. *Journal of Educational Psychology,* 1974, *66,* 811-816.
Cites studies that showed children think math is masculine and reading is feminine. Children's ratings of sex-appropriateness of the subject is related to their achievement in the subject, especially for boys sixth grade and up.

Epstein, C.F. *Woman's place: Options and limits in professional careers.* Berkeley: University of California Press, 1970.
The proportion of employed women who are married decreases as the status of the job increases. The conflict between career and family responsibilities is discussed.

Epstein, C.F. Changing sex roles: a review of sociological research developments and needs. *Current Sociology,* 1974, Special Conference Number, 283-315.
Economic or role changes (such as divorce) reduce a woman's power over certain areas of her life. Research on current pressures on women, as well as past history is needed. Women are kept out of positions of power and prestige and made economically dependent on men. Women are trained to "need" love more, so that they have less power in a love relationship.

Feather, N. and Raphelson, A. Fear of success in Australian and American student groups: Motive or sex role stereotype? *Journal of Personality,* 1974, *42,* 190-201.
Male subjects gave more "fear of success" responses to female success than to male success, and more than female subjects gave. Males seem to be more conscious of the sex-role stereotype that a female will be punished for success.

Feather, N.T. and Simon, J.G. Reactions to male and female success and failure in sex-linked occupations. *Journal of Personality and Social Psychology,* 1975, *31,* 20-31.

A study of high-school-age girls found successful males and unsuccessful females were rated more acceptable people than successful females and unsuccessful males. Males were seen as being personally responsible for success, females blamed for failure.

Feshbach, N.D. Student teacher preference for elementary school pupils varying in personality characteristics. In M.L. Silberman (Ed.), *The experience of schooling*. New York: Holt, Rinehart, and Winston, 1971, pp. 72-85.

Girls described as rigid and passive were rated by student teachers as more likeable and intelligent than boys so described. Boys described as flexible and assertive were rated more likeable and *much* more intelligent than girls so described.

Festinger, L. Informal social communication. In D. Cartwright and A. Zander, (Eds.), *Group dynamics.* Evanston, Illinois: Row, Peterson and Co., 1953, pp. 190-203.

Presents a theoretical formulation of pressures toward uniformity, communication and rejection of deviates.

Frieze, I., Fisher, J., McHugh, M., and Valle, V. Attributing the causes of success and failure: Internal and external barriers to achievement in women. Presented at conference *New Directions for Research on Women,* Madison, Wisconsin, 1975.

Reviews and interprets causal attribution studies and theory. Females failure to achieve is more often attributed to internal factors than external constraints. Success is attributed to external causes such as luck. This pattern reduces reinforcement of the person's efforts and expectations of future performance. This pattern is correlated with low self-esteem.

Frymier, J., Norris, L., Henning, M., Henning, W., Jr., and West, S. A longitudinal study of academic motivation. *Journal of Educational Research,* 1975, *69,* 63-66.

Women scoring high on an education motivation scale were less likely to go to college than men with equal scores.

Gavron, H. *The captive wife: Conflicts of housebound mothers.* London: Routledge and Paul, 1966.

An intensive observational study of British women found that conflicts were more due to children than to marriage per se. This was especially true in the working class family where play facilities, good housing, and nursery schools were scarce.

Gillespie, D.L. Who had the power? The marital struggle. *Journal of Marriage and the Family,* 1971, *33,* 445-458.

Reviews and reinterprets family power literature. The male's advantage in ten sources of power in the society at large operate to increase his power in the family.

Glass, D.C. and Singer, J.E. *Urban Stress.* New York: Academic Press, 1972.

Arbitrary social discrimination is equivalent to perceived uncontrollability.

Goldberg, P.A. Are women prejudiced against women? *Transaction,* 1968, *5,* 28-30.

Professional articles were rated less significant when attributed to female authors than when attributed to male authors.

Goode, W. *World revolution and family patterns.* New York: The Free Press, 1963.

Well educated men are more egalitarian in ideology than in practice. The importance of the man's career is used to justify his power in the family.

Gurwitz, S.B. and Dodge, K.A. Adults' evaluations of a child as a function of sex of adult and sex of child. *Journal of Personality and Social Psychology,* 1975, *32,* 822-828.
Adult subjects were shown video tapes of a child and told it was either male or female. Female subjects gave a more favorable rating when they thought the child was male and males were more favorable when they thought the child was female.

Hartley, R. and Klein, A. Sex-role concepts among elementary-school-age girls. *Marriage and Family Living,* 1959, *21,* 59-64.
Children's sex role stereotypes were found to be similar to those of adults.

Heer, D.M. Dominance and the working wife. In F.I. Nye and L.W. Hoffman (Eds.), *The employed mother in America.* Chicago: Rand McNally & Co., 1963, pp. 251-262.
Working wives had a greater role in family decision making than nonworking wives. The more children a wife had, the less power she had in the family.

HEW-National Council for Educational Statistics. Washington, D.C., 1974.
Women in university faculty positions earn less and less often hold tenured positions than males.

Hillman, J.S. An analysis of male and female roles in two periods of children's literature. *Journal of Educational Research,* 1974, *68,* 84-88.
A study of literature of the 1930s and 1960s found that main characters are seldom female. When included, female characters are shown as more affiliative and dependent while males are more aggressive and competent, in literature of both periods.

Hoffman, L.W. Effects on children: Summary and discussion. In F.I. Nye and L.W. Hoffman (Eds.), *The employed mother in America.* Chicago: Rand McNally & Co., 1963, pp. 190-212.
Reasons and conditions surrounding the employment of the mother are important in evaluating the effects on children. Male and female children may be affected differently.

Hoffman, L.W. Parental power relations and the division of household tasks. In F.I. Nye and L.W. Hoffman (Eds.), *The employed mother in America.* Chicago: Rand McNally & Co., 1963. Pp. 215-230.
Whether working mothers had more power in the family than matched housewives depended on sex role ideology, income, children, and reasons for working.

Hoffman, L.W. Early childhood experiences and women's achievement motives. *Journal of Social Issues,* 1972, *28,* 129-155.
Reviews literature on socialization. Concludes that girls are not encouraged to become independent. They are "protected" more and explore the environment less than boys and, therefore, continue to be dependent on adults to solve problems.

Horner, M.S. Sex differences in achievement motivation and performance in competitive and non-competitive situations. Unpublished doctoral dissertation, University of Michigan, 1968.
Reports the original "fear of success" studies. Unpleasant consequences of success were predicted for females in TAT stories. Women scoring high on "fear of success" did badly in competitive tasks.

Horowitz, M., Becker, S., and Malone, P. Stress: Different effects on patients and

non-patients. *Journal of Abnormal Psychology,* 1973, *82,* 547-551.
Stress was more disruptive of task performance for psychiatric patients than for "normals."

Jackson, P.W. and Lahaderne, H.M. Inequalities of teacher-pupil contacts. In M.L. Silberman (Ed.), *The experience of schooling.* New York: Holt, Rinehart and Winston, 1971, pp. 123-134.
Sixth grade teachers had more managerial and prohibitory interactions with boys than with girls.

Janeway, E. *Between myth and morning: Women awakening.* New York: Morrow and Co., 1974.
Chapter entitled, "The weak are the second sex." Power, not gender, is primary, but if power is defined as masculine, then nonpowerful males identify with and support powerful males rather than joining with nonpowerful females.

Johnson, P. Social power and sex role stereotypes. Presented at *Western Psychological Association,* San Francisco, 1974.
In group discussions, when women attempted to use power (influence the group), they were rated as "pushy" and not as more competent. Men who used power were seen as more competent than less active men.

Juhasz, A.M. The teacher and sex-role stereotyping. *School Health Review,* 1974, *5,* 17-22.
Excellent review of studies of stereotyping in the environments of children (media, teachers, peers).

Kagan, J. The child's sex-role classification of school objects. *Child Development,* 1964, *35,* 1051-1056.
Elementary school children label school and learning as "feminine."

Kedward, H.B. and Sylph, J. The social correlates of chronic neurotic disorder. *Social Psychiatry,* 1974, *9,* 91-98.
Neurotics were found to have many more practical problems such as illness or unemployment than "normals."

Kiesler, S.B. Actuarial prejudice toward women and its implications. *Journal of Applied Social Psychology,* 1975, *5,* 201-216.
Reviews evidence that as the percent of women in an occupation goes up, the prestige of the occupation goes down. Also, reviews evidence of how expectations and differential attributions affect performance.

Knudsen, D.D. The declining status of women: Popular myths and the failure of functionalist thought. *Social Forces,* 1969, *48,* 183-193.
Census data from 1940 to 1964 show that relative to men, women's occupational, economic, and educational status has declined. Status of both men and women has gone up some since 1940, but men have gone up much more than women.

Komisar, L. Where feminism will lead: An impetus for social change. *Civil Rights Digest,* 1974, Spring, 2-9.
Points out that both the employment and unemployment of women are considered by society as less socially significant than those of men. It is noted that government training programs officially give priority to male over female heads of households.

Latane, B. and Dabbs, J. Sex, group size and helping in three cities. *Sociometry,* 1975, *38,* 180-194.
Females were given more help, especially by males, and especially in the southern city.

Lavach, J.F. and Lanier, H.B. The motive to avoid success in 7th, 8th, 9th and 10th grade high achieving girls. *Journal of Educational Research,* 1975, *68,* 216-218.

Reviews studies showing that both males and females rated males or products of males as more significant than females. Reports "fear of success" study of black and white high achieving females, seventh through tenth grades.

Levitin, T., Quinn, R.P., and Staines, G.L. Sex discrimination against American working women. *American Behavioral Scientist,* 1971, *15,* 237-254.

Females' income was 68 percent that of males', when controlled for qualifications and experience.

Lewinsohn, P.M. A behavioral approach to depression. In R.J. Friedman and M.M. Katz (Eds.), *The psychology of depression: Contemporary theory and research.* Washington, D.C.: V.H. Winston, 1974, pp. 157-178.

Sees depression as due to lack of positive reinforcements.

Lippitt, R. and Gold, M. Classroom social structure as a mental health problem. In M.L. Silberman (Ed.), *The experience of schooling.* New York: Holt, Rinehart, and Winston, 1971, pp. 294-307.

Children were rated on social power by their classmates. Power and liking were found to correlate. Teachers responded most favorably to low status girls and high status boys.

Maccoby, E.E. and Jacklin, C.N. *The psychology of sex differences.* Stanford: Stanford University Press, 1974.

Reviews studies of sex differences in psychological traits. The higher verbal ability of females and mathematical and spatial ability of males does not occur until after age eleven. Studies of socialization processes find that males get more contingent reinforcement than females.

Maccoby, E.E. and Masters, J. Attachment and dependency. In P. Mussen (Ed.), *Carmichael's manual of child psychology,* Vol. 2. New York: Wiley, 1970, pp. 73-157.

Girls are seen as more fragile and in need of help, are helped more, and thus are socialized for dependence. Parents seem to pay more attention to boys' achievement behavior.

McArthur, L.Z. and Resko, B.G. The portrayal of men and women in American TV commercials. *Journal of Social Psychology,* 1975, *97,* 209-220.

Reviews evidence of the effects of television ads on viewers. Women in ads were portrayed as receiving social approval for using the product, while men got status advancement.

Miller, J. Sex roles in TV cartoons. *School Health Review,* 1974, *5,* 35-37.

In TV cartoons, females were portrayed with small, shapely figures and as helpless or upset. The males' physical build was more varied, and males were shown as cool, capable of handling situations, and assumed to be right unless proven otherwise.

Mischel, W. Sex-typing and socialization. In P. Mussen (Ed.), *Carmichael's Manual of Child Psychology,* Vol. 2, New York: Wiley, 1970, pp. 3-72.

Supports the view that females are socialized for dependence, males for achievement and autonomy.

Morgan, S.W. and Mausner, B. Behavioral and fantasied indicators of avoidance of success in men and women. *Journal of Personality,* 1973, *41,* 457-470.

Women underachieved in competition with men, regardless of "fear of success" scores. The females who did *not* underachieve had better educated parents but seemed tense during the task.

Mosher, E.H. Portrayal of women in drug advertising: A medical betrayal. *Journal of Drug Issues,* 1976, *6,* 72-78.
Sex role stereotyping was found to be prevalent in drug advertising. This reinforcement of stereotypes may lead to misuse of drugs by doctors.

Moss, H. Sex, age and state as determinants of mother-infant interaction. *Merrill-Palmer Quarterly,* 1967, *13,* 19-36.
Mothers reacted more contingently to girls than to boys. Suggests this produces more need for social attention and approval in girls.

Murphy, L.B. Infant's play and cognitive development. In M.W. Piers (Ed.), *Play and development.* New York: Norton, 1972, pp. 119-126.
Children raised in extreme poverty show different cognitive patterns in play. This may be because the people in the environment do not respond to the child's actions. The child does not learn that his actions can bring pleasant results.

Murray, A.D. Maternal employment reconsidered: Effects on infants. *American Journal of Orthopsychiatry,* 1975, *45,* 773-790.
Studies indicate that infants' emotional development is dependent on contingency of response to the infant's behavior.

Nash, S.C. The relationship between sex-role stereotyping, sex-role preference and the sex difference in spatial visualization. *Sex Roles: A Journal of Research,* 1975, *1,* 15-32.
Sixth and ninth grade girls who preferred to be boys were as high on spatial ability as boys who preferred to be boys.

Nye, F.I., Perry, J.B. and Ogles, R.H. Anxiety and antisocial behavior in preschool children. In F.I. Nye and L.W. Hoffman (Eds.), *The employed mother in America.* Chicago: Rand McNally & Co., 1963, pp. 82-94.
Children of matched working and nonworking mothers did not differ on a variety of negative characteristics, e.g. psychosomatic symptoms, antisocial behavior, withdrawal.

Pendergrass, V., Kimmel, E., Joesting, J., Petersen, J., Bush, E. Sex discrimination counseling. *American Psychologist,* 1976, *31,* 36-46.
Reports a case study of a sex discrimination suit. Anger, isolation, and emotional distress accompany awareness of and the fight against discrimination.

Piuck, C.L. Child-rearing patterns of poverty. *American Journal of Psychotherapy,* 1975, *29,* 485-502.
Childrearing practices may mediate the relationship between poverty, low achievement, and mental illness. Harsh unpredictable punishment may reduce the child's development of inner controls and communication skills.

Polk, B.B. Male power and the women's movement. *Journal of Applied Behavioral Science,* 1974, *10,* 415-431.
Sources of male power include norms (sex-role stereotypes), status, expertise, brute force, and control of options and reinforcers.

Powell, K.S. Personalities of children and childrearing attitudes of mothers. In F.I. Nye and L.W. Hoffman (Eds.), *The employed mother in America.* Chicago: Rand McNally & Co., 1963, pp. 125-132.
Children of working mothers were higher on need achievement. No signifi-

cant relationship was found between work and childrearing attitudes of mothers.

Radloff, L.S. Sex differences in depression: The effects of occupation and marital status. *Sex Roles,* 1975, *1,* 249-265.

Married women are consistently more depressed than married men of comparable age, education, income and number of children. Working wives are not consistently less depressed than housewives.

Rosen, B. and Jerdee, T.H. Reported in: The corporate double standard. *Human Behavior,* 1975, 47-48.

Questionnaires answered by business managers reveal attitudes and expectations which would make it easier for men than women to combine professional, social, and family lives.

Rosenthal, R. and Jacobson, L. Pygmalion in the classroom—An excerpt. In M.L. Silberman (Ed.), *The experience of schooling.* New York: Holt, Rinehart, and Winston, 1971, pp. 107-117.

Children's performance was greatly influenced by the expectations and attitudes of teachers.

Rubin, J.Z., Provenzano, F.J., and Luria, Z. The eye of the beholder: Parents views on sex of newborns. *American Journal of Orthopsychiatry,* 1974, *44,* 512-519.

Parents, especially fathers, see newborn infants in stereotyped ways. Girls were described as smaller, softer, finer features than boys, although they were equal on length, weight, and health indices. Reviews studies which show fathers see daughters as weaker and more in need of nurturance than sons.

Safilios-Rothschild, C. Cross-cultural examination of women's marital, educational and occupational options. *Acta Sociologica,* 1971, *14,* 96-112.

Women have more educational and vocational options in countries of mid-level development. The U.S. is among the most restrictive countries, perhaps because of the tradition that the mother has exclusive responsibility for child care.

Schachter, S. Deviation, rejection and communication. In D. Cartwright and A. Zander (Eds.), *Group dynamics.* Evanston, Illinois: Row Peterson and Co., 1953, pp. 223-248.

Experimental verification of theories of pressures to uniformity, communication, and rejection of the deviate.

Seligman, M.E.P. *Helplessness: On depression, development and death.* San Francisco: W.H. Freeman, 1975.

Reviews evidence for the impact of helplessness in depression. Discusses helplessness component in "risk factors" for depression, such as age, income, and race.

Serbin, L.A., O'Leary, K.D., Kent, R.N., and Tonick, I.J. A comparison of teacher response to the preacademic and problem behavior of boys and girls. *Child Development,* 1973, *44,* 796-804.

In this study of preschools, teachers' interactions with and discipline of boys and girls were very different. Overall, the teachers were much less likely to react to a girl's behavior, whether appropriate or not, thus teaching girls that their actions have little effect on their environment.

Shirreffs, J.H. Sex-role stereotyping in elementary school health education textbooks. *Journal of School Health,* 1975, *XLV,* 519-523.

Textbooks analyzed put much stress on male athletics and portrayed stereotypic play activities and chores.

Siegel, A.E., Stolz, L.M., Hitchcock, E.A., and Adamson, J. Dependence and independence in children. In F.I. Nye and L.W. Hoffman (Eds.), *The employed mother in America.* Chicago: Rand McNally & Co., 1963, pp. 67-81.
Dependence and independence were observed in kindergarten children of working and nonworking mothers. Sex differences were found, as well as some indication that boys and girls reacted differently to working mothers.

Smith, L.C. Women: Target of the mood-altering drug industry. *Sociological Research Symposium IV,* 1974, 901-911.
Reviews evidence that mood-altering drugs are prescribed more for women. The advertising of these drugs portrays very stereotyped pictures of women as depressed, weak, and unable to cope.

Stemple, D. and Tyler, J.E. Sexism in advertising. *The American Journal of Psychoanalysis,* 1974, *34,* 271-273.
Looks at the changing roles of women as depicted in magazine ads over the years. The current "liberated" woman is still portrayed as a sex object, amusing herself until marriage.

Sternglanz, S.H. and Serbin, L.A. Sex role stereotyping in children's television programs. *Developmental Psychology,* 1974, *10,* 710-715.
Females comprised only one fourth of major TV roles, most of which were in a love or family context. Men were more often shown as aggressive and constructive and received more positive reinforcement for acts. Females were more apt to receive no consequences at all.

Symonds, A. The myth of femininity: A panel. *American Journal of Psychoanalysis,* 1973, *33,* 42-65.
Suggests that submissiveness, fear of self-assertion, being a follower rather than an initiator, and other behaviors our culture calls feminine result from the "dependent solution" (Horney) accepted by girls.

Tavris, C. It's tough to nip sexism in the bud. *Psychology Today,* 1975, *9,* 58.
Report of Guttentag's program to train children to abandon stereotypes. Pretests showed that by age five, most children have adopted stereotypes very strongly. After the program, the boys tested as *more* sexist and the girls less so, compared with the pretest.

Terry, R. The white male club. *Civil Rights Digest,* 1974, *Spring,* 66-77.
Points out how within a racist/sexist power structure, white males are able to control important decisions by the control of economic, political, and technocratic resources. Cites evidence that white males do control resources.

Thibaut, J.W. and Kelley, H.H. *The social psychology of groups.* New York: Wiley, 1959.
Review of theory and data of the behavior of people in small groups, including attraction to the group as a source of power.

Thompson, C. . . . In M. Green (Ed.), *On women. New York:* Basic Books, 1971.
Points out that certain characteristics attributed to women are actually attributes found in any oppressed people deprived of direct expression of hostility.

Tresemer, D. Fear of success: Popular, but unproven. *Psychology Today,* 1974, *7,* 82-85.

Reviews "fear of success" studies. Questions the coding procedures and definition of "success." Suggests the point may not be fear of success but fear of "sex-role deviance."

Tuddenhan, R.D., Brooks, J., and Milkovich, L. Mothers' reports of behavior of ten year-olds: Relationships with sex, ethnicity, and mother's education. *Developmental Psychology,* 1974, *10,* 959-995.

Compares six studies of reports of mothers on behavior of ten-year olds. Sex differences found are in line with stereotypes of active, assertive boys and passive, submissive girls.

Unger, R.K. Status, power and gender: An examination of parallelisms. Presented at conference *New Direction for Research on Women,* Madison, Wisconsin, 1975.

Reviews theory and evidence of gender as status. Males are more powerful due to ascribed status. For men, failure is deviant; for women, success is deviant. Points out the barriers to changing this pattern.

Wahrman, R. and Pugh, M.D. Sex, non-conformity and influence. *Sociometry,* 1974, *37,* 137-147.

Competent nonconforming females have less influence and are more disliked than incompetent nonconforming males.

Warren, R. Primary support systems and the blue collar working woman. Presented at *Conference on New Research on Women II,* Ann Arbor, Michigan, 1975.

Blue collar husbands got more emotional support from their wives than the wives did from their husbands and the wives were more depressed.

Weissman, M.M. and Klerman, G.L. Sex differences and the epidemiology of depression. *Archives of General Psychiatry.* In press.

Review of evidence confirms that there is more depression among women than men, and that at least part of the difference is likely to be due to social roles.

Weissman, M.M. and Paykel, E.S. *The depressed woman.* Chicago: The University of Chicago Press, 1974.

The social functioning of depressed women was compared with matched "normal" controls. The depressed women had more interpersonal friction and inhibited communication, even after recovery from acute depressive symptoms.

Whiting, B.B. and Whiting, J.W.M. *Children of six cultures: A psychocultural analysis.* Cambridge, Massachusetts: Harvard University Press, 1975.

In many cultures, girls start helping the mothers at home very young. Boys begin responsible behaviors at a later age and then range farther from home with less adult supervision. This would encourage dependency in girls and self-reliance in boys.

Williams, M., Ho, L., and Fielder, L. Career patterns: More grist for women's liberation. *Social Work,* 1974, *July,* 463-466.

Reports well designed study of social workers. Women earn a lower salary than men even when controlled for qualifications, experience, and more subtle factors such as mobility and family responsibilities. Single as well as married women earn less than men.

Winchel, R., Fenner, D. and Shaver, P. Impact of coeducation on "Fear of Success" imagery expressed by male and female high school students. *Journal of Educational Psychology,* 1974, *66,* 726-730.

"Fear of success," i.e. social rejection predicted for successful females, was found in high school students. It was higher in female students in coed schools than in all-girl schools.

Wolfe, D.M. Power and authority in the family. In D. Cartwright (Ed.) *Studies in social power.* Ann Arbor: University of Michigan Press, 1959, pp. 99-117.
Study showed that as the wife's "need for love" increases, the husband's power in the relationship increases.

Wolman, C. and Frank, H. The solo woman in a professional peer group. *American Journal of Orthopsychiatry,* 1975, *45,* 164-171.
Women in otherwise all male groups of peers became isolates or deviants. Their attempts to influence the group were ignored and/or rejected. They finally gave up and became depressed.

Zanna, M.P. and Pack, S.I. On the self-fulfilling nature of apparent sex differences in behavior. *Journal of Experimental Social Psychology,* 1975, *11,* 583-591.
Studies find "conformity" to be more common in women than men. Suggests that this indicates that both men and women are *conforming* to the sex role stereotype.

Chapter 13

REPORT OF THE TASK FORCE ON SEX BIAS AND SEX-ROLE STEREOTYPING IN PSYCHOTHERAPEUTIC PRACTICE*

IN JULY 1974, responding to requests by the APA Committee on Women in Psychology, the Board of Professional Affairs established a task force to (a) examine the extent and manner of sex bias and sex-role stereotyping in psychotherapeutic practice as they directly affect women as students, practitioners, and consumers; (b) recommend actions both within the formal structure of APA and to psychotherapists generally to reduce sex bias and sex-role stereotyping in psychotherapy; and (c) develop materials and methods of dissemination of relevant information to members of the APA and to related professionals and institutions providing psychotherapeutic services.

There are two problems central to sexism in psychotherapeutic practice with women: (a) the question of values in psychotherapy and (b) the therapist's knowledge of psychological processes in women.

At a minimum, the therapist must be aware of ter[1] own values and not impose them on the patient. Beyond that, tey has a responsibility for evaluating the mental health implications of those values. That psychologists expect women to be more passive and dependent than

*Task Force members included Annette Brodsky and Jean Holroyd, Cochairs, plus Carolyn Payton, Eli Rubinstein, Paul Rosenkrantz, Julia Sherman, and Freyda Zell. Tena Cummings was an ex-officio participant, and Carolyn Suber was APA staff liaison: Julia Sherman was responsible for the review of literature, and the initial data analysis was voluntarily donated by Gayle Janzen of the University of Alabama, and Susan Pirhalla of Bryce State Hospital, Tuscaloosa, Alabama.

This study was authorized by the Board of Professional Affairs (BPA) of the American Psychological Association as an issue of sufficient concern to psychology at large to merit study; however, the report does not necessarily reflect the views of BPA or APA in general.

[1]Tey = he/she; ter = his/her; and tem = him/her. These neuter gender pronouns are substituted for the generic *he* throughout this report in order to raise the consciousness of the reader to the sexist effect of the structure of the English language.

men while acknowledging that these traits are not ideal for mental health has been empirically demonstrated (Broverman, Broverman, Clarkson, Rosenkrantz, & Vogel, 1970; Broverman, Vogel, Broverman, Clarkson, & Rosenkrantz, 1972; Fabrikant, 1974; Neulinger, Schillinger, Stein, & Welkowitz, 1970; Aslin, 1974).

The therapist must also be aware of the ways in which conventional beliefs have biased theory, scientific research, and psychological assumptions (Levenson, 1972; Bernard, 1972). Tey will need to reevaluate theories about women, especially those theories of Freud.

Because female topics and females as subjects for research have been neglected (Carlson & Carlson, 1960; Schwabacher, 1972), therapists may find that they are ignorant of important aspects of female psychology. The female patient, for example, may be struggling with her fear of success (Horner, 1972), yet the therapist may be totally unaware of the conflict. Seduction by her father may be overlooked because the therapist is fixated on Freud's Oedipal theory of the child as the source of the sexual impulse. Psychosomatic reactions such as "frigidity," infertility, spontaneous abortion, or amenorrhea may be seen as pathological without awareness of the protective, constructive features of these reactions. Uninformed or misinformed, the therapist may mishandle questions of emotional changes accompanying the menstrual cycle, pregnancy, childbirth, and menopause.

The whole question of "masculinity," "femininity," and adaptation to sex role has been rife with unexamined value problems as well as conceptual and empirical difficulties (Constantinople, 1973; Sherman, 1971). For example, a woman may be told that she is "too aggressive" when her deficit in social skills is the result of anxiety about self-assertion. The psychological problems of "masculine" women have been found to relate more to the inconsistent quality of their "masculinity," that is, unadaptive "feminine" traits, than to their masculinity (Sherman, 1971). Rather than reporting a difficult transition for masculine women in middle age, Bart (1972) found that it was the excessively feminine woman who encountered trouble.

Biased treatment may occur differently for special groups of women, though little data are available. Intelligent women may have their intelligence unrecognized or in some manner discounted. There are certain prejudices about lower-class women. For example, a lower-class female client (bogus description) was seen by therapists as less self-confident, less well liked, less independent, less assertive, more conforming and submissive to authority, and less permissive and democratic with respect to the family than a middle-class female client (Briar, 1961).

Black women are caught in a double bind. Swartz and Abramowitz (1974) found that white psychiatrists viewed black patients, especially female ones, as having a better prognosis than white patients. The authors suggest that the psychiatrists may attribute the psychopathology to external rather than internal sources, and therefore assign a better prognosis. The stereotyped attribution of inner strength to the black woman, sometimes exaggerated into a matriarchal and/or castrating caricature, is experienced by black women as a cruel farce and gross misinterpretation of their family role (Carkhuff, 1972; Chesler, 1972; Hare & Hare, 1972; Hernandez, 1974).

Lesbians are likely to be labeled as emotionally disturbed and to encounter the belief that a good heterosexual experience will solve their problems. Even fairly knowledgeable, well-intentioned therapists may find that their helpfulness is limited by a lack of knowledge of such experiences as "coming out" and the nuances of the social interactions of the gay and bisexual communities in the nexus with straight society (Chesler, 1972; Reiss, 1974).

Because most therapists are male and most patients are female, the problem of handling sexual attraction and sexual intimacy is of special concern. Many therapists are unprepared to handle these problems skillfully, thus contributing to antitherapeutic results, unnecessary marital discord, and even divorce. The most dramatic aspect of this problem is when a male therapist has sexual relations with his female patient. The percentage of therapists engaging in sexual relations with their patients is unknown but believed to be small (Kardener, Fuller, & Mensh, 1973). However, numbers do not reflect the salience of the problem or the bitterness of many women who have had sexual relations with their therapists. Sexual relations between patient and therapist reflect sex bias in at least three ways: (a) Nearly all complaints are from women patients regarding male therapists; (b) stereotypic feminine qualities, especially passive dependence, are exploited (Belote, 1974); and (c) the male therapist has considerably more power in the therapy situation than the female patient, a classic situation for the operation of sexual politics. In addition to the sex-bias consideration, sexual intimacy makes it difficult if not impossible for the therapist to remain objective and to conduct the course of therapy in a manner beneficial to the patient's interests.

The question has been raised as to whether sex between a female patient and male therapist can be assumed to be harmful. In one study, 25 women who had sexual relations with their therapists reported that they were nonorgasmic both before and after therapy with all men, including their therapists (Belote, 1974). Thus far, the literature review has failed to reveal even anecdotal cases in which sex with the therapist was reported as beneficial.

Some may argue that intercourse between a therapist and a patient that does not involve force or deceit is a private matter. The question of deceit is central because patients assume that therapists will act in the patient's best interests. However, the position that women who enter therapy are fully responsible for their behavior would at least require that we educate the female public so they may choose the kind of relationship they wish to pay for before a transference relationship obscures their objectivity.

Good process studies of sex bias and sex-role stereotyping during the therapy hour are lacking, but studies of clinical judgment are suggestive. Although two recent studies have found clinical judgments of women generally no different from those of men, in one of the studies the more conservative examiners found left-of-center political deviancy more indicative of maladjustment when the purported patient was female than male (Abramowitz, Abramowitz, Jackson & Gomes, 1973; Swartz & Abramowitz, 1974). Of course, left-of-center deviance is particularly associated with feminism. There is some evidence, too, that female therapists may be freer of bias, though findings are contradictory on this point (Delk & Ryan, 1975; Fabrikant, 1974; Aslin, 1974; Abramowitz & Dokecki, 1974).

Some indications of differential treatment were found by Fabrikant (1974), who reported that female patients were in therapy more than twice as long as male patients. Fabrikant concluded that "the overall results most strongly support the feminist viewpoint that females in therapy are victimized by a social structure and therapeutic philosophy that keeps them dependent for as long as possible" (p. 96).

Fabrikant also measured patients' perceptions of therapists' attitudes. Female patients perceived that therapists believe husbands should dominate the marital relationship, and both male and female patients perceived that therapists have a double standard of sexual behavior. While both male therapists and male patients agreed that the majority of women can be fulfilled by the wife-mother role and thought abortion should be a joint marital decision, neither female therapists nor female patients agreed with these views. Whether or not a patient perceives ter therapist's views correctly, these findings raise the question of whether a therapist may need to make ter values explicit in areas of rapidly changing social values.

Some additional insight into sex-biased and sex-role-stereotyped therapy can be gained by contrasting it with feminist therapy (Barrett, Berg, Eaton, & Pomeroy, 1974; Brodsky, 1973; Kirsch, 1974; Rice & Rice, 1973; Tennov, 1973). Hannah Lerman (1974) characterizes feminist therapy as distinctly nonauthoritarian and claims that it denies the philosophical position of being an expert about the client. The personal is viewed as political, and the client must learn to differentiate between what are *her* problems and what are society's problems, what behaviors are considered socially appropriate and what may be appropriate for her. She is taught to be self-nurturing, is freed from the indiscriminate nurturing of others, and is shown that normal self-interest need not be viewed as "selfishness." Interestingly, making clients into feminists is not a goal of treatment, but rather helping them "'become the best person they can, within the limits of their personal circumstances and the patterns of society in general" (Lerman, 1974).

Research that explicitly addresses the issues of sex bias and sex-role stereotyping in therapy is in its infancy. As a first step, and until more empirical data are amassed, the Task Force attempted to identify concerns of female consumers and practitioners as gleaned from their own experiences.

A SURVEY OF WOMEN PSYCHOLOGISTS

An open-ended questionnaire was developed to elicit descriptions of incidents or circumstances that were perceived as indicative of sex bias or sex-role stereotyping in psychotherapy with women. The questionnaire was mailed to 2,000 women in APA Divisions 12, 17, 29, and 35[2] with the assumption that they had experience both as consumers and practitioners of psychotherapy and had a vested interest in responding in numbers.

Three hundred and twenty replies were received and categorized by themes involving issues of sexism affecting women as clients in psychotherapy.

Four general areas of perceived sex bias and sex-role stereotyping affecting women as clients of psychotherapy emerged: (a) fostering traditional sex roles; (b) bias in expectations and devaluations of women; (c) sexist use of psychoanalytic concepts; and (d) responding to women as sex objects, including seduction of female clients. The themes within these areas and selected verbatim responses are presented to illuminate the issues.

Fostering of Traditional Sex Role

Theme: The Therapist Assumes That Problem Resolution and Self-actualization for Women Come from Marriage or Perfecting the Role of Wife

"My therapist suggested that my identity problems would be solved by my marrying and having children; I was 19 at the time and in no way ready for marriage. This stereotypic solution was unfortunately typical of the kind of response I later heard from my patients about their experiences with male therapists."

---

[2]Division 12 = Clinical Psychology; 17 = Counseling Psychology; 29 = Psychotherapy; 35 = Psychology of Women.

"My woman therapist pushed for 'adjustment of my marital problems' —exploration of major changes was quite hard—the message was 'stay in the marriage.' My male therapist teases 'Just like a woman'—claims awareness, professes he will (should) stop it—and does not."

"As a state hospital intern, I was appalled at the treatment given women—usually 'go home and do more of what a wife should do—clean house, etc.'—live lives of a kind that sent them to the hospital in the first place."

Theme: The Therapist Lacks Awareness and Sensitivity to the Woman Client's Career, Work, and Role Diversity

"I know of a therapist, seeing a married couple, who asked questions about the husband's work, then went on to other matters and never found out that the wife was an eminent biologist."

"Spent six years in psychoanalysis. My major problem then as now, that is, the major source of my anxiety, was my sense of self-worth as a psychologist. I want to do a good job and enjoy status, prestige, money, etc., that comes from being a productive worker. Situational factors which thwart these ends such as sex discrimination are thus highly threatening and frustrating. In spite of the fact that my dreams, associations, day-to-day crises were job centered, my analyst never did accept this. It seemed impossible to him that a woman could place such high value on her competence, creativity, achievement. He considered my occupation a pesky, irrelevant resistance used to avoid facing early memories, 'basic identity' problems, etc. 'When are you going to quit talking about your job so that we can get down to the real trouble?' "

"Although I was encouraged to pursue my interests, I was at the same time made to feel less than adequate as a female because of my dissatisfaction with the role of 'homemaker.' The traditional role of a woman with respect to her husband and children was one I felt I had to deal with simultaneously with my career. I was never helped to see that there were viable alternatives."

Theme: The Female Client's Attitude toward Childbearing and Childrearing is Viewed as a Necessary Index of Her Emotional Maturity

"My femininity was 'questioned' by a male therapist colleague when I disagreed with him over marital and child-rearing principles."

"My therapist, who was also a woman, argued strongly for me to have a child and not get my tubes tied. She finally conceded that maybe for me it was not necessary to have a child in order to be fulfilled as a woman."

Theme: In Family Therapy or Treatment of Children, the Therapist Supports the Idea That Childrearing and Thus the Child's Problems Are Solely the Responsibility of the Mother

"Many of my friends have reported experiences . . . [in which] it will be the mother who is brought into therapy with the implication that it is her responsibility more than the responsibility of the father for whatever difficulties the child may be having . . . current practice tends to imply that the 'blame' for a child's problems is attributable primarily to the mother."

"Frequently the woman is scapegoated in family therapy. Implicit or explicit therapeutic goal often is strengthening husband's power in family constellation and weakening woman's power in family. Woman is 'controlling' whereas man is 'strong.' "

"A family therapy case—[juvenile delinquent] daughter, father a trained carpenter who had not sought employment for five years. Mother had gone out and gotten a job and had supported the family for most of that time. Interpretation—girl was disturbed because of sex-role reversal of family—father was exhorted to seek a job, which he did, and mother then described as hostile and castrating because she didn't quit her job."

Theme: The Therapist Defers to the Husband's Needs in the Conduct of the Wife's Treatment

"Female psychiatrist asked me if I had my husband's agreement for me to see therapist twice a week. (I earn more money than he and am capable of making that decision with or without his agreement.)"

"I shouldn't work, I shouldn't go to school, all the problems in the marriage were mine. . . . I was not supposed to get angry or hurt my husband's feelings—In the meantime he was (always in private) threatening to kill my youngest kid—wouldn't have done it but plenty of things he did do. . . . First time I've ever mentioned it except to my female analyst—and still feel like I'm quite crazy for even putting it down on paper and no one will believe it."

"I have had several women patients in therapy who complained that male therapists didn't understand them. One example was a woman whose alcoholic husband would leave the house for several days each time she disagreed with him. The male therapist told her that she was being too assertive, trying to be too dominant, and rejecting her role as a woman."

Bias in Expectations and Devaluation of Woman

Theme: The therapist or colleague denies the adaptive and self-actualizing potential or assertiveness for female clients and fosters concepts of women as passive and dependent

"I was in psychoanalytic therapy and was constantly reminded the man should run the home . . . that women were naturally bitchy and need to be controlled."

"Three of the male psychologists . . . actually encouraged the client to continue to be 'docile'—'passive'—'seductive'—'nonassertive'—and to stay in professions 'open to women.' "

"Whenever a female becomes active, assertive, and aggressive in group situations the label 'castrating bitch' is applied to her.

Theme: The Therapist Uses the Theoretical, e.g. Masochism, to Ignore or Condone Violence Toward and Victimization of Women

"Though my husband . . . was beating me periodically and we were in joint marital therapy with a well-known psychologist, he never questioned, probed, or interpreted the acting out behavior. What passed for humanistic nonintervention therapy actually seemed to cover implicit acceptance of 'lots of women are slapped around by their husbands in our society so it's nothing to be concerned with.' "

"A psychoanalytically oriented male therapist, with some agreement from some of the other males [therapists], insisted that there was no such thing as rape—that the woman always 'asked' for it in some way."

"My co-therapist [male] and the male patients [in a psychoanalytically oriented group] made it clear that they assumed a woman patient had encouraged an unknown male to attempt to rape her. This was within one-half hour of the actual incident. The woman patient was extremely frightened and upset. Myself [female therapist] and other female patients saw the incident as potentially dangerous to the woman and having occurred without seductive motivation on the part of the patient. The male therapist interpreted my support . . . and view . . . as penis envy."

Theme: Sexist Jokes and Off-hand Comments by the Therapist Have the Effect of Demeaning Women

"If one assumes that how a male clinician talks about women and 'women's lib' at parties reveals something of what happens in the office, we've got a *really* pervasive problem here!"

"In a recent staff conference to discuss the direction of therapy, I found my colleagues [male] chuckling over their decision that all a client needed was a 'good man' banging her once in awhile. When I disagreed, one psychologist said, "Don't give us any more of that liberation crap.' "

"One of my major professors once bragged in my presence about how he had ridiculed a patient about her anxiety over her sexual functioning and then he made comments on her qualities as a sex object. I was more shocked than angry at the time, for this man had written several books about the importance of honest, mutually respectful communication. To this day I have no respect for him."

Theme: The Therapist Employs Inaccurate or Demeaning Labels (Seductive, Manipulative, Histrionic, etc.) When Describing Female Clients

"I have merely noticed a tendency in psychiatry to apply the label 'histrionic' and 'manipulative' but especially 'seductive' much more frequently to women than to men patients—even when I personally have seen no clear evidence to justify the label."

"A tendency among male therapists to attribute the anxiety of female patients stereotyping the women as 'hysterical' and feeling very derogatory to them. Accompanied by frequent discussion of female patients 'being controlling' of the therapist. Male therapists seldom talk about male patients being 'controlling.' If a woman is assertive this is viewed as a negative."

"Disparaging attitudes about 'hysterical' women and depressed women. Somehow, it's the idea that it's a woman with these symptoms who is obnoxious and unpleasant to treat. Taught that female psychiatric wards are more dangerous than male wards."

Sexist Use of Psychoanalytic Concepts

Theme: The Therapist Insists on Freudian Interpretations

"I underwent psychoanalysis because I was told that all psychologists should have the experience, and I was very Freudian at the time. After eight months of the effort, I began to realize that I was tailoring my responses to fit the Freudian concept of the female . . . and I realized that all of this had nothing to do with ME—either as an individual or a woman."

"I picked my therapist very carefully with regards to attitudes toward women, but his Freudian "transference" training is a real problem. He feels this aspect of the therapy is not moving along quickly enough. I know if I say, 'You're nice and you help me but you're twice my age and just *don't* turn me on,' he'd say I was resisting. I don't think I can win!"

"In my own therapy with a male analyst, I often felt that interpretations were consistent with his value—that a woman *is* dependent, frightened, irrational. Particularly in the area of childrearing—his attitude was that he as a psychiatrist could better evaluate my infant's needs than I myself. . . . Dream occurring prior to first pregnancy (A kitten jumped on a table on which was standing a glass of milk). Despite my report of pleasant surprise as the major affect in the dream, the psychiatrist's interpretations focused on conflict over nursing a baby, fright, in the face of a dangerous and unpredictable animal."

Theme: The Therapist Maintains That Vaginal Orgasm is a Prerequisite for Emotional Maturity and Thus a Goal of Therapy

"I was told the need to have clitoral stimulation stuck out like a sore thumb in an otherwise well-integrated, feminine person."

"Surprisingly many colleagues (male and female) still define maturity in women as the capacity for vaginal orgasm. My feeling is that women who do not experience or report this are seen (and therefore subtly treated) as emotionally limited."

"Inordinately prolonged treatment aimed at achieving vaginal orgasm and contentment with motherhood as therapeutic goals (in the mind of the male therapist), with consubsequent guilt and frustration."

Theme: The Therapist Labels Assertiveness and Ambition with the Freudian Concept of "Penis Envy"

"Friends of mine in treatment experience the frustrations associated with therapists who interpret frustrations arising from the very real inequities that exist in our society as being nothing more than male envy or penis envy on the part of the female patient."

"Everything was interpreted in terms of penis envy and my wanting to sleep with my father. My problems would decrease if only I would submit to the 'male' society."

"I had a classical analysis '61–66, four times per week. . . . I could write for hours on this: The interpretation of penis envy, questions regarding feeling that I was, in fact, a penis—honestly—when I reported my rapture on first standing on my toes in dancing as a child, 'difficulties' accepting the 'female' role, questioning me why I identified with male heroes primarily (although I pointed out that research indicated that women with female heroes were reported to have problems), implicit encouragement that now that I was divorced . . . that I should look for another man, etc."

Responding to Women as Sex Objects Including Seduction of Female Clients

Theme: The Therapist Seduces the Client

"I know of many abuses of women patients–hasty 'termination' in order to have an affair with the patient, sexual seduction represented as "therapeutic,' with disastrous consequences."

"In my years as a psychotherapist, many women have come to me with stories of seduction and sexual intimacies with male therapists. In most instances the patients were deeply disturbed by these relationships, saw them as exploitative (although sometimes they justified the therapists' role and protected them) and sometimes resulted in psychotic breaks. This is the ultimate of sex-role bias: the rationalization of the therapist that his exploitation of the doctor-patient relationship for his gratification could be construed as therapeutic 'for a woman.' "

"Sorry to say it, but I know of too many cases of actual seduction of female clients by their male therapists usually justified by the view that frigidity is a fate worse than death which can be 'cured' by the 'right male' (the therapist). I know of *no* cases of young impotent males whose female therapists take the same stance. Also there is the tendency to think of lesbians not as a sexual choice but as inevitably 'sick' . . . I know personally of two women (now both therapists themselves) who were seduced (one case) or propositioned (the other) by [name of therapist]. I have no reason to disbelieve their stories, but despite the anger which both of these women have now gotten in touch with (as a result of therapy and supervision) neither will formally complain or *consider* lodging a complaint with the ethics committee."

Theme: Therapist Has a Double Standard for Male and Female Sexual Activities

"My husband and I separately saw a male marriage counselor . . . for one session each. The counselor dismissed my husband's extramarital affairs as 'natural' extracurricular activities, yet he felt my having extramarital affairs was a sign that I was not happy in my marital relationship. My husband and I discussed the counselor's assessment and decided that we would not continue seeing him because we both felt he was 'sexist.' "

"Woman should not be promiscuous but have sex with love. My therapist (a woman) tried to make me regret an episode of sex without love or commitment."

"At VA Hospital, as the only woman trainee, was told to be aware of my impact on patients because I was a woman, to dress discreetly, etc. I do not believe a male in an all-female installation would have been given these tips. Also, one male supervisor was interpreting my impact on patients because of my sex as if this was the only variable."

Theme: The Therapist Heavily Weights Physical Appearance in the Selection of Patients or in Setting Therapeutic Goals

"We wasted an awful lot of time arguing about whether I should wear eyeshadow or not, misunderstanding each other grossly about what self-esteem means—until the women's movement came along and suddenly it became more acceptable to wear slacks and no makeup, as I had been doing for years."

"The male counselors in the clinical area would reject the physically unattractive client who was female, in preference for her opposite."

"My own therapist's concept of a woman was that she should be 'feminine'—that is, slim, well dressed, good posture, soft voiced, etc.—a regular charm school or airlines image. The therapist, whom I later changed, was a woman also. She believed any woman who resisted such an image was therefore 'aggressive and unfeminine' (her own quotes)."

OTHER ASPECTS OF THE SURVEY

Respondents also provided information on treatment techniques they considered beneficial in particular for women clients and gave suggestions as to how professional psychology can respond to problems of sex bias and sex-role stereotyping in psychotherapy. They listed a variety of circumstances as evidence of sex bias and sex-role stereotyping that influenced their training and employment as psychotherapists. They were actively discouraged from completing the PhD, directed away from (or into) clinical psychology because they were women, and accused of using graduate school or a job as a temporary stop gap until they got married (or if married, until they got pregnant). They were regarded as subordinate, overemotional, dependent, and decorative by some supervisors and colleagues. They were frequently expected to assume a passive and nurturing role when doing cotherapy with a male, or else supervisors interpreted their therapeutic interactions in sexist terms, that is, that they would be automatically nurturant or would encourage dependency because they were women.

Sex-role stereotyping was cited particularly in the referral or case-assignment process. Women and children were preferentially referred or assigned to female therapists and men to male therapists. Extremely difficult or penniless cases were referred to women therapists for "mothering," while interesting or unusual cases were more likely to be assigned to male therapists.

The women reported that men often stated a preference for male therapists and were surprised or taken aback when their therapist turned out to be a woman, and also that some people in treatment responded negatively to a female therapist being unmarried.

Many respondents thought that there were no special techniques applicable to therapy with women. Indeed, some respondents indicated that the request for specific techniques that would be helpful with women was itself sexist. However, others mentioned specific techniques or areas of focus, such as encouraging independent and achievement-oriented behaviors, thus building self-esteem; accepting nonstereotypic feelings and behaviors; use of a female therapist as role model and as a more adequate source of empathy; assertiveness training; use of consciousness-raising groups or all-female groups; and sexual reeducation. Many people advocated particular schools of therapy, though there was no consistency of response except a frequent rejection of the psychoanalytic approach.

The inquiry as to how professional psychology can respond to sex bias and sex-role stereotyping in psychotherapy provided the following three major groups of suggestions:

1. The main thrust was toward an educational effort primarily on graduate school level but also in the form of a variety of postgraduate workshops, lectures, and consciousness-raising sessions. A part of this effort would be reexamination of theories, texts, etc.
2. Another direction would be an ongoing effort to sensitize psychotherapists through a variety of group processes which, in the minds of the respondents, would help to change attitudes of psychotherapists.
3. Finally, many respondents urged sanctions within and outside the profession to compel modification of sexist behaviors on the part of the psychotherapists. A frequent message was one expressing frustration both with the state of affairs currently in the discipline and with the prospect of improvement. Most urged modification of the APA Code of Ethics to deal with this question. Others asked for public legal sanction.

TASK FORCE RECOMMENDATIONS

The following recommendations derive from an examination of the results and from the overall work of the Task Force.

The most immediate need is for consciousness raising, increased sensitivity, and greater awareness of the problems of sex bias and sex-role stereotyping in psychotherapeutic practice. This need must be responded to within APA at all levels, and by other organizations concerned with psychotherapy practices, as well as by therapists and clients. Specific activities should include (a) workshops for therapists and therapists in training sponsored by relevant groups within APA, for example, by the Board of Social and Ethical Responsibility in Psychology and by the APA Ethics Committee with funds also made available to local and regional groups interested in running such workshops; (b) requesting relevant APA divisions (12, 17, 29, and 35) to develop programs directed toward problems of sex bias and sex-role stereotyping in psychotherapy; (c) convening of cross-disciplinary workshops and conferences among professionals in psychotherapy, psychiatry, social work, and other therapy professions to discuss sexism in psychotherapy; (d) developing training materials to sensitize therapists and therapists in training to sexism in psychotherapy.

A second important need is for development of guidelines for nonsexist psychotherapeutic practice. Funds have been requested for this project.

Third, formal criteria and procedures are needed to evaluate the education and training of psychotherapists in the psychology of women, sexism in psychotherapy, and related issues. This would include such things as presence of female role models as supervisors, training for increased competence in the handling of sexual attraction and seductive behavior by therapist and/or client, and sexist practices in psychological testing and diagnosis. The Education and Training Board should disseminate such training criteria.

Fourth, the Ethical Standards of Psychologists should include statements regarding sexism and the *Casebook on Ethical Standards of Psychologists* should provide illustrative case material.

Finally, the Task Force should be continued to carry out the following activities: (a) the development of guidelines for nonsexist psychotherapeutic practice, (b) the development of criteria for education and training, (c) development of procedures for obtaining information from consumers about sexist practice in psychotherapy, and (d) the investigation of the ethical and therapeutic issues regarding sexual intimacy within psychotherapy.

REFERENCES

Abramowitz, S., Abramowitz, C., Jackson, C., & Gomes, B. The politics of clinical judgment: What nonliberal examiners infer about women who do not stifle themselves. *Journal of Consulting and Clinical Psychology,* 1973, *41,* 385-391.

Abramowitz, C.V., & Dokecki, P.R. *The politics of clinical judgment: Early empirical returns.* Paper presented at the meeting of the American Psychological Association, New Orleans, September 1974.

Aslin, A.L. *Feminist and community mental health for women.* Unpublished manuscript, University of Maryland, 1974. (Mimeo)

Barrett, C., Berg, P., Eaton, E., & Pomeroy, E.L. Implications of women's liberation and the future of psychotherapy. *Psychotherapy: Theory, Research and Practice,* 1974, *11,* 11-15.

Bart, P. Depression in middle-aged women. In J. Bardwick (Ed.), *Readings on the psychology of women.* New York: Harper & Row, 1972.

Belote, B. Personal communication, November 27, 1974.

Bernard, J. *Sex differences: An overview.* Paper presented at the meeting of the American Association for the Advancement of Science, Washington, D.C., December 1972.

Briar, S. Use of theory in studying effects of client social class on students' judgments. *Social Work,* 1961, *6,* 91-97.

Brodsky, A. The consciousness-raising group as a model for therapy with women. *Psychotherapy: Theory, Research and Practice,* 1973, *10,* 24-29.

Broverman, I.K., Broverman, D.M., Clarkson, F.E., Rosenkrantz, P.S., & Vogel, S.R. Sex-role stereotypes and clinical judgments of mental health. *Journal of Consulting and Clinical Psychology,* 1970, *34,* 1-7.

Broverman, I.K., Vogel, S.R., Broverman, D.M., Clarkson, F.E., & Rosenkrantz, P.S. Sex-role stereotypes: A current appraisal. *Journal of Social Issues,* 1972, *28*(2), 58-78.

Carkhuff, R.R. Black and white in helping. *Professional Psychology,* 1972, *3,* 18-22.

Carlson, E.R., & Carlson, R. Male and female subjects in personality research. *Journal of Abnormal and Social Psychology,* 1960, *61,* 482-483.

Chesler, P. *Women and madness.* Garden City, N.J.: Doubleday, 1972.

Constantinople, A. Masculinity-femininity: An exception to a famous dictum? *Psychological Bulletin,* 1973, *80,* 389-407.

Delk, J.L., & Ryan, T.T. Sex role stereotyping and A-B therapist status: Who is more chauvinistic? *Journal of Consulting and Clinical Psychology,* 1975, *43,* 589.

Fabrikant, B. The psychotherapist and the female patient: Perceptions and change. In V. Franks & V. Burtle (Eds.), *Women in therapy.* New York: Brunner/Mazel, 1974.

Hare, N., & Hare, J. Black women 1970. In J. Bardwick (Ed.), *Readings on the psychology of women.* New York: Harper & Row, 1972.

Hernandez, A. Small change for black women. *Ms,* August 1974, 16-18.

Horner, M.S. Toward an understanding of achievement related conflicts in women. *Journal of Social Issues,* 1972, *28*(2), 157-176.

Kardener, S.H., Fuller, M., & Mensh, I.N. A survey of physicians' attitudes and practices regarding erotic and nonerotic contact with patients. *American Journal of Psychiatry,* 1973, *10,* 1077-1081.

Kirsch, B. Consciousness-raising groups as therapy for women. In V. Franks & V. Burtle (Eds.), *Women in therapy.* New York: Brunner/Mazel, 1974.

Lerman, H. What happens in feminist therapy? In A. Brodsky (Chair), *Feminist therapy: In search of a theory.* Symposium presented at the meeting of the American Psychological Association, New Orleans, September 1974.

Levenson, E.A. *A fallacy of understanding.* New York: Basic Books, 1972.

Neulinger, J., Stein, M.I., Schillinger, M., & Welkowitz, J. Perceptions of the optimally integrated person as a function of therapists' characteristics. *Perceptual and Motor Skills,* 1970, *30,* 375-384.

Rice, J. & Rice, D. Implications of the women's liberation movement for psychotherapy. *American Journal of Psychiatry,* 1973, *130,* 191-196.

Riess, B. New viewpoints on the female homosexual. In V. Franks & V. Burtle (Eds.), *Women in therapy.* New York: Brunner/Mazel, 1974.

Schwabacher, S. Male versus female representation in psychological research: An examination of the *Journal of Personality and Social Psychology,* 1970, 1971. *JSAS Catalog of Selected Documents in Psychology,* 1972, *2,* 20. (Ms. No. 82)

Sherman, J. *On the psychology of women: A survey of empirical studies.* Springfield: Thomas, 1971.

Sherman, J. Social values, femininity and the development of female competence. *Journal of Social Issues,* (1971).

Swartz, J.M., & Abramowitz, S.I. *Effects of psychiatrist values and patient race and sex on clinical judgment.* Paper presented at the meeting of the American Psychological Association, New Orleans, September 1974.

Tennov, D. Feminism, psychotherapy and professionalism. *Journal of Contemporary Psychotherapy,* 1973, *5,* 107-116.

Chapter 14

PERSPECTIVES ON COUNSELING BIAS: IMPLICATIONS FOR COUNSELOR EDUCATION*

NANCY K. SCHLOSSBERG AND JOHN J. PIETROFESA

WE ARE concerned about the ease with which educators, and counselors in particular, adopt as "god-given" certain notions about appropriate behavior. For example, when counseling a fifty-five-year-old widow about entering college, a black man about becoming a banker, or a single adult male about adopting a female child, the counselor's "god-given" notions about appropriate behavior can play an unconscious part in counseling. Counselors defend themselves as being conveyors of reality and not decision-makers for their clients. Yet client self-reports contain many references about the negative impact counselors have had on career development. For some counselors, dispensing discouragement rather than encouragement has been the order of the day. Many minority group members and women have been limited by inappropriate counseling and testing.

Counselor bias is here defined as an opinion, either unfavorable or favorable, which is formed without adequate reasons and is based upon what the bias holder assumes to be appropriate for the group in question. Bias is evident whenever it is assumed that someone can or cannot take a certain course of action because of her or his age, social class, sex, or race. The difference between bias and prejudice is the ease with which bias can be discarded when a new reality is made evident. Bias becomes prejudice when the role ascription serves a deep-seated need of its holder. Prejudice is resistant to information which might lead to a changed belief. Some people need scapegoats, and reeducation is often impossible in instances like this. Allport (1958, p. 12) states, "In most cases prejudice seems to have some 'functional significance' for the bearer." A great deal has been written

From The Counseling Psychologist, 1973, 4, 44-54.

about prejudice and its relationship to personality disorder; but little has been written about bias and its effects in the helping relationship.

We are assuming that counselors are like people-in-general—no better, no worse. We all share one thing: We make judgments about appropriate behaviors for different groups of people. Such prejudgments may be important in influencing the behavior of others.

Rosenthal and Jacobson's studies (1968) illustrate the degree to which attitudes about particular children's competency do, in fact, affect performance. As expectancy rises, so does performance. One person's expectations of another's behavior come to act as a self-fulfilling prophecy. Thus, if a counselor assumes that sixty-five-year-olds should not enter doctoral work, forty-five-year-olds should not begin to produce and raise children, twenty-five-year-olds should not be college presidents, women should not be corporate executives, men should not do laundry, bed cleaning, diaper changing, or combing of little girls' hair, lower-class blacks should not live side by side with millionaires—then this will probably be reflected in the counseling interview.

Even though a large percentage of women work, and a large percentage of workers are women, their position has startlingly declined in recent years. The facts are alarming: women work at lower-level, lower-paying jobs than men. While more women are working than ever before, they are under-represented in the professional technical categories. Women also receive proportionately fewer advanced degrees than in the 1920s (Millett, 1968; Manpower Report of the President, 1967).

Complicating the picture is the fact that each sex occupies different levels on the status hierarchy and the sexes are unevenly distributed as to field of endeavor. It has been substantiated that

> American education is blighted by a sex-split in its curriculum. At present the whole field of knowledge is divided along tacit but well understood sex lines. Those subjects given the highest status in American life are 'masculine'; those given the lowest are 'feminine' . . . thus math, the sciences . . . business administration . . . are men's subjects . . . and the humanities are relegated . . . 'suitable to women' (Millett, 1968, p. 14).
>
> Discrimination in the world of work can be easily seen when one examines the number of women in certain high-status fields. For example, only 208 women are listed among the 6,597 members of the American Institute of Physics. One half of the women are employed as physics teachers. Of the 600,000 people classified as in engineering and related technical fields, only 6,000 are women. About 7 percent of chemists, 3 percent of all dentists, and 4 percent of the doctors are women (Cassara, 1963, p. 77).

This unbalanced occupational distribution of the sexes needs to be critically examined from the vantage point of counselors.

This paper offers no incontrovertible data, but merely tries to bring perspective to a topic which we need to acknowledge and act upon. We are educable. We can help ourselves with new perspectives. We can free ourselves from ideas which restrict our thinking and which, in turn, may restrict our client's behavior. As one counselor educator said to a class, "men may marry women who are willing to be kept barefoot, pregnant, and behind the plow; it's quite another thing for counselors to impose these views on counselees."

COUNSELOR BIAS AND SEX ROLE ASCRIPTION

Sex bias appears to be an important component of some individuals' emotional makeup. Traditionally, women have been viewed as biologically inferior human beings. Because of this discrimination, women have maintained a position secondary to men in family life, education and work. Ginzberg (1971) stated, "The increasing acceptance of women as workers represents a clear challenge to guidance. The field has paid inadequate attention to women at every stage of the career process: in curriculum and course selections, in career planning, and in assisting those who seek to return to the labor force after a period of homemaking and childbearing (p. 318)."

Since people-in-general hold strong beliefs about sex-appropriate behavior, we can assume that counselors also hold to these notions. Since these notions are currently being challenged as biased, counselors need to be aware of the degree to which they try to push counselees into certain directions because of their own sex biases. Gardner (1971) states, "Right now, in our excessively sexist society, it is unlikely that anyone without special training in feminism can create conditions which would encourage females to 'exercise their right to select goals of the counselor.' The goals of counselors trained in traditional programs can hardly be expected to do other than reflect the sexist values . . . (p. 173) ."

Counseling Interview

While it can be assumed that counselors "support" equality for both sexes, several works have dealt with sex-stereotyping attitudes of clinicians. These works will be described in some detail to examine the generally untested notion that counselors do in fact counsel from a stereotyped framework.

In a landmark study, Broverman et al., (1970), utilizing a sex-role stereotype questionnaire, studied actively-functioning clinicians. They hypothesized that "clinical judgments about the characteristics of healthy individuals would differ as a function of sex of person judged, and furthermore, that these differences in clinical judgments would parallel stereotypic sex-role differences." They also felt that behaviors and characteristics considered to be healthy for a sex-unspecified adult will resemble behaviors judged healthy for males and differ from behaviors judged healthy for their female counterparts. The subjects were 79 clinically-trained psychologists, psychiatrists, or social workers (46 males, 33 females)—all working in clinical settings. Ages ranged from 23 to 55 years, while experience covered the spectrum from internship to extensive professional work. The authors utilized the Stereotype Questionnaire composed of 122 bipolar items—each pole characterized as typically masculine or feminine. The results indicated that high agreement existed among clinicians—both male and female—about the attributes characterizing healthy adult men, healthy adult women, and healthy adults with sex unspecified.

It appears that a "double standard of health" exists among clinicians. The researchers note that:

> More likely, the double standard of health for men and women stems from clinicians' acceptance of an 'adjustment' notion of health, for example, health consists of a good adjustment to one's environment. In our society, men and women are systematically trained, practically from birth on, to fulfill different social roles. An adjustment notion of health, plus the existence of differential norms of male and female behavior in our society, automatically leads to a double standard of health. Thus, for a woman to be healthy, from an adjustment viewpoint, she must adjust to and accept the behavioral norms for her sex, even though these behaviors are generally less socially desirable and considered to be less healthy for the generalized competent, mature adult (p. 6).

Clinicians are significantly less likely to attribute traits which characterize healthy adults to a woman than they are to attribute these same traits to a healthy man. The clinicians appear to reflect stereotypes no different from the general population. This tends to support our earlier contention that counselors are no better or worse than other societal members in terms of sex bias. Obviously, clinicians need to critically examine their attitudes and position with respect to the adjustment notion of health.

Thomas and Stewart (1971) tried to "determine whether secondary school counselors respond more positively to female clients with traditionally feminine (conforming) goals than those with traditionally masculine (deviate) goals" . . . Information concerning the home, school, self-description, and personal values of high school girls were presented on audiotape to 64 practicing counselors and their responses were analyzed by sex and experience. The findings are as follows: "(a) Female counselors gave higher Acceptance scores to both deviate and conforming clients than did male counselors; (b) counselors, regardless of sex, rated conforming goals as more appropriate than deviate; (c) counselors, regardless of sex, rated female clients with deviate career goals to be more in need of counseling than those with conforming goals" (p. 352).

Hawley (1972) found that the feminine model held by 52 female counselors-in-training allowed a wider range of educational and career choices than the feminine model held by 45 female teachers-in-training. She suggested that counselors such as those represented in the study can help female clients become aware of a variety of life styles and career choices, without implying that any one choice is superior to any other.

Naffziger (1971) studied attitudes towards woman's roles among counselors, counselor educators and teachers of both sexes. He found that women described their ideal woman as one who is more extra-family oriented than the ideal projected by men. Although both men and women rejected the intra-family oriented ideal woman, women more strongly rejected her. Women were more accepting of working mothers. Women projected the ideal woman as being more responsible for the success of the marriage. Men suggested that career women are less attractive to men. On the other hand, men supported ideal women who would argue against authority. Naffziger found no significant differences by age (under 35, over 35) in the definitions of their ideal woman.

In another noteworthy study, Friedersdorf (1969) explored the relationship between male and female secondary school counselor attitudes toward the career planning of high school female students. The subjects were 106 counselors in Indiana schools. Twenty-seven male and 29 female counselors role-played a college-bound high school girl while 23 male and 27 female counselors role-played a non-college-bound high school girl. The Strong Vocational Interest Blank for women was completed. The following conclusions were drawn:

1. Male and female counselors responded differently when role-playing as a college-bound high school girl versus role-playing as a non-college-bound high school girl.
2. Counselors perceived college-bound high school girls as identifying with cultural activities and skills involving verbal ability.
3. Items which reflected differences between college-bound versus non-college-bound girls were not the same for male and female counselors.
4. Both male and female counselors have at least some relatively distinctive attitudes toward which levels and types of occupations are realistic and appropriate for both college-bound and non-college-bound girls.
5. Male counselors associated college-bound girls with traditionally feminine occupations at the semi-skilled level; female counselors perceived the college-bound girl as interested in occupations requiring a college education.
6. Male counselors tended to think of women in feminine roles characterized by feminine personality traits.

7. Female counselors tended to expand the traditional image of female work roles and projected women's roles into careers presently occupied.
8. Male counselors perceived the college-bound girl as having positive attitudes toward traditionally feminine occupations regardless of the classification level of the occupations. Occupations traditionally engaged in by men were not considered by male counselors as occupations that college-bound girls would like as careers.

The implication, obviously, is that some of the counselor attitudes reflected might have great impact on the goals of the female clients as expressed in counseling sessions.

In order to test the hypothesis that counselors were biased against women entering a "masculine" occupation, Pietrofesa and Schlossberg (1970) arranged interviews between counselor trainees and a coached female counselee in the counseling practicum at an urban university. During the counseling session the counselee informed the counselor that she was a transfer student to the university, that she was entering her junior year of college and could not decide whether to enter the field of engineering, a "masculine" occupation, or enter the field of education, a "feminine " occupation.

Each interview was tape recorded. At the end of the interview, the counselor was informed that the counselee had been coached and that the sessions and tapes were to be used for a research study. Counselors were requested not to mention their interviews to other counselors. After all counselors had conducted interviews, a brief discussion was held among the counselor group concerning their feelings about the counseling sessions. No other information was given the counselors. The subjects (counselors) in the study were students in a practicum during fall and winter quarters, 1968-69. The counselor group, then, consisted of 29, i.e. 16 males and 13 females. Tapes were reviewed and tabulated as to their bias by a male graduate student in guidance and counseling, a male counselor educator experienced in supervision of the counseling practicum, and a female college professor who was a former school psychologist with a research specialty. Frequencies and percentages were calculated and chi square was then used in a variety of configurations. The final stage of the project involved a content analysis of all biased statements.

The raters designated a counselor's statement as biased or prejudicial against the female counselee when she expressed interest in the "masculine" field and the counselor rejected this interest in favor of the "feminine" vocation. Statements of rejection then included disapproval of the female counselee's desire to enter the "masculine" field—comments that implied disadvantages in entering that field, etc. A counselor's statement was considered biased for the female counselee when she expressed interest in the masculine occupation and the counselor supported or reinforced this expressed interest. Statements of positive bias toward females ranged from direct approval to statements that subtly implied advantages in entering the masculine field.

The results of this study indicated that counselor bias exists against women entering a masculine occupation. Female counselors, interestingly enough, displayed as much bias as did their male counterparts. Percentage results strongly reinforce the conclusion that counselors are biased against women entering masculine fields. Of the total bias statements, 81.3 percent are against women, whereas only 18.7 percent are biased for women. A content analysis of the 79 biased statements made by the counselors in this study reveals that most negatively biased statements emphasized the masculinity of the field; working conditions and promotional opportunity were mentioned, but with less frequency. Thus, the pressures against women working in a field stereotyped as masculine were prevalent among this group.

In order to tabulate the statements, ten categories were devised so that negative bias (NB) and positive bias (PB) statements could be classified as to content. The following examples of bias statements will give the flavor of the kinds of pressure counselors imposed.

Salary—Amount of monetary return
(NB) Money isn't everything.
(PB) You could make much more money as an engineer.

Status—Perception of self in vocation
(NB) The status of a woman is higher in the field of teaching.
(PB) There is more prestige in becoming an engineer.

Marriage and Family—Family attachment
(NB) Would your husband resent your being an engineer?
(NB) You would only be gone from home during school hours if you taught school.
(PB) Being an engineer would not interfere with your becoming married.

Parents—Parental support
(NB) How do your parents feel about your entering engineering instead of education?
(PB) I am glad your parents want you to become an engineer.

Educational Time—Amount of time necessary for preparation to enter the vocational field
(NB) Engineering would take five years and elementary education would be four years . . . These are things you might want to consider.

(PB) It may take longer to become an engineer but it is well worth it.

Educational Preparation—Classes one must take to enter the field and the kinds of classes already taken

(NB) The course work in engineering would be very difficult.

(PB) Your classwork up to now shows that you would do well as an engineer.

Promotional Opportunities—Advancement in position

(NB) There might be a holding of you back because you are a woman.

(PB) Your chances of promotion would be good in engineering.

Hiring—Opportunity to enter field

(NB) They are not supposed to discriminate against women, but they still get around it.

(PB) The opportunities for a woman in engineering are good.

Working Conditions—Where, with whom, what kinds of work, and/or under what conditions work is done

(NB) Engineering . . . it is very, you know, technical, and very, I could use the term 'unpeopled'.

(PB) You could work at a relaxed pace as an engineer.

Masculine Occupation—Identification of occupation as masculine

(NB) You normally think of this as a man's field.

(PB) There is no such thing as a man's world anymore.

Pietrofesa and Schlossberg drew the following conclusions:

1. Counselors display more bias against females entering a so-called "masculine" occupation than for females entering a so-called "feminine" occupation.
2. Female counselors display as much bias against females as their male counterparts.
3. Content analysis of bias statements indicate that major stress is placed upon the "masculinity" of the occupation.

Several other studies have looked at in-counseling behaviors of counselors and their impact on women clients. Parker (1967) noted a relationship between directive and nondirective responses of male therapists and the sex of the counselee. Therapists made significantly more nondirective responses than directive responses to female clients than to their male counterparts. Heilbrun (1970) developed this thesis one step further when he tested the hypothesis that female clients' dependency needs were frustrated by the nondirective approach of male therapists, and as a result, they left therapy prematurely. The results of the study supported this contention. The Parker and Heilbrun research involved male counselors, and yet the sex of the counselor may be a most important ingredient. Pringle (1972), in an incomplete study, analyzing the interaction effects of (1) the sex of the high school client, (2) the sex of the high school counselor, and (3) the client behavior presented in the initial stages of the counseling interview, has preliminary findings which suggest there are significant differences occurring as a function of the match between counselor sex, client sex, and client behavior.

From the studies cited, it appears that counselors do ascribe roles to men and to women, and that counselor interview behavior reflects these biases.

Counseling Materials

When discussing counselor bias, it is essential to examine materials which are commonly used and relied upon in the counseling interview. Counselors need to evaluate critically every tool they use—whether it is description of fields in the **Occupational Outlook Handbook,** an interest inventory, a career brochure, or a college catalog. Does the information being presented or the test content reflect stereotyped roles for men and women? Do the materials contain biased statements which could lead a counselee in one direction rather than another? Do the materials reflect the past rather than the future? Are the materials reinforcing outmoded views of "women's place"?

Since interest inventories play a crucial role in career counseling, stemming partly from clients' continual insistence for specific feedback and answers, we must certainly assess the inventories to determine whether they are a freeing or restricting influence. Cole (1972), in a scientific description of present interest inventories, sees them as restricting: "The use of traditional women's occupational scales may have a severely limiting effect on the careers women consider" (p. 8). Harmon (1973), in a paper delivered at the American Personnel and Guidance Association Convention, listed and discussed the major interest inventories which contained "characteristics which may contribute to sexual bias."

Despite the growing awareness among leaders in the area of tests and measurements, practitioners—both men and women—are often unaware of the sexual bias inherent in the major inventories as presently constructed. In a recent meeting, the authors asked if the trained counselors present felt that the two most widely-used inventories, The Strong Vocational Interest Blank and the Kuder, were biased. A minority felt the inventories were biased. The counselors, generally considering the inventories as unbiased, seemed amazed by the presentation of a detailed description of the bias inherent in each test.

The extent of bias has been documented for one of the best inventories available, The Strong Vocational Interest Blank, by Schlossberg and Goodman (1972b). They point out four major limitations of The Strong Vocational Interest Blanks.

> *First,* the Strong includes thirty-three occupations for men which are not listed for women—such as psychiatrist, author, journalist, physicist; it also includes thirty-seven occupations listed for women but not available for men including elementary teacher, art teacher and medical technologist. Since four hundred members of an occupation are an appropriate norm group for a SVIB scale, and census data indicate that in most instances at least four hundred persons of the opposite sex are employed in an occupation reserved for one sex on the SVIB, no justification exists for differential norm groups of each sex.
>
> The *second* major limitation stems from the fact that when the same person takes both forms of the SVIB, the profiles turn out differently. For example, in a pilot study of which twenty-eight men and women took both forms of the SVIB, one woman scored high (A or B+ standard score) as a dental assistant, physical therapist, occupational therapist on the women's profile, and physician, psychiatrist, psychologist on the men's form. One man scored high on personnel director, rehabilitation counselor, social worker, physical therapist, and community recreation administrator on the men's form, and guidance counselor, medical technologist, engineer, dietician, occupational therapist, physical therapist, registered nurse, licensed practical nurse, radiologic technologist, and dental assistant on the women's form.
>
> The *third* major limitation stems from the current manual and handbook which offers guidelines to counselors which, if followed, could be harmful. For example, the current manual states, "Many young women do not appear to have strong occupational interests, and they may score high only in certain 'premarital' occupations: elementary school teacher, office worker, stenographer-secretary." "Such a finding is disappointing to many college women, since they are likely to consider themselves career-oriented. In such cases, the selection of an area of training or an occupation should probably be based upon practical considerations—fields that can be pursued part-time, are easily resumed after periods of non-employment, are readily available in different locales."
>
> *Fourth,* the use of The Strong Vocational Interest Blanks may also be attacked on legal grounds—that the SVIB deprives women of their right to the Equal Protection of the Law and that the use of the SVIB is in violation of Title VII of the Civil Rights Act of 1964 (Schlossberg & Goodman, 1972b).

This detailed analysis is merely illustrative of one instrument. However, an equally biased picture becomes apparent no matter what guidance material one examines. For example, the opening paragraph in American College Testing Program's brochure describing their Career Planning Program reads:

> We all make career decisions—decisions affecting our educational and job futures. Sometimes we make these decisions by default because of what we didn't know or didn't do. Sometimes we are able to take charge, to discover our possibilities and weigh our choices. This report is designed to help YOU take charge.

However, at the bottom of the profile, there is a special note addressed to counselors:

> Counselors Notes: When a student is unlike other students entering an educa-

tional program, predictions for that program should be used with caution. For example, care should be used in interpreting predictions for a student of one sex in a program in which the other sex predominates (American College Testing, 1971).

A forthcoming revision of The Strong Vocational Interest Blank is an attempt to eliminate sexual bias. Clearly, we need further studies and revision of all guidance tests, materials, and occupational information. Analysis of these materials should be in terms of bias —not just against women but against all groups.

IMPLICATIONS FOR TRAINING

Counselors, both male and female, have biases about female counselees. Counselor education programs must accept counselor bias as a fact and attempt to bring biased feelings into the open, so that counselors are able to control them, or better yet, remove them from their counseling and human encounters. Westervelt (1963) writes:

> . . . counselors who express the conviction that women's primary and socially essential roles are domestic and maternal and take place in the home may be reflecting a covert need to keep them there.
>
> Girls and women in the lower socioeconomic brackets who particularly need counseling help to recognize and plan for paid employment will get little assistance from such counselors. Nor, of course, will these counselors help intellectually and educationally privileged girls to use their gifts and training to best advantage.
>
> . . . No formal, university-sponsored graduate-level, degree-awarding program in counselor education requires even a one-semester course in social and psychological sex differences which effect development or provides focus on sex differences in a practicum or internship in counseling. . . .
>
> Trends toward the integration into counselor education, at basic levels, of more subject matter from social psychology, anthropology, sociology, and economics would also provide more exposure to materials on psychosocial sex differences and changing sex roles. Again, however, the effect of such exposure will depend on the students initial sympathetic interest, since the material will be only a small part of a much larger whole (pp. 21-22).

Westervelt (1963) make references to the role, and more so, the importance of the practicum in the training of counselors:

> Counselors, guidance workers, and student personnel workers . . . should have as many opportunities as possible to counsel with females—and, ideally, with females of all ages, in order that, no matter what the age level with which they eventually work, they get an opportunity to observe first hand the patterns of continuity and discontinuity in feminine development. Counseling experience should not, however, be limited to working with females; opportunity to counsel with boys and men is most important, both because it will provide insights into psychosocial sex differences and because it will provide a chance to explore useful variations in approaches to counseling the two sexes. All counselors-in-training should be helped to identify, understand and work with sex differences in their counseling practicum or internship . . . (pp. 26-28).

Before one can implement these notions spelled out by Westervelt, the first task is to convince counselor educators that they, too, probably hold biases about age, sex, social class, and color. Each person might not hold biases in all four areas, but it is unquestionably true that each one of us holds certain beliefs about what is appropriate behavior for these groups. It is difficult to face these beliefs in ourselves; once recognized, it is difficult to control them in our counseling and programming.

The second task is for counselor educators to build this into training counselors. In which classes do we discuss these notions? How do we make explicit aspects of counselor behavior about which we know so little? While cognitive dimensions of age and sex bias can be integrated throughout a counselor education program, the practicum experience might afford the best opportunity to effectively deal with the more basic feelings of counselors. It also provides a vehicle where counselors come face-to-face with girls and women of all ages.

The third task is to begin developing materials for use in training counselors. One possibility would be the development of a self-administered instrument which might yield several bias scores. A more fruitful one, however, would be the use of situational vignettes where counselors are more likely to express what they truly feel. Paper and pencil inventories seem to allow for a more superficial, simply verbalized, egalitarian point-of-view than do situational experiential tasks.

A TRAINING MODEL

We suggest and have implemented a four-pronged training model. The goal is simple—to enable counselors and teachers to participate with their constituency in an unbiased fashion. The following components are simply suggestive and obviously have to be adapted to specific settings in order to be operational.

1. Expanding the cognitive understanding of participants regarding the role of women through lectures and readings.
2. Raising the consciousness of participants regarding sexual bias through group techniques.
3. Promoting the acquisition of nonbiased helping skills among participants through audio-video taping and role playing.
4. Fostering skill development in program planning and implementation among participants through tutorial projects.

Each of these components will be briefly summarized so that the nature of training can be envisioned. This approach is based on fifty-six hours of training. We have found the most effective approach to be an intensive period of one week followed by sixteen hours of follow-up sessions during the year.

Expansion of Cognitive Understanding

The intellectual dimension provides a convenient initial component. The approach must be interdisciplinary in nature. For example, experts in the fields of medicine, law, education, psychology, sociology, etc., have much to contribute to an understanding of women in our world. Lectures, panels, readings, and discussion provide the beginning steps of our training model.

Consciousness Raising

After intellectual awakening, and before skill acquisition, counselors need to personalize their learnings. It is not enough to know intellectually that dentistry is a female occupation in Greece and could become a reality in our culture. Counselors must begin to look at their consciousness and deal with their values, attitudes, beliefs, and biases about sex roles.

A starting point might be to read "Woman Which Includes Man, Of Course" (Wells, 1970), which is a description of sex-role reversal. This becomes the basis for self-exploration in group discussion. One technique we have found effective during this stage is the inner circle–outer circle or "fishbowl technique." In a recent workshop, seven members volunteered to sit in the inner circle with two coleaders. In addition, the inner circle contained an empty chair. Each outer circle participant observed one member of the inner circle; the focus, in this case, was a discussion of Wells' book. The observer's reactions to the inner circle participant's behaviors were to be fed back to that circle member at a later time. In addition, outer circle participants could move freely into the empty chair when impelled to speak. After consciousness-raising experiences, including the "fishbowl" exercise, one male participant decided he could best attack sexual bias by applying for a job as a first-grade teacher in his school district.

Acquisition of Helping Skills

Once a cognitive and affective base has been established, attention can be directed to specific skill acquisitions. Educational experiences are incomplete unless the participants can do something more effectively than when they began. Role playing and supervised practice provide the vehicle from which specific skills can emerge.

STEP ONE: Participants role play situations which may elicit sex-biased behaviors. The trainers develop a paragraph which describes a specific situation involving two or more people. For example, one situation might involve a mother pressuring her daughter to become a teacher, while the daughter would like to become a doctor. The mother and daughter seek the help of a counselor to resolve the conflict. The scenario is role-played through to resolution and then discussed.

STEP TWO: Participants pair-off as "helper" and "helpee." The helpees present situations in their lives in which sex role is an issue, while the helpers attempt a facilitative intervention. For example, one male helpee might discuss his relationship to his children while his wife works, or even his feelings about his wife's working. Another helpee might discuss the pressure she feels at work or a conflict with her children. The helper responds using attending, responding, and initiating skills according to the Carkhuff model (1972a, 1972b). Discussion follows each exercise, starting with the feelings of the helpee, helper, the other participants, and the supervisor. Evaluations, in terms of helper effectiveness, are made immediately using the five-point Carkhuff Scale.

STEP THREE: Counselors participate in video and audio taping of actual counseling sessions. The tapes are shared and immediately critiqued in terms of implementation and acquisition of counseling skills. Special attention is paid to situations where counselor biases might affect the counseling interaction and counselee decision making.

Program Development

In addition to understanding intellectually the role of women, raising one's consciousness, and developing more effective human relationship skills, counselors must foster change in their own work settings. Consequently, participants are asked to release their creative potentials to foster innovative programs resulting in better situations for women.

STEP ONE: Supervisors work with participants in outlining systematic steps of program development.

STEP TWO: Participants work in groups with the task of zeroing in on a specific measurable, observable program which will improve conditions for women and which can be implemented in their own work settings.

STEP THREE: Participants return four months later with an outline of their goals, activities, and evaluation to share with their counterparts.

In summary, participant experiences then would range from reading to actual supervised practice. Training would move from the usual cognitive vehicles, i.e. reading and listening, to learning through modeling, observation, and discussion. Actual participation in role playing and supervised practice would be included in the formal program. Training would be followed with continuous evaluation of field practice and program development.

Evaluation would involve (1) participant self-evaluation and (2) program evaluation. Participant evaluation could include paper-and-pencil tests, observation of self and others, and peer and supervisor feedback. The typical pre-post testing and participant critiques would be part of the evaluation of program development. All individual evaluation of participants would be confidential. Group data would be available for research.

SUMMARY

Sexual bias, whether displayed knowingly or not, affects counselor performance. Several studies have supported this fact. Counselors reflect such bias through in-counseling behaviors and through some of the materials they use.

This article discusses the relevant research surrounding this problem and proposes a model of training to help counselors reduce sex bias.

REFERENCES

Allport, G. *The nature of prejudice.* New York: Doubleday and Company, Inc., 1958.

American College Testing. Career planning program. 1971.

Broverman, I.K., Broverman, D.M., Clarkson, F.E., Rosenkrantz, P.S. & Vogel, S.R. Sex-role stereotypes and clinical judgments of mental health. *Journal of Consulting and Clinical Psychology,* 1970, *34,* 1-7.

Carkhuff, R.R. *The art of helping.* Amherst, Massachusetts: Human Resource Development Press, 1972(a).

Carkhuff, R.R. The development of systematic human resource development models. *The Counseling Psychologist,* 1972(b), *3*(3), 4-11.

Cassara, B. *American women: The changing image.* Boston: Houghton-Mifflin, 1963.

Cole, N.S. On measuring the vocational interest of women. No. 49, March, 1972, *The American College Testing Program,* P.O. Box 168, Iowa City, Iowa 52240.

Friedersdorf, N.W. A comparative study of counselor attitudes toward the further educational and vocational plans of high school girls. Unpublished study, Lafayette: Purdue University, 1969.

Gardner, J. Sexist counseling must stop. *Personnel and Guidance Journal,* 1971, *49,* 705-714.

Ginzberg, E. *Career guidance: Who needs it, who provides it, who can improve it?* New York: McGraw-Hill, 1971.

Harmon, L.W. Sexual bias in interest testing. *Measurement and Evaluation in Guidance,* 1973, *5,* 496-501.

Hawley, P. Perceptions of male models of femininity related to career choice. *Journal of Counseling Psychology,* 1972, *19,* 308-313.

Heilbrun, A.B. Toward resolution of the dependency-premature termination paradox for females in psychotherapy. *Journal of Consulting and Clinical Psychology,* 1970, *34,* 382-386.

Manpower Report of the President. Washington, D.C.: Department of Labor, 1967.

Millett, K. *Token learning: A study of women's higher education in America.* National Organization for Women, New York, 1968.

Naffziger, K.G. *A survey of counselor-educators' and other selected professionals' attitudes toward women's roles.* (Doctoral dissertation, University of Oregon) Ann Arbor, Michigan: University Microfilms, 1972, No. 72-956.

Parker, G.V.C. Some concomitants of therapist dominance in the psychotherapy interview. *Journal of Consulting Psychology,* 1967, *31,* 313-318.

Pietrofesa, J.J. & Schlossberg, N.K. Counselor bias and the female occupational role. Detroit: Wayne State University, 1970, ERIC Document, CG 006 056.

Pringle, M. The responses of high school counselors to behaviors associated with independence and achievement in male and female clients: An interaction analysis. Ann Arbor: University of Michigan, unpublished dissertation, 1972.

Rosenthal, R. & Jacobson, L. *Pygmalion in the classroom.* New York: Holt, Rinehart and Winston, Inc., 1968.

Schlossberg, N.K. & Goodman, J. Imperative for change: Counselor use of the Strong Vocational Interest Blanks. *Impact,* 1972a, *2,* 26-29.

———. Revision of the Strong Vocational Interest Blanks. Resolution to the American Personnel and Guidance Association, March 29, 1972, Mimeographed, College of Education, Wayne State University, 1972b.

Stewart, N.R. & Hinds, W.C. Behavioral objectives to direct simulated experiences in counselor education. Videotape presentation at APGA, New Orleans, March, 1970.

Thomas, H. & Stewart, N.R. Counselor response to female clients with deviate and conforming career goals. *Journal of Counseling Psychology,* 1971, *18,* 352-357.

Wells, T. Woman which includes man, of course. *Newsletter, Association for Humanistic Psychology,* 1970, *7.*

Westervelt, E. The recruitment and training of educational/vocational counselors for girls and women. Background paper for Sub-Committee on Counseling, President's Commission on the Status of Women, 1963.

Chapter 15

TRENDS IN COUNSELOR ATTITUDE ABOUT WOMEN'S ROLES*

PATRICIA AUER ENGELHARD, KATHRYN OTTO JONES, AND RICHARD J. STIGGINS

Counselor attitudes regarding women were measured three times over a span of six years in the state of Minnesota to chart attitude changes that have accompanied increasing career development interests on the part of women. An eighteen-item survey was constructed to tap three dimensions of attitude, including attitudes regarding the dual role of mother and worker, perceptions of sex role definition, and expectations regarding the societal impact of women. Changes from 1968 through 1971 to 1974 suggest more acceptance of the dual role and broader sex role definitions. Differential attitude changes based on sex and age of counselor are examined.

THE RAPID emergence of women into the work world presents guidance personnel with new professional challenges. As Westervelt (1973) has pointed out, both the percentage of unmarried women and the average age of women at the time of marriage are increasing, the birth rate is the lowest on record, the number of women 30 years of age or older who are students in higher education has doubled in the past decade, and the proportion of women in the labor force continues to grow. For women, who are remaining single longer, having fewer children, and returning to school after fulfilling their family responsibilities, information on work and career opportunities is becoming essential for decision making.

These changes have been accompanied by equally important changes in the nature of counseling services provided to women. Guidance counselors are responsible for being aware of and dealing

*The authors are indebted to W. Wesley Tennyson of the University of Minnesota for his help with the original study, to the Minnesota State Department of Education for their support of this study, and to Richard L. Ferguson, Nancy S. Cole, and Dale J. Prediger of the American College Testing Program for their constructive and supportive suggestions in the completion of this report.

with potential sex role biases and conflicts. Koontz (1970), Cooperman (1971), and Pringle (1971) indicated that counselor attitudes about women are crucial considerations in the delivery of effective guidance service. After a review of research on the topic, Pringle (1971) suggested that the counselor who is truly supportive of women must " (1) recognize the changing roles of women in American society; (2) recognize and evaluate his own sex role biases; and (3) develop some level of expertise with the growing body of recent research on sex differences and on the psychology of women" (pp. 13–14).

To chart the extent to which awarenesses such as these characterized Minnesota counselor attitudes, Engelhard (1969) and Otto (1973) administered attitude surveys focusing on women's roles during the 1968–69 and 1971–72 school years, respectively. These data have been combined with 1974–75 attitude measures to enable an analysis of the development of counselor attitudes over a period of six years.

METHOD

Subjects

Three cross-sectional random samples of Minnesota guidance counselors were selected at three-year intervals: 1968, 1971, and 1974. The characteristics of each sample are reported in Table 15-I. The distributions of subjects according to size of community, age, and sex suggest that comparable samples were obtained with each selection. The data gathered in 1968 and 1971 were not originally collected to facilitate comparisons between years. Specifically, no provision was made to permit matching of subjects across years. This prevents the study of attitude changes within subjects over time. Given these limitations, it was also impossible to determine the amount of overlap, if any, that occurred across samples. Nevertheless, for purposes of this analysis, each sample is considered independent.

An additional note on the selection procedures is warranted. Both the 1971 and 1974 data were gathered by mailing survey forms to randomly selected respondents. The return rates are listed in Table 15-I. However, the 1968 data represent the attitudes of a randomly selected subset of 139 of 871[1] counselors who participated in a statewide comprehensive study of guidance personnel attitudes.

Instrument

Guidance counselor attitudes about women's roles were initially measured by Engelhard (1969) in 1968 by means of a sixty-eight-item Likert attitude questionnaire (five-point scale: strongly agree to strongly disagree). These items were readministered in their entirety

[1]This figure represented 96% of all Minnesota counselors in 1968.

TABLE 15-I
SUMMARY OF SAMPLE CHARACTERISTICS

Characteristic	1968	1971	1974
Survey return rate			
Forms sent	139	175	200
Forms returned	139	143	179
Return rate	100%	82%	90%
Size of counselor's community*			
Twin Cities area	49%		46%
Out-state (15,000 and up)	13%		12%
Out-state (4,000 to 15,000)	15%		12%
Out-state (less than 4,000)	23%		30%
Counselor's age			
21-30 years	17%	12%	11%
31-40 years	48%	37%	39%
41-50 years	23%	34%	27%
51 years and up	12%	17%	23%
Sex of Counselor			
Female	22%	24%	26%
Male	78%	76%	74%

*Data on the size of counselor's community are not available from the 1971 study.

by Otto (1973) in 1971. However, a principal components factor analysis of the 1968 data suggested that the most prominent attitude dimensions of the survey could be efficiently measured with 18 of the original 68 items. This conclusion was reinforced when the factor analysis was repeated using 1971 data. The results of varimax rotations of the analyses are reported in Table 15-II. Consequently, the

TABLE 15-II
VARIMAX ROTATED FACTOR STRUCTURE MATRIX OF SURVEY ITEMS BASED ON 1968 DATA WITH LARGEST 1971 LOADINGS IN PARENTHESES

Item	Factor loadings			
	Working Mother	Sex Role Definition	Societal Impact	h^2
1. A woman who works full time cannot possibly be as good a mother to her grade school age children as one who stays at home.	.73 (.71)	.15	.16	.58
2. Women tend to respond emotionally, men by thinking.	.14	.55 (.56)	.05	.33
3. There should be a sex advantage to boys, other things being equal, on the granting of graduate fellowships.	.23	.59 (.60)	.06	.41
4. Women with ability should feel a responsibility for using their talents for the betterment of mankind.*	.05	—.10	.71 (.70)	.51

TABLE 15-II—(continued)

Item	Factor loadings			
	Working Mother	Sex Role Definition	Societal Impact	h^2
5. The values and ideals held by women will have more impact on society if women are encouraged to get sufficient education and professional training.*	.11	.02	.68 (.67)	.46
6. Men are meant to lead, and women, except in extreme circumstances, to follow.	.09	.73 (.72)	.11	.55
7. A married woman with preschool age children is justified in working simply because she wants to.*	.76 (.75)	.11	.01	.59
8. Many emotional and adjustment problems in children are primarily due to working mothers.	.71 (.68)	.15	.07	.53
9. Many women have a responsibility to put their humanizing talents to work outside the home.*	.20	.01	.59 (.58)	.38
10. Man is traditionally the breadwinner and woman is the homemaker, and we should attempt to maintain a definite role separation.	.34	.60 (.60)	.09	.48
11. Courses in math and physics should be considered by more girls than are considering them today.	.06	.14	.60 (.60)	.38
12. Mothers of children under 3 should not work either full or part time unless there is serious economic necessity for so doing.	.74 (.72)	.14	—.02	.56
13. Women should decorate and enhance their homes and leave the larger world to men.	.29	.56 (.57)	.21	.45
14. A choice between being a wife and mother and working full time is no longer necessary as the two can be integrated.*	.66 (.66)	.20	.29	.56
15. One of our greatest untapped resources of competent professionals, in many areas, is women.*	.12	.34	.55 (.54)	.43
16. Boys need to be educated so that they will be more cognizant of the broader role of today's women.*	.09	.27	.51 (.51)	.34
17. Few women have the fortitude and ability to compete in a man's world, such as in economics and politics.	.01	.62 (.61)	.09	.39
18. A married woman with children at home should not become involved at the career level of work.	.66 (.66)	.30	.19	.56
Percentage of variance	18.8	14.9	13.7	
Eigenvalue	5.10	1.90	1.51	

Note. All items without asterisks were scored strongly agree (1) to strongly disagree (5); all items with asterisks were scored strongly agree (5) and strongly disagree (1).

1974 administration included only these eighteen items. Further, year to year changes were traced in the three attitude dimensions tapped by these eighteen items. The three dimensions are defined in the following paragraphs.

The first dimension is the Working Mother factor, which reflects the expected impact of working on the mothering of school-age and pre-school-age children. A high score on this factor indicates support for the dual role of full-time worker and mother, while a low score reflects the attitude that children will not fare well in instances where mothers work (internal consistency reliability = .88).

The second dimension is the Sex Role Definition factor, which reflects attitudes regarding roles assigned to the sexes. In this case, a high score reflects a rejection of rigid, narrowly defined roles and support for broader role definitions. A low score, on the other hand, indicates a more traditional attitude about sex role differences with fixed and clearly defined roles, including a secondary professional role for women (internal consistency reliability = .74).

The third major dimension is the Societal Impact factor, which focuses on the perceived utility of women's special talents. A high score indicates the expectation that women have a contribution to make that will improve social circumstances, while a low score reflects little special impact for women (internal consistency reliability = .69).

Analysis

The individual item responses made by each subject to the eighteen items were transformed into cluster scores by averaging the responses to the six items that were associated with each of the three factors described previously. The resulting scores, which ranged from 1 to 5, were therefore not statistically independent. In fact, the correlations between variables across all 461 subjects were as follows: Working Mother–Sex Role Definition, .53; Working Mother–Societal Impact, .32; and Societal Impact–Sex Role Definition, .29. Consequently, the three cluster scores were used as multiple dependent measures in a three-way multivariate analysis of variance employing year (1968) 1971, and 1974), age of respondent (20s, 30s, 40s, 50 and older), and sex of the respondent as independent variables.

RESULTS

The results of the multivariate analysis of variance, as reported in Table 15-III, indicate statistically significant differences for all three main effects. For two effects, year and sex, this significance carries through each cluster score. However, age differences are not as clearly reflected in the three cluster scores.

TABLE 15-III
RESULTS OF MULTIVARIATE ANALYSIS OF VARIANCE

		Univariate *F*		
Source	Multivariate *F*	Working Mother	Sex Role Definition	Societal Impact
Year (A)	14.8589***	10.68***	40.86***	.01
Age (B)	2.3736*	1.33	1.89	4.57**
Sex (C)	29.1416***	73.78***	43.15***	31.83***
A × B	1.0735	1.25	.86	.44
A × C	.9521	2.25	1.58	.06
B × C	1.2191	2.24	1.35	.84
A × B × C	.8935	.92	1.21	1.38

* $P < .05$.
** $p < .01$.
*** $p < .001$.

Because of the lack of significance of the interactions among the main effects, mean attitude scores have been reported separately in Table 15-IV for the two most prominent independent variables. It is apparent that attitudes about the working mother and about sex role definition are changing rapidly over time. Further, there are reliable and prominent differences between male and female counselors on all three attitude dimensions.

TABLE 15-IV
SUMMARY OF CLUSTER SCORE MEANS BY YEAR AND SEX

	1968			1971			1974		
Sex	$\bar{X}$	σ	n	$\bar{X}$	σ	n	$\bar{X}$	σ	n
	Working Mother Factor								
Female	3.66	.69	31	4.02	.79	34	4.07	.76	46
Male	2.89	.86	108	2.82	.84	109	3.33	1.03	133
Total	3.06	.82	139	3.11	.83	143	3.52	.96	179
	Sex Role Definition factor								
Female	3.91	.62	31	4.47	.56	34	4.52	.46	46
Male	3.37	.70	108	3.73	.74	109	4.13	.69	133
Total	3.49	.68	139	3.91	.70	143	4.23	.63	179
	Societal Impact factor								
Female	4.47	.39	31	4.48	.49	34	4.48	.41	46
Male	4.10	.56	108	4.08	.53	109	4.07	.61	133
Total	4.18	.52	139	4.17	.52	143	4.18	.56	179

The data suggest that males' attitude scores start at levels significantly lower than females' attitude scores and, though they continue to remain lower, are changing at about the same rate. Hints of a leveling of female growth in the Working Mother and Sex Role Definition factors and acceleration in male growth in these same factors are found in observing 1971 to 1974 patterns. However, verification of these trends will have to await additional data in subsequent years.

DISCUSSION

Three major dimensions of counselors' attitudes regarding women and women's social roles were isolated in this study. These included attitudes toward the dual role of mother and worker, attitudes toward sex role definition, and attitudes regarding the expected impact of women on society. Each was reliably measured and traced over a six-year span. The framework of the discussion of the results will be to consider each major attitude factor separately and then to summarize by integrating the three.

The Working Mother Factor

In the past, there has been considerable opposition to women assuming major career commitments when these commitments interfered with mothering. Pre-school-age children particularly were and are thought to need constant maternal care. The amount of time spent with a child has been considered the key to sound development. Today, however, the concept of quality of time spent with a child is being given due consideration, and a working mother is viewed by some as a living example of independence and responsibility (U.S. Department of Labor, 1972). Items reflecting this dimension of thought about women's roles in society compose the first factor.

The Working Mother factor yielded the lowest cluster scores of the three factors for both men and women counselors, indicating the most conservative counselor attitudes. In addition, male and female counselors are farther apart in their attitudes on this factor than they are on either of the other two factors, with the average score for men at 3.0 and women at 3.9 on a five-point scale. Women counselors who might be working mothers could very well be affirming their own lives in this score.

The factor appears to have been resistant to change between the first and second surveys. The average cluster score went up less than .1 point on a five-point scale between 1968 and 1971. After 1971, attitude change appears to have accelerated, as the average score went up about .4 point between the second survey in 1971 and the third survey in 1974. This would certainly suggest more rapid acceptance of the dual role on the part of counselors.

The attitudes of male and female counselors were about as far apart in 1974 as they were in 1968, but both have become significantly more open to the combined worker–mother role. Their growth patterns seem to differ slightly, however. Men's scores began to increase slowly and have accelerated. Women's scores grew rapidly and appear to be slowing. However, since there was no significant interaction between sex and year, a claim of differential growth patterns would merely be speculation. Although the authors suspect such a trend, verification of our hypothesis must await the collection of additional data.

The Sex Role Definition Factor

First, some discussion of the social aspects of this factor seems warranted. Women have traditionally been considered passive and dependent in comparison to men, who are perceived as active and aggressive. As a result of cultural heritage, human traits have acquired a dimension of appropriateness associated with sex.

The traits that have been considered appropriate for women have been very narrowly defined in the past. Women have been concentrated in a few jobs at both professional and nonprofessional levels. It is unlikely that all women are satisfied with being homemakers, nurses, secretaries, and teachers while men have so many more options. Only within the last decade have women in this country in any large number entered schools preparing them for such male preserves as law and medicine.

Although women have been returning to work in larger numbers for some time, it has been reported that the motivation for many of them is economic necessity rather than self-fulfillment (Richards, 1966). However, the psychological literature increasingly ties guidance in career development to self-fulfillment and personal growth for both men and women (Schlossberg & Pietrofesa, 1973; Westervelt, 1973).

The data presented here suggest change in the guidance personnel perceptions paralleling this new social awareness. Counselors' attitudes about sex roles changed significantly from an average cluster score of 3.5 in 1968 to 4.2 in 1974.

Again on this factor, male and female attitudes are significantly different. The women counselors are much more open to diverse sex role definition. The average score for women was 4.3 and for men was 3.7.

Comparing men and women counselors over time is enlightening. However, the same cautious interpretation applied to the previous factor applies here due to the lack of a significant interaction. Males scored significantly lower in 1971, but their scores have increased steadily since then. Females changed their attitudes more quickly between the 1968 and 1971 surveys and showed signs of leveling off between the 1971 and 1974 administrations. As with the Working Mother factor, men and women seem to converge on the Sex Role Definition factor. The reliability of this trend will have to be tested with subsequent data.

The dimension of counselor attitude seems to be changing in a positive direction. Such change could facilitate client growth through the promotion of expanded sex role definition during formative years. A cornerstone of counseling philosophy has been the treatment of clients as unique individuals. This would seem to fit in naturally with the need to give people room to follow their unique talents and interests regardless of sex.

The Societal Impact Factor

The items that compose the Societal Impact factor focus on attitudes about the unique contributions women can make to society. Unlike the others, this factor may be less sensitive to social pressures. It has never been against traditional values to contend that women have a contribution to make. The social valence has come from the definition of the contribution. It is precisely that definition which the first two factors reflected.

Like the other factors, the Societal Impact factor tends to differentiate between male and female counselors, with females scoring higher. However, the gap between males and females was slightly smaller here than on the other factors.

A more pronounced, and perhaps significant, response pattern is reflected in the high level of stability of the attitudes over the six-year span of the study. This seems to support the contention that this factor is the umbrella of the other two. That is, men and women counselors agree that women are valuable to society. But, considering the changes taking place in the other two factors, guidance counselors are reassessing and redefining the true nature of that value.

The Age Variable

The independent variables of interest in this study were selected in the hope that they would help explicate the nature of guidance personnel attitudes with respect to the roles of women. Two of the variables were of considerable value. These were the sex of the counselor and the year of the response. The third variable, age of counselor, showed little relationship to the attitude measures employed. There are at least two viable explanations for this. It may be that guidance personnel are resistant to the hardening of social values that is so frequently said to accompany years of experience. In other words, regardless of age, guidance personnel continue to grow and remain sensitive to the social milieu within which they and their clients are functioning. An equally plausible explanation is that, over the years, guidance counselors who are not sensitive to such social evolution do not remain in the profession. Thus, those who do not reflect the growth apparent to these data may have selected themselves out of the sample. In either case, benefits accrue to the client.

Overview of the Results

Most of the outcomes of this attitude study are consistent with what might have been expected and with what might be considered appropriate by those concerned with the delivery of optimal guidance services. Male and female counselors in Minnesota differ on all three dimensions of attitude toward the female role. But there are signs of significant attitude growth on the part of both male and female counselors that, if appropriately translated into behavior, will ensure maximally open-minded guidance to male and female clients.

Most of the currently popular "awareness-increasing" activities have been designed for women. However, in the segment of the population reflected here, males tend to be paralleling female growth or emergence.

In 1968, the dual role of mother and worker was considered much more acceptable by Minnesota's female guidance counselors than males. Though this was still true in 1974, both males and females had become more accepting of the dual role in 1974 than they were in 1968.

Narrow, unnecessarily restrictive sex role definitions are no longer considered appropriate by either male or female guidance counselors. Once again, men and women differ significantly, but both are rapidly growing to accept a variety of roles. Both male and female counselors expect women to make a significant and unique contribution to society. This expectation has remained strong over the years spanned by this study.

The benefactors of these changing attitudes will undoubtedly be the clients or recipients of the Minnesota guidance service. In particular, the female clients should expect their options to be vastly increased with this emerging awareness of diversity in the role of women.

REFERENCES

Cooperman, I.G. Second careers: War wives and widows. *Vocational Guidance Quarterly,* 1971, *20,* 103-111.

Engelhard, P.A. A survey of counselor attitudes toward women. Unpublished master's thesis, University of Minnesota, 1969.

Koontz, E.D. Counseling women for responsibility. *Journal of the National Association of Women Deans and Counselors,* 1970, *34,* 13-17.

Otto, K.M. Attitudes of selected high school counselors toward women. Unpublished master's thesis, Mankato State College, 1973.

Pringle, M. Counseling women. *Counseling and Personnel Services Information Center (CAPS) Capsule,* 1971, *4,* 11-15.

Richards, C.V. Discontinuities in role expectations of girls. *National Society for the Study of Education Yearbook,* 1966, *1,* 164-188.

Schlossberg, N.K. & Pietrofesa, J.J. Perspectices on counseling bias: Implications for counselor education. *The Counseling Psychologist,* 1973, *4,* 44-53.

Westervelt, E.M. A tide in the affairs of women: The psychological impact of feminism on educated women. *The Counseling Psychologist,* 1973, *4,* 3-26.

U.S. Department of Labor, Women's Bureau. *Twenty facts on women workers.* Washington, D.C.: Author, 1972.

Section IV

THE MEANING OF WORK IN WOMEN'S LIVES: MYTHS, TRENDS, AND REALITIES

THE MEANING of work in women's lives is an area that needs much exploration. While it has been established that most women work for the same reasons men do—largely economic—diverse occupational motives of women have not been fully investigated. There has been concern that many of the efforts to open up options for women have been focused on middle-class women and professional occupations. While there is underrepresentation of women in the professions, there is also underrepresentation in the skilled trades.

This section focuses primarily on the current status of women in the world of paid work in American society. The chapters included present many facts about women's participation and distribution in both professions and skilled trades. Like all aspects of female development, the career development of women has its share of myths. As occupational barriers imposed by sexist attitudes slowly crumble, some obvious truths are revealed. Women differ widely from one another in terms of interests and values; when opportunity is open, women aspire to success in virtually the full range of occupations.

The special problems and concerns of women working in or planning to enter skilled trades receive considerable emphasis in this section. It is important for counselors and others working with women to learn more about occupations in the trades and the unique problems faced by blue-collar women. Hedges and Bemis point to the effects of reducing sex stereotyping in the skilled trades and document the interest of women in these jobs. On a more pessimistic note, Raphael points out that the percentage of female membership in labor unions actually declined in the late sixties.

Her data strongly suggest that the labor movement has not served to protect or advance the economic and vocational welfare of women workers to the same extent that it has benefited men. In spite of legislative action, women compared to men still tend to be underpaid, underemployed, and underprotected from exploitation. Raphael also believes that the so-called protective laws for women do more to protect the status and advancement of male positions than to protect women. She also points out the fact that women have minimal influence within labor unions, as very few hold top union positions.

Raphael discusses some of the differing perceptions of work and the women's movement held by middle-income and blue-collar women. Middle-income women may view work as a means to develop their potential and have choices as to working full or part-time; they tend to identify with the women's movement as a source of support in meeting their goals. In contrast, blue-collar women have few choices; they have to work. They tend to mistrust the women's movement as a source of assistance in bettering their work environments. While these groups currently represent two different forces for change, both would emphasize each woman's right to develop her capabilities in any direction she chooses.

Next, Kievit vividly dramatizes the dilemmas confronting women who seek recognition of their talents and contributions on the job. She uses the situation faced by female vocational educators to exemplify the problems faced by employed women in general. Negative discrimination toward women in pay, promotion, and granting of tenure is still painfully present. She also discovered that female vocational educators are found in traditionally feminine areas such as health occupations, home economics, and office occupations, while males are found in traditionally masculine areas such as agriculture, technical and distributive education. Kievit also notes that even in the "feminine" departments, males are found in the high status positions. She relates these inequities to both occupational discrimination and the socialization process.

Finally, a report from the Women's Bureau describes some of the myths in contrast to the realities of women's motivations for work and participation in the work force.

Chapter 16

SEX STEREOTYPING: ITS DECLINE IN SKILLED TRADES*

JANICE NEIPERT HEDGES AND STEPHEN E. BEMIS

EARLY IN 1973, American Telephone and Telegraph Co. (AT&T) adopted a series of personnel policies to end the "sex stereotyping" of jobs. Major elements of these policies were the goals and timetables for placing women in almost one third of the skilled jobs in the parent company and its subsidiaries.

"Ma Bell" was the first but not the only industrial giant to display a new commitment to equal employment opportunity irrespective of sex. Other employers, large and small, and labor organizations as well, are moving in the same direction.

The activity was sparked by a consent decree signed in January 1973 by American Telephone and Telegraph on behalf of Bell System companies and by the U.S. Department of Labor and the Equal Employment Opportunity Commission on behalf of the Government. The decree signaled the arrival of employment discrimination on the basis of sex as a matter of concern equal to employment discrimination on the basis of race. It called for an end to the domination of either sex in any occupation and underscored the point by levying financial settlements for alleged discrimination. And it identified the skilled trades as one of two major areas in which women were suffering discrimination (management positions were the other).

For the nation as a whole, each decennial census from 1900 through 1960 showed women holding between 2 and 3 percent of all skilled jobs.[1] The dominance of men in the crafts was comparable to the dominance of women in private household work. Even during World War II, when women in defense industries achieved high visibility in traditionally male occupations, they filled no more than 5

**From Monthly Labor Review*, May, 1974, pp. 14-22.*

[1]The term "skilled trades" or "skilled jobs" as used in this article conforms to the Bureau of the Census classification. For a complete listing, see table 16-II. The term is used interchangeably with "craft occupations."

percent of all skilled jobs (Pidgeon, 1947; Wool and Pearlman, 1947).

The absence of any substantial number of women in most of the skilled trades raised questions whether commitments to end sex stereotyping in those occupations would be frustrated by lack of interest on the part of women. But when occupational data by sex for the decennial census of 1970 became available, they suggested that an acceleration in the employment of women in the skilled occupations had been underway before the dramatic governmental and corporate actions of 1973.

DECADE OF GROWTH

In 1970 almost half a million women were working in the skilled occupations, up from 277,000 in 1960. The rate of increase (about 80 percent) was twice that for women in all occupations. (See Table 16-I.) It was eight times the rate of increase for men in the skilled trades. As a result, women in 1970 again held as high a proportion of the jobs in the skilled occupations as they had during World War II.

Moreover, women registered gains during the 1960s almost across the board: in construction, mechanic and repair, and supervisory blue-collar occupations (see Table 16-II). Of roughly eighty trades listed in the census, most showed rates of increase for women that exceeded the rate of increase for men; some exceeded the numerical increase as well. Even in many trades in which the employment of men remained stable or declined, the number of women increased. As late as 1960, women were such a tiny minority in nine trades that the census reported them filled entirely by men. A decade later, no trade was so dominated by men.

Data for 1973 from the Current Population Survey, although not strictly comparable with data from the decennial census,[2] indicate that the movement of women into skilled occupations is continuing.

THE WOMEN IN SKILLED OCCUPATIONS

What are the characteristics of the women who have been attracted to the trades? Do they differ from other women workers? What changes in their traits, if any, have taken place in recent years?

Women employed in the skilled trades in 1970 were several years older on the average than all employed women (see Table 16-III). They had a little less schooling as a group, but two fifths had completed four years of high school and about one tenth had one year of

[2]In recent decennial years, the Current Population Survey has reported from 67 to 80 percent as many women in the trades as the decennial census for the same year. For a discussion of the comparability, see *Accuracy of Census Data as Measured by the 1970 Census Match,* Report PHC (E)–10 (Bureau of the Census).

TABLE 16-I
EMPLOYMENT OF WOMEN IN MAJOR OCCUPATIONAL GROUPS, 1960 AND 1970
(Numbers in thousands)

Occupation	1960		1970		Change, 1960-70	
	Number	Women as percent of total	Number	Women as percent of total	Number	Percent
Total[1]	21,172	32.8	29,170	37.7	7,998	38
Blue-collar workers:						
Craft and kindred workers	277	3.1	495	5.0	218	79
Operatives	3,173	28.0	3,842	30.5	669	21
Nonfarm laborers	173	5.2	269	8.4	96	56
White-collar workers:						
Professional and technical	2,683	38.4	4,314	39.8	1,631	61
Managers and administrative	829	14.7	1,014	16.5	185	22
Sales workers	1,652	35.6	2,000	38.0	348	21
Clerical workers	6,204	68.0	9,582	73.5	3,378	55
Service workers:						
Private household	1,657	96.4	1,052	96.6	—605	—47
Other service workers	2,963	51.5	4,424	54.9	1,461	49
Farm workers:						
Farmers and farm managers	118	4.7	62	4.6	—56	—47
Farm laborers	248	16.7	141	15.2	—107	—43

[1]Includes occupations not reported.
Source: 1970 Census of the Population, Detailed Characteristics, U.S. Summary, Report PC(1)—D (Bureau of the Census), table 221.

college or more. As for their marital status, they were as likely as all employed women to be married, less likely to be single, and more likely to be widows or divorcees. These educational and marital differences probably were associated with their age differences.

Women in the trades differed little from all women workers in regard to race or region. Nationally, about nine out of ten were white, the same proportion as among all women workers. The probability of any employed women being in a skilled job in 1970 (about 1 out of 60) was not significantly different in the South, for example, than in the West, the Northeast, or the North Central States.

About one half the married women in the skilled trades in 1970

TABLE 16-II
WOMEN EMPLOYED IN THE SKILLED TRADES, BY DETAILED TRADE, 1960 AND 1970

Trade[1]	Number of women employed			Women as percent of total	
	1960[2]	1970	Change, 1960-70	1960	1970
Total	277,140	494,871	217,731	3.1	5.0
Automobile accessories installers	....	297	297	...	4.4
Bakers	20,283	32,665	12,382	18.0	29.8
Blacksmiths	101	249	148	.5	2.4
Blue-collar worker supervisor, n.e.c.	77,728	127,751	50,023	7.2	8.0
Construction	206	1,608	1,402	.2	1.1
Durable manufacturing	14,724	25,539	10,815	4.1	4.6
Nondurable manufacturing, including not specified	40,882	52,193	11,311	13.9	14.4
Transportation, communications, and other public utilities	2,480	5,676	3,196	1.2	3.7
All other industries	19,436	42,735	23,299	9.1	11.8
Boilermakers	41	371	330	.2	1.3
Bookbinders	16,513	19,461	2,948	57.9	57.1
Brickmasons and stonemasons	722	2,049	1,327	.5	1.3
Bulldozer operators	....	1,151	1,151	...	1.3
Cabinetmakers	891	3,429	2,538	1.3	5.1
Carpenters	3,312	11,059	7,747	.4	1.3
Carpet installers	....	754	754	...	1.7
Cement and concrete finishers	100	908	808	.2	1.4
Compositors and typesetters	15,494	23,962	8,468	8.2	15.0
Crane, derrick, and hoist operators	656	1,952	1,296	.5	1.3
Decorators and window dressers	23,566	40,408	16,852	46.3	57.6

Trade[1]	Number of women employed			Women as percent of total	
	1960[2]	1970	Change, 1960-70	1960	1970
Machinists	6,685	11,787	5,102	1.3	3.1
Mechanics and repairers	18,329	49,349	31,020	.9	2.0
Air conditioning, heating, and refrigeration	125	1,065	940	.2	.9
Aircraft	1,668	4,013	2,345	1.5	2.9
Automobile body repairers	....	1,332	1,332	...	1.2
Automobile mechanics	2,270	11,130	8,860	.4	1.4
Data processing machine repairers	....	864	864	...	2.7
Farm implement	....	420	420	...	1.2
Heavy equipment mechanics, including diesel	3,345	10,768	7,423	1.2	1.8
Household appliance and accessory installers and mechanics	....	2,550	2,550	...	2.1
Loom fixers	208	437	229	.9	2.1
Office machine	279	688	409	.9	1.7
Radio and television	1,688	5,032	3,344	1.7	3.7
Railroad and car shop	332	510	178	.6	.9
Other	8,414	10,540	2,126	1.2	4.2
Millers, grain, flour, and feed	64	161	97	.7	2.3
Millwrights	80	903	823	.1	1.2
Molders, metal	1,452	5,757	4,305	2.9	10.6
Motion picture projectionists	390	670	280	2.2	4.2
Opticians and lens grinders and polishers	3,045	6,121	3,076	15.0	22.3
Painters, construction and maintenance	6,449	13,386	6,937	1.9	4.1

Dental laboratory technicians	641	6,057	5,416	4.3	22.7
Electricians	2,483	8,646	6,163	.7	1.8
Electric power and cable installers	1,648	1,457	–191	2.1	1.4
Electrotypers and stereotypers	72	283	211	.8	4.0
Engravers, except photoengravers	1,948	2,333	385	17.3	26.6
Excavating, grading, road machine operators except bulldozer operators	688	2,513	1,825	.4	1.1
Floor layers, except tile setters	882	364	–518	4.9	1.7
Forge and hammer operators	769	724	–45	6.4	4.7
Furniture and wood finishers	768	3,600	2,832	3.5	16.9
Furriers	1,936	461	[3]–1,475	40.4	17.3
Glaziers	227	783	556	1.3	3.1
Heat treaters, annealers, and temperers	293	598	305	1.4	2.9
Inspectors, scalers, and graders, log and lumber	798	1,877	1,079	3.9	11.0
Inspectors, n.e.c	5,670	8,865	3,195	5.8	7.5
Construction	100	334	234	.7	1.5
Railroads and railway express service	76	247	171	.3	1.0
Jewelers and watchmakers	2,239	4,285	2,046	6.0	11.5
Job and die setters, metal	322	2,221	1,899	.6	2.6
Locomotive engineers	85	396	311	.1	.8
Locomotive firemen	104	151	47	.3	1.2
Paper hangers	1,455	1,111	[3]–344	6.0	10.3
Pattern and model makers, except paper	647	1,858	1,211	1.6	4.8
Photoengravers and lithographers	2,847	3,851	1,004	10.4	11.8
Piano and organ tuners and repairers	153	330	177	2.5	4.8
Plasterers	158	435	277	.3	1.5
Plumbers and pipe fitters	952	4,110	3,158	.3	1.1
Power station operators	1,375	557	[3]–818	5.1	3.0
Printing press operators	4,818	13,374	8,526	5.8	8.5
Rollers and finishers, metal	802	1,264	462	4.2	6.4
Roofers and slaters	107	749	642	.2	1.3
Sheetmetal workers and tinsmiths	1,530	2,902	1,372	1.1	1.9
Shipfitters	....	123	123	...	1.2
Shoe repairers	2,759	6,359	3,600	6.7	20.3
Sign painters and letterers	1,286	1,614	328	4.6	8.5
Stationary engineers	1,563	2,472	909	.5	1.4
Stone cutters and stone carvers	132	445	313	2.0	7.0
Structural metal workers	909	883	–26	1.5	1.2
Tailors	21,728	21,265	[3]–463	26.5	31.4
Telephone installers and repairers	3,018	8,289	5,271	2.0	3.5
Telephone line installers and repairers	824	762	–62	2.0	1.5
Tile setters	....	378	378	...	1.2
Tool and die makers	1,128	4,197	3,069	.6	2.1
Upholsterers	5,668	9,980	4,312	9.4	16.0
Craft and kindred workers, n.e.c	5,777	7,339	1,562	6.7	8.5

[1]Some of the occupational titles that appear in this table and elsewhere in the article are recent modifications of older titles which denoted or connoted sex stereotyping. The new titles were accomplished by a subcommittee of the Interagency Committee on Occupation Classification, under the auspices of the Office of Management and Budget. (See "Removal of Sex Stereotyping in Census Occupational Classification," *Monthly Labor Review*, January 1974, pp. 67-68.)

[2]Adjusted to 1970 occupation classifications. See John A. Priebe, Joan Heinkel, and Stanley Green, *1970 Occupation and Industry Classification Systems in Terms of Their 1960 Occupation and Industry Elements*, Technical Paper 26 (Bureau of the Census, 1972).

[3]Also showed a decline in *total* employment.

Source: *1970 Census of Population, Detailed Characteristics, U.S. Summary*, Final Report PC(1)–D1 (Bureau of the Census), table 221.

TABLE 16-III
AGE AND EDUCATION OF WOMEN EMPLOYED IN ALL OCCUPATIONS AND IN THE SKILLED TRADES, 1970 AND 1973
(Persons 16 years of age and older)

Age and years of schooling	1970		1973	
	All occupations	Skilled trades	All occupations	Skilled trades
Age				
Percent under 35 years	41.7	32.2	46.6	38.0
Median years of age	39.2	42.9	36.9	40.4
Years of School Completed[1]				
Total (percent distribution)	100.0	100.0	100.0	100.0
Elementary, 8 years or less	14.0	21.3	10.4	15.7
High school	61.2	67.9	63.2	72.0
1 to 3 years	20.6	27.6	17.8	23.6
4 years	40.6	40.3	45.4	48.4
College	24.8	10.8	26.4	12.3
1 to 3 years	14.0	8.3	14.0	9.3
4 years or more	10.8	2.5	12.4	3.0
Median school years	12.4	12.0	12.5	12.2

[1]March.

Note: Data for 1973 from the Current Population Survey are not strictly comparable with 1970 data from the decennial census. For further explanation, see text footnote 3.

Source: For 1970, *Census of Population: 1970* (Bureau of the Census); for 1973, Current Population Survey.

were wives of blue-collar workers—25 percent married to men who worked in the trades, 23 percent to operatives in factories or transportation, and 6 percent to nonfarm laborers. Almost one fourth were married to men in one of the white-collar occupations. The remainder were wives of men in farm or service occupations.

EDUCATIONAL GAP NARROWS

Perhaps the most significant change in characteristics between 1960 and 1970 was in level of education. During the decade, the average years of schooling completed by women in skilled occupations had risen by one year, three times the average rise for all women workers. Average age declined by about one-half year from 1960 to 1970, less than the decline for all employed women.

Current Population Surveys provide the most recent data on the characteristics of women in the trades: for 1973, an educational level of 12.2 years, slightly higher than had been reported in the 1970 census. The increase brought the educational level of women in the skilled trades within 0.3 years of the level of all women workers. Median age in 1973 was about 40 years, approximately 2.5 years lower than the average age reported in the 1970 census.

The characteristics of women employed in skilled occupations are of interest to those seeking to hire or train more women for work in the trades. But they provide little insight into the reasons for the growth of this group since 1960.

Over this period, women were entering one of the slower growing occupational groups at a rate that far exceeded their entry into professional, clerical, or service occupations (in which total employment was growing more rapidly). Powerful forces apparently were at work; these forces, however, did not seem to be operating through channels.

Like work institutions, most educational institutions have been firmly wedded to sex stereotyping. Counseling, hidden quotas, and scholarship and loan provisions posed obstacles to the entry of college-educated women into "masculine" professions such as medicine, law, science, and architecture. (U.S. House of Representatives, 1970–71; Women's Bureau, 1971a). But the larger group of women—those whose formal education ended with graduation from secondary school or earlier—had even less opportunity to break out of the circle of "women's occupations."

A national blind spot vis-à-vis women in skilled trades was illustrated by the report on secondary schools in the United States, prepared in 1967 by a committee of the National Association of Secondary School Principals (Conant, 1967). The report focused on unequal opportunities for education from one community to another, but was oblivious to the need for equal opportunity, irrespective of sex, *within* a community. It recommended that all "academically able students" study mathematics and science, but reinforced sex stereotyping of vocational and technical education by urging that "programs should be available for girls interested in developing skills in typing, stenography, the use of clerical machines, or home economics. . . For boys, depending on the community, trade and industrial programs should be available."

REBIRTH OF A MOVEMENT

It was in this atmosphere that the feminist movement resurged in the mid-1960s. Broadly based, including reformists and more radical groups, it demonstrated a force unknown for half a century in its drive to remove the limitations on women's activities in every sphere. In a return to the philosophy of the earliest feminists, before the suffragists brought about "a narrowing of vision" (Chafe, 1972), the movement enveloped every front: social, legal, economic, and psychological. Each had consequences for the skilled trades.

Social

On the social front, the women's movement demanded that a rational division of work in the home as well as in the workplace supersede the traditional division along sex lines. The demarcation between men's and women's activities in the home had already shown signs of weakening under the long-term employment of many wives. The sharing of household tasks, which husbands of working wives undertook "as a favor," became a routine, then an obligation (Chafe, 1972). Women in turn began to try their hand at more of the "masculine" skills: carpentry, plumbing, and auto repair, as well as painting, paperhanging, and furniture refinishing.

For some women, the "do-it-yourself" movement paved the way by providing amateurs with instructions for some of the simpler home maintenance and repair jobs usually performed by skilled tradesmen. Familiarity with the tools and techniques of a trade sometimes led to an interest in developing a higher level of skill. Adult education programs introduced special courses for women in the maintenance and repair of homes and automobiles. Courses for housewives in taking care of their own property sometimes evolved into occupational training.

The extent to which women's penetration of the trades was a break with their traditional activities, either in the home or in the workplace, was revealed by the list of fourteen trades with increases of 5,000 women or more from 1960 to 1970. Only two (baker and decorator) fit the standard explanation offered for women's participation in the labor force and their occupational distribution—namely, that women followed their homemaking duties out of the home. Two occupations on the list were blue-collar supervisors, representing an upgrading of some working women from less skilled occupations. But the other ten trades in the group were a departure from women's traditional activities—automobile mechanic, carpenter, compositor and typesetter, dental laboratory technician, electrician, heavy equipment mechanic, machinist, painter, printing press operator, and telephone installer and repairer.

Legal

On the legal front, Title VII of the Civil Rights Act of 1964 provided the framework to assure equal opportunity for women to enter any occupation. Claims of sex discrimination now constitute more than one-fifth of all charges filed with the Equal Employment Opportunity Commission (EEOC), which enforces Title VII.[3] The prohibition of discrimination in employment based on sex is enforced as vigorously as the prohibition of discrimination on the basis of race.

Further federal support for equal employment opportunity for women in every type of work was provided by Executive Order 11375, which added sex discrimination to other types of discrimination prohibited earlier in Executive Order 11246. The orders apply to most firms furnishing goods or services to the federal government or doing federally funded construction. The Office of Federal Contract Compliance (OFCC) was set up in the U.S. Department of Labor to administer these orders (U.S. Department of Labor, 1971a).

Provisions of state protective labor laws that operate against equal employment opportunity for women were held by the EEOC to be in conflict with Title VII and not available to employers as a defense against charges of discrimination. Very few if any of them are enforceable today, except where they provide benefits that can be extended to men.[4] The state laws, intended to protect women from overtime, shift work, or heavy physical demands, had in effect excluded them from many jobs.

Economic

On the economic front, the drive for equality with men was of critical importance in the skilled trades. With two fifths of all women already employed, their right to paid work was no longer at issue. The point at issue was women's low earnings relative to those of men.

Equal pay for equal work was an initial objective of the women's movement. Passage of the Equal Pay Act of 1963 helped to ameliorate this problem. But the difference between men's and women's earnings was due only in part to some employers paying women less than men for the same job. The concentration of women in relatively few occupations (Hedges, 1970) contributed to the disparity. Some "women's occupations" paid less because the skill level assigned to them was underrated (University of Wisconsin Extension, 1974), others because the skill level actually was low relative to "men's occupations." Shorter work experience and other factors also played a part (Council of Economic Advisors, 1973). But it seemed evident that economic equality would require the occupational dispersion of women (Cohen, 1972).

With their legal right to equal employment opportunity estab-

[3]*Seventh Annual Report of the Equal Employment Opportunity Commission* (Washington, 1973).

[4]"Effect of Sex-Oriented State Employment Legislation," *EEOC Guidelines on Discrimination*, 37 FR 6835, Sec. 1604. 2B, Apr. 5, 1972. For resolution of conflict between State protective laws and Title VII by requiring women's benefits to be extended to men, see *Hays v. Potlatch Forests, Inc.*, 465S. 2d, 1081, 1972.

lished, women were drawn to work that paid well.[5] For those with a high school education, such jobs were most likely to be found in the skilled trades.

In addition to higher pay scales,[6] the trades offer other economic advantages over many of the occupations in which women are concentrated. Apprenticeship systems offer beginners paid employment, along with two to four years of progressive on-the-job training and related classroom instruction. Apprentices receive pay increases at stated intervals, as well as paid vacations and holidays, sick leave, and workmen's compensation.

Psychological

The women's movement and the economic advantages of the skilled trades have been important forces leading women into the skilled occupations, but other forces as well have played a part. Among them has been the search for work more satisfying than that offered in many of the occupations traditionally open to women with a high school education.

As long as most women viewed paid employment as an interlude between the completion of their formal education and marriage, job satisfaction tended to be of minimal interest. But in 1960, the work-life expectancy for women at birth was twenty years, up from twelve years in 1940 (Wolfbein, 1963). With the prospect of a further extension in the years that women spend in the labor force, the satisfaction that could be found in a job was of increasing importance.

Jobs in the skilled trades generally present a striking contrast to the controlled and fragmented jobs of many factory and office workers. Many offer more independence and freedom, as illustrated by the opportunity to develop particular ways of working and to move about while performing the work, and individual ownership of tools. The work itself, which may involve producing a finished product, brings a sense of achievement.

In addition, some women find the outdoor work that typifies some skilled occupations more satisfying than work in offices, factories, or

---

[5]*Economic Report of the President, 1973,* p. 103. A shift in occupational distribution in the direction of higher earnings occupations has been noted for both men and women. During the 1950s the shift was more rapid for men than for women, but during the 1960s it was similar for men and women.

[6]Average hourly rates in male–and female-dominated occupations, based on annual and monthly averages reported in the *Occupational Outlook Handbook,* are illustrative: In 1972, the union minimum hourly wage rate for carpenters was $7.14, for construction electricians $8.19, and for hand compositors in the day shift in newspaper plants $5.94. Journeymen automobile mechanics in automobile dealerships had average hourly rates of $6.15. In contrast, general stenographers had an average hourly rate of $3.22, experienced accounting clerks $3.93, and licensed practical nurses in public health agencies $3.17. *Occupational Outlook Handbook, 1974-75 Edition,* Bulletin 1785 (Bureau of Labor Statistics, 1974).

stores. And some women like to work with their hands, a characteristic of all the skilled trades.

A prime factor in bringing women into the skilled trades was employer confidence in their ability to perform those jobs. Such confidence has been building for several decades. The employment of women in skilled jobs in aircraft plants, shipyards, foundries, and other defense industries during World War II had a strong and lasting effect on attitudes. The women who worked in those jobs captured the imagination of the public. More important, their work was compared favorably with that of men with equivalent training and experience (Women's Bureau, 1942). Many of the women left the skilled trades in the postwar period, as defense industries cut back employment or as returning veterans reclaimed their jobs. But the ability of women to function in those occupations had been demonstrated.

Many women have the aptitudes to perform jobs that have been dominated by men. Extensive studies by the Human Engineering Laboratory of the Johnson O'Connor Research Foundation in the area of aptitudes, dating back to 1922, indicate no significant sex differences in the majority of the aptitude and knowledge areas studied (Durkin, 1972). Of the remaining areas, men excel in two and women in six (see Table 16-IV).

The aptitudes of job applicants have been related to occupational requirements by the U.S. Employment Service (USES) over a period of years. The primary tool used is the General Aptitude Test Battery (GATB), which yields assessments in nine areas (U.S. Department of Labor, 1970; Droege, 1967). In the seven areas which are important to success in the skilled trades, two reveal no sex differences, women excel in four, and men in one. The aptitude differences found in the research of these two organizations are similar to those found in research in other countries (Australian Department of Labour and National Service, 1970; Karvonen, 1971).

The U.S. Department of Labor (1965) has established levels of strength required in various occupations, including the skilled trades. However, sufficient data are not available on the ability of the average man or woman to meet those physical demands.[7] In a number of trades, physical requirements are no higher than for housework; in others, they are within the capabilities of many women and beyond the capabilities of some men. Increasing mechanization has reduced and continues to reduce requirements of strength and stamina. In some skilled jobs, laborsaving devices could make the work more tolerable for workers now employed as well as remove unnecessary barriers to employment for men or women of lesser physical stamina.

[7]However, a Swedish study of aerobic power (oxygen uptake) compared the stamina of men and women. See discussion in Karvonen, 1971.

TABLE 16-IV
COMPARISONS OF THE PERFORMANCE OF MEN AND WOMEN IN SELECTED APTITUDE AREAS

Aptitude	Group with higher average performance
U.S. Employment Service	
Numerical reasoning	—
Spatial reasoning	Male
Form perception	Female
Clerical perception	Female
Motor coordination	Female
Finger dexterity	Female
Manual dexterity	—
Human Engineering Laboratory	
Abstract visualization	Female
Analytical reasoning	—
Eyedness	—
Finger dexterity	Female
Foresight	—
Grip	Male
Graphoria (accounting aptitude)	Female
Ideaphoria (flow of ideas in verbal pursuits)	Female
Inductive reasoning	—
Memory for design	—
Number memory	—
Observation	Female
Objective personality	—
Pitch discrimination	—
Rhythm memory	—
Silograms (word association)	Female
Structural visualization	Male
Subjective personality	—
Timbre discrimination	—
Tonal memory	—
Tweezer dexterity	—
Vocabulary (English)	—

Note: Dashes indicate no significant difference. Although the differences shown are statistically significant, in most cases they would be of little practical significance. To illustrate, USES research has found spatial reasoning to be important for many of the skilled trades. But the level required exceeds an employed worker average for only one trade. Studies of seniors in high schools throughout the country showed that 67 percent of the boys and 62 percent of the girls equal or exceed this average. This means that more than half the girls have at least the minimum amount of spatial reasoning needed for most skilled trades.

Physical requirements established by employers often are higher than the actual demands of the job. Guidelines issued by both the Office of Federal Contract Compliance (1971) and the Equal Employment Opportunity Commission (1970) prohibit such artificial barriers if they adversely affect minority or women applicants.

THE FUTURE

The employment of women in the skilled trades can be expected to increase as widespread reappraisal and rejection of the sex stereotyping of jobs are reflected in institutional changes.

Government

Prohibition of sex discrimination in employment has become a standard provision of legislation, executive orders, and regulations on equal employment opportunity.

The federal government is not satisfied with passive nondiscrimination. Acting under authority derived from Executive Orders 11246 and 11375, the Office of Federal Contract Compliance has issued an order (Revised Order No. 4) which requires contractors to take "affirmative action" to place women and minorities in jobs in which they are underrepresented. Goals and timetables are an important part of this affirmative action requirement.

At the local level, a number of Human Relations Commissions or Fair Employment Commissions have been established throughout the country. While the authority of these state, city, or county commissions varies considerably, some require goals and timetables from employers operating within their jurisdictions.

The consent decree signed by AT&T in 1973 promises to have a substantial impact throughout industry. The unison with which several federal agencies acted under the combined authority of the Civil Rights Act, the Equal Pay Act, and Executive Order 11246, as amended, together with the financial settlements for alleged discrimination, have alerted employers to the fact that sex stereotyping of occupations must be ended promptly through affirmative action.

Apprenticeship

The Bureau of Apprenticeship and Training (BAT) of the U.S. Department of Labor (1971b) requires all trades, including those in construction, to establish equal opportunity standards for the recruitment, selection, and employment of apprentices without discrimination because of race, color, sex, religion, or national origin.

Joint efforts to increase apprenticeship opportunities for women were undertaken by the Bureau of Apprenticeship and Training and the Women's Bureau (1971b) in 1968, bringing to the attention of employers, unions, and women the opportunities available in apprenticeship as a route out of low-paying, dead-end jobs. Apprenticeship programs for women have been established in several federal agencies—the Armed Forces, Government Printing Office, and others—to supply their own needs for skilled personnel.

A project conducted from 1970 to 1973 by the Wisconsin State Division of Apprenticeship and Training (1973) and the University of Wisconsin Extension Service, in collaboration with the Wisconsin Governor's Commission on the Status of Women, isolated, analyzed, and to some extent minimized barriers to apprenticeships for women. Among the project report's recommendations were the development of outreach programs to interest women in apprenticeship and admission of girls to preapprenticeship classes in public schools.

Some believe that further federal affirmative action requirements are needed to assure opportunities for women in many apprenticeable trades, especially in construction trades. The Office of Federal Contract Compliance requires (1) equal employment opportunity without regard to race, creed, color, national origin, or sex, and (2) that goals and timetables be established for employment of minorities in construction trades covered by Hometown Plans developed in about seventy cities and counties. But the goals and timetables requirements do not extend to women. (Revised Order No. 4 does not cover the construction trades.) Although the equal employment opportunity requirements of the Bureau of Apprenticeship and Training cover women, the requirements that the trades take affirmative action steps toward the indenturing of minorities (including the establishment of goals and timetables) do not extend to women. The precedent has been established, however, and perhaps the future will see one or both of these agencies requiring goals and timetables, and other affirmative action steps, for the employment of women in the construction trades.

Education and Training

Women still face rigid sex stereotyping in secondary education (U.S. Department of Health, Education, and Welfare, 1972a). However, vocational and technical schools are playing a somewhat larger role than in previous years in preparing women for skilled work.

In public school trade and industrial programs (many of which are considered preapprenticeship training), enrollments of women increased nationally from 116,000 in fiscal year 1966 to 280,000 in 1972 (U.S. Department of Health, Education, and Welfare, 1972b). Women were 12 percent of total enrollments in the latter year, with an overall rate of increase since 1966 half again that for men. In 1973, 500 or more women were enrolled in air conditioning, appliance repair, auto body and fender repair, auto mechanics, aviation occupations, carpentry, electricity, construction and maintenance, electrical occupations, electronic occupations, metalworking occupations, small engine repair, and woodworking.

In view of the prohibition of sex discrimination in training programs financially assisted by the Federal Government (contained in the Education Amendments of 1972), it seems reasonable to expect additional enrollments of women in trade and industrial training in the years ahead.

Although inadequate skill training has been a barrier to women's employment in the skilled occupations, general education is not a problem. In professional, managerial, sales, and operative occupations, men have an educational advantage over women (from 0.2 to 0.5 years of schooling in 1970). But in the skilled trades, men and women have the same level of education.

The growing interest in skilled occupations among women is illustrated by the variety of organizations that offer or sponsor training programs. The National Association of Women in Construction has a twelve-week course in the basics of construction, designed to upgrade women already working in the industry and to train high school girls. The United Community Services Demonstration and Development Fund in San Diego, Calif., offers an intensive twenty-week program (Project Repair), endorsed by the San Diego-Imperial Counties Central Labor Council, AFL-CIO. The YWCA in Denver (Better Jobs for Women) and Advocates for Women in San Francisco (an apprenticeship outreach program) are of particular significance. Both work with employers and unions to place women in apprenticeship programs and apprentice-type jobs.

Employment

Employment growth in the trades will affect the number of jobs available for either men or women. The level of employment in skilled occupations is influenced by many factors, including growth in the manufacturing and construction industries, which employ large numbers of craft workers, and trends toward automation and work simplification. An increase of 2.2 million jobs in the skilled trades has been projected for the period 1972–85. This increase would bring total employment to 13.0 million in 1985 (Rosenthal, 1973). Additional openings will occur from deaths and retirements among those employed. With growth and replacement combined, job openings during the period are projected to total 5.3 million, or more than 400,000 a year.

Women seem well placed to realize a more equal share of employment in the skilled trades. Many of the occupations into which substantial numbers already have moved employ from 100,000 to well over 800,000 workers. In occupations of that size, replacement needs alone require many new workers. In addition, women have moved into a number of trades that are both large and expanding.

Theoretically, given the similarity of aptitudes among men and women, the only limits to an equal division of jobs in the skilled trades are the ratio of women to men in the labor force and the physical requirements of some trades. The importance of the latter will decline with increasing mechanization.

In practice, a combination of social, legal, economic, and other factors is effecting a significant increase in the relative importance of the skilled trades for women vis-à-vis both their traditional occupations and their share of the skilled jobs.

REFERENCES

Australian Department of Labour and National Service, *Sex Differences in Performance on Test VG-S;* Vocational Guidance Technical Paper 1 (Melbourne, Australian Department of Labour and National Service, 1970).

William Henry Chafe, *The American Woman: Her Changing Social, Economic, and Political Roles, 1920-70.* (New York, The Oxford University Press, 1972).

Malcolm S. Cohen, "Sex Differences in Compensation," *The Journal of Human Resources, Fall* 1971, pp. 434-47, and *Fact Sheet on the Earnings Gap* (Washington, U.S. Department of Labor, Employment Standards Administration, Women's Bureau, 1972).

James B. Conant, *The Comprehensive High School: Report of the Committee for the Study of the American Secondary School* (New York, McGraw-Hill Book Co., 1967).

Council of Economic Advisers, "Economic Role of Women," *Economic Report of the President, 1973* (Washington, Council of Economic Advisers, 1973), ch. 4, p. 104.

Robert C. Droege, "Sex Differences in Aptitude Maturation During High School," *Journal of Counseling Psychology,* 1967, pp. 407-11.

Jon J. Durkin, *The Potential of Women,* Research Bulletin 87 (Washington, Johnson O'Connor Research Foundation, 1972).

Education Amendments of 1972, Public Law 92-318, Title IX, U.S. Congress, June 23, 1972.

Equal Employment Opportunity Commission. *Guidelines on Employee Selection Procedures* (Equal Employment Opportunity Commission, 1970), 29 CFR, 1607.

Janice Neipert Hedges, "Women workers and manpower demands in the 1970's," *Monthly Labor Review,* June 1970, pp. 19-29. BLS Reprint 2678.

M.J. Karvonen, "Women and Men at Work." *World Health,* Geneva, January 1971.

Office of Federal Contract Compliance, *Employee Testing and Other Selection Procedures* (Office of Federal Contract Compliance, 1971), 41 CFR 60-3.

Mary Elizabeth Pidgeon, "Women Workers and Recent Economic Change," *Monthly Labor Review,* December 1947, pp. 666-71.

Neal H. Rosenthal, "The United States economy in 1985: projected changes in occupations," *Monthly Labor Review,* December 1973, pp. 18-26.

University of Wisconsin Extension, *Report of the Dictionary of Occupational Titles Research Project* (Madison, Wisconsin Department of Industry, Labor, and

Human Relations and the University of Wisconsin Extension. In process).
U.S. Department of Health, Education, and Welfare, *A Look at Women in Education: Issues and Answers for HEW* (Washington, U.S. Department of Health, Education, and Welfare, Office of Education, 1972a).
———. *Summary Data, Vocational Education, Fiscal Year 1972* (Washington, U.S. Department of Health, Education, and Welfare, Office of Education, 1972b).
U.S. Department of Labor, *Dictionary of Occupational Titles, Vol. II* (Washington, U.S. Department of Labor, 1965).
———. *Manual for the General Aptitude Test Battery, Section III: Development* (Washington, U.S. Department of Labor, 1970).
———. *Affirmative Action Programs* (U.S. Department of Labor, Office of Federal Contract Compliance, 1971), 41 CFR 60-2, Dec. 4, 1971a (known as Revised Order No. 4).
———. *Equal Employment Opportunity in Apprenticeship and Training* (U.S. Department of Labor, Manpower Administration, Bureau of Apprenticeship and Training, 1971b.) 29CFR 30.
U.S. House of Representatives, *Discrimination Against Women*, Hearings before the Special Subcommittee on Education of the Committee on Education and Labor on Sec. 805 of H.R. 16098. U.S. House of Representatives, 91st cong., 2d sess., June-July 1970, Vol. I, 1970; Vol. 2, 1971.
Wisconsin State Division of Apprenticeship and Training et al., *Women in Apprenticeship: Why Not?* (Madison, State of Wisconsin, Department of Industry. Labor, and Human Relations, Division of Apprenticeship and Training, 1973).
Seymour L. Wolfbein, *Changing Patterns of Work Life* (U.S. Department of Labor, Manpower Administration, 1963), p. 13.
Harold Wool and Lester M. Pearlman, "Recent Occupational Trends," *Monthly Labor Review*, August 1947, pp. 139-47.
Women's Bureau; *"Equal Pay" for Women in War Industries*, Bulletin 196 (U.S. Department of Labor, Women's Bureau, 1942), pp. 5-7.
———. *Continuing Education Programs and Services for Women*, Pamphlet 10 (Washington, U.S. Department of Labor, Employment Standards Administration, Women's Bureau, 1971a).
———, *Why Not Be an Apprentice?* Leaflet 52 (U.S. Department of Labor, Employment Standards Administration, Women's Bureau, Reprint 1971b).

Chapter 17

WORKING WOMEN AND THEIR MEMBERSHIP IN LABOR UNIONS*

EDNA E. RAPHAEL

LABOR union membership affects the status of women in many ways. Perhaps most important is the fact that the large and pervasive income disparities between employed men and employed women are less when the women are union members. On the whole, this advantage probably derives less from union membership as such than from the fact that women are more likely to be union members when employed in industries where men predominate—where, by and large, wages are higher than in industries where women predominate.

Despite advantages which accrue to women through union membership, however, between 1966 and 1970 the proportion of working women who were members of labor unions declined, even as women's participation in the labor force increased. The proportion of working men who were union members also declined, but the decline was greater among women.

The following discussion documents the difference in earnings of women who are union members and those who are not, as well as the recent proportional decline in union membership. Other sections review the current status of legislation to guarantee equal rights for women and the stance of labor unions with respect to equal employment opportunities for women.

EARNINGS DIFFERENCES

Recent government surveys provide evidence of the higher earnings of union members, both men and women. However, and without

*More recent data from the Bureau of Labor Statistics biennial report on membership in labor unions and employee associations indicates that the proportion of working women who were union members was the same in 1972 as in 1970, despite the increase in the number of working women. More detailed information has been presented in the BLS Bulletin, *Directory of National Unions and Employee Associations, 1973.*

From Monthly Labor Review, May 1974, pp. 27-33.

exception, in all broad occupational categories and in both 1966 and 1970, the earnings of men were disproportionately higher than those of women. This held for union members and nonmembers, for the country as a whole, and for its four major regions.[1]

In the aggregate, among women who by occupation of longest job held in 1966 and 1970 were employed as private wage and salary workers (including both full-time and part-time workers), union members had higher earnings than nonmembers. The advantage was greater for women than for similarly employed men. The median income of women union members was roughly 80 percent higher in 1966 and 70 percent in 1970 than that of nonunion women (Table 17-I). The comparable advantage for male union members was only 30 percent in both 1966 and 1970.

For both men and women, the earnings advantage of union members was greater in blue-collar and service occupations than in white-collar occupations. In 1970 white-collar women union members had a 44 percent income advantage over nonunion women, but among white-collar men union members earned 8 percent less than nonunion workers.

Comparisons between men and women reveal that whether in unions or not, and in 1966 as well as in 1970, men earned more than women. In 1970, the earnings gap between men and women was narrower among union members who are white-collar or service workers, but wider among union members who are blue-collar workers. For example, among white-collar workers in 1970, nonunion men earned 180 percent more than nonunion women; union men earned 80 percent more than union women. Similarly, among service workers in 1970, nonunion men earned 120 percent more than nonunion women, union men 70 percent more than union women. Among blue-collar workers, income disparities between men and women were higher for union members than for nonmembers. In 1970, among nonunion blue-collar workers, men earned 90 percent more than women; among union members, men earned 100 percent more. This pattern holds when the comparison is limited to operatives (where women are more likely to be employed): among nonunion operatives in 1970, men earned 80 percent more than women; among union members, 90 percent more.

Since larger proportions of women than of men work part time, the earnings gap between men and women was less among full-time year-round private wage and salary workers than among all wage and salary

[1]*Labor Union Membership in 1966,* Current Population Reports, P–20, No. 216 (Bureau of the Census, 1971); *Selected Earnings and Demographic Characteristics of Union Members, 1970,* Report 417 (Bureau of Labor Statistics, 1972); *Directory of National Unions and Employee Associations, 1971,* Bulletin 1750 (Bureau of Labor Statistics, 1972).

TABLE 17-I

RATIO OF EARNINGS OF PRIVATE WAGE AND SALARY WORKERS, BY UNION MEMBERSHIP AND SEX, 1966 AND 1970

Occupation group of longest job	Ratio of median earnings								Labor union membership							Women private wage and salary workers (in thousands)	
	Men to women, by union membership				Union member to non-member, by sex				Percent with union membership				Percent change, 1966-70				
	Union		Nonunion		Men		Women		Men		Women		Men	Women			
	1966	1970	1966	1970	1966	1970	1966	1970	1966	1970	1966	1970	Direct	Direct	Adjusted[1]	1966	1970
Total	2.0	2.0	2.8	2.5	1.3	1.3	1.8	1.7	31.4	28.5	12.9	10.3	−2.9	−2.6	−5.5	26,065	28,632
White-collar workers	[2]	1.8	2.8	2.8	1.0	0.9	[2]	1.4	12.7	10.4	7.8	6.4	−2.3	−1.4	−2.3	13,517	15,352
Blue-collar workers	[2]	2.0	2.2	1.9	1.6	1.6	[2]	1.5	45.4	43.0	31.8	28.2	−2.4	−3.6	−5.2	[3] 5,780	[3] 5,749
Operatives	1.9	1.9	2.0	1.8	1.6	1.6	1.7	1.5	48.7	46.9	35.2	29.4	−1.9	−5.8	−8.0	5,444	5,002
Service workers, including private household	1.8	1.7	2.1	2.2	2.5	2.6	2.9	3.3	19.3	17.3	4.5	4.6	−2.0	.1	.4	6,195	7,129

[1]Adjusted values represent change in percent of women with union membership from 1966 to 1970 which would obtain if, in 1966, the percent of women in each occupational group who were union members had been the same as the percent of men who were union members:

$$\frac{\text{Percent of men with union membership, 1966}}{\text{Percent of women with union membership, 1966}} \times \text{Change in percent of women with union membership, 1966-70}$$

[2]The 1966 data on earnings were not published by white-collar and blue-collar categories. Data on earnings of union women by specific occupational groups cannot be aggregated to blue-collar and white-collar totals, because data are not published if the base is less than 100,000.

[3]In 1966, nonfarm laborers and farm workers are combined into a separate category. In 1970, nonfarm laborers are reported as a separate blue-collar category.

Source: For 1966 computations, *Labor Union Membership in 1966, Current Population Reports,* Series P-20, No. 216 (Bureau of the Census, 1971); For 1970 computations, unpublished background materials for *Selected Earnings and Demographic Characteristics of Union Members,* 1970, Report 417 (Bureau of Labor Statistics, 1972).

workers. Nevertheless, marked disparities in earnings remain, and here again union membership was not always associated with reduction of the disparity. Among year-round full-time blue-collar workers in the Northeast and South, in both 1966 and 1970, income disparities between men and women were greater among labor union members than nonmembers. This disparity between men and women increased in 1970 (Table 17-II). In the North Central region, on the other hand, the income disparity between men and women union members in blue-collar jobs was reduced in 1970 so that it was lower than among nonunion men and women.

Within industries, men were more likely than women to be labor union members (Table 17-III). This finding holds equally for white-collar and blue-collar workers and, where adequate data are available, for service workers as well. Both men and women were more likely to be labor union members if employed in industries predominantly composed of male workers. Or, to put it another way, an industry is more likely to be unionized if most of its workers are men.

Among white-collar workers, men and women were equally likely to be union members in the transportation, communications, and public utilities industry group, where 30.1 percent of white-collar men and 30.1 percent of white-collar women were union members. In public administration, 27.7 percent of the men and 10.7 percent of the women in white-collar jobs were members. In the same industry group—transportation, communications, and public utilities—among blue-collar workers who are operatives men are more likely than women to be labor union members (58.6 and 11.2 percent, respectively). In other industries as well, relatively large proportions of male blue-collar workers were union members. Among women in blue-collar jobs, this was characteristic only of manufacturing.

With few exceptions, membership in labor unions declined between 1966 and 1970. For the country as a whole, for all private wage and salary workers, and for blue-collar workers, the declines in union membership were greater among women than among men. Membership gained slightly (0.4 percent) among women service workers. The decline was about the same (– 2.3 percent) among men and women white-collar workers. Among women workers, the decline was greatest among operatives (– 8.0 percent).

Some of the gains and losses in labor union membership by sex and occupational class are more sharply differentiated in data by region and on year-round full-time private wage and salary workers. The gains and losses were not uniform in size or direction. Among both men and women, losses in union membership were greatest in the West. In that region, losses were greater among women than among men, and among women blue-collar workers (– 22.5 percent) than

TABLE 17-II

RATIO OF EARNINGS OF YEAR-ROUND FULL-TIME PRIVATE WAGE AND SALARY WORKERS, BY UNION MEMBERSHIP, SEX, AND REGION, 1966 AND 1970

Region and occupation group of longest job	Ratio of median earnings								Labor union membership						
	Men to women, by union membership				Union member to non-member, by sex				Percent with union membership				Percent change, 1966-70		
	Union		Nonunion		Men		Women		Men		Women		Men	Women	
	1966	1970	1966	1970	1966	1970	1966	1970	1966	1970	1966	1970	Direct	Direct	Adjusted[1]
NORTHEAST															
Total	1.6	1.6	1.8	1.7	1.0	0.9	1.0	1.0	35.5	34.8	22.3	19.8	–0.7	–2.5	–4.0
White-collar workers	1.3	1.4	1.9	1.9	.8	.8	1.2	1.1	12.3	16.7	12.9	12.8	4.4	–.1	–.1
Blue-collar workers	1.8	1.9	1.7	1.8	1.1	1.1	1.1	1.1	54.6	53.6	53.9	44.4	–1.0	–9.5	–9.6
Operatives and kindred workers	1.6	1.7	1.6	1.6	1.1	1.1	1.1	1.1	60.1	59.2	56.8	45.9	–.9	–10.9	–11.5
Service workers, including private Household	(2)	1.7	1.6	1.6	1.2	1.2	(2)	1.1	30.6	37.0	22.9	20.3	6.4	–2.6	–3.5
NORTH CENTRAL															
Total	1.8	1.6	2.0	1.8	1.0	.9	1.1	1.1	41.0	37.5	18.4	16.5	–3.5	–1.9	–4.2
White-collar workers	1.7	1.4	2.1	2.0	.9	.8	1.1	1.1	13.8	14.3	8.7	10.7	.5	2.0	3.2
Blue-collar workers	1.8	1.7	1.7	1.8	1.2	1.1	1.1	1.2	61.2	59.1	49.3	45.9	–2.1	–3.4	–4.2
Operatives and kindred workers	1.7	1.6	1.6	1.7	1.2	1.2	1.1	1.2	64.1	66.9	51.8	49.2	2.8	–2.6	–3.2
Service workers, including private Household	(2)	1.8	1.5	1.8	(2)	1.2	(2)	1.2	38.7	37.8	7.4	12.1	–.9	4.7	24.6
SOUTH															
Total	1.6	1.6	1.7	1.7	1.2	1.1	1.3	1.2	21.5	81.4	9.3	6.8	–3.1	–2.5	–5.8
White-collar workers	(2)	1.5	2.0	1.8	1.0	1.0	(2)	1.2	8.9	7.9	6.6	5.1	–1.0	–1.5	–2.0
Blue-collar workers	1.7	1.8	1.5	1.6	1.4	1.3	1.2	1.1	31.3	29.2	21.3	16.3	–2.1	–5.0	–7.3
Operatives and kindred workers	1.6	1.8	1.4	1.5	1.4	1.3	1.2	1.1	32.9	30.2	21.4	16.1	–2.7	–5.3	–8.1
Service workers, including private Household	(2)	(2)	1.7	1.8	(2)	1.4	(2)	(2)	17.7	12.8	1.0	3.7	–4.9	2.7	47.8
WEST															
Total	1.7	1.5	1.9	1.6	1.0	1.0	1.1	1.1	36.1	31.6	17.6	13.9	–4.5	–3.7	–7.6
White-collar workers	1.8	1.5	2.1	1.8	.9	.9	1.1	1.1	15.9	15.1	11.7	11.5	–.8	–.2	–.3
Blue-collar workers	(2)	(2)	1.8	1.7	1.2	1.2	(2)	(2)	57.0	52.2	46.9	26.0	–4.8	–20.9	–22.5
Operatives and kindred workers	(2)	(2)	(2)	1.5	1.2	1.2	(2)	(2)	61.0	57.4	42.9	27.3	–3.6	–15.6	–22.2
Service workers, including private Household	(2)	(2)	2.2	1.8	(2)	1.1	(2)	(2)	36.3	34.0	17.9	16.4	–2.3	–1.5	–3.0

[1]See footnote 1, table 17-I.

[2]Data not published for fewer than 100,000 members in 1966 or 75,000 in 1970.

TABLE 17-III

UNION MEMBERSHIP OF PRIVATE WAGE AND SALARY WORKERS, BY OCCUPATION OF LONGEST JOB, INDUSTRY, AND SEX, 1970

(Numbers in thousands)

Sex and occupation of longest job	Total		Industry: Manufacturing		Industry: Transportation, communications, public utilities		Industry: Wholesale trade		Industry: Retail trade		Industry: Services		Industry: Public administration	
	Number of workers	Per-cent union mem-bers	Number of workers	Per-cent union mem-bers	Number of workers	Per-cent union mem-bers	Number of workers	Per-cent union mem-bers	Number of workers	Per-cent union mem-bers	Number of workers	Per-cent union mem-bers	Number of workers	Per-cent union mem-bers
MEN														
Total	48,631	27.8	15,589	38.4	4,353	49.4	2,223	13.6	6,616	12.6	10,059	11.7	3,143	27.7
White-collar workers ...	18,442	12.5	4,429	11.1	1,278	30.1	1,309	6.1	2,845	9.1	6,004	8.0	1,812	26.5
Blue-collar workers	24,356	42.1	10,695	49.9	2,923	58.6	893	24.4	2,711	17.7	1,985	16.2	517	29.2
Operatives and kindred workers	9,914	46.4	5,844	53.7	1,233	57.7	412	27.4	1,115	17.9	540	22.0	83	37.3
Service workers	4,646	20.1	466	35.2	152	34.2	31	16.1	1,060	9.0	2,070	17.8	813	29.5
Farm workers	1,188	1.8	—	—	—	—	—	—	—	—	—	—	—	—
WOMEN														
Total	35,624	10.4	6,914	23.3	1,289	29.2	814	5.2	7,115	7.4	17,056	5.4	1,619	11.3
White-collar workers ...	20,962	7.4	2,231	6.1	1,096	30.1	656	4.1	4,580	7.4	10,546	5.3	1,492	10.7
Blue-collar workers	5,936	27.8	4,634	31.7	124	12.9	151	9.3	424	13.9	536	15.1	(1)	(1)
Operatives and kindred workers	5,154	29.0	4,226	31.8	116	11.2	122	9.8	265	17.0	398	18.3	(1)	(1)
Service workers	8,324	5.7	(1)	(1)	(1)	(1)	(1)	(1)	2,111	6.2	5,974	4.8	108	17.6
Farm workers	402	1.0	—	—	—	—	—	—	—	—	—	—	—	—

[1]Data not published for fewer than 75,000 workers.

Source: Unpublished data from the Bureau of Labor Statistics. Data on agriculture, mining, and construction not presented because of small numbers of women workers.

among women white-collar or service workers. While losses were not so large in other regions, nevertheless, declines were greater among women in blue-collar jobs than among male blue-collar workers. This loss of union membership among women blue-collar workers was lowest in the North Central region (– 4.2 percent). Marked gains appeared among women service workers in the North Central region (24.6 percent) and South (47.8 percent). Gains in union membership among men service workers appeared only in the Northeast.

These findings suggest that the large and even increased disparity in wages between men and women union members in blue-collar occupations was associated with the greater decline in labor union membership among women blue-collar workers. Some of the same data indicate that, among women workers in general, where labor union membership increased the disparity in wages decreased. For example, in the North Central region and among white-collar workers, labor union membership increased between 1966 and 1970 by 0.5 percent among men and 3.5 percent among women. During the same period, among labor union members, the ratio of men's to women's median earnings declined from 1.7 to 1.4. In the United States as a whole, among service workers, labor union membership increased for women (0.4 percent) and the ratio of men's to women's earnings declined from 1.8 to 1.7. Some of these declines are probably associated with relocation of industry to smaller towns and rural areas where wages are lower than in large urban areas. Data are not sufficient to indicate whether there is any causal relationship between the declines, or in which direction causation flowed.

THE LEGISLATIVE APPROACH

The labor movement has been slow to support equal rights legislation, and not until its October 1973 convention did the AFL-CIO go on record in support of the Equal Rights Amendment. As of March 1974, 33 of the 50 states had ratified this amendment (38 are required for passage).

Until recently, many unions vigorously opposed state laws passed in recent years to supersede long-established "protective" legislation for children and women—concerned with hours, lifting, nightwork, and so on. The women's liberation movement should be credited with alerting labor unions, and women generally, to the fact that state protective laws have often been used by employers, and by some labor unions, to prevent women from holding better paying jobs, from working overtime, and from accumulating plant-wide security and seniority by limiting their right to open access to the better jobs.

The Equal Employment Opportunity Commission has expressed concern that such laws do not take into account the capacities, preferences, and abilities of individual women and therefore are discriminatory on the basis of sex. The removal of even one such discriminatory practice, hours restrictions, may combine with other factors to introduce profound changes in the sexual composition of the American labor force, particularly in the blue-collar and service occupations, and to modify modes of operation in labor unions.

Labor union women, however, seem reluctant to resort to resources outside of the labor movement for help with problems resulting from discriminatory practices. Caucuses of women are emerging in several unions—though as yet hardly visible—some in combination with other unions and some confined to one union, across cities, states, and regions. A few skirmishes have taken place at national conventions and under special circumstances, but remain out of the public's eye.

Union women, concerned with the protection of the labor movement's achievements, may hesitate to place these in the jeopardy which might attend conflicts brought into the courts or before the public. There is always the chance that the courts, which test the legality of discriminatory practices, may entertain the notion that collective bargaining agreements which perpetuate discriminatory practices are themselves illegal. Legal actions already are being brought by employers to invalidate collective bargaining agreements with labor unions in some of the printing trades where separate locals for men and women have obtained for a long time. Some women unionists, also, may see constraint in the use of courts as a means to reach higher rungs of the union leadership ladder, reasoning that once there, they could help women as a whole to make strides in the blue-collar sector.

Recent guidelines of the Equal Employment Opportunity Commission have almost obligated labor unions to support Title VII of the Civil Rights Act. On April 5, 1972, the Commission issued guidelines holding that sex-oriented state employment laws, such as those requiring special rest and meal periods or physical facilities for women, are in violation of Title VII. An employer now is

> deemed to have engaged in an unlawful employment practice if (i) it refuses to hire or otherwise adversely affects the employment opportunities of female applicants or employees in order to avoid provision of such benefits, (ii) it does not provide the same benefits for male employees. (Equal Employment Opportunity Commission, 1972).

The Commission requires that to do otherwise the employer must prove that his business necessarily precludes extending these benefits to both. If so, it cannot provide them to either sex. Cases which involve interpretation of these guidelines are in the courts.

A number of national organizations other than labor unions currently subscribe to the view that the motivation for protecting child and female labor was more the protection and advancement of the male's status at work than a humanitarian attitude. The National Safety Council, for example, describes unreasonable statutory limitations and tacit unfair employment practices as a deliberate attempt to exclude the possibility that a large group of workers (women) may enter into competition with those already in the trade (men) (Ross, 1970).

Susan Deller Ross (1970) points out that the so-called protection of the state laws has been very uneven. Further,

> It is no accident that labor unions are often codefendants with employers in suits charging sex discrimination under Title VII, since they engineer collective bargaining agreements which clearly discriminate against their women members. In a number of recent cases the collective bargaining agreements reserved the highest paid jobs for men only. A few examples are illustrative of the way unions through adherence to State laws, or independent of these laws in collective bargaining agreements, have contributed to job discrimination. In one case an employer denied a woman's application for a job and gave it to men with less seniority because a union contract required two 10-minute rest periods for women. . . . Such benefit laws hurt women by denying them job opportunities and hurt men by denying them the 'benefit.'

Despite legal and contractual obligations imposed on the unions to provide equal treatment, women have turned to the Equal Employment Opportunity Commission rather than to their unions for redress of alleged grievances. Of approximately 400 such cases before the commission in 1970, the majority concerned seniority and layoff, rates of pay, demotions, and transfers.

Cases brought by the Commission often involve adherence by the employer and the union to state laws which still restrict women's employment; for example, a case brought against National Venders, a division of U.M.D. Industries and International Association of Machinists regarding over-time, in view of a Missouri state law which forbids women to work more than nine hours out of twenty-four (Daily Labor Report, June 5, 1972). Suits against company and union have become relatively frequent; while these generally refer to one state or region, they effectively introduced change in national practices of large firms and labor unions.

THE WOMEN'S MOVEMENT

In view of women's increasingly large role in the labor force, their small role in the labor movement is discouraging. Some 20 percent of AFL-CIO membership is female, but only a few women hold top-level jobs in American labor unions. Labor organizations—even those with the largest female membership—have few, if any, women in executive positions, and labor feminists consider these few a form of token representation.

In the areas of protective legislation and equal opportunity, the interests of the women's liberation movement and women in the labor movement have begun to join. But it is a tenuous friendship, limited to shared interest in law as an instrumentality for change in women's job rights. Beyond this joining of forces over legislative issues, it is doubtful that the liberation movement will ever gain a large following among women blue-collar workers, whether or not they are union members.

The middle-income woman's interest in work as a career, or as a device for self-actualization, is something only remotely related to the blue-collar worker's interest in improvements to the quality of her work life. Further rapprochement between the two forces for change seems as yet very remote. But the liberation movement has had an important if only indirect effect on women in the labor movement, through the encouragement it has given to all women to accept themselves as capable and competent to engage in all action on all fronts.

Overtures to working-class women by the women's liberation movement still largely are met with rebuffs. Mistrust on both sides explains the rebuff, but there are other problems as well. Women in the middle-income group, who largely compose the liberation movement, have choices which working-class women do not have: to work or not to work, the kind of work, part-time or full-time work, to further her education and thus upgrade her occupational level, and so forth. Most women employed in blue-collar jobs have no choices; they work because they must do so. To them, many of the issues so important to the women's liberation movement seem removed and even frivolous compared with their own bread-and-butter issues.

The liberation movement is further separated from women union members by its frequent hostility to labor unions. Some of the recent court actions in behalf of women's job opportunities—brought by organizations affiliated with the liberation movement—have pitted the women plaintiffs against the employer *and* the union, and the unions repeatedly have been on the employer's side in such cases.

In a review of women in unions, Alice Cook (1968) claimed that unions are paying less attention to special problems of women now than sixty years ago, a time when the Trade Union League and the Labor Education Services held important places in the American labor movement. She noted too that women's pages in labor journals are almost exclusively devoted to consumer problems, recipes, and household hints.

A few labor unions, on the other hand, have established women's departments with much wider concerns than those reflected in the labor journals. The most notable is that of the United Automobile Workers. While the Auto Workers "is an overwhelmingly male union, the 200,000 women members [in 1970] of the UAW exceed in number the total membership of many International Unions" (Haener, 1972). The union has an official position on women, recorded in convention proceedings. Its women's department has worked effectively and cooperatively with women in some of the organizations affiliated with the liberation movement. It is staffed by full-time paid workers; its first director now is a vice-president of the international, one of the few top-level union executive positions held by women in the United States. Through its women's department the Auto Workers has been aggressive in the use of and support given to legal instrumentalities for women available through the offices of government. It has supported amendments to legislation which would extend coverage or otherwise improve conditions pertinent to all working women, not only its own members. It was in the vanguard of the battle to remove from state statutes the so-called protective laws for working women. Other international unions, the Electrical Workers (IUE) in particular, have also established women's departments which are beginning vigorously to pursue women's interests.

Some other labor unions—such as the International Ladies 'Garment Workers' Union, the Amalgamated Clothing Workers, and the Textile Workers—which have predominantly women members and which earlier had actively combatted discrimination, are relatively inactive in these areas.

Within the labor movement, however, women union activists are on the move. The first state AFL-CIO women's conference was held in Wisconsin in March 1970. By the end of 1972, similar conferences had been held in Illinois, Arkansas, California, and Iowa *(U.S. News and World Report, 1972),* and by several internationals, specifically the Auto Workers, Communications Workers, Electrical Workers (IUE), American Federation of Teachers, and American Newspaper Guild. The Wisconsin conference called attention to the small role women play in the labor movement. Emphasis was directed toward women becoming more aware of their rights under Title VII. By passage of resolutions, the conference recognized that "protective laws for women passed in 1900 may well have met the needs of the time, but today serve only to limit opportunity in employment for women and discriminate against both men and women" (Proceedings 1970) and went on record as favoring passage of the Equal Rights Amendment.

An organization called WAGE (Women's Alliance to Gain Equality) has been established among union women in California. In the summer of 1973, 200 women—rank-and-file members and staff and officers—representing twenty national and international unions in eighteen states met in Chicago to set the stage for a national meeting (*AFL-CIO Federation News,* July 1973). Similar regional meetings of union women on the East and West Coasts were planned in preparation for the national conference. These women intend to pursue their organizational goals within the existing structure of the labor movement.[2] The Chicago conference moved cautiously. It passed no resolutions and established no policies. It perhaps was a second step, beyond the state conferences, to gain access to top leadership positions and thus to more effective representation of women's interests through labor union organization.

---

[2]In late March 1974, more than 3,000 women members of 58 unions voted into existence a national organization to work for women's rights within the trade union movement. The Coalition of Labor Union Women (CLUW) was headed by Olga Mader, a vice-president of the United Automobile Workers, with Addie Wyatt, director of women's affairs for the Amalgamated Meat Cutters and Butcher Workers Union, as vice president.

Among the organization's stated objectives are increased union efforts to organize women workers; increased participation of women in union affairs, particularly in policymaking positions; positive action by unions against sex discrimination in pay, hiring, job classification, and promotion; support of legislation to provide adequate child care facilities, a "livable" minimum wage, improved medical and pension benefits, improved health and safety laws, and better enforcement of these laws; and mass action in behalf of ratification of the Equal Rights Amendment and for legislation to extend to all workers the protection of statutes originally aimed at protecting women, such as maximum-hours limitations, breaks in the workday, and seating of workers.

A critical problem left unresolved is whether membership should be limited to women union members or opened to other women who work. This and other organizational problems are under study by a national coordinating committee of over 200 members and a 25-member steering committee.

REFERENCES

Alice Cook, "Women and American Trade Unions," *Annals,* January 1968, pp. 124-32.

Equal Employment Opportunity Commission, *Guidelines on Discrimination Because of Sex,* Part 1604 (Washington, Equal Employment Opportunity Commission, Office of the General Counsel, 1972).

Dorothy Haener, "What Labor is Doing About Women in the Work Force." In Mildred E. Katzell and William C. Byham, eds., *Women in the Work Force* (New York, Behavioral Publications, Inc., 1972), p. 44.

Proceedings, Women's Conference, Labor Temple, Wisconsin Rapids, Wis., Mar. 7, 1970.

Susan Deller Ross, *Sex Discrimination and "Protective" Labor Legislation* (New York, New York University Law School, 1970).

"Women Workers: Gaining Power, Seeking More," *U.S. News and World Report,* Nov. 13, 1972.

Chapter 18

WILL JILL MAKE DEPARTMENT CHAIRMAN?*

MARY BACH KIEVIT

TWO PORTLY businessmen walk, down the corridor of an office building. One nudges the other and looks skeptical as they pass a door with the sign: *W. J. Millwright and Daughters, Construction.* "Hm . . . why not?" the other responds thoughtfully.

Jill Ingenue enters a classroom one evening a week to learn the nuts and bolts of carpentry. At 7 AM the next day she dons hard hat and jeans to work as an apprentice carpenter on a 3.5 million dollar high school.

Jack Armstrong describes the conflicting values and attitudes of a fictional family and prepares students in the family relations class for a role-playing session.

"Out of the way, Mac!"—and a woman engineer in hard hat and coveralls working on a field site in south Jersey steps aside to allow passage. In a classroom some miles away a young woman instructs an industrial arts class in the use of selected drafting equipment.

The publicity generated when women move into traditionally male occupations testifies to its infrequency. Women are nevertheless making their way into a greater number of occupational areas. Conversely, men have challenged the exclusive hiring of women for certain kinds of jobs.

SIGNS OF DURABILITY

Although some people may be inclined to view the employment of women in all-male domains as a passing fad, there are significant economic, political, and social forces that suggest otherwise. In a period of rising economic aspirations combined with rising inflation, many

*From *American Vocational Journal, Nov. 1974, 49(8), 40-43.*

*Oppenheimer, Valerie, K. See References at end for this and other authors cited in this article.

families are becoming increasingly dependent on two incomes. Data from the 1970 census on women's participation in the labor force indicate that the presence of children, whatever their age, is becoming less and less a deterrent.

As more women work at all stages of the family life cycle, more women are going to view work as a major adult role. Under these circumstances, women are likely to become dissatisfied with the poorly paid, low-advancement work traditionally open to them (Oppenheimer, 1973).

Add to the above factors a decline in the birth rate, legislative support for enforcing equal opportunity in employment and education, decrease in traditionally female occupations, increased organization to protect the rights of women—and a climate emerges with powerful forces for change. This is not, of course, to minimize the counterforce of a tighter labor market and higher unemployment.

Vocational-technical education at all levels—secondary, postsecondary, adult, college, and university—can contribute significantly to eliminating the artificial barriers that deny employment to women (and men) in occupations for which they have the basic aptitudes and abilities. As vocational-technical educators, we need to ask: Are we more a part of the problem than of the solution?

Certainly, the question bears looking into at the college and university level. What is the status of women vocational educators at this level?

INFORMATION STILL MEAGER

In December 1972, AVA's resolution regarding professional opportunities for women in vocational-technical education stated that few facts were available concerning the numbers of professional men and women employed in vocational education, much less the salaries paid to each category. In mid-1974, facts were still scarce. In a search for descriptive data, I could find no comprehensive nationwide studies for four-year colleges and universities which gave data on the number of men and women in specific vocational fields.

In 1968, the National Center for Educational Statistics reported on teaching and research staffs in institutions of higher education, by academic field, but sex was not included as a variable. The composition of secondary vocational teachers by area and sex is given in the Center's 1970 report, *Vocational Education: Characteristics of Teachers and Students, 1969*. But data on college and university teachers are analyzed in a manner that makes it impossible to determine what proportion of all university and college vocational educators are women.

Anyone concerned with the status of women as professional vocational educators in higher education is forced to rely on observation, deduction, and specific cases which may or may not be generalizable. University colleagues in agriculture, distributive education, health, home economics, office, technical, and T&I education tend to corroborate the impression that distribution of the sexes follows somewhat the pattern of the occupations involved.

According to an HEW survey of secondary vocational teachers (1972), high school teachers of agriculture, technical- T&I, and distributive education are predominantly male (100 percent, 89 percent, and 77 percent, respectively). Approximately 89 percent of all health occupation teachers and 98 percent of home economics teachers are women, as are 72 percent of office occupation teachers.

It can be predicted that the composition of professional educators at college and university levels will tend to favor males even in those areas where women normally predominate. Two factors support this premise. First, even where men are a numerical minority, they tend to be disproportionately represented in higher level positions. Second, a lower proportion of women earn the advanced degrees required for employment in colleges and universities. Ann Sutherland Harris reports in the *AAUP Bulletin* that women earned about 13 percent of all Ph.D.'s awarded in the 1960s. Of the 216 EPDA fellowships granted to vocational educators between 1970 and 1973 for three years of doctoral study, 32 or about 15 percent were awarded to women.

Alice Cook reports that women students are distributed very unevenly within the various colleges, with relatively high enrollments in the colleges of arts, home economics, social science, and in professional schools of library science, education, nursing, and social work. Women represent a minority, sometimes very small, in agriculture and medicine. And rarely does the proportion of female to male faculty correspond favorably with the proportion of female to male students.

In the College of Human Ecology at Cornell where 90 percent of the students are women, only 58 percent of the faculty are women. In the College of Arts and Science, 28 percent of the students, but only 5.2 percent of the faculty, are women. Suggesting that conditions at Cornell probably do not differ from those in similar institutions, Ms. Cook reports the following figures on rank of faculty on the Ithaca campus:

Full professor: 658 men, 22 women (12 in the College of Human Ecology).

Associate professor: 317 men, 47 women (25 in the College of Human Ecology).

Assistant professor: 349 men, 42 women (16 in the College of Human Ecology).

Of the total faculty, 7.5 percent were women.

DEGREES AND TENURE ETC.

In the March 1974 issue of *Change,* Alan Bayer reports on a study conducted by the American Council on Education which surveyed a representative national sample of more than 300 two– and four–year colleges and universities. The study showed that in 1968-69, in all types of institutions, substantially more men than women held senior-level ranks.

In 1972-73, 32 percent of faculty women and 55 percent of faculty men were either associate or full professors. Women were less likely to have tenure, 45 percent in four-year colleges as compared with 69 percent of the men.

In 1968-69, 19 percent of all college and university faculty were women. By 1972-73, the proportion had increased to 20 percent. In universities, the proportion was 15 percent in 1968-69 and 16.5 percent in 1972-73. The proportion in four-year colleges declined over this period.

In terms of advanced degrees, the survey found that in four-year colleges, 62 percent of the women and 48 percent of the men held master's degrees or less. In universities, the ratios were 67 percent for women and 31 percent for men. Women spent more time in the classroom than did men, and carried substantially more of the undergraduate load.

The meager evidence available indicates that the position of women in vocational-technical education in colleges and universities closely approximates the position of women in higher education generally. This position will be subject to modification (though admittedly slow) through the efforts of colleges and universities to comply with Title IX of the Education Amendments of 1972; Title VII of the Civil Rights Act of 1964; and Executive Order 11246 as amended. The proposed rules for interpreting Title IX, published in the *Federal Register* of June 20, 1974, explicitly cite vocational courses, programs, and institutions.

SOCIAL CONSCIOUSNESS WAVE

Complex social forces have raised the consciousness of many to decry the limited opportunities for women. Government has responded with legislation designed to encourage equal opportunity. Litigation where violations occur has led to increasing enforcement. But complying with the law is primarily a reactive response, whereas the situation calls for committed, persevering, and creative leadership.

The actions of college and university faculties reflect the values and contribute to the aspirations of other groups and individuals. Thus a breaking away from rigid adherence to sex stereotyping in professional vocational education can have a positive impact at other levels. But it will call for active recruitment of women and men to programs traditionally reserved for one sex. My best estimate at this time is that there are few women employed as teacher educators in vocational agriculture or industrial arts and equally few men employed as home economics teachers. Yet under Title IX, industrial arts, vocational agriculture, and home economics courses must be open to both sexes.

Most of us believe, however, that one effect Title IX will *not* have is the stampeding of boys into home economics classes or girls into the industrial arts shops. Not because home economics has little to contribute to boys or industrial arts to girls, but because societal expectations, though changing, have defined such choices as inappropriate to their sex roles.

In Sweden, expectations are being altered. Between the ages of 7 and 10, boys and girls learn to sew and do woodworking, between 10 and 12, they learn cooking and keeping a family budget, and between 15 and 16, caring for young children.

COMMUNICABLE DISEASE

Sex role expectations are transmitted in diverse subtle and not-so-subtle ways. To the extent that professionals in vocational technical education are representative of the traditionally female and male occupational roles, the field lends reinforcement to the status quo.

Consider the likely change in the tenor of faculty discussions on instruction and curriculum if home economics, industrial arts, and trade and industrial education all offered co-ed courses taught by both men and women. And consider the impact on T&I teachers completing certification programs if one or more of their "profs" were a woman who had become a teacher educator after working as a journeyman in the carpentry trade for a number of years.

But where are those persons?

Persistent and perceptive recruitment combined with encouragement and guidance at each level is essential to achieving a redistribution of women and men among the various disciplines. Small numbers of women are now enrolling in undergraduate programs in industrial education, industrial technology, and vocational agriculture.

Federal legislation, among other factors, is opening some apprenticeship programs to women. In a 1970 issue of *Monthly Labor Review,* Janice Hedges reports that in 1968 a total of 906 women were enrolled in auto mechanics, 142 in automotive specialization, 539 in aircraft maintenance, and 977 in radio-television repair.

An effort is currently underway to develop and test a recruitment package designed to enroll women in a mechanical technology program. Some of these recruits should be embryonic professional vocational educators for positions in higher education.

Programs for teachers, administrators, and teacher educators should provide some educational experiences which lead to a reexamination of the values and attitudes that undergird the practices of channeling boys and girls into a circumscribed range of jobs, occupations, and careers. Study of the social-cultural, cultural-biological factors that have influenced definitions of sex roles can lead to greater insights.

LEANING TOWARD LIBERALISM

In August 1974, Arlene Hantjis surveyed graduate students in the Department of Vocational-Technical Education at Rutgers to assess attitudes regarding men and women in work roles. The 37 Likert-type response items were formulated to tap out four components:

(1) Personal characteristics (women talk too much on the job).

(2) Men and women working together (women who work with men waste too much time worrying about their looks).

(3) Appropriateness of occupations based on sex (men are better for jobs requiring concentration and precision).

(4) Legislative and moralistic viewpoints (enrolling women in expensive trade and technical courses is a foolish waste of taxpayers' money).

A total of 189 usable responses was obtained, 130 from men and 59 from women. The possible score ranged from 37 to 148, with a theoretical mean of 92.5. The total mean score for men was 118.5 as compared with 128.9 for women. The difference was significant at the .01 level.

Both men and women exceeded the theoretical mean, indicating that they leaned toward liberal attitudes, but the women more so than the men. These variations remained consistent when analyzed in relation to age and position.

Administrators, both men and women, had the highest mean scores when compared with classroom teachers, full-time students, and teacher/administrators. In all cases but one, the higher mean scores for women were statistically significant at the .01 level.

Another survey compares attitudes of vocational-technical teachers in vocational schools with teachers in comprehensive high schools. Because the subjects of these studies are strategically located to recruit students at the point of initial vocational choice, these and similar studies will help assess the extent to which the attitudes and opinions of professional vocational educators impede the achievement of goals implicit in federal legislation and the basic tenet of equal opportunity for all.

FALLACIOUS STEREOTYPE

Stereotypes concerning women in professional (and nonprofessional) roles exist—too numerous to consider here. One that particularly merits attention, however, is the stereotype that disparages investment in advanced degrees for women because "women aren't seriously motivated" or "women will marry, have children, and be distracted from full contribution."

In a 1969 study, Helen Astin found that 91 percent of women who completed doctorates in 1957 and 1958 were in the labor force, and 81 percent were working full time. Of those employed full time, 79 percent reported that their careers had not been interrupted.

Those who had had graduate assistantships during their doctoral studies were more likely than others to be working full time. Seventy-five percent of the women had published at least one article, and 13 percent had published eleven or more. The women who produced the most scholarly work (primarily in research) were very active professionally, earned above the median income, and felt they had been discriminated against by their employers.

L. A. Simpson's 1970 study of attitudes of administrators and faculty toward selecting men or women for academic appointments showed that women were chosen over men applicants only when their superior qualifications could not be ignored. Reports resulting from affirmative action programs suggest similar discrimination in evaluations for promotions.

WHAT CAN BE DONE?

College and university departments can take action to combat such discrimination. For example, each department chairman and faculty might set some goals for employing fully competent women. Once on the staff, these women should have equal access to the resources necessary for production requisite to promotion. Among the needed resources are time, clerical support, and *acceptance for full participation in informal discussions.* These informal exchanges have been identified as the channels through which the most current, still unpublished information and ideas are expanded and incorporated into the work of others.

One study attributed exclusion from these informal discussions as a serious impediment to scholarly achievement by women in academic disciplines dominated by men. The norms most appropriate for governing behavior in these encounters are norms for colleagues rather than the traditional codes governing male and female relations.

Steps can be taken by professional organizations, also. Professional groups in each vocational field, for example, might provide scholarships to recruit persons of the sex currently in the minority. Goals could be set for changing the sex composition of the organization and a program of work developed toward that end. The maintenance of membership data could be systematized to provide a source of up-to-date information on progress made.

WILL JILL MAKE IT?

What changes will we as professional vocational educators produce during the next decade in the distribution of women and men in the various occupational areas at each educational level?

Will there be Jack Armstrongs in home economics and health occupation classrooms at secondary, college, and university levels—as students and as teachers? Will there be a number of Jill Ingenues in the vocational shops and technology classrooms, and in the teacher education programs? Will we reluctantly comply but not lead? Or will we lead with compliance?

REFERENCES AND SUGGESTED READING

Astin, Helen. *The Woman Doctorate in America.* New York, New York: Russell Sage Foundation, 1969.

Bayer, Alan E. "College Faculties: Le Plus Ca Change." *Change,* Vol. 6 (March 1974), pp. 47-48, 63.

Cook, Alice. "Sex Discrimination at Universities: An Ombudsman's View." *American Association of University Professors Bulletin.* Vol. 58 (September 1972), pp. 279-282.

Fogarty, Michael P. et al. *Sex, Career and Family.* Sage Publications, Inc., 275 South Beverly Drive, Beverly Hills, California, 1971.

Hantjis, Arlene. "Attitudes of Vocational-Technical Educators Toward Men and Women in the World of Work." Unpublished manuscript, August 1974.

Harris, Ann Sutherland. "The Second Sex in Academe." *American Association of University Professors Bulletin.* Vol. 56 (September 1970), pp. 283-295.

Hedges, Janice N. "Women Workers and Manpower Demands in the 1970's." *Monthly Labor Review,* Vol. 93 (June 1970), pp. 19-29.

Kievit, Mary B. *Women in the World of Work: Review and Synthesis of Research.* Information Series No. 56, VT 014 690. ERIC, U.S. Superintendent of Documents, Government Printing Office, 1972.

Oppenheimer, Valerie K. "A Sociologist's Skepticism." *Corporate Lib: Women's Challenge to Management.* (Edited by Eli Ginsberg and Alice M. Yohalem.) Policy Studies in Employment and Welfare Number 17. The Johns Hopkins University Press, Baltimore and London, 1973.

Ray, Evelyn R. *Vocational Education: Characteristics of Teachers and Students, 1969.* National Center for Educational Statistics, U.S. Department of Health, Education and Welfare, Washington, D.C. OE-80073.

Rossi, Alice and Ann Calderwood. *Academic Women on the Move.* New York, Russell Sage Foundation, 1973.

Simpson, Lawrence A. "A Myth Is Better Than a Miss." College and University Business, Vol. 48 (February 1970), pp. 72-73.

Westat, Inc. *Survey of Vocational Education: Student and Teacher Characteristics in Public Secondary Schools, 1972.* National Center for Educational Statistics, U.S. Department of Health, Education and Welfare, Washington, D.C. 1977.

Chapter 19

THE MYTH AND THE REALITY*

THE U.S. WOMEN'S BUREAU

The Myth	*The Reality*
A woman's place is in the home.	Homemaking in itself is no longer a full-time job for most people. Goods and services formerly produced in the home are now commercially available; laborsaving devices have lightened or eliminated much work around the home. Today more than half of all women between eighteen and sixty-four years of age are in the labor force, where they are making a substantial contribution to the nation's economy. Studies show that nine out of ten girls will work outside the home at some time in their lives.
Women are not seriously attached to the labor force; they work only for extra pocket money.	Of the nearly 34 million women in the labor force in March 1973, nearly half were working because of pressing economic need. They were either single, widowed, divorced, or separated or had husbands whose incomes were less than $3,000 a year. Another 4.7 million had husbands with incomes between $3,000 and $7,000.[1]
Women are out ill more than male workers; they cost the company more.	A recent Public Health Service study shows little difference in the absentee rate due to illness or injury: 5.6 days a year for women compared with 5.2 for men.

*Women's Bureau, Employment Standards Administration, U.S. Department of Labor: *The Myth and the Reality*. Washington, D.C., U.S. Government Printing Office, May 1974.

[1]The Bureau of Labor Statistics estimate for a low standard of living for an urban family of four was $7,386 in autumn 1972. This estimate is for a family consisting of an employed husband aged 38, a wife not employed outside the home, an 8-year-old girl, and a 13-year-old boy.

Women do not work as long or as regularly as their male coworkers; their training is costly — and largely wasted.

A declining number of women leave work for marriage and children. But even among those who do leave, a majority return when their children are in school. Even with a break in employment, the average woman worker has a worklife expectancy of twenty-five years as compared with forty-three years for the average male worker. The single woman averages forty-five years in the labor force.

Studies on labor turnover indicate that net differences for men and women are generally small. In manufacturing industries the 1968 rates of accessions per 100 employees were 4.4 for men and 5.3 for women; the respective separation rates were 4.4 and 5.2.

Married women take jobs away from men; in fact, they ought to quit those jobs they now hold.

There were 19.8 million married women (husbands present) in the labor force in March 1973; the number of unemployed men was 2.5 million. If all the married women stayed home and unemployed men were placed in their jobs, there would be 17.3 million unfilled jobs.

Moreover, most unemployed men do not have the education or the skill to qualify for many of the jobs held by women, such as secretaries, teachers, and nurses.

Women should stick to "women's jobs" and should not compete for "men's jobs."

Job requirements, with extremely rare exceptions, are unrelated to sex. Tradition rather than job content has led to labeling certain jobs as women's and others as men's. In measuring twenty-two inherent aptitudes and knowledge areas, a research laboratory found that there is no sex difference in fourteen, women excel in six, and men excel in two.

Women do not want responsibility on the job; they do not want promotions or job changes which add to their load.

Relatively few women have been offered positions of responsibility. But when given these opportunities, women, like men, do cope with job responsibilities in addition to personal or family responsibilities. In 1973, 4.7 million women held professional and technical jobs, another 1.6 million worked as nonfarm managers and administrators. Many others held supervisory jobs at all levels in offices and factories.

The employment of mothers leads to juvenile delinquency.

Studies show that many factors must be considered when seeking the causes of juvenile delinquency. Whether or not a mother is employed does not appear to be a determining factor.

These studies indicate that it is the quality of a mother's care rather than the time consumed in such care which is of major significance.

Men do not like to work for women supervisors.

Most men who complain about women supervisors have never worked for a woman.

In one study where at least three-fourths of both the male and female respondents (all executives) had worked with women managers, their evaluation of women in management was favorable. On the other hand, the study showed a traditional/cultural bias among those who reacted unfavorably to women as managers.

In another survey in which 41 percent of the reporting firms indicated that they hired women executives, none rated their performance as unsatisfactory; 50 percent rated them adequate; 42 percent rated them the same as their predecessors; and 8 percent rated them better than their predecessors.

Section V

NEGOTIATING AND PLANNING FOR MULTIPLE ROLES

As we have noted in earlier chapters, the ultimate reality for women, married or single, in today's world is the presence of multiple role expectations, opportunities, and aspirations. The myth that marriage and occupation represent an either/or choice, long unfounded in fact, is also disappearing from women's perceptions of their options. Instead, the central concerns facing many women are those of marriage *and* occupations, affiliation *and* achievement, self-fulfillment *and* family nurturance. The questions then are no longer those of a dichotomous choice, but rather have to do with negotiation, compromise, resolution of conflict and management of time, talents, and resources. Hall et al. (1972), in studying adult women in one, two, three, and four roles, found that the more roles a woman had, the greater sense of power she felt; at the same time, she also felt a heightened sense of conflict in trying to fulfill the multiple roles. The need for support systems to carry out multiple roles of women and men was stressed. The chapters included in this section explore some issues related to multiple and sequential roles and life-style alternatives. Implications for both female and male roles are discussed. Male attitudes and expectations continue to influence women's career development. On the other hand, women cannot redefine themselves and their roles without tremendously influencing male roles. The complexity of our society dictates multiple roles for both sexes, and changing work and family patterns are needed to make these multiple options possible.

In the first chapter in this section, Hedges and Barnett examine changing patterns of division of household labor. About two thirds of the women in the labor force live with husbands or dependent children or both; a frequently stated need of employed women is that of shared household tasks. A large-scale survey of husband-wife families revealed that family work roles of women and men may have changed less than has often been suggested. When the mother was employed, a proportion of the household tasks tended to be shifted to children rather than to the spouse. Husbands of employed or nonemployed wives spent about the same amount of time each day engaged in household chores. Also, the division of labor between husbands and wives tended to split along traditional lines: wives did most of the inside work while husbands did more home maintenance and yard work; husbands "helped" with marketing, record keeping, and child care. It would be interesting to study a sample limited to younger couples to see if this group had been more influenced by recent social changes. However, change in sex-role expectations may have occurred more in theory than in practice. One study of university students in Norway, for example, found that while both females and males expressed emergent or nontraditional attitudes about female-male roles, when a careful study was made of time utilization and division of labor, the female partner carried most of the household tasks. In Norway, as in American culture, it is often expected that "Employed Mom is Supermom."

Difficulties typically reported by women attempting to combine family and paid work responsibilities are discussed, and several suggestions for reducing conflict and increasing efficiency in management of time and resources are presented. It is clear that change is required on both societal and individual levels in order to meet the complex needs of individuals with multiple roles. For example, more and better day-care facilities are needed. A recognition of life cycle patterns by employers and educational and training institutions would be helpful so that interrupted educational and employment patterns of both women and men would be accepted and facilitated. Also, the need for men to assume fuller responsibility for *sharing* household tasks has quite a different implication than "helping" the woman with *her* work.

Lowenthal and Weiss provide an intriguing analysis of the relationship between interpersonal intimacy and life stages and crises. Although interpersonal intimacy has been proposed as an essential developmental task in achievement of adulthood, very little systematic research has been done in this area due to the theoretical and operational complexity of the concept. The authors believe that the American male's fear of intimacy also has discouraged study of the topic.

Lowenthal and Weiss contend that "most individuals find motivation to live antonomous, self-generating, and satisfying lives only through one or more mutually intimate dyadic relationships." Furthermore, they feel that close relationships can be an important resource during life crises or transitions such as planning for the first child, having the youngest child leave home, or retiring. In a preliminary analysis of an ongoing research project, marked life stage and sex differences were reported. For example, after the youngest child leaves home, both males and females anticipate a closer relationship with their spouse. However, soon after this change many women wish to become committed to some activity or interest beyond the family. In contrast, husbands continue to desire attention and "pampering" from their wives. The intimacy needs and developmental tasks for women and men appear to be at cross purposes during this life stage.

Lowenthal and Weiss propose a theoretical framework for studying psychosocial change, capacity for interpersonal intimacy, and several areas of commitment. Their formulation leads to a flexible stage theory in which several tasks or commitments must simultaneously be examined at each life stage. The ideas of Lowenthal and Weiss seem especially significant because the relevance of intimacy in the lives of both women and men is recognized and explored; too often affiliation is viewed as a female variable, and implications for males are ignored. Hopefully, increasing sex-role flexibility will allow males to openly accept their need for love and support as well as allow females to accept their need for achievement beyond the family sphere. Longitudinal research is needed to further investigate potential problem stages. Two populations at risk have tentatively been identified: (1) middle or lower middle-class family-centered women who are facing or who are in the early phases of the postparental stage and (2) middle-aged men. Some of the stages of crisis and transitions described by Gail Sheehy (1976), while not research-based, provide a useful departure point for thinking about life career planning, especially in relation to chronological age and life stage.

Finally, Hawley examines some of the immediate and practical problems related to life-style planning frequently encountered by counselors who work with women. After completing a large-scale study of high school women, Hawley concluded that these students need considerable assistance in formulating long-range plans. Although most of the women expected they would work, the majority saw work as part-time and subordinate to other goals. The presence of a male in their lives was clearly more valuable to their self-concept than any other measure of accomplishment, yet many of the young women seemed to have difficulty recognizing the influence of male views on their occupational choices. Most appeared to have trouble anticipating future possibilities such as divorce or widowhood. It seems clear that women need assistance in preparing for the complexities of the multiple and sequential roles they will almost certainly face and choosing alternatives that will result in satisfying life-styles, including the alternative of not marrying or not having children.

Hawley raises some very basic questions about the nature of work. She suggests that the satisfactions of paid employment may have been oversold, while emphasizing only the negative aspects of the homemaker role. She points out that much work is routine and dull, and not all individuals are qualified for challenging, high level occupations. We would add that an important goal is to expand the range of life-style alternatives and help each individual realize that he/she does have choices; not to create an equally restrictive cultural imperative that states that all women must have a paid job—even though increasing numbers do so and, if Labor Department projections are accurate, will continue to do so. Hawley cautions that it is not helpful to raise aspirations without concurrently stressing the heavier demands on personal energy, time, and commitment that go along with better jobs and multiple roles. Another goal that seems to be implied here is the need to help individuals clarify their work values so that they can know which roles are most meaningful and satisfying for them and the means to attain them.

Hawley concludes with an urgent plea for counselors to discard both the old and the new stereotypes and rigid ideologies and to approach their clients with an open problem-solving framework. She favors an androgynous point of view which encompasses both female and male behaviors, attitudes, and emotions. We can only agree with Hawley that androgynous people are most likely better equipped to face the developmental tasks and multiple options and demands of a complex technological society. For a more detailed discussion of androgyny, see Bem (1975). Bem, who has conducted a series af androgyny studies, points out that while androgyny may lead us toward a more liberated sexual identity, it will eventually "self-destruct," as the need for such masculine-feminine dichotomies diminishes.

REFERENCES

Bem, S.L. Beyond androgyny: some prescriptions for a liberated sexual identity. Keynote address for APA-NIMH Conference on the Research Needs of Women, Madison, Wisconsin, May 31, 1975. In Sherman, K. and Denmark, F. (Eds.), *Psychology of Women: Future Directions of Research*. Psychological Dimensions, in press.

Sheehy, G. *Passages: Predictable crises of adult life*. New York: Dutton, 1976.

Chapter 20

WORKING WOMEN AND THE DIVISION OF HOUSEHOLD TASKS*

JANICE NEIPERT HEDGES AND JEANNE K. BARNETT

WOMEN with family responsibilities are entering the labor force in increasing numbers. In the population as a whole, the proportion of women who are married has remained stable over the past twenty years, at about 60 percent. In the same period, however, the proportion of women workers who are married has risen by 10 percentage points, to 59 percent. While much of this increase is among married women without children, the number of working women with children has increased also. By 1971 one third of the women in the labor force had both husbands and dependent children.

These increases, along with "women's liberation" and its call for a new look at traditional roles in the family and in the workplace, have focused increased attention on the ways in which family responsibilities are handled in homes where both husband and wife are employed outside the home. Against a background of selected data on American working women,[1] this chapter reports on a number of surveys that show how—and how much—women with jobs share their household tasks with other members of their families.

FAMILY RESPONSIBILITIES OF WORKING WOMEN

In all, about 65 percent of the women in the labor force in March 1971 (about 20.6 million women) were living with husbands or dependent children,[2] or both (see Table 20-I). In addition, substantial

*This article is based on a paper prepared under the auspices of the U.S. Women's Bureau at the request of the United Nations Commission on the Status of Women.
From Monthly Labor Review, April 1972, pp. 9-14.

[1]For further detail, see Elizabeth Waldman and Kathryn R. Gover, "Marital and family characteristics of the labor force," *Monthly Labor Review*, April 1972, pp. 4-8.

[2]The terms "dependent children" and "children under eighteen" are used interchangeably in this article. Throughout, "mothers" refers only to those with dependent children, and "children" refers only to dependent children.

though unknown numbers had parents or other relatives living with them.

TABLE 20-I
NUMBER AND DISTRIBUTION OF WOMEN IN THE LABOR FORCE LIVING WITH HUSBANDS OR DEPENDENT CHILDREN, OR BOTH, MARCH 1971

Presence of husbands or children	Number (in thousands)	Percent distribution
Total female labor force	31,681	100
With husband or children	20,633	65
Husband and children	10,098	32
Husband only	8,432	27
Children only	2,103	7
Without husband or children	11,048	35

Note: Numbers may not add due to rounding.

Husband-wife families with children and working wives averaged about 2.2 children.[3] Working mothers who headed fatherless families averaged 2.1 children. One tenth of the white women who headed families and almost one fourth of the black women had four children or more:

	White	*Black*
Number (in thousands)	1,397	563
Percent distribution, by number of children:		
Total	100	100
1 child	45	39
2 children	33	22
3 children	13	15
4 children	7	10
5 children or more	3	14

An important indicator of the extent and nature of a mother's responsibilities toward her children is their age. Almost a third (31 percent) of mothers with preschool children were in the labor force in March 1971, compared with over half (52 percent) of mothers with only schoolage children.[4] The difference is largely explained by preschoolers needing more constant parental attention and care. Moreover, as children grow older, current and future needs for funds for education and training draw more mothers into the labor force. Whatever their husbands' incomes, mothers of preschool children are less

[3]For further information on the children of working women, see Elizabeth Waldman, "Children of women in the labor force," *Monthly Labor Review,* July 1971, pp. 19-25.
[4]Following the usual practice, school age is defined as six to seventeen years.

likely to be in the labor force than mothers of schoolage children (see Table 20-II).

TABLE 20-II
LABOR FORCE PARTICIPATION OF MOTHERS, BY PRESENCE AND AGE OF CHILDREN, MARCH 1971, AND BY INCOME OF HUSBAND IN 1970

Presence and age of children	Husband's income in 1970				
	Under $3,000	$3,000-4,999	$5,000-6,999	$7,000-9,999	$10,000 and over
Number (in thousands):					
With children 6-17 only	376	576	947	1,904	2,623
With children under 6	268	441	772	1,223	965
Participation rates:					
With children 6-17 only	52	56	58	55	43
With children under 6	36	35	36	32	22
Difference	16	21	22	23	21

Working women with particularly heavy family responsibilities include mothers who head families[5] or whose husbands are low earners or not employed. About 2.0 million of the mothers who were in the labor force in March 1971 were heads of families. About nine tenths of them were divorced, separated, or widowed; the balance were single women. During the past decade, the number of all families headed by women with children increased by 33 percent (or .9 million), compared with an increase of only 7 percent (1.6 million) in husband-wife families with children.[6]

In March 1971, 2.1 million wives in the labor force had husbands who were not working; 1.4 million of these husbands were not in the labor force because of age, disability, illness, or other reason. The remainder were unemployed.

For about 2.0 million of the wives who were working in March 1971, their husband's incomes the previous year had been less than $3,000; for another 2.2 million, their husbands' earnings had ranged from $3,000 to $5,000.

RACIAL MINORITIES

Of all women in the labor force in March 1971, a larger proportion of minority[7] women than white women had dependent children (44

[5]Includes those who are legally separated, those whose husbands are absent for military service or other reasons, and single women.

[6]The labor force participation rates of mother without husbands reflect their financial responsibilities. In March 1971, 69 percent of all divorcees with children and 52 percent of all widows with children were in the labor force, compared with 40 percent of all mothers with husbands present. See also Robert L. Stein, "The economic status of families headed by women," *Monthly Labor Review,* December 1970, pp. 3-10.

[7]Includes Negro, American Indian, and Oriental. Negroes constituted more than nine tenths of this part of the population.

and 37 percent, respectively), and a smaller proportion had a husband living at home (49 and 60 percent, respectively).

In all, about .8 million of the black and other minority women who were in the labor force in March 1971 were heads of families. But even in husband-wife families, women of the minority races are more likely to carry heavy financial responsibilities. Black men are more vulnerable than white men to unemployment, more likely to be out of the labor force because of disability or illness, and more likely, even if working year round full time, to have low earnings.[8]

SHARING OF HOUSEHOLD DUTIES

Working women with families must achieve a balance between commitment to their jobs and to their responsibilities at home. Many working wives and mothers have difficulty finding sufficient time for the myriad of tasks associated with home and family. A number of surveys have sought out the various ways in which these responsibilities are accommodated.

Household tasks or duties are variously defined. They may include, for example, chauffeuring of children and teacher conferences. Activities such as sewing and flower arranging illustrate another difficulty—that is, drawing the line between household tasks and leisure time pursuits. Umpiring a Little League game or taking children to a museum might be classified as child care or as recreation.

Measurement of time spent at household tasks also presents a problem, since more than one task may be carried on simultaneously, and the time spent on a particular task may be fragmented into short irregular units of time. Since there are no productivity norms for household tasks, judgments as to time required and time spent must be highly subjective.

The sharing of household tasks was surveyed in 1,300 husband-wife families of varied socioeconomic status in Syracuse, N.Y., and its suburbs in 1967-68 (Walker, 1970). The results indicate that wives employed more than thirty hours a week spent, on the average, thirty-four hours a week or almost five hours a day on household tasks. Women who were not employed reported spending fifty-seven hours a week on household tasks. Thus, the working wives apparently substituted thirty hours or more on the job for twenty-three hours of household work. The survey did not reveal whether the same "output" of household work was accomplished in the lesser time, or

---

[8]For a further discussion of earnings and income differentials by race, see Robert L. Stein and Janice N. Hedges, "Blue-collar/white-collar pay trends: Earnings and family income," *Monthly Labor Review,* June 1971, pp. 13-24.

whether (and which) household tasks were truncated or given up entirely.[9]

Paid and volunteer work plus household work in these Syracuse families averaged sixty-three hours a week for women and sixty-four hours for men. Husbands averaged about 1.6 hours a day on household jobs, whether or not their wives worked. Teenagers whose mothers were employed fifteen hours or more a week (and who had no younger brothers or sisters) worked an average of 2.7 hours a day on household jobs. This constituted nearly 30 percent of the total time spent by the family on household work. Those whose mothers were employed less than fifteen hours a week (including those whose mothers were not employed) contributed on the average 20 percent of the time the family spent on household duties. In this group, at least, it would appear that when a mother takes a job, a portion of her chores are shifted to her children rather than to her husband.

A study of time budgets in forty-four metropolitan areas in the United States in 1965-66 (Robinson and Converse, 1966) found that the total time spent by married workers on paid work, commuting to work, housework, and family tasks averaged 66.5 hours a week for men and 71.4 hours for women. Married men spent 2 hours a day more than married women, on the average, at paid work and commuting, but 2.7 hours less on housework and family tasks. Among working couples with children, fathers averaged 1.3 hours more free time[10] each weekday and 1.4 hours more on Sunday than mothers. Among childless married couples both of whom were employed, husbands averaged .7 hours more free time a weekday and 1.1 hours more on Sunday than wives.

ROLES OF FAMILY MEMBERS

Family work roles of men and women may have changed less than has often been suggested. The Syracuse study mentioned earlier found that wives did most of the inside work, while husbands did home maintenance and yard work. Husbands helped with marketing, recordkeeping, and child care.

In families in which the wife is employed in a profession that requires a high level of education, the division of home tasks seems to follow that in families in which she is employed in less skilled occupations. A case study was made of twenty couples in the Boston-Am-

[9]A report on Seattle, Wash., homemakers (based on a 20-percent response from a random sample of 1,200 homemakers) found that the average weekly hours spent on all home-associated tasks ranged from 39 for those who worked for pay 40 hours or more a week, to 54 for those who were not employed. See Florence Turnbull Hall and Marguerite Paulsen Schroeder, "Time Spent on Household Tasks," *Journal of Home Economics*, January 1970, pp. 23-29.

[10]"Free time" was defined as time spent in resting, education, radio, television, reading, social life, conversation, walking, sports, and spectacles.

herst area in 1968-69, all of them with wives employed in a profession that typically requires a doctorate (Holmstrom, 1970). As in other families, wives were more likely than husbands to prepare dinner, shop for groceries, and do the laundry, while husbands were more likely to do repairs and heavy yard work and to empty garbage and trash. Cooking breakfast and washing dishes were most often shared. Mothers were assisted by their husbands or by hired help, or both, in child care. Usually either husband or wife had full responsibility for keeping accounts, paying bills, and figuring taxes.

Children played a very small role in household tasks in these families in which the mother worked in a highly skilled profession. Household help generally was hired on a regular basis, particularly for ironing and cleaning.[11]

OBSTACLES TO EMPLOYMENT

Paid employment cannot always be reconciled with family responsibilities. An unemployment rate in March 1971 of 7.0 percent for married women (husbands present) with children, compared with a rate of 4.5 percent for those without children, indicates difficulties in reconciling the needs of children with the needs of employers. The exceptionally high unemployment rate for mothers of preschoolers (10.2 percent) suggests the special problems this group faces in locating or holding jobs compatible with their home responsibilities.

Family responsibilities are a major factor also in a woman's decision to leave her job or not to seek work. In 1970, of the 6.5 million women who had stopped working during the previous twelve months, over half cited home or school responsibilities as the reason (Flaim, 1971). About one third of the 2.7 million women who wanted a job but were not seeking employment also cited home responsibilities (unpublished data, Bureau of Labor Statistics).

Married women workers who are employed full time, year round are likely to have lesser family responsibilities than those employed part time or part year. For example, in 1970, 44 percent of the former, but 65 percent of the latter, had dependent children. Similarly, only 12 percent of those employed full time, year round had children under six, compared with 31 percent of the part-time or part-year workers.

SOME TYPICAL DIFFICULTIES

Surveys of the attitudes of working women and the extensive literature on the subject suggest several areas in which women commonly

[11]Paid help has become less and less of an option for women workers. The ratio of private household workers to all women workers has steadily declined:

1940	.169
1950	.086
1960	.079
1970	.052

experience difficulty in combining employment with home responsibilities.

Isolation of Families

The predominance of "nuclear families"—that is, families composed only of parents and dependent children—generally precludes the sharing of household duties and child care with grandparents or other adult relatives. In March 1971, relatively few households included a nonemployed adult woman in addition to a working mother: in the case of a working mother with dependent children, one out of fifteen, and if the children were under six, only one out of twenty-five.

Task Sharing

According to a Harris public opinion survey, in 1970,[12] many women feel the need for more help with household and family tasks. Almost one half the working women polled felt that men should do more repair work, and more than one third felt they should help more with childcare, cleaning, and shopping. About one fourth of the working women surveyed wanted men to help more with dishwashing.

Child Care

Lack of adequate care for the children of working mothers is not only a serious obstacle to the employment of women, it is a matter of social concern as to the welfare of the children. Results of a national survey of child care arrangements made by mothers who worked twenty-seven weeks or more (full time or part time) in 1964 and who had children under fourteen years of age (Women's Bureau, 1965) are shown in Table 20-III. Eight percent of these children looked after themselves.

A nationwide survey of day care in 1970 (Westinghouse, 1971) reported that day care was an institution lagging far behind the social change that brought about the need for it. According to the survey, over 350,000 working mothers in families with incomes of less than $8,000 reported they were very dissatisfied with their child care arrangements. Another estimated 750,000 mothers in families at this income level found lack of child care an obstacle to their employment.

An interview survey of 6,000 welfare recipients in 1970 (Thompson and Miles, 1971) revealed that nine out of ten of the mothers who were working at the time of the survey believed that their children were being cared for adequately, while only three out of five of those

[12]Virginia Slims, American Women's Opinion Poll, 1970, a study conducted by Louis Harris and Associates. The sample included both married and single women; 29 percent were working women.

TABLE 20-III
CHILD CARE ARRANGEMENTS MADE BY MOTHERS WORKING 27 WEEKS OR MORE, WITH CHILDREN UNDER 14 YEARS, 1964

Type of arrangement	Percent distribution
Total	100
Cared for by mother[1]	28
Cared for at home by other than mother	46
Cared for away from home	18
Group care	2
Other	16
No care	8

[1]Mother either cared for the children while working or worked only during their school hours.

not working believed that their children would be adequately cared for if they went to work. About three fifths of the white mothers on welfare and half of the black mothers preferred to be at home because they believed their children needed them there. Over one fourth of the white and one fifth of the black mothers gave the need to care for their children as a reason for leaving their last job.

Work Schedules and Practices

Present schedules and practices do not easily accommodate to family responsibilities. Opportunities for part-time work, for example, still fall short of the needs of working women. In the case of professional workers, part-time work may be associated with a reduction in status.

Sickness in the family and other family emergencies that may require a parent's presence are not routinely acceptable reasons for absence from work with—or without—pay. For some women, the problem is not only the absolute number of hours worked, but the inability to adjust work schedules to the demands of home. For example, lunch breaks may not be long enough to permit mothers to go home at lunchtime even though their school children are sent home at noon.

Transportation

Lack of convenient transportation sometimes impedes the meshing of home and work responsibilities, especially for part-time workers. Public transportation often is inadequate and erratic in off-peak hours, while in many urban areas parking space is scarce by midmorning.

The Effect of Role-attitudes

Husbands and wives often hold different views of women's role in marriage and in society, and these views are sometimes obstacles to employment. Studies of the labor force experience of women showed a strong correlation between husbands' attitudes and their wives' anticipation of labor force activity.[13] For example, of white married women under 25 years of age whose husbands had positive attitudes toward their working, two thirds indicated they would accept a job offer. Of those whose husbands had strong objections, only one fifth said they would work. The pattern for blacks was similar, but the sample was too small to generalize. Among white married women age 30 to 44, women who reported that their husbands strongly favored their working were three times as likely to have permissive views about working as those whose husbands opposed their working. The relationship was even stronger among black women.

One fourth of all married women age 30 to 44 were described as having permissive attitudes toward the employment of mothers with school-age children, while two fifths had ambivalent attitudes and slightly more than one third were opposed. Black women were half again as likely as white women to have permissive attitudes, and white women were 50 percent more likely than blacks to be opposed. The attitudes of husbands toward their wives working is the factor most strongly associated with the women's attitudes toward the employment of mothers.

A small study of couples where all the wives and most of the husbands were employed in professional occupations found that the women generally felt it possible to combine a profession and marriage as long as the husband was not threatened by his wife's capabilities and achievements, as long as he viewed it as adding to his stature and not as diminishing it, and as long as the wife was not ambivalent toward her role. Nonetheless, these wives were found to have limited their career ambitions in order to promote the smooth running of their homes (Poloma, 1970; Poloma and Garland, 1970).

SOLUTIONS

The following suggestions to better accommodate the needs of working women with family responsibilities have been compiled from attitudinal surveys and other literature.

[13]Herbert S. Parnes et al, *Years for Decision,* Vol. 1, and *Dual Careers,* Vol. 1 (Washington, U.S. Department of Labor, Manpower Administration, 1971). Another study, of men in blue-collar occupations, also indicates that the ease with which a wife carries out dual roles may be influenced by her husband's attitude. Harold Sheppard, *Who are the workers with the blues?* (Kalamazoo, Mich., W. E. Upjohn Institute for Employment Research, 1970).

Day Care

One of the most frequently mentioned needs is more day care facilities providing adequate services at feasible prices. The Administration-initiated welfare reform legislation now before Congress authorizes $700 million to provide child care opportunities for 875,000 children.

Some groups, maintaining that child care is a legitimate business expense, have long advocated extension of tax allowances for such expenses to workers at all income levels. Recent tax reform legislation substantially liberalized allowed deductions. Previously, U.S. tax laws allowed a working woman a maximum deduction of $600 for child care expenses for one child under thirteen years and $900 for two or more. In order to claim the deduction, married women were required to file a joint return with their husbands and any deduction was reduced $1 for each $1 of combined adjusted gross income exceeding $6,000.

The new law permits a maximum deduction of $400 a month for care in the home of a child under 15 years. In the case of child care outside the home, up to $200 of the $400 may be used for one child, up to $300 for the care of two children, and up to $400 for the care of three children or more. The deduction is available to a single taxpayer whose annual adjusted gross income is not over $18,000 and to married taxpayers who file a joint return if the combined annual adjusted gross income is not over $18,000. The deduction is reduced by 50 cents for each dollar of income above $18,000.

Upgrading Household Employment

Still another means that has been suggested to promote the smooth running of households in a nuclear family situation where the wife is employed outside the home is upgrading household employment to attract more workers into that occupation. Experimental and demonstration projects in the late 1960s funded by the U.S. Department of Labor indicated that trained household employees can provide needed services that command decent wages and good working conditions.

More Efficient Home Management

Planning and organizing housework, utilizing labor-saving devices and convenience products, determining priorities, and taking a relaxed attitude toward chores of lesser importance have also been suggested as ways to reduce the demands of housework.

Adaptable Work Rules

The development of more part-time jobs has been suggested, as well as time off without loss of pay for such child-related activities as teacher conferences, doctor visits, or similar obligations,[14] and liberal maternity leave.

Recognition of Life-cycle Pattern

The problems of working women can be eased if employers (as well as educational and training institutions) come to accept and make provision for interrupted education and employment patterns.

Fuller Sharing of Family Responsibilities

A more egalitarian family style, one in which the careers of husband and wife are equally important and the burdens of household tasks and child care are equally shared, has been pointed out as a way to enable more women to cope with responsibilities at home and on the job.

REFERENCES

Paul O. Flain, *Employment in Perspective* (BLS Report 396, 1971).

Lynda Lytle Holmstrom, "Intertwining Career Patterns of Husbands and Wives in Certain Professions," Ph.D. dissertation (Brandeis University, 1970), prepared under a grant from the Manpower Administration. (PB 191917, National Technical Information Service, Springfield, Va.)

Margaret M. Poloma, "Role Conflict and the Married Professional Women," paper presented at the annual meeting of the Ohio Valley Sociological Society, 1970.

Margaret M. Poloma and T. Neal Garland, "The Myth of the Egalitarian Family," paper presented at the annual meeting of the American Sociological Association, Washington, D.C., 1970.

John P. Robinson and Philip E. Converse, *Summary of U.S. Time-Use Survey* (Ann Arbor, University of Michigan, 1966), Survey Research Center Monograph.

David L. Thompson and Guy H. Miles, *Self-Actuated Work Behavior Among Low-Income People* (Minneapolis, Minn., North Star Research and Development Institute, 1971).

Kathryn E. Walker, "Time-use patterns for household work related to homemakers' employment," speech, Agricultural Outlook Conference, Washington, D.C., February 18, 1970.

Westinghouse, *Day Care Survey*, 1970 (Washington, D.C., Westinghouse Learning Corp. and Westat Research, Inc., 1971).

Women's Bureau, *Childcare Arrangements of Working Mothers* (Washington, Women's Bureau, U.S. Department of Labor, and Children's Bureau, U.S. Department of Health, Education, and Welfare, 1965).

[14]The collective bargaining agreement signed in 1967 between the Preway Co. (Wisconsin Rapids, Wis.) and the Office and Professional Employees International Union provides working mothers up to forty hours a year off without loss of pay for such purposes.

Chapter 21

INTIMACY AND CRISIS IN ADULTHOOD*

MARJORIE FISKE LOWENTHAL AND LAWRENCE WEISS

Abstract

Even though interpersonal intimacy has been proposed as a vital developmental task in the achievement of adulthood (Erikson, 1963) there has been little systematic study of intimate relationships as a psychological resource in transactions and crises of the adult life course, including those resulting from sociohistorical change. Both the high degree of complexity and relativity of the concept of intimacy, as well as the American male's traditional flight from intimacy, contribute to its lack of exploration. It is the thesis of this article that in the absence of overwhelming external challenge, most individuals find the motivation to live autonomous and satisfying lives only through one or more mutually intimate dyadic relationships. Some preliminary evidence in support of this thesis is presented showing marked life stage and sex differences. In addition a theoretical framework for the study of psychosocial change in adulthood focusing on areas of commitment, juxtaposed with some evidence, suggests a more flexible life stage theory than that proposed by Erikson (1963). The implications of intimacy as a resource are discussed for two adult risk groups: middle-aged women in the post-maternal stage of life and middle-aged men who are "overwhelmed" by life stresses.

Background

WITH A FEW exceptions, notably the psychoanalytic theorists, psychological and social scientists have left the concepts of love and intimacy to philosophers, poets, novelists, artists, and the humanists. The assumption seems to be that such essentials to life and growth, both individual and societal, cannot be studied scientifically. The exceptions are notable, including Freud and many of the neo-Freudians such as Spitz and Wolf (1946). More recently, Bowlby and his colleagues (1969), Chevalier-Skolnikoff (1971), and Harlow (1971) have conducted important work with animals. The bulk of this theoretical and empirical work, however, was on the relationship be-

*Research data reported within this article supported by Grant No. AG00002, National Institute of Aging (formerly HD03051 and HD05941, National Institute of Child Health and Human Development).

From The Counseling Psychologist, 1976, 6(1), 10-15.

tween mother and infant, and its implications for future relationships and other dimensions of development.

Erikson (1963) and Sullivan (1953) have made the capacity for intimacy a vital component of their developmental theory, identifying it as the critical developmental task in the transition from adolescence to adulthood. In classical analytic theory, the assumption is that such a developmental stage could not be successfully negotiated without the firm underpinnings of a satisfactory infant-mother relationship. Erikson's work is not quite so dogmatic on this point. While brilliantly illuminated in case studies and in his biographical works (1958, 1969, 1975), Erikson's developmental theory and the role of intimacy within it have proven difficult to define succinctly and to put to empirical test (Gruen, 1964). Many clinicians, on the other hand, have found his insights "true" in a therapeutic relationship, and among others, the case studies of healthy people as well as of patients by Robert Coles reveal Erikson's strong influence (Coles, 1967).

Research has been done on the process of acquaintanceship, affiliation, courtship, and marriage on the one hand, and social networks on the other. There have been very few systematic studies of the significance of intimate dyadic relationships across the adult life course, however, even though sensitive adults are aware of their importance for growth in adulthood, and as a rich psychological resource in the inevitable transitions and crises of the life course.

Interpersonal intimacy is a complex concept, both theoretically and operationally. The major components contained in an intimate relationship, as reported in our earlier work, include similarity, reciprocity, and compatibility (Weiss & Lowenthal, 1975). These components are in turn manifested through various verbal, nonverbal, and physical modalities. Verbal manifestations of intimacy range from the sharing of intellectual ideas, similar attitudes (Byrne, 1971) and guarded exchanges of information to totally free, open, and spontaneous interchanges and self-disclosures that involve reciprocal expressions of affection and love. Nonverbal manifestations of intimacy range from the similarity of behaviors such as gestures or dress, to sustained eye-contact (Argyle & Dean, 1965) as well as spatial distancing or positioning (Hall, 1966; Kiesler & Goldberg, 1968), to an occasional and often totally unexpected sense of being pleasurably shaken by the presence of another. Physical manifestations of intimacy range from a casual handshake or hug, to the kind of "earth-moving" sexual encounter described by Hemingway in *For Whom the Bell Tolls.* Morris (1971) describes twelve stages necessary for a man and a woman to pass through in order to establish an intimate "bond," which in turn is necessary for survival. In this schema (which we feel needs more rigor), sexual intercourse is the final stage, and itself in turn strongly influences the depth of the "bond." As reflected in the above ranges, there are a variety of degrees or levels that may exist in an intimate relationship. Of particular importance here are those qualities within a relationship that emphasize emotional support or dependability, trust, and mutual empathy or understanding. Dahms (1969) reports a study in which he asked university students to whom they would turn for help with severe crises. The majority of the students took their problems to their peers, faculty, or others rather than to helping professionals. It appears, then, that in times of extreme crises, one's close friends or significant others may be an important resource in the adapting process. The degree of resourcefulness that various levels of intimacy may have on the adaptation process is an intriguing question that clearly needs additional exploration.

Close dyadic relationships consist of varying mixes of all the above forms or manifestations of intimacy, sometimes one far outweighing the others. In our opinion and based on what little evidence is available, the question of the conceptual usefulness of scales or levels of intimacy, contrary to Dahms (1972), should be left open. For example, from a subjective point of view, the concept of intimacy is a highly relative one. As some of our earlier work has shown (Lowenthal & Haven, 1968), one person's confidant is another's casual acquaintance. Jean Paul Sartre, in a recent "Sartre at Seventy" interview (Sartre & Contat, 1975) spends considerable time ruminating about such complexities. He discusses the subtleties of nonverbal, nonsexual physical intimacy, on one hand, and verbal on the other, and centers his hopes for the future of mankind around an increased willingness of individuals to yield their subjective selves to others, above and beyond any expectation of reciprocity. The relativity of the concept of intimacy is further reflected in our work on friendship patterns across the life-course (Weiss & Lowenthal, 1975). The middle and lower middle-class people in our sample of various life stages, when asked to describe the nature of their relationship with their three closest friends, not only attributed different functions to each (reflecting a heterogeneous pattern), but also often expressed a desire for closer, more reciprocal and emotionally laden relationships than they actually had.

In the four adult life stages studied, these needs were expressed much more frequently among women than among men. This comes as no surprise to those familiar with our cultural, and especially our literary, tradition. From *Moby Dick* and *Huckleberry Finn* to *Death in the Afternoon* and *The Great Gatsby* (and beyond), a main theme has been the urge (or necessity) to escape from what is construed as a yoking intimacy with women, to escape into parallel work, parallel play, or fighting with men. Intimacy between men is warded off as though in fear of homosexuality, and the exploration of intimacy between men and women is left to the women, writers and otherwise. This fear of intimacy is found much less often among English and European writers of earlier and concomitant vintage. Flaubert, Stendal, the early Tolstoy, and the great poets and essayists of nineteenth century England did not leave themes of "sense and sensibility" entirely to the insights and gifts of the Austens. Nor have they written only about the nuances of intimacy between sexes: from Shakespeare on, male friendships, homosexual or otherwise, have been subjects for literary homage, with no noticeable signs of guilt. Indeed, even today, it is frequently observed (though to our knowledge not empirically studied) that close friendships among European men are as frequent as among women. In some strata of our own society, relationships among men are qualitatively different from that of women (Lowenthal, Thurnher, Chiriboga, & Associates, 1975).

It remains to be seen whether Sartre is a true prophet, but he does seem to be holding a sensitive finger to the winds of change. Research, the mass media, and in between, the popularizers of "psychology," share an increasingly pervasive theme of complaint: lack of "real" communication between the sexes, between the generations, and among humankind in general. Indeed, the remarkable, if not frightening, proliferation of various kinds of encounter groups is perhaps the most dramatic consequence of the pervasive and tragic emotional frustration, if not malaise, among middle-class Americans. Some recent research done at Stanford on the impact of encounter groups on its participants found that 13 percent of the participants could be deemed "casualties" or entered into psychotherapy as a result of the experience, as compared to 3 percent of the controls, signifying a high risk situation. On the other hand, however, most of the participants were satisfied (61%) with their experience and reported positive change with respect to inner understanding and sensitivity to others, but with negligible effect on one's social networks, including degrees of intimacy (Lieberman, Yalom, & Miles, 1972). This latter finding seems somewhat contradictory to alleged objectives of most encounter groups, namely to facilitate interaction with others on a more meaningful, open, and intimate level. It may be that the often rather forcefully arranged possibilities for "instant intimacy" are so overwhelming that they actually inhibit the usually slow-growing development of a close relationship under less artificial circumstances.

The striving for interpersonal intimacy is not, in our opinion, the result of nostalgia among the various generations and age cohorts making up our current population. Rather, it seems to be a conscious or preconscious realization that the traditional norms of our society, and the frontier atmosphere within which these norms developed and continue to influence our educational and familial systems, as well as our communications media, have resulted in the repression or suppression of what, next to the dire necessities of life, is perhaps the basic human need. Except for such groups as the New England Brahmins and their Southern counterparts, our culturally varied ancestors, of whatever generation American, were so caught up in the challenges and grueling work of Western expansion, power dreams, and women having yet more children to till the soil and later build the factories, that they had no time or inclination for introspection.

It is our thesis that in the absence of overwhelming external challenge, most "average" men and women find the energy and motivation to live autonomous, self-generating, and satisfying lives only through one or more mutually supportive and intimate dyadic relationships. In addition, we suspect that the development of "crises," both personal and societal, could, under optimal circumstances, have a unifying effect and facilitate the further development of existing intimate relationships. Such crises may also provide the setting for the initiation of new close relationships among persons directly involved in them. At our present stage of evolution (as Maslow's, 1954/1970, search for self-actualizing people indicates), a relatively small proportion of the population (including, but not only, the geniuses) are born with or develop early the capacity for living autonomous, self-actualizing lives. We agree with Sartre (Sartre & Contat, 1975) that many others may become autonomous if our social institutions and norms begin to loosen up the sanctions against the expression of subjective experience, especially interpersonal, and each finds his own way of giving and yielding to others.

There is, as we have noted, relatively little research on the subject of intimacy, and even less from the perspective of the adult life course through old age. The Human Development Program at the University of California, San Francisco more or less stumbled onto its importance as a critical intervening resource between life stress and adaptation many years ago. In reviewing the research literature, we will therefore be drawing somewhat immodestly on our own work. At the same time, we are in a position to know and are pleased to report that there is something like a groundswell of theoretical and research interest in the subject among young, as yet unpublished, psychologists, sociologists, and anthropologists.

After a brief review of what is known in this relatively new field, we shall then sketch out some relevant aspects of a conceptual framework which we are developing, primarily for research purposes. We believe that this framework may, as it becomes refined with empirical data, be useful for clinicians, and will therefore conclude with some suggestions in regard to its implications for counseling psychologists.

Insights from Research

Almost none of the relatively little research literature on intimacy, has been devoted to close relationships as a resource in life crises as these are usually defined. On the other hand, all of us, from clinical, personal, and observational experience, and from the reading of life histories and case studies, could supply a wealth of anecdotal material about how the availability of an intimate other can help ease one through the stressful periods of life. One of our few research-based observations is that widowerhood is often more traumatic for men than widowhood for women (Lowenthal, Berkman, & Associates, 1967), and we explain this on the basis that men are less likely to have other persons with whom they are intimate. In fact, men name their spouses as their confidantes far more often than women do (Lowenthal & Haven, 1968). In addition, Jourard (1964) and Taylor (1968) elaborate on these sex differences and claim that man's inability to disclose himself intimately contributes to his shorter life expectancy. The process of disclosing oneself to another during particular periods of crises may be the only "therapeutic" action necessary, whether it be "cathartic" in the Aristotelean sense, or self-validating (Sullivan, 1953) in form.

In any case, it has long been established within the research literature on animals that the "herding instinct," or the tendency for affiliation among the same species, serves as a definite survival mechanism (Lorenz, 1966) and directly reduces fear or anxiety (Latane & Glass, 1968). Schachter (1959) performing several experiments with humans dealing with anxiety and affiliation, found that people preferred to affiliate with others when presented with an anxiety-provoking situation—not just anyone, but others in a similar plight. He interpreted his findings in terms of the need not only for anxiety reduction, but also for self-evaluation and social appraisal. In other words, people are attracted to those who fulfill their needs and desires, and provide them with protection and security. This, however, is true only to a certain degree. When the crises are overwhelming, then reactions may sometimes be just the opposite, with the individual seeking privacy and isolation. An extreme example of this would be the retreat into a psychotic depressive reaction under a serious loss, or even worse, a catatonic state with total blockage of external reality and communication.

It has long been traditional among the medical profession to ignore the need for closeness with others among sick or dying patients. Some psychiatrists, primarily geriatric, recognize this need and are able to transcend the classical Freudian "do not touch" code and employ the therapeutically important modality of touch. Physical manifestations of intimacy, such as the holding of hands, the stroking of the patient's head, or even an arm around the shoulder is extremely important in helping the older person deal with severe crises, including the prospects of dying (Simon, personal communication). In fact, in a recent doctoral dissertation (Weiss, 1975), it was found that the importance of touch was not just in the frequency of the act, but in the quality of the touching experience, as reflected through its location, duration, intensity, sensation, and the extent of the body touched. In addition, the differences between men and women in the quality of touching were quite marked, reflecting different tactile needs for men and women. These differing tactile needs have to be taken into consideration not only in the helping relationships, but also in other social relationships that are closer or involve more intimate interaction.

While it is clear that some animals may prefer to be sick and die in solitude, or, conversely, that some die as result of the tremendously strong desire to flock together (Lorenz, 1966), we know far too little about the needs of human beings in this respect. Indeed, it may well be that even people who have been undemonstrative all their lives have a very deep-seated need for the physical warmth of human contact when their defenses are weakened by being critically ill or dying —a need which family and friends may or may not sense, and which medical staff are explicitly trained to disregard along with any other verbal or physical signs of "emotional involvement" with patients. These needs, however, have to be recognized and incorporated into the health care of the ill, as well as those significant others who are affected by the stress. How often does one see a situational crisis where the only focus of the "helping" personnel is on the patient, totally ignoring the mother, spouse, or friend who may also be present? They too need support to overcome the burden of the stressful situation.

In the case of death or even divorce, the loss of the significant person creates a void, resulting in a strong need to replace the intimate. The proliferation of "singles" groups all over the country, many geared specifically to the needs of the recently widowed and divorced of all age groups, provides dramatic testimony to the growing acceptability of the acknowledgment of the needs of men, as well as women, for the replacement of a lost intimate.

Before shifting our attention to the more ordinary stresses of the adult life course, and how the presence of, or capacity for, an intimate relationship affects them, we first have to emphasize that intimacy, as we have defined it, goes beyond Schachter's (1959) concept of selective affiliation. In fact, as our earlier work on friendship reflects (Weiss & Lowenthal, 1975), the important qualities in a close relationship are more reciprocal or mutual in form, involving trust, support, understanding, and the sharing of confidences. We are still working on this defining process in our present research. Nonetheless, in a preliminary longitudinal analysis of our data of the role of the capacity for intimacy or mutuality as a mediator between the stresses of normative life course transition (leaving home, having or planning for the first child, having the youngest child leave home, and retiring), we have found that there are marked life stage and sex differences. This was also true of the baseline data reported in Lowenthal et al. (1975) where, for example, the capacity for mutuality proved a greater resource for highly stressed but well-adapted middle-aged men than for anyone else. Five years later, when nearly three-fourths of the sample as a whole had undergone the anticipated transition, we find that the happiest people and those having the fewest psychological (and physical) symptoms are those with a high baseline rating on mutuality, in this instance, intrafamilial. This is the kind of generalized finding that usually gets reported in studies of adults.

There are, in fact, notable variations by stage and sex which make the overall correlation relatively meaningless. Among the former high school seniors there was no relationship between mutuality and these indicators of adaptation at any of the three periods of interviewing, possibly because they had not yet reached Erikson's postulated intimacy stage. This interpretation is partially confirmed by the fact that, at the initial contact, newlywed women ranking high on both intra– and extrafamilial intimacy were significantly happier than those who had low ratings. That this was not true eighteen months and five years later, when the majority had at least one child, may well be due to the often-noted alteration in the marital relationship with the advent of the first child—or, equally plausible, that the glow of the honeymoon phase had worn off. Interestingly, newlywed men, who were noted at the baseline as having a surge of exuberant energy and often were involved in a phrenetic range of activities, revealed no relationship between the assessed capacity for mutuality and our adaptive measures at any of the three periods of contact.

On the other hand, among men who were anticipating the empty-nest stage at the initial contact, there was a high correlation between intrafamilial mutuality and happiness eighteen months later when the youngest child had left home, perhaps because they felt they would now get more attention from their wives. Women at this stage resembled the men in this respect. This relationship between mutuality and happiness among the middle aged does not hold, however, five years later. Possibly the effects of a *second* honeymoon had worn off. Our interpretation, however, based on in-depth analysis of intensive life histories of these subjects, is rather different. During these baseline interviews, men and women had hoped for a closer relationship with their spouses after the youngest child had left home, and perhaps had attained it when the house first became free of the distractions caused by the presence of an adolescent. The longer-range goals of these men and women, however, were often on a collision course, many women hoping to become committed to some activity or interest beyond the family, and many men hoping to be yet more pampered by their wives, to ease them through another ten or fifteen years of boredom on jobs to which they had relatively little commitment and even less hope of changing (Lowenthal, 1975).

This original detailed analysis (Lowenthal et al., 1975) also showed that mutuality was a significant resource for a certain type of "challenged" men, those who were having or had had much stress but were not preoccupied or obsessed by it. Thus we are not surprised to find that eighteen months later the happiest men among those facing retirement were those with a high initial mutuality rating. That this was not true five years after the initial contact may well be due to the already mentioned disparate long-term goals of men and women at this life-stage, as if, in support of Jung's (1933) thesis, to make up for what each of them had missed in earlier life stages. The implications of these findings for the interpretation of research data which do not take into account variations between the sexes at various ages or stages of adulthood are self-evident.

Toward a Conceptual Framework

For the early phases of life, psychologists have emphasized the developmental task of the establishment of same-sex dyadic relationships in the pre-puberty and early puberty stages. And we have already noted Erikson's formulation of intimacy with a member of the opposite sex as the critical developmental task of late adolescence and early adulthood. Scholars studying later phases of adulthood, however, have tended to by-pass dyadic relationships in favor of research on participation in social networks, familial and otherwise (Lowenthal & Robinson, in press). The emphasis is on behavioral involvement and activity patterns, rather than on the quality of interpersonal relationships.

As a result of our previous empirical work, we are beginning to develop a theoretical framework for the study of psychosocial change, centered around four areas of commitment. Shifts from one type of commitment to another may prove functional for adaptation in various stages of the adult life course (Lowenthal, in press). The five foci of commitment are interpersonal; mastery or competence; creativity; moral; and self-protective. In our concept of interpersonal commitment, we steer a middle course between nineteenth century romantic ideas of lifelong commitments to dyadic heterosexual and same-sex relationships, and the predictions of Lifton (1967/1969) of an emerging new human type who will make many smooth and fluid transitions across the life course, with inconsistency in self-image and commitments the norm, rather than, in Lecky's (1969) terms of self-consistency, the exception. Nor do we completely abjure nineteenth century romanticism—on the contrary, we strongly suspect that former intimate relationships, disrupted by death, distance or interpersonal conflict, may continue to be a resource in terms of crisis, chronic and acute, throughout the life course, such as is described by Sartre (Sartre & Contat, 1975) in discussing his earlier relationship with Camus. Knowing through past experience that one is capable of having an intimate relationship, romantic or otherwise, may prove nearly as important a resource in difficult life situations as actually having an intimate at the time of crisis: a former relationship is reinforcing and at the same time sustains hope for a future one.

The proposed framework for studying psychosocial change in adulthood includes coping not only with the inevitable crises of life, but with the more insidious psychological and social changes involved in the growing awareness of becoming mature, then, as is the norm in our culture, becoming obsolete, and finally confronting the imminence and inevitability of death. Incidentally, and relevant to the theme of this paper, we are convinced, though we cannot yet demonstrate, that individuals who have worked through the death of an intimate other between late childhood and early adulthood are better equipped to cope with the prospective loss of the most intimate of intimate others, the self, than are those who have not.

Implicit in Erikson's (1963) stage theory is that there is a main task for each stage, and that, once mastered, one is then free to go on to the next. While he states (1975) that each mastered capacity has continuing importance throughout adulthood, he has not as yet elaborated on the nature of their significance. Nor does Erikson explore differences between the sexes in great detail (much of his work has focused on men), which in many areas of life, including intimacy, we have found to be more important than life stage differences within the same sex. High school boys resemble pre-retiree men more than they resemble high school girls, for example, and on many counts.

If we juxtapose the aforementioned evidence from our longitudinal study into a theoretical commitment framework, we seem considerably to modify Erikson's (1963) stage theory. While he focuses on a sequence of tasks for successive life stages, our findings, as those of other adult longitudinal studies (e.g., Britton & Britton, 1972), strongly suggest that one must simultaneously examine several "tasks" or commitments, how they periodically wax and wane, and how these rhythms differ, and possibly conflict, between the sexes. Erikson's formulations relate essentially to interpersonal commitments, from dyadic (intimacy) to the more broadly interpersonal implied in his concept of generativity, to an almost pan-human level ("integrity"), a sense of being at one with one's fellow men and one's place in human history. In other words, he tends to focus on one commitment per life stage, which, with successful completion, enables one to move on to the next.

Highly relevant to our concept of intimacy as a continuing and vital necessity for a satisfying and growth-oriented existence through old-age (an essential component of intimacy, as we see it, is concern with growth of the other) are one's concept of self and the feeling of hope. It has generally been accepted, at least since the work of George Herbert Mead (1934), Harry Stack Sullivan (1953), and to some extent since the earlier inception and development of classical psychoanalytic theory, that close interpersonal relationships are essential not only to the beginnings of a concept of one's self, but to its continuing change across the life course, for better or for worse. An exception to this would be the person who never experienced any, or enough, of the types of intimacy we have suggested in infancy, adolescence, or young adulthood, and whose self-concept seems to be sustained only through a more or less random kind of social feedback. Indeed, this may well be a common personality configuration in our culture, people whose energies are devoted almost exclusively to the procuring of indiscriminate feedback (and they might well resemble Lifton's Protean Man). So all-absorbing is the need for the reinforcement provided by adulation that there is no room for the kind of interpersonal commitment that intimacy requires, or for the genuine substantive concerns involved in commitment to competence, mastery, creativity, or to moral, spiritual or religious values.

We have called these people, whose sheer survival depends on constant generalized reinforcement, a variant of the life-long self-protective. This is to be distinguished from the self-protectiveness that often develops with age and its concomitant dependencies, as well as from that of lifelong isolates, who, were they to allow themselves to be "caught" by a psychotherapist, a circumstance from which their very isolation protects them, might well be labeled schizoid (Lowenthal, 1964). The kind of narcissistic self-preservation we are referring to also differs from what we have elsewhere (Lowenthal et al., 1967) called the *marginally isolated,* individuals who keep trying, but continuously fail to establish intimate relationships. Unlike the narcissistic self-protective, both the life-long and marginally isolated may have commitments to competence or mastery, and to moral or religious precepts and faiths which are sustaining. They have no need to manipulate the adulation of others to survive.

As to hope, while we have good evidence for its being closely related to time perspective, that is, preoccupation with past, present, or future, and the individual's projection of his or her lifespan, at this point we can only say that we are convinced that, for many people, intimacy is a sine qua non for the sustainment of hope. The exceptions are the life-long self-protectives who for whatever reason are incapable of it. We know from the work of Spitz and Wolf (1946) that infants and children deprived of a close relationship became withdrawn, unenterprising and despondent. Some die. We know that schizophrenics long confined to mental hospitals increasingly withdraw and grow old there, unless they sustain relationships with family, friends, or staff. We know that people in nursing homes, which are generally not distinguished by personal warmth on the part of staff, become rapidly depressed, enclosed in a cocoon, and some die without known cause. In fiction and autobiography we also can read about the liberating, hope-inspiring effect of a new close friendship or of falling in love. From the same sources, as well as from our own lives, we know that this kind of renewal is not limited to one stage of life—it can happen, even for the first time, in old age.

Implications for the Counseling of Adults

One of the generalizations we should like to draw from this paper is that one cannot generalize about counseling adults past the age of thirty, any more than one can assume that every disturbed young woman is a hysteric, or that every disturbed child grew up in a "schizophrenic family." The day may come when longitudinal research, extending throughout adult life, will enable us to locate various populations at risk and provide some inkling of the psychological, social, and cultural-historical factors involved. At this stage of our knowledge, we can venture to suggest only two such risk groups, both middle-aged. From our own research, we have learned that one such group at risk is made up of middle and lower middle-class women facing, or actually in, the early phases of the post-parental stage. Most of these women, who have mainly been family-centered, can anticipate another twenty-five or thirty years of reasonably healthy life. Many have not very clearly thought through the urge to find commitments, often related to a need for mastery or competence, beyond the family sphere. Yet they are caught in a bind, because they also yearn for a renewal of intimacy with their spouses, often expressed in terms of "better communication." Many of their husbands, increasingly dependent, are demanding more of their wives' time, mainly in pampering to their own physical comfort, and such men are often jealous of any actual or potential outside interests on the part of their spouses. Further, the social milieu in which these women live still places many obstructions in the way of those who want to "do" something, whether educational, creative, voluntary, or paid. It is all too easy for these women to use their husbands' demands as an excuse for not taking any initiative. Over and above this conflict, as we are beginning to see in the follow-up material, many of these women are reaching the age when they have increasingly dependent parents, sometimes their own, sometimes their spouses', and occasionally all four. It is, of course, the women in our culture who primarily bear the burden of the psychological and physical needs of the dependent parents, at least while their husbands are still working. Altogether these women facing the empty nest stage were the most poorly adapted of our eight age and sex subgroups. For reasons of their socioeconomic class, and perhaps its accompanying prejudices, few would voluntarily seek counseling.

The second high risk population are the middle-aged men. As current statistics show, they have a high rate of heart attacks and other cardiovascular problems, as well as mental health problems, dramatically reflected in the upward swing of the suicide percentages. It is precisely this group in which we found that the existence or absence of close interpersonal relationships was an important factor in the extent to which men were preoccupied with their stressful experiences. In addition to the fact that men in general do not have, but want, more emotional qualities within their close relationships, the middle-aged men who are "overwhelmed" rate themselves low on the capacity for intimacy and mutuality. These findings support the proposition presented here: close interpersonal relationships serve as a resource against life's crises. Therefore, this risk group, the middle-aged men, needs special attention in counseling in the form of focusing in on their interpersonal milieux as a resource. It is our intention to explore this resource area further to bring more knowledge and understanding to bear on its clinical application.

In addition to the above fairly well-supported suggestions, we can only summarize impressions which we as yet can only tentatively suggest may have important implications for the counseling of adults, and hope that they will be supported in future research.

Perhaps most important among these is the promise of a more flexible life stage theory than that initially formulated by Erikson. First, there may be marked cultural and class differences in the developmental stages of adulthood. Second, even among the largely privileged individuals whom he clinically or biographically studied in depth, presumably drawing on this experience in the development of his important theoretical contribution, there may be additional or more pertinent developmental tasks. For example, Berezin (1963) offers the possibility of a consultative stage as a late extension of the stage of generativity, one involving less responsibility than Erikson's concept implies. We are also willing to venture the hypothesis, with less hesitancy, that within each socioeconomic group in each culture, the developmental trajectories of men and women differ. For example, among some of the middle and lower middle-class women we are studying longitudinally, a generative stage (in Erikson's sense) seems to develop after the more literal generative phase of childbearing and rearing. Erikson's (1968) essay on women strongly implies, in true Freudian tradition, that the former is the principal if not the only form of generativity available (and satisfying) to women. His afterthoughts on this subject (1975) since the advent of the women's liberation movement are more open, but his thesis about psychological sex differences being to a considerable extent determined by biology (with which the authors of this article have no quarrel) remains intact.

Even more important, we believe, is flexibility about the stage concept and its implication that each successive stage must be attained before the next can be reached. We suggest more attention to the simultaneous examination of the individual's commitments to all of Erikson's stage-tasks (and some other forms of commitment as well) at each successive stage of the adult life course. For example, we suspect either for developmental or circumstantial reasons, that many people may achieve true intimacy only long after young adulthood. We also have some evidence which leads to a firmer conclusion: that the salience of intimacy waxes, wanes, and waxes again across the life course and that the rhythms vary between the sexes, often with disruptive consequences. At the same time, we may, in our culture at least, be experiencing sociohistorical change toward more self-revelation among both sexes, which may eventually mitigate such disruption.

REFERENCES

Argyle, M. & Dean, J. Eye contact, distance, and affiliation. *Sociometry,* 1965, 28, 289-304.

Berezin, M.A. Some intrapsychic aspects of aging. In N.E. Zinberg & I. Kaufman (Eds.), *Normal psychology of the aging process.* New York: International Universities Press, 1963, pp. 93-117.

Bowlby, J. *Attachment and loss.* Vol. I. New York: Basic Books, 1969.

Britton, J.H. & Britton, J.O. *Personality changes in aging.* New York: Springer, 1972.

Byrne, D. *The attraction paradigm.* New York: Academic Press, 1971.

Chevalier-Skolnikoff, S. *Ontogeny of communication in Macaca Speciosa:* Unpublished doctoral dissertation, Dept. of Anthropology, University of California, Berkeley, 1971.

Coles, R. *Children of crisis.* Boston: Little, Brown, 1967.

Dahms, A. Preferred sources of help in time of crisis as related to conceptual systems of college students (Doctoral dissertation, University of Northern Colorado, 1969). Ann Arbor, Mich.: University Microfilms, No. 69-15, 720.

Dahms, A. *Emotional intimacy.* Denver, Colorado: Pruett, 1972.

Erikson, E.H. *Young man Luther: A study in psychoanalysis and history.* New York: W.W. Norton, 1958.

Erikson, E.H. *Childhood and society* (2nd ed.) New York: Norton, 1963.

Erikson, E.H. Womanhood and the inner space. (Ch. 7) *Identity: Youth and crisis.* New York: Norton, 1968, pp. 261-294.

Erikson, E.H. *Gandhi's truth.* New York: Norton, 1969.

Erikson, E.H. *Life history and the historical moment.* New York: Norton, 1975.

Gruen, W. Adult personality: An empirical study of Erikson's theory of ego development. In B.L. Neugarten & Associates, *Personality in middle and late life.* New York: Atherton Press, 1964, pp. 1-14.

Hall, E.T. *The hidden dimension.* New York: Doubleday, 1966.

Harlow, H.F. *Learning to love.* San Francisco: Albion, 1971.

Jourard, S. *The transparent self.* Princeton: Van Nostrand Reinhold, 1964.

Jung, C.G. The stages of life. In *Modern man in search of a soul* (trans. by W.S. Dell & C.F. Baynes). New York: Harcourt, Brace and World, 1933, pp. 95-114.

Kiesler, C.A. & Goldberg, G.N. Multidimensional approach to the experimental study of interpersonal attraction: Effect of a blunder on the attractiveness of a competent other. *Psychological Reports,* 1968, *22,* 693-705.

Latane, B. & Glass, D. Social and nonsocial attraction in rats. *Journal of Personality and Social Psychology,* 1968, *9,* 142-146.

Lecky, P. *Self-consistency: A theory of personality.* Garden City, N.Y.: Doubleday Anchor, 1969.

Lieberman, M.A., Yalom, I.D., & Miles, M.S. *Encounter groups: First facts.* New York: Basic Books, 1972.

Lifton, R.J. *Boundaries: Psychological man in revolution.* New York: Random House (Vintage Books), 1969. (Originally published, 1967.)

Lorenz, K. *On aggression.* New York: Harcourt, Brace, and World, 1966.

Lowenthal, M.F. Social isolation and mental illness in old age. *American Sociological Review,* 1964, *29*(1), 54-70.

Lowenthal, M.F. Psychosocial variations across the adult life course: Frontiers for research and policy. *The Gerontologist,* 1975, *15*(1), Part 1, 6-12.

Lowenthal, M.F. Toward a sociopsychological theory of change in adulthood and old age. In J.E. Birren & K.W. Schaie (Eds.), *Handbook of the psychology of aging.* New York: Van Nostrand Reinhold, in press.

Lowenthal, M.F., Berkman, P.L. & Associates. *Aging and mental disorder in San Francisco: A social psychiatric study.* San Francisco: Jossey-Bass, 1967.

Lowenthal, M.F., & Haven, C. Interaction and adaptation: Intimacy as a critical variable. *American Sociological Review,* 1968, *33*(1), 20-30.

Lowenthal, M.F. & Robinson, B. Social networks and isolation. In R.H. Binstock & E. Shanas (Eds.), *Handbook of aging and the social sciences.* New York: Van Nostrand Reinhold, in press.

Lowenthal, M.F., Thurnher, M., Chiriboga, D., & Associates. *Four stages of life: A comparative study of women and men facing transitions.* San Francisco: Jossey-Bass, 1975.

Maslow, A.H. *Motivation and personality.* New York: Harper, 1970. (Originally published, 1954.)

Mead, G.H. *Mind, self, and society* (C.W. Morris, Ed.). Chicago: University of Chicago Press, 1934.

Morris, D. *Intimate behavior.* New York: Random House, 1971.

Sartre, J.P. & Contat, M. Sartre at seventy: An interview. *New York Review,* Aug. 7, 1975, 10-17.

Schacter, S. *The psychology of affiliation.* Stanford, CA: Stanford University Press, 1959.

Spitz, R.A. & Wolf, K.M. Anaclitic depression. *Psychoanalytic study of the child,*

2, New York: International Universities Press, 1946, pp. 313-342.

Sullivan, H.S. *The interpersonal theory of psychiatry* (H.S. Perry & H.L. Gawel, Eds.). New York: W.W. Norton, 1953.

Taylor, D.A. The development of interpersonal relationships: Social penetration processes. *Journal of Social Psychology,* 1968, *79,* 75-90.

Weiss, L., & Lowenthal, M.F. Life-course perspectives on friendship. In Lowenthal, M.F., Thurnher, M., Chiriboga, D., & Associates, *Four stages of life: A comparative study of women and men facing transitions.* San Francisco: Jossey-Bass, 1975, pp. 48-61.

Weiss, S. *Familial tactile correlates of body image in children.* Unpublished doctoral dissertation, School of Nursing, University of California, San Francisco, 1975.

Chapter 22

EMPIRICALLY BASED COUNSELING PRACTICES FOR WOMEN*

PEGGY J. HAWLEY

AS A COUNSELOR educator, my task is to attempt to send students off to their various professional settings equipped insofar as possible with the knowledge and skills they will need as practicing counselors. One important emerging area of knowledge is the understanding of the great social movements of our times, as Matthews (1974) has observed, in which various groups—women, minorities, the handicapped, and the aged—are seeking ways to move out of their state of powerlessness into the ranks of full citizenship, especially insofar as their right to work is concerned. Their quest is simple enough—they are asking to be evaluated on the basis of the work they can perform, not by their class membership. It is an interesting paradox that they must use the solidarity of the group to win the right to be treated as individuals.

Although the study of all of these struggling groups is fascinating, my interest has focused upon the so-called women's movement for several reasons. First, my own life story has been a study in transition as I moved from my very traditional role as homemaker and mother to professional woman with all of the accompanying anxieties and rewards of each role. Second, few groups of people have experienced such rapid role redefinition, conflicts in societal expectations, pressures and counter-pressures as have women in the last decade. Finally, the very size of the group undergoing change has meant that everyone is potentially affected by it. Most individuals live and work in close proximity with members of the opposite sex so that it becomes apparent that one sex cannot redefine itself without affecting the other. This makes sexual redefinition a very immediate process as well as an intimately personal one. Changes and potential changes in something as close to home as this are certain to bring out an army of opponents,

---

**From Focus on Guidance, February 1976, 8(6), 1-10. Courtesy of Love Publishing Company.*

some of whom might be expected to be found on the same team. Loyalties converge and disintegrate depending upon how feminism is interpreted. Women will group around different issues that are important to them at various times in their life cycles. At one time it could be abortion, at another discrimination in promotion practices, and at still another access to equal credit under the law.

Those who call themselves feminists claim that the movement has much in common with humanistic movements of all kinds and prophecy that new options opening for both sexes will provide the world with "person power" heretofore unavailable. Opponents, however, view with alarm the blurring of the sexual dichotomy and see it as causing a disintegration of the family, the basic unit of society. They warn of the dangers of a "unisex" world.

HOW HAS THE FEMINIST CONTROVERSY AFFECTED THE HIGH SCHOOL?

As vitally interested as I have been in this issue for the last ten years, I have become increasingly uncomfortable with my attempts to provide student counselors with the knowledge and skills needed to help girls sort through the confusion and come to some sense of their own identities as women and as workers. Unless one keeps up with the changing realities of the field, the temptation is strong to get caught up in righteous indignation over issues that are long since dead. Whatever else can be said of the media, it does facilitate the spread of ideas to the extent that it is difficult to know whether findings which turned up in empirical research five years ago have survived even that short period.

So, armed with a generous Ford Foundation grant releasing me full time from teaching responsibilities, I left the security of my ivory tower to spend a strenuous and productive year in the high schools of a large school district in a Southern California city of 750,000 inhabitants. I talked endlessly with girls and counselors, teachers and administrators, groundsmen and cafeteria workers. I tried to be a careful observer of the trivial and apparently inconsequential as well as a critical examiner of hard data. Each campus, it seemed, had its own temperament; each was imbued with an aura of its own which could be sensed although not documented in any concrete way. My intent was to discover if and how new definitions of femininity were related to young women's career development, how girls were currently being counseled, and how counselors perceived themselves in this process. This information could then be used in inservice as well as preservice education of counselors for the ultimate benefit of young people of both sexes.

Random selection of over 17 percent of tenth, eleventh, and twelfth grade girls based upon the ethnic distribution of each of thirteen high schools yielded 2,234 usable questionnaires from students. Over 85 percent of the counselors responded on identical questionnaire forms providing a sample of sixty-five from the counselor group. Data were then analyzed using multivariate statistical techniques.

FROM DICHOTOMY TO ANDROGYNY: A NEW ATTITUDE SCALE

A major tool in this investigation was a scale I had developed for previous research on women which measures the tendency of some people to dichotomize human characteristics into male/female categories and of others to view characteristics simply as *human* expressions, without the need to use a sex referent. Each respondent earns a score on this sex-based (dichotomous) to non-sex-based (androgynous) continuum. Such an instrument eliminates the disadvantages of scales labeling people "conforming or nonconforming," "traditional or non-traditional," or the familiar "masculine or feminine." Implications of sexual deviancy in the case of male/female, scales have long been a problem.

Recent research suggests that, contrary to earlier theories of personality, individuals who have psychological access to a wide range of both masculine and feminine behaviors—in short the *androgynous* ones—may indeed reflect a higher standard of mental health than those masculine men and feminine women so long held as ideal. Bem's (1974, 1975) investigations of behaviors in actual situations show that strongly sex-typed people may be "seriously limited in the range of behaviors available to them as they move from situation to situation."

The Relationship of IQ to Androgyny

Of great practical importance for the counseling profession is the finding that there is an extremely strong, nonchance relationship between girls who score high on IQ tests and androgynous views of life as reflected in questionnaire scores. The higher the IQ, the more apt a young woman is to resist being tracked into conventional modes of thinking. Although she may eventually choose what has been considered appropriate for women in the past, she will be quick to inform you that her selection was not based upon the assumption that it was "women's work." Such students will be also more likely to attend college than their less academically capable sisters, a selective process contributing to previous results showing college women to be more androgynous than those without college educations (Hawley, 1971). Counselors should certainly encourage these girls to continue to widen their horizons personally, educationally, and vocationally.

At this point it is important to state that, no matter where a person finds himself/herself in the "Great IQ Controversy" (Eysenck, 1973; Sowell, 1973) and after the behaviorists and geneticists have had their say, all agree that an IQ score is far from being a "pure" variable (if such a thing can be said to exist at all in social science research). It is a construct made up of many things—heredity, experience, persistence, plus such seemingly unrelated phenomena as the sort of topics discussed at the family dinner table. Whether IQ is relatively fixed or environmentally modifiable, regardless of its correlation (or lack thereof) to success outside of the academic setting, its relationship to attitudes toward sex-roles is important.

Of greater concern than the connection between high IQ and androgyny is the *inverse* relationship, that between girls with low IQ scores and dichotomous views of sex-roles. Probabilities of these girls seeking some of the most rewarding positions are further reduced because their definition of femininity does not lend itself to the consideration of high paying jobs already heavily male-dominated. I found that some counselors *were* informing female students of good job possibilities that do not require heavy academic preparation, such as skilled crafts in construction and manufacturing industries and in the expanding service industries. Little was being done, however, to help girls rethink their stereotypical views of work options, an experience which could help them construct a totally new life view instead of the piecemeal approach of judging each alternative separately. Investigators in search of facts upon which to build career theory for women have found vocational choice and life style closely related. Women tend to choose within societal restraints (despite the fact that these may be incompatible with personal values), and they do not pick an occupation by itself but rather select it along with a whole life style that allows some flexibility to juggle work with marriage, children, and other personal interests (Angrist, 1975).

Haener (1972), speaking from her long experience as an employment counselor and as a union official, warns of the hard realities of the working world and asks if counselors can take the heat. Especially pertinent are her observations on conditions at the lower end of the economic scale. The farther down you go, she warns, the greater the discrimination; yet these problems are "frequently overshadowed by the far more serious consequences of women's low level of aspiration and their lack of motivation." She notes that the feminist movement has been dominated by middle class women and the "awareness of self-limiting role concepts for the most part escaped disadvantaged women." Strong social disapproval of women entering the "non-female" occupations must be counteracted by counselors alert to the situation and willing "to take the heat."

This is not to suggest that counselors should in any way coerce girls into moving into heretofore male-dominated areas, but only that they need to find ways to break through the psychological barriers which prevent a thoughtful look at nontraditional opportunities as well as the ones long considered acceptable. The insidious thing about psychological barriers is that they are often so subtle and located at such an unconscious level that they are not recognized as barriers at all but are seen as evidence of "the way things are."

The counselor's trained ear—his or her ability to "hear" beneath the counselee's words to unvoiced (perhaps unrecognized) assumptions and implications—is an invaluable skill in feminist counseling. This assumes, of course, that the counselor has worked through his or her own sexual conditioning at least to the point where it is not passed along unconsciously to the counselee.

The Relationship of Ethnicity to Dichotomy and Androgyny

Although only about one half as effective a predictor as the variable of IQ, there was a significant relationship in this sample of high school girls between ethnic background and attitudes toward women's roles. The sample size of female high school students grades ten through twelve, it will be recalled, was 2,234. This group was comprised of approximately 12 percent Chicanas, 12 percent Black, 1 percent Asian American, and 72 percent Anglos. There were not enough students of Native American extraction or of other groups to constitute a 17 percent sample. The approximation of the sample to the racial distribution of the entire school district was very close. A slightly greater (2%) representation of Chicanas was an artifact due to the omission of males and all tenth graders.

Worth emphasizing is the fact that ethnicity, although a significant variable, was much less powerful a predictor than IQ. Another way of interpreting this finding is to say that a high scoring Chicana, Black, or Asian American girl would be more likely to hold androgynous views of sex roles than would an Anglo girl with a low IQ score. It is of utmost importance, furthermore, to keep in mind that the counselor is concerned with the growth and well-being of the *individual,* even in the interaction with *groups* of individuals. All of us must continually guard ourselves against the tendency to see people in terms of their group membership. Knowing that group data obscure individual differences, we still occasionally fail to realize that any member of a group may be radically different from other members on all but the variable upon which they are being classified.

With the above caveat in mind, let us turn to additional findings, particularly as they might be applicable to minority girls.

Discussions with high school girls, supported by questionnaire data, revealed that minority girls and/or those from low income groups tended to view feminism in its most stereotypical form, an actual caricature of the movement at its responsible best. One young woman asked, "Why do these women's libbers think that we all should go into men's jobs like running a jackhammer to break up streets?" Such a view is, no doubt, a reflection of many people's opinions who, listening to the rantings of a militant few, take them to be representative of the main theme.

Counselors can help all girls make the connection between the efforts of feminists to win equal treatment under the law and the "quest by all minorities—the handicapped, the economically depressed, the culturally different, and the aged—for a greater dignity and position within society" (Matthews, 1974).

Another serendipitous, albeit unhappy, discovery gained during a year's experience in the schools was the incredibly strong need on the part of girls to establish a relationship with a male. Comments written in margins of questionnaires provided an unexpected bonus and a better basis for questions during follow-up interviews. Statements about the need to protect the male ego were frequent whenever the subject of competition between the sexes was mentioned. Apparently the warning "Fragile, Handle with Care" is still pasted to the male psyche. None of the respondents mentioned such a thing as a female ego—perhaps they thought female egos did not need protection, or if they did, no one expected that the opposite sex was responsible for its protection.

While this was more apparent in schools with a high percentage of minority students and for those located in low-income sections of the city, I am confident that it is not strictly a function of race and income. Middle-class Anglo girls from affluent homes may have been less open about their feelings, yet they exhibited the same tendency. Without statistical data and on the basis of counselors' statements and my own observations, I came to the conclusion that the need for a relationship with the opposite sex was plainly greater for girls than for boys. The social necessity to "have a man" was so compelling that many girls would endure physical abuse rather than go "manless." As a source of feelings of self-worth, the presence of a male was clearly more valuable to their self-concept than any other measure of accomplishment.

None of these observations are new, of course, yet I am hopeful that they are more indicative of the past than the future because historically women have felt less in control of their own fates than men. Their station in life, the house and neighborhood in which they live, the social group with whom they interact, all depended in the past upon the men they married. Seven recent studies quoted by Maccoby and Jacklin (1974) show that boys display a greater sense of personal power emerging as early as grade school. Perhaps women's feelings of powerlessness will change as they move into the work world with greater assurance of equal pay and equal opportunity under recent protective legislation. Yet at the present time, as Hansen (1974) points out, the special focus upon career planning is widely needed during these years of transition.

All girls, and minority girls in particular, need to have recent affirmative action mandates interpreted in such a way that it has *personal* meaning for them. This should not be too difficult as we see daily reports in the media of heavy judgments against businesses, industries, and governmental agencies whose employment practices were ruled to be in violation of the civil rights of their employees. Certainly, no one would claim that racial and sexual discrimination have been eliminated by any standards, yet the point to be emphasized is that competent young women of minority backgrounds are in demand in the work world for the first time in history.

Girls' Perceptions of the Relative Importance of Marriage and Work

Most high school girls anticipate that paid employment outside of the home will play some part in their future lives. Over 89 percent of this sample said that they expected to work, a statistic remarkably close to the U.S. Department of Labor's estimate that nine out of ten women will work sometime during their lives (Maymi, 1975b). Approximately 60 percent stated that they saw work as a part-time activity, an indication that, although work is increasingly receiving a higher priority in investigations like this, it is still subordinate to other activities in the eyes of girls. In the light of the present economic situation, many may find that part-time work is insufficient to maintain their needs. Department of Labor figures show that more than four out of ten women workers and more than half of all minority women workers today are single, divorced, or separated from their husbands. Even for those married, many husbands' incomes are insufficient to maintain a home. In March, 1974, there were 5.5 million married women workers whose husbands earned less than $7,000 in the previous year. Despite the fact that women heads-of-households carry full responsibility for care of children and other dependents, their wages are still far behind those of male family heads. As of May 1974, the difference in pay averaged $80.00 per week, with women earning only 63 percent of men's earnings (Maymi, 1975a).

In full realization that responses to the question of the relative importance of marriage and work might be only loosely connected to actual future behavior, an item asking just that question was included in the questionnaire. Responses disclosed that 51 percent rated marriage above work, 23 percent saw work more important than marriage, and 26 percent valued them equally. Written comments were again enlightening. In the case of the importance of work and marriage, one comment appeared most frequently in various forms. Typically, the student wanted to know why marriage was mentioned and other living arrangements were ignored.[1] Many volunteered the information that they planned to live with a man before even considering marriage. ("You don't need a piece of paper to make a good relationship.") Children would not be born unless they were "really wanted." Marriage was judged much more important if children were part of the picture.

When asked to assess their chances of success in their chosen areas of work, nearly 80 percent estimated their chances to be good or excellent. This is an encouraging contrast to a similar question fourteen years ago on the Report of the President's Commission on the Status of Women (1962) which showed 42 percent of the high school girls in a random sample felt their chances were poor. Nevertheless, perhaps because work has been a lower priority for girls than for boys, girls are still inclined to be less realistic in their career planning than their male counterparts (Flanagan & Jung, 1971).

Mean scores for girls generally were toward the androgynous end of the continuum. They believed in equal pay for equal work, believed in equal educational opportunities, were convinced it is possible to combine home and work responsibilities successfully, and were convinced that intellectual capabilities were just as important for women as for men. With impressive sophistication they reprimanded women who "wanted it both ways"—demanding advantages with men in the world of work, yet insisting upon special privileges at the same time. They were equally scornful of women who played "sex games," strongly disagreeing with the statement that "feminine wiles" should be used to get one's own way. This item brought out a rash of such comments as, "This is a stupid way to act . . . it's dishonest" and "People should talk things over, not insist on their own way."

Midst all of this *androgyny,* however, one response alerts us to the possible susceptibility of young people caught up in a sense of the "cause." Mean scores fell on the dichotomous side of the scale for a number of items; one is particularly noteworthy because of strong general agreement with the statement, "A woman should work only if she can do so without interfering with her domestic duties." Scribbled notes often interpreted "domestic responsibilities" to mean child-

[1]My research design had to be evaluated by the district research review board to receive official sanction. The suggestion that any living arrangements could be an alternative to marriage on a questionnaire for high school students would most certainly have been censored.

rearing, but apparently few questioned the assertion that domestic duties, with or without children, were the primary responsibility of the woman.

In an economy where women are often the only breadwinners and in which many families need two breadwinners to survive, the idea that women must earn the "right" to work by first fulfilling their "primary" responsibility is, to say the least, discriminatory. Schedules where parents share equally in responsibilities of childrearing, household duties, and work outside of the home are no longer uncommon in our society, especially among the college educated. This is not to argue, of course, that such arrangements fit the needs of all families; but the possibility—the fact that it is a viable life style for some people —should not be denied or ignored.

The Effect of Religion on Attitudes

Early in the inquiry it became apparent that an important variable was missing. It came to my attention during the pilot phase through girls' written comments which have proved so valuable throughout this undertaking. Reactions to the statement "The best guarantee of a good marriage is for the wife to be submissive to her husband" were most often in disagreement. However, a check mark beside the response "very strongly agree" was often accompanied by such assertions as "The Bible tells us so." This established the need to expand the design to include one new variable, religion. To test the effect of religion on girls' attitudes toward sex-roles, a large Catholic high school was added to the previous list of twelve public high schools to be tested.

Interestingly enough, the girls told me that their religion (98% of whom were Catholic) would not affect their views—and they were right. As a matter of fact, this school was the third most androgynous school in the city. Admittedly, this only ruled out the effect of the one denomination; a measure of a different church-supported school (perhaps a more fundamentalistic one) might have yielded a different outcome.

Before leaving the discussion of the results of the investigations on high school girls and turning to the results about their counselors, a final comment about reactions to the question of male influence on career-related decisions is offered. Pressures on females in this culture to please males is self-evident and well-documented (Farmer & Vohn, 1970; Hawley, 1971; Kaley, 1971; Horner, 1972). So, one could predict that girls might be aware of male influence in their career development. This was not the case for most of them. A majority, almost 74 percent in fact, checked the response "not at all influential" or "slightly influential." Comments such as "No one really influences me, I make up my own mind" suggest that at this level of maturity there is a tendency to be oblivious to the numerous forces at play in shaping the daily decisions made by all of us. The assumption that even adult women have not always been aware (at least in the past) of the extent of male influence was substantiated in earlier research (Hawley, 1971). A study of three groups of women in different categories (Homemaker Career, Feminine Career, and Androgynous Career) showed that women's perceptions of male views of the feminine ideal have played an important, although often unrecognized, part in careers women choose.

COUNSELORS CRITICIZED

Counselors have been widely criticized by professionals outside and inside the field of counseling for their lack of sensitivity and minimal knowledge of women's career development. An engineering professor at Illinois Institute of Technology asserts that the big reason women accounted for a mere 6 percent of first-year engineering students in 1974 is that "secondary-school teachers, counselors, and parents do not direct women toward engineering." She states further, "A girl who is good at math is still likely to end up being directed into teaching" (Graham, 1975).

Professionals within the field have been even more critical of counseling practices, contending that pervasive sex bias results in a perpetuation of the status quo, which in turn prolongs the old division-of-labor doctrine (Epstein, 1970; Freidersdorf, 1969; Schlossberg & Pietrofesa, 1973; Thomas & Stewart, 1971).

Not only have counselors been found wanting in the skills department, they have been found uninformed and even misinformed about pertinent facts crucial to girls in the process of career planning. Bingham and House (1973) in two studies, one of factual knowledge and the other of attitudes, found both sexes poorly informed about the number of working women, extent of sex discrimination, and salary discrepancies. Male counselors were less knowledgeable than females in regard to occupational alternatives needed by women, their ability to combine the roles of home and work, and general ability of women. It was suggested in conclusion that negative attitudes toward working women could possibly have contributed to a denial of obvious information.

ANDROGYNOUS COUNSELORS

Whether a heightened sense of professionalism supported by efforts of feminists, accompanied by a general quickening of social conscience, or any combination of these forces—whatever the reason—counselors appear to be making progress toward the elimination of sex bias. Most encouraging is the discovery of a significant difference between attitudes of girls and counselors. Counselors, as a group, scored substantially more androgynous than did the girls they counsel. If it follows then that counselors' behaviors match their self-reported attitudes, they should be in a better position than ever before to help girls use the leverage provided by affirmative action mandates to gain a new foothold in the job market. This is not to say that all evidence of dichotomous views of counselors related to work roles have disappeared; the picture will be balanced eventually with more negative outcomes.

Counselors agreed that intellectual competence and a college education were equally important for men and women, that women should follow any line of work their interests and talents lead them into, that it was possible for women to successfully combine home and outside work, and that it would be appropriate for a woman, if qualified, to be President of the United States. In concert with girls, they almost totally rejected the "dumb blond, sex symbol" image of womanhood. They rejected also mother's traditional warnings against "beating a man at his own game" along with the use of feminine wiles, the wisdom of playing helpless, submissiveness as a guarantee of a good marriage, seductive behavior in business settings, and the myth that a woman's place is in the home.

Effects of Age and Sex Upon Attitudes

Results support the bulk of existing information about the effects of counselor's age and sex upon their attitudes toward sex roles. Attitudes showed differences in an androgynous to dichotomous direction as responses were measured in age groups from 20 to 60+ years. Males and female were roughly parallel in this progression.

This certainly does not mean that counselors necessarily grow more dichotomous with age; without having longitudinal data, one can only speculate. Actually, there is no reason why older counselors should hold traditional views and there is reason to believe that nonstereotypical attitudes are more a function of recent exposure to the more liberal college climate than to age (Hawley, 1972). Engelhard (1969) using a "traditional to emergent" continuum found sex differences (with females more emergent), but discovered that younger counselors were, in fact, *more traditional* then older ones. It should come as no surprise that women are more aware of the repressive aspects of sex stereotyping. They have more to lose by its survival and much more to gain by its demise.

LOYAL AND NOT-SO-LOYAL OPPOSITION

Lest we forget that counselors are not representative of American women in general, we must remind ourselves that what some women label "repressive" others see as advantageous, of positive benefit to self and society. The growth of such groups at Total Woman, Fascinating Womanhood, and Stop ERA all testify to the strength of the opposition. A recent telephone interview survey conducted on a cross-section of American women for the National Commission of the Observance of International Women's Year (1975) revealed that only three out of ten women think the women's rights movement has helped them personally, and just over one-half were aware of the Equal Rights Amendment.

Certain aspects of this "counter revolution" can partially be explained as a reaction against the radical rhetoric of the few who seem to despise children, men, and housewives as well as against the naive, starry-eyed among them who claim the women's rights movement will bring peace to the world and order to our lives. The wise heads have noted and deplored the widespread and insidious "putdown" of homemakers. Repudiation of those who make a career of homemaking implies that self-actualization cannot take place in the private sector, only in the public one. Bardwick (1975) in a recent lecture said, "Feminists' almost total focus on the negative aspects of homemaking is frightening because women will continue to play traditional roles. Feminists who further strip the role of wife and mother of status are trying to substitute a paycheck—"You are what you earn!" She spoke of "existential anchors" especially needed in a technological society and noted that parenthood is the most permanent anchor. Work success? It is frought with danger, competition, and a changing economy.

It is certainly possible that we have oversold work outside the home to women in the same way some career theorists have romanticized it for men. The majority of the workers of the world, male and female, labor at jobs that are repetitive and often dehumanizing. The most prestigious and well-paying careers carry with them no guarantee of self-actualization, and it is misleading to the young and inexperienced to draw too sharp a contrast between the lives of housewives and those who work on the "outside."

LET US NOT EXCHANGE SEX STEREOTYPES, BUT DISCARD THEM

An androgynous life view encompasses both "male" and "female" behaviors, attitudes, and emotions. This is a very different premise from a life view which advocates *exchanging* a set of feminine characteristics for a set of masculine ones. Women who try to "out-man the men" by whatever means succeed only in alienating others and making themselves look foolish. This reversal of roles is an example of dichotomous thinking at its worst.

Only by discarding outmoded sex referents which are attached to many of our attitudes and behaviors can we allow for an expansion of psychologically available thoughts and actions. Men can be free to be gentle, tender, and even weak on occasions when they really *are* weak (it must be difficult always to have to be the strong one) ; and women can be intellectually aggressive, adventuresome, and even angry when the occasion calls for it. Hopefully, sooner or later, both sexes can react to the *situation* rather than to a preconceived role.

What has all this to do with career development? Everything! Signs of the approaching acceptability of an androgynous way of life can be seen in such unlikely and pragmatically oriented places as the world of commerce and business. Androgynous people may be better equipped than dichotomous ones to engage in work in the future. As an example, merchandising—once thought to require the aggressive "hard sell" so-called masculine approach—is beginning to change. "Companies are finding out that women are ideally suited to the new more individualized and problem-solving approach to a client," says one California consultant on business psychology and management (Hegarty, 1975). A psychologist at Georgia State University predicts that organizations previously valuing traditional male characteristics —capacity to be hard and maintain a psychological distance from other people—will in the next ten years come to value traditional female characteristics—emotionality, sensitivity to others, more compassion (Jewell, 1975). Possibly, it is a sign of social maturity that the world is opening, not only to women but to the softer human characteristics which women have been taught to internalize and exhibit. Effective counselors are known to possess these attributes and, it must be added, this is reflected in their consistently higher scores on the feminine side of most personality measurements. Their inclinations, reinforced by their training, help them break the confines of tight rational boundaries and recognize the legitimacy of feelings necessary to augment linear patterns of thought.

My year on research leave is over; as I think back trying to recount what I learned during that time, several major themes emerge which have implications for practice.

- Women need special help at this point in time with career plans. They need help, moreover, with the *underlying* attitudes which will contribute to their ability to envision the wide array of life styles which will support these career plans. In short, they must learn to think androgynously.
- Girls at formative life stages must be encouraged to keep traditional

feminine attributes and at the same time augment them with the traditionally masculine behaviors of independence, self-assertiveness, ability to channel energies toward a goal, and self-confidence.

- It is important for women to think in terms of long-range goals rather than to limit their thinking to short-range plans. They tend to define a career in very personal terms–compatibility with an accommodation to family needs. This should remain but be expanded to include such long-range, concrete, "masculine" thinking patterns as attention to promotion prospects, overt *and* covert rewards, and proper sequencing.
- Counselors, in their roles as consultants, can urge teachers to establish the same performance standards for female as for male students. Girls should not be rewarded with high grades because they are appealing, conforming, cute, or *female.* The standard must be based upon demonstrated performance, and it must be single, not double.
- A focus upon behaviors (as opposed to traits) will help to make behavior *situation-specific* and free both sexes to act spontaneously and appropriately instead of reacting to a role. A good example of a learned role is the "female" tendency to smooth things over in conflict situations . . . to neutralize strong feelings when problem-solving calls for confrontation.
- Counselors and teachers can improvise ways to help girls imagine what life would be like at forty or fifty, how it would feel to be single for a lifetime, divorced, or widowed. I found that divorce has been experienced second-hand enough to have meaning but that it was nearly impossible for sixteen-year-olds to imagine themselves dealing with the problems of widowhood at fifty-five. Small group settings in which girls write and enact their own scripts are good vehicles for this.
- It is not helpful to raise aspiration levels without, at the same time, stressing the correspondingly heavier demands of personal energy, time, and commitment which go along with "better" jobs. Although patently obvious, this warning is particularly applicable to the counseling of girls right now because of the promise of new opportunities for women. Heretofore, nearly unattainable opportunities now exist for minority women and low socioeconomic women of all ethnic backgrounds, but certainly they cannot be won without effort.
- Finally, although the relationship between low IQ scores and dichotomous views of sex-roles is a strong one, evidence on the relationship between IQ scores and *success* outside of the academic setting is unclear. The work world is full of successful people with undistinguished academic records. Girls who have not "found themselves" in the school environment may very well do so outside of it

and need help to consider androgynous ways of looking at self in the work world.

> There is no reason why qualified women should not be able to work where and when they want, at whatever jobs suit their fancy. Every American has that basic right. Our task must be to turn rights into reality, and eliminate barriers to nontraditional occupations for women in business, industry, and government at all levels.
>
> *Secretary of Labor, Peter J. Brennan*

REFERENCES

Angrist, S.S. Review essay: An overview. *Signs: Journal of Women in Culture and Society,* 1975, *1,* 175-183.

Bardwick, J. An evening with Judith Bardwick. University of California Extension, University of California at San Diego, October 9, 1975.

Bem, S.L. The measurement of psychology and androgyny. *Journal of Counsulting and Clinical Psychology,* 1974, *42,* 155-162.

———. Sex-role trap: Fluffy women and chesty men. *Psychology Today,* 1975, *9,* 58-59.

Bingham, W.C. & House, E.W. Counselors view women and work: Accuracy of information. *Vocational Guidance Quarterly,* 1973, *21,* 262-268 (a)

———. Counselors' attitudes toward women and work. *Vocational Guidance Quarterly,* 1973, *22,* 16-23. (b)

Engelhard, P.A. A survey of counselor attitudes toward women. *Minnesota Guidance Bulletin,* winter, 1969, pp. 7-11.

Epstein, S.F. *Woman's place: Options and limits in professional careers.* Berkeley: University of California Press, 1970.

Eysenck, H.J. IQ, social class, and educational policy. *Change,* September, 1973.

Farmer, H. & Vohn, M. Home-career conflict reduction and the level of career interest in women. *Journal of Counseling Psychology,* 1970, *17,* 228-232.

Flanagan, J.C. & Jung, S.M. *Progress in education: A sample survey (1960-1970).* Palo Alto, CA: American Institutes for Research, 1971.

Friedersdorf, N.W. A comparative study of counselor attitudes toward further educational and vocational plans of high school girls. Unpublished study, Lafayette, IN: Purdue University, 1969.

Graham, L. Special section: The American woman. *U.S. News & World Report,* December 8, 1975, pp. 54-74.

Hansen, L.S. Counseling and career (self) development of women. *Focus on Guidance,* 1974, *7*(4).

Hegarty, S. Special section: The American woman. *U.S. News & World Report,* December 8, 1975, pp. 54-74.

Haener, D. The working woman: Can counselors take the heat? *Personnel and Guidance Journal,* 1972, *51,* 109-112.

Horner, M. Fail: Bright women. *Psychology Today,* 1969, *3,* 36-41.

Horner, M. Toward an understanding of achievement-related conflicts in women. *Journal of Social Issues,* 1972, *28,* 157-175.

Hawley, P. What women think men think: Does it affect their career choice? *Journal of Counseling Psychology,* 1971, *18,* 193-199.

Hawley, P. Perceptions of male models of femininity related to career choice. *Journal of Counseling Psychology,* 1972, *19,* 308-313.

Jewell, D. Special section: The American woman. *U.S. News & World Report,* December 8, 1975, pp. 54-74.

Kaley, M. Attitudes toward the dual role of the married professional woman. *American Psychologist,* 1971, *26,* 301-306.

Maccoby, E.E. & Jacklin, C.N. *The psychology of sex differences.* Stanford: Stanford Press, 1974.

Maymi, C. *Woman and work: News from the U.S. Department of Labor.* April, 1975. (a)

Maymi, C. *Woman and work: News from the U.S. Department of Labor,* August, 1975. (b)

Matthews, E. A perspective on the vocational guidance of girls and women in the mid-1970s. Invitational paper prepared for the National Vocational Guidance Association 60th Anniversary Theme Session, New Orleans, April, 1974.

National Commission on the Observance of International Women's Year Survey, conducted by Market Opinion Research of Detroit. Reported in the *San Diego Union,* December 6, 1975.

Report of the President's Commission on the Status of Women. *American Women,* Washington, D.C.: U.S. Government Printing Office, 1962.

Schlossberg, N.K. & Pietrofesa, J.J. Perspectives on counseling bias: Implications for counselor education. *Counseling Psychologist,* 1973, *4,* 44-53.

Sowell, T. Arthur Jensen and his critics: The great IQ controversy. *Change,* May, 1973.

Thomas, A.H. & Stewart, N.R. Counselor response to female clients with deviate and conforming goals. *Journal of Counseling Psychology* 1971, *18,* 352-357.

Section VI

MANAGING EMERGING LIFE PATTERNS

In Section V, trends toward multiple and concurrent roles for both women and men were discussed. Building on the preceding discussion, Section VI includes articles which reflect a variety of life patterns representing various means of coping with individual needs and societal demands and managing the inevitable conflict between the two. Emerging life patterns for women include a number of single person or two person alternatives such as the equal partnership marriage, the dual career family, or living as a divorced person, a widow, or a single person. Some of these life-styles reflect conscious decision making and planning while others, such as divorce or widowhood, may be roles, sometimes transitory, which a woman is forced to adopt. It is clear that we must examine women's roles both with and without males as significant parts of their lives. Bailyn (1970) makes an important point about women's perceptions of their life-style alternatives. She suggests that although a wide range of options currently exists in principle, the range of choices which exists psychologically for most women is much narrower. For example, the decision to remain single and/or not have children is often viewed as the result of unfortunate circumstances and still results in social stigma. Hopefully, women will increasingly recognize that all life-styles represent legitimate options and result in satisfaction for some individuals. While the full range of alternatives is not covered in this section, the papers do provide stimulus for thinking about some new life-style patterns.

In the first chapter, Neugarten examines some of the elemental tasks and conflicts that confront human beings as they live out their lives. She points out that many of the stresses and conflicts that human beings encounter are time-specific, related to their particular life stages, and that these often pass and are replaced by the new problems of a succeeding phase of the life cycle. She also notes that unanticipated, life events, e.g. divorce and widowhood, are the most traumatic. Major stress is also likely to be present when the timing of events in the life cycle occurs earlier than normal, for example, when death of a parent occurs in childhood rather than in old age.

Of particular interest to this volume are Neugarten's findings on the stresses encountered by women in menopause. She found little evidence to suggest that menopause was itself the trigger for a life crisis. Similarly, she reports that the "empty nest" phenomenon of the home-leaving of children is not in itself a cause for crisis. Even the crisis of widowhood was handled very differently by different women. The overwhelming message in this chapter is that women who grow and develop themselves as fully intact and human individuals can cope readily with the changes built into the latter phases of the life cycle. Women need not fear age and the changes of time if they build the foundations of full development and appropriate life-styles.

In the second chapter, Holmstrom compares two-career and traditional families with respect to perceptions about marriage, parenthood, and work. Professional women often find themselves in a double bind in relation to marriage and career decision making. As stated in earlier sections, the choice may not be either/or, but it may be that the combination of professional career and homemaking results in the expectations of a "superwoman." Holmstrom discusses some of the changes in the family life cycle that are required for the successful functioning of what she calls the two-career family. For example, many professional women marry late, have no children or fewer children than nonprofessional women, and space the birth of their children in relation to points in their lives where they may be able to take convenient breaks or have extra time. In spite of the complexities involved in participating in a two-career family, both females and males reported that they were able to achieve very satisfying life-styles.

In the final chapter in this section, Rapoport and Rapoport report an intensive sociological study of sixteen dual-career families in Great Britain characterized by high levels of occupational commitments and qualifications in both partners. The assumption underlying the dual career family is that *both* males and females have dual roles; no activities with the exception of pregnancy and childbirth are viewed as belonging primarily to only one sex. Particularly interesting is their description of the kinds of dilemmas faced by these husbands and wives. A microsocial analysis of the dual-career family unit generated a framework for classifying five focal areas of stress. The authors believe that most of the problems encountered by these families are the result of outmoded social norms and structures. For example, one area of stress is the clash between personal and social norms. For women this often occurs around the area of maternal employment.

Many women become uncomfortable with their work roles if their relatives and friends believe that "good mothers don't work." (See Wallston [1973] for a more complete discussion of the effects of maternal employment on children and the way in which women perceive this issue.)

Finally, Rapoport and Rapoport indicate some of the social changes needed to facilitate the successful functioning of the two-career family. Changes in the organization and structure of work, environment, and marital roles are needed which recognize, accept, and facilitate the interconnectedness of domestic and occupational roles.

Two important limitations on this section should be noted. First, the papers focused primarily on professional women and men. The perceptions and attitudes of sex roles and the nature of work and achievement may be quite different at other socioeconomic levels, resulting in different ideas about what would constitute the most adaptive and satisfying life-style. Ethnic differences also need to be explored. A second limitation is that while variants of the two-person family were explored, further attention should be directed toward problems and coping mechanisms associated with the single person life-style.

It seems clear that multiple roles and increased range of choice provide avenues for increased growth, development, and fulfillment for individuals. Yet role conflict, stress, and overload on time and energy will inevitably continue until social norms and institutions become more consistent with recent social change. We have identified some life-styles both for meeting individual needs and coping with complex societal demands. It is likely that individuals will experiment with an increasingly diverse array of life patterns in order to facilitate functioning within a complex society. Communal living or a variation of the dual-career family in which each partner works half-time provide examples of other life-styles not previously discussed.

BIBLIOGRAPHY

Bailyn, L. Career and family orientations of husbands and wives in relation to marital happiness. *Human Relations,* 1970, *23*(2), 97-114.

Wallston, B. The effects of maternal employment on children. *Journal of Child Psychology and Psychiatry,* 1973, *14,* 81-95.

Chapter 23

ADAPTATION AND THE LIFE CYCLE*

BERNICE L. NEUGARTEN

A LIFE history can be understood only by considering its historical setting. The life cycle of a man born in 1910 differs from that of a man born in 1950. Any historical economic, or political event varies in personal significance according to the point in the life cycle at which the event occurs. For example, the effects of the Great Depression or the Vietnam War on a young man just finishing school and entering upon economic adulthood differ greatly from those on a middle-aged man at the height of his occupational career. This chapter is concerned with adaptation through time and with life time as differentiated from calendar or historical time.

The interweaving of historical time and life time occurs in the context of a third dimension, that of socially defined time. Every society is age-graded, and every society has a system of social expectations regarding age-appropriate behavior. The individual passes through a socially regulated cycle from birth to death as inexorably as he passes through the biological cycle: a succession of socially delineated age-statuses, each with its recognized rights, duties, and obligations. There exists a socially prescribed timetable for the ordering of major life events: a time in the life-span when men and women are expected to marry, a time to raise children, a time to retire. This normative pattern is adhered to, more or less consistently, by most persons within a given social group—although the actual occurrences of major life events are influenced by various contingencies and although the norms themselves vary somewhat from one socioeconomic, ethnic, or religious group to another. For any social group it can easily be demonstrated that norms and actual occurrences are closely related. Age norms and age expectations operate as a system of social controls, as prods and brakes upon behavior, in some instances hastening an event, in others, delaying it. Men and women are aware not

*From *The Counseling Psychologist, 1976, 6(1), 16-20.*

only of the social clocks that operate in various areas of their lives but also of their own timing; and they readily describe themselves as "early," "late," or "on time" with regard to the major life events.

From this perspective, time is at least a three-dimensional phenomenon in charting the course of the life cycle, with historical time, life time (or chronological age), and social time all intricately intertwined.

The social change that occurs with the passage of historical time creates alterations in the rhythm and timing of the life cycle, leading in turn to changes in age norms and in expectations regarding age-appropriate behavior. Within the family cycle, there are points at which the individual moves from "child" to "adolescent" to "adult" and where, after physical maturity is reached, social age continues to be marked off by relatively clear-cut biological or social events: marriage, the birth of the first child, the departure of children from the home, and the birth of grandchildren. At each of these points, the individual takes on new roles in the family, and his status in relation to other family members is altered.

Changes in timing of the family cycle have been dramatic over the past several decades: age at marriage has dropped; children are born earlier in the marriage; longevity has increased, thereby increasing the duration of marriage. Marriage and parenthood imply adulthood within the family cycle, so it may be said that adulthood is reached earlier than before. The average modern woman marries before her twenty-first birthday, gives birth to her first child within the first year or so thereafter, bears all her children in the next six to eight years, and sees her last-born child in school by the time she reaches age 35. Active parenthood is becoming shorter, for children are leaving home at an earlier age. It follows that grandparenthood also comes at an earlier age now than in preceding generations. At the same time, widowhood tends to occur later.

The historical trend, therefore, has been toward a quickening of events through most of the family cycle, followed by an extended post-parental interval (now some 15 to 17 years) in which husband and wife are the remaining members of the household.

Marriage, although it defines maturity within the family, is no longer synchronous with the attainment of economic maturity. With the increasing needs of the American economy for technical and professional workers, the length of time devoted to education has increased for young people, but without a comparable delay in marriage.

Changing sex-role patterns with regard to the timing of economic maturity are reflected in the rising proportion of young married women in the labor force. In 1890, only 6 percent of married women aged 14 to 24 were working; by 1970 it was over 40 percent. While the percentages reflect marriages in which husbands are working, as well as those in which husbands are still in school, they reveal in both instances that young wives are increasingly sharing the economic burdens of new households and that they are doing so at younger and younger ages. Economic maturity is being deferred for men, but not for women.

The new rhythms of social maturity impinge, of course, upon other aspects of family life as well. Parent-child relationships are influenced in many subtle ways by the fact that half of all new fathers are under 23 and half of all new mothers under 21. Changes in parental behavior, with fathers reportedly becoming less authoritarian and with both parents sharing more equally in tasks of homemaking and child-rearing, may be reflections of this trend. The relative youth of parents and grandparents may also be contributing to the complex patterns of help between generations that are now becoming evident, including the widespread financial help that flows from parents downward to their adult children. Similarly, with more grandparents surviving per child and with an extended family system that encompasses several generations, new patterns of child-rearing are emerging in which child-grandparent relations take on new significance.

In a recent study of three-generation families in which various styles of behavior by grandparents were delineated, we found that younger grandparents (those under age 65, as compared with those over 65) more often followed what we called the *fun-seeking* pattern. The *fun-seeker* is the grandparent whose relation to the child is informal and playful and who joins the child for the specific purpose of having fun, somewhat as if he were the child's playmate. Grandchildren are viewed by these grandparents as a source of leisure activity, as an item of "consumption" rather than "production," and as a source of self-indulgence. The relationship is one in which authority lines are irrelevant and where the emphasis is on mutual satisfaction.

Another new trend among the middle-aged is for women to go back to work. The proportion of working women in their early twenties is high; it drops off somewhat from age 25 to 35 and then rises again. More than 50 percent of all women aged 35 to 44 are now in the labor force and more than 50 percent of those aged 45 to 54. The young child is likely to have his mother at home but his grandmother out working; the adolescent, to have both mother and grandmother working.

A few generations ago, with children spaced further apart, the last child married and the nest emptied when women were in their mid-50s. Today, this event occurs when many women are in their late 40s, at about the same time they experience the menopause and the biological climacterium. This is the same age when the census data show the number of women on the labor market taking its sharpest upturn.

These are but a few examples of the way in which historical time and social change are affecting the course and rhythm of the life cycle, affecting in turn social expectations with regard to age-appropriate behavior.[1]

Although there have been many changes in the life cycle, there also remain many regularities and continuities. While it is true that the rapidity of social change is unprecedented and that the explosion of knowledge occurring in the social, psychological, physical, and biological sciences may upset many of our present assumptions about human nature, people's lives in the next few decades are not likely to be transformed as drastically as some of our newspaper writers would lead us to believe. Despite the contraceptive pill and the increased freedom with regard to the occurrence and timing of parenthood, despite the organ transplants and the promise of greater control over death, and despite space travel, the human life cycle is likely to retain its major features for some time to come. Biologists seem to believe, for instance, that the human life-span is relatively fixed by genetic factors; and even as they begin to separate the effects of aging from those of injury or disease, and as greater proportions of the population live to the biological limits, it is likely to be a long time before the life-span itself can be lengthened.

New methods of biological engineering may alter the genetic composition of the human species, yet for the foreseeable future we are likely to deal with human organisms who will grow and develop to biological maturity in the first third of the life-span, who will continue to change psychologically and socially in the second and third parts of the life-span, and who will age and die. Accordingly, men and women will continue to experience many of the same biological, social, and psychological regularities of the life cycle.

Some of these regularities will continue to arise from the social controls related to age-norms and age-appropriate behavior. Because individuals live in contact with persons of all ages, they learn what to anticipate. There is a never-ending process of socialization by which the child learns what facets of his childhood behavior he must shed as he moves into adolescence; the adolescent learns what is expected of him as he moves from school to job to marriage to parenthood; and the middle-aged learn approved ways of growing old. Thus the social ordering of age-statuses and age-appropriate behavior will continue to provide a large measure of predictability.

There are certain other regularities of the life cycle which may be said to arise more from within the individual than from without. To draw a dichotomy between "inner" and "outer" is, of course, merely a

[1]The effects of social change upon the timing of major life events and the creation of new age norms are described at great length in an earlier paper (Neugarten & Moore, 1968).

heuristic device, given a transactional view of personality. As the result of accumulative adaptations to both biological and social events, there is a continuously changing basis within the individual for perceiving and responding to new events in the outer world. It is in this sense that orderly and predictable changes occur within the personality as well as in the social environment.

People change over time as the result of the accumulation of experience. As events are registered in the organism, human individuals inevitably abstract from their experiences and create more encompassing and more refined categories for interpreting new events. The mental filing system not only grows larger but it is reorganized over time, with infinitely more cross-references and classifications. Not only do middle-aged parents differ from their adolescent children because they, the parents, were born in a different historical period and were therefore subject to different formative experiences, but they differ also because of the effects of having lived longer, of having therefore a greater apperceptive mass or store of past experiences (or, again, a more complex filing system) by which to evaluate any event.

(It is not being cynical to suggest that young people who demonstrated on college campuses all over the world are subject to the same imperatives of change that stem from the course of the life cycle. This is not to say that people as they age become more conservative politically, for the evidence on this point is moot, but rather that with increasing age, perspectives inevitably lengthen and, as a consequence, attitudes and behavior change. Only a few hippies have remained hippies into their thirties and forties, not only because the social issues have changed and hippie culture itself has altered, but because there are internal pressures to change that stem from movement through one's own life cycle.)

A few such alterations that occur with age can be illustrated from some of our studies carried out in the Committee on Human Development at the University of Chicago over the past decade, where we have been making studies of personality, of adaptational patterns, of career lines, of age-norms and age-appropriate behavior in adults, and of attitudes and values across social class and generational lines. While this set of inquiries has not involved longitudinal research on the same subjects (except for one group of 300 older persons who were followed over a seven-year period), it represents a related set of investigations in which the number of men and women participating now totals well over 2,000. Each study is based upon a relatively large sample of normal people, none of them volunteers, all living in metropolitan communities in the Midwest.

In one set of investigations of persons aged 40 to 70 from varied walks of life, based upon both interviews and projective data, we found that different modes of dealing with impulse life become salient with increasing age. In middle age, there is an emphasis upon introspection and stocktaking, upon conscious reappraisal of the self. There is conscious *self-utilization* rather than the self-consciousness of youth. Preoccupation with the inner life seems to become greater; emotional cathexes toward persons and objects in the outer world decreases; the readiness to attribute activity and affect to persons in the environment is reduced; there is movement from outer-world to inner-world orientation. A constriction seems to occur in the 60– and 70-year-olds in the ability to integrate wide ranges of stimuli and in the willingness to deal with complicated and challenging situations in the environment. We have referred to this increased saliency of the inner life as an increased "interiority" of personality. We regard it as reflecting certain intrinsic as well as responsive processes of change, since it was measurable in well-functioning adults by the mid-40s, well before the social losses of aging occurred and well before there was any measurable change in competency of performance in adult social roles.

In the present context this increased interiority is to be regarded as one of the "inner" psychological regularities of the life cycle. Interiority seems, however, to be relatively independent of adaptation or *purposive* behavior. Our studies suggest that interiority is age-related and adaptation is not (Neugarten et al., 1964). In more general terms, adaptational abilities are to be distinguished from age-related personality changes.

A related finding appeared in a different sample of middle-aged adults. In this instance we interviewed at length 100 highly placed men and women concerning what they regarded as the most salient characteristics of middle-adulthood. These persons were university graduates: business, professional, and artistic leaders, some of whom appeared in *American Men of Science* and *Who's Who in America.* Both men and women talked of the difference in the way time is perceived. A particularly conspicuous feature of middle age is that life is restructured in terms of time left to live rather than time since birth. Not only is there a reversal in directionality but also an awareness that time is finite. Middle-aged people look to their positions within different life contexts—changes in body, career, family—rather than to chronological age for their primary cues in clocking themselves. It was at first a surprise, then a commonplace, that middle-aged persons when asked their age could not immediately give their exact age but stopped to think, often saying, "Let's see . . . 51? No, 52. Yes, 52 is right."

Yet responses like the following were characteristic: "Before I was 35, the future just stretched forth. There would be time to do and see and carry out all the plans I had . . . Now I keep thinking, will I have time enough to finish off some of the things I want to do?" Or, "Time is a two-edged sword. In some of my friends, it brings anxiety that there won't be time enough. To others, it adds a certain challenge in seeing how much pleasure can still be obtained. But all of us figure backward from the end . . . and estimate how much time we can expect."

The change in time-perspective is intimately related to the personalization of death. Death in middle age becomes a real possibility for the self, no longer the magical or extraordinary occurrence that it appears in youth. In women there is the rehearsal for widowhood which becomes characteristic (one which rarely occurs in men); and in men there is the "sponsoring" issue with regard to young associates as well as with regard to one's children, an issue we called "the creation of social heirs."

Increased interiority, changed time perspective, and personalization of death are only a few of the psychological changes which have emerged from our own studies and which we regard as characteristic of men and women as they move through adulthood.

The fact that regularities of change through the life cycle are demonstrable along biological, social, and psychological dimensions leads to the questions of adaptation and the concept of the "normal, expectable life-cycle."

Adults carry around in their heads, whether or not they can easily verbalize it, a set of anticipations of the normal, expectable life cycle. They internalize expectations of the consensually validated sequences of major life events—not only what those events should be but when they should occur. They make plans, set goals, and reassess those goals along a time-line shaped by these expectations.

The individual is said to create a sense of self very early in life. Freud, for example, in describing the development of the ego, and George Mead, in describing the differentiation between the "I" and the "me," placed the development of self very early in childhood. But it is perhaps not until adulthood that the individual creates a sense of the life cycle, that is, an anticipation and acceptance of the inevitable sequence of events that will occur as men grow up, grow old, and die. Adulthood is when he understands that the course of his own life will be similar to the lives of others and that the turning points are inescapable. This ability to interpret the past and foresee the future, and to create for oneself a sense of the predictable life cycle, presumably differentiates the healthy adult personality from the unhealthy.

From this point of view, the normal, expectable life events do not themselves constitute crises, nor are they trauma producing. The end of formal schooling, leaving the parents' home, marriage, parenthood, occupational achievement, one's own children growing up and leaving, menopause, grandparenthood, retirement—in our society, these are the normal turning points, the markers or the punctuation marks along the life cycle. They call forth changes in self-concept and in sense of identity, they mark the incorporation of new social roles, and accordingly they are the precipitants of new adaptations. But in themselves they are not, for the vast group of normal persons, traumatic events or crises that trigger mental illness or destroy the continuity of the self.

That we often err in construing a normal life event as a crisis can well be illustrated in one of our own recent studies of middle age. Wishing to study patterns of adaptation, we began with a study of women, reasoning that women's lives in the middle years were characterized by two major crises: the biological climacterium evidenced by the menopause and the change in roles that follows upon children leaving home. We felt that these two crises for women in their forties and fifties might have measurable effects upon their psychological well-being.

Accordingly we selected a population of 100 normal women aged 43 to 53 from working-class and middle-class backgrounds, all of whom were in good physical health, all married and living with husbands, all mothers of at least one child, and none of whom had had hysterectomies. Five to six hours of interviewing and projective testing were carried out, and we obtained data on a large number of psychological and social variables, including measures of anxiety, life satisfaction, and self-concept. Because this period of life has been relatively unexplored by psychologists, and because psychiatrists have shown special interest in the menopause and in questions of the possible relation to so-called involution depressions, this study perhaps warrants relatively full description.

Like puberty and pregnancy, the climacterium is generally regarded as a significant turning point in a woman's psychosexual development—one that reflects profound endocrine and somatic changes and one that presumably involves a variety of psychological and social concomitants. Because it signifies that an important biologic function, woman's reproductive life, has come to an end, the menopause has often been described as one of the most critical events of the middle years—as a potential threat to a woman's identity.

Although there is a large medical and popular literature on the climacterium, there is a conspicuous lack of empirical research with normal, or nonclinical, women. While an estimated 75 percent of women experience some disturbance or discomfort during the climacterium, only a small proportion receive medical treatment, suggesting that conclusions about the menopause drawn from clinical observations can not be generalized to the entire population.

In the present study, several approaches were employed in exploring the menopause as a focus of concern. Women were asked about their expectations regarding menopause, what they had heard or read about it, what they had observed in other women. Each woman was asked also whether she regarded herself as premenopausal, menopausal, or postmenopausal; what was the basis of her assessment; and what, if any, were the symptoms and reactions she had experienced.

We first divided the 100 women into three groups: those who reported no changes or irregularities in their menstrual patterns and were evaluated as premenopausal; the menopausal; and those who had stopped menstruating for at least two years, the postmenopausal. We discovered at once that menopausal or climacteric status was an insignificant variable: that is, it did not differentiate among these women with regard to any of our other variables.

Moving on, we found that these women as a group tended to minimize the significance of the menopause and to regard it as unlikely to produce much anxiety or stress. For instance, when asked to select those which worried them most from a list of possible events or sequelae of middle age, only four women of the 100 regarded menopause as a major source of worry. (More than half indicated that "losing your husband" was the greatest concern; "just getting older" and "fear of cancer" were also frequent responses.) When asked, at another point in the interview, what was disliked most about middle age, only one of the women mentioned the menopause. When questioned further, at still another point in the interview, about the best thing and the worst thing about menopause, only 12 women could not mention anything good about menopause but 30 could not think of anything bad about it.

These women were unusually cooperative and eager to talk about themselves, yet even after considerable time was given to the topic on two different interview occasions, only one-third could think of any way that a woman's physical or emotional health was likely to be adversely affected by the "change of life." Some expressed the view that the menopause served to improve a woman's state of health. A majority maintained that any changes in health or emotional status during the climacteric period were caused by idiosyncratic factors or individual differences in capacity to tolerate stress generally. "It depends on the individual. Personally, I think if women look for trouble, they find it." Similarly, when asked about how the menopause affects sexuality, 65 percent maintained there was no effect and that any alteration in a woman's sexual life during climacterium must be a function of her attitudes prior to the menopause. (Of the 35 women who thought there was change in sexual activity associated with climacterium, half thought sexual activity becomes less important and half thought sexual relations become more enjoyable because menstruation and fear of pregnancy were removed.)

In a specially devised checklist of attitudes toward menopause

(Neugarten, Wood, Kraines, & Loomis, 1963), the overwhelming majority (over 80 percent) attributed little or no change or discontinuity in a woman's life to the menopause. About three-fourths took the view that, except for the underlying biologic changes, women have a relative degree of control over their symptoms and need not have even symptomatic difficulties.

In addition to studying attitudes, we devised a checklist of menopausal symptoms based on a careful review of the medical literature (the 28 most frequently reported somatic, psychosomatic, and psychological symptoms—hot flashes, paresthesia, vertigo, headache, insomnia, irritability, depression, and so on) and asked women to report the frequency and intensity of their symptoms (Neugarten & Kraines, 1965). We found that overall these women held relatively favorable views of the menopause and did not regard it as a major loss of feminine identity, irrespective of the severity of their symptoms.

We obtained also from each woman a brief psychosexual history, then assessed the degree to which each reported physical or emotional difficulty regarding the first sex information, menarche, menstrual periods, first sexual experience, pregnancy, and childbirth. The result was that difficulties with menarche, menstrual periods, and pregnancy were related to severity of menopausal symptoms. Those women who reported the most symptoms and who viewed the menopause as disturbing, unpleasant, and unpredictable were those who expressed more negative affect regarding their earlier psychosexual experiences.

Our general conclusions were, then, that there was little evidence in these data to support a "crisis" view of the climacterium and that the crisis theory in the literature probably reflects basic differences between clinical samples and a community sample.

We then moved further in the analysis. To measure psychological well-being, we used several different measures: a set of ratings of life-satisfaction, a self-cathexis scale and a body cathexis scale, the Taylor Manifest Anxiety scale (taken from the MMPI), the IPAT Anxiety Questionnaire (from Cattell's 16-factor test), and a set of measures based on the TAT. The correlations between climacteric status, menopausal symptoms, and attitudes toward menopause, on the one hand, and each of the various measures of psychological well-being, on the other, were very low (most ranged from 0.11 to 0.35). We concluded, just as we had from the first part of this study, that the menopause was not a crisis event; for if it were, it should have shown a significant relation to the psychological well-being or mental health of these women.

With regard to our second presumed "crisis," the empty nest, our findings were similar. We divided the women according to family stage: the intact stage, in which none of the children had left home;

the transitional stage, in which one or more had left, but one or more remained; and the empty nest, or postparental stage, in which all the children were living outside the home. We looked also at those women who had children under age 14 at home, as compared with those whose youngest child was 15 or older. We worked out a set of life-styles or role orientations and separated the sample into those who were primarily home-oriented, community-oriented, work-oriented, or mixed home-community-oriented. We studied these women also for *change* in pattern of role activities, assessing the extent to which each woman had expanded or constricted her activities in family roles (wife, mother, homemaker, grandmother, daughter) and in nonfamily roles (worker, church member, club member, citizen, friend, user of leisure time) over the past five to ten years and grouped the women into "expanders," "shifters," "statics," and "constrictors."

The relationships among these social role variables and our measures of psychological well-being were all low and showed again that our initial hypothesis was wrong. Rather than being a stressful period for women, the empty nest or postparental stage in the life cycle was associated with a somewhat *higher* level of life satisfaction than is found among other women. Evidently for women in this sample, coping with children at home was more taxing and stressful than having their children married and launched into adult society. Neither was life satisfaction correlated with *role-change* patterns—although the latter finding may be an artifact of our data. (It was of some interest that, in this sample, life satisfaction was highest in the home– and community-oriented women, and lowest in the work-oriented.)

Now that the study is completed, we wonder that we should ever have formulated such naive hypotheses; yet it seemed tenable enough to predict that women who showed high symptomatology at menopause and whose children had left home would be those women who would have shown lower levels of life satisfaction than the other women in the sample.

That this was not so is evidence for the normal, expectable life cycle. Women in their forties and early fifties expect the menopause to occur and see it, therefore, as a normal and natural event. They may have listened to old wives' tales and may have some mild anxieties which they project on other women, but they know the climacterium is inevitable; that all women survive; and they take it in stride or, as one of them put it, regard it merely as "a temporary pause that depresses." Many welcome it as relief from menstruation and fear of unwanted pregnancies.

The normal, expectable life event too superficially viewed as a crisis event can be illustrated in the researches of other investigators as well as in our own. For example, to an increasingly large proportion of men, retirement is a normal, expectable event. Yet in much of the literature on the topic, it is conceptualized by the investigator as a crisis, with the result that the findings from different studies are at variance, with some investigators unprepared for their discovery of no significant losses in life satisfaction or no increased rates of depression following retirement. The fact is that retirement is becoming a middle-aged phenomenon, with many workers, for instance, now offered the opportunity to withdraw from work at age 55. The latest national survey indicates that a surprisingly large proportion of workers in all industries are choosing to retire earlier and earlier, with the main, if not the single, determining factor being level of income—as soon as a man establishes enough retirement income he chooses to stop working. Even more pertinent is the fact that nearly 70 percent of persons who retired *as planned* were content in their retirement, compared with less than 20 percent of the unexpected retirees—those who retired unexpectedly because of poor health or loss of job (Barfield & Morgan, 1970).

Death, too, becomes a normal, expectable event to the old, and there are various studies which describe the relative equanimity with which it is anticipated (Munnichs, 1966). The fact that old people do not necessarily fear death comes to the young graduate student as a surprise—evidence of an age-graded perception—but the surprise disappears when he discovers that old people more often than not talk calmly and freely about death once the interviewer himself overcomes his reluctance to discuss it. Judging from the many interviews with old people that are now in our files at Chicago, the crisis is not death, but for some, *how* one will die, whether in the accustomed home and family environment or elsewhere. Some recent findings (Lieberman & Coplan, 1970) are of interest on this point. They studied matched groups of old people (matched for age, health, ethnic background, education), one group living in their homes in the community; the second, persons on a waiting list to be admitted to a home for the aged; the third, a group who had survived relocation and who had been living in the institution for two years or longer. Each group was divided into those who were near death and those who were not —or "death-imminent" and "death-distant." This determination was made by following the groups over a three-year interval to see who died and who survived and then going back and studying their interviews and test performances. Among the death-imminent, it was the second group who showed evidence of fear of death, not the first nor the third group, that is, neither of the groups who were living in familiar and stable surroundings. It would appear that it is the prospect of dying in a *non*-normal, *un*expected circumstance that creates the crisis.

The situation with regard to widowhood is more equivocal; yet even here, as shown in a study by Parkes (1964), while somatic symptoms increased somewhat for both younger and older widows in the months following bereavement, consultation rates for psychiatric symptoms were very high for women under 65 but not in women over 65. Is this because by the time a woman reaches old age, death of a husband—a husband several years her senior, in most cases—moves into the category of the expected? On this same point, Baler and Golde (1964), in reviewing some of the epidemiological data regarding the widowed as a high-risk group in terms of mental illness, physical illness, and mortality, indicate that there is excess risk at younger rather than at older ages for both sexes.

All these findings are not to deny that the expectable life event precipitates crisis reactions in some persons, especially in those who come to the attention of the mental health professional; but this reaction is probably true for the minority, not for the majority. Even for the minority, it is more often the timing of the life event, not its occurrence, that constitutes the salient or problematic issue. This observation is not a denial, however, of the fact that the major life events in middle age and old age are losses to the individuals concerned or that grief is their accompaniment. It is to say, rather, that the events are anticipated and rehearsed, the "grief work" completed, the reconciliation accomplished without shattering the sense of continuity of the life cycle.

In drawing the distinction between illness and health, between the clinical and the normal, the psychology of grief is not synonymous with the psychology of mental illness. The relationships between loss, grief, physical illness, and mental illness are complex, although "loss" itself is a multidimensional factor. Some of Lowenthal's work (Lowenthal, Berkman, & Associates, 1967) seems to support the point being made here; old persons who had experienced retirement or widowhood in the three years prior to being interviewed were not more frequently diagnosed by psychiatrists as mentally ill, nor did they find their way into mental hospitals with any greater frequency than others. Mental illness, on the other hand, was associated with self-blame, with reports of having missed one's opportunities, of having failed to live up to one's potentials; in short, with intrapunitiveness.

In summary, then, there are two distinctions worth making: first, that it is the unanticipated life event, not the anticipated—divorce, not widowhood in old age; death of a child, not death of a parent—which is likely to represent the traumatic event. Moreover, major stresses are caused by events that upset the sequence and rhythm of the life cycle —as when death of a parent comes in childhood rather than in middle age; when marriage does not come at its desired or appropriate time; when the birth of a child is too early or too late; when occupational achievement is delayed; when the empty nest, grandparenthood, retirement, major illness, or widowhood occur *off-time*. In this sense, then, a psychology of the life cycle is not a psychology of crisis behavior so much as it is a psychology of timing.

REFERENCES

Baler, L.A., & Golde, P.J. Conjugal bereavement: Strategic area of research in preventive psychiatry. In *Working papers in community mental health.* Vol. 2, No. 1. Boston: Harvard School of Public Health, Department of Public Health Practice, 1964.

Barfield, R.A., & Morgan, J.N. *Early retirement: The decision and the experience.* Ann Arbor, Mich.: Institute of Social Research, University of Michigan, 1970.

Lieberman, M.A., & Coplan, A.S. Distance from death as a variable in the study of aging. *Developmental Psychology,* 1970, *2,* 71-84.

Lowenthal, M.F., Berkman, P.L., & Associates. *Aging and mental disorder in San Francisco: A social psychiatric study.* San Francisco: Jossey-Bass, 1967.

Munnichs, J.M.A. *Old age and finitude: A contribution to psychogerontology.* Basel: Karger, 1966.

Neugarten, B.L., & Associates. *Personality in middle and late life.* New York: Atherton Press, 1964.

Neugarten, B.L. & Kraines, R.J. Menopausal symptoms in women of various ages. *Psychosomatic Medicine,* 1965, *27,* 266-273.

Neugarten, B.L., & Moore, J.W. The changing age-status system. In B.L. Neugarten (Ed.), *Middle age and aging.* Chicago: University of Chicago Press, 1968.

Neugarten, B.L., & Wood, V., Kraines, R.J., & Loomis, B. Women's attitudes toward the menopause. *Vita Humana,* 1963, *6,* 140-151.

Parkes, C.M. Effects of bereavement on physical and mental health: A study of the medical records of widows. *British Medical Journal,* 1964, *2,* 274-279.

Chapter 24

THE LIFE CYCLE OF THE FAMILY*

Lynda Lytle Holmstrom

I always thought that I would get married, but it wasn't the goal.
Professional wife

Marriage for me had priority. The best thing was to get married and then think about professional life later.
Traditional wife

Our present society has many expectations regarding family life. For one thing, the life cycle of the family is to follow a certain timetable. Not only are you to marry, but you are to do so by a given age. Not only are you to have children, but you are to have them by a given age. Our society gives more latitude in these matters than many other societies do. But, even so, eyebrows are raised if the wife is still childless by her late twenties, and certainly if she is over thirty! And if no children are born, people will keep asking why.

Families are also expected to have a certain structure. We expect today that the household will consist of father, mother, and their children, but no other relatives, and we presume the couple will follow a division of labor in which each sex is assigned its special tasks.

All these current expectations have behind them the assumption that there will be only one career in the family. Our ideas about the life cycle make it difficult to launch two careers while still marrying and having children "on time." Our type of family structure—especially its isolation and its division of labor—makes it difficult for both spouses to work while raising children.

The two-career family thus goes counter to the family customs that now prevail. It therefore would not be surprising to find a different life cycle in such cases. That is what this chapter is about.

---

*From Holmstrom: *The Two-Career Family*. Cambridge, Schenkman Publishing Co., 1972.

THE DOUBLE BIND

Our present family customs leave professional women in a double bind. No matter which alternative they choose, they lose. On the one hand, if they marry they step into the role of wife. This role as presently defined is incompatible with the full pursuit of one's own career. On the other hand, if they remain single, they face the stigma of spinsterhood. People, as they become adults, are expected to found families of their own. They are not expected—indeed hardly permitted—to go through life as single, unattached individuals, lacking spouse and children. These pressures toward marriage and parenthood are especially forceful for women. The stereotypes abound that a woman cannot develop her humanity to the fullest extent without fusion with a male personality, that the female personality by nature is destined to domestic pursuits, and that a woman must fulfill herself as a person through marriage and motherhood.[1]

The labels attached to the unmarried woman, unless in a convent, have been derogatory. The unmarried girl soon becomes the spinster, and the spinster the old maid. The woman deliberately may have turned down marriage, but she will be criticized by others who say that she is shirking her responsibilities as a woman or that marriage has passed her by. "No positive values whatever are attached to spinsterhood within the accepted framework of roles. The spinster is regarded as having failed in the essential effort of women: to find a husband and raise a family" (Caplow, 1964). The stigma of being unmarried may be removed in the future, but it is still with us today.

Not only single women, but occupationally successful women in general find their claims to recognition limited by the sacred values attached to the housewife role (Caplow, 1964). The only way out of the impasse may be to try to do everything. This is the "superwoman" solution in which career, wife, and mother roles are all combined. The trouble is that this solution is seldom practicable.

This indeed leaves women in a double bind. If they remain single and opt solely for careers, they will be accused of having failed as women. If they try through marriage and motherhood to succeed "as women," they impose severe occupational handicaps on themselves.

MARRIAGE

When They Married and How They Viewed It

In view of this double bind, it is interesting to note that the marriage rate among certain groups of career women is often quite low. Female business executives often do not marry. In a recent study of

[1]The pervasiveness of these stereotype is reported by Baker. He also questions them (Baker, 1968).

women with successful careers in business, half married and half did not. And, incidentally, even those who did marry remained single until at least age thirty-five (Hennig, 1970). The marriage rate among female doctorates has been similar. Women who received doctorates in 1957-58 were studied several years later when many were in their forties, and even by then only 55 percent[2] had married (Astin, 1969). This rate of marriage is low, both in comparison to males with similar education and occupations and in comparison to women in the general population.

The attitudes of the professional women interviewed in the present study reveal that they were less oriented toward marriage than most women are. All twenty were married, since this was one of the characteristics by which they were chosen. But it is clear—both in attitude and deed—that an early marriage was not their sole preoccupation. This is not surprising in view of the low marriage rates described above and the difficulties of combining marriage and career.

Although most of these twenty professional women did marry while in their twenties, four "married late." These four married for the first time when they were thirty years or older. Furthermore, slightly over one third were thirty years or older when they married their present husband.

As to attitude, a third of the professional women either expressed some reservation over getting married or they explained that marriage was not *the* goal. They said that they had not seen themselves as getting married. They were very ambivalent about taking the step of marriage. They turned down some men who were opposed to careers for women. They had especially long courtships because of apprehension about how two careers would mesh. Or they did not see marriage as the first priority. One woman explained:

> *I always thought that I would get married, but it wasn't* the *goal. I took it as a very natural thing that eventually I would meet the right person. . . . At that time, being young and foolish, I saw no difficulty whatsoever in attempting to combine (laughter) marriage and career. . . .I wasn't going to go out and* look *for a man or worry if a man didn't appear, if the right man didn't appear, because I had the feeling that there would be somebody appearing who would agree that I should go on and do my graduate work, or, if I had finished it, that I should go on and pursue my own interests.*[3]

Another woman explained that there had been a previous man whom she had dated very seriously, but she had never been convinced that a marriage with him would work out. When asked if she had ever

[2]Another survey, done of people who received doctorates between 1958 and 1963, reports that 50% of the women married, in contrast to over 95% of the men (Simon et al., 1967).

[3]The occasions of laughter are reported because they occurred in patterned ways throughout the interviews. They were most often associated with problems or hard times, a point of tension, an earlier naive view, or an opinion at variance with others.

changed her career plans because of such previous men, she explained:

> *No. And that was one of the bones of contention with this man that I say I dated seriously but was never convinced. I was determined that I would want to go on having my career. And what he wanted was what I used to call a nice Jewish housewife.*

Rather than give up her career, she gave up the relationship.

One woman, although atypical, is of particular interest because she lived much of her adult life as a divorcee. The description of her life style when she was divorced—or, as she phrased it, when she was single—shows that such a life can have advantages for a professional woman. In discussing her eventual remarriage, she said that just by a stroke of luck, she and her second husband were employed in the same area; had he been elsewhere, the situation would have been very difficult.

> [*Would you have moved if the man you wanted to marry did have to be in another city?*] *I liked being single. I abandoned it only after long thinking. I wasn't desirous of marrying again. . . . My career commitment was strong. I enjoyed it. I've worked all my life. This is how I chose to live my life. To abandon this for someone who has to be somewhere—well, if confronted with this, I just can't say.*

Having spoken so positively of single life, she was asked to elaborate on what she saw as its advantages. Being single gave her more control over her own life. In her words, it was for "the most selfish of reasons—you do what you want when you want." Her one regret, in connection with single life, was not having had children. She said, "I regret it very much. But this is what happens, since my desire to have a child was not overwhelming enough to marry for that reason."

Her implication that she would have had a child only within marriage is of interest. Of course up to now, marriage has been required for parenthood to be socially acceptable. But now many people are experimenting with a variety of family structures and life styles. Variations are becoming more acceptable. It will be of interest to see whether single women will have and rear children if social definitions continue to change and they are "allowed" to do so. Several steps in the direction of single parenthood have already been taken. Adoption agencies in some places have changed their rules and now allow a single person of either sex to adopt. Also, more unwed mothers are keeping their babies rather than giving them up. These changing attitudes will undoubtedly increase the single woman's opportunities for fulfillment.

Though single life may be seen as desirable by the individual concerned, there is always the issue of how the status is viewed by others, or how one thinks it is viewed by others. One woman who had reservations about getting married, felt that students perceived her more favorably after her marriage.

The fact that I was single until my early thirties I think has affected my career in a positive way. . . . I think here at [the university] the fact that I am *married—and I think [this is true] in general in dealing with young people, for a woman, anyhow—the fact that I* am *married, and have more or less of what is considered a normal life, evokes a favorable reaction from youngsters. I can talk about a lot of things, and they will believe me more than if I were not married. I was unmarried long enough to test that, you see. Maybe I wasn't an old old-maid, but you know (laughter), I was beginning to be considered one.*

Whether the students' attitudes really changed or whether she just thought they did, this is still an example of the current stereotype that a woman is not seen as fulfilled without marriage and motherhood.

Was the Wife's Career Discussed Before Marriage?

One might expect a couple to discuss, prior to marriage, the issue of the wife's career. After all, having two careers in the family will pose many problems for them. Half the wives said they did discuss the issue. The position the wives took was that they wanted to continue their education and work. One of the more firm statements was:

I made the point—which he completely agreed with and obviously completely understood—that career was my way of life. And, that although I wanted a family also, I in no way considered this a matter of alternatives or substitutes, but a matter of both. And he completely agreed.

The other half of the wives reported that they did not discuss, prior to marriage, the issue of the wife's career. The reasons for lack of discussion of the issue varied. In a few early marriages, the women married first and became professionals later; that is, the wife did not have explicit career plans at the time she married. One said:

All of these sort of life decisions were not discussed, and, as I say, the whole thing of a career didn't present itself as a plan at that time.

In a few late marriages, the issue was not discussed because it was taken for granted that the wife would continue with her career. For example, one of these women said, "It was simply assumed. It was a simple matter of knowledge." They had known each other for a long time before marrying. And since he had a position similar to hers, she felt that she did not have to explain to him what having such a job meant. A few said they did not discuss their careers because it just was not their style to plan life so explicitly. One said that her husband planned his own life, but that she had never been capable of that. She said, "That's just not my style." Incidentally, this inattention to planning, on the part of some women, was not correlated with low involvement in career or lack of success. There were women who did not plan, but who were very committed to their work and very successful in it.

The men, although very much affected by being in a two-career family, had given little attention to the issue before meeting their wives. For example, the men were asked if, prior to meeting their wives, they had thought about whether they wanted to marry a woman primarily devoted to homemaking or a woman who had some career interests. Most men said that they had not thought about it, and only a few had explicitly considered the issue. Those who had thought about it said they preferred a woman with intellectual interests, with a professional orientation, or with a career of her own.

PARENTHOOD

The Desire for Children

In the view of most people in our society, marriage and children go together. Children have become obsolete as producers, and thus economic liabilities rather than assets. The reasons for wanting children may have changed, but people are still very much interested in having them. A survey done in the Detroit area shows the value placed on children. In the survey, almost all the couples wanted children. Marriages which were childless by choice were practically nonexistent. Further, wanting only one child was as rare as wanting none. The childless wives, except for recently married ones, expressed frustration over their fate. Thirty-six percent of them could think of nothing good at all about the fact that they had not had children (Blood and Wolfe, 1960).

Like most Americans, the professional couples placed a value on having children. Most of the wives said that having children was important to them and that they had expected to have them. This attitude was expressed not only by the mothers, but also by a couple of women who had remained childless. They said, "We wanted children, there was no doubt about it." "We definitely wanted a family." "We thought we should reproduce." Or, "I wanted a child intensely." For some, having children was unquestioned; it was just assumed. Only one woman, a mother, was completely negative about the idea of children; she saw no purpose in having them. Most of the men also said that they had wanted to have children. A few were rather neutral about the idea of fatherhood until the child actually was born, whereupon their enthusiasm grew. Only a few said that children were unimportant to them.

Although wanting to become mothers, a few of the women either had felt concern over how they would manage once the child was born or had felt hindered in their work during the pregnancy itself. One woman was finishing up some work in graduate school at the time, and said:

I got pregnant, and I was concerned for fear the schedule wouldn't work out. I mean I had these things to do and I didn't want this dratted baby to interfere with it.

And another woman stressed the fatigue she experienced in the early months of pregnancy. She was so tired she could not get anything else done. She said, "I remember I was terribly discouraged at that time because it was cutting into everything—my whole way of life." For her, the fatigue passed after a couple of months and then she became quite happy about it. Because the above statements sound somewhat rejecting, perhaps it should be stressed once again that they were from women who in general had very positive attitudes toward motherhood and who were very devoted to their families.

Childbearing

Combining motherhood and career poses certain difficulties. It is not surprising that—despite their desire for children—these professional women differed both from the traditional wives and from the population as a whole in their actual childbearing patterns.

The life cycle of the family in the United States is more or less as follows. At first marriage, the husband is typically about twenty-two years old and his wife about twenty. The wife will bear her first child within about one and one half years after marriage. Young women now bear about 2.8 children in their lifetimes. They complete their childbearing, on the average, by age twenty-six or twenty-seven; this is about six years younger than their grandmothers were when they completed their families.[4]

In contrast, the childbearing of the professional women interviewed was atypical in three ways. First of all, they tended to have small families. Most (three quarters) of them had zero to two children. Secondly, there was likely to be a relatively long interval between marriage and birth of the first child. Not quite half of these wives had their first child within four years of marriage. Slightly over half waited five or more years before having their first child. Third, most of the professional wives who were mothers had their first child at a relatively late age. Although most had their first child when they were in their twenties, usually it was in their late twenties. Furthermore, six wives were thirty-one years or older at the birth of their first

---

[4]It is difficult to make exact comparisons with the general population at any given point in time because when interviewed in 1968, the women in the present study ranged in age from 35 to 55. Nevertheless, comparison with the figures presented here gives some indication of how they differ from the general population. The figures are taken from Goode (1964) and he relies heavily on Glick's (1957) analysis of 1950 census data.

child; indeed, one woman was thirty-six, and one was thirty-seven.[5]

Thus many of these professional women did not even *begin* their families until as late or later than the age at which women on the average *complete* their families. This suggests that it is age at birth of the first rather than the last child which is of greater relevance for women at the professional level. The question is, how established are the women in their careers prior to the time they also are responsible for the care of children. This focus is somewhat different from that usually found in the literature. Typically, attention has been given to the age of the mother at the birth of the last child, or when the last child enters school; and, the suggestion has often been made that since women are now completing their families earlier than in previous generations, they will therefore have additional years after the children are in school during which they can accept employment or engage in other activities outside the home. This line of thought does not seem to apply to the professional women interviewed; most worked even while raising a family. The difference between the two patterns of female employment—the nearly continuous and the severely interrupted—becomes important when one considers policy. Helping some women work when their children are young and helping other women return to the labor force after their children are in school would require two different types of institutional change.

The atypical childbearing patterns of professional women—found both in this and other studies—do not in themselves answer the question of whether "biology is destiny." A correlation, for example, between a small number of children and high involvement in career does not in itself tell you which of the following interpretations to choose. Is it that women who just happen to have few children are free to pursue careers? Or do women who want careers deliberately limit the size of their families? Nevertheless, a common approach by researchers has been to see how women's employment correlates with the composition of their families and then either to state or imply the "cause-effect" direction is that the composition of the woman's family determines whether or not she participates in the labor force. One example of this approach[6] is provided by Eli Ginzberg, a professor of economics, in his study of educated women. He implies that the woman is passive in this process:

> Children are the *primary* factor influencing a woman's work decisions. . . .

---

[5]Other studies have reported similar deviations between the childbearing of professional women and those of the general female population. For example, Astin found that the married woman doctorate was more apt to be childless than her counterpart in the general population, her family was smaller (she had an average of two children), and her childbearing started and terminated much later (Astin, 1969).

[6]As another example see Astin who states that "the number and ages of her children and her husband's income are important determinants of the woman doctorate's decisions regarding employment." Astin, (1969).

> The data indicate that a woman's involvement in work will be determined first by her family situation and second by such factors as her educational achievement, her field of specialization, her location and her career plans (Ginzberg et al., 1966).

Ginzberg's approach has been attacked by Alice Rossi, a well known sociologist and advocate for women's rights. She criticizes Ginzberg for not raising the important possibility that things such as the kind of men these women married, where they lived, whether they had children or not and how many, are the *effects* of the values they held and the balance they wanted between work and family, rather than the *determinants* of their life styles (Rossi, 1966). The difference in interpretation is crucial. The issue at stake is whether women are passive in the process—at the mercy of their biology—or whether they actively influence their procreative function and adapt it to suit the kind of life style they want to lead.

With this issue in mind, the professional couples were asked about family planning. Their answers show the women were not necessarily at the mercy of their biology. Half the women with children reported that their career was one factor which influenced their childbearing. It influenced the size of their family or it influenced the timing and spacing of the children.

Some of these women were mostly concerned about how many children they had. For example, one woman explained the influence of her career on this as follows:

> *I've always thought that if I did not have a career, then I'd like a large family. . . . We jointly agreed two children at least. And we had a boy and a girl so now there's no need to have any more—especially because of our work load. We don't think we want one now because of work.*

Her husband stressed the time it took to bring up children. With both of them working, time was limited. He said that if they had more children, the proportion of time they could spend with each child would be less.

Other women were mostly concerned about when they had children. For example, in one couple the woman's career plans influenced the timing of her children in several ways. She said she had wanted a child intensely. She deferred having the first child with the notion that she would have it right after completing her professional education. Concerning the spacing of her children she stated:

> *We space them that way in terms of when I don't want to do anything else. I make calculated guesses of when I can get time off. I calculate on time off* before *I get pregnant—I mention that in ten months or so there may be a child coming and see what can be arranged.*

Her husband commented more about postponing the first child. "It was eight or nine years before the first child and we were well established. . . . When we were established, then we decided we'd try one."

The women's logic of what would be most beneficial for their careers was not always the same. For example, one woman spaced her children with several years in between, fitting pregnancies into her work schedule. But another woman had all her children close together because she felt she would be freer if the children had each other for companionship.

For some women, the importance they attached to controlling pregnancy varied over time and depended on what was happening in their professional life. The following quote is interesting in this connection. This woman described how at one point in her career she was established and holding a secure job so it was not necessary to plan her family in terms of her career. But later, in a less secure job, she became concerned about controlling the timing of her pregnancy.

> *We had decided with the first child that we very much wanted to have a child and that I would simply take a chance, whenever the pregnancy would occur. I suppose I would have to say that I was on tenure in my post at the time, and I was very well known and established there and I realized that if anything did go wrong—say I had to miss school for a month—why this would be called standard sick leave. I had no concern about problems. When we planned our second child, however, which was just after we came here, such was not the case; and I timed the pregnancy so that it could occur only with a summer birth. I didn't want to take that sort of gamble. And fortunately everything went well.*

The fact that careers were, for some women, one factor in planning their families indicates that women do not necessarily lead life styles that are merely the result of how many children they have. The experiences of these twenty professional women suggest that the correlations researchers find between family composition and labor force participation of women may be due to two opposite processes. On the one hand, there were a few women who had fewer children than desired because of physical problems and who expressed very ambivalent attitudes about working mothers. They suffered miscarriages, were unable to conceive at all or for as many times as desired, or suffered prolonged illness during and because of the first pregnancy. It would appear that for these few women it is their inadventently limited families which have allowed them to work as much as they have. On the other hand, there were eight women in which the "cause-effect" went in the opposite direction. These eight planned their childbearing partially in terms of their careers.[7]

The Childless Wives

There were only four childless wives among the twenty professional women. All four expressed some regrets about this fact. It was a sacri-

[7]Among the twenty there were also some women who saw the issue as completely irrelevant.

fice; they would have enjoyed children. The two who were childless because of biological reasons had both considered adoption. But each gave several reasons for not having followed through with an adoption; for example, ambivalence about rearing a child, not being considered appropriate prospective parents by adoption agencies' criteria, involvement in career. One explained her situation as follows:

> *We talked of adopting, but it would have been such a chore because my husband isn't* [the same religion] *and because of our age. We would have had two major strikes against us, so that would mean scrounging around and not being able to adopt through a regular agency. Plus the fact that we were already beginning to be somewhat ambivalent. So it just meant taking enormous initiative and I think that's what one has to do if you're going to adopt. . . . We didn't really explore it the way younger couples often do.*

This quote shows how adoption agencies, by accepting ideas prevalent in the society about who makes good parents, make it harder for couples like these to adopt. Or, at the very least, such rules play into people's psychological problems if they are ambivalent about having children.

The regrets of the four childless women, however, seem to have been tempered by other satisfactions and interests in life. The most ambivalent of the four explained her situation as follows. One of the reasons she married was because she thought she wanted kids. But then she just did not get pregnant.

> *But, you know, I was 39 when I got married so I was already very ambivalent. . . . I began to wonder more and more, whether I would really be able to be tolerant and be able to handle all the responsibilities of a small child. . . . I don't think it's been as major a disappointment as I might one day in the past have thought it would be. . . . If there's one thing I've missed, by marrying late, it's that. My major regret I guess would be that I haven't had kids. But I don't feel very sad about it.*

In general, the comments of these childless wives were in keeping with the findings reported in a recent study of women who had never married. Luther Baker, a professor of family life, administered personality tests to women who had never married and to women who were married and had children. The tests showed that these two groups were very similar to each other in their personal and social adjustment. His conclusion was that personal fulfillment does not depend on marriage and parenthood. The unmarried women, for example, did not express feelings of "not being a whole person" because they were single. "Their sense of personal worth comes not from their biological function as a female but from their social function as a human being, from what they perceive as a creative contribution to their significant society" (Baker, 1968). The women in both groups were selected from Business and Professional Women's Clubs. In searching for an explanation of the similarity of their adjustment,

Baker notes that women in both groups listed work at the top of their sources of personal accomplishment and satisfaction. He cautions against generalizing to women without such creative jobs. His caution is probably justified. Childless wives in a survey of families in the Detroit area stressed the negative aspects of their situation. Above all, they missed the companionship children would have provided. They emphasized the loneliness of being a childless wife (Blood and Wolfe, 1960).

THE TRADITIONAL COUPLES

The traditional couples—especially the women—saw the woman's role as oriented more exclusively toward marriage and children. This can be seen both in their actual childbearing patterns and in the attitudes they expressed.

Even these traditional wives began their families relatively late. They all had their first child when they were in their late twenties. But whereas six professional wives were over thirty at the birth of their first child, none of the traditional wives waited this long. Professional wives were more likely to wait a longer number of years than traditional wives between marriage and birth of their first child. Not quite half the professional wives had their first child within four years of marriage. Almost all the traditional wives had their first child within this amount of time; the sole exception was one case where the woman's first child died at birth and thus her first surviving child was not born within four years of marriage. Most of the professional wives had zero to two children. In contrast, all the traditional wives had two or more children.

In general, the traditional women seemed more exclusively oriented to the family and less concerned about what effect a family would have on their career. Prior to marriage, these couples tended not to discuss the issue of the wife's career. All the traditional women married while in their twenties, and if they got divorced, they remarried while still in their twenties. Late marriage where the wife was thirty or over did not occur. One woman said, "Marriage for me had priority. The best thing was to get married and then think about professional life later." All traditional women reported that they simply assumed that they would have children or that having children was important to them in their present marriage. Most of their husbands also took this view. Only one woman expressed any career-related regrets over being pregnant. Hardly any of these women reported that their career was a factor influencing how many children they had or when they had them. There was one woman who had hoped to finish her graduate education before having children, but did not do so; she said if she thought about it at all, it was in terms of,

"I must get this damn Ph.D. finished so that I can have my kids." And there was one other woman who began to think in these terms—but only after having children and returning to school.

The comments of a few traditional wives are interesting in that they imply that involvement in a large family and involvement in a career may serve as alternatives to each other. One said:

> *I suppose if I had embarked on a serious career of my own at an earlier age, I wouldn't have wanted, wouldn't have needed, to have a spread-out family or so much of a family.*

This woman solved the problem of what to do with her life by having more children. Another solved it the opposite way. After three children, she and her husband felt that was all they could manage. It was depressing to her to think that her family was finished. To overcome the depression, she began to do other things. And this was one of the factors that got her back to work. To the extent that women see work and continued childbearing as alternate sources of satisfaction, the implications for people worried about the world's population explosion should be obvious.

A few traditional women expressed considerable pleasure in feeling needed by the family and having others dependent upon them. Like the others who had been away from their careers, these two were asked if they felt any lack of confidence because of rusty skills. They did worry over the adequacy of their professional knowledge and abilities, but they also said that they felt more confident in another way after having a family. As one said:

> *I wished to get married and I found in marriage certain things that I was looking for. . . . Before I was married, I felt a different kind of lack of confidence in myself which I don't have any more now that I am married and have the children and so on and have so many (laughter) people depending on me in some way.*

She implied that she now had a greater feeling of security as a woman. And, as so many traditional women, she gave greater priority —both in word and in deed—to the domestic role than to the career.

REFERENCES

Helen S. Astin, *The Woman Doctorate in America: Origins, Career, and Family* (New York: Russell Sage Foundation, 1969).

Luther G. Baker, Jr., "The Personal and Social Adjustment of the Never-Married Woman," *Journal of Marriage and the Family,* 30 (August, 1968), pp. 473-79.

Robert O. Blood, Jr. and Donald M. Wolfe, *Husbands and Wives: The Dynamics of Married Living* (New York: Free Press, 1960).

Theodore Caplow, *The Sociology of Work,* "Occupations of Women" (New York: McGraw-Hill, 1964). (First published in 1954: University of Minnesota.)

Eli Ginzberg et al., *Life Styles of Educated Women* (New York: Columbia Uni-

versity Press, 1966).
Paul C. Glick, *American Families,* "The Life Cycle of the Family" (New York: Wiley, 1957).
William J. Goode, *The Family* (Englewood Cliffs, New Jersey: Prentice-Hall, 1964).
Margaret Hennig, "Career Development for Women Executives" (unpublished Doctor of Business Administration dissertation, Harvard University, 1970), p. VII-10 and p. VI-15.
Alice S. Rossi, "Review of Ginzberg: Life Styles of Educated Women," *American Sociological Review,* 31 (December, 1966), pp. 874-75.
Rita James Simon, Shirley Merritt Clark, and Kathleen Galway, "The Woman Ph.D.: A Recent Profile," *Social Problems,* 15 (Fall, 1967), p. 222.

Chapter 25

THE DUAL CAREER FAMILY: A VARIANT PATTERN AND SOCIAL CHANGE*

Rhona Rapoport and Robert N. Rapoport

Families in which both husband and wife pursue careers (i.e. jobs which are highly salient personally, have a developmental sequence, and require a high degree of commitment) and at the same time establish a family life with at least one child concern us in this investigation. This is part of a larger interest in the relationship between work and family life (Rapoport & Rapoport, 1966) and a specific interest in factors affecting highly qualified women's participation in the world of work (Fogarty, Rapoport, & Rapoport, 1967).

Massive changes are underway as contemporary society enters the post-industrial era. These changes affect the patterning both of work and family life. The dual-career family is instructive to study in relation to these changes because while this is a variant pattern now it may become more prevalent given current trends. Assuming that post-industrial society emerges structurally as a presence based on advanced technology, it is likely to be followed by a variety of consequent structural and value shifts. At work, the new values are likely to emphasize self-expression, personal development, and rewarding interpersonal relationships in place of individual achievement and the capacity to endure distress while continuing to perform competitively as an individual. In the face of rapid social change, individuals may be expected increasingly to pursue serial careers and to be required to readapt to new situations continuously throughout the life cycle. The pre-industrial emphasis on kinship as a fundamental social institution in the area of family life gave way in industrial society to an increased emphasis on the nuclear family and a sharp sex-role differentiation

*The research on which this paper is based has been sponsored by the Leverhulme Trust in a grant to Political and Economic Planning (P.E.P.). We have collaborated in this research. For a preliminary statement on the research, see Fogarty M.P., Rapoport R. & Rapoport R.N. *'Women and Top Jobs'*, P.E.P. 1967. The couples in the study must remain anonymous so cannot be thanked except generally.

**From Human Relations, 1969, 22(1), 3-30. Courtesy of Plenum Publishing Corporation.*

between men and women. In post-industrial society, however, the emphasis is increasingly on partnership in family life: equality between husband and wife, joint activities, and collaboration in decision-making so as to maximise the possibilities of each member of the family sharing the benefits of participation external to the family—leisure, political, educational, as well as occupational. Thus external relationships of the post-industrial family are likely to be more diverse. Aspects of these points have also been argued by Bell (1967), Goode (1963), Trist (1968), and Wilmott (1968).

The dual-career family, though a tiny minority in contemporary society, expresses both in structure and values one variant that may be expected to emerge in the post-industrial society which is in the making. The value systems of contemporary society are incompletely evolved to support social structural changes of the kind under examination. Indeed, as Trist (1968) points out, there is not only cultural lag but strong resistance to value changes even though the old values are maladaptive to the new structural requirements. The dual-career families illustrate this in the pattern of strains they encounter at the present point in the change process. These strains are not intrinsic to the phenomenon of the dual-career family, but in the relationship between this phenomenon and its present social context. Given this, an analysis of strains may be useful for indicating short-term social change processes. Planning implications are touched upon briefly.

THE INCREASE IN MARRIED WOMEN AT WORK

Following the industrial revolution in Western countries, there was a radical separation of work and family spheres (Weber, 1947). This was accomplished partly in the interests of fiscal accounting important for the enterprises of the emergent capitalist society and partly to minimize particularistic bases for employment so that competitiveness could be maximized. The net effect of this pulling apart of work and family has been to consolidate the world of work under the control of men and the world of home and child-care under women. The attitude of many people toward married women working (in Victorian England) is expressed by Tennyson in "The Princess":

> Man for the field and woman for the hearth;
> Man for the sword and for the needle she;
> Man with the head and woman with the heart;
> Man to command and woman to obey;
> All else confusion.

Both in Western and Eastern European countries, sex roles are becoming somewhat more egalitarian. In both groups of countries, for somewhat different reasons, there has been an increase, following World War II, of married women in the labour force (ILO, 1958; Hunt, 1968; Wrochno, 1966). This has been accompanied by the trend toward a higher proportion of women marrying, younger marriage, and compression of fertility into a narrower band in the life cycle. Consequently there has been a tendency for married women to re-enter the labour force while still relatively young and vigorous.

While the proportions of married women working have risen, women's ascent into higher status positions and occupations has lagged behind the general trend (Jefferys & Elliot, 1966; Sommerkorn, 1966; Fogarty, Rapoport & Rapoport, 1967). Women still tend to favour occupations which are traditionally sex-typed as 'feminine' (the arts, nursing, teaching); entry into or advancement in the business, industrial, and science worlds require a considerable "pioneering" orientation (Robbins, 1962; Rossi, 1964; Baude & Holmberg, 1967).

Many reasons have been put forward in explanation for women not rising to the top occupationally in great numbers. Polemical single factor arguments (e.g. economic exploitation by men or men's vested psycho-biological interests in domination) have given way to a more complex analytic framework. Myrdal & Klein (1956) and Wrochno (1966) stress role conflicts and incompatibilities between expectations placed on women in the two spheres of work and family. Alice Rossi (1964, 1968) depicts the interplay between psychological and socio-cultural factors at different stages of the life cycle to produce the observed behaviour.

At the point of graduation from University in Britain, the differences between the level of men's and women's aspirations are clear. In our survey of 1967 graduates, we found that while about a quarter of the men indicated that their ambition was to "get to the top" in their line of work, only 5 percent of the women indicated this level of aspiration. Another 45 percent of the men aspired to hold high positions, as compared with only 30 percent of their fellow graduates of the opposite sex. These differences become much more marked over time, as our survey of "eight-year out" graduates shows. Women tend to shift their levels of aspiration downward as they encounter difficulties in trying to pursue careers and family life at the same time, while these experiences act in the reverse for men.

Furthermore our data indicate that men's ambitions tend to be channelled into specific fields of work and toward success in a material and public recognition sense, while women's are more diffuse and orientated to service or personally meaningful and aesthetic goals. Some data for the U.S.A. show similar patterns (Turner, 1964; Rossi, 1968).

CHANGES IN FAMILY STRUCTURES

While more married women have been entering the labour force, there have been concomitant changes in the organisation of the family. Looking at the structure of families in relation to their environments, some social scientists have emphasised the isolation of the nuclear family as an adaptive response to the necessity for increased mobility in industrial society and the increased differentiation of interests and involvements of members of the ascriptive kin group (Parsons, 1943; Rosser & Harris, 1965). Parallel to the same broad cultural trends manifested in the educational experiences of boys and girls, there has been a trend toward the more democratic or "companionship" type of family life. This has been evident both in the husband-wife relationship and in the child-rearing patterns of the modern family, where there has been a trend away from authoritarian bases for organising all of the family role relationships.

The process of change in the direction outlined has been uneven. Many writers have marked out residual extended functions, i.e. as reference groups (Litwak, 1960), mutual support groups in financial and other crises (Bell, 1967), and local community functions reminiscent of more folk-like situations (Young and Willmott, 1957; Mogey, 1963; Fried, 1963; Gans, 1965).

Obviously the structural and cultural dimensions of the change process in marital role relationships are interlaced. Recent British studies show an increase in "joint" participation in the family division of labour as families move from relatively well integrated, urban, working class neighbourhoods to new, individualistic housing developments in surburbia or other urban districts. Bott, for example, stresses the structural interpretation indicating how, when individuals are freed from the constraints of the more tightly-knit community with its traditionally defined sex-types patterns of expectation and behaviour, new patterns of sharing between husband and wife may emerge (Bott, 1957). Young & Willmott and Mogey tend to place more emphasis on the importance of historical and class-cultural factors which differentiate life in the new communities from that in the old (Young & Willmott, 1957; Mogey, 1963). Willmott points out that the change, toward a partnership type of family structure, does not follow the simple paradigm of dissemination of changes downward through the class system from the upper to the lower classes. Some "successful" middle class families show less partnership than do some working class families (Willmott, 1968).

To summarise, recent social changes have brought about a change of traditional kin-centered, locality-based social networks; various substitutions have replaced or developed alongside the traditional pattern. In some situations, there has been a superficial continuation of the old pattern; in some it has been done away with and, in still others, there have been substitutions of different patterns for the traditional close-knit extended family and friendship networks (Rosser & Harris, 1965; Bott, 1957; Laumann, 1968). The trend has been one of diversification. Similar diversification has occurred in the internal relationships of families. The old pattern of male authority and female subservience and a segregated division of labour has become increasingly untenable as equality of access to education and to the world of work have increased. However, this has not always led to partnership in the sense used here. The ideal of an egalitarian partnership is one that is increasingly held but as Leach has pointed out, the gap between sentiment and reality remains great and is not easily bridged (Leach, 1968). Leach has indicated some of the sources of strain in juxtaposing an outdated traditional set of family norms to the complexities of contemporary life.[1] It is the purpose of this paper to fill out the picture somewhat and to indicate (on the basis of an intensive study of several dual-career families) some of the stresses and strains that are being experienced as well as some of the satisfactions enjoyed in experimenting with post-industrial social structures in the contemporary environment which is for the most part still geared to the values of industrial society.

STRESS AND SOCIAL CHANGE: A MICROSOCIOLOGICAL APPROACH

Some kinds of social change occur through interventions at a macroscopic level, some through changes of a diffuse kind at the microscopic levels of social organisation. Some occur through self-conscious, deliberate, and purposeful goal-directed action, others through adaptive responses to dissatisfactions or strains intrinsic in the situation. The analysis reported here is a microsociological one though we are concerned with larger societal implications.

The essence of the *dual-career* family as a variety of the partnership family is that there is a division of labour in relation to family functions that is distributed between the partners on an equal-status basis. Thus (aside from pregnancy and child-birth) the division of functions in relation to household cleaning, shopping, child-care and discipline, supervision of domestic help, food preparation, and so on may be arranged according to the skills and inclinations present in the specific partnership. We do not accept the traditional view that

[1]The cultural lags in the Eastern European countries also resemble those in the West. Sokolowska reports, for example, that when working hours were shortened this resulted in an increase in leisure for working men and in an increase in *housework* for working wives. This was presumably based on the traditional assumption that housework is a feminine area of responsibility (Sokolowska, 1963).

this set of activities is and always has been "expressive" in nature and therefore feminine in role allocation. The argument that women have always performed the household activities and men the work activities is considered irrelevant. In technological innovation after all, new forms are continually emerging. The couples we studied did, in fact, tend to see themselves as partners in social innovation.[2]

In analysing the ways in which our families have divided their activities and social network involvements, we concentrate on stresses or structural sources of strain. However, we are aware of the total situations within which the stresses occur. This includes positive as well as negative aspects. After all, these are families who have remained intact despite the stresses. A study of families which have succumbed to the strains might show additional or more severe stresses, or they might lack the supports present in the families studied. In every case, the overall patterns were evolved from choices which were made, often to avoid what may have been perceived by the couple as still more severe stresses. It is important to note that we do not assume that these stresses are peculiar to the dual-career family. Many of them may exist, perhaps in less poignant form, in single-career families. Such stresses may represent issues of our culture and the dual-career family represents a particular context within which the specific dilemmas are played out. The controls we have been able to use, e.g. the "drop-out" families, are inadequate to provide definitive conclusions. Our impression, however, is that dual-career families show the patterns of stresses in particularly acute form; the ways in which they coped with them may represent future solutions for a larger proportion of the population. We see each of the families studied as engaging, in a sense, in a microscopic experiment with social change. They are working out patterns of living-together—in relation to their network of relationships—that are without clear precedent.

The study is based on thirteen functioning dual-career families and three in which the dual-career aspect was given up by the wife breaking off her career, at least temporarily. People may drop out for various reasons and for differing amounts of time and effort at different points in their careers—men as well as women. In some situations special provisions are made for career interruptions by women which may obviate the need to "drop-out" in the sense of resigning from a position in an organisation. In other situations "dropping out" may simply mean a slackening of the pace of activity or output, e.g. in the career of an artist or sculptress. We use the term drop-out to refer

[2]The couples in our study valued the rights of women as well as of men to pursue careers. However, the general line of our analysis is in agreement with Goode's point that ". . . .the kernel of the psychological problem of extending human rights to a given group. . . .(is) that each right is someone else's obligation, that to grant a right requires that someone loses what he had formerly considered his right. . . ." (Goode, 1966).

to an indefinite cessation of activity—whether from an organisational post or less formal position.

The sixteen families studied were interviewed by a pair of interviewers (one male, one female); the interviews were tape recorded and transcribed verbatim. The course of interviews, which served as the basis for a preliminary write-up, ordinarily consisted of one or two joint interviews (husband and wife together interviewed by the pair of interviewers) and one or two separate interviews with the husband and wife separately by individual interviewers. The validity of the case write-ups was checked to some extent by presenting a preliminary form of write-up to the couples for discussion. In this further interview, the "feed-back interview," corrections were made for gross omissions and distortions. Where there were differences of perceptions, either between the couple or between the couple and the interviewers, these were discussed so that a statement might be made that would encompass the different possibilities. Each interview was approximately three hours long. The couples were chosen to represent a range of occupations for the women; they had to be intact families with at least one child still living at home.[3]

The current discussion is preliminary and tentative. We remain close to the phenomenological level in reporting the stresses and the patterns of resolution to them. Our own propositions drawn from this limited data can then be treated with appropriate skepticism and the data used for other propositions should this seem merited on further investigation.

Five foci of stress in the couples studied are indicated. They are neither exhaustive nor more than a preliminary grouping of complexes of stress as appreciated by ourselves in interaction with the couples studied. Subsequent analyses and further research will doubtless refine the list. We believe, however, that it encompasses major dimensions of stress and that it is useful at this point to state them descriptively. They are: overload dilemmas, personal norm dilemmas, dilemmas of identity, social network dilemmas, and role cycling dilemmas. In each area we shall discuss the sources of stress and the ways in which the couples have adapted to the enusing strains.

Overload Dilemmas

The old folk-expression "behind every successful man there is a woman" stands not only for a social-psychological situation where the wife gives emotional support, advice, etc., but also for a whole culture complex of activities and relationships within which the wife is a help-

[3]Couples who fitted our criteria for inclusion were obtained through Establishment or Personnel Officers in the Civil Service, BBC, and large Industrial Organizations, through Professional and Business Association Representatives for the architects and small business women.

mate—attending to the shopping, child-rearing, housekeeping, and general social tasks necessary to provide a smoothly operating base to which the male can retreat after the rigours of a day's work and from which he can sally refreshed and emotionally supported. One of the couples studied began the interview by reversing the expression, stating that "behind every successful woman there is a man." What they meant by this, however, was that the man encouraged his wife to face and cope with problems arising in her work, provided consultation on financial matters, and co-operated in various ways. They did *not* mean to indicate that the husband gave the same sort of backing —through shopping, mending, cooking, child-minding, and so on that would be the obverse of the traditional picture.

In fact, when only the man is following a career, it is possible for his wife to provide the domestic "back-up," but when there is a dual-career family, it is not usually possible for the man to provide this kind of total reversal of the traditional roles (though role reversals are by no means non-existent). The most usual situation among our couples where both husband and wife pursue a career is a rearrangement of the domestic side of their lives. Some of the household tasks are delegated to others, part is reapportioned between husband and wife and children. In effect, each member pursues a career and performs some household and child-rearing activities. Among the couples we studied, the overload experienced seems to have been a function of at least four factors.

THE DEGREE TO WHICH HAVING CHILDREN AND A FAMILY LIFE (AS DISTINCT FROM SIMPLY BEING MARRIED) IS SALIENT. With the exception of one of the couples studied, family life in general and children in particular were highly salient. The couples were very concerned with the possible effects on their children of their both pursuing careers. This implied a limitation in the degree to which the couples were willing to delegate child-care, even assuming the availability of satisfactory resources. Aside from the sheer number of things to be done by the conjugal pair who are both working and at the same time value interaction with their families, there is an element of psychic strain involved in allowing two major areas of life, so different in their demands and characteristics, to be highly important. The overload, then, is not a simple arithmetical one of increased number of tasks to be accomplished, but one far more difficult to assess, which is related to the duality of emotional commitment and concern.[4]

---

[4]It is interesting to note that this duality of emotional commitment is put into practice by only a small number of people. It would appear, however, that many more highly qualified people value this duality than are actually able to carry it out. Preliminary analysis of a sample of 1960 graduates shows the relative salience of work, family, and leisure in relation to marital status and family stage. Degree of satisfaction was used as a rough index of salience and respondents were asked which area of life gave them greatest satisfaction, which next greatest

THE DEGREE TO WHICH THE COUPLE ASPIRE TO A HIGH STANDARD OF DOMESTIC LIVING. Most of the couples aspired to a high standard, pleasant home and garden, high standards of decor, cleanliness, cooking, and so on. This made the problem of management of the domestic side of their lives more complex, albeit by choice, than if they had kept to a lower standard. The notion of a lower standard materially, though, is almost a contradiction in terms to the notion of career success, for a certain standard of life is implied in occupational achievement; the process tends to become circular in that once having acquired a taste for the high standards, the impetus to continue working and career development is increased.

THE DEGREE TO WHICH SATISFACTORY ARRANGEMENTS FOR THE REAPPORTIONMENT OF TASKS IS POSSIBLE. Here we found various combinations of conjugal role reorganisations and delegations of parts of the domestic work to children and helpers of various kinds.

THE DEGREE TO WHICH THE SHEER PHYSICAL OVERLOAD OF TASKS AND THEIR APPORTIONMENT IS ADUMBRATED BY A SOCIAL-PSYCHOLOGICAL OVERLOAD. These arise from struggling with the following conflicts: normative conflict, sex role identity maintenance, network management, and role-cycling. Couples vary enormously in the degree to which these other sources of tension feed into the family system and the degree to which they can manage them once present.

For all the couples the overload issue was salient; they all emphasised the importance of physical health and energy as a prerequisite for making the dual-career family a possibility. They regarded it as important for their children to be healthy too. Generally speaking there was little room for illness in the systems that were evolved.

To deal with the overload issues, all of the dual-career families studied spent much thought and effort on arranging a system of domestic help. This problem can be seen as having two sides to it—the availability of different kinds of domestic helpers on the one hand and the preferences of the couples as to which elements of the

---

satisfaction, and which the most dissatisfaction. For men there is a sharp contrast between those who are single and those who are married and have children. For the single men, "career" is the most frequently chosen as the area giving most satisfaction (55 percent), with "leisure" second (17 percent) and "family" third (12 percent). For married men with children, "family" is the most frequent chosen area (55 percent), with "career" second (30 percent) and "leisure" dropping alongside the other areas as of little importance, i.e. under 5 percent choosing it as the most satisfying. Single women like single men choose "career" as the most important (45 percent) with "leisure" second (22 percent) and "family" third (15 percent). For married women without children, the pattern is like that of the married men with children; 57 percent indicate that "family" is the most important area of satisfaction, 19 percent indicating "career" and 10 percent "leisure." The married woman with children, however, overwhelmingly look to family as their greatest satisfactions, with over 80 percent indicating that this is the main area. It is interesting that only 4 percent indicated "career" as their main area of satisfaction; this is about the same proportion of the married women with young children who work at jobs for over thirty hours a week.

domestic roles they wish to delegate.

Our survey data indicate that at a point seen after graduation domestic role tasks become differentiated into different types. Graduate women become aware that they would like to delegate the activities which are impersonal—the washing, cleaning, ironing, etc.—tasks which can absorb a great deal of time particularly in households with a high standard of living.[5] They tend to wish to retain the more people-orientated activities, particularly in relation to childcare and feeding. Among the couples studied intensively, the delegation of the less desirable aspects of domestic labour was both the expected and the observed tendency. Given the low value placed on domestic work as an occupation in our society, the dual-career couples have all had to devote considerable energy to improvising viable arrangements. A wide range of domestic help arrangements is found: short term and long term; full-time and part-time; live-in and live-out; nannies, *au pairs,* dailies, students, secretaries-doubling-as-baby-sitters, domestic help couples with husband and wife dividing up the domestic part of the employing couples' household affairs, unmarried mothers and their babies taking over part of the premises, and so on. Most of the couples used at least a duplex system; often they would shift from one type of a system to another following a major transition like having a child, having the last child enter school, etc. Sometimes the shift was associated with a difficult experience with the prior system; sometimes it was based on the couples' conception of a better arrangement for the particular stage, e.g. the dropping of a nannie and the taking on of an *au pair* instead as the infant reaches school age. Simple as the tasks of household maintenance may be, the difficulties in obtaining reliable personnel to whom to delegate them is so great in contemporary British and American society as to call for all sorts of perquisites. In the couples studied, domestic helpers were not only offered the usual salary and private room arrangements (often with TV) but in addition were sometimes given the use of one of the family cars and in one case a specially built flat. Few of the couples studied used their parents in a major way, though many used them occasionally to look after children while they were away, say for a conference or a long weekend.

As indicated above the area of childcare presents special problems. While most of our couples valued interaction with their children and felt that their children's welfare and development were of primary importance, they had to delegate at least part of the childcare to pursue

---

[5]From a communication with Alice Rossi, it appears that this pattern holds even in the U.S.A. where there are a great many labour-saving devices in the home. In countries where households are less mechanised and shopping is less rationalised, e.g. no "supermarkets" and shopping centres, the burden of overload in the situation is even greater.

their careers. Precisely because the children were so important to them, the issue of how to arrange childcare contributed heavily to the overload picture for these couples. As many of them put it, if the house got dirty it was unfortunate but could be ultimately remedied and anyway was not crucial. However, serious lapses in relation to the children's care simply could not be allowed to occur. Most of the families were aware of and concerned with modern conceptions of child development and the importance of parental involvement in it. As one couple put it: "We are all victims of our culture in the Spockean age," i.e. this child-centered age. While compromises could and often were made in the domestic care areas, none of the couples were willing self-consciously to adopt a policy which would have meant possible harm to their children's physical or psychological development. It was not possible within the scope of the study to assess the effects of the dual-career couples' child-rearing practices on their children. However, in detailed interviews it was striking how low the level of reported disturbance appeared to be.[6] Although the couples were quite aware of potential negative effects, they also pointed to some of the positive effects of their pattern of life. Thus, their pattern was seen as possibly fostering independence and responsibility, e.g. in getting children to help with household chores: redistributing domestic role allocations resulted in fathers spending more time with their children; providing a student companion for the children was seen as useful in giving them someone to "talk nonsense" with—something enjoyable to the children when their parents were away or preoccupied with work tasks, and so on. Most of the families interviewed had read or heard about the relevant research work and were concerned with the issue of whether or not a mother working would constitute for the child a potentially harmful "maternal deprivation" situation.

The majority of the couples studied took precautions against placing complete reliance on any one helping figure and they tended to monitor very carefully the interaction between children and domestic helpers. One mother describes the degree to which she had to rely on help and how distasteful it was to a strong and independent minded person to have to be made to feel dependent in this way: "I had no one, so I had to go from hand to mouth. I never knew, in fact, when I could make appointments ahead. It was such a strain that I got not ill but terribly upset, unable to cope, you know, and I put a high

[6]Terence Moore's work, though not on dual-career families specifically, supports the impression that the maternal separation entailed in mothers' working does not per se produce disturbance (Moore, 1968). American research reported in Nye & Hoffman (1963) leads to a similar impression. We are aware that we are unable to make scientifically conclusive statements on the effects of the dual-career family structure on childrens' development. We hope, however, to study this more closely in a subsequent project.

value on being able to cope . . ."

The vulnerability of the woman, in particular, to malfunctioning in the domestic help area is expressed by Mrs. Y. who indicated that, even when she is working or travelling, there is a "little corner of my mind somewhere that is thinking and worrying about the management of the children." Mr. Y, in contrast, reserves the comparable "little corners" in the back of his mind for forward planning of their work and the family's finances. The general tendency among the couples studied was to place high value on having children and developing a close relationship with them. Even in the rare instances where children were sent to boarding school, the reason for doing so (with one possible exception) was not to unload the care of the children onto an institution but rather because of tradition (father and grandfather had gone to that school) or the child's own wishes.

In general, most of the couples interviewed thought that the main consequence of their both working was that there was "very little slack left in the system." Several indicated that they were both "whacked" by the time they got home and that they had very little energy left over for extra activities, particularly on week-nights. The following quotes indicate the kinds of expression frequently used:

> A husband : . . . after a hard day in the office she is sometimes very spiky in the evening . . ."
>
> A wife, speaking of their situation where her husband's job keeps him out days as a producer and her job keeps her out evenings, as a performer: ". . . (talking of shared leisure) it's something that strongly has to struggle for existence, really. It's a matter of a night off every now and then and a weekend that we try and organise every few weeks to try and keep something apart from our work . . . We's like to have more time off when we can see one another, but what happens is that when I'm off he might be on and it creates a sort of tension . . ."

While leisure activities tend to be sacrificed first under the impact of overload, the repercussions may spill over into the work lives of one or both of the partners. Couples vary in the degree to which they protect this as a higher priority than other areas, like activities with the children, or the reverse.

> Mr. S. illustrates part of this pattern of spill over into work (in discussing how he concerns himself with his wife's business problems): ". . . one takes up time during the day thinking over these problems instead of perhaps dining with someone one ought to dine with for one's own business career . . . or, one comes home to commiserate to work out a problem, or even to have a quiet

evening and one can't because the wife is really worn out and exhausted and can't cope with it. . ."

Thus, the overload issue seems to arise acutely as a stress when both members pursue careers. The strains are felt first, in relation to leisure and recreational activities which are often sacrificed very early; second, in relation to the children and the degree and quality of relationships with them or in relation to one's work. Characteristic patterns of coping with these strains are:

1. Deliberately to "work" at leisure—to discipline oneself to take holidays, weekends in the country to "unwind," frequent trips away, etc. To conserve health and energy deliberately as a human resource.
2. To delegate as much as possible of the less desired domestic chores and to provide adequate care for child-rearing—"suitable mothering" influences and other relevant companionship as seen to be needed by the growing child. Strategies to provide the child with the best possible environments—home, school, etc.,—consume major proportions of the time of the couples studied. Some of this is described in greater detail below under "dilemmas of personal norms."
3. To modify one's work involvements in such a way as to be compatible with the other partner's and to diminish the strain of "overspill," e.g. from an excessively complicated, demanding, or otherwise difficult work situation. If one travels or gets too deeply involved with complex relationships at work it is likely to impinge more on the other's capacity to function at work. Thus, most of the couples made choices that attempted to avoid unnecessary involvements of this kind so as to optimise participation of both partners in work and family spheres. Some of this is described in detail under conflicts in role-cycling.

Dilemmas Arising from the Discrepancy Between Personal Norms and Social Norms

The women in the intensive case study reported here have found ways to continue their careers even after childbirth, stopping work only for a minimal period which did not interfere with their career development. In doing so they have had to deal with dilemmas arising from the clash between their personal norms, i.e. what they felt was right and proper behaviour for themselves, and social norms, i.e. the norms they felt people around them held (Bott, 1957).

These dilemmas arise, as indicated above, because of the fact that most women, even highly qualified ones, tend to drop their careers to fulfill traditional domestic roles even if this is accompanied by personal frustration (Gavron, 1966). It is accepted as the right and proper thing to do by the majority of people in our society, and supported from childbirth by a pervasive set of cultural symbols and manifestations: the importance attributed to "mothering" (assumed to be always by the biological mother except in abnormal cases), the sanctity of the home and the housewife role, etc. The men and women in our study have deliberately adopted a variant pattern, extending the universalistic elements of their educational experience, i.e. where boys and girls were assumed to have similarly valuable potentials and were assumed equally to be able to realise them in work. For various reasons and under various circumstances they arrive at this pattern and the dilemma for them becomes resolved and dormant.

Under some circumstances, however, the dilemmas become reactivated. Three examples are given of instances which reactivate the normative dilemmas causing the variant norms to collide with the more traditional norms and requiring a resolution again. These examples are (1) at critical transition points in the family life cycle (particularly birth of the first child); (2) at critical transition points in the career (or occupation) life cycle of *either* partner (role enlargement or contraction); and (3) at critical events in the life space of the children, e.g. illness, school problems, etc.

A critical point in the family life cycle that reactivates these dilemmas is the birth of the first child.[7] For example, when Mrs. O's baby was born, she had to overcome the feeling of distress when "well meaning" neighbours who had got to know her better while she was at home during the final phase of pregnancy and expected her to remain at home following the birth of the baby made such remarks as: "Oh well, I suppose you won't mind when your baby doesn't recognize you as its mother." It took her some time to overcome the heightening of the conflict aroused by such remarks before she resumed her preferred pattern of pursuing both career and family interests.

These remarks are manifestations of a larger set of cultural norms related to child-rearing practices. Most of the couples studied experienced pressure from these norms. Mrs. O, a civil servant with a good social science degree, sums up how she resolved her dilemma as follows:[8]

[7]Our survey data also support this, showing that while nearly 90 percent of single women graduates are working 30 hours a week or more eight years after they leave university and this pattern is sustained for 65 percent of the married women without children, only 4 percent of the married women with children continue working this amount.

[8]While all of the dual-career families made similar resolutions, sometimes less scientifically based, the "drop-out" cases differed in this. Two of the three drop-outs resolved this dilemma in favour of the traditional norms at the point of the birth of the first baby. The third drop-out was occasioned by a crisis in the area of the childrens' life space (breakdown of care facilities accompanied by incipient signs of disturbance in the child).

When I first went back to work (after having the baby) there were the women who quoted (a noted child-psychiatrist) to me, you know. I got so fed up with this man. I got all his books out before I went back permanently. Really it made me feel a criminal. . . but I came to the conclusion that he was taking for his children those who had been in institutions on the one hand and comparing them with the kind of children who were in an ordinary mother's care. . . and it seemed to me to be such a long way off from what I was going to do. . . I think a lot of mothers have gripped onto him to justify staying at home. I went to see a number of friends of mine who have combined both and whose children are, in the main, older and who have turned out into well-adjusted, independent, happy, thoroughly sort of normal children who seem to have a perfectly normal relationship with their parents, as far as one could judge. I was a bit unconvinced.

An example of how a critical transition in the occupational situation can reactivate this dilemma is seen with the Ss. Mrs. S, a clothing designer, discussed how she had been thrown into conflict (which immediately became a family-conflict) when an offer was received from a large fashion group of companies to take over her firm and promote her products in a really "big" way. Mrs. S says that this conflict was exacerbated by its timing, coming at a period of her life (age about 40) when she was in any case reviewing her personal norms and values (Jaques, 1965). She felt that before she would realise it, the children would have grown up and left home. In attempting to resolve this, Mr. and Mrs. S each played devil's advocate with the other. When Mr. S was arguing in favour of maximising familial values, he would say it was bad enough that the father could not spend more time at home with the children but to have mother away so much in addition was "terrible." Mrs. S would counter this with how a more senior position would enable her to be more flexible with her work hours, have more assistance, and how they would have more and better holidays and be able to remove financial worries about the childrens' future. Then, when she took the position that she should stay at home, spend more time with the children, pursue cultural interests and so on, Mr. S would argue that it would be doing something to her which they would both regret later as she had so much invested in her career and derived so much satisfaction out of it, etc. They indicated that this was a period of "brinkmanship" in which each pushed the other over the brink until they had worked their way through the feelings of both of them about a new resolution to the dilemma. The resolution finally adopted was one in which she agreed to the take-over but with a number of new perquisites allowing for more time with the family and contractual safeguards against her being drawn too deeply into the firm's business involvements.

There are several instances reported of events in the childrens' life space reactivating this dilemma. This may occur around a major focussed crisis, e.g. the child's disturbance or poor performance at school. More usually it is aroused by small occurrences. Most of the working mothers cite the feelings aroused when they see other mothers wheeling their prams in the park, e.g. while they are at the office, but they tend to put down these feelings relatively easily saying that probably many of these mothers would rather be going to work, or that they would soon be bored with doing only this every day. Occasionally, however, the dilemma is made more acute, e.g. when the child "uses" the fact that the mother works for "playing up" the mother's guilt, e.g. by saying that she prefers her granny's house or the house of a non-working mum of a school friend. In continuing their work, most of these dual-career family mothers emphasised the positive elements of the situation with which the children are reported by and large to have agreed, e.g. having a happier and more interesting mum; having a mum who designs things—in one case the child's school uniform; having a mum who is on T.V., etc.

Dilemmas of Identity

We are concerned here with dilemmas arising within the person about the very fundamental characteristics of the self—whether one is a "good" person, a "good" man or woman and so on. This is at a deeper level and more internally generated than the conflicts arising over specific behavioural patterns, as in the discussion above on normative dilemmas. This set of dilemmas stems from the sociocultural definitions of work and family as intrinsically masculine and feminine. The quintessence of masculinity is still, in our culture, centered on work and competing successfully in the "breadwinning" roles. The quintessence of femininity is still centered on the domestic scene. While there are some occupations which have come to be defined as acceptable for women—even preferably feminine—such as nursing, primary school teaching, and social work—these tend to be as temporary, part-time, or for unmarried women. Conversely, where men enter these occupations it is probable that they encounter internal dilemmas of identity stemming from the same source of social stereotyping. In analysing the dilemmas observed in this area, it is important to note that we consider these dilemmas to be a product of our contemporary socio-cultural situation. They would be different under different circumstances or at different points in the social process.[9]

---

[9]For an interesting discussion of how cultural norms affect the role of psychotherapists, see Knoblochova & Knobloch (1965). In Czechoslovakia, the tendency in family physchotherapy (where identity problems of the type being described here are encountered) is to assume employment as a part of the feminine role concept. If there are marital difficulties associated with a dual-career situation, they are as likely to see the issues as problems of the husband's difficulties in allowing his wife equal opportunities as of the wife's deviance in relation to a narrow domestic role conception.

Taking the specifically sexual component of the identity dilemmas, i.e. whether the individual feels himself to be a "good" or a "real" man or woman, there seem to be at least three levels at which the issues are discussed in the literature—the physical, the psychological, and the socio-cultural. Some observers seem to assume that confusion arising at one level will necessarily be reflected in confusion at other levels. Thus we were told by one psychiatric colleague at the outset of the research that men and women who cross sex lines socioculturally (as have all of the women in our study to some extent) would be characterised by a psychological confusion of sexual identity as well. The assumption, furthermore, was that women who wanted to enter the male world of competition would be highly motivated by competitiveness with men and, as a consequence, would emasculate their husbands and there would tend to ensue a sex life characterised by impotence and frigidity. This would be enhanced by their tendency to choose mates who fit into their needs in this regard.

While we did not focus in the study on the sex lives of the couples in detail, the data that we have seem to indicate that while these stereotyped conceptions may be present in some cases (doubtless the types of cases most seen in clinical practices), this is not the universal picture by any means. Our impression of a "normal" range of types of sexual experience makes sense when one goes into greater detail about the actual patterns of motivation that seem to be present among these people and also their ways of coping with dilemmas and issues that arise in their relationships. We find that, while competitiveness with men may be a prominent motive among some of the women, it is only one of many that seem important among the women studied. Most of these women are involved (to the extent that they are fighting battles in relation to this) in issues relating to financial security, the need to be creative (in ways that are difficult for them if focussed on the household), and the desire to be effective as an individual person. However, while autonomy is a prominent part—financial, psychological, and otherwise—it is coupled with, rather than exclusive from, the wish to be interdependent with their husbands. The occupational world is used by all of our women as the area in which they develop their separate personal identities. This makes it possible for both husband and wife to relate as two individuals, *each* having a separate identity as a person. To the extent that each has a clear personal sexual identity associated with his physical make-up, the issues of physical relationships may even be enhanced in such a situation. But it would take a more focused and detailed study to investigate this.

What actually seems to happen in the couples studied is that they are able to go a certain way toward their ideal establishment of individual identities which are independent of socio-cultural definitions but in each case indications of discomfort arise at a certain point. They seem to say, in effect: "this is as far as I go in experimenting with a new definition of sex-roles without having it 'spill over' into my own psychological sense of self-esteem and possibly my physical capacity to carry on in this relationship." This point represents a limit to which an individual's psychological defences are felt to be effective, and in each of the couples studied one or more points seem to have evolved beyond which each knew it was dangerous to push the other. We have called these points identity "tension lines."

Manifestations of "tension lines" are as follows:

> In the O family, the matter of income is a crucial point. Mr. O encourages his wife to pursue her career and to be successful and effective in her work, but the amount of her income relative to his is a point of some tension between them.
>
> With the Xs the central issue is authority. Mr. X wanted his wife to follow her profession and to achieve the security that she wished in it; he even welcomed her earning more than himself and stabilizing the family income so that he could get on with what he valued more highly, namely, creative designing work. However, he did not wish actually to have her in authority over jobs on which he himself was working.

Manifestations of the sex-identity "tension line" are sometimes seen in subtle, often unrecognised, undercutting behaviour by the husband toward the wife. This seems to be an indication of strain and a defensive manifestation rather than the preferred mode as it occurs in couples where the husbands make such statements as

> "My wife has at least as good an education as I have; she earns as much as I do, I don't see any reason why we shouldn't regard ourselves as equal partners, and that is what we do. . ."
>
> "We see our family as a collection of individuals, each with different skills and interests and as having evolved the capacity to live together."
>
> "Our marriage is a form of partnership, and has to be understood in terms of the characteristics of partnerships. . ."

Clearly these are statements of fundamental ideals on which the dual-career family is based. In actually observed or reported interactions, when the tension point was approached the men tended to undercut their wives. Examples of this were seen in the way some husbands cut across their wives in the interview situation, not allowing them to answer fully, as though to say "I'm really better at this than you, dear." One husband actually prefaced his interruptions with statements of that type. Another example was when a husband described his wife's business practices; he tended to make a bit of a joke of them, not expecting her to deal with her management role as "for real" as he did himself. He expressed surprise when a larger firm thought his wife's business worth a take-over bid but was reassured when they offered a ridiculously low sum. In another instance the husband indicated that he thought that his wife was basically unemployable except for his help. It must be emphasised, however, that these manifestations were subordinated to the more dominant aspect of their relationship, which was that the husband did in fact support, sponsor, encourage, and otherwise facilitate his wife's career. It is to be expected that there would be some "backwash" of other feelings about it stemming from the sacrifices and threats that the pattern involved. These processes of "undercutting" and supporting are also present on the women's side of the symbiotic relationship. Where the dual-career situation persists, as it has in the couples studied, a balance is achieved which constitutes a resolution of the dilemma. In the families which are also a professional partnership (as with the Ys, an architectural husband-wife partnership) these processes are accentuated.

Where the working partnership is conducted at home there must be developed a way to soften the cut-and-thrust of critical competitive work-modes of relationship lest it erode the husband-wife relationship. The Ys recognise that criticism is important for the maintenance of work standards and to stimulate creativity. Mr. Y, indicating how they resolve this, says, "It is important if one is to preserve this kind of relationship to learn to criticise with love; and to accept criticism in work matters as different from attacks on the person. . ."

The Y's themselves recognise that it is easier said than done and have learned to accept a good deal more overt conflict in their relationship than, for example, their parents were accustomed to.

Some of the wives developed distinctive ways of handling their dilemmas in relation to the sex-role identity issue. Where their occupational roles called for aggressive behaviour or other patterns of behaviour sharply inconsistent with their conceptions of the wifely role, they more or less consciously segregated the two sets of roles: Examples of the segregation mechanism are "When I'm at work I'm very authoritarian. I wear a white coat at work and I try to hang up my working personality with it when I leave the office." To this was added her husband's view: "I once visited my wife's company on business and by chance I saw her there. She was so different, I hardly recognised her. She seemed like someone else—some sort of tycoon—certainly not my wife."

In another case, the switch-over was not so deliberate but nevertheless decisive: "My friends who know me in both capacities say that I am two different people at home and at work . . . I am much more domineering and aggressive in the office than I am at home in that I will fight a point in the office in a way that I would never fight in a domestic situation, or want to."

Another way that at least two of the wives dealt with identity dilemmas that would tend to arise if they gave too much emphasis to their career ambitions was to play them down almost deliberately. They presented their careers as a series of improvisations which allowed them to do something interesting rather than as a series of steps taken toward a career ambition or goal. A given couple may have more than one tension line operating and the tension lines may shift through time. When either individual is pushed into a pattern which is too discrepant with his or her sense of personal (and sexual) identity, defensive behaviour begins to develop. The form this takes —attack, withdrawal of support, etc.—varies according to the couple constellation.

Social Network Dilemmas

Each of the couples relates to its social environment through a network of relationships. This social network of each family is variously composed of kin, friends, neighbours, work associates, service relationships, and so on. The networks vary in their size, mutidimensionality, interconnectedness, and so on. Network composition is affected by many sorts of things, e.g. personal preferences, convenience, obligations, and pressures of various kinds. Family phase and occupational affiliation are of central importance in determining composition and the quality of relationships. At different stages in the life cycle one may add or drop people from the "active" network, some people being carried along from stage to stage in a relatively more "latent" capacity. For example, when a woman works, some of her work relationships may be important for the family in a way similar to the work relationships of her husband. (In both cases, these will vary according to the general importance of work relationships in the specific occupations and in the national cultures concerned.) When a family has children, they may enter into relationships with service personnel relating to children's care and activities and they may form relationships with families of their children's friends with whom they might otherwise not have related. As well as sheer quantity of relationships, there is the matter of quality of relationships, some being kept rather superficial and others "deeper," some relating only to a sector of one's interests and others being more general.

The population with which we are concerned has several characteristics. They are very busy people, committed to occupations which are very demanding. In addition they have their own families whom they value highly; as these families are at the stage where there are growing children at home, this creates yet another very demanding situation. Because of the heavy demands in these immediate spheres, the couples tend to have a relatively smaller amount of active involvement with kin and friendship relationships than may prevail among other professional middle class families, where there is a greater "slack" for visiting and sociability outside the round of pressing work and family duties (cf. "overload"). While some of the couples in our sample interacted frequently with relatives and some kin were drawn on to help with children occasionally, the more general pattern was for difficulties to appear in this area because of the divergence of the dual-career family from expected norms of kin behaviour. This is one of the areas in which network dilemmas tended to arise. The second area in which distinctive dilemmas arose was that of friendship formation. Each of these can be illustrated. They both involve difficulties in reciprocating conventional role expectations and they both give rise to dilemmas as in each case there is both a wish to sustain a relationship and also a wish to protect oneself from it because of the criticism that is usually entailed in the reactions a career wife and mother gets in these relationships.

The kin dilemma is illustrated in Mrs. O's experience. Because her husband was very close to his widowed mother, who lived with his spinster sister, she wished to be as nice to them as possible. On the other hand, Mrs. O's in-laws found it difficult to accept that she was not only a working wife but one with a very heavy demanding schedule. Mrs. O described a characteristic incident as follows:

> She (mother-in-law) will call up and ask if she can just drop around for a visit. I've got her pretty well trained now to realise that I cannot just have a chat with her or prepare things for her. . . Early on, even my husband didn't realise what a problem this was. When she telephoned once, I heard him say "yes, she'll be home on Thursday, drop in anytime in the afternoon." He didn't realise how precious that afternoon was for me. . . how many things I'd saved and planned to get done on that day, I couldn't spend it chatting with his mother. I've got her trained now to accept every third week-end.

Mrs. S describes similar difficulties with her husband's mother. Mr. S, as with most of the men in our study, felt that he had a special relationship with his mother. In his case, although Mr. S had four brothers, it was he who had always been close to her and in later years is was he who always carried the burden of his mother's difficulties. This was a recurrent source of conflict of loyalties in relation to his own wife and family and a high level of tension developed when his mother became seriously ill with a long terminal illness. Mrs. S says

> This was the first time I felt that my marriage might break up. He would return late at night from staying up with her and then be so disturbed about

it that we couldn't get any rest. This was at the same time as there were heavy demands being made on me to keep my business going. Even when none of the others in the family would lift a finger and he acted on doctors' advice to have her put into a home, he felt so guilty about it that it disturbed our own relationship.

In one of the couples where the husband's mother lived in a self-contained flatlet in a wing of their large house, the wife and mother have worked out a routinised daily contact for a few minutes between the wife's arrival home from work and the beginning of the television programme that the mother watches each evening in her own quarters. Aside from this contact, communication is largely by notes left by the wife in the morning about how to deal with the matters that might arise, e.g. with tradesmen expected.

The dilemma over friendship is less a matter of obligations being modified in the light of the wife's career demands than a matter of deviating from the usual choice patterns for friends. There seems to have been established, particularly among professionals and executives in the business world, a pattern of friendship based on the male's occupational associates (Lazarfeld & Merton, 1954; Babchuk & Bates, 1963). Typically, however, the male's occupational associates are married to women who do not themselves pursue careers, though there is some variation in this. It is far less likely that a businessman's associates would be married to women pursuing careers than might hold for the professionals. In both cases, however, there was a tendency for the women in our sample to report a discomfort with social situations in which the wives of the relevant couples were not themselves working or, if not working, at least positively orientated toward it and perhaps intending to work themselves later. In other situations there tended to be at best a lack of shared interests and at worst an awkward situation arising out of expressions of criticism.

The circumstances of the dual-career family tended to produce, among the couples studied, a situation in which friendships are formed in different ways from what might be expected in mono-career families. Aside from the general tendency for overload to crowd out many contacts with friends and to make relationships very selective (as with leisure activities generally) there are other tendencies too. Neighbourhood is perhaps less important than in the mono-career family because, as Mrs. O indicates above, casual visiting patterns are impossible. In only one family was the neighbourhood a source of friends and in this case the neighbourhood was a suburb and one with people of the same type as themselves, i.e. a high density of dual-career families or families in which the women had high qualifications and wanted to work at some point. A striking feature of the dual-career families in the study is the tendency to form their friendships on a couple basis. While traditional families, particularly in the middle class, assume a minimal degree of acceptance by both partners' of any friendships that they form, the tendency has been for the wife to accommodate to the husband's choice and for the women and men to relate separately according to traditional lines of division in activities and interests. In the dual-career families, because of the sharp difference in outlook and situation between the career wife and the non-career wives, most of our families have tended to associate primarily with other couples like themselves, in so far as the wife's involvement in an occupation went. This produces a situation in which it is the wife who has a determining role in selection of friendships, though the end product is a couple based relationship. This is because there is a greater range of acceptable couples purely from the man's point of view than from the woman's point of view, leaving the selection process to centre on her sense of comfort and acceptance. This is further accentuated by the fact, as mentioned above, of overload falling most heavily on the wife, making it up to her to indicate whether she can handle friendships which are both gratifying and demanding.

Role Cycling Dilemmas

There is a good deal of literature on the life cycle and on cycles within specific spheres of life, e.g. the family life cycle. The family, for example, goes through phases which are named in the culture—engagement, honeymoon, marriage, parenthood, and so on. Each culture distinguishes different sub-phases and not all possible phases are named and identified as separate. For example, in ordinary usage in our own culture we do not have a designation to distinguish the phase of the family life cycle before having children and, later, the phase in which children leave home. In our culture, we call them all "parenthood," referring not to the whole family situation but only to roles of the marital partners. In other spheres, e.g. the occupational, there is a plethora of terms depending on the specific occupation—training, apprenticeship (internship, residency), establishment, etc., to retirement. In complex organisations there are specific hierarchies that contain named stages, e.g. in the Administrative Class of the British Civil Service there are the stages of Assistant Principal, Principal, Assistant Secretary, Under Secretary, Secretary. Other classes of the Civil Service have other grades. Other organisations have other hierarchies and stages of the career associated with them. In both spheres sociologists have evolved a more precise terminology (Duvall, 1957; Hill, 1960; Rodgers, 1964). Alice Rossi indicates the utility of thinking in terms of role-cycles (Rossi, 1968). A young man marrying enters the role of husband and he has a cycle of experiences in the husband role. When he takes the additional role of father, he has another set of experiences which has its own cycle. In some of our earlier work (Rapoport, 1963; Rapoport & Rapoport, 1964 & 1966) we outlined the critical importance of events at the transition points from one role to another, discussing the processes of unorganisation, disorganisation, and restructuring that occur to accommodate the shifts in role. The life cycle of the larger units—families, careers, organisations of different kinds—is seen as punctuated by these points of reorganisation, which tend to be accompanied by a certain degree of turbulence and conflict. Put into a more general framework, the role cycle may be seen as having an *anticipatory* or preparatory phase; the establishment phase (called the "honeymoon" stage by Rossi) in which efforts are directed at stabilising ways of managing the role and is usually accompanied by heightened interest and involvement; and a *plateau* (or steady-state) stage during which "the role is fully exercised" (Alice Rossi, 1968, p. 30). Then there eventually comes a stage of *disengagement* from the role which is given up voluntarily or under the force of circumstances.

The couples studied and reported here were mostly in the stage of familial roles that would be termed the *plateau,* in that they were married, had children, and were functioning as parents in a family that was established and growing, with children still at home. In three instances, there were new first babies, so the plateau stage was barely entered at the time of the study. In all the others it was well established. Our data indicates two basic types of role cycling conflicts: between the occupational roles of husband and wife and their family roles; and between the occupational role of the husband and the occupational role of the wife. Two potential conflicts will be discussed: the career-family cycling dilemmas and the dual-career cycling dilemmas.

In relation to the career-family role cycling dilemmas, the parental role is one into which women are to some extent pushed by cultural expectations. The woman is, in addition, particularly vulnerable as she may be catapulted into becoming a parent accidentally, even with modern methods of birth control (Rossi, 1968). The parental role is largely irrevocable and one for which parents tend to be relatively poorly prepared. While none of our couples report having been catapulated into parenthood, it is clear that the pressures to become parents were more keenly felt by the women than by the men and several of the couples described the decision to have their first child as one that was pressed by the woman and with which the man tended to acquiesce. The timing of this step in relation to the career role cycle was something that received considerable attention from our couples and two points of view were expressed.

Some couples stressed the importance, in their continuing to work, of their having been occupationally established before having children.

This meant that they had a high income and a secure position with flexibility and perquisites of one kind or another, and they could therefore afford a great deal of domestic help and were able to take time off to see that things worked out well. Their commitment to work was, by this time, so well established that dropping out seemed unthinkable.

One of the "drop-out" couples argued, in contrast, that as they had both reached the plateau stage of their careers, there was no need for the wife to work any longer as her husband's earnings would be high and they had accumulated savings through having had a surplus income for so long. The couple felt that for those in the establishment phase, struggling to make the grade, the pressure on women to continue working after becoming a mother was greater. As Mrs. K had previously established herself, they felt she could re-enter occupationally whenever she wished; had she become a parent earlier she might not have had sufficient status and contacts to make this possible.

The differences between these viewpoints seem to depend to some extent on the specific occupational situation and to some extent on the values and style of life of the specific couple. An example of the latter is the style of life of the Ks (above) who lived at a level set by what one income would allow; other couples lived at levels that required both incomes. An example of the way the specific occupational situation affects whether or not women stay in after becoming mothers is seen in architecture. Martin & Smith (1968), in a survey of women architects, show that if they are married to architects they have a higher chance of continuing their careers than if they marry men of other occupations. The early marriers, restricted as their social lives tend to be to fellow students, are more likely to marry architects than are late marriers.

None of the couples expressed strong feelings about the degree to which women had to curtail career involvements in favour of family demands as compared with men. This might have been more pronounced had we studied a series of "captive housewives." For the most part the women felt fortunate that they had been able to work out a situation where they had as full a career as they had managed to achieve. They tended to accept as "inevitable" for the present that the women would have to bear the main brunt of child-care and domestic organisation, so that there would "naturally" tend to be more strain on the wife's career-family cycling problems than on the husband's.[10] The general tendency was to be "thankful for small

[10]For an account of how the ideal-real discrepancies are absorbed into everyday life in Finland and Hungary, see Heiskanen and Manilla, 1967. These writers distinguish between "formal ideology" and "everyday ethic," the former representing the "ideal" pattern, the latter the "real" one.

mercies," such as having a husband who did not invite guests home to dinner at the last minute or who did not mind running a vacuum cleaner over the carpets. There were only a few who were very outspoken about their views that "jointness" and equality in the marital relationship should be equality in the degree to which *each* must curtail the demands of career in favour of their joint familial commitments.

The second type of role-cycling conflict, i.e. between demands of the two careers, was expressed by most of the couples. When Mrs. O wished to diminish the demands being made on her by her career so that she could have more time to spend with her growing children and as she wished to continue in a senior professional job of some kind, she considered taking a different post in a remote part of the U.K. Mr. O, however, could find no job in that area comparable to the one he held. So Mrs. O had to give up that opportunity. When Mr. P. was offered a promotion with his industrial firm if he would move to the north of England, he turned it down because there was no chance there for his wife (a research scientist) to obtain a job comparable to the one she held in the London area. Mr. S gave up a promising career in politics in order to stabilise a home base and income to underpin the development of his wife's career as a designer.

An example of a dilemma arising between the woman's career role and the parental role is seen most crucially at the point of childbirth. As indicated this is when most women drop out, at least for an extended period. Our data from the 1960 graduates' survey indicate that there is a point following childbirth when the woman's occupation aspirations soar (having been depressed in the face of difficulties following graduation from university and kept down by the counterbalance of the glow of early parenthood).

In all these instances there was stress—both within the individual making the career sacrifice and to some extent between the pair. However, in all cases resolutions were made on the basis of a recognition of joint interest in optimising family-career decisions so as to keep the three sets of role systems functioning with minimal tension.

SUMMARY AND DISCUSSION

There is a trend toward increased participation of women in the work-force. Women are doing this not at the expense of marrying but along with it and increasingly expect to combine marriage and career. This is producing, more and more often, the phenomenon of the dual-career family in which husband and wife are not only companions and equal on different scales of evaluation but are both participating on the same evaluative planes. Thus, while there has been a good deal written about "women's two roles" (Myrdal & Klein, 1956), the point of reference of the present chapter is not the role of women but the family in relation to its social environment. The dual-career family is one in which both "heads" of the family pursue careers. The implication is not, as with the concept of women's two roles, that men do not also have two roles. Both men and women, in the dual-career family, have both career roles and familial roles and, with the exception of pregnancy and childbirth, there is no assumption that any of the activities are inexorably sex-linked. This is not to say that there are categorically no biologically linked sex-differences in the capacities of men and women to perform specific activities, e.g. "mothering." The probability is that there are "overlapping curves" of characteristics such that some men may have more of an attribute (say nurturance) than some women and, conversely, some women may have more of an attribute (say mechanical skills) than some men (Riesman, 1965). At the same time, more women may turn out to be more nurturant biologically than most men and more men may turn out to be biologically more "mechanical" than most women.

At present there are strongly held socio-cultural beliefs about sex-linked attributes which affect self-conceptions and interaction patterns. Different sub-systems within society change at different rates.[11] Within the socio-cultural domains, a very complex inter-relationship exists between ideology, social structure, and behaviour. In contemporary society, egalitarianism is a dominant ideological theme. This is expressed, for example, in the educational sub-system. Boys and girls at school are taught and compete with one another on a single set of evaluative scales. When they leave school or university however, the sex differentiation becomes more marked. It is to be noted that egalitarian education is a tendency not an actuality. Many graduate women accommodate to the traditional sex-differentiated norms of the post-university role systems without apparent strain. Some similarly highly educated women conform to the traditional pattern but show great strain (the "captive wife" syndrome). Others extrapolate the egalitarian norms of their educational period into the adult stage, working out new patterns as they go because role models and precedents for equality in the work-family relationships of married couples with children are largely lacking. For the men there would seem to be less discontinuity.

The level of analysis which we have conducted is "microsociological" in that we have concentrated on the small innovating units—the

[11]It seems to be generally assumed that technological sub-systems not only change more rapidly than socio-cultural sub-systems, but that they are "open ended." That is, they can change in ways that open up new possibilities never before experienced, e.g. for increased speed, power, and control over nature. At the socio-cultural level there seems to be a much greater assumption that socio-cultural changes are limited by the relatively unchanging biological condition of men.

dual-career partnership family. Though our study does not attempt to encompass a cross-section of such units so as to estimate the prevalence of each of the patterns observed, we believe that it covers a sufficiently broad range of examples to provide insight into some major contemporary processes of change. Because each of the units functions in a larger cultural system of norms and values and in a larger social system of relationships and interactions, the innovating patterns which are attempted may be seen as going "against the grain" of society in various ways. As society itself is changing, the strains outlined in this paper are not presented as permanent or intrinsic in the dual-career family situation but rather a matter of contemporary concern. The contemporary concern has policy implications but looking at the issue more theoretically we suggest that the analysis of structural sources of stress are relevant for social change. In Goode's terms, each couple strikes a series of "role bargains" to reduce or otherwise deal with the strains and dilemmas they experience (Goode, 1962). Taken altogether, these role bargains form new structures, which are more collaborative in the sense described for post-industrial society as a whole by Trist (1968).

The structures evolved by dual-career families of the type studied are more than of private interest. These are couples who are unusually visible and articulate. They provide models for a wide range of less distinguished members of the society and may be seen in varying degrees as exemplars, or at least 'trial balloons' for those who follow. In addition, they tend to participate in more complex and dispersed clusters of relationships (Trist, 1968).

In the immediate situation, the new behavioural models which are evolved may be evaluated in various ways. Personal satisfaction is a dimension which provides one element of evaluation but which is too diffuse and complex for our current form of analysis. It would involve matching specific personality constellations to the different structural models. For the present, a structural form of analysis is suggested. Structural sources of stress may be detected and the consequent patterns of strain described. Individual differences in capacity to absorb the strains will affect satisfaction but, as indicated, we do not go to this level here. Within limits, the economic metaphor of a cost-benefit analysis is useful. Each family works out for itself whether the "costs" of pursuing the variant life career of a dual-career family—in any of its various forms—is worth it to them in relation to the "benefits" they derive.

These costs and benefits may be summarised for the couples studied in relation to five structural dimensions of stress.

Role Overloads: Dual-career families benefit in taking on an additional set of occupational roles by the increased family income, the stimulation and personal development afforded the wife, her utilisation of her training, the closer relationship between father and the children, and so on. These benefits, which are consistent with the values of post-industrial society, are realised at the cost of taxing the energies of both members through role overloads and possibly restricting of the husband's career participation. The couples generally tend to reduce the overload effect by curtailing non-essential, particularly leisure and social, activities.

NORMATIVE DILEMMAS: These dilemmas arise through the discontinuities in ideology as between educational and adult roles, producing strains. One way of reducing this kind of strain is to extrapolate the earlier role ideals into the later behaviour—continuing the wife's career development. This leads to benefits for the woman (and indirectly for the husband) of a sense of integrity, of feeling "true to oneself," as distinct from having to "put the lid on" or to compromise one's ideals or waste one's capacities. This may be accomplished, however, at the "cost" of diverging from the norms and expectations representing the other side of the dilemma—the more traditional female role norms, holding it right and proper for a woman to be at home looking after her family. The strains, both intra-psychically and in significant social relationships, are dealt with by various devices of insulation and compartmentalisation.

MAINTENANCE OF PERSONAL IDENTITY: This becomes a problem when one departs from the standard patterns of behaviour that are institutionally supported in the traditional role structures. Where men and women continue to pursue their personal development through the same rather than different channels of roles with their different norms and sanctions, they may find themselves confronting the issue of how to maintain their distinct identity. The "benefits" of equal participation are in terms of fairness and equity in access to society's valued resources. The "costs" may entail competitive rivalries and their concomitants, interpersonal discord, difficulties in sexual relations, and so on. The couples studied seemed to deal with the identity issue by constructing (in their psychic and interpersonal world of reality) a "tension line" which demarcates areas within which they feel they can comfortably function as separate and distinct individuals.

THE SOCIAL NETWORK: These dilemmas provide structured sources of strain in reconciling obligations (e.g. in kinship relations) with desires (e.g. in friendship relations) and responsibilities (e.g. in erecting a network of effective service relationships), all in the face of overloads in the work and family role systems. The "benefits" of a fairly decisive limitation on network relationships and concentration of them on gratifying components (e.g. by eliminating unwanted relationships, delegating obligations to service personnel, etc.) may be reckoned in comfort and an enhanced capacity to function and develop in work and family roles. On the other hand, the process of network construction which this tends to represent may lead to feelings of guilt by the individual, and resentment by others, and these must be reckoned among the 'costs'.

ROLE-CYCLING: The husband and wife in the dual-career family are involved in three role systems: the work system of each spouse (except where they are partners, in which case the two work systems are merged) and the family system which they share. Each system makes different demands according to the position of the role in the system, and each role makes different demands on the individual according to phase. The tendency for heavy demands to be made on people in work roles is when working upward toward senior positions (more than once one actually reaches an established senior role) and within roles shortly after the initial ("honeymoon") period when the new structure of person-in-role is being worked out. In the family, the heaviest strain is at the time of having young children of pre-school age. There are different costs and benefits according to what the correspondence is between the peak demands on roles in these three spheres. If the couple arranges their lives so as to have the family role demands "peak" first, they may miss opportunities for career advancement. If they allow the two career role strains to "peak" first, they may pay the costs in family life of the additional strains imposed through fatigue as they are older, and a greater age gap between themselves and their children. If one spouse "peaks" while the other defers heavy involvement, the one that defers may have to pay a price in career development as well as perhaps bear a heavier brunt of family role strains. This is, obviously, an over-simplified picture and many combinations are possible, but the issue of role-cycling and the "fits" in the family among the various role cycles is only beginning to be understood (Rossi, 1968).

Finally, we are concerned with indicating briefly what social changes may facilitate diffusion of the dual-career family structure. The policy implications of these considerations are apparent but will not be dealt with in depth here. It is suggested that the dual-career family structure is likely to become more prevalent in our society to the extent that three arenas of change provide compatible arrays of factors to support the diffusion of the pattern:

the arena of work role relationships,
the arena of domestic role relationships, and
the arena of the built environment.

Many occupational groups and organisations are working toward a reduction of the crude forms of discrimination linked to archaic sex-role stereotypes. The issues of similarity or differences between men's and women's capacities is increasingly seen as part of the more general issue of individual differences, and the entire range of jobs in the world of work is becoming increasingly open to women on an equal basis with men. However, the capacity of women, particularly married women with children, to grasp the increasingly available opportunities and to exercise to their fullest capacities the available career roles will depend on the degree to which these roles can be made compatible with the demands of womens' other roles. Many current ways of organising the world of work are not intrinsically necessary and yet make participation difficult for women because of being based on "male" assumptions about times of accessibility, etc.

The arena of domestic role relationships, similarly, will provide a set of factors affecting the diffusion of the dual-career pattern. The greater diffusion will depend on the extent to which husbands as well as wives re-define the marital role relationship so as to give explicit recognition to the inter-connectedness of domestic and occupational roles. If the pursuit of a career by the wife is to become a possibility for more than the "amazons" of this world, it will depend on men having an attitude more supportive than "it's all right so long as it doesn't affect me." The whole area of child-care seems to be the most important element in this constellation of roles. To the extent that husbands can participate more in child care and that auxiliary roles and arrangements are developed, the pattern may diffuse more.

The "built-environment" can be expected to play an important part in the extent to which the dual-career family becomes more viable and pervasive in future. This seems to be most relevant in two areas: the journey to work and the pooling of services in the areas of domestic arrangements. The tendency following the industrial revolution to remove the work-place as well as the husband from the home is no longer as relevant given the more agreeable general conditions of work. To the extent that new complexes of living bring work and family into more easy interplay, as in some of the new towns organized with industry as well as housing in mind, the impediment of the arduous journey to work now placed on women and men and contributing to their role overloads, will be diminished. If housing developments are orientated in the future to the sharing of domestic care facilities—cleaning, food buying and preparation, child-care etc.—rather than simply multiplying individual living units as seems to be the present tendency, a greater diffusion of the pattern is possible. New mixtures of individualism and communalism may be expected in post-industrial society, with an increase in the latter for the Western countries (Bell, 1967).

The situation, in summary, is that the trend toward cultural norms which are compatible with the dual-career family seems to be well underway. In many instances the mono-career family structure will be chosen for self-expressive rather than traditional reasons. However, where there is the wish to choose the dual-career structure and there are normative conflicts these are partly due, in our view, to cultural lag and partly to defensive reactions from people in the environment who have not been able to succeed in evolving a dual-career family on a microsociological level. The structural changes which are necessary to fully implement these changes are not yet in effect, particularly in the areas of organization of work, organization of domestic role relationships, and the conception of the built-environment.

In conclusion, what is being suggested is that the availability of these facilities will be important in making it possible for individual families to have a choice of potential arrangements. It is not implied that the dual-career family is advocated as a universal pattern.

REFERENCES

Babchuk, N. & Bates, A.P. (1963). "The primary relations of middle class couples: a study in male dominance," *Amer. Socio. Rev. 28.*

Baude, A., & Holmberg, Per. (1967). The position of men and women in the labour market, in Dahlstrom, E. (ed). *The changing roles of men and women.* London: Duckworth.

Bell, C. (1968). Mobility and the middle class extended family. *Sociology 2* No. 2 (May, 1968).

Bell, D. (1967). Notes on the post-industrial society (I & II). *The Public Interest* Nos. 6 & 7.

Bott, E. (1957). *Family and social network.* London: Tavistock Publications.

Dahlstrom, E. (1962). *The changing roles of men and women.* London: G. Duckworth.

Duvall, E.M. (1957). *Family development.* Philadelphia: Lippincott. (revised 1962).

Fogarty, M., Rapoport, R.N., & Rapoport, Rhona (1967). *Women and top jobs.* London: Political and Economic Planning (P.E.P.).

Fried, M. (1963). Mourning for a lost home, in Duhl, L. (ed). *The urban conditions,* New York: Basic Books.

Gans, H. (1965). *The urban villagers.* New York: Free Press.

Gavron, H. (1966). *The captive wife.* London: Routledge & Kegan Paul.

Goode, W.J. (1962). Theory of role strain. *Amer. Sociol. Rev. 25*

Goode, W.J. (1963). *World revolutions and family patterns.* New York: Free Press.

Goode, W.J. (1966). Family patterns and human rights, *Int. J. Soc. Sci. No. 1.*

Heiskanen, V.S. & Haavio-Manilla, E. (1967). The position of women in society: formal ideology and everyday ethic. *Social Service Information, 6,* (December, 1967).

Hill, R.L. & Hansen, D.A. (1960). The identification of conceptual framework utilised in family study. *Marriage and Family Living. 22,* 229-311.

Hunt, A. (1968). *Survey of women's employment.* Government Social Survey. *55.379.* (March, 1968).

International Labour Organization. (Yearbooks of Labour Statistics 1958 & 1967).
Jaques, E. (1965). Death and the midlife crisis. *Int. J. Psychoanal. 46,* 502-514.
Jefferys, M. & Elliott, P.M. (1966). *Women in medicine.* Office of Health Economics. London.
Knoblochova, J. & Knobloch, F. (1965). Family psychotherapy In World Health Organisation. *Aspects of family mental health.* Public Health Papers, *28.* Geneva.
Komarovsky, M. (1940). *The unemployed man and his family.* New York: Dryden Press.
Laumann, E.O. Friends of urban men. (1968) mimeo. *Sociometry* (forthcoming).
Lazersfeld, P.G. & Merton, R. (1954). Friendship as a social process. In M. Bergerstal (ed). *Freedom and control in modern society.* New York.
Leach, E. (1968). *A runaway world.* Oxford University Press.
Litwak, E. (1960). Occupational mobility and extended family cohesion. *Amer. Sociol. Rev. 25.*
Martin, F. & Smith, H. (1968). Women in architecture. Political and Economic Planning (P.E.P.) Mimeo Memo. 1068.
Mogey, J. (1963). *Family and neighborhood.* Leiden: Bull.
Moore, T. (1964). Children of full-time and part-time working mothers. *Interna. Journ. of Soc. Psychiat.* (Special Congress Issue No. 2.)
Myrdal, A. & Klein, V. (1956). *Woman's two roles, home and work,* London: Routledge & Kegan Paul.
Nye, N.I., & Hoffman, L.W. (1963). *The employed mother in America.* Chicago: Rand McNally.
Parsons, T. (1943). The kinship system of the contemporary United States. *American Anthropologist, 45,* No. 1.
Parsons, T. & Bales, R.F. (1955). *Family Socialization and Interaction Process.* Glencoe, Ill.: The Free Press.
Rapoport, Rhona. (1963). Normal crisis, family structure and mental health *Family Process, 2.*
Rapoport, Rhona & Rapoport, R.N. (1964). New light on the honeymoon. *Hum. Relat. 17*(1).
Rapoport, R.N. & Rapoport, Rhona. (1966). *Work and family in contemporary Society. Amer. Soc. Rev. 30,* 381-94.
Riesman, D. (1965). Some dilemmas of women's education. *The Educational Record.* Washington.
Robbins. (1961-63). *Report on higher education.* H.M.S.O., 1961-63.
Rodgers, R.H. (1964). Toward a theory of family development *Journal of Marriage and the Family,* August, 1964.
Rossi, A. (1964). Equality between the sexes: an immodest proposal. *Daedalus,* Spring, 1964.
Rossi, A. (1968). Transition to parenthood. *Journal of Marriage and the Family, 30 No. 1.*
Rossi, A. (1968). *Head and heart,* manuscript in preparation.
Sokolowska, M. (1963). The household; unknown working environment. *Studia Socjologicze, 3*(10), pp. 161-182. M. Sokolowska (ed.). Warsaw: Ksiazka and Wiedza.
Sommerkorn, I. (1966). The position of women in the university teaching profession in England. University of London Ph.D. Thesis.
Trist, E. (1968). Urban North America: the challenge of the next thirty years. Keynote address to the Annual Conference of the Town Planning Institute of Canada, June, 1968. Tavistock Institute, H.R.C. Document 153.

Turner, R. (1964). *The social context of ambition.* San Francisco: Chandler.
Weber, M. (1947). *The theory of social and economic organisation.* London: Hodge.
Willmott, P. (1968). The influence of some social trends of regional planning. Mimeo. Centre for Community Studies.
Wrochno, K. (1966). Women in directing positions about themselves. *Kobieta* Wspolczesna.
Young, M. & Willmott, P. (1957). *Family and kinship in East London.* London: Routledge & Kegan Paul.

Section VII

FACILITATING WOMEN'S CAREER DEVELOPMENT

FROM the standpoint of the helping professional, all of the issues and concerns mentioned in the earlier chapters crystallize around one problem: How do we intervene to facilitate the optimal career development of each individual woman? Our view is that there is no single clear-cut prescription through which this goal can be accomplished. The factors that operate to inhibit the full development of women in our society are, as we have seen, multiple in nature; our efforts to help need to be delivered in a variety of settings, modes, and systems. Direct one-to-one counseling is only one approach. Basic changes in curriculum in our schools, consultation with teachers and parents, improved training programs for educators and other socialization agents, and basic reforms in business, industry, government, and other social institutions all represent avenues for change that must be explored. The trends toward developmental rather than only crisis counseling and toward counselor involvement in the mainstream of curriculum have important implications for expanding career options for women.

That young women and men need and want more help in career planning than they are getting has been well documented in a nationwide study (Prediger, Roth, and Noeth, 1974). In their study of 32,000 high school students, the investigators found significant differences in female and male occupational goals which have important implications for counselors. The kinds of help that counselors provide and the biases they bring with them to the counseling role also have been summarized by Guttman (1974).

In the first chapter in this section, Hansen outlines a unified curriculum framework through which counselors in collaboration with teachers can implement systemmatic career education programs designed to facilitate the optimal career development of each girl and boy. Drawing from a number of career development theorists and developmental psychologists, Hansen describes a set of vocational development tasks (later called management tasks) which need to be progressively mastered through the primary, intermediate, junior, and senior high years. This framework is firmly based on the assumption that career development is self-development over the life span and must focus on the issues of self-concept, marriage-career conflict and commitment, and civic and leisure pursuits, as well as occupational choice. Broad scale developmental interventions carefully planned to operate throughout the childhood and adolescent years probably offer our best hope for optimizing the career development of females. Given the powerful socialization process that channels women into traditional roles (see Section III), we cannot expect women to choose from the full range of occupational and life-style options without providing broad and early interventions which continue into mature adulthood.

The second chapter, by Harmon, focuses upon career counseling as an intervention that can be employed at crucial points in the development of women. After reviewing the literature on female career development, she concludes that women's career decisions are influenced primarily by external variables, although internal determinants are more likely to lead to satisfaction. In an intriguing analysis, Harmon draws on Maslow's hierarchy of needs to explain vocational behavior of women. For many women, physiological and safety needs are met through the association with a husband or father whose labor assures that her needs will be met. These women may not believe that they can independently gratify their own needs. This idea is related to Lipman-Blumen and Leavitt's concept of vicarious achievement. Maslow's framework is also useful in looking at the fear of loss of affiliation and fear of success phenomenon; women may have to compromise need for self-esteem in order to obtain love and esteem from others. Both esteem and love needs have to be met before self-actualization can occur. Unfortunately, many women do not reach this stage because they are conflicted about their love and esteem needs or even fixated at the level of physiological and safety needs.

Harmon questions whether or not women are prepared for career planning and decision making. She points out that it is necessary to assess the developmental level of each client and begin counseling at that stage.

Leonard, Hansen, and Knefelkamp discuss issues of unequal treatment of females in counselor preparation programs in a context which could be equally useful in analyzing other academic settings and departments. Using Blocher's (1974) process model for bringing about change in human systems, they apply the model to case studies of female experiences in graduate preparation programs. The article is unique in its application of systems change theory to common problems of women students in professional programs in higher education.

In the last chapter, Astin points to the role of continuing education in helping adult women change the direction and focus of their lives. As has been discussed in other parts of this volume, the point in the life cycle when children mature is a point at which many women desire redirection, accomplishment, and new work orientation. Continuing Education for Women (CEW) programs were developed to facilitate the entry or reentry of women past the traditional age of eighteen into the academic world. These programs were founded on the assumptions that learning can take place at any time and that education can be distributed over the life span, permitting the leisure, work, family, and educational roles to alternate or occur concurrently.

Astin studied the educational and occupational aspirations, self-perceptions, and family reactions of women participating in fifteen diverse CEW programs. The goals and backgrounds of women in these programs are varied, although some typical reasons for entering CEW programs include gaining or updating marketable skills, making midlife career changes, and searching for identity. Reentering the academic world can lead to institutional barriers and personal problems such as lack of confidence, time management, and guilt about diverting time and attention from the homemaker role. Support services within CEW programs must help women make the transition to new roles and manage stress accompanying the increased number of roles as well as help individuals determine direction.

One other point brought up by Astin deserves comment. It has been stated in other parts of this text that institutions need to change to better respond to the needs of the individual with multiple and complex roles. Within many CEW programs, beginning attempts at reorganization have been made. For example, time and place constraints have been restructured. The traditional fifty minute class which meets three times weekly has become a three-hour, once-a-week sequence. Also, available spaces in local churches or schools have been utilized to minimize transportation difficulties.

It is essential that counselors and others concerned with the career development of women examine their own biases and assumptions and rid themselves of stereotyped thinking. There is some evidence that counselors do stereotype work along male and female dimensions and have limited perceptions of the dual or multiple roles that many women can and must play. The issue of counselor bias is discussed briefly by both Hansen and Harmon. The chapter by Schlossberg and Pietrofesa included in Section III provides a more focused treatment of this issue.

REFERENCES

Blocher, D.H. *Developmental Counseling. 2nd ed.* New York: Ronald Press, 1974, chapter 16 pp. 291-308.

Guttman, M.A. Counselor bias in vocational guidance. *In Women and ACES: Perspective and Issues.* Washington, D.C.: Association for Counselor Education and Supervision. Muncie, Indiana: Accelerated Development Press, Inc., 1974.

Prediger, D., Roth, J., & Noeth, R. Career development of youth: a nationwide study. *Personnel and Guidance Journal,* October 1974, *53*(2), 97-104.

Chapter 26

PROMOTING FEMALE GROWTH THROUGH A CAREER DEVELOPMENT CURRICULUM

L. SUNNY HANSEN

THAT American girls and women need help at all stages of their lives in acquiring knowledge both about self and about the increasing range of options available to maximize their career opportunities has been clearly established. If they are going to "see things steadily and see them whole" through integrating their new awareness and information into more satisfying career decisions, they need more systematic help in the process.

How can counselors and other human services workers become catalysts for the positive growth of women? What can they do to intervene at various developmental stages of women's lives to facilitate that growth? It is the position of this chapter that counselor preparation programs, as well as other psychological training programs, ought to provide theoretical models and practical interventions for those in training to learn to become more effective in meeting the special needs of females of all ages. What follows is a description of a career development conceptual framework for curriculum through which counselors especially can facilitate female growth. It requires counselors to work with curriculum and consult with teachers, as well as to examine and modify their counseling techniques.

Rationale

The data on the increasing participation of women in activities outside the home are well known. The decline of motherhood as a full-time occupation is not something created by the women's movement but a phenomenon resulting from a variety of forces in society. Some of these include the domestic labor-saving devices made possible by technology; population control, with increasing couples deciding not to have children or only one or two; the increase in more human-ized day care centers; the accent on more part-time jobs, flexible schedules, and shared positions; the acknowledgement and greater acceptance of various family and career patterns and life styles; federal legislation and regulations opening up new opportunities for women; and perhaps most important, the new assertiveness and sense of personhood of women seeking and finding paths for their talents and abilities and greater meaning in their lives.

That women should have opportunities in whatever directions their potentials, motivations, circumstances, and goals indicate seems to be finally gaining greater acceptance as a reasonable goal. While the barriers to full equality for women in the economy have been increasingly acknowledged in the past decade, the psychological barriers to their growth and development have been less well-known. There is an increasing body of knowledge which speaks especially to counselors and counselor educators and suggests some directions in which they—as facilitators of human growth and development—should be moving. While space does not allow a comprehensive examination of the literature here, a brief summary of some of the more pertinent studies follows. Of particular relevance to career development are the studies on sex-role socialization, female aspirations, self-concepts, and career patterns.

That children are exposed in the early years to the female role as a passive, indoor housekeeper and to the male role as an active earner and breadwinner has been well documented (Hochschild, 1973; Weitzman, 1972; Hartley, 1960; Maccoby, 1966). Matthews and Tiedeman (1964) found that girls who had expressed strong vocational goals in the junior high had shifted to marriage goals in the senior high, although a more recent study by Rand and Miller (1972) suggested that a new "cultural imperative" for women was being perceived by females in junior high, senior high, and college—that of the dual role of career and marriage. Some studies have cited females' lack of vocational goals and realistic planning (Lewis, 1965; Zytowski, 1969; Rapoza and Blocher, 1976) though other recent studies reveal girls as showing more concern for career planning and wanting more control over their own lives (Flanagan and Jung, 1971). Several studies of female self concepts indicate that girls tend to devalue themselves (Goldberg, 1968; Smith, 1939; Rosenkrantz, 1968) and that they experience role conflict and "fear of success" in thinking about careers (Horner, 1968). While the evidence on female self-concepts is still conflicting, these studies seem to suggest a number of factors which mitigate against women feeling very good about themselves as achieving, motivated, participating human beings and, instead of freeing them to make choices, lead them to expect and accept the traditional role.

Women in the Work Force

Yet the present and projected facts about women in the work force suggest some new realities. While there are many myths about American working women, there is much data available about the nature and extent of women's participation in education and work (Streidl, 1972), facts which should be known by counselors, counselor educators, and other human services workers. It is well-known, for example, that women comprise one third of the labor force; that 42 percent of all women are working, over half of them married; that most women work for economic reasons; that the average woman will have from 25 to 35 working years after her children (if she has them) are in school; that three out of four of the intellectually qualified female high school graduates do not enter college; that by the ninth grade 25 percent of the boys but only 3 percent of the girls are considering careers in science or engineering; that women earn only one in ten of doctoral degrees; that they are concentrated in a limited group of occupations, namely secretary, retail clerk, elementary teacher, household worker, bookkeeper, waitress and nurse; and that they have been discriminated against in hiring, promotion, and salaries, will have to wait longer for promotion, and make three fifths of what a man makes for equal training and work (Crowley et al., 1973; Streidl, 1972). Thus, in addition to the psychological barriers which have thwarted women from being successful and effective participants, there are very real economic ones which keep them in lower level and sometimes dead-end jobs that deflate rather than enhance their self-image (Work in America, 1973).

Career Development of Women

Concern for women's career development is not a movement to get every woman into the labor force. Rather, it is concern for her uniqueness and individuality as a person and for her right to have some freedom of choice in both her personal and professional work life. It is a concern about the overwhelmingly subordinate nature of women's roles—as nurses rather than doctors, as teachers rather than principals, as assembly workers instead of supervisors, as secretaries rather than bosses, as telephone operators rather than telephone repair workers, as administrative assistants rather than deans. It is concern about the ancillary nature of women's occupations, with only infinitesimal numbers in medicine, engineering, management, and finance. It is concern about the passivity and dependence that keep her from finding room at the top of a competitive, aggressive world and for her lack of preparedness to deal with that organizational world (Robie, 1972). It is concern about not only fear of success (which may have been grossly overemphasized) but fear of competency and fear of loss of affiliation that keeps women from maximizing their potentials and from making what Tyler (1972) calls first-class rather than second-class contributions to society. It is concern about the complexity of demands, pressures, and conflicts facing women at different stages of their lives and the limited reward system which denies them the range of rewards and options available to men. Most important, it is concern about the increasingly documented negative self-images of women that result in denigration, depression and low motivation and keep them from developing and utilizing their potentials.

While it is true that most of the career development theory and research has been based on males, there have been modest attempts to postulate a theory for women. There is agreement that women's patterns in multiple ways differ not only from those of men but also from those of other women (Werner, 1969; Wolfson, 1972). For example, because of the traditional focus on marriage, the woman typically has moved from student to wife, mother, and employee, usually in that order; the man has moved from student to employee, husband, and father, usually in that order. Among those who have attempted to describe a theory of women's career development are Ginzberg, Super, Anastasi, Psathas, and Zytowski. Their formulations are briefly described below.

Ginzberg (1966) suggested three life style directions for women: the traditional (home, husband, and children-oriented); the transitional (combining home and job orientation in a casual, unplanned way); and innovative (actively planning and preparing for a home-job combination with a serious career commitment).

Super (1957), in his "logical scheme" of women's career patterns, prefaced his scheme with "Woman's role as childbearer makes her the keystone of the home and therefore gives homemaking a central place in her career." He then described seven patterns: (1) Stable homemaking, (2) Conventional, (3) Stable working, (4) Double-track pattern, (5) Interrupted, (6) Unstable, and (7) Multiple trial. In spite of his prescriptive statement, Super's classification was significant in that it was the first time any vocational theorist directed his attention toward female participation in the work world (Wolfson, 1972).

Anastasi (1969) assumed that women could follow a variety of patterns and used socioeconomic divisions to describe the following female careers: (1) Blue-collar, (2) Active volunteer; (3) Interim job; (4) Late-blooming career, and (5) Double-life pattern.

Zytowski (1969), assuming also that homemaker is the modal role, outlined a "contribution toward a theory of women's vocational development," characterized by three factors: (1) age of entry into an occupation; (2) span of participation (how long she continues to work); and (3) degree of participation (type of work). Combinations of these elements, he suggested, yield three different vocational patterns: (1) mild vocational—very early or late entry, brief span, and low participation; (2) moderate vocational—early entry, lengthy span, low degree of participation or multiple entries; and (3) unusual vocational—early entry, lengthy or uninterrupted span, and high degree of participation. (This latter fits the stereotype that females with high career commitment and achievement motivation are "odd" or "unusual"). He indicated that one's pattern of vocational participation is determined jointly by one's own preferences and by a combination of internal and external factors (Wolfson, 1972).

Sociologist Psathas (1968) emphasized the limiting influence of cultural and situational factors, chance elements, and social class. He also suggested that woman's vocational choice is not made independent from the role of wife and mother. While these are all partial theories of single aspects of women's career development and tend to give primacy to the homemaker role, they are significant in that they acknowledge the fact that women differ and indeed do have different life patterns. In spite of their uniqueness, however, the majority of women (78 percent) end up in virtually the same role (Streidl, 1972).

Counselors and Women

Counselors have come under frequent criticism for blocking development of women both through omission and commission. While there is a need for more careful research on counselor attitudes toward and impact on women's development, a few studies exist. Engelhard (1969), in a study of 871 Minnesota counselors, sought to determine differences between groups of counselors in their alignment on a traditional-through-emergent continuum expressing attitudes toward women's roles. She found (1) Female counselors were more emergent (liberal) than male counselors; (2) Married women counselors were most emergent, single men least emergent; (3) Male counselors with working wives were more emergent (tended to confirm their own circumstance); (4) Counselors in urban settings were more emergent than out-state counselors; and (5) Younger counselors were *not* more emergent than older counselors. The 21 to 30 age group were least emergent, over 51 most emergent (Engelhard, 1969). A report by the Citizens' Advisory Council on the Status of Women cited evidence of counselor sexism (1972). Guttman (1974) also summarized the then extant literature on counselor bias. The most encouraging data on changing counselor roles are reported in Project TALENT students from 1960-70 where it was found that (1) 67 percent of the adolescent girls were discussing post–high school plans with a counselor and (2) the percentages seriously examining vocational plans increased over a ten-year period (Flanagan and Jung, 1971). The burgeoning of special journal issues on counseling women attests to the growing awareness and concern of counselors and psychologists in this area (Fitzgerald and Harmon, 1973; Birk and Tanney, 1976).

But the question still remains, how can counselors better facilitate woman's career development? The rest of this chapter suggests some ways in which counselors can intervene systematically through curriculum and through counseling.

A CAREER DEVELOPMENT CONCEPTUAL FRAMEWORK

Utilizing a career development framework for facilitating women's growth seems totally appropriate if one accepts the broad definition, presented here, of career development as self development over the life span.[1] This model assumes that career development is self development (not merely job choice) and, as Super (1957) suggests, a process of developing and implementing a self-concept, with satisfaction to self and benefit to society. Career development is seen as a continuous, lifelong process, conscious and unconscious, from preschool to old age, with various developmental stages. It is seen as the sequence of positions one holds in a lifetime, the various choices and decisions one makes to implement a life style, and the ways in which work and leisure fit in with the kind of person one perceives oneself to be. This definition assumes that consideration of career is intimately related to family roles and patterns and to matters of employment-marriage choices and commitments. As is evident, it draws from a number of career development theorists and developmental psychologists. It includes such tasks as developing positive self-concepts, gaining control over one's life, and maximizing vocational possibilities; such goals as gaining self-awareness, occupational-educational informatoin, knowledge about the psychosocial aspects and impacts of work environments, employability skills, interpersonal skills, and a sense of planfulness (Tennyson, Hansen, Klaurens, 1970). While many parts of it apply to both women and men, the focus here is on women.

The University of Minnesota Career Development Curriculum (CDC) is a comprehensive unified curriculum model, K-12, to be used by counselors and teachers in implementing career education programs. The interdisciplinary staff has refined a set of vocational development, or, more appropriately, *career management*, tasks (tasks to be mastered progressively at different stages of the human life cycle) for the primary, intermediate, junior high, and senior high years. They have identified performance objectives (desired outcomes) ap-

[1]The framework presented in this chapter is an adaptation of a model developed jointly by the author, Mary Klaurens, W. Wesley Tennyson, and Mary Antholz in the Departments of Distributive Education and Counseling Psychology, College of Education, University of Minnesota and published by the Minnesota Department of Education (Tennyson et al., 1975).

propriate for the various vocational life stages and suggested enabling objectives (means) to reach the performance objectives. Seven Learning Opportunities Packages (LOPs) for use by senior high teachers and three for junior high teachers have been created. Although all of the packages are intended for all students, one which deals directly with the role and status of women is *Women and the World of Work* (Thoni et al., 1972). The CDC gives a useful framework for more systematic, as opposed to fragmented, approaches to career development.

Below is a special portion of the Career Development Curriculum model which is concerned primarily with women's development. It provides a vehicle through which counselors can work with teachers in creating curriculum experiences to facilitate female growth. It is a conceptual framework of sequential, developmental experiences for girls and boys from kindergarten through senior high. The objectives serve only as a guide from which creative teachers, counselors, and others can develop varied experiences to meet the needs of their particular students. Some activities might be integrated into regular subjects and some might require special courses, but it is intended that these would not be added on but infused into the regular curriculum. While these objectives are an integral part of a broader curricular framework concerned with human development, they could stand alone as a conceptual base for developing implementation strategies related to the special needs of women. Although there are many innovative women's programs, units, and courses emerging throughout the country at various levels of the school system, few have attempted to build their efforts around a systematic theoretical framework of career development. The following is such an attempt: the italicized phrases are the refined developmental tasks; the first indentation is the performance objective; and the second indentation is the enabling objective, i.e. the means to achieve the performance objective.

Objectives for Career Development Curriculum, K-12, Relating to Emerging Life Patterns of Women[2]

Primary Years (K-3)

Awareness of Self

Describes how health may affect work performance or be affected by it.

Identifies physical and mental abilities required by different occupations.

Acquiring a Sense of Control over One's Life

Identifies manipulative abilities that have relevance for work.

[2]These objectives have now been incorporated into the Career Development Curriculum.

Identifies ways in which the child is like workers he/she knows.

Identifies men and women who have entered and been successful in nontraditional occupations.

Acquiring Knowledge About Workers

Increases the range of workers about whom one has knowledge.

Identifies occupations which have been created in the last ten years.

Ability to Present Oneself Objectively

Shows a genuine concern for coworkers and expresses a shared responsibility for success or failure of the work group.

Describes how the activities of members in different families can affect the family unit.

Acquiring Respect for Other People and the Work They Do

Describes how the work of women is as important as the work of men.

Describes how the contribution of individuals both inside and outside the home is important.

Intermediate Years (4-6)

Developing a Positive Self Concept

Describes how one perceives self in terms of interests, abilities, values, and goals.

Describes ways in which one sees self as similar to or different from workers in occupations which traditionally have been stereotyped by sex.

Identifies own values as they relate to work situations.

Identifies values of workers in occupations which traditionally have been stereotyped by sex.

Acquiring the Discipline of Work

Demonstrates ability to organize self and situation in order to accomplish a variety of tasks.

Sets priorities for tasks to be done and allocates time.

Assesses energy and time required to complete a series of tasks within a given period and checks it out.

Identification with the Concept of Work as a Valued Institution

Describes how one's interests relate to broad occupational areas.

Identifies women and men with different work values.

Increasing Knowledge About Workers

Studies workers in various occupations to learn their satisfactions and dissatisfactions

Identifies women and men in new or unusual occupations which one would like to learn more about.

Identifies the reasons why many women will need the stimulation and rewards of a work role in addition to a family role.

Identifies life patterns of women and men which are different from the traditional societal one.

Identifies family patterns in which women and men have equal roles in work and in home management.

Describes the changing roles of women in the labor force.

Lists the advantages and disadvantages of mothers working outside the home.

Examines satisfactions of women who are not working outside the home.

Examines satisfactions of women who are working outside the home.

Increasing Interpersonal Skills

Describes how a person's welfare is dependent upon the well-being of all people in society.

Identifies clubs, organizations, and activities within the present and future school setting that might provide work-related experiences.

Increasing Ability to Present Oneself Objectively

Copes with authority exercised by others in the work environment in ways which lead to effective achievement of the task.

Valuing Human Dignity

Describes how one can contribute to society now.

Describes how work in America can help to overcome social problems which confront society today.

Identifies occupations in which women and men may help solve a major social problem.

Identifies community needs which might be met through creation of new jobs.

Junior High Years (7-9)

Clarification of a Self Concept

Describes own values as they relate to occupations, work situations, and personal work behavior.

Identifies compromises a woman or man may have to make in choosing to pursue an occupation.

Identifies ways in which one performs work roles at home that satisfy needs of the family.

Predicts and gives supporting evidence for the likelihood of achieving one's occupational goals.

Identifies societal barriers which may hinder achievement of one's occupational goals.

Identifies ways in which different work and family patterns may require different kinds and amounts of energy, participation, motivation, and talent.

Assumption of Responsibility for Vocational Planning

Describes how management of personal resources (talents, time, money) affects one's way of life and achievement of life goals.

Relates personal abilities, energies, goals, motivations, tastes, and circumstances to a variety of life patterns.

Demonstrates a commitment to the idea that one should have a plan for vocational-educational life.

Describes implications of a tentative plan for other aspects of life (marriage, family, leisure, community, etc.).

Plans current school experience so that it fits into the pursuit of one's occupational goals.

Describes vocational and avocational implications of subjects he or she is taking.

Acquires experience in a variety of tasks, including those typically stereotyped by one's sex.

Formulation of Tentative Career Goals

Identifies personal needs and sources of satisfaction which one should consider in planning a career.

Identifies from a variety of life styles those which at present appear to be most compatible with the kind of person one sees oneself to be.

Identifies personal goals or values which might be satisfied through a combination of work, community, social, and family roles.

Acquiring Knowledge of Occupations and Work Settings

Increases the range of occupations of which one has knowledge and examines their functions and requirements.

Identifies occupations which have been created in the last decade to help solve society's problems.

Identifies occupational areas increasingly open to both women and men.

Gathers information concerning the factors necessary for success on a job.

Identifies discriminatory practices in employment which may affect success in preferred occupations.

Describes those factors beyond one's control which operate within the modern work world to stimulate or retard vocational opportunities.

Describes sex stereotypes which may limit the opportunities for women and men in certain occupations.

Describes special problems of minorities and women in relation to power and authority.

Acquiring Knowledge of Educational and Vocational Resources

Identifies and utilizes those resources available for gathering information about occupational characteristics.

Identifies individuals in nontraditional occupations or work roles who might be information resources or role models.

Identifies and utilizes appropriate criteria for evaluating occupational information.

Identifies attitudes of adults (parents, teachers, counselors, relatives, etc.) which influence occupational opportunity.

Studies relationship between education and occupation.

Describes a strategy for career decision-making.

Identifies possible consequences of decisions facing one regarding senior high program.

Acquiring a Sense of Independence

Identifies those characteristics which make him or her a unique individual.

Identifies personal needs and values in relation to unique occupational preferences.

Selects from the advice given by significant others that which one can utilize in planning a career.

Identifies possible conflicts in selecting occupational goals different from the expectations of significant others.

Ranks own goal priorities in relation to goals of significant others for him or her.

Senior High Years (10-12)

Reality Testing of a Self Concept

Describes the social roles and social demands one must fulfill for successful performance in preferred occupation(s).

Describes the multiple roles one may fill and ways in which they affect and may be affected by occupational preferences.

Awareness of Preferred Life Style

Makes explicit one's own life style needs and priorities at this point in time.

Identifies several life patterns which might be followed by women.

Discusses the significance of each in regard to the personal development and family life of a woman.

Identifies from a variety of life styles those which seem most compatible with personal characteristics and needs.

Projects consequences of preferred life style on family, leisure, significant others.

Reformulation of Tentative Career Goals

Studies and projects a career plan that will enable one to pursue an occupation which will fulfill the personal needs and values one considers most important.

Describes power and authority relationships characteristic of preferred work setting and occupation.

Identifies three work environments compatible with his or her needs.

Increasing Knowledge of and Experience in Work Settings and Occupations

Describes work as a principal instrument for coping with and changing one's own environment.

Cites examples of change within the modern work society which have affected the traditional division of labor by sex.

Identifies discriminatory practices in the work environment which one might help to change.

Describes women's changing roles in the labor force.

Lists five career-family or life style patterns open to women and men.

Examines labor force data on women and men in different occupations.

Describes how the work contribution of woman is as socially significant as that of man.

Participates in and observes situations in which women are found in roles other than traditional ones.

Gathers information concerning vocational opportunities for women in various areas of work.

Clarification of the Decision-Making Process as Related to Self

Projects and describes the factors which may influence one's career decisions.

Identifies alternatives and possible outcomes of each.

Projects the potential satisfactions of preferred occupations in relation to priority values and needs.

Identifies alternate occupations if first preferences do not work out.

Commitment with Tentativeness Within a Changing World

Identifies the possible sources of the attitudes toward women held by oneself and the society in which one lives.

Reads and discusses relevant literature dealing with women, their traditional roles, and their place in the world of work.

Discovers elements within our culture which have contributed to the continuance of the traditional view of women.

Investigates the opinions that contemporary women hold of

themselves and their place in the world of work.

Identifies the changing meanings of work over time and between cultures.

Examines different career patterns of women and men and their potential effect on family patterns and life styles.

Compares work ethic at the turn of the century with contemporary work ethic(s).

Identifies the changing meanings of work in one's life in relation to other values.

Examines the extent to which one accepts the work values and career patterns of the predominant culture.

Describes the ways in which changing work and leisure values may bring about career shifts in adults.

Implications for Curriculum Change

Since the preceding is a conceptual model, the interventions have yet to be developed. It is apparent that most of the objectives are intended to be implemented through curriculum rather than through the traditional one-to-one counselor-student delivery system; some, however, might be achieved through individual and group counseling. Possible intervention strategies both through curriculum and counseling are briefly described below.

The CDC model assumes that career development is a continuing lifelong process; it also assumes that *career education,* which has become a significant national movement in education, consists of the modes used by teachers, counselors, and community to facilitate that development. In curriculum it may occur through units, courses, labs, mini-courses, learning modules, and group guidance procedures. In a creative elementary classroom, for example, Schmid (1972) uses "the teachable moment" to help her third graders become aware of sexism and sex-role stereotyping in their readers (and other curricular materials). She has girls and boys participating in such activities as baking cakes, working at the tool bench, rewriting stereotyped materials, and the like.

In a junior high English class Tallen and Allyn helped girls and boys to get more in touch with their own feelings, values, and self-concepts through study of a three-week unit focusing on Male-Female Images. Students' activities included analyzing sex-role images on TV commercials and reading short stories and female biographies and autobiographies. They became aware of barriers which limit opportunity for women through independent study of problems related to female and male development, e.g. sex stereotyping, discrimination in employment, discrimination in sports, education, law, etc. Vetter (1973) has developed and piloted a unit on "Planning Ahead for the

World of Work" for ninth grade students. Also tried out with seventh and eleventh graders, it focuses on knowledge of occupations and work settings.

In the senior high Erickson (1973) describes as one type of intervention a course on "Women in Literature" designed to promote moral development according to Kohlberg's cognitive developmental stages. Students read about women at different stages, including women such as Nora in "Doll's House" and "Antigone." The class, which served as a support group for the sophomores, juniors, and seniors enrolled, also included a career exploration phase and cross-age teaching. Other counselors have worked with English and social studies teachers in developing units or courses on "Women's Search for Identity" and "Women in History."

Besides programs in process, several educators have suggested a variety of interventions which could be tied to developmental goals. Hansen (1972) suggests that counselors work with teachers in creating, planning, and teaching courses and units at the elementary, junior high and senior high levels. Mitchell (1972) recommends that the miseducation of girls might be redressed through such career curriculum strategies as (1) examination and elimination of sex-stereotyped materials; (2) workshops for teachers; (3) curriculum content on women's studies and changing status of women, including preparing teachers to help girls develop instrumental competencies; (4) role models of achieving women brought into the elementary school; (5) parent education for improving opportunities for developing girls' potentials; and (6) special training for counselors to eliminate discrimination in educational-vocational counseling of girls. The Emma Willard Task Force on Sexism in Education presents a variety of technique and strategies (Emma Willard Task Force, 1972).

Simpson (1972) offers eleven specific steps in "Career Education—Feminine Version," including efforts by elementary educators to enlarge girls' vocational self-concepts; a variety of single and married role models as resources; new curriculum materials portraying women in a variety of constructive life styles and occupational roles; teacher orientation to vocational preparation of women; women's history courses in social studies; training programs including opportunity to prepare for dual roles; and alternatives and supplements to in-school instruction related to vocational preparation. Varenhorst et al. (1972) have developed junior and senior high materials on decision-making which help boys and girls through clarifying values; identifying, evaluating, and using information; and developing decision strategies. These could be related to a number of the developmental tasks and performance objectives and are merely illustrative of the ways in which developmental objectives can be translated into learning experiences and various kinds of intervention strategies to promote career growth.

Implications for Counseling

There are a number of trends which will help women to achieve greater equality of opportunity and greater freedom of choice. Important strides have been made through Federal legislation and executive orders and through the affirmative action plans of both industry and labor and educational institutions to change their practices regarding hiring, promotion, and status of women (General Electric, 1972). The increased consciousness is extending to men as well as to women. In Minnesota, for example, the State Board of Education has disseminated a position paper on "Eliminating Sex Bias in Education," suggesting several ways in which school boards, administrators, teachers, parents, and counselors can act to abolish sex discrimination (1972). It was not implemented, however, until a human relations consultant was hired to work directly with the schools in reducing sexism. Increasingly, women are looking to the work world as one means of possible fulfillment, and the notion of combining family and career has much greater acceptance today than in earlier times (Work in America, 1972).

The need for counselors and others to work with females and males in examining life role options and ways to achieve them is becoming increasingly important from early childhood to late adulthood. Individuals in our society need to know that roles are changing for women and men and that both can choose to have one role or many; that they may have *concurrent* roles, combining several at one time, or *sequential* roles, in which they focus more energy and time on a particular role at one life stage and then move on to another. They need to know both themselves and the options available so that they can make better decisions about which roles or combinations of roles in work and family are most satisfying and meaningful to them. They also need to know that the probability of both women and men fulfilling multiple roles is increasing.

Counselors can play a key but not the only role in counseling women and men for changing roles in society. Matthews et al. (1972) have addressed themselves to counseling girls and women over the life span and have discussed life stages, sex differences, and psychological development of girls and women from infancy through mature adulthood and old age. Tyler (1972) stresses the need for all individuals at various life stages to have counseling available regarding their many potentials. She stresses the need for help in developmental choice making and decision making, the need to learn the process of decision making in order to make a maximum contribution. Loughren and Hanson, counselors at Brooklyn Junior High in Osseo, Minnesota, developed counseling groups for girls, focusing on consciousness raising, building a support system, and providing role models.

Besides facilitating inputs into curriculum, the following are some counseling strategies of which prospective counselors, counselor educators, and other human services workers ought to be aware:

1. Help girls and women think of themselves as persons, to affirm their sense of personal worth, to face and work through their identity and role conflicts.
2. Help female clients consider a wide range of occupational options in addition to the traditional stereotypic ones. Do not raise eyebrows or look shocked when she says she wants to be a pilot or engineer. Encourage her to explore new and emerging occupations and expose her to contact with women in those nontraditional fields as well as traditional ones.
3. Help clients (girls and boys) think through and plan for multiple roles as workers and parents. The consequences of choices they make in terms of life styles and family patterns need to be stressed.
4. Make sure clients (girls and boys) have accurate information about women in the labor force, present and projected, and about alternatives available.
5. Help each girl to learn the process of decision making and to know that she *can* choose in accord with her values, ability, motivation, and preferences from a variety of life patterns.
6. Make both males and females aware of the variety of life styles and family patterns from which they can choose and of potential role conflicts involved in choosing one pattern (e.g. single life, multiple children, two-person career, equal partnership) over another.
7. Provide group guidance and group counseling experiences in which boys and girls can talk together about changing roles of males and females and the possible androgynous society of the future.
8. Involve parents in orientation sessions and information groups regarding career development of girls and ways in which they block or facilitate, since they still have the greatest impact on their children's career development.
9. Be aware of the developmental stage the girl is at and "where she is coming from" as a person and woman.
10. Be prepared to listen to and counsel female clients who are considering a great many alternatives both inside and outside the home and help them to choose the alternatives most consistent with the quality and style of life they prefer and most consistent with their emerging self-concept.

This kind of awareness and these kinds of curriculum and counseling strategies may help counselors and other human service workers in and out of the formal educational structure to become facilitators not only of female development but of the development of all persons for a variety of life roles.

REFERENCES

Anastasi, A. Sex differences in vocational choices. *National Catholic Conference Journal,* 1969, *13* (4), 63-76.

Birk, J. and Tanney, M.F. Counseling Women, II. *The Counseling Psychologist,* 1976, *7* (1).

Citizens' Advisory Council. Counselor attitudes sexist? Presidential panel thinks so in report on public school discrimination, bias. *APGA Guidepost,* September, 1972, *15,* 1-2.

Crowley, J.E., Levitin, T.E., and Quinn, R.P. Seven deadly half-truths about women. *Psychology Today,* 1973, *6,* 94-96.

Emma Willard Task Force. *Sexism in Education.* Minneapolis: Emma Willard Task Force, 1972.

Engelhard, P.A. A survey of counselor attitudes toward women. *Minnesota Guidance Bulletin,* Winter, 1969, 7-11.

Erickson, L.V. *Personal growth for women: A cognitive-developmental curriculum,* University of Minnesota, March, 1973 (mimeo).

Fitzgerald, L. and Harmon, L. Counseling Women, I. *The Counseling Psychologist,* 1973, 4 (1).

Flanagan, J.C. and Jung, S.M. *Progress in education: A sample survey* (1960-1970). Palo Alto, California: American Institutes for Research 1971.

General Electric. Women and business: Agenda for the seventies. *Business Environmental Studies.* New York, March, 1972.

Ginzberg, E. *Life styles of educated American women.* New York: Columbia University Press, 1966.

Goldberg, P. Are women prejudiced against women? *Transaction,* 1968, *5,* 28-30.

Guttman, M.A. Counselor bias in vocational guidance. *Women and ACES: Perspective and Issues.* Association for Counselor Education and Supervision. Muncie, Indiana: Accelerated Development, Inc., 1974.

Hansen, L.S. We are furious (female) but we can shape our own development. In J. Lewis (Ed.) Women and counselors. *Personnel and Guidance Journal,* 1972, *51,* 87-93.

Hartley, R.E. Children's concepts of male and female roles. *Merrill-Palmer Quarterly,* 1960, *6,* 83-91.

Horner, M.S. Women's will to fail. *Psychology Today,* 1968, 36-38.

Lewis, E.C. Counselors and girls. *Journal of Counseling Psychology,* 1965, *12,* 159-166.

Maccoby, E.E. (Ed.). Sex differences in intellectual functioning. In *The development of sex differences.* Stanford, California: Stanford University Press, 1966.

Matthews, E.E. et al. *Counseling girls and women over the life span.* Washington, D.C.: National Vocational Guidance Association, 1972.

Matthews, E.E. and Tiedeman, D. Attitudes toward careers and marriage and the development of life style in young women. *Journal of Counseling Psychology,* 1964, *11,* 375-384.

Minnesota State Board of Education. *Eliminating sex bias in education.* St. Paul, Minnesota: Minnesota State Department of Education, September, 1972.

Mitchell, E. What about career education for girls? *Educational Leadership,* December, 1972, *30,* 233-236.

Psathas, G. Toward a theory of occupational choice for women. *Sociology and Social Research,* 1968, *52,* 253-268.

Rand, and Miller, A. A developmental sectioning of women's careers and marriage attitudes and life plans. *Journal of Vocational Behavior,* 1972, *2,* 317-331.

Rapoza, R.S. and Blocher, D.H. The Cinderella effect: Planning avoidance in girls. *Counseling and Values,* 1976, *21* (1), 12-19.

Robie, E. Women: They'll manage, given half a chance. *Equitable Life Forum,* 1972, *1,* 12-16.

Rosenkrantz, P., Vogel, S., Bee, H., Broverman, I., and Broverman, D.M. Sex-role stereotypes and self-concepts in college students. *Journal of Consulting and Clinical Psychology,* 1968, *32,* 287-295.

Schmid, A.M. Let brother bake the cake. Sexism in the elementary curriculum and how to overcome it. *American Teacher,* 1972, *57,* CE 4-5.

Simpson, E.J. Career education—feminine version. Paper presented at Regional Seminar/Workshop on Women in the World of Work, Technical Education Research Centers, Chicago, Illinois, October, 1972.

Smith, S. Age and sex differences in children's opinion concerning sex differences. *Journal of Genetic Psychology,* 1939, *54,* 17-25.

Streidl, I. The composition of the nation's labor force. Paper presented at Regional Seminar/Workshop on Women in the World of Work, Technical Education Research Centers, Chicago, Illinois, October, 1972.

Super, D.E. *The psychology of careers.* New York: Harper Brothers, 1957.

Tennyson, W.W., Hansen, L.S., Klaurens, M.K., and Antholz, M.B. *Educating for career development.* St. Paul: Minnesota Department of Education, 1975.

Tennyson, W.W., Klaurens, M.K., and Hansen, L.S. *Career development curriculum.* Departments of Counseling Psychology and Distributive Education, College of Education, University of Minnesota, 1970 (mimeo).

Thoni, R., Hansen, L., Klaurens, M.K., Tennyson, W.W. *Women and the world of work.* St. Paul: Minnesota Department of Education, Pupil Personnel Services Sections, 1972

Tyler, L.E. Counseling girls and women in the year 2000. In E. Matthews (Ed.) *Counseling girls and women over the life span.* Washington, D.C.: National Vocational Guidance Association, 1972, 89-96.

Varenhorst, B., Gelatt, H.B., and Carey, R. *Deciding.* New York: College Entrance Examination Board, 1972.

Vetter, L. and Sethney, B.J. *Women in the work force: Development and field testing of curriculum materials.* Columbus, Ohio: The Center for Vocational and Technical Education, The Ohio State University, December, 1973.

Weitzman, L.J., Eifler, D., Hokada, E., & Ross, C. Sex-role socialization in picture books for pre-school children. *American Journal of Sociology,* 1972, *77,* 1125-1150.

Werner, J.E. *A study of Holland's theory of vocational choice as it applies to selected working women.* Unpublished Ed. D. dissertation, State University of New York, Buffalo, 1969.

Wolfson, K.T. *Career development of college women.* Unpublished doctoral dissertation, University of Minnesota, 1972.

Work in America. Perspectives on women and work. Report of a Special Task Force to the Secretary of Health, Education, and Welfare. Washington, D.C., December 1972, 47-53.

Zytowski, D.G. Toward a theory of career development for women. *Personnel and Guidance Journal,* 1969, *47,* 660-664.

Chapter 27

CAREER COUNSELING FOR WOMEN*

LENORE W. HARMON

WORK can be a way for individuals to express their identity and to explore their potential for competence and self-actualization. Women, however, seem unable to make choices about work in their lives. They literally live out Erikson's observations, that, "Young women often ask whether they can *have an identity* before they know whom they will marry and for whom they will make a home" (Erikson, 1968, p. 283). The important task in career counseling with women is to help them to maximize their potential choice and control of their lives.

Counselors are not responsible for the attitudes their clients bring to the counseling relationship, but they are responsible for their own responses to those attitudes (Smith, 1972). Thus, when women come to counseling without a strong sense of identity as a context in which to make career choices, the counselor may react in one of two ways. The first would be to assume that the situation is "natural" and one must work within the limitations it presents. The second would be to assume that the situation is painful and must be changed. The first reaction is analogous to regarding the bound feet of nineteenth century Chinese women as natural and the second reaction is analogous to assuming that everything will be fine if the bindings are simply removed. Both kinds of assumptions are being used in counseling women today and both assume that someone other than the client knows the "right" set of goals for her, whether it is raising outstanding children or winning a Nobel prize.

It is important to separate what is *now* from what is *possible* in the future and to view each woman's individual level of accomplishment as a product of her own choices which are not strictly rational or permanent. (The term *rational,* as used here, means uninfluenced by

*From E. Rawlings and D. Carter (Eds.): Psychotherapy for Women: Treatment Toward Equality, 1977. Courtesy of Charles C Thomas, Publisher, Springfield.

emotion and does *not* imply an evaluation.) Despite the romanticized visions of the potential roles available to women today, no life style is without its negative aspects. Each person must make choices on the basis of her own evaluation of the rewards available in a given situation.

THEORIES OF CAREER DEVELOPMENT

How people make career choices is a fascinating subject. Several types of theories have been proposed. They vary along two dimensions important to a discussion of career counseling for women. The first dimension extends along a sociological-psychological continuum. Theories at the sociological end of the continuum ascribe major importance to external events; theories at the psychological end of the continuum ascribed major importance to internal events. Psathas' (1968) outline of factors important in a theory of occupational choice for women is highly sociological with major emphasis on marriage and parental variables. Ginzberg, Ginsburg, Axelrad and Herma (1951) present a more psychological approach with emphasis on internal events such as fantasies. Super's (1951, 1963) approach also rests on a psychological basis emphasizing that individuals seek to implement a self-concept in making career choices. Obviously, no career choices made by either sex are purely sociological or purely psychological.

Findings show that men are more independent than women in their cognitive approach to tasks involving spatial perception (Sherman, 1967). It is tempting to generalize from these findings about the way women make vocational choices. To counselors, women seem to be extremely alert to external forces in making decisions. However, this perception itself may be influenced both by counselors' biases and by differences in the way men and women clients learn to talk about their choice process. For *anyone* making a career choice, the balance between external demands and internal factors is potentially conflict-ridden and deserves considerable attention in the counseling process. However, the author's hunch is that women, as a group, do take more account of external influences in making career choices than men do.

A second dimension of theories of career development extends from an emphasis on the developmental choice process to an emphasis on typology and content. Super's work (1957, 1972), for instance, emphasizes the process of career development with lesser concern for the content of the choices themselves. His (1957) approach leads him to suggest different career patterns for men than for women. While men's working patterns are limited to four, he suggests seven for women, including stable homemaking, double-track (women who are married and continuously employed) and interrupted (women who leave the world of work for homemaking, but return to it) patterns. Zytowski (1969), who attempts to understand the career development of women, emphasizes the homemaking role as an important aspect of their career development. It is interesting to note that no theorists, as yet, postulate homemaking or interrupted patterns for men. All assume a lifetime span of participation in the job market for men. Neither is the fact that most men fit Super's double-track category highlighted. While present developmental approaches may reflect accurately the way we currently conceptualize career development, they do not exhaust the possibilities.

The formulation of Roe (1957, 1972) falls near the middle of the developmental-content continuum because it relates childhood experiences to specific eventual choices.

The approaches which stress typologies such as Holland's (1966, 1973), underscore content rather than process. These approaches show clearly that the content of women's choices differs from men's choices. Holland (1974) reviews evidence that young women and girls choose predominantly social and artistic occupations while boys and young men choose predominantly realistic (manual, mechanical, agricultural, electrical and technical) and investigative (scientific) occupations.

These findings do not indicate that all women choose social or artistic occupations nor that all men choose realistic or investigative occupations. They do suggest that women choose within the norm for their sex in order to avoid conflict.

INTERNAL VS. EXTERNAL FRAME OF REFERENCE

Career decisions must be made with considerable attention to the internal frame of reference because internal determinants are more ultimately satisfying than the external ones (Herzberg, 1966). Thus, psychological determinants would be more important to career counseling than sociological determinants. Developmental and typological theories also depend on the ability of the individual to implement personal preferences without overwhelming influence from the outside. However, Bernice Sandler (1974), a counselor by training, who is now Director of the Project on the Status and Education of Women, Association of American Colleges, has argued, "Unless women come to grips with the conflicts and difficulties that being female presents in our society, I suspect that women's view of work will continue to be shaped primarily by externally caused factors. Traditional counseling, unless it deals with the contradictions of a woman's life, is not likely to have any great impact."*

*Sandler, Bernice, Personal Communication, 1974.

MOTIVATION TO WORK

Vocational behavior would be easier to understand and explain if everyone worked for the same reason, but of course they do not. Industrial and management psychologists have noted the value of Maslow's hierarchy of needs in explaining the behavior of workers (Herzberg, 1966; Rush, 1969). However, neither Maslow nor those who have applied his theory to work have given much attention to how it might apply to women and their vocational behavior.

Briefly, Maslow postulates a hierarchical order of five types of needs: physiological needs, safety needs, belongingness and love needs, esteem needs, and self-actualization needs (Maslow, 1970). He believes that people do not become conscious of or attempt to gratify the higher-order needs (esteem and self-actualization) until the lower order needs (physiological and safety) are gratified. For example, to a hungry person, food is all important and she/he will do anything to get it, even if it means being cast away by peers or violating a personal sense of morality. The needs of belonging and self-esteem mean little in the face of all consuming hunger which is a physiological need. We can explore the general dimensions of Maslow's hierarchy of needs to explain vocational behavior in a way which will be useful for career counseling for women.

Social and cultural factors which are not under the control of the individual often determine whether the lowest level needs in the Maslow hierarchy—physiological, safety, and to some extent, love and belonging—are met. These gratifications are related to the sociological end of the sociological-psychological dimension running through career theories.

Most people in our society are not deprived of gratification of their physiological needs. However, it is interesting to analyze the mechanisms through which the physiological needs are met. For men, the usual means of gratification of physiological needs is through labor which produces either the needed food and water or the money to purchase them. For women, however, the usual means of gratification of physiological needs is through association with someone, husband or father, whose labor assures that her needs will be met. This is not to say that women do not work or that no woman has independently satisfied her physiological needs. But since the Industrial Revolution, the role of woman as housewife and mother has removed her from the world of work, at least in the view of society (Lewandowski, 1973).

When men have been unable to fulfill their own physiological needs independently it has been because of unforeseen natural and economic events or cultural values which systematically excluded some subgroups, such as Blacks and Catholics, from adequate opportunity. While no one would argue that women cannot independently assume responsibility for gratifying their physiological needs, most women have grown up in a world where they were not expected to do so and where, in fact, the opportunities for them to do so were limited compared to the opportunities offered to men. Thus, counselors have observed that the typical American housewife does not believe she can independently gratify her own needs. Neither, apparently, do many of the young women who marry out of desperation for someone to *take care of me,* nor do their parents who breathe a sigh of relief once the wedding ceremony is over.

The same type of sexual dichotomy applies to the needs for safety and security once physiological needs are adequately gratified. Men can usually insure that in a stable society, their needs will be met directly by their labor. In contrast a woman usually works in the home to please a man who provides her a safe environment. However the newspaper advice columns are full of letters from women who begin, "My husband is a good provider and my life looks ideal to an outsider but . . ." That "but" is usually followed by "he doesn't love me," "he treats me like a child," or, "I am bored. There is no growth in my life." These complaints correspond to the three highest levels of needs in Maslow's hierarchy.

An interesting reaction occurs in the woman who is able to insure her own safety and security by direct labor. The low-level jobs which are available to a woman may gratify her needs for safety to a minimal extent but keep her from risking that stability in an attempt to reach a higher level of employment and potential gratification. At this level she is not deprived physiologically and feels fairly secure and safe. However, even though her work does not gain her much belongingness, love, or esteem, she does not attempt to improve her position because she cannot risk losing the security. The extent to which failure to fulfill love, esteem, and self-actualization needs are common for American women is an indication that there may be conditions in our society which contribute to fixation of women's gratification at the level of safety.

The woman who ventures beyond the home *and* the typical woman's job (secretary, nurse, or teacher) is risking the loss of whatever feelings of belongingness, love, and esteem she receives for filling the typical female role. While men are loved and esteemed more highly for their successes, women are not always loved for their successes, especially if their successes are atypical for women. Horner's work (1969, 1970, 1972) on the fear of success in women demonstrates the conflicts women face in their potential and actual achievement.

A woman may have to compromise her need for self-esteem in order to achieve her need for esteem from others. Most bright women can recall a time when they concealed their abilities in order to avoid losing the esteem of someone else. More recently some women have been able to express their anger at having made or being expected to make this type of compromise. For women, more than for men, there seems to be a conflict between the behaviors which would lead to self-esteem and esteem from others. This is not as apparent for the woman whose interests are traditional (for whatever reason) as for the woman whose interests are nontraditional.

Maslow postulates that needs for esteem must be gratified before needs for self-actualization can emerge. The needs for self-esteem and self-actualization are at the psychological end of the sociological-psychological continuum, although there are probably no behaviors which are purely self-determined. However, Maslow's hierarchy suggests that psychological needs emerge after the others are adequately gratified. He also implies that people who gratify their needs for self-actualization, i.e. have become what they can be, reach a higher level of existence than those who have not (Maslow, 1970). Most career counseling rests on the assumption that it is possible to meet the needs for self-esteem and selfactualization, at least partially, through good career planning and decisions. The process of helping people decide how to meet their physiological and safety needs is exciting only if they have been severely deprived! Then the problem is to find some source of income. Most career counselors specialize in helping people find work environments which will be satisfying and exciting in addition to providing daily bread. It would appear, then, that career counseling deals mainly with the gratification of higher-level psychological needs of the individual.

This author is not sure that most women are prepared for such career counseling. Only if a woman's physiological and safety needs have been met and she has resolved her conflicts of achievement and self-esteem versus belonging and the esteem of others, is she free to make career plans and decisions which will fulfill needs for self-actualization. One might add that not all men reach this level either, and one of the large factors in their failure is their responsibility for dependent women and children. Although it is not usually clear to those experiencing painful changes in the roles of women and men, it is apparent that the more that women are free to satisfy their needs directly, the freer men will be to gratify their needs.

When applied to vocational behavior and problems, Maslow's hierarchy of needs suggests that (1) basic needs are fulfilled differently by women and men, (2) there is more conflict involved for women than for men in meeting higher-level needs which keeps women at lower levels of gratification, and (3) most career counseling and many career development theories are aimed at the high-level gratifications as postulated by Maslow. One is left with the question posed by Sandler, "Are women ready for career counseling?"*

COUNSELING APPLICATIONS

In career counseling for women a process suggested by an analysis of Maslow's hierarchy of needs may overlap with counseling approaches which are not usually considered career counseling. Schlossberg (1972) suggests the importance of assessing the developmental stage of each woman client in relationship to Tiedeman and O'Hara's (1963) decision-making stages. In addition, it is important to assess for each woman client which of Maslow's basic needs she is meeting and how she is meeting them.

First, a career counselor should determine at what level the client is on Maslow's hierarchy and how she got there. It is important that every woman, adolescent or middle-aged, be sure that she can independently meet her needs for food and security. The old idea of having a skill *to fall back on* is not outmoded. In counseling young women, it is important that they realize what personal freedom they can insure for themselves by developing the most immediately valuable of their skills. It is not necessary to spend a lifetime as a computer programmer or dental technician. These skills can be used as a means to provide income and independence to do whatever a person wants: study nuclear physics, write a novel, or be a housewife. For the middle-aged woman the problem is often to help her reevaluate what skills she now has which would allow her to meet her own personal needs. Years of dependence on someone else have often convinced the adult woman that she really is helpless. Only major changes in her attitude toward herself will allow her to use the skills she already possesses or to learn new ones. In either case, it is true that until a woman can meet the lower-level needs through work, she will never be free to confront her higher-level needs.

One thing is clear: Many of the jobs society offers to women (and minority group members) are subsistence-level jobs which will barely meet their physiological and safety needs, much less go beyond them. A recent article in the *Milwaukee Journal* (Dembski, 1974) told the story of a woman reporter who worked as a nurse's aid in a nursing home for two weeks. She earned about two dollars an hour, and found it dirty, backbreaking work. She wrote, "But what really helped was the knowledge that I would not have to spend the rest of my life working in a nursing home." At a job like that, a woman will earn a little over $4000 a year. Even a woman without dependents would

*Sandler, Bernice, Personal Communication, 1974.

have little left over to devote to education, hobbies, or recreation after food, shelter and taxes. Too often job training programs prepare women for precisely this level of work. No counselor should consider such subsistence-level jobs as any more than a temporary solution when lower order needs must be filled. They and their clients should be seeking better, more rewarding solutions to the clients' career problems.

Women who are sure of their abilities to meet their basic physiological and safety needs present a different set of counseling problems. They often feel conflict between fulfilling their own needs and fulfilling the needs of others who are sources of love and esteem. For instance, the president of a business firm could not understand why one of his women employees was using irrational excuses to avoid promotion until he remembered that she also had declined her last pay increase to avoid making more money than her husband. Working through that kind of conflict, helping a woman to label the forces that make up her dilemma, and accepting her decision as to what she wants to do are also a part of career counseling. For a younger woman, the specter of such conflict makes her avoid certain nontraditional careers. It is important that a woman choose what she wants whether it is housewifery or surgery but she cannot choose until she is aware of the conflict. It is a counselor's responsibility to bring the conflict to her awareness. It is hard to imagine any one meeting her needs for self-actualization in a career into which she has been forced by a desire to meet the needs of someone else.

"What will make me happiest and allow me the most opportunities for personal growth?" is the kind of problem faced by the client who is attempting to satisfy needs for self-actualization. Such a question does not emerge until other types of needs are adequately satisfied. Career counselors are best prepared by their theories and measurement techniques to handle clients with that kind of problem. Unfortunately, few woman clients are at that stage in their hierarchy of needs. As a result, career counseling with women has been a hopeless task for which there has been no training. Until career counselors began to assess the hierarchical level of needs of women and vary their techniques accordingly, career counseling with them will be frustrating both for the client and the counselor.

COUNSELOR BIAS

Counselors will not be prepared to work in this way with their women clients until they assess their own biases toward women and careers. Schlossberg and Pietrofesa (1973) summarize much of the data on counselor bias and leave no doubt that both men and women counselors are biased by the sex of the client. Counselors must begin to look at most careers and jobs as androgynous. It may help in overcoming old biases to explore why individual counselors and society have labeled each career or job as *masculine* or *feminine*. It may also be worthwhile to explore the results of such labeling. Clearly the range of acceptable vocational behavior has been unnecessarily narrowed for both sexes. This situation is both a cause and effect of the low economic status women suffer.

Counseling aids such as occupational information and testing materials which imply sexual stereotyping must be revised. The same biases which shape counselor behavior were incorporated in producing these products. These biases will be altered as the market demand changes. However, that demand will not change without fundamentally restructuring the way counselors view the world of work. An interesting example of this process as applied to testing materials can be traced by reading the resolution introduced to APGA by Schlossberg and Goodman (AMEG Commission, 1973) and the proceedings of the National Institute of Education's recent Conference on Sex Bias and Sex Fairness in Career Interest Inventories (Diamond, 1974). Revisions in interest inventories follow the vocal protest of counselors and clients.

A final important observation for counselors is that the marriage-career dichotomy is overemphasized. To imply a forced choice between the two suggests that women must choose between independence and the kind of dependence which forces them to use someone else's labor to satisfy their most basic needs. The dichotomy also ignores the fact that most men have both careers and families. The whole question of combining a career and family should be explored with clients of both sees. The counselor's job is to help the client to clarify personal values and to recognize that those values and the decisions based on them, may change in time under new circumstances. Many of the middle-aged women a counselor sees today were convinced at age twenty that they never wanted to be anything but a housewife. At age forty, they are confused and frightened by their dissatisfaction with the role they expected to be satisfying for a lifetime.

Counselors should, after all, be helping clients to prepare for a world of changes. The old myth that career decisions can be made once for a lifetime has outlived its usefulness. Women (and men, too) need counselors who expect them to outgrow today's needs and decisions, who will help them to accept their changing selves, and who will provide them with a model for future decision-making. Career counselors themselves should expect to experience considerable change in the theories, techniques and materials they use in response to the needs of their clients.

REFERENCES

Association for measurement and evaluation in guidance commission on sex bias in measurement. AMEG Commission report on sex bias in interest measurement. *Measurement and Evaluation in Guidance, 6:*171, 1973.

Dembski, Barbara: Little time to give love. *Milwaukee Journal,* part 1, p. 1, January 27, 1974.

Diamond, E. (Ed.): *Sex Bias and Sex Fairness in Career Interest Inventories.* Washington, D.C.: National Institute of Education, 1974.

Erikson, Erik: *Youth and Crisis.* New York: Norton, 1968.

Ginzberg, Eli, Ginsburg, Sol. W., Axelrad, Sidney, and Herma, John I.: *Occupational Choice: An Approach to a General Theory.* New York, Columbia University Press, 1951.

Herzberg, Frederick: *Work and the Nature of Man.* Cleveland, World Publishing, 1966.

Holland, John L.: *The Psychology of Vocational Choice.* Waltham, Blaisdell, 1966.

Holland, John L.: *Making Vocational Choices: A Theory of Careers.* Englewood Cliffs, Prentice-Hall, 1973.

Holland, John L.: *The Use and Evaluation of Interest Inventories and Simulations.* Center for Social Organization of Schools, Report No. 167, Baltimore, John Hopkins University, January, 1974.

Horner, Matina S.: Fail, Bright woman. *Psychology Today, 3:*36, 1969.

Horner, Matina S.: Femininity and successful achievement: A basic inconsistency. In Walker, E.L. (Ed.): *Feminine Personality and Conflict.* Belmont, Brooks Cole, 1970.

Horner, Matina S.: Toward an understanding of achievement-related conflicts in women. *Journal of Social Issues, 28:*157, 1972.

Lewandowski, C.M.: The evolving power of women in western society. Unpublished master's thesis, University of Wisconsin-Milwaukee, 1973.

Maslow, Abraham H.: *Motivation and Personality,* 2nd ed. New York, Harper & Row, 1970.

Psathas, George: Toward a theory of occupational choice for women. *Sociology and Social Research, 52:*253, 1968.

Roe, Anne: Early determinants of vocational choice. *Journal of Counseling Psychology, 4:*212, 1957.

Roe, Anne: Perspectives in vocational development. In Whiteley, J.M., and Resnikoff, A. (Eds.) : *Perspectives on Vocational Development.* Washington, D.C., American Personnel and Guidance Association, 61-82, 1972.

Rush, Harold M.F.: *Behavioral Science—Concepts and Management Application.* New York, National Industrial Conference Board, 1969.

Schlossberg, Nancy K.: A framework for counseling women. *Personnel and Guidance Journal, 51:*137, 1972.

Schlossberg, Nancy K. and Pietrofesa, John J.: Perspectives on counseling bias: Implications for counselor education. *The Counseling Psychologist, 4:*44, 1973.

Sherman, Julia A.: Problems of Sex differences in space perception and aspects of intellectual functioning. *Psychological Review, 74:*290, 1967.

Smith, Joyce A.: For God's sake, what do these women want? *Personnel and Guidance Journal, 5:*133, 1972.

Super, Donald E.: Vocational adjustment: Implementing a self-concept. *Occupations, 30:*88, 1951.

Super, Donald E.: *The Psychology of Careers.* New York, Harper & Row, 1957.

Super, Donald E.: Self concepts in vocational development. In Super, Donald E.,

(Ed.): *Career Development: Self Concept Theory.* New York, CEEB Research Monograph No. 4, 1963.

Super, Donald E.: Vocational development theory: Persons, positions, and processes. In Whiteley, J.M. and Resnikoff, A. (Eds.): *Perspectives on Vocational Development.* Washington, D.C.: American Personnel and Guidance Association, 13-33, 1972.

Tiedeman, David V. and O'Hara, Robert P.: *Career Development: Choice and Adjustment.* New York, College Entrance Examination Board, 1968.

Zytowski, Donald G.: Toward a theory of career development for women. *Personnel and Guidance Journal, 47*:660, 1969.

Chapter 28

A PROCESS MODEL FOR CHANGING COUNSELOR EDUCATION DEPARTMENTS*

MARY LEONARD, L. SUNNY HANSEN, AND LEE KNEFELKAMP

THE PROACTIVE counselor is concerned with the development of women over the life span. It seems appropriate that women students in counselor preparation programs examine the system in which they are learning to be counselors and identify ways in which they can change it to facilitate their own development, as well as that of other women. It seems equally appropriate that counseling psychologists and counselor educators who are in the business of bringing about change in individuals, groups, and organizations take an inward look to determine how they are affecting students. It is important for both groups to act as change agents within the organization to eliminate the problems which stifle human development and effectiveness, e.g. sexism, racism, destructive competition, classism, and incompetence. It should go without saying that counselors learning to promote human development should have that kind of facilitative behavior modeled in their training programs, for men and women.

Counselors have been accused of being unresponsive to women's concerns, and even more important, of being the obstacle to rather than facilitator of this development. While their charge needs to be more fully documented, it would seem fair to assume that counselors (and counselor educators), like other educators, are affected by the pervasive conscious and nonconscious sexism in education. One of the needs is to help sensitize professors and other students to the special needs and problems of women. While choices of majors, occupations, marriage partner, and life style are concerns of both male and female students, the experiences of being a female undergraduate or

Reprinted from Women and ACES: Perspective and Issues, Mary Alice Julius Guttman and Patsy A. Donn, Editors, copyright 1974 by the Association for Counselor Education and Supervision and published by Accelerated Development Inc., Muncie, In. Reprinted with Permission.

graduate student are unique and demanding and need special attention at this point in time.

THE FEMALE UNDERGRADUATE STUDENT

The female college student exists in an environment dominated by males. Almost all of her professors are male, and more than half of her classmates are male. If she chooses a "traditionally male" academic major, e.g. engineering, she is likely to find that only a very few of her classmates are women and that she may more easily resolve her role conflict by changing majors rather than by persevering. She has few role models to emulate and a very limited support system if any.

The concerns that are traditionally a part of the college years—career choice, decisions about a family, and personal growth and development—are viewed very differently for males than for females. It is simply assumed, for example, that a male will choose a career, marry, and have a family. It is assumed that the male will be able to combine a career and a family with little trouble at all. Those assumptions do not hold when society views the female with career aspirations. The female who may choose to remain single is viewed as odd or unusual. Women who wish to combine a career and marriage face enormous pressures from their families, their university environment, and frequently from their prospective mates. Women graduates also face discrimination when they apply for jobs, for credit, and for graduate school, Affirmative Action notwithstanding. Today's college woman is aware of the difficulties facing her both in the educational setting and the world of work. She also faces on a day-to-day basis the difficult task of personal development and self-esteem with very little support.

THE FEMALE GRADUATE STUDENT

The problems of female college students are exacerbated among female graduate students. Existing as they do in an exceedingly competitive environment, they are subject to a highly developed and self-protective double standard. An assertive male graduate student is viewed as a "go-getter" and one who will likely contribute to his field, while an assertive female graduate student is viewed as an aggressive, unfeminine bitch. Job opportunities come more often to male graduate students, and they are more often "listened to" in class. Married male graduate students frequently are able to give a majority of their time and effort to their academic careers, because it is expected that they do so and because their wives are expected to care for the home front (and frequently the finances, as well). Female graduate students who are married face discrimination from the very beginning of their academic work. For example, admissions committees will discuss the marital status and number of children of a female applicant but will not consider those factors when making decisions on the male candidates; female students are expected to be "good" students and "good" wives, but with little recognition of the time and effort and pressures involved in doing both; female graduate students find that the job market discriminates against them when it comes to hiring; and women candidates are often dismissed from consideration because it is simply assumed that they will have to move if and when a husband's career provides an opportunity to do so. In short, the female graduate student (single or married) juggles a number of roles and often finds that she is punished interpersonally for the very qualities (determination, intelligence, assertion) that are rewarded in male students. These are among the issues that sensitive counselors and counselor educators need to address themselves to.

THE WOMAN IN COUNSELOR EDUCATION

Women in counselor education, as women in other fields of higher education, are faced with problems of discrimination and denigration, as the WEAL Report (1971) so clearly documents. Cross (1972) reports that the Newman Task Force on Higher Education found in a 1971 study that "discrimination against women, in contrast to that against minorities, is still overt and socially acceptable within the academic community." In spite of this negative situation, it would seem that graduate students in counseling, since they are now being equipped with the skills and competencies to change systems, should be able to identify needs and implement strategies for change in their own educational institution. The main portion of this chapter takes an organizational change model, applies it to a counselor education program, and suggests a variety of interventions through which women in these programs can not only improve their own learning conditions but transfer their learning regarding women's development to the systems in which they eventually will be employed.

The model adapted is Blocher's (1974) model for facilitating change in human systems.* It is briefly presented and is followed by discussion of some abortive approaches to change, as well as some interventions which used the model and were successful. The interventions represent a sampling of strategies using a process model to promote positive growth of women in counselor education programs.

Blocher and Rapoza (1972) described the purpose of this model as "to facilitate positive change in human systems." Within this framework, the client may be a single individual, a group, or social

*Used by permission of author.

system. The interventions available to the change agent include teaching, one-to-one counseling, group work, consultation techniques, laboratory learning approaches, and all verbal persuasion procedures —in essence, all the skills of a highly trained counselor/psychologist.

The model prescribes a series of nine activities initiated by a change agent who must be cognizant and skilled in various sources of gain in "relationship, cognitive, behavioral, and social psychological theories" (Blocher and Rapoza, 1972). The model is presented in flow chart form in Figure 28-1. The rationale is more fully explained in Blocher (1974).

FACILITATING CHANGE IN HUMAN SYSTEMS

1
Define professional goals in terms of institutional and/or population needs

2
Scan relevant environments (school, university, community) for opportunities to advance goals

3
Identify potential client systems; select on basis of feasibility and payoff

4
Build communication and relationship network within and around client system

5
Negotiate specific behavioral goals within client system and obtain public commitment to them

6
Introduce new concepts and model new behavior to client system

7
Shape specific new behaviors and integrate them through simulation or tryout

8
Transfer new behaviors to "real world" and attach to maintainers (reinforcers) in real environment

9
Evaluate process and outcome

Figure 28-1.

A few comments must be made about the model before its applications are described. The model has two advantages: (1) Since it is a process model, this allows it to be useful within any situation or with any problem; (2) Its structure gives the change agent an organized and planful approach to deal with the incredible complexity of issues involved in changing a human system.

The model makes several important assumptions. If either of these ingredients is missing, this systematic approach to changing an organization is next to impossible:

1. *The institution (or specific powerful people) is somewhat open to new ideas and if definite needs are articulated, change is seen positively.* If the institution or specific powerful people are actively working against the change agent or consistently passively resisting, other models of organizational change may be more appropriate, e.g. affirmative action plans, outside pressure groups, litigation, revolution, etc.
2. The change agents have the necessary relationship skills and psychological knowledge to implement and carry out the activities within the model. The skills of the change agent are more difficult to evaluate, especially if the change agent is female and the target client is male. Assertiveness in women is viewed and handled in many ways; not all are negative, but too often a woman who states her position clearly and articulates her needs is dismissed, shrugged off, and the nicest names given her are unprintable. It is often hard to decide if difficulties the change agents may have are due to their lack of skill and knowledge of the problems of the resisting people or an idiosyncratic interaction effect. This issue must be examined very carefully and not blithely overlooked. Sometimes a neutral third person can diagnose where the ownership of the problem lies.

Assuming the institution is relatively open to change and the change agents are knowledgeable and skillful in implementing the change process, the model itself can be examined. The following material is drawn from Blocher and Rapoza (1972), from discussions between the graduate students and Blocher, and experiences of many women in counselor education departments.

STAGES OF THE MODEL APPLIED

STEP 1. The change agent clearly understands her goals. These must be in relation to the needs of the client population of the institution or social system. If her goals are seen as having no bearing to the department, she can be written off as too idealistic, a troublemaker, or a radical "women's libber." Deciding to be a change agent in one's own department is a very difficult step. Factors which mitigate against involvement in long-range change goals include: (1) paranoia ("They'll get me on my master's paper, prelims, dissertation, final orals, or in my recommendations"); (2) lack of leadership and support; (3) lack of knowledge and skills to be successful; (4) a history of punishing experiences (prior risk-taking and putdowns); (5) little comprehension of the problem (either knowledge vacuum or rose-colored glasses perceptions); (6) an unsympathetic response to the issues; (7) little hope of success ("It's always been this way");

but, worst of all, (8) no time (which often means lack of commitment to the task or fear of risk-taking). The second major difficulty in step one is clearly articulating a goal. Too often individuals want things changed but are unable to specify what should be changed or how.

STEP 2. The change agent examines the environment to find opportunities to advance her professional goals in a "proactive versus reactive" fashion. She begins to build a communication and relationship network which is open and honest and allows straight messages to be transmitted. As Blocher and Rapoza (1972) state, "The way to begin to help any human system is to listen to it and help it listen to itself." In this step the change agent becomes totally familiar with all aspects of the system she wishes to operate within. If the system is the counselor education department, as in this instance, then she needs to know about the professors, the decision-making modes, the students, and the political system in which the department exists. In terms of professors, she needs to know who talks to whom, who is supportive of what, what their opinions are on a variety of topics and especially on women's issues (friendly, neutral, hostile, etc.). Concerning the decision-making process, she needs to know the explicit and implicit rules by which it operates and who makes and enforces these rules. In terms of students, she needs to know at least one student in each student group, their basic opinions on the specific topic of counseling women, and how easily mobilized they are. Concerning the general political climate of the department, she needs to know if the department is autonomous in major decision making; where the budget is controlled, and if hard and soft monies are reliable; whether the department is on shaky or stable ground within the college, graduate school, or university; and what the problems of the department are, internally and externally, and how these affect students, faculty, and policy decisions.

STEP 3. This step involves an open and direct negotiation upon clearly stated and mutually agreed goals. This is most potent when public commitment is obtained. Negotiation for goals should be approached from a feasibility and payoff perspective. Successive approximations should be seen as a viable approach. Unless the change agent is able to obtain the total change she would like to effect, she should obtain part of the goal first with her eye on future interventions and see the foot-in-the-door as an acceptable first step. For example, the change agent may only be able to get the faculty to give some time in a counseling class for a workshop on women and counseling. This is beginning success. As the change agent is persistent and willing to do the homework and as the worth of the material becomes apparent, the demand for the material and more class time by the students will increase.

Step 4-7. Blocher and Rapoza (1972) state that after the negotiation phase is over, a "whole-part-whole" learning sequence is initiated. This entails giving information, feedback with appropriate models, and practice in a safe place. This aspect of the change model is most appropriate when dealing with specific behavior change in individuals. In a counseling department, this might get translated into dealing with professors who are "chauvinistic" toward women or a counselor who would like to treat a female client as a whole person and not as a "wife" or "daughter" or in any role-specific manner. This aspect of the change model parallels what a counselor would do with a client who wanted to change some behavior.

Step 8. This sequence of activities is aimed at transfer of learning and the maintenance of the new learning in the actual environment of the client. This may be the most discouraging phase. Often a professor, student, or potential change agent will have concerns which are oriented toward some issue involved with women and counseling. They will say they are committed to these goals, and they act consistently with their words in the strategy meetings. However, when the admissions committee meets, the professor somehow "forgets" about the female candidate he was going to support; when a female client comes in, the male counseling student says he cannot understand why she wants to leave her child to come back to school; when faced with making a commitment to action, the potential female change agent is suddenly afraid of what her adviser will think of her participation.

Step 9. Professionals evaluate their work to learn from their failure and to repeat their success. It is imperative that consistent feedback be obtained on the effectiveness of various interventions into the system. Both formal and informal data should be collected. Failure or partial successes can then be retranslated into goal statements or set aside for a more feasible time to be approached. Failure will tell the change agent how well she either diagnosed the system's readiness for the intervention, the skill with which it was accomplished, or both.

EXAMPLES FROM COUNSELOR EDUCATION

The remainder of this section will give examples of successes and failures of different individuals and groups in making interventions regarding women's development in counselor education settings. The change model provides a framework for examining both the effective and ineffective strategies. Since the concern about female development in counselor education programs is relatively new, the authors are unaware of any systematic, comprehensive attempts to develop program interventions. A variety of individual strategies have been used to improve the status of women in higher education around the nation, including efforts to influence admissions committees, offering stipends and scholarships, hiring more female professors, creating women's studies and women's centers, and the like (Cross, 1972).

Within counselor education, the interventions have taken such forms as developing women's seminars and courses; creating units on women within courses where appropriate; workshops for teachers and counselors; developing multimedia presentations to increase awareness; creating special videotapes to be used in training counselors; developing assertive training courses and groups; creating and implementing women's courses to be piloted in practicum and internship settings; developing conceptual models for women's development; creating, implementing, and evaluating intervention models as part of M.A. or Ph.D. research; developing support groups; presenting programs at local, state, and national professional meetings; selecting research topics on aspects of women's development and counseling; developing units on sexism in human relations courses; creating a women's library; influencing staff through personal confrontations and feedback; and utilizing organizational development principles and skills to change the counselor education environment. What follows is a brief description of a few unplanned attempts and of two planned interventions in counselor education. The cases given move sequentially from less sophisticated to effective approaches analyzed within the Blocher model.

Case 1—Self-Defeating Strategies

In one department, women students often gathered in groups and complained about the "chauvinism" of particular professors, the lack of material on women in the curriculum, the scarcity of female professors as models, ad infinitum. The school year ended, the women went on to their counseling internships with none of their complaints or ideas ever directly heard or acted upon. Three basic problems halted the effectiveness of this group: There was a reluctance to clearly and specifically define what they disliked in the department (Step 3); They never decided to try to *do* something about the problem (Step 1); and the spokeswomen for the group tended to be perceived as abrasive, accusative, disorganized, and hostile in their conversations with faculty about their concerns (Step 4, and also skills and knowledge assumption).

Case 2—Getting Into Curriculum

A different group of women identified three areas for intervention. They were curriculum, staff development, and the admissions committee. The staff development goal was rejected as an immediate goal because of negative experiences and feelings the group feared would carry over from a prior staff development project on a different issue. The admissions committee intervention was labeled very important but very sensitive. It was decided that more information on how the department made decisions was necessary before any major moves were made. Successive approximations were achieved, however, in eliminating from female candidates' credentials the marital status and number of children (the same information had not been listed for men). Step 2 was enlarged.

Curriculum intervention appeared to be an immediately attainable goal (faculty had invited student participation in planning issues to be presented in class). The women obtained two class periods to do a unit on women and counseling. It was very effectively done and stimulated counseling students to request more information on the problems and on what they could do as counselors. The unit material was expanded to a workshop on women in counseling and was also presented at a national convention. One means of evaluation and feedback was use of the Spence and Helmreich questionnaire (1972) on faculty and student attitudes toward male and female roles, with feedback on results provided to each individual and to the workshop group.

Case 3—Changing Male Professors' Treatment of Female Graduate Students

This intervention focused on the relationship between student and professor and is described according to the change model.

Steps 1-4: Two female graduate students felt ignored in a seminar by a particular professor. They decided to talk to him about this concern. *Step 5:* When they met with the professor, he denied the existence of the problem saying he treated all students alike. The students then produced frequency charts from the last four classes counting the number of times male and female students volunteered to speak and were called on. The data supported their feelings. The professor agreed to call on more female students. *Step 6:* The students talked with the professor about the problem of selective perception concerning female students and their achievement. Relevant articles were given to him. They suggested he sit in on another seminar conducted by a female professor to see the difference in interaction among the female students. *Step 7:* During the next two class meetings the students kept a frequency count and fed the results back to the professor. *Step 8:* It took another quarter of work with a new class and new female graduate students to shape the professor's behavior. It was not until the professor finally began to respect the contributions of the female graduate students that his "calling-on-female-graduate-students" behavior was maintained at a high level. *Step 9:* The professor sought out the first two graduate students and thanked them for their initiative and feedback. They considered the whole project a success. They asked him ways the processes could have been facilitated and then fed the information back to their support group so the other women could share and learn by the success.

Case 4—Building Departmental Support Groups

Women who have chosen counseling as a career are sometimes disillusioned when they discover that their department, dedicated to development of human effectiveness, does not always seem to be applying those principles in its treatment of women. They sometimes need to know that there are others who share their feelings and concerns. This intervention was designed to meet that need.

Step 1: After talking among themselves, one female professor and three female graduate students decided to try to identify and create a group of individuals who would be sympathetic and willing to get involved in the concerns of women in counseling and counseling women. *Step 2:* In scanning the environment, they decided to decrease the complexity of the issue and look for those within the department (instead of the university). They did get information from other departments on their strategies for creating support groups of women. They then talked to many professors and students within the department concerning the development and counseling of women. *Step 3:* The client population was identified. The females of the department (professors and students) would be contacted for a general meeting. The decision to include only females was made on two grounds: (a) feasibility, for in talking to people in the department, on the whole the females were more interested in and sympathetic to the concerns of women; and (b) openness, because the females expressed concern about talking about these issues in front of men. In terms of payoff, it therefore seemed best to begin with just females with the end goal being to gather as much support from all people as possible. (This is a good example of successive approximations toward the desired goal.)

Step 4: Building a communication and relationship network was accomplished over a span of a school year. Through meetings, seminars and classes on women developed, informal support groups emerged, and new professional and personal relationships among the women students were created. Trust was slowly built. *Step 5:* Specific goals were defined and public commitment obtained. A core of fifteen women committed themselves to working on specific projects and to team up with others on large, visible projects. Another group of about twenty women gave their moral support to the efforts of the fifteen and committed themselves to show up if numbers were ever needed, and emergency required their presence, or their specific talents could be used in small one-shot projects. *Step 6:* New concepts were introduced and behavior was modeled. Through the support groups and classes, the fifteen women learned more about the problems of women in society, in education, and in counseling. Views, feelings, and experiences were shared, and evidence of effective action and change in behavior was reinforced. *Step 7:* Not applicable. *Step 8-9:* Transferring new behaviors to real environments and attaching reinforcers was often hard because it was difficult to find support for the women's class or support group outside of the women students. They were mostly ignored. It was not until they reflected upon how far they had come that they began to feel good about their efforts and became self-reinforcers. As they shared their experiences with women from other departments and universities, they realized how far they had progressed on their own. This knowledge helped to maintain the behavior. Then, as the group of fifteen turned from a think and support group to an action group, the rewards of the intervention became propelling. Many individual women began making interventions on their own in their specific work or educational sphere. In one of the major projects under development at the time of writing a female faculty member knowledgeable in career development and a counseling graduate student employed by a central Office for Student Affairs tried to enhance women's opportunities by getting counseling and career development inputs into a campus Women's Center, a university-wide agency. Although the coordinated efforts are still in progress, a process analysis would reveal that Steps 1-4 have been followed and that Steps 5-9 will come after enactment of the plan.

DISCUSSION

Once a group of women become organized, knowledgeable, and successful, they usually turn their attention to outreach projects in the community, the university, and their professional groups and journals. The biggest problem is usually Step 2, obtaining knowledge of the system—Who can understand a university or APGA?—and Step 4, building a communication relationship network around the client system. If the women know people in the university, community, or professional groups and have established relationships with them, this process is accelerated.

A dozen more examples of women's concerns could be given to demonstrate how each of these problem areas has been dealt with. All of the successful attempts incorporated the essentials of the change model plus a considerable amount of knowledge and skill on the part of the women involved in the interventions. There is no way the complexity or difficulty of changing human systems can be minimized. But the probability for effecting change for the positive growth of women seems greater if the interventions are based on a solid conceptualization of women's needs and development, as well as on a systematic model for change process. In the early stages, nonetheless, there is likely to be a certain amount of "trial and error."

But planful, successful change is possible in counselor education programs and can facilitate the career development of the students, especially the women. One of the biggest steps is deciding to become a change agent in one's own department/institution and risking/delighting in the consequences of the involvement. The decision entails putting oneself personally and professionally on the cutting edge.

It has been proposed that systems interventions on behalf of women be based on a conceptual model of human development such as the career development model described in Hansen (1974), as well as on a knowledge and application of principles of organizational change such as the process model presented here. Counseling students and counselor educators grounded in both should have enormous potential for making educational systems more responsive to the developmental needs of women, to give them greater freedom of choice, more positive self-concepts, and greater control over their own decisions and their lives. These would seem to be appropriate goals for counselor education.

REFERENCES

Blocher, D. *Developmental counseling.* Second edition. New York: Ronald Press 1974.

Blocher, D.H., and Rapoza, R.S. A systematic eclectic model for counseling—consulting. *Elementary School Guidance and Counseling,* Dec., 1972, *7,* 106-112.

Cross, K.P. Women want equality in higher education. *The Research Reporter,* Center for Research and Development in Higher Education, 1972, *7,* 5-8.

Hansen, L.S. A career development curriculum framework for counselors to promote female growth. In M.A.J. Guttman and P. Donn (Eds.): *Women and ACES: Perspective and issues.* Muncie, Indiana: Accelerated Development Inc., 1974.

Women's Equity Action League. Facts about women in education. Washington, D.C., 1971 (mimeo).

Chapter 29

CONTINUING EDUCATION AND THE DEVELOPMENT OF ADULT WOMEN*

HELEN STAVRIDOU ASTIN

IN THE late 1960s and early 1970s, interest in nontraditional education, with its diverse students and new goals and programs, emerged in higher education. Today, nontraditional study is growing: College and university espousal of innovative approaches is reflected in external degrees, flexible curricula and requirements, and open universities.

As institutions have opened their doors to new populations—veterans, housewives, second-careerists—they have been challenged to provide appropriate and flexible curricula. However, little information exists about the specific needs and interests of these populations or about their personal characteristics and modes of learning.

About one-and-a-half years ago, the National Coalition for Research on Women's Education and Development sponsored a study to address some of the issues concerning the characteristics, interests, and needs of one of these populations: adult women returning to higher education. Colleges and universities have responded to this group with continuing education programs for women (CEW).

This chapter focuses on the women in this study, describing their needs, interests, aspirations, goals, and views about education, work, and social action. It also shares perceptions of how families view the wife and mother who is returning to school. What have been some of the changes in the family and in the women themselves which permit them to assume new responsibilities and to combine new roles with old? In what ways have the educational development and aspirations, occupational status and plans, and personal growth of these women been directly affected by their experiences in programs of continuing education?

Fifteen diverse CEWs were selected for this study: they represent rural versus urban settings, two- versus four-year institutions, coed

*From *The Counseling Psychologist*, 1976, 6(1), 55-60.

versus primarily single-sex institutions, sectarian versus non-sectarian status, mixed versus homogeneous populations, state versus institutional bases, and large, multi-faceted versus small, single-focus programs.

In the spring and summer of 1974, case studies of the fifteen programs were conducted through site visits and in-depth interviews with administrators in the parent institutions, program directors, and members of the staff. In addition, about 300 women who had participated or were participating in various programs, such as group counseling, credit or noncredit courses, and certificate or degree programs, were randomly selected and interviewed. We also conducted interviews with spouses and children.

In the fall and winter of 1974, a mail survey of about 1,000 participants, 300 of their spouses, and 1,000 alumnae (women who had participated three to five years earlier) of the 15 programs was conducted. The discussion here is based primarily on responses from 649 women (68%) participating in the programs during the survey period and from 153 spouses (54%). Some data from the interviews are also presented.

ADULT DEVELOPMENT AND EDUCATION

Scholars in the field of adult development (Flavell, 1970; Neugarten, 1973; Simon, 1968) have generally agreed that adults passively accommodate experiences, whereas children and youth actively assimilate them. While children's cognitive development is based on physical and maturational aspects, adults cognitive style is based on unprogrammed experiences, such as psychotherapy and adult education.

While youth is described as a search for identity, adulthood is depicted as a search for "integrity" and a denial of despair. However, adult women in continuing education are searching not only for integrity but also for identity, in that they are asking themselves who they are other than wife and mother.

Differences have been observed in the coping styles of men and women in later life. Although men become more affiliative as they mature, women show a great need for independence, become more outward and assertive, and remove themselves somewhat from the role of nurturer (Brim, 1974; Lowenthal & Chiriboga, 1973). Baruch (1967) found that a temporal cycle in the achievement motive is associated with the age and family situation of college-educated women. The high achievement need that a woman experiences before she begins a family appears to be followed by a decline in achievement need. However, once the children are grown, the need for achievement returns to the previous high level. Changes in the life cycle of women suggest a need for redirection, accomplishment, and new work orientation.

Although they are defining self in terms of new roles and experiences, adult reentry women also typify the adult learner in that they are conscious of their reason for learning and understand the benefits of education (Tough, 1968).

Even though the literature on adult development has described the developmental differences between youth and adulthood and between adult men and women, it has not differentiated adult women by past roles and experiences. Adult women described in the literature have primary roles of wife and mother. There is no information on the similarities and differences between women with career commitments and those primarily with family commitments. Also, do women who had careers, who were involved in scholarly, scientific, and artistic endeavors, have adult crises similar to those of men? Do adult women who have always been outwardly oriented show needs for affiliation in adulthood similar to those of adult men?

The largest proportion of the population in this study was adult women who are searching for identity and integrity, who have new outwardly defined goals, and who are actively assimilating new experiences. However, the study includes a small proportion of women who have always had careers, and who have returned to college to update or to develop skills for a second career.

The study also addressed the complex interactions between familial variables and educational and occupational outcomes. Questions central to the study were: How do the internalized sex roles and the support—or lack of it—from significant others (spouses and children) affect women's self-concept, achievements, and aspirations? What kinds of attitudes and behaviors, exhibited by the immediate family, elicit differential perceptions and behaviors by women about their self-concept, sense of personal worth, emotional well-being and mental health, need achievement, motivation, and educational-occupational accomplishment?

Since adult women in continuing education programs are a unique population (age span, diverse education, career continuity and discontinuity), we could examine the complexities in the educational and career development of women. For example, because of the age range, we were able to analyze the interests, aspirations, and concerns of women between 20 and 65 or over. Thus, we could examine interests and status as they appear for women 30 and under, between 31 and 40, between 41 and 50, and 51 or older.

In the literature on adult education, four basic terms, which are often used interchangeably but which communicate specific ideas and concepts, frequently occur. They are adult education, continuing education, recurrent education, and lifelong learning. Adult education, offered primarily by secondary institutions and community agencies, refers to vocational and avocational courses and experiences specifically for adults. Continuing education, offered in postsecondary institutions, refers to programs that enable adults to upgrade their education and occupational skills. Recurrent education and lifelong learning refer to learning for learning's sake or to training for better jobs.

Recurrent education is a European idea largely pioneered by the Centre for Educational Research and Innovation of the Organization for Economic Cooperation and Development. It provides for "new relationships between individuals, educational opportunities, and working careers that would lead to more equity between social classes, ethnic and age groups, men and women" (Gass, 1973). Recurrent education implies the distribution of education over a life span, permitting leisure, work, and education to alternate throughout life.

The important premises of recurrent education are

1. Learning can take place at any time.
2. Learning should be equitable; the goal of recurrent education is to achieve educational and social equality.
3. The need for recurrent education results from rapid change and growth in knowledge and information.
4. Work and social experiences should be important considerations in admissions and curricular designs.
5. Recurrent education expands the concept of educational opportunity to include all of one's life.

Since the primary purpose of recurrent education is to reduce inequality and offer a second chance, women's interest in recurrent education is closely allied to their concern for equal opportunity in the form of equal rights, chances, and achievement. Moreover, since recurrent education provides opportunities for career development, it is a way to update skills obsolete because of long-term interruptions for family.

Recurrent education epitomizes the public concern for equal educational opportunity which began in the 1960s and paralleled the efforts of women leaders of CEW. Even though it was only recently that a national conference took place (the 1973 National Institute of Education conference on recurrent education) and a publication was issued (*Lifelong Learners—A New Clientele for Higher Education* in 1974), the efforts of CEW directors were evident in the early 1960s.

However, women in continuing education programs constitute only one part of the adult population seeking education. In 1962, a national study (Johnstone & Rivera, 1965) sponsored by the Carnegie

Corporation inquired into adult education in America. Specifically, the study examined educational activities, reactions to continuing education, and facilities.

About 25 million adults were active in some form of learning during the year of the study. About one-half had enrolled in courses part time. Their activities ranged from vocational to recreational to academic. Their median age was 36.5. They were about equally divided between men and women. They were somewhat better educated than the typical adult and more likely to hold white-collar than blue-collar jobs.

When rates of study were examined among men and women at different age levels, a substantially higher proportion of men than women under 35 were engaged in learning activities. In general, more adults were taking courses because of interest than because of specific occupational objectives. However, more men than women were participating in educational activities directly related to occupational goals.

The more facilities available in a given community, the more likely were the adults to pursue educational activities. Johnstone and Rivera concluded in 1962 that the audience for adult education would increase more rapidly than the population as a whole and that learning-for-work and learning-for-leisure together would dominate the adult education scene in the future.

A close examination of studies of the educational needs of adult women and the programs designed to serve them reveals parallels to the findings of this study. Johnstone's and Rivera's 1962 predictions have been realized and one can now forecast that the growth will continue.

CONTINUING EDUCATION PROGRAMS FOR WOMEN

Continuing education programs for women were originally developed to facilitate the entry or reentry of women past the traditional age of 18 into the academic world. A recent publication by the Women's Bureau, *Continuing Education for Women: Current Developments* (1974), highlights the historical development of women and continuing education. The first CEWs emerged in the early 1960s. Although by 1963 there were only about twenty such efforts, the Women's Bureau identified about 100 programs in 1966. In 1971, 376 institutions with special programs or services for adult women were listed with a brief description in *Continuing Education Programs and Services for Women.* However, research efforts by both Mattfeld (1971) and Mulligan (1973) have indicated that these programs vary considerably in quality and services. Mulligan received 190 responses to her survey of the 376 programs; 61 indicated no special services for mature women. She surmised the programs were included in the publication either because they offered courses of interest to women or courses at times convenient for women.

Continuing education programs for women have expanded rapidly. To a large extent, this expansion has resulted from the increasing numbers of women seeking employment, technological changes that have reduced housework, declining birth rates, longer life spans, rising living costs, and encouragement and support by the women's movement.

The literature highlights some of the characteristics of those in continuing education. Women who continue their education can be roughly divided into two groups: those whose goal is a career or work and those whose goal is further education or a degree but not employment.

Women who need to work come to continuing education programs to gain or to update marketable skills. Some women have jobs but have discovered that without a college degree they have no opportunity for advancement. Also in continuing education are men and women who have been employed for a number of years and who are now preparing for midlife career changes. For the largest proportion of women in continuing education, family demands have decreased and work is an appealing prospect.

Non-career-oriented women are attracted to continuing education for various reasons. Generally, they wish to keep abreast of the advances in so many fields; rapid proliferation of knowledge has made an education a life-long endeavor. Precisely what motivates them to enter these programs? Avocational interests often lead individuals to enroll in courses. Some women find they are bored; their children are in school or gone, their husbands have an active social life, and philanthropic activities no longer seem satisfying. For a few women, enrolling may serve as an excuse to refuse the community agencies trying to enlist their services or as a refuge from marital and family problems. Some women in degree programs left college to work or marry and now find that they can complete their degrees.

As women reenter the academic world, they are confronted with both personal problems and institutional barriers. The first problem a woman faces is how to go about returning to school or beginning a career. Another problem is the lack of confidence which a woman invariably feels after being out of school for some time, particularly if she has been a homemaker in the interim. She is apprehensive about taking notes, remembering material, using the library, and writing papers and exams. Afraid she will not be able to keep up with the 18- to 22-year-olds, she hesitates to enter competitive academic situations. Arranging a schedule to include both academic and household responsibilities is a problem for many women, particularly those with families. A return to college involves not only classes, but also library work and study, which all require a major time investment.

Guilt is another problem with which these women must cope. Because of an internalized concept of their primary role as wife and mother, they feel guilty about leaving their homes and families to undertake a time-consuming venture so personally fulfilling. Sometimes they feel selfish for neglecting their families or spending money that could have gone toward a family trip or the children's college educations.

CEWs were established by individuals who recognized that these problems were major impediments to women contemplating a return to college or work. The programs were developed to help women make the transition with a minimum of extraneous complications, as well as determine the direction they wished to take.

THE WOMEN AND THEIR FAMILIES

The women in continuing education programs vary a great deal in age, socioeconomic and marital status, religious background, and so forth. To view them only as adult middle-class women whose family responsibilities have been reduced so they can return to education for personal development would be shortsighted and quite erroneous. Unfortunately, colleges have often viewed these women as dilettantes who have come back to take a course here and there. They have not been considered persons who need to develop their talents so they can have greater access to occupations and support themselves or their families. The study included women who were young and single. Some were very poor, some had high educational attainment, and some had not completed high school. For example, among women enrolled during the past academic year, one-third were under age 30, with one in seven under 25. One in seven were also over 51 years of age. The women's educational level prior to entry varied: one in seven had never been to college while one in 10 had graduate degrees.

The women also differed in family status. Seventeen percent had never married while 15 percent were separated or divorced. About one-third were childless.

Education and Job Aspirations

What are the educational and occupational aspirations and plans of women in continuing education programs?

When asked why they sought continuing education, the women most often mentioned becoming more educated, achieving independence and a sense of identity, and preparing for a job. Job preparation was a much more important objective for single, separated, divorced, or widowed women than for married women.

A little less than half of the women were involved in some kind of academic or training program. Financial barriers seem to prohibit access to education. Women who indicated that their ability to finance their education was a major concern were less likely to be in a degree or certificate program.

Women in degree or certificate programs had come to continuing education because of job dissatisfaction. These women may have been in dead-end and low-paying jobs; thus, dissatisfaction with their status motivated them to seek further education and training to improve their occupational status. Certificate programs are usually intensive courses of short duration which provide training for paraprofessional jobs, e.g. legal assistant, landscape architect, and counseling aide. Such programs permit women to get jobs without spending a lot of time in training. This preparation also provides for interim work experience before a woman makes a long term commitment. In an interview, one woman said, "I'll try the legal work. If I like it and feel competent in it, then I can consider the longer and more expensive training to become a lawyer."

In general, women in academic programs have a great sense of direction, feel independent, and have mapped out a plan of action. The continuing education program provides the means for them to reenter college and to work toward their goals without the usual obstacles of a regular program, i.e. admissions requirements, inflexible programming as to time and place, and restrictions on part-time study.

Occupational Status

At the time of the survey, over one half of the women in the programs were also working. Of them, two thirds were working full time. The majority of these were again in clerical, secretarial, and teaching jobs. Nearly half of all working women were making less than $10,000. Working women often utilized the program primarily to get information about career possibilities.

Whether a woman worked or not related to several independent factors; being single, and for married women, being childless and having a husband with a relatively low income, were factors in her being employed.

Working women reported that their mothers worked while they were growing up, that their husbands approved of their working, and that they perceived themselves as independent. They held liberal views about the appropriate age for children before the mother returns to college or work, i.e. a mother's decision does not depend on a child's age.

For a married woman to work, unless she has an economic need, the conditions must be right. She must have had early experiences that socialized her to value independence. A working mother could have provided a model, as well as contributed to personal development and a sense of independence. The married woman also needs to feel that her husband supports her in her activities outside the home. Other important conditions are a childless marriage or children who have grown up.

Further analyses identified the characteristics of women who had a strong career orientation and of those who aspired to nontraditional fields. Career orientation was identified by an item in which women indicated the importance of a career to their personal fulfillment. The career-oriented women were more likely to aspire to careers in nontraditional areas for women, were more liberal in their views about age of children and mother's involvement outside the home, were more positive toward the women's movement, rated themselves high on intellectual self-confidence, and were more likely to be working and to have worked in the past. Career-oriented women were also more likely to have been discontent at home. However, their husbands approved of their working.

Benefits to Women and Families

How have the woman and the family been affected by the woman's return to college? What changes have taken place in these women, or their families, work, and interpersonal experiences and relationships? Have their lives changed and, if so, in what ways?

Overall, women see great benefits to themselves. Invariably, they feel increased self-awareness and self-esteem. They are more confident and more open to new ideas and to a variety of new people. In open-ended interviews with more than 200 women, a question asked was, "In what way have you changed?" Here are some typical comments:

> "The Program was a turning point for me. It showed me what was available. I had been vegetating while married. The program made a significant change in the direction of my life."
>
> "I am not stupid. I lived with that image for 28 years. In the last 3 years that image has changed."
>
> "It gave me my whole future. It kept me from a nervous breakdown. I thought after marriage had failed me I had nothing and I was very unsure of myself. The program has made me realize that there was more to the world than just my little bit of trouble."

The women also value the newly acquired knowledge and skills.

> "I don't feel inadequate anymore. I can approach issues critically and evaluate things, situations properly."
>
> "I really look forward to the mornings of school and to thinking about *just me*."
>
> "I like me better. I am more worthwhile, more realistic, honest."

Not only has their own self-respect increased, but their respect for other women has also grown. Of course, these two go hand-in-hand: A woman cannot like and respect herself as a woman unless she has positive feelings toward other women and vice versa.

Fewer than 3 percent of the women reported negative effects from continuing education, such as greater confusion or decreased self-confidence.

As to consequences for the family, the overall effects of continuing education were positive. Family members became more organized and self-reliant:

"The family has become closer."
"We interact to a greater extent."
"Marriage has improved."
"The children's respect for me has increased."

Of course, some women and their families experience some negative consequences, such as more tensions in the marital relationship or disapproval by neighbors.

Women's Self-Perceptions

What views do these women hold about themselves and their roles as wives, mothers, and workers?

In addition to motivation, self-concept is an important variable in a woman's decision to pursue higher education or to go to work. For some women who have been away from school for a long time and who were skilled in other than educational or occupational areas, the sense and acceptance of self are important determinants in whether they will venture outside the home.

Unfortunately, this study could not examine changes in the self-concept prior to the decision and entry into continuing education. Also, it could not compare these women with a group similar in other respects which opted to remain at home.

In responding to the question, "Where do you rate yourself on various traits compared to the typical woman of your age?", the women emerge with a positive self-image: at least one-fifth rated themselves in the highest 10 percent of their peers on effectiveness on the job, independence, academic ability, and drive to achieve. They rated themselves similarly on success as a mother and as a wife. Only four ability traits were consistently rated low: mathematical, athletic, artistic, and public speaking. Comparing the women's self-ratings with those of their spouses revealed differences on these self-ratings similar to those for college populations of men and women. In this study, the men's overall self-concept emerged higher than the women's.

More husbands than wives rated themselves high on self-confidence, leadership, job effectiveness, and public speaking and writing ability. More men also rated themselves higher on mental and emotional well-being and on physical stamina. Differences favored women on skills that relate to their family roles, i.e. success as a wife and mother, on physical attributes, such as appearance, and on popularity with men and women.

Self-perceptions differ from the perceptions of others. We asked the husbands to rate their wives on these traits. Even though the women rated themselves higher on physical appearance and on popularity than the men rated themselves, husbands tended to rate their wives even higher. The husbands also rated their wives higher than the women rated themselves on such competencies as mathematics ability, success as a wife and mother, and self-confidence. However, women rated themselves higher than their husbands rated them on drive to achieve, stamina, independence, mental and emotional well-being, and athletics. One wonders whether societal stereotypes indicating that these traits are not exhibited as often by women biased these men so they rated their wives in stereotypic ways.

In another analysis, we further estimated the actual agreement or disagreement between a husband's perceptions of his wife and the wife's self-ratings on each trait. Overall, husbands and wives disagreed quite extensively in perceptions. The most disagreement was over physical stamina (66%) and drive to achieve (66%) and the least disagreement was over physical appearance (45%).

In the analyses of education and occupational status and plans the most significant self-ratings were "independence," "intellectual self-confidence," and "leadership ability." Whether these women were characterized by such traits all along and thus were able to make the break from wife and mother for education or a job or whether work and recent educational involvement provided experiences that enhanced their selfconcepts is hard to ascertain with these data. However, autonomy and self-confidence are important characteristics of career-oriented adult women who decide to pursue educational activities.

Effect of the Women's Movement

How do these adult women view the women's movement? What effect has the movement had on self-assessment, motivation, and clarification of interests and needs?

We asked the women if they had been affected by the women's movement and, if so, in what ways. Their responses from the most frequent to the least frequent were as follows:

Their most frequent response was "it increased my awareness of the various issues, e.g. equality of opportunity, pay, sex roles." (49%)

"It reinforced my views, encouraged me to do what I am doing." (24%)

"I have greater respect for and understanding of other women, including myself." (20%)

"I don't like the extremes of the women's movement." (5%)

"It interferes in the relationships with the opposite sex—it is antiethical to femininity." (3%)

To quote one woman, "The movement has made me aware that I am one of the untapped resources that should be utilized. This means both being given an opportunity and accepting a responsibility."

Another woman said: "The women's movement freed my potential. I realized I had leadership ability. For many years I felt I was a derailed train; now I am on the track."

Another one said, "Before I was not sure about women. I thought they were dull and sneaky, but now I have a high regard for them."

Sixty-nine percent of the women had raised their goals and had become more ambitious as a result of the women's movement: "I feel that I can go in any direction I want." Some women reported that the women's movement had made them feel restless and discontent or that their "marriage had been threatened or dissolved." Whether these outcomes can be viewed as positive or negative, it is hard to say; I am sure it depends on the individual case.

There is some disagreement between the women's and husband's views about how the wives have been affected by the movement. Even though some husbands indicated that their wives have gained self-awareness and increased their self-esteem, a greater proportion believe that their wives' traditional views have been reinforced and that their wives have no respect for aggressive feminists. Similarly, fewer indicated that their wives are more interested in encouraging girls to pursue all kinds of careers or to think girls should be able to join boys' organizations. One wonders to what extent their views and projections interfered with their perceptions of how their wives might actually have been affected by the movement.

A related question was whether the woman had been active in the women's movement. At least one-fifth said that they participated actively. Moreover, there were 7 percent who said they were members of national women's organizations (NOW, WEAL); 15 percent said they participated in consciousness-raising groups; 10 percent had participated in feminist meetings, conferences or demonstrations; 10 percent belonged to women's caucuses, coalitions, or special commissions; and 20 percent had done community, legal, or political work on behalf of women.

Who were the active women and what were their demographic and personal characteristics? Women active in the movement had done volunteer work in the past. In essence, they had always had an interest in group activities and in "causes." They were likely to have had group counseling. Their experience with counseling can be interpreted in several ways: on one hand, group counseling may have been important because it provided an opportunity to discuss and share problems, concerns, feelings, and views with other women. It could reflect that women who were searching for a self-identity and a new life style sought out counseling. On the other hand, women who have had a positive experience in counseling might be more likely to become active in the women's movement as a result of that experience. Some evidence supports this latter view, since the "active" women indicated that one outcome from their participation in the programs had been an increase in respect for other women.

The "active" women in the movement rated themselves high on academic ability and had received high grades in high school or college. They viewed their husbands as supportive; they had also had a working mother while growing up. The nonwhite women were most likely to be active in the women's movement.

Reaction of Husband and Family

How do husbands and children feel when the mother asserts herself outside the home? Are they supportive? Do they feel threatened?

A relatively large proportion of the women had been away from school for a long time—almost one fourth of them for at least eleven years. Thus, the decision to return to academia and to prepare for a career or even to take courses for personal development is not only a new experience for the women but it also affects the whole family. She is satisfying herself not by concentrating on the family alone, but by doing things for herself. As one woman put it, "I really look forward to the mornings of school and to thinking about just me." This new view is bound to create a variety of feelings in the rest of the family. It is a new experience for them to see "mother" or "wife" excited about going to school, or to listen to her talking about her experiences as a student. She is a new person who feels more competent and knowledgeable.

The majority of husbands had positive feelings about their wives' activities. They saw the wife's new role as not only making her a happier, more actualized person, but also as benefiting the whole family intellectually and financially. Husbands believed that as wives increased their earning potential, they would assume part of the financial load. They also reported positive effects on the children, who became more independent and more willing to share household responsibilities. They also became more interested in their school work; mother as a student provided a role model for them.

Of course, apprehensions developed too. Some spouses thought that the marriage suffered and that there were more tensions in the family as a result of the wife's new involvement. In response to an open-ended question, "How do you think your wife's educational plans and/or future work will affect you?" they indicated from the most frequent to the least frequent the following outcomes:

Make her happier, more fulfilled	92%
I'll benefit from her experience	74%
Improve our marriage; make it a better partnership	58%
Would lessen the burden on me to support the family	41%
Give us less time together	27%
Put strain on our marriage	10%
Make her restless	3%

Husbands realized that it was important for their wives to have a career in addition to the family. Thirty-four percent considered it essential for her fulfillment and another 30 percent said it was very important. Only 12 percent considered it unimportant. Moreover, a little over half the husbands believed that both husband and wife should share as breadwinners.

During the study, we interviewed 88 children—50 girls and 38 boys. Although they ranged from 9 to 31 years of age, the majority (73%) were under 18. Children's views about why their mother was going to college differed somewhat from the views of their fathers. Only 29 percent mentioned "personal growth," while 58 percent believed their mother went to college to prepare for or to get a better job. To a similar question, 58 percent of the husbands indicated "personal growth" and 38 percent to prepare for a job. One wonders whether these differential perceptions result from generational differences in values or whether the children receive different reasons from their mothers for interests outside the home. When I discussed these differences in perceptions, some women mentioned that it is easier to give practical reasons or reasons that indicate benefits to the total family than to give personal reasons—another outcome of the sex socialization process that reinforces the women's role to nurture.

The children unanimously agreed that their mothers were good students. To the question, "How have things changed around the house?" the two most frequent answers were: "I spend less time with her" and "I have more household chores." Few (between 6% and 9%) voiced any disapproval of their mother's working before, now, or in the future.

We asked the children sixteen years or older what they might have done differently if they were in their mother's place with her life to live again. Sixty-one percent said that they would have lived differently: they would have gone to school earlier, had fewer children or spaced their children differently, asked their husbands to share more household responsibilities, or married later or not at all. All the responses reflect the known barriers to a woman's educational and occupational development: marriage and children.

If we were to ask the children the same question about their fathers, I would expect that marriage and children would not have been mentioned as barriers to their father's development or self-actualization. I would predict that the children would probably have mentioned aspects of the educational preparation or work and career activities.

SUMMARY

To summarize briefly the highlights of our empirical findings so far: women who participate in continuing education programs are an exceedingly diverse group that does not fit the stereotype of the bored housewife dabbling in a little culture. These women are serious, determined, and very frequently pragmatic in their goals. Those women who enter continuing education with a strong career orientation differ in many respects from the other participants: they express less traditional views about the role of women, are more supportive of the women's movement, and have more self-confidence. Although they are also more likely to be dissatisfied at home, their children and husbands are generally supportive of their work and educational activities. Practically all the women see their continuing education as being highly beneficial both personally and professionally. Many report profound changes in their self-concepts. Although only a minority of these women could be labelled activists, they are uniformly supportive of the women's movement and see it as a positive force in their lives.

Whereas the women's movement has given women the freedom to "be," continuing education has provided the support and training that adult women need to develop their talents and to acquire skills that enable them to enter or reenter the labor market. The same might be said about other campus efforts, such as women's studies, women's centers, and programmatic research.

The very existence of these programs provides a psychological boost to a woman considering venturing from her home. The programs are proof that she is not alone and that she will be meeting and attending classes with women in similar positions with similar concerns. The programs indicate that, as an adult, she can go to college or begin a career; others like her have done it successfully.

The programs offered by continuing education are strongly based on the job market and organized to develop skills for competent performance. Most provide skill-oriented courses, as well as liberal arts curricula, to meet the diverse needs and interests expressed by their clients. Counseling and career guidance play key roles in the educational process.

Time and place constraints have been greatly reduced by restructing the delivery of courses from, for example, 50 minutes three times a week to a three-hour sequence once a week, and by using available space in churches and schools to reduce transportation hassles. Admissions procedures and traditional performance criteria have been altered so they are more appropriate for adults.

While many colleges and universities have recognized the demand for continuing education and have developed programs, support is often qualified. The programs are frequently self-supporting rather than university financed; their existence depends on the income from the courses. While this arrangement is good in that a program must meet the needs of its audience to survive, it is unfortunate in that it necessitates a high price for courses and allows little funding for financial aid or program development. Moreover, the programs are not completely autonomous; they depend on the continued support of an administrator in the parent institution. Administrative favor and financial success are two key determinants of a program's continuation.

Continuing education programs for women clearly point out the need for institutional change. College and universities must adopt a more flexible attitude to accommodate individual differences. They must relax nonessential academic regulations and requirements that do not apply to older women returning to school. These programs are in the forefront of higher education innovation, demonstrating how changes can be made with no sacrifice of educational quality. They have tried to remove structural and institutional barriers, as well as to alleviate some of the problems and concerns of the populations they serve. They deserve our support.

REFERENCES

Baruch, R. The achievement motive in women: Implications for career development. *Journal of Personality and Social Psychology,* 1967, *5,* 260-267.

Brim, O.G. Jr. *Selected theories of the male mid-life crisis: A comparative analysis.* Paper presented at the meeting of the American Psychological Association, New Orleans, 1974.

Flavell, J. Cognitive changes in adulthood. In L.R. Goulet & P.B. Baltes (Eds.), *Lifespan developmental psychology.* New York: Academic Press, 1970.

Gass, J.R. Recurrent education—The issues. In *Recurrent Education.* Washington: National Institute of Education, 1973.

Johnstone, W.C., & Rivera, R.J. *Volunteers for learning: A study of the educational pursuits of American adults.* Chicago: Aldine Publishing Co., 1965.

Lowenthal, M.F., & Chiriboga, D. Social stress and adaptation: Toward a life-course perspective. In D. Eisdorfer & M.P. Lawton (Eds.), *Psychology of adult development and aging*. Washington: American Psychological Association, 1973.

Mattfeld, J.A. *A decade of continuing education: Dead end or open door?* mimeographed, 1971.

Mulligan, K.L. *A question of opportunity: Women and continuing education*. 1973. (ED 081 323).

Neugarten, B.L. Personality change in late life: A developmental perspective. In C. Eisdorfer & M.P. Lawton (Eds.), *Psychology of adult development and aging*. Washington: American Psychological Association, 1973.

Simon, A. Emotional problems of women—Mature years and beyond. *Psychosomatics*, 1968, *9*, 12-16.

Tough, A. *Why adults learn: A study of the major reasons for beginning and continuing a learning project*. Ontario: Ontario Institute for Studies in Education, 1968.

Women's Bureau, U.S. Department of Labor. *Continuing education programs and services for women*. Washington: U.S. Government Printing Office, 1971.

Women's Bureau, U.S. Department of Labor. *Continuing education for women: current developments*. Washington: U.S. Government Printing Office, 1974.

Section VIII

ASSESSMENT OF FEMALE CAREER INTERESTS

One of the problems that has plagued career counselors in their attempts to work with women has been that of using fair and appropriate instruments to measure the vocational interests of women. Major questions exist around how and when interest inventories can be utilized with women to broaden options and produce exploration of new areas. Limitations and biases in interest inventories also have relevance for theoreticians, as methodological inadequacies may build unintentional bias into research and contribute to an inaccurate picture of women's vocational behavior.

In the first chapter in this section, Cole and Hanson raise basic questions about the objectives, assumptions, and methodology of interest measurement. As a starting point they provide an excellent overview of theoretical formulations and relevant research related to the concept (construct) of interest, goals of measurement, and dominant rationales used to construct and validate interest inventories. Some of the following questions are discussed: Should we attempt to compare directly the interests of women and men within the same occupational group? Should separate or combined norm groups be used? Should women be told their position within both female and male norm groups? Cole and Hanson also discuss two issues which result in a set of problems particularly relevant for today. First, interest measurement was predominantly developed for and about men. We are now clearly concerned about women, and the applicability of traditional approaches for women must be examined. Second, interest measurement has depended on a relatively stable social situation in which no large breaks or changes have occurred during the socialization process within an individual life history or during a point or period in the society's history. This assumption no longer fits either society or the individual as indicated in other parts of this volume.

An illustration of these problems can be seen by looking at one common method of test construction and validation which is based on the rationale that if people now like to do activities similar to the activities of a job, they will like those job activities and consequently be satisfied with their job. Due to differential socialization, not liking an activity might have quite a different meaning for a man who had tried the activity and liked it and been allowed to like it than for a woman whose socialization ruled it out. We know that sex differences in interests exist, but the relevance and implications of these differences for predicting occupational satisfaction are not known. Current inventories reflect the socialization process; the challenging question raised by Cole and Hanson is whether the socialization process of females is as predictive of job satisfaction as the same process for males when females have not been socialized to examine as wide a range of possible interests.

Cole and Hanson describe two hypotheses which generate widely divergent implications on which to base future action in relation to interest measurement. The "socialization dominance" hypothesis suggests that "until the areas of socially accepted interest options become broadened during a person's development, the careers in which such people will be satisfied will not broaden." In contrast, Cole favors the "opportunity dominance" hypothesis which states that "when career opportunities widen, people will find satisfaction in a wider range of careers in spite of limiting aspects of their earlier socialization." Implications of these hypotheses for theory and practice are discussed.

It is recognized that past experiences influence vocational interests. In the next chapter, Prediger and Cole suggest means to insure that measures of vocational interests do not simply reflect sex-role stereotypes resulting from past socialization. Unfortunately, little information exists about how to predict future satisfaction of women or men in new (nontraditional) occupational areas. The methodological implications of the socialization dominance and opportunity dominance hypothesis, described by Cole and Hanson, are further explored. They examine methods for reporting vocational interests which do and do not reflect differences in the socialization of males and females. Second, the problems and issues involved in using current employment patterns as criteria for validating and evaluating interest inventory results are discussed. Some of the suggestions made by Prediger and Cole may be controversial, as they contradict some of the procedures employed in some frequently used popular inventories. However, it is heartening that we have gone beyond obvious superficial criticisms of interest measurement and that creative and well-considered technical innovations are being discussed. For further discussion of the issues raised by Prediger and Cole, see Holland, Gottfredson, and Gottfredson (1975) and Prediger and Cole (1975).

In the final chapter in this section, the National Institute of Education has proposed a set of guidelines for the assessment of sex bias and sex fairness in interest inventories. "The working definition of sex bias expresses the primary concern that career alternatives not be limited by bias or stereotypical use of sex roles in the world of work." This chapter generates a checklist of considerations that is based on the issues raised in the previous two chapters in relation to the inventory itself, technical information, and interpretive information. The comments on interpretive information should be especially useful to counselors.

Considerable disagreement as to what constitutes sex bias, or, conversely, sex fairness, in interest measurement remains. The chapters included in this section provide only a sample of some current thinking on interest measurement, and the reader should go beyond the readings in this section to obtain a comprehensive understanding of this area. Despite controversy, we have at least made a start in raising relevant questions, providing guidelines for appropriate use, and generating technical improvement for minimizing sex bias. Cole and Hanson conclude that, if used appropriately, interest inventories can be useful tools within a developmental counseling context. They point out that with proper guidelines, two primary objectives of interest inventories can be met: broadening the options of both sexes throughout the full range of career areas and stimulating exploratory behavior in relation to self and occupation. The suggestions made in the articles in this section for the development and use of interest inventories have important implications for facilitating the career development of both women and men by expanding choices and options for both sexes.

BIBLIOGRAPHY

Holland, J.L., Gottfredson, G.D., and Gottfredson, L.S. Read our reports and examine the data: a response to Prediger and Cole. *Journal of Vocational Behavior,* 1975, *7,* 253-259.

Prediger, D.J., & Cole, N.S. It is time to face some issues: a response to Holland, Gottfredson, and Gottfredson. *Journal of Vocational Behavior,* 1975, *7,* 261-263.

Chapter 30

IMPACT OF INTEREST INVENTORIES ON CAREER CHOICE*

NANCY S. COLE AND GARY R. HANSON

Abstract

This chapter begins with two fundamental questions: What are interests and why do we measure them? The answers provided are that interests are a constellation of likes and dislikes leading to consistent patterns or types of behavior, and we measure them in order to predict some types of job satisfaction. Our theories of what interests are, however, tell us very little about how interests are linked to satisfaction. These issues are judged especially important in measuring women's interests because the prominent methodologies for interest measurement (the similarity of a person to people in an occupational group or the similarity of liked activities to activities required in an occupation) have possible severe limitations in predicting job satisfaction for women.

The authors argue that we are at a time in which present data do not tell us how to validly proceed with measuring women's interests. In the interim we are forced to accept one of two working hypotheses: either (1) the socialization of a woman's past will dominate and limit her to satisfaction in the limited range of careers acceptable in the past or (2) expanded career opportunities will dominate and women will find satisfaction in a wide range of careers in spite of past socialization. The authors strongly favor the interim use of the second hypothesis because they view it as less potentially destructive if wrong, especially when interest inventories are viewed as a stimulus to further career exploration within a broader career-guidance process.

Finally, within this context, the authors argue that interest inventories should be expected to demonstrate, as a kind of interim validity, that they broaden the exploratory options for both sexes and that they stimulate exploratory behavior. These interim requirements should not, however, replace the more basic need for research to better understand the relation of interest to types of job satisfaction.

---

*This research was funded under a contract to the ARIES Corporation (#OE-C-72-5240) from the National Institute of Education of the U. S. Department of Health, Education and Welfare. The views expressed do not necessarily reflect those of the ARIES Corporation, the National Institute of Education, or any agency of the U. S. government.

From National Institute of Education: Issues of Sex Bias and Sex Fairness in Career Interest Measurement. Washington, D.C., U.S. Dept. of Health, Education, and Welfare, 1975, pp. 1-36.

INTRODUCTION

NEW SITUATIONS and events often force reexamination of established institutions and beliefs. For example, the two decades following the 1954 Supreme Court decision on school desegregation have been marked by the reevaluation of societal institutions and beliefs in the light of increased awareness of the needs and rights of minority racial-ethnic groups. More recently, but with potential effects no less dramatic, the women's movement has aroused consciousness of another set of injustices and again forced reexamination of previously unquestioned actions and beliefs. Because of the power that derives from a person's occupation in this society, through both money and status, a focal area of the women's movement has been the career opportunities of women. One specific concern in this area is the effect that interest inventories have on women's career choices and, in particular, the possibility of a negative, limiting effect.

Thus interest measurement has become one of those established institutions whose basic tenets require scrutiny and reexamination. It is the purpose of this paper to raise again, in the light of our current understandings, questions about the principal objectives of interest measurement and the assumptions, rationales, or theories on which it is based, and to examine the implications of those objectives and assumptions for the career choices of women and men in a time of social flux and change.

INTEREST MEASUREMENT IN PERSPECTIVE

The problems, issues, and concerns that are emerging with regard to interest measurement are many and complex. Our own ideas and opinions on these topics have been in a state of change for several years and we doubt that the ideas in this paper will represent our final thoughts. At this point in our thinking we have been forced to reconsider some very fundamental aspects of interest measurement: what are interests and why are we trying to measure them? We believe such reconsideration is basic to an examination of the questions that relate to the usefulness or bias of interest inventories. Therefore we begin this paper by examining interest measurement in the perspective of its historical theories, purposes, and methods.

What Are Interests?

William James was one of the first psychologists to deal with the concept of interest. To James, "Only those items which I notice shape my mind—without selective interest, experience is an utter chaos. Interest alone gives accent and emphasis, light and shade, background and foreground—intelligible perspective, in a word" [1890, p. 403].

Thus James saw interests as a cognitive function of the mind, instrumental in selecting and organizing an individual's experience.

Kitson (1925) perceived the concept of interest in terms of the psychological constructs of "identification" and "self." To Kitson, "To be interested in a thing is to endeavor to identify one's self with it [p. 141].

In a classic review of interest measurement, Fryer (1931) distinguished between "subjective" and "objective" interests. Subjective interests were defined as *feelings* of pleasantness and unpleasantness toward certain experiences, and objective interests as observable *reactions* to such experiences. Both subjective and objective interests were viewed as acceptance-rejection activities.

In discussing interests, W. V. Bingham (1937), head of a group of individual psychologists at the Carnegie Institute of Technology, defined an interest as a tendency to become absorbed in an experience and to continue in it: "We therefore define interest not only in terms of the objects and activities which get attention and yield satisfaction, but also in terms of the strength of the tendencies to give attention to and seek satisfaction in these competing objects of interest" [p. 62].

Strong's early conception of interests revolved around an empirical definition based on the differentiation of men in various occupations by the Strong Vocational Interest Blank. Later, however, in the introductory chapter of *The Vocational Interests of Men and Women* (1943), Strong presented his views on the nature of interests somewhat differently. Simply stated, his definition of interests was as follows: "They [interests] point to what the individual wants to do, they are reflections of what he considers satisfying" [p. 19]. In more recent work Strong stated:

> What are interests? . . . They remind me of tropisms. We go toward liked activities, go away from disliked activities [1960, p. 12].
> Interest scores measure a complex of liked and disliked activities selected so as to differentiate members of an occupation from nonmembers. Such a complex is equivalent to a "condition which supplies stimulation for a particular type of behavior," i.e., toward or away from participation in the activities characteristic of a given occupation. Interest scores are consequently measures of drives [1955, p. 142].

The concept of interest was further refined by Carter (1944), who extended the concept of interest to include the ideas of "developmental growth," "the self-concept," and "identification." The main impact of his ideas can be gleaned from the following sample of his writing:

> . . . the individual derives satisfaction from the identification of himself with some respected group; by this method he seizes some sort of status. This identification leads to an interest in restricted activities and experiences; to the extent that this is true the person learns about the vocation and the vocational group [p. 185].

Darley (1941) suggested that interest types represented outgrowths of personality development and that occupational selection and elimination were functions of personality type as well as functions of abilities or aptitudes. Darley concluded that ". . . occupational interest types grow out of the development of the individual's personality" [p. 65].

The concept of interest type was further elaborated by Bordin (1943) in terms of self-concept and identification. He maintained that in answering an interest inventory an individual expresses his acceptance (or rejection) of a particular view or concept of himself in terms of his occupational stereotypes. For Bordin, interests encompass certain patterns of likes and dislikes that are expressions of personality, and as the self-concept fluctuates and changes so too will the pattern of likes and dislikes.

A somewhat different approach to the concept of interest has been provided by Berdie (1944): "When interests are considered as expressions of liking and disliking, attention can be paid to the objects liked or disliked. These objects form constellations; they have characteristics in common that enable us to place them in classes" [p. 153].

Berdie maintained that such constellations are relatively constant and can be considered fundamental aspects of personality. The specific interests or objects involved in the constellations can change and learning and emotional experiences can affect them, but the constellations (or patterns of interest) themselves are not as susceptible to experience and are probably determined by constitutional and early social factors.

Super (1949) formulated a conceptual definition much like Bordin's:

> Interests are the product of interaction between inherited aptitudes and endocrine factors on the one hand, and opportunity and social evaluation on the other. Some of the things a person does well bring him the satisfaction of mastery or the approval of his companions, and result in interests. Some of the things his associates do appeal to him and, through identification, he patterns his actions and interests after them; if he fits the pattern reasonably well he remains in it, but if not he must seek another identification and develop another self-concept and interest pattern [p. 406].

Holland's view of interests can be seen in the following excerpts from a recent book (Holland, 1973a):

> In short, what we have called "vocational interests" are simply another aspect of personality [p. 7].
>
> Just as we are more comfortable among friends whose tastes, talents, and values are similar to our own, so we are more likely to perform well at a vocation in which we "fit" psychologically . . . In the present theory, the congruence of a person and his environment is defined in terms of the structure of personality types and environmental models [p. 9].

In summary, we can note several important common features of these conceptions of interest. First, they are a constellation of likes and dislikes leading to consistent patterns or types of behaviors. Second, they may involve some mix of genetic and environmental causes, but they are certainly related to environmental influences. Third, although the explanations of interest relate to satisfaction with activities, they are not derived from a clear explication of the link between interests and satisfaction.

Why Measure Interests?

As described in the preceding section, interests are a pervasive part of a person's personality and an important guide to behavior. For this reason alone, it would be "interesting" to these theorists to measure interests. We are concerned here, however, not with researchers or theorists but with the implications of interest measurement for the people whose interests are being measured. When interest measures are used as feedback to such people, the basic goal or purpose of the interest measurement has been clear, even when only implicitly stated. *That goal has been to provide people with information that would help them identify careers in which they would be satisfied.* The word *satisfied* is used here to refer to various forms of satisfaction, including happiness and personal fulfillment.

Strong (1943) indicated this important link between interests and happiness or satisfaction: "The more happiness is stressed, and not mere efficiency, the more concern educators must have for interests; for they are indicators of what activities bring satisfaction" [p. 3].

The same basic goal remains today, as can be seen from Campbell (1971): "The Strong Blank is designed to help guide the student and the employee into areas where they are likely to find the greatest job satisfaction" [p. 2]. Similarly, according to Kuder (1968): "Interest scores . . . can be used to help [an individual] set goals likely to bring him personal fulfillment" [p. 3].

Interests and Satisfaction

Interests have been defined in varying ways: characteristic constellations of likes and dislikes, patterns of behavior, drives, self-concepts, or personality. The basic goal of measuring interests has been given as providing information to help identify occupational situations which will be satisfying and those which will not. Thus we must examine the link between interests as a characteristic of a person and the occupational environment as a source of a variety of types of satisfaction. As can be seen from the foregoing discussion of interests, this link is elusive at best.

The link between interests and satisfaction is provided by a primary theoretical theme of vocational psychology: that congruence between an individual and the environment leads to satisfaction in a job. This theme can be seen in different forms in both trait and factor theories and psychodynamic theories, the two lines in the historical development of vocational psychology identified by Crites (1969). The roots of the theme can be seen in the man-job matching model of Parsons (1909), and it has been emphasized in the writings of numerous other authors (e.g. Dawis, England, & Lofquist, 1964; Holland, 1966, 1973a).

Though espousing the congruence notion, interest inventory developers have not been directly concerned with the relation between personal and environmental characteristics. Instead, interest measures have been built around personal characteristics alone—namely, constellations of likes and dislikes that describe a person's behavior pattern or personality type. Thus the problem of the link between measured interests and job satisfaction remains a central problem for interest-measurement methodology.

Interest Measurement Methods

In this section we briefly survey the dominant rationales for interest-measurement methods and how they provide the link to job or career satisfaction, the stated basic goal.

People-similarity Rationale

Historically, the dominant method of interest measurement has derived from the observation that people in the same job have similar characteristics, similar likes and dislikes. As Darley and Hagenah (1955, p. 19) noted, "The most general clue to an understanding of interest measurement is found in the old adage that birds of a feather flock together." From this occurrence a logic or rationale for interest measurement can be stated:

> RATIONALE 1. If a person likes the same things that people in a particular job like, the person will be satisfied with the job.

According to this rationale, one measures the degree of similarity between a person's likes and dislikes and those of people in a number of jobs and concludes that the person will likely be most satisfied in the job for which the similarities are the greatest. The two dominant interest inventories, the Strong Vocational Interest Blank (SVIB) and the more recent Kuder Occupational Interest Survey (OIS), are implementations of this rationale. For simplicity of discussion, it will be referred to in this paper as the people-similarity rationale.

As stated, the people-similarity rationale is more an empirical observation than a rationale. And, in fact, interest measurement in its most widely used forms (the SVIB and the OIS) has been primarily an empirical science. Although the question "Why is a person who has interests similar to those of people in a job likely to be satisfied with that job?" has not been entirely ignored, it has received far less attention than the observation itself that such a person is likely to be satisfied. The apparent answer to this very basic question "Why?" can be gleaned from the conceptions of interest described above: People who stay in and are satisfied with a particular job do so because the job provides an environment that is, in some unspecified way, congruent with their constellation of likes and dislikes. Thus a person with interests similar to those of such people would have similarly congruent interests for that job environment.

Activity-similarity Rationale

A derivative of the people-similarity rationale that has received greater emphasis in recent years could be called the activity-similarity rationale. In its purest form, this rationale answers the question "Why?" that intervenes between similarity and satisfaction in a very direct way.

RATIONALE 2. If people like activities similar to the activities required by a job, they will like those job activities and consequently be satisfied with their job.

Under this rationale, one measures a person's likes and dislikes for common activities similar to those required on a job and concludes that the person will probably be most satisfied in the job requiring activities similar to those which the person now most likes to do.

A number of recent efforts have placed great emphasis on types of activities as they relate to job activities. The Ohio Vocational Interest Survey (D'Costa, Winefordner, Odgers, & Koons, 1970) emphasizes the data, people, things dimensions of job activity and uses actual job activities from the *Dictionary of Occupational Titles*. Holland's Self-Directed Search (Holland, 1973a) classifies past job-related activities into categories derived from and related to the structure of the world of work. Prediger and Roth (1974) provide a direct link from a job-activity orientation to a personality orientation seen in the structure of interests pervasive in present interest measures (Cole & Hanson, 1971; Holland, Whitney, Cole, & Richards, 1969). And recent interest inventory development at The American College Testing Program (ACT, 1974; Hanson, 1974) has relied on common, familiar activities with an apparent relation to job activities as the basis for two new inventories. None of these approaches, however, relies on a pure form of the activity-similarity rationale. Instead, activities have been used more as an indicator of the constellation or type of personality of the person than as a direct indicator of likely satisfaction with particular job activities.

How Have Interest Measures Been Validated?

If the basic goal of interest measurement is to relate to the many aspects of job satisfaction, the obvious way to validate interest measures is to empirically relate them to measures of job satisfaction. In fact, each of the two rationales described suggests a different ideal validation.

People-similarity Validation

For the first rationale, based on people similarity, the obvious validation procedure is to relate interest scores to measures of satisfaction on the job. However, a number of problems immediately arise. First, the concept of job satisfaction is complex and difficult to measure. As Strong (1958) observed,

> Years ago I contended that there was "no better criterion of a vocational interest test than that of satisfaction enduring over a period of years [p. 385]." . . . I have never used satisfaction as a criterion on the ground that there seemed to be no good way to measure it. Such correlations as have been reported between interest scores and satisfaction have been for the most part too low to be of practical significance [p. 449].

Strong was no exception in having these views, and today interest inventories have still not used measures of job satisfaction as criteria for validation (except in terms of global satisfaction ratings in defining occupational criterion groups), just as the rationales of interest measurement have not directly involved the why and how of job satisfaction. But the measurement of job satisfaction has progressed over the years, and we believe a fruitful area for future research is a more thorough examination of the relation of interests to various sources of job satisfaction (some of which we would expect to be related to interests and others not).

A second problem with this ideal validation concerns the prediction of relative satisfaction in different occupations when people can be in only one occupation (or a very few occupations) at one time. Thus we can usually observe only the degree of relationship of the interest scores to satisfaction in one job—the one the person has chosen to enter.

Because of these problems with these ideal validations, interest inventories have been validated in terms of group membership. Strong (1943) listed four propositions needed to establish the predictive value of his vocational interest measures (p. 388):

1. Men continuing in occupation A obtain a higher interest score in A than in any other occupation.

2. Men continuing in occupation A obtain a higher interest score in A than other men entering other occupations.
3. Men continuing in occupation A obtain higher scores in A than men who change from A to another occupation.
4. Men changing from occupation A to occupation B score higher in B prior to the change than in any other occupation, including A.

All four conditions rely on the occupational group to which a person belongs as an implicit indicator of the job in which that person would be most satisfied. And, in fact, empirical results have tended to confirm that people's interest scores (whether on occupational scales or general scales) are consonant with the occupation in which they are employed and with which they state a general level of satisfaction.

The group-membership criterion poses an important technical problem aside from the fact that it only indirectly addresses job satisfaction. The problem is that social influences can make the relation between interests and group similarity high even when people would have been much happier in other occupations. As long as the society channels people with particular characteristics into particular occupations, interest inventories validated against group membership will be considered highly valid whether or not the people in an occupation are happier than they would be in other occupations and whether or not there are many people with other characteristics who could be happiest in that occupation.

Activity-similarity Validation

Under the activity-similarity rationale, an inventory measures the liking of a person for activities related to job activities. Thus the first step in ideal validation is to relate empirically the inventoried likes and dislikes for common, familiar activities with the likes and dislikes for actual job activities. Since the common goal is to relate to job satisfaction in a more global sense, the second step is to discover the extent to which liking particular job activities is important to more general job satisfaction. Although the purpose of inventorying likes and dislikes for such activities has commonly been to indicate general personal characteristics, as in the people-similarity procedures, it would appear to us to be very useful to perform some of the steps of the ideal activity-similarity validation to learn more about the relative importance of various sources of job satisfaction and the link to interests.

NEW PROBLEMS FOR INTEREST MEASUREMENT

The perspective of interest measurement given in the preceding section involves additionally two dominant elements not yet discussed.

First, interest measurement has been predominantly developed by, for, and about men. Conceptions of interests have been largely based on data about men's interests; interest-measurement methodology has arisen out of interest measures on men; and interest measures have been validated primarily on men. Second, interest measurement has depended on a relatively stable social situation in which no large breaks or changes in the socialization process occur within an individual life history or at a point or peroid in the society's history.

These two elements raise special problems in the 1970s. First, we are clearly concerned with women as well as men and we must examine the applicability for women of approaches based on men. Second, we are in a time of a rather dramatic break in the continuity of the socialization process for women as it relates to careers, self-concepts, and occupational roles. Thus we must examine interest-measurement approaches in the light of this discontinuity. In this section we examine some of these new problems for interest measurement.

Problems with the People-Similarity Method

The people-similarity rationale stated above relies very heavily on a stable socialization process and is tied very closely to the past. Two special problems of this method arise from its highly empirical orientation and its reliance on the status quo.

Limits of Empiricism

Interest measurement has historically been a highly empirical science. The thing we know most about it is that it has tended to work in the past. We know much less about why it has worked. To know something has worked in the past is very useful as long as the future is like the past. When the future is dramatically different, then we need to know *why* something has worked in the past in order to judge if and how it might work in the future. Thus the empiricism of interest measurement, which has been one of its great strengths, is, we believe, at this time in history a weakness.

Reliance on the Status Quo

The people-similarity methodology, which uses group membership as its primary criterion, relies heavily on the status quo. The group-membership criterion, which undoubtedly properly includes elements of satisfaction (groups are usually limited to those expressing some level of satisfaction), also may, and almost certainly does, include elements extraneous to job satisfaction but resulting from the existing social situation. For example, when a physician scale is constructed by the people-similarity method, the scale is defined by the likes and dislikes of current (at the time of construction), satisfied physicians. Since in the past many physicians have come from relatively high socioeconomic status (SES) backgrounds, the Physician scale of the Strong, for example, reflects these backgrounds, as can be seen from the following list of selected positively scored items from the SVIB Physician scale for men, from Campbell (1971). (The entire SVIB Physician scale for men includes a total of 76 items: 8 amusements, 22 occupations, 12 school subjects, 6 types of people, 9 activities, 13 preferences between items, 6 abilities and characteristics.)

> *Amusements:* tennis; chess; bridge; art galleries; symphony concerts; skiing
> *Occupations:* orchestra conductor
> *School subjects:* literature
> *Types of people:* musical geniuses

Although these items might relate to one's satisfaction in associating with people with similar high SES interests, they seem highly questionable as interests essential to satisfaction as a physician, especially when the field of medicine itself is taking steps to break this traditional physician mold and encouraging the enrollment of a more diversified group of students.

In the case of women, the problem of reliance on the status quo becomes especially pronounced. It appears in obvious fashion in the lack of some occupational scales for women. Under the status quo there are many occupations with few or no women in them, and therefore under the people-similarity method the potential of women for satisfaction in these jobs cannot be predicted.

Problems with the Activity-Similarity Method

Although the activity-similarity method avoids some of the problems of the people-similarity method by relying on the activities required on a job rather than the people who happen to be in the job, it raises a different set of problems.

Experiental Effects on Interests

The activity-similarity method relies on people's liking or disliking common activities similar to those required on jobs. However, the socialization process results in quite different exposure to activities by men and women. For example, in a nationwide study, Prediger, Roth, and Noeth (1973) found wide differences in the career-related experiences reported by girls and boys in grades 8, 9, and 11. These data indicated that the expressed interests of men and women in such activities differ markedly in ways that parallel the experiential differences. Thus, while we know that only 17 percent of the 1969 Strong Women-in-General sample (Campbell, 1971, p. 403) liked "repairing electrical wiring," we do not know whether more would have liked it if the social setting encouraged rather than restricted such an activity for girls or, more importantly, whether more girls would learn to like it if they were encouraged. Because of the differences in socialization, *not liking* an activity might have quite a different meaning for a boy who had tried it and been "allowed" to like it than for a girl whose socialization ruled it out. The activity-similarity method therefore must deal, in general, with the differences in socialization, and, in particular, with their implications for predicting job satisfaction.

Problem of Sex Differences

The types of items that have historically appeared in interest inventories are subject to systematic sex differences. The previously noted "repairing electrical wiring" is a case in point. In contrast with 17 percent of the women, as cited above, 39 percent of the 1969 Strong Men-in-General sample reported liking that activity (Campbell, 1971, p. 400). Because of these sex differences, occupational scales were constructed separately by sex, masculinity-femininity scales based on items that differentiated the sexes came into being, and even separate forms of the inventory were constructed. There are, however, pitfalls into which this historical pattern has led us.

First, in the case of empirically constructed occupational scales, the historical pattern has limited the information an inventory provides women, since occupational scales are based on people already in occupations and many occupations have few women. For the same reason there are similar but fewer restrictions on the information given men. By leading us to separate the sexes in this way, this historical pattern has limited the direct comparison of men and women in many occupations (e.g., auto mechanic, nurse) to determine to what extent there are differences in likes and dislikes and whether there are crucial likes and dislikes, regardless of sex, in relating to job satisfaction. Thus we are left knowing that there are sex differences presently without knowing their relevance or irrelevance or their implications for predicting job satisfaction.

There are similar problems with scales measuring general-interest dimensions such as those of Holland. Holland has documented sex differences on his logically based scales and argued (1974) that he is intentionally measuring the socialization process, which differs now for girls and boys and results in different interests. We agree that he is measuring the socialization process and that it does now differ for girls and boys. We doubt, however, that Holland's basic intention is to measure the socialization process per se, as can be seen from the statement, "The SDS provides a method for locating groups of occupations where a person is most likely to find satisfaction [1973b, p. 1]."

We believe to be unanswered the question whether the socialization process for girls is as predictive of job satisfaction as the same process for boys when girls have not been socialized to examine as wide a range of possible interests as boys and yet rather suddenly have access to that full range. In the past the socialization process matched the career process in terms of the range of experiences and options. If we are in a state of transition, as we believe, the present can be illustrated by a mismatch: career options are opening before the early socialization process can be changed accordingly. Although hopefully the future could be characterized by the full circle of options for both sexes, that situation will not be reached immediately. In the interim we must make some decisions and take some kind of action.

Although the implications of the situations are unknown, at least two different hypotheses on which to base action are possible. One hypothesis derives from the argument of Holland noted above and will be discussed here as the hypothesis of socialization dominance.

> HYPOTHESIS OF SOCIALIZATION DOMINANCE. Until the areas of socially accepted interest options become broadened during a person's development, the careers in which such people will be satisfied will not broaden.

An alternative hypothesis emphasizes the importance of career opportunities rather than socialization. This hypothesis is implicit in the work of Cole (1973) on the structure of women's interests and will be referred to here as the hypothesis of opportunity dominance.

> HYPOTHESIS OF OPPORTUNITY DOMINANCE. When career opportunities widen, people will find satisfaction in a wider range of careers in spite of limiting aspects of their earlier socialization.

Although neither hypothesis can be proved at this time, the one to which a person subscribes has important implications for the treatment of sex differences in interest measurement.

Basically, the sex difference problem raises an issue that has been emphasized throughout this chapter—that the goal of interest measurement is to predict satisfaction in a job or career. Because the methodology and the validation of interest measurement are only indirectly related to that goal, it is easy to replace that goal with prominent means and similarity of people or activities. The similarity methodology tends by its nature to support the hypothesis of socialization dominance. But the problem of sex differences forces us to recall the more basic goal. Men and women are not now similar in all their likes and dislikes, but an unanswered question is which of those dissimilarities are directly related to satisfaction or dissatisfaction. When we recognize this goal of predicting satisfaction, it becomes clear that we do not know which hypothesis is correct. Since our actions are likely to be based on one or the other, in the interim we must judge the value of the two hypotheses not by their correctness but by the results of the action to which they lead.

Problems of Norms and Reference Groups

One of the important implications of the two hypotheses concerns the norms or reference groups used in interest inventories. Holland reports interests as raw scores. No norm or reference group is used. Instead the reference is the logical basis of the items. This results in scales that reflect the socialization process very clearly, and women tend to score highest on the Social and Artistic scales and very low on the Realistic scale. Such score reporting is consistent with the hypothesis of socialization dominance.

By contrast, recently developed interest instruments at The American College Testing Program (as part of the ACT Career Planning Program and the ACT Assessment) and the much older Kuder Preference Record homogeneous scales use a different approach consistent with the opportunity-dominance hypothesis. For those inventories the raw general scale scores are compared with norms of the same sex as the person taking the inventory. Thus a woman's score on a Technical scale, which may be low when compared with scores of men, is reported as high if it is higher than the Technical scores of most women. The logic here is that for each occupation in the full range of occupations there will be some women who will be able to find satisfaction in it (hypothesis of opportunity dominance), and the best bets in the previously unentered areas are those women who have higher interests than the mean produced by the socialization process. Some support for these procedures is found in the structure of women's interests reported by Cole (1973), in which referencing women's scores to women's norms produced the full range of interest patterns and occupational profiles; these, where comparable, closely paralleled the occupational profiles based on men's interest scores.

These two cases are based on the use of general interest scales. Occupational scales present even greater problems, although in somewhat different forms. The application of the socialization-dominance hypothesis would lead to the continued use of available occupational scales for women along with the construction of new occupational scales as women entered new occupations in sufficient number. However, both the Strong (at least, the new Strong-Campbell Interest Inventory) and the Kuder Occupational Interest Survey attempt to broaden the information given by reporting scores for women on occupational scales developed for men, which seems at least a step in the direction of the opportunity-dominance hypothesis. According to the latest information available to us, the Strong-Campbell will report the general Basic scales using a combined-sex reference group that will result in interest patterns more nearly corresponding to Holland's raw score patterns and the socialization-dominance hypothesis than to the same-sex reference patterns.

Vocational Development and Career Guidance

Historically, interest inventories have been viewed as a source of information input at the time of career-choice decisions. Career choice was often viewed as an "event" occurring at a single point in time. Thus students who had to select a college major or decide on a job might go to a college counselor, take an interest inventory, and try to make a decision. The inventory was designed to assist in making such a choice at a pressing decision point.

Today, however, the prevailing view of career decisions and career guidance is distinctly different. First, career decisions are viewed not as an event but as part of a process that begins very early in a child's development and continues throughout life in a variety of career-decision activities. Career-education programs being developed for the schools emphasize these developmental aspects and are designed to promote career-related experiences—both "hands on" and vicarious—in the full range of career options. Career knowledge and exploration are emphasized in the schools with the basic goal of avoiding sudden, pressured "choices" at a time when some decision must be reached. Such programs of career education and career guidance offer many helpful possibilities in the broader experiences they provide and encourage for women at a time of transition.

Career guidance as it exists today emphasizes the use of information, including interest inventories, to stimulate career exploration and the exploration of self in relation to careers (Prediger, 1974). This process of exploration should lead people to discover new things about themselves and about the world of work. Using such information, people can begin to consider a broader range of career options. The usefulness of this type of stimulation is that it provides focused exploration. Appropriate use of interest inventories with women may well lead to focused exploration in totally new areas.

Career-guidance programs also emphasize the importance of transforming guidance information into action. That is, interest inventories should no longer be merely reported or interpreted. They should change behavior. The change may take the form of students seeking new job experiences, involving parents in their career decision making, and participating in volunteer work experiences. Thus there are new problems and altered roles for interest inventories in this broadly conceived career-guidance framework.

WHERE DO WE GO FROM HERE?

A primary feature of the perspective emerging from the preceding section is the lack of simple answers to the difficult problems raised. There are, however, both discouraging and encouraging elements to be noted. The following statements are representative of our present beliefs after a reexamination of basic tenets and methods.

1. Interests still seem to us to be an important concept, with considerable potential value for understanding differences between people and their characteristic ways of behaving. Further, we suspect that interests will continue in the future to relate in many meaningful ways to various types of career satisfaction.
2. We believe that the goal to provide people with information that will help them choose careers in which they will be happy and satisfied is timely and worthy. The need to open wider career options for women and for men makes the goal perhaps even more important than before.
3. We believe that present interest measures give important information about characteristic patterns of likes and dislikes and their historical occupational membership correlates.
4. We feel that if the link between interests and job satisfaction had been more explicitly examined during the last quarter century, then we would know more now about predicting job satisfaction in a changing social environment and in particular about predicting job satisfaction for women.
5. We believe that we are in a situation in which many basic questions about validity of interest inventories cannot yet be answered completely or well. In the interim we must make decisions with incomplete information.

When we are in a situation of not knowing what action is "valid" in terms of ultimate goals, possible courses of action must be evaluated in terms of possible advantages and disadvantages. One possible course of action would be to stop using interest inventories until we know more about the implications of recent social change for their ultimate validity. This action would avoid possible wrong predictions, but it would also eliminate any possible positive role inventories might play. Another course would be to continue to use inventories but to take whatever actions are necessary to minimize the possible negative effects. The remainder of this paper deals with interim actions designed to maximize positive and minimize possible negative effects and the assumptions on which these actions are based.

A Proposed Context for Interest Inventory Use

In an earlier section we described current conceptions of vocational development and the career-education and career-guidance programs that correspond to those conceptions. According to these views, career guidance occurs as a process rather than at a single decision point, involves providing a person with career experiences of various types and with information about self and careers, and emphasizes the importance of exploratory behavior in the career decision process. Prediger (1974) has focused on this important role of career exploration in the career-guidance process. Within that context he views tests or inventories primarily as stimuli to that exploration.

We believe that implementation of a broad career-exploration program provides the proper context in which interest inventories can serve a very valuable role as a stimulus for exploration. Such a use of interest inventories provides an interim course of action that maximizes the benefits of the inventories and minimizes the possible detriments.

Our belief in the value of this interim course of action is based on at least three assumptions. The first assumption is that people need some form of stimulus or organizing assistance in making career plans. Second, the best way for people to make judgments (or predictions) about whether or not they will be satisfied in an occupation is to obtain all the information they can about themselves and about the occupation. Third, by embedding interest inventory results in a broad career-exploration process in which further exploration follows any inventory results, the negative impact of incorrect inventory predictions can be minimized.

What Can We Expect an Interest Inventory to Do?

In the context of the career-exploration process, we have two primary expectations for an interest inventory. These two expectations are expressed here as guidelines for interest measurement, with several subordinate guidelines encompassed by the two general areas.

Broadened Options

The first area of expectation for interest inventories concerns the broadening of career options:

1. Interest inventory scores should suggest occupations that broaden the options of both sexes throughout the full range of career areas.

There are several important aspects of this desired broadening. The first concerns the relation of inventory results to previous job preferences. As we view the career-exploration process, a person with some job preference would explore that job in many ways and on the basis of that exploration would reach some sort of decision about the appropriateness of the job in relation to various personal goals. Thus we view the predominant role of interest inventories as a broadener of options—to suggest reasonable possibilities for exploration that people might otherwise have failed to explore. While a traditional distinction has been made between this exploratory role and a confirmatory role, we place far greater importance on the former. One way to examine the degree to which options are broadened is to compare inventory results with previous job preferences in accord with the following guideline:

1a. For a given group, it is desirable that there be some variation between original occupational preferences and inventoried occupational suggestions and that an inventory produce several occupational options for each person.

The second aspect of the broadening of options concerns the type of alternative options an inventory suggests. For example, guideline 1a. could be met by the inventory suggestions of "medical technologist" and "dental hygienist" for a woman whose original job preference was "nurse." This type of broadening within sex-career stereotypes is insufficient. Similarly, it is inadequate to broaden options only within sex-related career areas—for example, by suggesting primarily social types of occupations for women.

1b. Interest inventories should produce approximately equal distributions of scores for men and women throughout the full range of possible general scale and occupational scale scores.

This guideline has important implications for the norming of interest scores. Preliminary data presented in Table 30-I, from a report in preparation at The American College Testing Program, show the distributional implications of three types of general scale scores from the ACT Interest Inventory for the type of two-point codes used by Holland. Both the raw scores and scores referenced to a norm group composed equally of women and men produce vastly different two-scale code options for women than for men. By contrast, the distributions of codes are quite similar for women and men when separate sex norms are used. Only the scores produced by the separate sex norms meet guideline 1b. With present instruments, people's scores will probably have to be reported in terms of their relation to the distribution of scores obtained by people of the same sex in order to accomplish the balanced distributions required under this guideline.

TABLE 30-I
DISTRIBUTION OF PERCENTAGES OF HOLLAND CODES FOR WOMEN AND MEN FOR DIFFERENT TYPES OF SCORE REFERENCING

Holland code	Codes based on raw scores		Codes based on separate sex norms		Codes based on combined sex norms	
	W	M	W	M	W	M
Social total	67.3%	26.3%	17.9%	14.3%	28.8%	4.1%
SE	14.3%	6.9%	5.1%	3.8%	6.6%	1.3%
SC	11.3	1.8	2.2	1.5	6.0	0.3
SR	1.6	7.2	2.7	2.2	1.3	1.1
SI	11.8	4.5	3.3	2.4	5.6	0.8
SA	28.3	5.9	4.6	4.4	9.3	0.6
Enterprising total	3.1%	9.6%	13.6%	13.3%	11.1%	14.0%
ES	1.7%	3.8%	2.9%	2.9%	3.4%	2.0%
EC	0.4	2.2	3.8	4.8	2.8	4.3
ER	0.1	1.8	2.0	2.0	0.2	3.9
EI	0.1	0.7	0.9	0.9	0.6	1.5
EA	0.8	1.1	4.0	2.7	4.1	2.3
Conventional total	9.7%	8.7%	18.0%	16.2%	20.0%	11.9%
CS	5.8%	2.5%	2.8%	1.4%	5.4%	0.6%
CE	2.2	2.6	6.8	6.2	7.4	4.6
CR	0.2	2.1	4.8	4.0	1.7	3.9
CI	0.4	1.2	1.8	2.9	2.4	2.2
CA	1.1	0.3	1.8	1.7	3.1	0.6
Realistic total	0.2%	18.9%	14.4%	19.4%	2.8%	35.8%
RS	0.2%	6.1%	1.8%	2.0%	0.7%	2.9%
RE	0.0	2.8	2.2	4.2	0.3	8.7
RC	0.0	2.9	3.2	4.3	0.8	6.5
RI	0.0	5.5	3.8	5.7	0.2	14.5
RA	0.0	1.6	3.4	3.2	0.8	3.2
Investigative total	9.1%	30.0%	19.3%	21.2%	13.5%	24.7%
IS	5.5%	11.7%	4.9%	5.1%	5.2%	2.5%
IE	0.1	1.5	1.2	1.7	0.4	1.7
IC	1.0	2.5	3.3	3.9	2.0	2.7
IR	0.2	10.1	5.1	3.9	1.4	12.8
IA	2.3	4.2	4.8	6.6	4.5	5.0
Artistic total	10.8%	6.4%	16.7%	15.3%	24.1%	9.4%
AS	7.8%	3.2%	5.0%	5.1%	12.0%	2.5%
AE	0.5	0.9	2.8	3.4	4.0	1.8
AC	0.7	0.2	1.9	1.3	3.0	0.8
AR	0.3	0.8	3.8	1.4	1.7	2.5
AI	1.5	1.3	3.2	4.1	3.4	1.8
Grand total	100%	100%	100%	100%	100%	100%

Note: Based on the scores of 3,439 college-bound high school students (2,009 women and 1,430 men) who took the ACT Interest Inventory in October 1972.

Thus we come back to the discussion of the hypotheses of socialization dominance and opportunity dominance. Guideline 1b is clearly an expression of the latter hypothesis. As already noted, the validity of either hypothesis is not now known. Therefore, guideline 1b is an expression of a belief, first, in the eventual validity of the implied methods of prediction of satisfaction and, second, in the maximal positive aspects and minimal negative aspects of the suggested interim course of action. If the opportunity-dominance hypothesis is supported eventually, inventory results consistent with the socialization-dominance hypothesis will have reinforced incorrect and inappropriate stereotypical views and minimized further exploration. On the other hand, if the socialization-dominance hypothesis is supported, inventory results consistent with the opportunity-dominance hypothesis will have led people to waste time exploring new career areas; but probably nothing more harmful will have occurred, since that exploration should result in the elimination of inappropriate inventory suggestions. Thus we justify 1b by our belief not only in the opportunity-dominance hypothesis but, more importantly, in its high potential for positive social effect and its low potential for negative social effect.

Although we see great social value and minimal harm in expanding options as described, this interim action should not serve as a substitute for more thorough attempts at validation. Further, these validation attempts should not be limited to the people-similarity approaches described earlier in this paper. Instead they should be aimed at the use of interest measures to predict some aspects of job satisfaction or fulfillment. While it will be impossible to validate the predictions of job satisfaction deriving from the two hypotheses within a short time, initial steps should be undertaken and primitive initial types of validating data should be sought. Even crude initial data could give valuable information about the appropriateness of suggesting that a woman consider the occupation electrician, for example.

1c. Tentative, short-term forms of validation should be undertaken to determine user reaction to the appropriateness of inventory results, especially reaction after exploration of the suggested occupation.

1d. Studies of the types of job satisfaction and their relation to vocational interests should be initiated.

Inventories As Stimuli

Within our conception of the career-guidance process, interest inventories serve primarily as stimuli to exploration. The second major area of expectation that we have for interest inventories concerns this role:

2. Interest inventory results should stimulate exploratory behavior.

If we expect interest inventories to serve as stimuli, then we must examine the exploratory steps and actions people take as a result of the inventory. Although the study of inventory impact could have been useful and informative at any time in the history of interest measurement, we have found only limited and very recent empirical examinations of such impact. Holland and his colleagues showed concern with the behavioral impact in the design of SDS. Zener and Schnuelle (1972) empirically examined the impact of the SDS on the number and type of occupational options considered. They reported an increase in the number of options considered after the SDS was taken, but no broadening of the type of option. Redmond (1972) reported that both boys and girls were likely to seek more vocational information after the SDS experience.

Note that when the goal is to produce certain types of behavior, then various aspects of an inventory must be examined in the light of that goal. For example, for the goal of widening options an inventory might result in 40 possibilities. Within the present concern with the behavioral impact, 40 options would probably be overwhelming and produce little exploration. Thus the two goals interact in determining the best characteristics of an inventory. Note also that another implication of trying to produce exploratory behavior concerns the supporting materials and score reports. For this goal such materials should be designed to have maximal impact on exploratory behavior.

In the study of inventories as stimuli, information must be collected about the number and types of jobs explored after inventory use and about the forms that exploratory behavior took. Such studies, though not now available, can be accomplished in reasonable periods of time; they involve no long-term followup, and supporting materials that may influence the results are relatively easy for publishers to modify. Thus we are led to two specific elements of guideline 2:

2a. An interest inventory, its supporting materials, and its score reports should be designed to maximize exploratory action by the person taking the inventory.

2b. Studies should be reported in inventory manuals to show the effect or lack of effect of the inventory on exploratory behavior.

SUMMARY AND CONCLUSIONS

We have described some expectations for interest measurement that can be examined at least in preliminary ways in a short time period. Accomplishment of those expectations will not answer all the ultimate questions about interest inventories as predictors of job satisfaction. It will, however, put us in a position of beginning to answer those questions while maximizing benefits and minimizing ill effects of present procedures.

The usefulness of an interest inventory for any group (different age groups, racial-ethnic groups) can be evaluated in terms of how well the expectations in these two areas are met within that group. If an inventory does not broaden options or produce exploration in the particular group, then we would question its use with that group. Similarly, the appropriateness of any type of interest scale (occupational or general, empirical or logical) would be judged in terms of whether it meets the stated expectations for broadening options and producing exploration.

REFERENCES

American College Testing Program. *Handbook for the ACT Career Planning Program, grades 8-11.* Iowa City: Author, 1974.

Berdie, R.F. Factors related to vocational interests. *Psychological Bulletin,* 1944, *41,* 137-157.

Bingham, W.V. *Aptitudes and aptitude testing.* New York: Harper & Row, 1937.

Bordin, E.S. A theory of vocational interests as dynamic phenomena. *Educational and Psychological Measurement,* 1943, *3,* 49-65.

Campbell, D.P. *Handbook for the Strong Vocational Interest Blank.* Stanford, Calif.: Stanford University Press, 1971.

Carter, H.D. Vocational interests and job orientation. *Applied Psychology Monographs,* 1944, *2.*

Cole, N.S. On measuring the vocational interests of women. *Journal of Counseling Psychology,* 1973, *20,* 105-112.

Cole, N.S., & Hanson, G.R. An analysis of the structure of vocational interests. *Journal of Counseling Psycholgy,* 1971, *18,* 478-486.

Crites, J.O. *Vocational psychology.* New York: McGraw-Hill, 1969.

Darley, J.G. *Clinical aspects and interpretation of the Strong Vocational Interest Blank.* New York: Psychological Corporation, 1941.

Darley, J.G., & Hagenah, T. *Vocational interest measurement.* Minneapolis: University of Minnesota Press, 1955.

Dawis, R.V., England, G.W., & Lofquist, L.H. A theory of work adjustment. *Minnesota Studies in Vocational Rehabilitation,* 1964.

D'Costa, A.G., Winefordner, D.W., Odgers, J.G., & Koons, P.B., Jr. *Ohio Vocational Interest Survey.* New York: Harcourt Brace Jovanovich, 1970.

Fryer, D. *The measurement of interests.* New York: Holt, Rinehart & Winston, 1931,

Hanson, G.R. *Assessing the career interests of college youth: Summary of research and applications.* (ACT Research Report No. 64) Iowa City: American College Testing Program, 1974.

Holland, J.L. *The psychology of vocational choice: A theory of personality types and model environments.* Waltham, Mass.: Ginn/Blaisdell, 1966.

Holland, J.L. *Making vocational choices: A theory of careers.* Englewood Cliffs, N.J.: Prentice-Hall, 1973. (a)

Holland, J.L. Sexism, personal development, and the Self-Directed Search. Unpublished paper, Center for Social Organization of Schools, Johns Hopkins University, 1973. (b)

Holland, J.L. Some guidelines for reducing systematic biases in the delivery of vocational services. *Measurement and Evaluation in Guidance,* 1974, *6,* 210-218.

Holland, J.L., Whitney, D.R., Cole, N.S., & Richards, J.M., Jr. *An empirical oc-*

cupational classification derived from a theory of personality and intended for practice and research. (ACT Research Report No. 29) Iowa City: American College Testing Program, 1969.

James, W. *The principles of psychology.* New York: Holt, Rinehart & Winston, 1890.

Kitson, H.D. *The psychology of vocational adjustment.* Philadelphia: Lippincott, 1925.

Kuder, G.F. *General Manual, Kuder Occupational Interest Survey, Form DD.* Chicago: Science Research Associates, 1968.

Parsons, F. *Choosing a vocation.* Boston: Houghton Mifflin, 1909.

Prediger, D.J. The role of assessment in career guidance. In E.L. Herr (Ed.), *Vocational guidance and human development.* Boston: Houghton Mifflin, 1974.

Prediger, D.J., & Roth, J.D. *The data/ideas, people/things dimensions of work and Interests: Summary of research and applications.* (ACT research Report No. 67) Iowa City: American College Testing Program, 1974.

Prediger, D.J., Roth, J.D., & Noeth, R.J. *A nationwide study of student career development: Summary of results.* ACT Research Report No. 61) Iowa City: American College Testing Program, 1973.

Redmond, R.E. Increasing vocational information seeking behaviors of high school students. Doctoral dissertation, University of Maryland, 1972.

Strong, E.K., Jr. *The vocational interests of men and women.* Stanford, Calif.: Stanford University Press, 1943.

Strong, E.K., Jr. *Vocational interests 18 years after college.* Minneapolis: University of Minnesota Press, 1955.

Strong, E.K., Jr. Satisfactions and interest. *American Psychologist,* 1958, *13* (8), 449-456.

Strong, E.K., Jr. An eighteen-year longitudinal report on interests. In W.L. Layton (Ed.), *The Strong Vocational Interest Blank: Research and uses.* Minneapolis: University of Minnesota Press, 1960. Pp. 3-17.

Super, D.E. *Appraising vocational fitness.* New York: Harper & Row, 1949.

Zener, T.B., & Schnuelle, L. *An evaluation of the Self-Directed Search.* (Report No. 124) Baltimore: Center for Social Organization of Schools, Johns Hopkins University, 1972.

Chapter 31

SEX-ROLE SOCIALIZATION AND EMPLOYMENT REALITIES: IMPLICATIONS FOR VOCATIONAL INTEREST MEASURES*

DALE J. PREDIGER AND NANCY S. COLE

Methods for reporting vocational interests which do and do not reflect sex-role stereotypes are examined. Interest inventory validation procedures based on the prediction of occupational preference and group membership are shown to favor inventories providing scores that reflect past sex-role stereotypes and current employment inequities. Reporting and validation procedures minimizing these shortcomings are suggested. These procedures, which are supported by past practice and recent research, result in similar interest score distributions for men and women. Finally, career counseling problems arising from the confounding of reports of human interests with current employment realities are discussed.

THE EXISTENCE of sex-role stereotypes in the vocational preferences of students is widely recognized. Its extent was vividly demonstrated in a recent nationwide study (Prediger, Roth, & Noeth, 1974) which found that the vocational preferences of more than half of the nation's eleventh-grade girls fell in 3 of 25 job families (education and social services, nursing and human care, and clerical/secretarial work) —job families preferred by only 7 percent of the nation's eleventh-grade boys. By contrast, the vocational preferences of boys greatly outnumbered those of girls in the technologies/trades, engineering, natural science, and business management job families. Using U.S. Census data, Gottfredson, Holland, and Gottfredson (1974) recently demonstrated the extent to which sex-role stereotypes are also reflected in employment patterns.

These data present a challenge to the guidance profession particularly because the social, economic, and political barriers to nontraditional careers are being eliminated, one by one, as a result of both increased public concern about sex discrimination and the impact of

*From *Journal of Vocational Behavior, 1975, 7, 239-251.* Courtesy of *Academic Press, Inc.*

Federal legislation (e.g. Title IX of the Education Amendments of 1972) and regulations (Equal Employment Opportunity Commission, 1970). Progress is being made on many fronts. Federal agencies such as the National Science Foundation and the National Institute of Education are devoting large sums of money to studies of barriers to nontraditional careers and how these barriers can be overcome. Publishers are producing textbooks that show men and women in nontraditional work roles. The U.S. Department of Labor has begun to use sex-neutral titles for occupations. Employers are initiating affirmative action employment programs. The American Personnel and Guidance Association is conducting a series of more than 200 state workshops to help counselors become aware of and, hopefully, eliminate sex-biased career guidance practices ("Sex Equality Trainers," 1974). All of these activities are accompanied by a steady increase in the number of persons entering nontraditional areas of the labor force.

Although it is not the purpose of this paper to review the many efforts, nationwide, to help students consider and enter nontraditional careers, the characteristics and use of vocational interest inventories must be viewed in the context of these efforts. Indeed, interest inventories have recently become the subject of considerable attention because of the key role they can play in career exploration and planning. Definitions of sex bias in interest inventories have been formulated by the AMEG Commission on Sex Bias in Measurement (1973) and the National Institute of Education (Diamond, 1975). Both organizations are seeking ways to make practitioners and publishers aware of the recently developed guidelines for assessing sex bias (Diamond, 1975).

Implicit in all these activities is the desire to insure that measures of vocational interests do not simply reflect sex-role stereotypes resulting from past socialization. Instead, the hope is that interest inventories can be used to help men and women consider the expanded career opportunities now beginning to open to them. The purposes of this paper are (a) to examine methods for reporting vocational interests which do and do not reflect differences in the socialization of females and males and (b) to explore the problems and issues involved in using current employment distributions as criteria for validating and evaluating inventory interest results.

DERIVING MEANING FROM INTEREST INVENTORY RESPONSES

Although few people question the influence of past experiences on vocational interests, few people want measures of vocational interests simply to reflect the effects of sex-role socialization. Instead, the basic goal of interest measurement is to identify the types of work in which a person is likely to experience satisfaction. Unfortunately, in a time of increasing career options for both sexes, there is little clear information about how to predict the future satisfaction of women or men in new (to them) career areas. Cole and Hanson (in press) argue that in the absence of appropriate information one must accept one of two hypotheses concerning the relationship of interests to occupational satisfaction. These two hypotheses are defined below.

1. SOCIALIZATION DOMINANCE HYPOTHESIS. Until the socially accepted activity and choice options of males and females are broadened during the developmental years, the occupations in which males and females will be satisfied will be restricted to those consistent with their early sex-role socialization.

2. OPPORTUNITY DOMINANCE HYPOTHESIS. When socially accepted activity and choice options broaden and nontraditional career opportunities increase, people will find satisfaction in a wider range of occupations, in spite of any limitations imposed by their earlier socialization.

Current approaches to the measurement of vocational interests are consonant with one of the two hypotheses, particularly in the choice of a reference group on which to base score interpretations. There is no question that sex-role socialization differentially influences the activity and occupational preferences of men and women and, hence, their responses to many interest inventory items. The problem lies in how to use these responses in reports to counselees.

One approach, an approach based on the socialization dominance hypothesis, is simply to report raw scores. The reasoning is that if a person prefers certain types of activities and not others, for whatever reason—sex-role socialization, past experience, or the lack thereof—raw scores will appropriately reflect this as well as the likelihood that the person will find satisfaction in corresponding occupations. Stated another way, the interest inventory responses of men and women (considered as groups) differ. According to the socialization dominance hypothesis, these responses reflect personal orientations that are not likely to change; hence, the responses indicate potential satisfaction in different types of occupations. When this application of the socialization dominance hypotheses is followed, as in Holland's use of raw scores in the Self-Directed Search (SDS), many more men than women are referred to scientific and technical occupations and many more women than men are referred to social service and artistic occupations (Holland, 1972). Holland (1974b) views these differential results for men and women as a natural outcome of interest assessment since "interest inventories simply tally the effects of one's life history and heredity" (p. 215). Apart from the question of whether the socialization dominance hypothesis warrants support, it would appear that there are several serious psychometric problems involved in the use of raw scores to represent human interests.

Quite early in the development of psychological assessment, psychologists recognized that raw scores have no meaning in and of themselves—that a zero score on an interest inventory (or aptitude test) does not mean zero interest (or ability). It was only by determining the standing of a person's characteristics in a relevant norm group that psychologists were able to assess the relative strength of the characteristics in human terms. (Recent efforts to implement criterion-referenced interpretation as a substitute for norm referenced interpretation have largely been confined to domains of educational achievement amenable to thorough specification, e.g. mathematics.) Closely associated with the above principle was the recognition that a test (or inventory) is, at best, a sample of behavior and that test scores, although they appear to be numerically precise, may not correspond closely to quantities of whatever it is that is being measured. That is, a raw score of 6 on an interest scale does not necessarily indicate twice the interest of a raw score of 3; nor does a raw score of 6 on one scale necessarily indicate more interest than a raw score of 5 on another scale, even assuming perfectly reliable scales. Thus, comparisons of interest level from scale to scale are not warranted when raw scores are used. Indeed, the average raw scores of women and men on a set of interest scales are largely determined by the inventory author's choice of items for the scales, as recently demonstrated by Rayman (1974). The raw score means of men and women on each of Rayman's Holland-type scales were much more similar than raw score means on Holland's SDS (Holland, 1972).

If one agrees that norms are necessary, the next question that arises is "what norms?" Our reading of the literature indicates that the choice of a norm group is a compromise—a compromise that weighs theory, practicality, and the need for specificity. Past practice, as represented in the Strong Vocational Interest Blank (Campbell, 1971), the Kuder General Interest Survey (Kuder, 1964), and the Ohio Vocational Interest Survey (D'Costa, Winefordner, Odgers, & Koons, 1970), suggests that in the assessment of human interests, same-sex norms represent the minimally desirable standard from all three standpoints. Although the new Strong-Campbell Interest Inventory (Campbell, 1974) uses combined-sex norms to obtain standard scores on the basic and theme scales, same-sex norms are also used in reporting results for these scales. Thus, past practice in interest assessment has been to use norms in reporting results, typically same-sex norms.

The use of same-sex norms in reporting interest inventory results conforms to the opportunity dominance hypothesis described above and produces comparable interest score distributions for women and men. Thus, suggestions for career exploration are not restricted by sex-role stereotypes, and both women and men are provided with a greater variety of career alternatives than are provided by reporting procedures following the socialization dominance hypothesis (Prediger & Hanson, 1974).

Recent research on the structure of men's and women's interests (Cole, 1973; Cole & Hanson, 1971) and research on the interest scores of men and women in the same occupations (Prediger & Hanson, 1975) and college majors (Hanson, 1974) support the same-sex norm tradition. For example, Prediger and Hanson compared the raw score and standard score (same-sex norms) interest profiles of 19,096 women and 19,939 men in the same 104 occupations and found, contrary to expectations based on Holland's theory of careers (Holland, 1973), that there are substantial, systematic, and stereotypic differences in the raw score profiles of women and men, especially for nontraditional occupations. The nature and extent of these differences raise serious questions concerning the use of raw score profiles to represent the career interests of women and men. By contrast, the standard score profiles of women and men in the same 104 occupations exhibited few systematic differences, thus supporting expectations based on Holland's theory. Furthermore, occupational profiles based on standard scores generally meet intuitive expectations. Taken as a whole, results of the study suggest that same-sex norms provide relatively accurate indices of the interests of men and women; and, as noted above, interest score distributions based on these indices do not reflect the sex-role stereotypes observed in raw score distributions. Hanson (1974), in an analysis of the interests profiles of 10,000 college senior men and women in the same 18 majors, also obtained results supporting the use of same-sex norms.

The use of same-sex norms, in effect, treats the results of sex-role socialization as the appropriate baseline against which to compare the interests of an individual. Thus, a woman whose mechanical interests are high relative to other women is reported to have high mechanical interests since her interests are exceptional, given the social norms for female behavior in our society. This approach to reporting interest results recognizes that the social climates for mechanical interests among females and males are possibly as different as the January climates of Minnesota and Mississippi, and that it may be as inappropriate to compare the raw scores of females and males on a mechanical interest scale as it would be to compare the raw scores of residents in the two states on a scale assessing "interest in snow." Of course, the scores (numbers) could be compared, but the psychological meaning of score differences would be in doubt. The use of combined-sex interest norms, a procedure analogous to the use of combined-state norms in the example above, would appear to be equally inappropriate. We propose that the scores reported for interest inventories should, as a minimum requirement, take into account the different social/environmental climates that males and females experience in American society. Same-sex norms, which compare the responses of women to those of other women and the responses of men to those of other men, have been the traditional approach to accomplishing this goal.

EMPLOYMENT PATTERNS AS CRITERIA FOR INTEREST PATTERNS

The consequences of following the socialization dominance hypothesis in the assessment of vocational interests are vividly illustrated in the recent article by Gottfredson et al. (1974) referred to above. In this article, Holland and his coworkers suggest that the interest score distributions of men and women should correspond to the occupational distributions of men and women. That is, the proportion of women (or men) scoring highest on each scale in a set of interest scales should be similar to the proportion of women (or men) in occupations corresponding to those scales. Census data are used to show the percentage of women and men employed in occupations categorized according to Holland's six types. The distribution by Holland type for women (men in parentheses) in occupations requiring "some college and above" is given as follows–Social: 70% (20%); Enterprising: 15% (42%); Conventional: 4% (6%); Realistic: 1% (6%); Investigative: 5% (21%); and Artistic: 5% (6%). (It should be noted that these data, because they are based on the entire adult labor force, do not necessarily represent the employment opportunities of women and men entering the labor force in the last few years.)

Holland and his coworkers use the interests of several samples of high school and college youth, as assessed by Holland's SDS and the ACT Interest Inventory (Hanson, 1974), to classify students into the above six categories according to their highest interest score. The distributions of men's and women's interests reported as raw scores are shown to more closely correspond to the occupational distributions than do interest distributions derived from normed scores. On the basis of these results, interest inventories using same-sex norms are said to be "unrealistic because they create score distributions that diverge greatly from the distribution of actual employment" (p. iii). In addition, the correspondence between raw score and occupational distributions is cited as suggesting that "the infrequent occurrence of some . . . [interest codes] is not an anomaly of assessment but corresponds to the uneven distribution of kinds of work in society" (p. 8).

This interpretation and application of the socialization dominance hypothesis, an extension of Holland's previous assertion that interest inventories simply tally the effects of one's life history and heredity, raises several important issues. If occupational distributions are to be used in judging the adequacy of interest score distributions, it would follow that a society's occupational structure should, ideally, determine the distributions of interest scores—a proposal of far-reaching import for interest inventory authors and users. Or, stated another way, the guidance provided by interest inventory scores at a given time should reflect the employment distributions of men and women at that time. By this standard, interest inventories of the 1850s would have suggested farming to nearly all males and homemaking to nearly all females.

Conversely, this application of the socialization dominance hypothesis supposes that the distribution of human interests conforms, theoretically, to the occupational structure of society, in this instance to the industrial/technological society of the United States. We know of no theory (psychological or psychometric) or research to support this supposition.

OCCUPATIONAL GROUP MEMBERSHIP AS A VALIDATION CRITERION

Occupational group membership, as reflected in the employment distributions of men and women, has sometimes been used as a criterion in studies of the predictive validity of interest inventories. More often, occupational preference (choice) has served as a substitute criterion. In this approach to validation, predictive validity is indicated by the accuracy of predictions of occupational preference or entry (e.g. see Gottfredson and Holland, 1975). Length of time in an occupation is sometimes used in refining the definition of occupational membership.

As explained below, interest inventories providing scores which reflect sex-role stereotypes and expectations will generally produce more accurate predictions of occupational preference and membership than inventories which do not. However, the former inventories may be "successful" only because they replicate the occupational status quo resulting from sex role expectations.

It is no great feat to accurately identify large numbers of women who will later enter certain occupations, for example, social service occupations. According to the 1970 census data tabulated by Gottfredson et al. (1974), 70 percent of the employed women in the United States who have "some college or above" are in social service occupations. Hence, if one simply used the occupational base rates to predict, thirty or forty years ago, that *all* girls who went to college and later became employed would be in social service occupations, 1970 census data would prove the predictions to be correct for 70 percent of the cases, i.e. the "hit rate" would be 70 percent.

If occupational entry (or preference) is accepted as an appropriate criterion in interest inventory validation, then, in order for an interest inventory to demonstrate respectable validity, it would have to improve upon the "hit rate" achieved through the use of occupational base rates illustrated in the example above. An interest inventory that does not suggest social service, nursing, or clerical occupations to large numbers of women and business, technical, or trades occupations to large numbers of men would produce a relatively low hit rate because of the very nature of current occupational distributions. Its predictive validity (hit rate) would be suspect. On the other hand, the hit rate could be relatively high for an interest inventory providing predictions that closely parallel current employment distributions. The base rates can be hard to beat, however, as recently demonstrated by Gottfredson and Holland (1975) in an attempt to predict the occupational preferences of college women attending two different types of institutions (*N*s = 432 and 557). Base rate predictions (hit rates = 72 and 62%) were more accurate than predictions obtained from Holland's SDS, even though the SDS predictions reflected essentially the same sex-role stereotypes as the occupational preferences.

Because occupational group membership (or preference) predictions must reflect employment (or preference) distributions in order to achieve high hit rates, the hit rates obtained by this use of group membership as a criterion variable in predictive validity studies would appear to have questionable bearing on interest inventory validity. The assumption in such predictive studies is that people enter and persist in occupations because they are satisfied with them. However, there are multiple causes of occupational entry and persistence, only some of which are directly relevant to satisfaction. Thus, when group membership is used as a validation criterion, it is important to distinguish between factors influencing satisfaction with work (the commonly accepted criterion for interest measures) and factors influencing occupational entry and persistence (e.g. the expectations of society, labor market needs, the contingencies of life).

To those who maintain that the primary goal of psychological science is to predict human behavior, we can only suggest that a prior goal is to determine which behavior it is appropriate to predict. Given the counseling context in which interest inventories are used, it would appear that potential satisfaction with the activities required in a job is a more appropriate criterion than occupational entry. The latter criterion might be preferable in research on the psychosocial determinants of job seeking behavior, for example.

Thus, we propose that in validating interest inventories for use in vocational counseling, the goal should not be to predict what people will do (or prefer). As already noted, pursuit of this goal will force one into a numbers game in which the winning strategy will be to produce interest score distributions which correspond with the preference and employment base rates for men and women. Because these base rates in part result from sex-role socialization and expectations, this strategy uses what could be called the *socialization approach to validation.*

We propose an alternative strategy for validation, one which avoids some of the problems inherent in the socialization approach by distinguishing between those factors influencing occupational entry and those influencing satisfaction. This strategy requires one to accurately and separately describe the interests of those women and men who have and will become engineers, nurses, chemists, etc.—regardless of the base rates. Validity is determined by the degree to which the interests of satisfied members of occupations actually match the descriptions used in counseling. Because current occupational base rates are ignored and all occupations are considered to be equally likely options, depending on the person's vocational interests, goals, and other characteristics, the arbitrary channeling of counselees into high base rate occupations is avoided. The validation strategy we are proposing recognizes that many persons may not actually enter occupations corresponding to the options suggested by an interest inventory. For a number of very practical reasons, people will continue to find their way into high base rate occupations. The proposed strategy places emphasis on "should consider" not "will enter" (or prefer) and can be called an *opportunity approach to validation.*

The opportunity approach to validation does allow for the use of occupational group membership predictions as an indicator of validity. However, in the assessment of hit rates, the occupational groups for which membership is predicted should be treated as if they were of equal size. (For example, the individual group hit rates, expressed as proportions, could be combined and averaged to obtain an overall hit rate, assuming each group is large enough to provide stable results.) Whenever possible, employment stability and intrinsic satisfaction should be used as criteria in selecting group members. When all groups are treated as if they were of equal size, hit rates will not be affected by occupational base rates reflecting sex-role expectations or employer needs at a particular point in history.

Both approaches to interest inventory validation require one to identify the vocational interests characterizing people in given occupations. However, there is a crucial difference in the way in which persons pursuing nontraditional careers are treated. The predictive efficiency of the socialization approach to validation will be little affected if the interest patterns of the comparatively few (by definition) persons in nontraditional occupations are ignored. Given the employment status quo and sex-role expectations, persons with such interests are not likely to enter nontraditional occupations—and occupational entry is the criterion to be predicted in the socialization approach. On the other hand, the opportunity approach to validation requires identification of characteristics associated with occupational satisfaction (membership being an intermediate criterion), regardless of the base rates. When differences are found in the interests of men and women in any occupation (traditional or nontraditional), this information must be reflected in the occupational suggestions provided by the interest inventory.

Application of the opportunity approach to validation to two popular interest inventories will illustrate its implications for validity evidence. For example, the opportunity approach would require evidence justifying the use of the same Holland raw score code on the SDS to characterize members of an occupation, regardless of sex (Holland, 1974a). Because of the substantial differences in the SDS raw score profiles of men and women (i.e. men score high on the Investigative and Realistic Scales and women score high on the Social and Artistic Scales), it is possible that the Holland raw score codes for traditionally male occupations may not accurately reflect the vocational interests of women in those occupations (Prediger & Hanson, 1974). If this is true, women counselees with interests that are similar to the interests of women in traditionally male occupations might, instead, be referred to traditional female occupations, thus perpetuating the employment status quo. Holland (1974b) has acknowledged the need for research comparing the interests of men and women in the same occupation. The recent study by Prediger and Hanson (in press) summarized above provides evidence bearing directly on these points.

Likewise, the opportunity approach would require evidence justifying the use of men's scales with women (and vice versa) on the new Strong-Campbell Interest Inventory (Campbell, 1974). That is, the appropriateness of comparing the interests of women with those of men in an occupation predominantly consisting of men would have to be shown. Again, the basic question is whether women in an occupation really score as men do on the occupational scale for males (and vice versa). If not, different score standards and interpretations are required when interests are reported on opposite-sex scales as opposed to same-sex scales.

The difference between the socialization and opportunity approaches to the use of occupational group membership as a criterion for interest inventory validation is crucial. The former can result in reinforcement of the status quo, as represented by current occupational preferences and employment distributions of men and women. The latter can facilitate the exploration of career opportunities that are only just developing.

TRADE-OFFS IN INTEREST MEASUREMENT

Two conflicting approaches to reporting vocational interest inventory results have been discussed. The approach based on the socialization dominance hypothesis provides quite different distributions of career options to men and women, distributions corresponding to current occupational sex-role stereotypes. Validation of this approach relies heavily on the use of occupational entry as the criterion for prediction. Hence, it is closely tied to current employment base rates. By contrast, reporting and validation procedures based on the opportunity dominance hypothesis result in similar distributions of career options for men and women, thus encouraging the exploration of a greater variety of careers, including nontraditional careers.

A possible negative effect of the opportunity dominance approach is the possibility of suggesting that a counselee explore a career area that will be rejected as inappropriate because of internalized sex-role stereotypes or lack of employment opportunities. Holland and his co-workers (Gottfredson et al., 1974) argue that when interest score distributions and employment distributions are highly discrepant, "large numbers of people are misleadingly told their interests resemble those appropriate for jobs that they usually do not get" (p. 11). This is intended to support their previous assertion that the "use of sex norms may be misleading in vocational guidance, especially for women" (p. 11). But, is it not possible that women's interests *could* be appropriate to jobs they usually do not get? Could sex-biased employment practices and stereotypes about what is "woman's work" affect the types of jobs which women obtain? In the case of women and blacks, would it be misleading for an interest inventory to suggest exploration of apprenticeship trades, even if both sex and race discrimination were widely practiced?

We believe that it makes no practical sense to confound a report of measured interests with information on the occupation structure and that, indeed, troublesome counseling problems will result. In career counseling, both measures of interests and information about the labor market should be considered—and separately weighed.

The opportunity dominance hypothesis provides an alternative approach to helping counselees take into account the realities of the work world. We see the primary purpose of interest inventories as helping counselees to organize their preferences for work-related activities into basic areas of interest that suggest (through the opportunity approach to validity) occupations, college majors, etc., for exploration. This exploration should not be restricted to traditional careers through use of inventories based on the socialization dominance hypothesis. We believe that the individual, during the process of exploration, should be helped to take into account and weigh the realities of the social and economic structure (employment trends, opportunities, etc.), particularly in his/her own locale. In this approach, information about interests and information about the work world are considered separately by the counselee.

The problems of providing appropriate career guidance when wide discrepancies exist between interest distributions and occupational distributions should not be minimized. Too often occupational "reality" has played the role of restricting the options for certain groups, whether or not interest inventories are involved. For example, when a counselor dwells on the difficulties a woman may encounter in an engineering career because few women are now in engineering, the "reality" may become an unrealistic barrier. At the same time, it would seem to us foolish for a woman with high technical interests and related abilities to consider a career in engineering without also considering the barriers to women's employment which do exist in technical fields. Providing realistic occupational information yet not letting it become a psychological block is a delicate matter indeed, certainly not one that can be handled well by interest scores.

Although there are trade-offs one must make in choosing any approach to interest measurement, the most desirable course for the future seems clear to us. The price to be paid in the opportunity dominance approach—the suggestion of career areas which may be rejected as inappropriate because of internalized sex-role stereotypes or lack of opportunities—seems small indeed in comparison with the potential cost of adhering to the socialization dominance hypothesis —that is, frequent failure to identify otherwise suitable career options that do not conform to current sex-role stereotypes or employment distributions. The data on the characteristics of men and women in the same occupations that are now beginning to accumulate (Prediger & Hanson, 1975) also support the opportunity dominance approach to interest measurement.

REFERENCES

Association for Measurement and Evaluation in Guidance Commission on Sex Bias in Measurement. Report on sex bias in interest measurement. *Measurement and Evaluation in Guidance,* 1973, *6,* 171-177.

Campbell, D.P. *Handbook for the Strong Vocational Interest Blank.* Stanford, CA: Stanford University Press, 1971.

Campbell, D.P. *Manual for the Strong-Campbell Interest Inventory.* Stanford, CA: Stanford University Press, 1974.

Cole, N.S. On measuring the vocational interests of women. *Journal of Counsel-*

ing Psychology, 1973, *20,* 105-112.

Cole, N.S., & Hanson, G.R. An analysis of the structure of vocational interests. *Journal of Counseling Psychology,* 1971, *18,* 478-486.

Cole, N.S., & Hanson, G.R. Impact of interest inventories on career choice. In E.E. Diamond (Ed.), *Issues of sex bias and sex fairness in career interest measurement* (National Institute of Education report). Washington, D.C.: U.S. Government Printing Office, 1975.

D'Costa, A.G., Winefordner, D.W., Odgers, J.G., & Koons, P.B. *Ohio Vocational Interest Survey, manual for interpreting.* New York: Harcourt, Brace, and Jovanovich, 1970.

Diamond, E.E. (Ed.). *Issues of sex bias and sex fairness in career interest measurement* (National Institute of Education report). Washington, D.C.: U.S. Government Printing Office, 1975.

Equal Employment Opportunity Commission. Guidelines on employment selection procedures. *Federal Register,* August 1, 1970, *35,* 12, 333.

Gottfredson, G.D., & Holland, J.L. Vocational choices of men and women: A comparison of predictors from the Self-Directed Search. *Journal of Counseling Psychology,* 1975, *22,* 28-34.

Gottfredson, G.D., Holland, J.L., & Gottfredson, L.S. *The relation of vocational aspirations and assessments to employment reality.* Research Report No. 181. Baltimore: Center for Social Organization of Schools, The Johns Hopkins University, 1974.

Hanson, G.R. *Assessing the interests of college youth: Summary of research and applications.* ACT Research Report No. 67. Iowa City, IA: American College Testing Program, 1974.

Holland, J.L. *Professional manual for the Self-Directed Search.* Palo Alto, CA: Consulting Psychologists Press, 1972.

Holland, J.L. *Making vocational choices: A theory of careers.* Englewood Cliffs, NJ: Prentice-Hall, 1973.

Holland, J.L. *The occupations finder.* Palo Alto, CA: Consulting Psychologists Press, 1974. (a)

Holland, J.L. Some guidelines for reducing systematic biases in the delivery of vocational services. *Measurement and Evaluation in Guidance,* 1974, *6,* 210-218. (b)

Kuder, G.F. *General Interest Survey manual.* Chicago, IL: Science Research Associates, Inc., 1964.

Prediger, D.J., & Hanson, G.R. The distinction between sex restrictiveness and sex bias in interest inventories. *Measurement and Evaluation in Guidance,* 1974, *7,* 96-104.

Prediger, D.J., & Hanson, G.R. Holland's theory of careers applied to women and men: Analysis of implicit assumptions. *Journal of Vocational Behavior,* in press.

Prediger, D.J., Roth, J.D., & Noeth, R.J. Career development of youth: A nationwide study. *Personnel and Guidance Journal,* 1974, *53,* 97-104.

Rayman, J. Sex and the single interest inventory: An empirical validation of sex balanced vocational interest inventory items. Unpublished doctoral dissertation, University of Iowa, 1974.

Sex equality trainers are active in states. *Guidepost,* November 23, 1974, p. 8.

Chapter 32

GUIDELINES FOR ASSESSMENT OF SEX BIAS AND SEX FAIRNESS IN INTEREST INVENTORIES*

THE ATTACHED guidelines have been developed as part of the NIE Career Education Program's study of sex bias and sex fairness in career interest inventories. During the development of the guidelines, the following working definition of sex bias was used:

> Within the context of career guidance, sex bias is defined as any factor that might influence a person to limit—or might cause others to limit—his or her considerations of career solely on the basis of gender.

The working definition expresses the primary concern that career alternatives not be limited by bias or stereotypical use of sex roles in the world of work. The guidelines, by what they require and preclude, represent a more specific definition of the many aspects of sex bias or, conversely, sex fairness in interest inventories and related interpretive, technical, and promotional materials.

The term "career interest inventory," as used in these guidelines, refers to various formal procedures for assessing educational and vocational interests. The term includes but is not limited to nationally published inventories. The assessment procedures may have been developed for a variety of purposes and for use in a variety of settings. The settings include educational and employment related settings, among others, and the uses include career counseling, career exploration, and employee selection (although the latter may also involve other issues of sex bias in addition to those discussed here).

THE GUIDELINES DO NOT REPRESENT LEGAL REQUIREMENTS. They are intended, however, as standards to which developers and publishers should adhere in their inventories and in the technical and interpretive materials that American Psychological Association (APA)

*Prepared under contract from the National Institute of Education at a workshop on sex bias in interest testing held in March, 1974.

Standards for Development and Use of Educational and Psychological Tests[1] require them to produce, and by which users should evaluate the sex fairness of available inventories. It should be clear that there are many essential requirements for interest inventories in addition to the requirements relating to sex fairness. These guidelines do not replace concerns for fairness with regard to other subgroups such as various ethnic or socioeconomic-status groups. Neither are these guidelines a substitute for other technical requirements for tests and inventories such as those found in the APA Standards, EEOC testing guidelines,[2] and the Title IX testing guidelines.[3] The guidelines presented here represent supplementary, additional requirements with respect to sex fairness.

These guidelines directly address interest inventories and related services and materials. However, it is possible for sex bias to enter the career exploration or decision process in many ways other than through interest inventory materials. Several of the guidelines have clear implications for other materials and processes related to career counseling, career exploration, and career decision-making. The spirit of the guidelines should be applied to all parts of these processes if sex bias is to be eliminated.

Guidelines are presented here in three sections: (1) the inventory itself, (2) technical information, and (3) interpretive materials.

I. The Inventory Itself

A. The same interest inventory form should be used for both males and females unless it is empirically demonstrated that separate forms are more effective in minimizing sex bias.

B. Scores on all occupations and interest areas covered by the inventory should be given for both males and females, with the sex composition of norms for each scale clearly indicated.

C. (a) Insofar as possible, item pools should reflect experiences and activities which are equally familiar to both females and males. In instances where this is not currently possible, a minimum requirement is that the number of items favored by each sex be balanced. Further, it is desirable that the balance of items favored by each sex be achieved within individual scales within the limitations imposed by validity considerations. (An alternative statement has been submitted by E. Belvin Williams of ETS. In slightly edited form it reads: (b) "Insofar as possible, items within any given occupational dimension should reflect experi-

[1]Third draft.

[2]Equal Employment Opportunity Commission Rules and Regulation Guidelines, Guidelines on Employee Selection Procedure August, 1970.

[3]Title IX of the Education Amendments of 1972.

ences and activities familiar to both females and males. An item should be included within a given scale if and only if either the endorsement proportions for each sex group are nearly equal or, if unequal, the item is counterbalanced by one with similar endorsement proportions in the opposite direction.")

D. Occupational titles used in the inventory should be presented in gender-neutral terms (e.g. letter carrier instead of mailman) or both male and female titles should be presented (e.g. actor/actress).

E. Use of the generic "he" or "she" should be eliminated throughout the inventory.

II. Technical Information

A. Technical materials provided by the publisher should describe how and to what extent these guidelines have been met in the inventory and supporting materials.

B. Technical information should provide the rationale for either separate scales by sex or combined-sex scales (e.g. critical differences in male-female response rates that affect the validity of the scales versus similarity of response rates that justify combining data from males and females into a single scale).

C. Sex composition of the criterion and norm groups should be included in descriptions of these groups. Furthermore, reporting of scores for one sex on scales normed or constructed on the basis of data from the other sex should be supported by evidence of validity—if not for each scale, then by a pattern of evidence of validity established for pairs of similar scales. (Chuck Johannson suggested, for the second sentence, "Furthermore, implications of reporting scores for one sex on scales normed or constructed on data from the other sex should be explained.")

D. Criterion groups, norms, and other relevant data (e.g. validity, reliability, item response rates) should be examined at least every five years to determine the need for updating. New data may be required as occupations change or as the characteristics of persons entering occupations change. Test manuals should clearly label the date of data collection for criterion or norm groups for each occupation.

E. Technical materials should include information about the distribution of suggested career options produced by the inventory for samples of typical respondents of each sex.

F. Steps should be taken to investigate the validity of interest inventories for minority groups (differentiated by sex). Publishers should describe comparative studies and should clearly indicate whether differences were found between groups.

G. Unless it is empirically demonstrated that separate inventory forms are more effective in minimizing sex bias, the same vocational dimensions should be provided for each sex.

III. Interpretive Information

A. The user's manual provided by the publisher should describe how and to what extent these guidelines have been met in the inventory and the supporting materials.

B. Interpretive materials for test users and respondents (manuals, profiles, leaflets, etc.) should explain how to interpret scores resulting from separate or combined male and female norm or criterion groups.

C. Interpretive materials for interest inventory scores should point out that the vocational interests and choices of men and women are influenced by many environmental and cultural factors, including early socialization, traditional sex-role expectations of society, home-versus-career conflict, and the experiences typical of women and men as members of various ethnic and social class groups.

D. Manuals should recommend that the inventory be accompanied by orientation dealing with possible influences of factors in B above on men's and women's scores. Such orientation should encourage respondents to examine stereotypic "sets" toward activities and occupations and should help respondents to see that there is no activity or occupation that is exclusively male or female.

E. Interpretive materials for inventories that use homogeneous scales, such as health and mechanical, should encourage both sexes to look at *all* career and educational options, not just those traditionally associated with their sex group, within the broad areas in which they score high.

F. Occupational titles used in the interpretive materials and in the interpretation session should be stated in gender-neutral terms (e.g. letter carrier instead of mailman) or both male and female titles should be presented (e.g. actor/actress).

G. The written discussions in the interpretive materials (as well as all inventory text) should be stated in a way which overcomes the impression presently embedded in the English language that (a) people in general are of the male gender and (b) certain social roles are automatically sex-linked. For specific writing guidelines see Birk et al. *A Content Analysis of Sexual Bias in Commonly Used Psychology Textbooks* and Scott, Foresman and Company, *Guidelines for Improving the Image of Women in Textbooks.*

H. The user's manual (a) should state clearly that all jobs are appropriate for qualified persons of either sex and (b) should attempt to dispel myths about women and men in the world of work that are based on sex-role stereotypes. Furthermore, ethnic stereotypes should not be reinforced.

I. The user's manual should address possible user biases in regard to sex roles and their possible interaction with age, ethnic group, and social class and should caution against transmitting these biases to the respondent or reinforcing the respondent's own biases.

J. Where differences in validity have been found between dominant and minority groups (differentated by sex), separate interpretive procedures and materials should be provided that take these differences into account.

K. Interpretive materials for respondent and user should encourage exploratory experiences in areas where interests have not had a chance to develop.

L. Interpretive materials for reentry persons and persons changing careers or entering post-retirement careers should give special attention to score interpretation in terms of the effects of years of stereotyping and home-career conflict, the options congruent with current goals and past experiences and activities, and the norms on which the scores are based.

M. Case studies and examples presented in the interpretive materials should represent men and women equally and should include but not be limited to examples of each in a variety of non-stereotypic roles. Case studies and examples of mature men and women and of men and women in different social class and ethnic groups should also be included where applicable.

N. Both user's manuals and respondent's materials should make it clear that interest inventory scores provide only one kind of helpful information, and that this information should always be considered together with other relevant information—skills, accomplishments, favored activities, experiences, hobbies, influences, other test scores, and the like—in making any career decision. However, the possible biases of these variables should also be taken into consideration.

Defining Sex-bias in Interest Inventories

1. Sex-bias can occur both in what is *presented* to persons taking interest inventories (e.g. the inventory items, interpretive leaflets, etc.) and in what is *reported* to persons taking interest inventories (e.g. their scores and/or the career options they are invited to consider). The guidelines cover both aspects of sex bias. However, the characteristics of interest inventory reports are especially important because of the direct influence these reports presumably have on career explora-

tion, planning, and decision-making.

2. Degree of sex-restrictiveness is a crucial characteristic of the information reported to persons taking interest inventories. Because sex-restrictiveness does not necessarily indicate sex bias, it must be considered separately from sex bias.

3. *A definition of sex-restrictiveness:*

An interest inventory is sex-restrictive to the degree that the distribution of career options suggested to males and females is not equivalent for the two sexes. Conversely, an interest inventory is *not* sex-restrictive if *each* career option covered by the inventory is suggested to similar proportions of males and females. (Although interest inventories should cover the full range of career options in American society, the *degree* of coverage must be considered independently of the degree of sex-restrictiveness.)

(*Note.* This is simply the guidelines' definition of "sex bias" stated in operational terms and applied to reporting procedures.)

4. In the above definition, "suggested career options" result from the application of scoring or interpretation procedures used or advocated by the interest inventory publisher.

5. *So that degree of sex restrictiveness in reporting procedures can be easily judged by users, the publishers of interest inventories should show the distribution of career options suggested by their inventory to a cross section of males and females.* (This is not an unreasonable requirement since norm group data could be used to develop the distributions.)

6. Sex-restrictiveness is a potential indicator of sex bias and, because of its serious social implications, the publisher of a sex-restrictive inventory must demonstrate, in order for the inventory to be called "sex fair," that sex-restrictiveness is a necessary concomitant of validity. That is, if an interest inventory discriminates between the sexes in the career options it suggest, it must do so *only* as a requirement of validity. Hence, the following definition of sex bias in interest inventory reporting procedures is warranted.

7. *A definition of sex-bias in reporting procedures:*

An interest inventory that is sex-restrictive, as previously defined, can be considered to be sex-biased when the publisher uses or advocates arbitrary rules or procedures (rules or procedures unsupported by validity evidence) for determining which career options will be suggested to an individual. Conversely, in order for a sex-restrictive inventory to be called "sex fair," the publisher must demonstrate that sex-restrictiveness is a necessary concomitant of validity. The burden of proof is on the publisher.

Section IX

CROSS-CULTURAL PERSPECTIVES ON FEMALE CAREER DEVELOPMENT

RECOGNIZING that sex roles have a cultural foundation, we look at the career development of women from an international perspective in this section. The chapters present perspectives on women in the world of work in a variety of developed and developing countries. Many cross-cultural parallels can be seen in terms of trends in the labor market, inequality of treatment in the world of work, and stress related to demands of multiple roles. The relationship between economic systems and the roles assigned to women and men becomes more clear when examined from a cross-cultural perspective. This part seems to both document and dramatize the enormity of the social changes needed to provide equal opportunities for both sexes and create a world in which women and men can live and work together in a climate of equality, respect, freedom of choice, and participation in the larger society.

Steinmann presents the results of a cross-cultural project designed to investigate feminine and masculine perceptions of the feminine role in six cultures including the United States, England, Czechoslovakia, Brazil, Greece, and Israel. Women of diverse cultural backgrounds were found to share specific values regarding feminine roles and behaviors. Most women indicated a desire to combine self-achievement and familial responsibilities and saw themselves moving toward multiple roles. However, the women believed that the men in their cultures desire a traditional family-oriented woman who places family needs above her personal needs. It was found that men also share values about women's role but desire a woman more self-achieving than the ideal woman attributed to men by the women in the study. Preliminary data from research on perceptions of the male sex role in the United States reflected the same paradox: both sexes had the same ideal image, yet neither sex had an accurate picture of the feelings of the other sex. Role confusion apparently exists for both women and men, and implications are discussed.

Next, Kievit examines the data on women's participation in the international labor force. Several trends appear to be occurring worldwide: The proportion of women workers has increased and the proportion of employed married women has increased, as has the employment of middle-aged women. Cultural, social, and economic factors related to employment patterns are discussed; five main patterns of urban female labor force participation are identified.

Examination of the data on women's participation in the labor force also reveals similar inequities from culture to culture. While there are some cultural differences as to which occupations are associated with a particular sex (e.g. 25 percent of the dentists in Norway are women), women around the world are employed in a narrow range of traditional occupations. In the Soviet Union a high proportion of women have entered professional and technical occupations traditionally dominated by men; however, their prospects for advancement are not equal to those of males. Kievit also points out that although dual roles for women are increasing, there has yet been no satisfactory way to more evenly distribute the burdens of homemaking and child care tasks unless men are willing to share more equally in these roles. The problems of economic and time resources are even more crucial when there is no particular support system to share in the tasks.

Holter provides a theoretical analysis of the consequences of social changes for sex roles. She assumes that the extent and mode of sex differentiation are more the result than the determinants of social change and that the ultimate explanation is economic. The needs of the economic system with respect to labor and consumption are viewed as promoting a change from traditional sex roles to quasi-egalitarianism. Some ideas on the question of strategies for sex-role change within this context are offered.

The concluding chapter ties together a worldwide picture of basic inequality between women and men in the world of work. Women are still under-represented in many fields, underpaid compared to males doing the same work, and denied access, sometimes in subtle ways, to training and educational opportunities. Women's right to equality of opportunity is on fragile ground and will covary with the economy. However, there are some signs for optimism. Some countries, particularly in Scandinavia, are making tremendous changes in reorganization of work and family roles. In Sweden an effort is being made to break down occupational sex typing by providing training grants to employers who train women for traditionally male jobs and vice versa. Employment subsidies for new jobs will be contingent upon at least 40 percent of new jobs going to each sex.

The parallels between distribution of women in the work force in Norway and in the United States are striking. While the Norwegian occupations are different, women are still in the lower-paying, dead-end jobs in canning, textiles, and fisheries. With some jobs disappearing due to the discovery of oil off the west coast and the resultant closing of the less lucrative fisheries that have been major employers of women, it is the women who are first displaced. Analysis of women in science majors in the *gymnasium* and of women in top positions in the universities indicates that Norway has a long way to go in achieving true equality.

Cross-cultural counseling and equal treatment of the sexes have become an important topic in counseling psychology. Ways to help males become less defensive about female culture and to recognize their biases have to be found.

The universality of the phenomenon of sex role as a culture is pointed out very well in the articles which make up this section. It is hoped that this kind of international perspective will help counselors and other helping professionals to identify those factors which inhibit and those which facilitate career development of women around the globe. Institutional policies as well as individual behaviors must be changed if women are to share in the economic benefits of society, more fully utilize their resources, and integrate in more actualizing ways their various life roles.

Chapter 33

FEMALE AND MALE CONCEPTS OF SEX ROLES: AN OVERVIEW OF TWENTY YEARS OF CROSS-CULTURAL RESEARCH*[1]

ANNE STEINMANN

THE LAST several decades have witnessed much confusion and even more controversy regarding women, their place in society, and men's place in a society that is in the midst of a social, technological, and sexual revolution. Males, as well as females, in our society continue to face severe ambiguity in defining the so-called "appropriate" feminine and/or masculine roles.

The conflicts that exist in women as a consequence of these sex role ambiguities have been studied by many investigators. Farmer and Bohn (1970) studied one conflict experienced by women, the conflict between home and career. Based upon their experimental paradigm, these authors concluded that the source of this conflict is "the cultural lag between social opportunity and social sanction." In a study of college-educated women, Gordon and Hall (1974) found that "the most common conflict was that between a home role and a nonhome role."

Coser and Rokoff (1971) noted that the conflict experienced by working women is that they are at the same time expected to be committed to their work and to give priority to their families. In another examination of the career-family dilemma, Bailyn (1970) found support for the hypothesis that "a husband's mode of integrating family and work in his own life is crucial for the success—at least in terms of marital satisfaction—of any attempt of his wife to include a career in

*From *International Mental Health Research Newsletter, Winter 1975, 17(4), 2-4, 8-11.*

[1]Data in this paper are from the United States, England, Brazil, Czechoslovakia, Greece and Israel. The Maferr Foundation has also gathered data in the following 12 countries: France, Finland, Germany, Austria, the Philippines, Peru, Argentina, Mexico, Japan, India, Iran and Turkey.

her life." Tomlinson-Keasey (1974) investigated women's conflict about achievement or success and concluded that "the conflict between general societal roles and personal aspirations" was responsible for the "fear of success" observed in women.

All too few investigators have focused upon the conflicts experienced by men. Komarovsky (1973), in a study of 62 college seniors, found a significant amount of ambivalence toward the traditional masculine role is a source of "role strain." Steinmann and Fox (1974), over a period of twenty years of investigation, have documented the dilemmas facing men (and women). Some of the findings of this research appear in this chapter.

In order to examine ambiguities empirically, the Maferr Foundation has conducted research for over twenty years on male and female perceptions of feminine and masculine roles. What follows is a report on cross-cultural research that has been conducted on male and female perceptions of the *feminine* role in the United States, England, Czechoslovakia, Brazil, Greece and Israel (Maferr Bibliography, 1957-1975) as well as a brief report of findings of research that has been conducted in the United States on male and female perceptions of the *masculine* role.

The instrument employed in this phase of the research on feminine roles, the Maferr Inventory of Feminine Values, is based upon the following conceptions of woman's role:

The *traditional* family-oriented concept of the feminine role is that the woman conceives of herself as the "other," the counterpart of the man and children in her life. She performs a nurturing role. Her achievement is to help others achieve. Her distinguishing feature is that she fulfills herself by proxy (Steinmann, 1963).

The *liberal* self-achieving concept of the feminine role is that concept held by the woman who embraces a self-fulfilling orientation. She strives to fulfill herself directly by realizing her own potentialities. Her distinguishing feature is that she seeks fulfillment through her *own* accomplishments (Steinmann, 1963).

The basic hypotheses of the research are, first, that women of varied backgrounds, of different professional and life status positions, of different ages, ethnic backgrounds, and varied national origins and present nationalities will, nevertheless, share specific values regarding feminine roles and behavior. Among these values is the belief that men desire an extremely family-oriented woman, a woman who derives her major satisfactions from her role and responsibilities as wife and mother. The second hypothesis tested was that men also share values about women's role, and that these shared values would reflect a woman significantly more self-assertive and self-fulfilling than the ideal that women attributed to men. To test these hypotheses, the objective instrument, the Maferr Inventory of Feminine Values, has been administered to samples of women and men deliberately selected to vary on psychosocial variables. Samples were selected on the basis of data availability in various countries so that similar populations within different cultures might be studied. We have held the instrument constant, while varying nationality, age, professional status, occupation, and ethnic status.

Data have been collected in the United States and abroad from over 110 samples of women, totalling approximately 14,000 female respondents and from over 55 samples of men, totalling more than 7,000 male respondents (Steinmann & Fox, 1974). This is a report on one set of data from 14 selected samples. Similarities and differences in the response patterns will be discussed.

METHOD

Subjects

The subjects came from 14 cluster samples: three from the United States, two from Czechoslovakia, four from Brazil, one from England, three from Greece, and one from Israel. Ages ranged from the late teens to the mid-sixties, although the majority of subjects were under forty. The samples represented a reasonable cross section of better educated segments of these populations, and as noted in Table 33-I, include college students, graduates, professionals, nonprofessionals, and the general population at large. We shall consider the overall pattern of responses from these samples in order to obtain insight into cross-cultural male and female perceptions of woman's role (Steinmann, 1974).

Instrument

The Inventory of Feminine Values,[2] developed by the Maferr Foundation, consists of 34 statements, each of which expresses a particular value or value judgment related to woman's activities and satisfactions. The respondent indicates the strength of his or her agreement or disagreement to each statement on a five-point Likert scale, ranging from "strongly disagree" to "strongly agree," through the midpoint of "I have no opinion." The statements are sometimes stated positively, sometimes negatively, to avoid a respondent being able to adopt one position by always agreeing or disagreeing.

Seventeen of the 34 items are considered to provide a respondent with the opportunity to delineate a value we call family-oriented and

---

[2]Devised originally by Alexandra Botwin, Ph.D., San Francisco, California. Developed and copyright, Maferr Foundation, Inc. 1966.

nurturant. That is, a woman who sees her own satisfactions coming second after those of her husband and family, and who sees her family responsibilities as taking precedence over any potential activity or occupation. This corresponds to the *traditional* concept that was mentioned above. The other 17 items delineate a self-achieving woman who considers her own satisfactions equally or more important as those of husband and family, and who wishes to have opportunities to realize any latent ability or talent. This corresponds to the *liberal* concept of woman's role.

The Inventory was designed to encompass five major areas in male-female relationships. The first group of statements consists of items such as "I am energetic in the development and expression of my ideas," or "When I am doing something with a group of people, I often seem to be drifting into a position of leadership." These and others like them are concerned with the personal and social characteristics of women. A second group of items concerns the inter-relationships between husbands and wives. This group includes such items as "I would like to marry a man whom I could really look up to," or "I would rather not marry than sacrifice some of my essential beliefs and needs in order to adjust to another person." A third area is concerned with motherhood, such as the item, "I will have achieved the main goal of my life if I rear normal, well-adjusted children." The fourth group of items is concerned with the inter-relationships of work and family responsibilities for women, including such items as "I believe the personal ambitions of a woman should be subordinated to the family as a group." The fifth area involves a woman's self-realization, i.e. "I would like to create or accomplish something which would be recognized by everybody."

The score on the inventory represents the difference in strength of agreement to the 17 family and 17 self-achieving items. A respondent who took equal but opposite positions each time would have a score of zero; a respondent who consistently took diametrically opposite positions on the item types would have a score of minus 68 if she always took the strongest possible family-oriented position, and a score of +68 if she always took the strongest possible self-achieving position. Positive scores between zero and +68 thus represent intermediate degrees of a self-achieving orientation, and negative scores between 0 and minus 68 represent intermediate degrees of the family-orientation.

The reliability of the inventory has been estimated through the split-half technique and, when corrected through the Spearman-Brown procedure, is .81. The items have face validity in that they are statements with generally accepted connotations, but they have also been submitted to validation by seven judges who agreed on the nature of the categorization as family or self-oriented.

Three forms of the Inventory were used in the research with females: Self-Concept (A), Own Ideal (B), and Woman's Concept of Men's Ideal (C). The men in these samples responded to one form of the Inventory, the one asking them to answer as their Ideal Woman would (BB).

RESULTS AND INTERPRETATION

An examination of Table 33-I reveals the following:

On Woman's Self-Concept (Form A)

In all countries but Greece, college undergraduates have a self-concept that is self-achieving ($\bar{X}$ +3.2 for the United States, $\bar{X}$ +6.2 for Brazil, $\bar{X}$ +4.7 for England, and $\bar{X}$ +10.7 for Israel). The Mean for Greek undergraduates is –2.6. Professional women studied have a self-concept which is more self-achieving than the female undergraduates (+28.9 for the United States, +11.4 for Czechoslovakia, and +6.8 for Brazil). The mean for Greek professional women (0.0) is seen to be balanced between family-oriented and self-achieving strivings, but is more self-achieving than the mean for Greek undergraduates. The non-professionals in the United States and the non-professionals and teachers in Brazil have a family-oriented self-concept (–1.2 for the United States, –4.1 and –1.3 for Brazilian nonprofessionals and teachers, respectively). It is interesting to note that the nonprofessionals in Czechoslovakia and the college undergraduate females in Israel have strong self-achieving self-concepts (means of +9.4 and +10.7) respectively. One interpretation might be that these women need a strong self-concept in order to balance the dual roles that the structure of their society demands: that of middle class mother and proletariat worker. This interpretation was corroborated by our interviews with these women.

On Concept of Woman's Own Ideal (Form B)

It is interesting to note that among professionals, the ideal woman is either very close to the self-concept or more self-achieving than the self-concept. There was no significant difference found between self and ideal for the Greek professional woman. The ideal of the other groups is slightly more family-oriented, but quite close to the self-concept. The ideal woman of the group of Israeli college undergraduates (+12.8) is slightly more self-achieving than their self-concept (+10.7). However, the sample of Greek undergraduates is significantly more family-oriented in their ideal (–6.5) than in their self concept (–2.6).

It is possible that this reflects a shift in social values and/or opportunities in the Greek culture. In times of transition, the concept of

TABLE 33-I

Means & Standard Deviations of Women's Concept of Self (A), Ideal Woman (B), and Man's Ideal Woman (C)
Means & Standard Deviations of Man's Concept of His Ideal Woman (BB)

+ = achievement oriented concept
— = family oriented traditional concept

		Female Forms							Male Form	
	No. of	A		B		C		No. of	BB	
Sample Studied	Subjects*	X	S.D.	X	S.D.	X	S.D.	Subjects†	X	S.D.
United States										
Undergraduates	285‡	+ 3.2	11.34	+ 2.7	14.19	—15.1	13.49	182	+ 1.5	12.91
Professionals§	54	+28.9	9.63	+32.2	11.13	—23.8	21.30	54	+14.6	10.42
Non-professionals	31	— 1.2	9.98	+ .4	9.10	— 9.7	13.24	34	+ 2.2	15.29
Czechoslovakia										
Professionals	32	+11.4	9.21	+10.1	9.85	—14.7	16.11	45	+13.6	10.34
Non-professionals	33	+ 9.4	7.52	+ 8.3	9.73	—13.5	9.52	30	+ 2.9	8.95
Brazil										
Undergraduates	100	+ 6.2	13.69	+ 5.8	11.03	— 6.4	17.09	100	+ 1.2	12.65
Professionals	58	+ 6.8	14.61	+10.2	12.81	—14.2	22.71	91	+ 4.9	15.04
Non-professionals	78	— 4.1	18.61	— 1.0	13.90	— 6.0	15.83	68	— 2.2	12.62
Teachers	78	— 1.3	10.46	+ .9	13.84	—10.1	17.25	¶		
England										
Undergraduates	43	+ 4.7	8.23	+ 3.8	14.09	—17.8	12.36	36	+ .2	12.19

Greece										
Undergraduates	73	— 2.6	11.20	— 6.5	13.70	—14.4	14.55	¶		
Professionals	24	0.0	9.02	— .8	9.40	—24.8	12.00	43	— 6.5	13.24
Athens Representative Sample	‖							172	—17.3	14.33
Israel										
Undergraduates	62	+10.7	6.4	+12.8	8.38	— 9.9	9.4	31	+ 9.9	3.48

*951 Total Females
†886 Total Males
‡206 for Form B
§Psychologists
‖No female sample
¶No male sample

one's own ideal might be a reflection of those "old" social values which are in the process of changing. This was found to be the case in questioning female college undergraduates in the past. Almost all of our samples exhibited a more family-oriented woman as their ideal at the onset of this research in 1952. However, after 1968, the trend reversed, and female college undergraduate samples began to evidence an even more self-achieving ideal than their own self-perception, a self-perception which itself is becoming more self-achieving over the years.

On Woman's Concept of Man's Ideal Woman (Form C)

Of greatest significance are those data which reflect woman's concept of man's ideal woman. It is well to bear in mind that what is being considered is more than a twenty-year research span and that the results reveal an amazing consistency on woman's concept of man's ideal woman. In all populations studied, women believe man's ideal woman is one who is home-oriented, putting her own growth and development second to her role in the home and family. The mean scores range from –9.9 for Israeli college undergraduates to –24.8 for the Greek professional women. Further, one notes that the higher the educational level of the woman questioned, the more family oriented and traditional her perceptions of man's ideal woman are likely to be.

On Man's Concept of His Ideal Woman (Form BB)

In contrast to woman's perception of man's ideal woman, the concept of man's ideal woman as reported by men in the United States, Czechoslovakia, England, Israeli, and Brazilian undergraduate and professional samples was one evidencing varying degrees of a self-achieving orientation (Table 33-I).

Professional men queried in the United States and Czechoslovakia indicated that their ideal woman was strongly self-achieving (+14.6 and +13.6 respectively). Israeli undergraduates also delineated a strongly self-achieving ideal woman (+9.9). *Undergraduates* and *nonprofessionals* in the United States, Czechoslovakia, and England indicated as their ideal a woman more balanced between self-achieving and family orientations, but still on the self-achieving side of the scale (Table 33-I). The mean for Brazilian nonprofessionals is more family oriented (–2.2).

In opposition to the above findings, a different picture is presented by the samples of Greek men. Both Greek professionals and the large sample of Greek urban males residing in Athens delineate as their ideal woman one who is family-oriented, with mean scores of –17.3 for the latter and –6.5 for the former. A follow-up study is currently underway in Greece.

COMPARISONS:

On Women's Concept of Man's Ideal (C) Compared to Man's Ideal Woman (BB)

All samples reported revealed dramatic differences between woman's concept of man's ideal woman (C) and man's actual ideal (BB). The largest disparities occur in the sample of United States and Czech professional men and women. United States professional women rate their concept of man's ideal as strongly family-oriented, while the professional males' actual ideal woman is strongly self-achieving. Czech professional women's concept of men's ideal is strongly home-oriented. However, their professional male counterparts' concept of their ideal woman is strongly self-achieving. In the first instance, a difference of 38.4 points is seen, and in the second, there is a discrepancy of 28.3 points (Table 33-IIA).

TABLE 33-IIA

Absolute Point Difference in Mean Scores on Women's Concept of Man's Ideal Woman (Form C) and Man's Concept of His Ideal Woman (Form BB)

Sample Studied	No. of Subjects Female	Male	Form C $\overline{X}$	Form BB $\overline{X}$	Point Difference
United States					
Undergraduates*	285	182	—15.1	+ 1.5	16.6
Professionals	54	54	—23.8	+14.6	38.4
Non-professionals	31	34	— 9.7	+ 2.2	11.9
Czechoslovakia					
Professionals	32	45	—14.7	+13.6	28.3
Non-professionals	33	30	—13.5	+ 2.9	16.4
Brazil					
Undergraduates*	100	100	— 6.4	+ 1.2	7.6
Professionals	58	91	—14.2	+ 4.9	19.1
Non-professionals	78	68	— 6.0	— 2.2	3.8
England					
Undergraduates	43	36	—17.8	+ .2	18.0
Greece					
Professionals	24	43	—24.8	— 6.5	18.3
Israel					
Undergraduates*	62	31	— 9.9	+ 9.9	19.8

*College Undergraduate Students

Large differences between woman's and man's concept of Man's Ideal Woman are also evidenced by United States college undergraduates and nonprofessionals (Table 33-IIA). The male and female Greek professional sample is also widely split, with means of –6.5 for the men's concept of ideal woman, and –24.8 for the women's concept of men's ideal woman. Israeli male and female college undergraduates also evidence a strong disparity in Man's Ideal Woman with interestingly divergent scores of +9.9 for man's ideal woman and –9.9 for woman's concept of men's ideal. Scores on Table 33-IIA are revelatory of all samples discussed.

A lack of communication between men and women is consistently demonstrated, since the data show that all samples of women report man's ideal woman as one who is home-oriented, but men report that man's actual ideal woman is one who possesses varying degrees of home orientation and self-achieving concepts.

It is clear from the data that the widest discrepancies are found in the samples of professional males and females. There seems to be a reverse correlation in operation here. It was noted above that the data reveal that the higher the educational level of the woman questioned, the more family-oriented her perception of man's ideal woman is likely to be. Conversely, it seems that the higher the educational level of the man questioned, the more self-achieving his own ideal woman is likely to be, but still the professional man is not in agreement with his female counterpart. These results are reinforced in a study by Maureen M. Kaley. Dr. Kaley's study revealed that married professional men expressed a negative attitude toward the professional woman's ability to cope with home and work roles (Kaley, 1971).

On Man's Concept of Ideal Woman (BB) Compared to Woman's Own Ideal (B)

The data show that woman's perception of her ideal woman is actually very close to man's perception of his ideal woman. An examination of Table 33-IIB reveals that, in the comparison between woman's concept of her ideal and man's concept of his ideal, for the samples tested, there is but one group having absolute point differences greater than 5.7 points. This group is the United States professionals, whose point difference between woman's ideal woman and man's ideal woman is +17.6. Both mean scores, however, are strongly self-achieving (+32.2 for the women and +14.6 for the men), and so the difference is primarily one of degree, not orientation (Table 33-IIB).

TABLE 33-IIB

Absolute Point Difference in Mean Scores on Women's Concept of Ideal Woman (Form B) and Men's Concept of Ideal Woman (Form BB)

	No. of Subjects		Form B	Form BB	Point
Sample Studied	Female	Male	$\overline{X}$	$\overline{X}$	Difference
United States					
Undergraduates*	206	182	+ 2.7	+ 1.5	1.2
Professionals	54	54	+32.2	+14.6	17.6
Non-professionals	31	34	+ .4	+ 2.2	1.8
Czechoslovakia					
Professionals	32	45	+10.1	+13.6	3.5
Non-professionals	33	30	+ 8.3	+ 2.9	5.4
Brazil					
Undergraduates*	100	100	+ 5.8	+ 1.2	4.6
Professionals	58	91	+10.2	+ 4.9	5.3
Non-professionals	78	68	—1.0	— 2.2	1.2
Greece					
Professionals	24	43	— .8	— 6.5	5.7
Israel					
Undergraduates*	61	31	+12.8	+ 9.9	2.9
England					
Undergraduates*	43	36	+ 3.8	+ .2	3.6

*College Undergraduate Students

DISCUSSION

Conclusions and Implications

What conclusions might be drawn from an examination of these data?

In examining Table 33-I, one pattern in the data is very clear. In all samples, these women are saying, "I am pretty much what I would like to be, but I am not what men would like me to be." This pattern, moreover, is one wherein women attribute to men a concept of an ideal woman who is strongly family-oriented. On the other hand, men when questioned state that their ideal woman is either strongly self-achieving (United States and Czech professional men) or balanced between intra-family and extra-family strivings (all other samples except for the Greek men). The discrepancy between the family-oriented woman that women believe men desire and the ideal woman that men actually delineate may be accounted for in at least four ways.

In responding as they do (a) both men and women are telling the truth as they see it, and the data reflect serious lack of communication; (b) women are projecting what they really might be feeling and what they would like men to believe; (c) men are talking a current liberal stereotype and may neither believe nor behave as they responded; and (d) when the men espouse a liberal concept of woman's role, they are exposing an ambivalence that may or may not be the result of their own use of projection and denial of an active role.

Research still underway has not yet revealed which of these four interpretations is the most sensible explanation of the discrepancy. It is likely that all the factors mentioned are involved. However, at this time, it is possible to state that in the eyes of these women, men desire a type of woman that they have no wish to be. The discrepancy between ideas is so great, the gap is so wide and deep that, even more than a lack of understanding, this discrepancy suggests almost a closed path of communication between men and women. Evidently both men and women do not understand each other's desires as to what role a woman should assume.

Data gathered at an Eastern college in 1974-75 present a recent example of this communication barrier. A live-in, coeducational community was set up at the college and it was hypothesized that closeness and a natural exchange and sharing of ideas and feelings between men and women would lead to more accurate perceptions of themselves and each other. The data did not support this hypothesis. Apparently communication channels were not opened sufficiently, or words and behavior used in exchange were not reflective of actual feelings. A first analysis of the data appears in Table 33-III. A full report is being prepared.

Our research into male and female concepts of the *masculine* role (Steinmann, Farkas & Fox, 1968) has revealed that this communication barrier exists as much for the masculine role as it does for the feminine role. The samples for this study included 441 males and 635 females in the United States. The initial data from the research on perceptions of the male sex role reflected the same paradox identified in our research on female roles: Both sexes had the same ideal image, yet neither sex had an accurate perception of how the other feels. The discrepancy between the image of an ideal man which men attributed to women and the ideal to which women actually aspire is particularly dramatic, since men's prediction is as far on the family-oriented side of the midpoint as women's actual ideal is on the self-oriented side. Thus, the original hypothesis that this kind of sex-role confusion would exist for male roles as well as for female roles is supported by these data.

However, these data permit us to go beyond the previous research

TABLE 33-III

New Jersey College Experiment in Coeducational Community Living — Pre-Post Study
Means & Standard Deviations of Women's Concept of Self (A), Ideal Woman (B), Man's Ideal Woman (C), and Man's Concept of His Ideal Woman (BB)
Means & Standard Deviations of Men's Concept of Self (H), Ideal Man (D), Woman's Ideal Man (E), and Woman's Concept of Her Ideal Man (DD)

Maferr Inventory of Feminine Values	Females									Males		
	A			B			C			BB		
	#	X	S.D.	#	X	S.D.	#	X	S.D.	#	X	S.D.
1973 "Pre" Study	40	+15.32	8.48	40	+19.0	14.60	40	— 7.30	14.20	30	+10.13	13.24
1974 "Post" Study	38	+19.79	12.08	38	+23.68	18.16	38	— 4.00	17.84	27	+11.38	11.60

Maferr Inventory of Masculine Values	Male									Females		
	H			D			E			DD		
	#	X	S.D.	#	X	S.D.	#	X	S.D.	#	X	S.D.
1973 "Pre" Study	31	+ 3.61	9.16	31	+ 3.61	13.44	31	— 4.93	12.16	40	+ 7.40	11.32
1974 "Post" Study	28	+ 5.43	10.52	28	+ 5.48	12.36	28	— 5.08	16.00	40	+ 8.56	11.72

on women for this study of males has available one set of data not previously obtained for women—and that is the women's prediction of how men would respond. These data enable us to note that not only are men confused as to what kind of man woman wanted, but women are also confused as to how men would like to be. For men also say, "Women want us to be less assertive and self-oriented (−6.0) than we would like to be" (+5.4) (Table 33-IV). If the data are interpreted this way, one may state that men are hearing women correctly in relative terms but erroneously concluding that women therefore want a man who, overall, is more family than self-oriented.

TABLE 33-IV

Means on Men's Concept of Self (H), Ideal Man (D) and Women's Ideal Man (E)
Means on Women's Concept of Her Ideal Man (DD) and Women's Concept of Man's Ideal Man (F)

	No. of Subjects	Male Forms			No. of Subjects	Female Forms	
		H	D	E		DD	F
Mean Score	441	+1.7	+5.4	−6.0	633	+5.4	+10.7

What is suggested by the data is that the preoccupation in recent years in both lay and professional circles with the role confusion of women as they move into new areas of interest and activity has ignored comparable confusion on male roles. These data suggest further that the communication between the sexes as to what they indeed do want for themselves and for each other has been no more effective for males than it has been for females. Finally, it is our belief that the data strengthen the need for the establishment of programs bringing together men and women, and particularly husbands and wives, in candid consideration and discussion of their needs and expectations in the area of sex-role behavior. The virtually identical male ideal revealed in this current study combined with the comparable female ideals previously reported indicates the basic agreement on which these discussions could be based.

Summary

In this study of women and men on a cross-cultural level, the data supported the initial hypotheses. First, women of varied backgrounds were found to share specific values regarding feminine roles and behavior. Among these values is the belief that men desire a family-oriented woman. Further, it was found that men also share values about women's role and that these shared values reveal a woman more self-achieving than the ideal woman that women attribute to men. In addition, one particular finding appears most relevant; namely, that most women sampled indicated on the Maferr Inventory that they perceive themselves to be well balanced between self-achieving and family orientations (although there do tend to be relative cultural differences and variability within each sample and, as we have seen, both the highly educated and/or professional women are more self-oriented and self-achieving.) In other words, the women indicate a strong desire to combine, in harmony, both duties related to the family and worthwhile self-achieving activities outside of the family context. Furthermore, the data also reveal that women worldwide currently are attempting to approach this new double identity. However, while most women indicate that they are becoming pretty much what they would like to be, they do not feel that men approve of their new roles outside of the family. Cross-culturally, women indicate that they feel that the men in their particular cultures desire a woman who is extremely nurturant and places her own personal growth and development second to the family. Women report that there are still stereotypes and restrictions of one sort or another to block or limit their total development. Women appear to be moving towards the combination of self-achievement and familial responsibilities, but continue to feel frustrated in light of the various discriminatory practices designed to hinder their progress and freedom. This frustration in women must be recognized by men and resolved for their own male well-being. Society and societies are in a transitional period. Men and women must keep on working to find each other, and to get in touch with each other's true feelings.

The disparity in concept of self and concept of the other reflects a lack of communication, but this disparity is not simply a male-female breach in communication. The breakdown in communication is society's problem. Our data suggest that one factor which might be contributing to the male-female confusion in role concept is woman's push toward higher education. Cross-culturally, women indicate that they feel that the men in their particular cultures desire a woman who is extremely nurturant and places her wifely and familial duties before her own personal growth and development. The Maferr studies have shown that, as the woman's level of education rises, the gap in communication between the sexes seems to become greater. This raises an obvious question: "To alleviate the problem, do we curtail education for women?" Of course not; that is a ridiculous solution. What we must do is raise and increase levels of education within society as a whole and particularly among men as to the content, cause, and possible solutions for the discrepancies in masculine and feminine role concepts. Perhaps then society's enlightenment might tend to close the communication gap between the sexes. It is well to remember that society is made up of men and women, and each man and woman is society.

In sum, the research tends to indicate that the conflict for women attempting to combine both family and self-achieving roles exists. It is not just a plank for Women's Liberation. It is a problem shared by women *and* men. Men, too, must try to combine family and self-achieving roles. The conflict will remain until both men and women change static and stereotyped attitudes about male and female roles that do not benefit them and, further, the conflict will remain until they change social institutions to make it easier for men and women to communicate and understand each other better.

REFERENCES

Bailyn, L. Career and family orientations of husbands and wives in relation to marital happiness. *Human Relations*, 1970, *23*, 97-113.

Coser, R.L. & Rokoff, G. Women in the occupational world: social disruption and conflict. *Social Problems*, 1971, *18*, 535-554.

Farmer, H.S. & Bohn, M.J., Jr. Home-career conflict reduction and the level of career interest in women. *Journal of Counseling Psychology*, 1970, *17*, 228-232.

Gordon, F.E. & Hall, D.T. Self-image and stereotypes of femininity: Their relationship to women's role conflicts and coping. *Journal of Applied Psychology*, 1974, *59*, 241-243.

Kaley, M.M. Attitudes toward the dual role of the married professional woman. *American Psychologist*, 1971, *26*, 301-306.

Komarovsky, M. Presidential address: some problems in role analysis. *American Sociological Review*, 1973, *38*, 649-662.

Maferr Bibliography. New York: Maferr Foundation, Inc., 1957-1975.

Steinmann, A. A study of the concept of the feminine role of 51 middle-class American families. *Genetic Psychology Monographs*, 1963, *67*, 275-352.

Steinmann, A., Farkas, R., & Fox, D.J. Male and female perceptions of male sex roles. *Proceedings* of the 76th Annual American Psychological Association Convention, 1968.

Steinmann, A. & Fox, D.J. *The Male Dilemma*. New York: Jason Aronson, 1974.

Steinmann, A. Cultural values, female role expectancies, and therapeutic goals. In V. Franks and V. Burtle (Eds.), *Women in therapy: Contemporary approaches*. New York: Bruner/Mazel, Inc. 1974.

Tomlinson-Keasey, C. Role variables: their influence on female motivational constructs. *Journal of Counseling Psychology*, 1974, *21*, 232-237.

Chapter 34

WOMEN AT WORK: AN INTERNATIONAL PERSPECTIVE*

MARY BACH KIEVIT

LABOR FORCE PARTICIPATION

Numbers and Trends

HUMAN resources are an important factor in economic development. Women throughout the world constitute roughly one-half of those resources. At a period when nations vary greatly in the levels of economic development, it is not surprising to find manpower analysts in most countries considering the labor force participation of women. The comparability of census procedures, including periods in which data are collected, type of data collected, and definition of terms, pose limitations upon the precision of systematic comparisons in labor force participation from one country to another. Economists, however, taking this difficulty into account have arrived at approximations.

Johnstone (1968) stated that over the world as a whole, 30 out of every 100 women are economically active. In some countries women form more than two-fifths and nearly one-half of the labor force. Variations in participation rates of different countries are considerable however. Klein (1965), reporting data from 21 countries (see Table 34-I), pointed out some of the variations in statistical methods of reporting. Some countries, such as Denmark, Luxemburg, the Netherlands and the United Kingdom do not include unpaid family workers —often a high percentage of whom are women—whereas some countries do, such as Turkey and Greece. Thus while reporting women as a proportion of the total labor force, the proportion of unpaid women workers, i.e. work in addition to housework, is also indicated in Table 34-I.

Klein pointed out that women have at all times and in all countries taken part in the economic activities of their countries. In industrial-

*From Kievit: Women in the World of Work. Columbus, Ohio State University Press, 1972, pp. 3-17. Courtesy of The Center for Vocational Education, The Ohio State University.

TABLE 34-I

Women as a Percentage of the Civil Labour Force of the Organization for Economic Cooperation and Development Member Countries, and Proportions of Working Women Who Are Unpaid Family Workers[1]

Country	Year	Women as percent of Civil Labour Force	Unpaid family members as percent of working women
Austria	1961	41.3	24.2
Belgium	1962	31.6	15.1
Canada	1962	27.1	5.1
Denmark	1962	35.3	
Eire	1961	26.7	
France	1962	34.9	18.9
Germany (F.R.)	1962	36.9	22.3
Greece	1961	32.8	55.1
Italy	1962	29.0	24.3
Luxemburg	1962	20.0	
Netherlands	1957	24.9	
Norway	1961	22.9	
Portugal	1960	18.4	28.2
Spain	1961	18.5	16.5
Sweden	1962	36.5	8.0
Switzerland	1960	30.1	
Turkey	1960	40.9	
United Kingdom	1961	34.4	
United States	1962	34.1	4.2
Yugoslavia	1961	33.4	25.7

[1]Klein, 1965, p. 16.

ly advanced countries women now constitute a major labor force reserve. Stating that economic growth depends on enlisting more women, she cited that technological advance, including mechanization, has brought many more jobs within the range of women's physical abilities and created many new jobs. Observing that in the face of manpower needs, public attitudes have become accepting of women being employed, she noted that women have responded to the need not simply because of existing opportunities but for potent personal reasons as well. These reasons are an intermingling of economic, social, and psychological elements.

Klein reported that within the past fifteen years, the proportion of women workers has increased almost everywhere. This has been particularly so in highly industrialized countries, but also in those on the threshold of industrialization. Steady and sometimes steep growth in female employment occurred in the 21 countries studied except

France, Portugal, and Turkey.

Another trend is the increase in the employment of married women. To illustrate, Klein reported the increases for selected countries as shown in Table 34-II.

TABLE 34-II

Married Women as Proportions of Total Female Labor Force[1]

Country	Year	Percent	Year	Percent
Canada	1951	37.9	1962	58.3
France	1954	49.0	1962	53.2
Norway	1950	12.0	1960	24.6
Sweden	1950	30.0	1962	50.0
Switzerland	1950	16.3	1960	25.1
United Kingdom	1950	41.0	1960	52.0
United States	1950	52.0	1960	60.0

[1]Klein, 1965, p. 19.

A related trend reported by Klein is the increasing employment of middle-aged women as a result of more education, earlier marriages, steadily improving standards of health and living, and greater longevity. This trend offers the new opportunity of a large reserve of mature reliable workers, often with previous work experience and special qualifications. Special problems affect women in the more highly qualified occupations, who may have lost some competencies and confidence during the years at home. She reported that schemes for refresher courses with a variety of sponsors were increasing in many countries. The demand for skilled personnel, however, still exceeds the supply of these schemes.

Demographic aspects in female employment in eastern Europe and the U.S.S.R. were analyzed by Berent (1970). Rates of employment for all women fifteen years and over were specified as reported in Table 34-III).

From Berent's data on age and employment it is apparent that rates tend to be comparatively stable in the 20-54 years of age categories and exceed the rates for all women 15 years of age and over reported in Table 34-III. Rates decline for the marginal age groups of 15 to 19 and 55 to 60 years and over. Berent reported a generally high economic participation rate for married women, at 40 percent in Hungary, whereas in Eastern Germany, Czechoslovakia, and Poland the figure exceeded 60 percent.

Relative to employment rates in relation to the number of chil-

TABLE 34-III

Proportion of All Women Age 15 and Over Employed At Population Census Date by Country[1]

Country	Census date	Percent of women 15 years and over
Bulgaria	1965	60.7
Czechoslovakia	1961	50.4
Eastern Germany	1964	48.4
Hungary	1960	43.4
Poland	1960	58.9
Rumania	1966	62.5
U.S.S.R.	1959	66.8

[1]Derived from Berent, 1970, Table IV, p. 181.

dren, Berent noted that a comparison of data from 1949 to 1960 for Hungary indicated family size to be somewhat less of an obstacle in 1960. However, the impact of family size was strong. For eastern Europe and the U.S.S.R., Berent concluded that the data show generally high levels of employment and raised the question of whether the contribution of women to the future growth of the labor force can be sustained on this scale. Policies continue to insist on fuller utilization of women, with the more comprehensive development of child-care facilities, improvement of public catering, further rises in levels of skills and qualifications among women, and more widespread availability of part-time work, facilitating employment.

He projected, however, that

> . . . it is not unlikely that the currently held views and policies on the desirability of female economic participation will be modified in the near future, in light of the dramatic fall in the birth rate (and even in the number of births) that has occurred all over eastern Europe since the mid-1950s and of the clear contribution of female employment to this trend (Berent, 1970, p. 191).

In a report from the International Labour Office (1969) relative to manpower aspects of recent economic developments in Europe, the implications of trends of the labor force participation of women were discussed. The following points were stated:

1. The average duration of women's occupational life will increase; thus greater attention should be given to choosing a satisfying occupation with opportunities for advancement than has been given by many expecting a short work life.
2. With larger proportions of women reentering the labor force in

the 40 to 45 years of age period, there is need for counseling and training for reentry.

3. The proportion of married women workers is increasing, thus more workers are combining domestic and work obligations.
4. Decrease of proportion of workers in the lower age categories reflects the fact that girls are continuing their education; which is in keeping with the increased need for skilled workers.

Related Cultural, Social, and Economic Factors

A number of cultural, social, and economic factors are related to the participation of women in the labor force. Some of the factors which came to the fore in this review were the stage of economic development of the country studied; the geographical dispersion of population in urban centers, small towns, and rural areas; types of family systems; and religion. These factors are not mutually exclusive but in any specific society are intricately related. Any effort to understand the variations in the employment of women which exist throughout the world must include consideration of such factors.

The relationship between female labor force participation rates and stage of economic development has been noted and studied by Wilensky (1968), Denti (1968), and Thormann (1969), among others. Wilensky, using per capital income in U.S. dollars as an index of economic development, compared the proportions of women workers in 33 countries, excluding unpaid women workers in agriculture. The data were from 1953 or the nearest year. Participation rates ranged from 38 percent of women aged 14 or 15 and over in the United Kingdom to 1 percent in Pakistan. Wilensky pointed out that the three great industrial powers, the United States, the United Kingdom, and the Soviet Union were among the top five on one of two measures of occupational opportunity, i.e. proportion of women in the labor force, or proportion of the labor force who are women. He analyzed variations in rates among countries in relation to feminist ideology, rated as more egalitarian and less egalitarian, and concluded that the level of economic development was far more important than feminist ideology as a determinant of female participation in the urban economy.

Denti (1968) in a study of urban and rural labor force participation provided data which points up: (1) the complexity of studying relationships between labor force participation and cultural, social, and economic factors; and (2) the types of variations in urban labor force participation rates which result from cultural, social, and economic factors. Relative to the first, he emphasized the lack of precisely comparable data from the 40 countries studied, and stated that statistics for economically active females are more influenced by differences in national statistical reporting and classification procedures than those for males. This difference is linked principally to the treatment of unpaid family workers, composed largely of women in farm households, as a census category.

Relative to types of variations, Denti discerned five main patterns of urban labor force participation evident in the statistical data in Table 34-IV.

TABLE 34-IV

Urban female Activity Rates (Percentages), by age group, for selected groups of countries according to type of pattern

Type and country	Age group (years)					
	15-19	20-24	25-44	45-54	55-65	65 and over
Type I:						
More developed countries in Europe other than Eastern Europe[1]	48.8	61.6	39.4	42.2	34.2	8.4
Japan	50.3	66.4	44.1	45.3	34.2	15.2
Canada	38.5	54.2	33.3	37.2	25.6	7.3
United States	30.8	48.3	41.6	50.3	38.3	11.3
Type II:						
Latin American countries	27.9	34.9	30.5	25.2	17.7	9.4
Less developed countries in Europe other than Eastern Europe[2]	36.2	41.5	25.9	19.4	14.0	5.9
Ceylon	19.1	26.0	18.6	15.6	12.4	2.9
Type III:						
Eastern European countries	37.3	59.3	53.3	46.7	27.1	11.3
Finland	45.5	66.8	60.5	59.1	44.0	8.9
Type IV:						
(a) India and Indonesia	17.4	25.0	32.1	30.6	22.3	10.0
(b) Burma, Ghana and Liberia	27.9	31.9	36.7	42.7	38.5	19.5
Type V:						
Moslem countries[3]	9.0	9.7	9.7	10.7	8.2	4.6

[1]Denmark, France, Norway and Sweden.
[2]Greece, Portugal and Spain.
[3]Iran, Morocco, Syria and Turkey. Denti (1968) from Table XI, p. 539.

Type I is characterized by two peaks occurring in the age groups 20-24 and 45-54. The pattern is prevalent in more developed countries of Europe other than eastern Europe, Canada, the United States, South Korea, Japan, and the Phillipines. Variations among countries are linked to variations in school participation levels, age at marriage, completion of childbearing, and opportunities for employment.

Type II, prevalent in the Latin American countries, Ceylon, and some southern European countries, is characterized by a peak of activity at 20 to 24 years of age with rates decreasing thereafter.

Type III, found primarily in eastern European countries and Finland, is characterized by increasing activity rates to the 20-24 years of age group with a very gradual decline thereafter until the category of 55-65 years. The comparatively high activity level between 25-44 years can be explained by the greater access to child-care facilities.

Type IV is found in the non-Moslem countries of Africa and Asia. Activity rates increase from the age of 15 up to the age group of 45-54 and drop sharply thereafter. Data from Burma, Ghana, Liberia, India, and Indonesia show a similar pattern with slight variations.

Type V which is typical of Moslem countries shows generally low work rates for all age groups and no sharp peaks.

Denti also reported that participation rates for the various age groups in the less developed countries vary more widely than in the more developed ones.

Relative to labor force participation patterns in rural areas, Denti reported serious limits on the possibility of arriving at any conclusive statement about different levels of age-specific work rates and the shape of patterns prevailing in the rural areas of various countries. He divided the 40 countries into two groups, with the first comprising countries where the numbers of female unpaid family workers in the agricultural labor force are relatively low; the second comprising countries where they are relatively high.

In the first group three major patterns were discernible: the first existing in Canada and the United States and resembling the first urban pattern described earlier, but with lower level of activity. The second exists in northern Europe and is characterized by high activity in the younger age groups, a constant decline to the age of 25, stability to the age of 54 and declines thereafter. The third pattern is found mainly in the Latin American countries, Portugal, and the Moslem countries, and is characterized by very low levels of activity at all ages and generally a gradual decrease with increasing age. Denti projected that with increased economic development and the improvement of educational and retirement practices, countries with the second and third patterns will move closer to those with the first.

Three types of patterns were evident, also, for countries in the second group. Denti stated:

> In the first the activity rates for the age group 25-44 are lower than those for

> the age groups 20-24 and 45-54 and therefore resemble to a certain extent the first pattern in group I. The second pattern is found in Japan and the eastern European countries. Again the levels of activity are very high for all age groups, and with the exception of the high rate in Japan for the age group 20-24, the pattern resembles a bell curve, i.e., the rates for the very young and the old are lower while those for the middle span (25-54) are higher. The third pattern is represented by the non-Moslem countries of Asia and Africa. It is similar to the second but is skewed towards the higher age groups, i.e., the rates of activity increase at successive age levels generally to the age of 50 or so and decline thereafter. (Denti, 1968, p. 544-545)

In summary, Denti found a greater variety of levels and patterns of the female age-specific work rates in rural areas than in urban areas and these different patterns and levels appear to be associated with the level of economic development.

Bean (1968, p. 405) analyzed the utilization of women in the labor force in Pakistan and concluded that

1. women are underutilized;
2. varying rates of participation in East and West Pakistan are interrelated with a) the proportion of non-Moslems, b) the type of cultivation, rice rather than wheat, c) higher rates of widowhood, and d) higher literacy.;
3. the same values that have restricted the employment of women in the past will produce greater opportunities in the future; as long as medical treatment for women is given only by women physicians and related medical personnel, and as long as sex-segregated schools are maintained, the expansion of these services will require larger numbers of professional women.

Bean reported that provision was, in fact, being made for the training of such professional women.

Thormann (1969) comparing Portugal's rate of female labor force participation of 18 percent with a rate of 46.5 percent for north-west Europe, attributed it to cultural factors as well as the low standard of education for girls.

Kim (1970) reported that 30 percent of all females in non-farm households in South Korea were gainfully employed in contrast to 41 percent in farm households. Rates for urban women peak at 20-24 years of age category and again at the 40-44 years of age category; whereas those in farm households rise gradually until the early 40s and then drop rapidly. He attributed these differences to the prevalence of the extended family system in rural areas in which women are expected to find time to engage in gainful employment as well as their normal family duties. In contrast, urban women withdraw from employment to rear their children.

Occupations

Women are employed in a variety of occupations throughout the world. Viewed, however, within the perspective of the total range of existing occupations, women are employed, in large part, in a narrow range of traditional occupations.

Wilensky (1968, p. 235) indicated that the concentration of women workers is in jobs that involve one or more of the following characteristics: (1) traditional housewives' tasks—cooking, cleaning, sewing, canning; (2) few or no strenuous physical activities and hazards; (3) patience, waiting, routine (receptionists, sales workers, telephone operators); (4) rapid use of hands and fingers, such as in office machine operating and electrical assembling; (5) a distinctive welfare or cultural orientation; (6) contact with young children, and (7) sex appeal. Johnstone (1968) stated women are concentrated in a limited number of technical and professional fields to which they are drawn by tradition, e.g. nursing, teaching and childcare, and in the lower range of traditional occupations such as textiles and dressmaking. Myrdal and Klein generalized about employment of women in France, England and Wales, Sweden, and the United States in this statement:

> Everywhere the development in recent times has been characterized by a reduction in domestic service, a relative decrease in industrial work (relative, that is, to the total number of women working) and an increase in the number of women in clerical, distributive, and professional services. The proportion of women in employment rose more significantly among the salaried employees than among the manual workers . . . (Myrdal and Klein, 1968, p. 75).

They noted that in skilled and professional occupations a certain division of labor between the sexes seems to have developed, very much along traditional lines. Myrdal and Klein asked a critical question: Is this new specialization along sex lines characteristic only of our period of transition or has it come to stay? They expressed the view that there is doubtless a danger that the modern distribution of labor between the sexes may establish a pattern which isolates women in positions where their chance of independence and responsibility is low.

From the data on these same four countries, Myrdal and Klein pointed to several aspects in which sex divisions within the professionals differ. In France and Sweden, dentistry and pharmacology are becoming feminine fields of work. While in the United States, a relatively large number of women are employed in finance, insurance, and real estate, in Great Britain they have hardly made an impact. Thus, they concluded, innate sex differences are not the basis of the narrow range of occupations, but rather a complex of opportunities and prevailing social customs.

With regard to Eastern Europe and the U.S.S.R., Berent (1970, p. 179) reported that

> as in Western countries the extent of female employment in industry varies considerably between the branches with women workers predominating in such traditional domains as textiles, clothing, food processing, and in some other consumer industries, but it is by no means negligible in heavy industry.

The share of women in total employment in trade and public health increased between 65 and 75 percent. In the U.S.S.R., women constitute an overwhelming majority in the service sector.

Dodge (1966) indicated that in 1959 almost 80 percent of the total number of women employed in the Soviet economy were engaged in what is officially termed physical labor. Agricultural work accounted for 63 percent of women employed in physical labor. He pointed out that of the remaining occupational groupings, only three would be considered women's occupations by American standards—communal and household services, nursing, and public dining. High proportions would be expected also in the garment, textile, and food categories. Metalwork (15 percent of all workers), construction (18 percent of all workers), and railway work (31 percent of all workers), however, are not occupations in which many women could be found in the United States or in other Western industrial nations. He related the high percentage of women in these occupations to the shortage of males of working age, combined with the regime's determination to maintain high rates of growth.

Relative to semi-professional and professional occupations, Dodge noted the high percentage of women in areas traditionally dominated by men as a major accomplishment of the Soviet regime. Occupations considered in this group include administrators, managers, supervisory personnel, scientists, engineers, and technicians; educators, doctors, lawyers, and accountants; journalists, artists, and performers; and white-collar workers, bookkeepers, clerical personnel and others. The above category refers to those who are engaged in "mental" work as opposed to "physical" work. Women constituted slightly more than one-half (11.1 million) of this important segment of the labor force in 1959. About half of these women have had a specialized secondary or higher education. Dodge analyzed the relationship to education, and stated that the largest advances in the number of women specialists with specialized secondary or higher education were from 1941 to 1964. Health, education, and the statistics-economics field were soon dominated by women specialists. The predominance of women among persons engaged in "mental" work is partially explained by the high female enrollment in specialized secondary and higher educational institutions during and after World War II, and by the number of men in the 20-34 age category with specialized secondary or higher education who served in the military. The proportion of women in this area declines with each successive level of education, about 30 percent of all persons holding the candidate degree, and only 10 percent of those holding doctorates. Women in these occupational categories are in the less demanding occupations, and the proportion tends to decrease with successive increase in rank, even in education and health fields where women predominate, and in science and technology where there are fewer women. Dodge concluded that prospects for a woman entering and succeeding in a professional career in the Soviet Union appear to be much more favorable than in the United States or in other Western countries, but the prospects for advancement are not equally favorable to prospects for men.

VOCATIONAL AND TECHNICAL TRAINING

Access to vocational and technical training, as well as lower level general education, is an important factor in determining the degree and type of economic activity of women. Johnstone (1968) reported that in principle, girls in most countries have the right to full and free access to vocational guidance and training. In actuality, however, little thought is given to their occupational choice. The advice they receive is influenced by pressures of tradition, parents, teachers, the immediate environment, and marriage possibilities. In most countries, there still exists limited practical access to training for many occupations, and also in many, to training at higher levels of skill and responsibility. According to Johnstone, some older industrial countries or developing countries have segregated education, and opportunities for girls do not equal those for boys. Training is provided in only a few trades considered "suitable to the nature of girls" and standards of such training tend to be low.

Findings of a study by UNESCO (1968) provide statistical data on vocational and technical education from responses by 98 countries to a 1964 survey. Responses were incomplete, however, attesting to the variability in the availability of pertinent information. Specific data from this study tend to support Johnstone's generalizations. Variations in vocational and technical education reflected the stages in the economic development of the various countries and to some degree differing political structures. The UNESCO report (1968, p. 90) indicated, for example, that

> the distribution of girl and boy students according to type of training for different branches of activities displays major discrepancies . . . of one to the other. In all countries considered, there is a massive enrollment of girls in training for jobs in the service sector, both at the skilled worker and technician levels. The proportion of girls in total enrollments is, in general, over 50 percent. This finding holds true for all countries regardless of the level of development. However, in the new and developing nations, these types of vocational and technical training are, with few exceptions, the only ones in which girls are actually enrolled, while many other varied types of training are given to boys. In the industrialized countries despite the fact that to varying degrees there is more diversification in type of training given to girls, these are still the branches of training in which, with addition of training for jobs in food technology and textiles, most girls are found and in which their rate of participation is highest.

The report continued that this is also true in the socialist industrialized countries included in the study, although survey responses from these countries show that girls are in fact trained in all branches of activity not prohibited for reasons of health, and do in fact have a higher rate of participation in "unusual training" than in other countries.

The International Labour Office (1969) provided some interesting observations relative to education and vocational-technical training of girls in European countries. Accordingly, it was noted that the occupational choices of girls and provisions for their training are less responsive to emerging opportunities than are those of boys. Therefore, more adequate attention should be given to vocational guidance and training.

Relative to the participation rate of girls in apprenticeships and other vocational training programs, the report stated that as a general rule, all countries in Europe over the past 10 to 20 years were experiencing an upward trend. This trend is particularly evident in apprenticeship, although the number of girls entering full-time training as apprentices is still relatively small, e.g. 20 percent in France, 26 percent in Switzerland, 32 percent in Denmark, and 43 percent in East Germany.

Girls were found to tend more towards general education rather than vocational, in contrast to boys. This is partially attributed to their greater academic competence which facilitates admission to general secondary programs. When they do seek vocational training it is within a narrow range of traditional occupations. Although noting that teacher training is a popular choice in colleges and universities, the report indicated that many girls still seek general education that does not prepare for a profession. In many countries, however, a rising proportion of students selecting science and medicine are girls; i.e. 34 percent in France in 1959, 23 percent in Sweden in 1960, 58 percent in Poland in 1959, 55 percent in the U.S.S.R. in 1966-67.

Few girls in market economies are in technical programs. They represent a minority in these programs in centrally planned economies but are represented in higher proportions. In analyzing the factors which contribute to this, the differentiation of curriculum for boys and girls at lower levels of basic education was noted. Curricula for girls, the report stated, makes time for cooking, sewing, and homemaking often at the expense of mathematics and science. Thus early levels of education do not prepare girls as adequately for some types of vocational training. Therefore they seek preparation in nursing, teaching, textiles, clothing, wholesaling, retailing, clerical, and personal services. Retraining programs for older women are frequently in this same narrow range. Courses in mechanical trades or repair of telecommunications equipment, however, when organized exclusively for women, have had extremely good results.

The International Labour Office reported that it has been chiefly in a tight employment market that the education and training of women and girls have received new impetus towards achieving parity with boys. The report concluded with an emphasis on the need for better dissemination of occupational information to girls, their parents, teachers, and those in authority to develop new training programs in order to assure that women make the most of new employment opportunities.

Organizations in various countries periodically publish reports on the employment of women as it relates to the availability of vocational and technical education. In England, The Association of Teachers in Technical Institute (1970) issued a report citing the limited opportunities for women in seeking employment and gaining more training, in utilizing short vocational courses to prepare for reentry after a period of absence from the labor force. The Association sought to assess the progress made in vocational education since The Industrial Training Act passed in 1964. One intent of the Act was to improve training of women at work. They noted the surprising dearth of statistics relevant to their concern, and using what was available reported that with an increase to 9 million working women in the country, the proportion in skilled, technical, and managerial positions was declining. Further, although women workers increased 13.9 percent, the increase in low level skilled jobs was 23 percent. The report concluded with a series of recommendations including:

1. Teachers should be trained to help children become vocationally aware, and to encourage children to look at themselves as persons rather than as members of one sex or the other;
2. Career guidance should start earlier and encourage girls to think outside the traditional feminine occupations;
3. Career guidance should be available to women seeking reentry;
4. Parents' horizons of vocational possibilities for their daughters should be expanded;
5. Colleges should encourage girls to prepare for careers where women have heretofore been rarities.

The Canadian Association for Adult Education (1969) sent a "Brief to the Royal Commission on Status of Women in Canada," detailing the changes in women's lives relative to employment and family life and recommending various courses of action to facilitate reentry into education and employment. These included reexamination of admission regulations, greater flexibility in scheduling, dispersal of training opportunities, and refresher courses for professional women seeking to reenter their profession.

Cockburn and Raymond (1967) studied the needs of Canadian women university graduates for continuing education. Webster (1968) directed her attention to adult education for married women in lower socioeconomic levels in Vancouver. They reported a conflict between *priorities* as perceived by resource personnel and clients, the former stressing organizational objectives, the latter wanting preparation for employment. Both groups agreed on the need for study in family relationships, nutrition, home management, and employment.

The City and Guilds of London Institute (1964) issued the second of three monographs concerned with part-time courses to prepare persons in skilled crafts. One section considered "Craft Courses for Girls."

Bookman (1964) prepared a booklet to suggest some opportunities for training of mature women entering or reentering the Canadian labor force. Job descriptions, training requirements, and sources of additional information were provided for 19 occupations. These included: cashier, dental assistant, food service supervisor, hairdresser, medical laboratory technologist, medical record librarian, nursing assistant, occupational therapist, office worker, radiological or x-ray technician, power sewing machine operator, real estate agent, sales clerk, seamstress, teacher, waitress, and visiting homemaker.

Bell (1969) reported on the operation of the Women's Bureau Careers Center of the Ontario Department of Labor. Data are reported for the 732 women who came to the center for guidance in order to prepare for returning to work.

DUAL ROLES

Most analysts of women's employment consider the domestic responsibilities, which seemingly, without exception for the majority of women, irrespective of country, are additional to their work in the marketplace. Klein (1965) described conditions in 21 countries which affect the degree of ease or difficulty with which women manage employment in combination with domestic responsibilities. Among the conditions described were length of the work week in various occupations; hours and length of the work day; community services available to assist employed women with family responsibilities; special arrangements and facilities for expectant mothers and those with young infants; the opening and closing hours of retail shops, public service agencies, such as post offices, schools, and banks, and shops providing personal services, e.g. beauty shops. She stressed the importance of coordination among these different "compartments" in which employed women have needs to fulfill, and emphasized that many problems result from the lack of synchronization.

Markus (1970, p. 61) attested to the limitations imposed by the dual obligations to work and family when she wrote:

> The movement towards the emancipation of women, which depends upon their having economic independence and full equality with men in the world of work, is at a dead end, brought up sharply by the fact that though women now do take paid employment as a matter of course, they have not been released from their traditional burden of home and child care. In consequence, they remain basically a low-level, low-paid labour force, still largely financially dependent on men.

Noting that two trends are in evidence to ameliorate this situation, Markus stated that neither provides a satisfactory solution. The one trend evident in the United States is for women to work, marry and bear children, withdraw for 10-20 years, and then return to work. The second trend evident in the socialist countries, but not only there, is that the majority of women stay in employment until they retire, but receive various aids and concessions from the State and from the enterprises where they work to help them during the child-raising period. The inadequacy of the trend in the United States in assisting the emancipation of women is linked to the outcomes of discontinuous labor force participation, such as loss of skill, unable to keep up with technical changes, and loss of experience viewed as essential for advancement to higher ranks. Consequently women continue to be employed in low paid jobs at the lower ranks. She noted that it can be argued that the Socialist pattern is a more positive solution since labor force participation has continuity, but she asserted that analysis of the present actual situation shows otherwise. For due to the lower level of technical development and prevailing standard of living, the tremendous burden of household responsibilities take up even more time than in the highly developed capitalist countries. The majority of women work because of purely economic pressures and hold low level jobs which are often more monotonous and done under worse conditions than average.

Dodge (1966), in describing the low proportions of women in higher levels in science and the professions in the Soviet Union, referred frequently to the continuing conflicts between career, marriage, and motherhood. He noted that if the Soviet regime should choose to divert a greater proportion of its investment funds towards child care facilities and consumer goods to lighten the burden of housework, creative energies might be channeled in greater productivity and subsequent advancement.

Auvinen (1970, p. 73) echoed both Klein and Markus when she stated:

> Equality of opportunity for women in education and employment is legally a fact and factually a fiction — because social attitudes are more constraining

than law. Attitudes about woman's role and marriage not only constrain a girl throughout her entire education towards 'feminine' fields and away from 'masculine' fields — such as science and engineering — but strongly inhibit her aspirations towards high achievement in her chosen career and towards positions of leadership in competition with men. Women's traditional burden of housework and child care, though she may be employed or studying, puts her at a further unfair disadvantage, so the husband and society itself should take over some of the domestic load.

With seeming consensus that the combination of domestic and employment responsibilities impedes women in achieving full economic equality with men, some conclusions have been drawn and recommendations made.

Markus (1970) emphasized the need for a continuing struggle against the prejudices that hinder a more even distribution of the burdens of homemaking. She recommended that a major financial effort be made to provide an extensive range and network of service organizations and establishments to take over a large share of the household work, with the cost of services so low that all women can take advantage of them. She raised the question as to whether certain aspects of housework could not be turned into trades or professions to create realistic alternatives both for women who wish to remain within a family environment and those who wish to escape from it.

Klein (1965) concluded and recommended the following:

1. Although most governments recognize that no women with family responsibilities should be forced to work, abundant incentives to work do exist now and even more women would work outside the home if certain obstacles were removed.
2. Present work weeks permit both men and women more free time. As working hours are reduced, they should be equitably distributed between men and women, assuring women equal status in the work force and contributing to equal status of men in the home.
3. Efforts should be directed to utilizing more part-time workers and to the inclusion of these workers in unions to protect their interests.
4. Adjustments in the domestic sector are occurring through mechanization and modernization of households, with some greater participation of husbands and fathers in domestic functions.
5. The field most in need of improvement is in the synchronization in areas where occupational and domestic tasks converge, e.g. shopping hours, day care centers, services by public and private agencies.

Klein noted that a prerequisite for all the measures recommended is a change of public attitude to provide moral as well as practical support for the woman worker in what she is trying to accomplish. Her recommendations included home help at nominal cost (necessitating subsidizing) particularly for emergencies; increased day care centers with diverse sources of funding; regularized part-time work; extended service hours in shops, banks, post offices beyond regular working hours; employee allowances for a limited number of odd days (or half-days) off at their convenience, and provision of more training schemes for late entrants and refresher courses for those wishing to return to work after a long break.

In conclusion, one might liken the conditions confronting women workers in specific countries of the world to variations on a theme. In developing countries today, as in the history of developed countries, when agriculture requires the major portion of the labor force, women work in the fields, forests, and rice paddies often as unpaid family workers, sometimes as paid agricultural workers. Some work in "cottage industries," others in service capacities. With industrialization and urbanization, labor force participation rates, with some exception start to decline, but with increasing mechanization and changes in economic structure, different economic and social pressures emerge. With development comes an increase in the rate of labor force participation, first for the single, perhaps, and then for the married. Women are resuming a role in economic activity diminished somewhat during the transition from a predominantly agricultural to industrial economy. The cultural heritage, contemporary social values and norms, as well as past or recent economic and political crises will mediate the specific conditions under which women seek employment, the type of employment, and the duration of employment in relation to their function of bearing and rearing children.

REFERENCES

Association of Teachers in Technical Institute. *Education, Training and Employment of Women and Girls.* London, England: Association of Teachers in Technical Institute. February, 1970. 13 pp.

Auvinen, Rita. Women and Work (II): Social Attitudes and Women's Careers. *Impact of Science on Society,* Vol. 22 (January, 1970) pp. 73-83.

Bean, Lee L. Utilization of Human Resources. *International Labour Review,* Vol. 97 (April, 1968) pp. 391-410.

Bell, Linda. *Women Returning to the Labour Force: A First Report, Women's Bureau Careers Centre.* Toronto, Canada: Ontario Department of Labour, Women's Bureau, 1969.

Berent, Jerzy. Some Demographic Aspects of Female Employment in Eastern Europe and the U.S.S.R. *International Labour Review,* Vol. 101 (February, 1970) pp. 175-192.

Bookman, Celia. *Job Training for the Mature Woman Entering or Re-entering the Labor Force.* Ottawa (Ontario): Canada Department of Labor, Women's Bureau, 1964.

Canadian Association for Adult Education. Brief to the Royal Commission Status of Women in Canada. *Continuous Learning,* Vol. 8 (January-February, 1969) pp. 27-30.

City and Guilds of London Institute, Inc. *Further Education for Craftsmen.* London, England: 1964.

Cockburn, Patricia and Raymond, Yvonne R. *Women University Graduates in Continuing Education and Employment, An Exploratory Study Initiated by the Canadian Federation of University Women, 1966, and Le Femme Diplomee Face

A L'Education Permanente Et An Monde Du Travail. Toronto, Canada: Canadian Federation of University Women, 1967.

Denti, Ettore. Sex-Age Patterns of Labour Force Participation by Urban and Rural Populations. *International Labour Review,* Vol. 98 (December, 1968) pp. 525-550.

Dodge, Norton T. *Women in the Soviet Economy.* Baltimore, Maryland: The Johns Hopkins Press, 1966.

Hall, D.T., and Gordon, F. Career choices of married women: effects on conflict, role behavior, and satisfaction. *Journal of Applied Psychology, 58*(1), (1973), 42-48.

International Labour Office. *Manpower Aspects of Recent Economic Developments in Europe.* Geneva, Switzerland, 1969. 177 pp.

Johnstone, Elizabeth. Women in Economic Life: Rights and Opportunities. *The Annals of the American Academy of Political and Social Science,* Vol. 375 (January, 1968) pp. 102-114.

Kim, Kivan S. Labour Force Structure in a Dual Economy: A Case Study of South Korea. *International Labour Review,* Vol. 101 (January, 1970) pp. 35-48.

Klein, Viola. *Women Workers—Working Hours and Services.* Employment of Special Groups 1. Washington, D.C.: Organization for Economic Cooperation and Development Publication Center, 1965.

Markus, Maria. Women and Work (I): Feminine Emancipation at an Impasse. *Impact of Science on Society,* Vol. 22 (January, 1970) pp. 61-72.

Myrdal, Alva and Klein, Viola. *Women's Two Roles.* London, England: Routledge and Kegan Paul Ltd. (revised), 1968.

Sheehy, Gail. *Passages—Predictable Crises of Adult Life.* New York: E.P. Dutton and Co., 1976.

Thormann, Peter H. Employment and Earnings in Portugal, 1953-1967. *International Labour Review,* Vol. 99 (June, 1969) pp. 589-606.

United Nations Educational, Scientific and Cultural Organization. *Comparative Study on Access of Girls and Women to Technical and Vocational Education.* Paris, France: United Nations Educational, Scientific and Cultural Organization, December, 1968.

Webster, Daisy. *The Need for Adult Education of Married Women in the Lower Socioeconomic Levels in Vancouver.* Unpublished M.A. thesis. Vancouver, British Columbia: British Columbia University, May, 1968. 104 pp.

Wilensky, Harold L. Women's Work: Economic Growth, Ideology, Structure. *Industrial Relations,* Vol. 7 (May, 1968) pp. 235-248.

Chapter 35

SEX ROLES AND SOCIAL CHANGE*

HARRIET HOLTER

Some points made by authors addressing themselves to theories of changes in sex roles are first summarized, the economic character of their ultimate explanations being noted. The assumption is stressed that the modes and extent of sex differentiation are more resultants than determiners of social change, although gender differentiation contributes to the maintenance of given social orders. The second and main part of the article contains theoretical considerations about the consequences of social changes for the extent and modes of sex differentiation. The needs of the economic system with respect to labor and consumption are seen as promoting a change from traditional sex roles to quasi-egalitarianism, and mechanisms for masking of sex differentiation are discussed. A certain contradiction between covert sex differentiation at large and strong awareness in limited groups is pointed out. The author describes certain shifts in the maintenance of sex roles and other characteristics accompanying the main charges. Finally, some reflections on the question of strategies for sex role changes are offered.

Introduction: Theories and Strategies

THE FOLLOWING is a tentative outline of perspectives on changing sex roles in present-day society. First, a brief summary of some theories on sex roles and social change is given. It is of course impossible here to give justice to the great variety and depth of sex role theories, but attention is drawn to a few systematic descriptions of how and why sex roles are established and maintained. Secondly, an elaboration of important points of theoretical descriptions, as seen by this author, contains the substance of this article. The focus is here on fairly recent changes in sex roles and their links with society at large. Finally, questions of strategy, i.e. questions as to where in the social structure—in the light of theory—actions towards change should be directed in order to result in desired consequences, are discussed.

SOME THEORIES OF SEX ROLE CHANGE

Most theories about change in sex roles have a global character. They are often formulated with a view to understand the very exist-

*Reprinted with permission from *ACTA SOCIOLOGICA, Vol. 14, No. 1-2 1971.*

ence of gender differentiation, and at the same time purport to explain changes in the position of women especially.

A considerable number of authors simply point to changing "traditions" or "attitudes" as the main basis for changes in sex roles. Since traditions and attitudes are among the phenomena to be explained, only theories that attempt to do so are mentioned here. Also theories of sex roles that give constitutional features of men's and women's psychology a main explanatory status must necessarily be excluded here, since they do not lend themselves to an understanding of changes in the system.

The sociological, anthropological, or social psychological theories all seem to point—ultimately—to changes in the requirements of the economic system as the prime moving forces of shifts in sex roles or changes in the status of women.

The American sociologist Goode, for example, points to industrialization as a main explanation for a trend towards egalitarian relations within and outside the family. The industrialized economy and its need for a mobile, flexible, labor force is best served with a small, independent family. Goode postulates a "fit" between the conjugal family and the modern industrial system, stressing the individual's right to move about and the universalistic evaluation of skills. The increasing demand for skill and mobility tend to eliminate barriers of race and sex, and, in addition, forces within the conjugal family press for equality between husband and wife.[1]

Bott, especially, has shown how the social network of a family—that is, its total web of friends and social contacts—may influence the division of tasks in the family.[2] The families with looser social ties cannot count on stand-ins in traditional roles, and husband and wife are forced to give up a traditional arrangement and to share more than the families with more close-knit networks. Mobility combined with urbanization, which is likely to produce socially isolated families, may thus develop more egalitarian relations between spouses.

"The crisis theory of women's equality" furnishes another illustration of a view of changing sex roles. Rapid modernization as well as war and crisis often seem to bring women into "male" positions, at least for some time,[3] a fact which may be interpreted as a national mobilization of all resources, even secondary ones. In times of crisis, the economic or military demands may, at least temporarily, lead to a breakdown of cultural norms and ideals pertaining to men's and women's tasks. The fact that gender differentiation is reestablished, although often in novel forms, when crisis conditions disappear does not render the "crisis-theory" useless. It serves to illustrate the importance not only of material resources but also of the time necessary for changing ascribed roles. The possibilities and limitations for sex role change inherent in a society are likewise demonstrated during crisis.

Also relevant is the notion that sex differentiation is caused by gender differences in physical strength, which suggests that when technological development renders physical strength unimportant, as in highly mechanized production, this will eventually diminish sex differentiation.

In Marxist thinking, strategy can hardly be separated from theoretical descriptions without doing injustice to both. Nevertheless, for the sake of analysis and since Marxist theory is the theory of social change par excellence, a few points concerning Marxist ideas on changes in sex roles are presented here, rather than in the last section. Marx never formulated a comprehensive view on the subject, although his works contain several references to it; traditional Marxist theory is mainly developed by Engels[4] and later by Bebel[5] and Lenin[6]. In general, Marxist analyses of sex differentiation and sex discrimination are, of course, formulated in terms of historical development, starting with changes in the material conditions. With the development of surplus capital in prehistoric times, man—who through a natural and non-discriminating division of labor with women had access to the surplus—took possession and instituted private property. Private property again necessitates individual as opposed to collective households and rules of inheritance. This is the foundation of the patriarchical family in which the father rules and in which women and children are subjugated to the father.

Engels as well as Lenin saw women's participation in modern, collective forms of production and the disappearance of individual household work as a condition for equality and liberation of women. Lenin strongly advocated the establishment of child-care institutions and partly collective household functions in the Soviet Union, and seemed to believe that the USSR was on the road to the liberation of women.

It is recognized, however, also among Marxists, that important elements of traditional gender discrimination have survived in eastern Europe, and that additional theoretical considerations must be brought to bear on Marxist ideas about the subject. Simone de Beauvoir[7] Evelyn Sullerot,[8] Juliet Mitchell[9] and others have started this work, bringing forth rather different conceptions of sex roles and the forces which influence them. Most important is de Beauvoir's attempt to link historical materialism to a conception of man as a being of transcendence, seeking always to dominate the other, to exercise his sovereignity in an objective fashion. Men would not have used their early material advantage to dominate women had this not been embedded in their existential condition. According to de

Beauvoir then, a change in sex roles requires not only changes in the economic and social order, but first of all women's attainment of authenticity.

Recent Marxist theories on women's position are all very vague with respect to the crucial distinction between equality in a capitalist versus a socialist society. This is perhaps most evident in Mitchell's analysis, which focuses on the situation of women with respect to production, reproduction, socialization, and sexuality. Only changes in all these four structures can bring about equality between men and women, but they are at present in different stages of development. The problem of structures in which women are *not* integrated, e.g. the political power structure and the relation between class-struggle and sex equality, is left undiscussed in Mitchell's article. One is further lead to forget that some of the repression and manipulations to which women are subject are shared by men.

One of the difficulties of a strict Marxist analysis of gender differentiation is that such differentiation is common to all productive relationships, but is less important than the more specific relationship expressed by social classes.[10] Gender differentiation as such cannot be linked to capitalism. The task of Marxists is to place gender differentiation as an element in the productive relationship and in the superstructure, not as a property of the productive forces. The Marxist's specific, historical elaboration of the differentiation must, however, be seen in light of the class-structure, a question to which we may return in the discussion of strategy.

The—mainly sociological—analyses of sex roles cited above offer a natural mixture of pessimism and optimism with respect to the possibility of changes in sex differentiation in current society. The same is true of writers who have developed theories in which sex roles are seen as consequences of specific biological and sexual differences between men and women. Montagu[11] for example postulates women's biological superiority over men, and the unconscious striving of men to dominate and take revenge on women. The Norwegian psychologist Nissen[12] maintains a different sexual cycle for the two genders, and shows some of the implications of such a possibility in terms of male dominated societies.

Such deeper psycho-social elements of sex differentiation are not discussed in the following. The present modes and the present maintenance of sex roles, rather than their ultimate origin, causes, and historical development, are the themes in what follows. Furthermore, the discussion builds on the assumption, among others, that sex roles are of secondary importance as a force of social change in general. Also, the importance of basically economic forces, combined with technological developments and ideological shifts, is recognized. The analysis stresses, however, a trend towards *latent sex differentiation* and *latent discrimination* in industrial societies, as opposed to manifest differentiation in traditional society. It differs from some theories of changing sex roles in viewing sex differentiation, not as something which either exists or is eliminated, but as a social arrangement which may take on different forms and functions.

Theoretical Elaborations

Sex Differentiation and Potentials for Change

Anthropologists have labelled gender differentiation "the primary division of labor," and with good reason. Gender differentiation is more ancient, more stable and more widespread than any other type of social differentiation. It appears under all known economic systems and political orders. The very existence of sex roles cannot be attributed to special forms of production or subsistence conditions.

But the *extent* to which sex—or, rather, gender—constitutes a differentiating element in society varies considerably culturally and historically. This is true of the modes and substance of gender differentiation as well. It may be maintained for example that the degree of task differentiation between men and women have been kept stable over the last hundred years, since a number of "new" job openings for women actually are extensions into modern work life of their traditional tasks. At the same time, this shift in women's production from a primary to a secondary social frame for their work constitutes a change in the mode of sex differentiation. Such shifts also point to changes in those social forces which maintain sex differentiation.

Gender differentiation is here used primarily to include a division of tasks between men and women which is accompanied by a consistently different personality formation of the two genders. Such differentiation usually also discriminates against women, and it is the contention of the present author that discrimination of women necessarily follows from most known gender differentiations.[13]

The consequences of social changes for the extent and modes of sex differentiation practiced in a society—including degree of discrimination—is a main theme in the following discussion. It is an assumption, then, that the extent and modes of sex differentiation are more resultants than determiners of changes in other social and economic relations. This does not imply that changes in gender differentiation are without consequences for social structure and cultural conditions. The opposite is the case since gender differentiation contributes to the maintenance of a number of other social arrangements.[13] But sex differentiation contains less of a dynamic potential for conflict and change than, for example, social classes, or technological change. The very stability of sex differentiation should therefore also be exposed, at least in part, by the analysis presented here.

Sex Differentiation and Social Structure

The modes and degree of sex differentiation are partly a reflection of requirements of the economic system at large and of more specific demands for a suitable labor-and-consumption-force. Sex differentiation is also directly influenced by technological changes, such as the invention of contraceptives. The changes in cultural values which have developed, partly in harmony with and partly in opposition to the post-industrial economic demands, sometimes have a direct bearing on the current ideas about differentiation, ideas which to a large extent are contradicted by sex differentiating practices.

The shift from a production-oriented to a consumption-oriented economy have changed women's position more than men's, and in at least two ways. First, women's services have increasingly been extended directly to production outside the home, and employers take a novel interest in the female labor force. Secondly, the "consumption-and-fun-ethos" has brought women into focus as consumers—and as fun. The last pattern is supported by the inventions of a number of contraceptives, which has also implied new freedom for women as well as men.

A modern economy requires a mobile, partly well-trained labor force, and men are more mobile than women. Young women, however, have proved willing to move in great numbers to the urban centers, a development that has created population imbalances in the cities as well as in the rural areas. The changes in the structure and function of the family facilate mobility for men as well as women, and the changes in the family have probably provided increased sex-role equality between husband and wife. Physical strength has become less important for unskilled and half-skilled jobs, which should tend to eliminate sex differences in the lower echelons in industry. The expansion in white-collar jobs and the stagnation in blue-collar work favor women to a certain extent; the same may be true of a shift from labor-conflict and industrial struggles to an atmosphere of negotiation, human relation skills, and attempts at psychological manipulation of employers.

Most of these changes in the desired properties of the labor force should favor women in the lower positions in firms and corporations and may in time produce a certain pattern of equality in these sectors. The development, however, has not at all been conducive to equality in the middle and higher levels of industrial work units. The demands for leadership, devotion, education, efficiency, and stress-taking, when higher level work is concerned, effectively shut out women from the business elite and other types of elite.

Women's confinement to routine and service work is balanced, as it were, by their important function as consumers who are flexible and sensitive to advertising and status consumption. Women are even increasingly consumers of education, which partly serves to solve a main problem of modern economy: the absorption of surplus.[14] This is the more evident since women to some extent make no use of their education. But there is still a large group of women who work all day because they have two jobs, and another group who are full time consumers.

Women's work in the home constitutes part of the infra-structure of modern economy. Women's poorly paid, isolated work with children and family is clearly one of the conditions for the efficient, collective organization of "official" production. In both production spheres, and in the main, men still have the leadership positions, and women do the serving.

Since a large number of women are fairly isolated housewives, their conceptions of themselves and each other are mediated to them through "a third party"—especially the mass media. Such stereotyped self-images of women are less conducive to feelings of solidarity among women than direct contact and cooperation.

At the same time, new values constantly question this lack of changes in the basic differentiation according to gender. Ever since women came to be regarded as human beings, a comparison between the situations of men and women has been legitimate. Secularization and universalism have furnished new standards for such comparison; equality, scientific rationalism and "criticism is a duty" have strengthened these ideas.

The main effects of economic and social changes outlined above point to some forms of increased equality, but also to strong elements of inequality and covert sex differentiation. An elaboration of the changes that have taken place in sex differentiation may furnish some explanations for this situation.

From Traditional Sex Roles to Quasi-egalitarianism

The first type of change to be discussed is one from an openly recognized and accepted differentiation which is expressed in legal rules or other codes, to a more covert differentiation, a quasi-egalitarianism.[13] Present day sex differentiation is neither officially accepted nor manifested in legal codes, but constitutes a contrast to the official ideology. This discrepancy between ideology and reality is a "modern" phenomenon, the maintenance of which is closely related to the complexity of industrialized society.

The term quasi-egalitarianism refers to elements of latency in present-day sex differentiation as well as to certain mechanisms for covering sex differentiation.

Latent structures are potentials for which there exists a psychological and social preparedness, and which come into operation under certain circumstances. For example, some kinds of sex differentiation in the labor market or in education appear only under conditions of scarcity. When jobs are abundant, that is, when the business cycle is rising, women are in demand and may get jobs which would be denied them under economic down-turns. When parents can afford to give all children an education and they don't have to choose between sons' and daughters' education, the fact that parents would usually give priority to the education of a son is not expressed in action. There exists, nevertheless, a constant psychological propensity for sex differentiation—should the situation change.

The mechanisms of "covering" sex differentiation are numerous. An emphasis on legal definitions or official ideology may distract attention from actual practice, and the same is true of ritualized selection of women to a small number of official positions.

It may also be suggested that one of the covering processes is a tendency to increase women's influence in institutions which are, in some respects, becoming obsolete in present-day society.

At the same time as the family has lost its importance as an economic and political institution, egalitarianism between spouses has become increasingly common. Women are today probably the main decision-makers in a large number of families in which the father is a rather absent and diffuse figure. The father's absence is dictated by the demands of his work which again necessitates the mother's role as decision-taker. Nevertheless, this coincides with the decline of the family as an important social and political unit.

Educational institutions may furnish another example of female influence in obsolete institutions. The first years of elementary schools have—at least in Scandinavia, although similar trends are found in the USA[15]—changed over the last decades, from being oriented towards children's acquiring of knowledge, to more diffuse purposes of primary socialization and personality formation. At the same time, the male schoolmaster or teacher has moved away from these beginner classes of the elementary school system; female teachers are now in an overwhelming majority as teachers during the first years. Later, when the "real" acquisition of knowledge is in focus, the male teacher takes over. From a strictly educational point of view, the first steps have become, if not obsolete, at least more an extention of the family's primary socialization. The fact that there is a great number of female teachers does not imply that the educational tasks are distributed in an equal manner, but rather that female teachers continue the mother's family tasks.

One may, finally, consider certain aspects of women's political activity in the light of an hypothesis about female influence in institutions which are in the process of losing influence. In Scandinavian political discussions, it has been recurrently asserted that parliament as an institution is becoming less powerful, that important decisions to an increasing degree are taken outside this body, and that the parliament is loosing influence vis-a-vis a strong governmental apparatus, as well as powerful economic forces. This seems to be a typical postwar development. It is interesting to note that at the same time the percentages of women representatives are increasing in all the Scandinavian countries—although slowly. The number of women on the boards of banks, insurance companies, or industrial concerns remains nil.

From Unreflectedness to Self-awareness

With respect to sex roles, the development from traditional to industrialized society is also one from unawareness to self-reflection. This is true in the sense that sex roles in older societies were seen as unproblematic, God-given, and unchangeable, whereas the roles today—for example in Scandinavia—represent a constant subject of discussion, of reflection, and also of social research. The above description also suggest that some of the reasons for this change are to be found in the movement from legitimate to illegitimate differentiation. A social differentiation which is declared illegitimate, but which nevertheless occurs, will be reflected upon by some, although, almost by definition, covered up by others. Today there can be no doubt that the status quo is questioned, discussed, and criticized.

Such awareness of social injustices in certain groups is, however, also a more general characteristic of modern society than of traditional society. The idea that the present is not good enough permeates conservative as well as radical thought in Western society—although the premises for desires for change, as well as the changes advocated, may be quite different. It would be strange indeed if sex differentiation should be exempted from examination in this culture. It may be suggested, nevertheless, that the discrepancies between the criticism and reality illustrate the status of opinions in current society: the lack of consequences of opinions or ideas held is apparent.

The discrepancies between ideology and reality also indicate a powerlessness on the part of the official authorities in a society. In Scandinavia, most political parties state explicitly their desire to obtain equality between men and women, but their power to influence the development seems more limited than indicated by their programs. Furthermore, as can be seen in connection with a number of social problems, a "right" has become something which politicians, administrators, and "the law" would *like* people to have, not something people have. If this is true, rights may be increasingly generously issued to the losers in current Western society.

From Ideological to Psychological Maintenance of Sex Differentiation

The development from a commonly accepted sex differentiation to an almost-illegitimate one has had a number of consequences. One of them is, of course, that legal or open sanctions cannot be brought to bear upon those who deviate from the sex-role pattern. An employer is not free to fire women because they marry, no school or university may bar women's entrance, nobody could formally deny a female politician from running. Formal sanctions have been substituted for informal ones, and this has come to constitute a special pressure on psychological sex differentiation. In traditional society, *ideology, division of tasks,* and *personality formation* were to some extent harmonized for men and for women to form two distinct patterns of life, one male and one female. In industrialized society, ideology does not justify sanctioning of deviance from the essence of sex differentiation which is differentiation of tasks. The maintenance of task differentiation has thus become heavily dependent on different personality formation of boys and girls. This does not necessarily mean that the socialization of boys and girls is more segregated now than it was before, but that those differences which are the outcome of socialization have another social significance. Conformity must, for example, be important as a general characteristic.

From Supernatural to Rational Premises

The ideological changes which have accompanied an increasingly urbanized industrialized capitalist society have already been mentioned. The idea of a discrepancy between an official egalitarian ideology and actual differentiating between men and women is seen as an important aspect of sex roles in current society. The presence of an official egalitarian value system does not imply, however, that the actual practices have no ideological premises. Beliefs in sex differentiation, which are in conflict with the ideas of equality and which are more or less implicitly formulated, may sometimes be found as remnants of previous religious values. But even the ideas that constitute arguments *for* sex differentiation have undergone changes, in that more rationality, more systematic proofs, and sophistication are required of them. When research indicated that the old belief in superior male intelligence had no scientific basis, that was a blow to the arguments for a social differentiation of men and women. Other psychological data have, however, furnished arguments in favor of differentiation; this is the case with research regarding the infant's need for motherly care. In addition, more or less well-founded ideas about psychological sex differences have gained in importance as support for differentiation, whereas religious beliefs have lost much of their force in this respect.

From Role Homogeneity to Role Heterogeneity

The development from manifest to latent sex differentiation has a number of facets, of which only a few may be mentioned here. A shift from cultural homogeneity to cultural heterogeneity with respect to sex roles, should, however, not be overlooked. Although in traditional society the substance of sex roles may have varied somewhat within a population, at least they varied in fairly predictable ways. To be a woman in the feudal lower class was probably a fairly well-established role, even if it was somewhat different from the role of an aristocratic lady. Today the variations in sex roles with subgroups are probably considerable, and this is true within and sometimes across class boundaries.

Sex differentiation has however always assumed a different character in different social classes and it still does. Liberation is one thing for an educated middle class woman and another for a working class wife with only the prospect of unskilled labor if she wants to work outside the home. The trend is however to increase women's influx in white collar jobs and thus to decrease the class differences between women. On the other hand, new psychological dividing lines are separating women, such as married versus unmarried, or more subtle choices between various versions of the feminine role.

Shifts in the Domain of Male and Female Value Orientations

There can be no doubt about the fact that the—in a sense somewhat limited—entrance of women into secondary institutions in present-day society has taken place on male premises. Women have accepted the dominant norms and values of secondary affairs, be it "efficiency" or "competition" or "universalism," and these very values have often in the debates provided the justifications for women's participation in work, education, and politics. No wonder then that the male values persist in the face of female participation.

In primary relations, however, there seems to be a decline in the influence of traditional male values. As maintained by Dahlström,[16] a feminization or humanization of the relations in the family, in the class room, and in the work group may be observed.

The development may thus be interpreted as an increased polarization of male and female values, feminization of primary values being compensated, as it were, by an increased dominance of male values in secondary affairs. If this interpretation is reasonable, it indicates that the structure of primary groups are such that even with an influx of male participation, traditional female orientations not only prevail but are strengthened. In the same vein, the structure of secondary institutions are kept more or less unchanged in the face of increased female participation.

Strategies of Sex Role Change

In questions of sex roles and especially changes in sex roles, problems of strategy often take precedence over problems of theory, and sometimes, but not always, to the advantage of the two.

The first question to be asked concerns, of course, the aims of the movements towards equality between men and women. Whereas there is general agreement about the insufficiency of formal equality, expressed in laws and administrative rules or in "empty rights" of women, the content of equality is still vague.

One may roughly distinguish at least between equality within the framework of the present Western societies on the one hand, and equality in a radically changed society on the other. The first may be termed equality on masculine premises, or briefly "masculine equality"; the other—or others—is equality in a qualitatively different society, that is, a society which is not dominated by masculine values as we know them.

Masculine equality would be a situation accomplished in the present type of economy and political order, expressed as a 50-50 percent distribution of men and women in almost all positions, be it care of home and children or the business elite. Such a goal, combined with an assumption that present society and institutions remain by and large intact, obviously require women to become more similar to current masculine ideas of efficiency, profit, competition, and power, according to which Western societies operate. Half of the power, so to speak, would have to be handed over to women, with the burden which is implied in male power today—and in the female tasks that would be taken over by men.

The main strategies for attainment of this situation would be awakening of women's political consciousness and an increase in women's educational level, but above all an introduction of a number of specific detailed laws and regulations which secured for women the possibility and ability to compete, fight, and excercise power.

The thesis that obtaining equality is first and foremost a question of women seizing half of the power which men have now has a ring of reasonableness but is nevertheless an expression of a static view.

It is still a question whether equality in a reasonable sense can at all be attained within a society that builds on a capitalist economy, and perhaps at all in a society which is not both socialist *and* above a certain level of technology. The interests of children as a group would be contradictory to, and heavily set aside under, a combination of market economy and gender equality. The practicality of full equality under the present economy must be questioned.

A long-range perspective on equality contains the establishment of an economy subordinated to the goal of equality. In addition, a number of political and educational measures would be necessary.

Starting with today's economy, however, and with an eye to the description of sex differentiation offered in the previous paragraph, two examples of problems to be attacked may be mentioned. One is the problem of latent or covert sex differentiation, the other consists of breaking the psychological maintenance of sex roles. Both are closely related to the question of women's self-respect and ability to advance their own interest. The covert discrimination leads to a feeling of defeat since the official rights are all there, and gives the illusion that it is a matter of the single woman's ability and energy to use the rights. The psychological maintenance of sex differentiation also consists of encouraging women's devaluation of themselves in various ways, a devaluation which is clearly reflected in the wages paid for women's work.

The money and prestige paid for one's work are in current society the main road to self-respect for men. Women have been advised to seek their rewards in love and childrearing, which may be inherently as valuable—if it was paid and respected. To get out of this vicious circle for women, all work with children, especially in childcare institutions, should be paid somewhat more than, say, the production and maintenance of cars. This would increase the self-respect of large groups of women and, in addition, change radically the desirability of childcare work. Such a manifestation of changes in a society's values and priorities would lower the prestige of competitiveness and technological advancement.

Increased higher education for women is another road to changes in women's working conditions and in their self-respect. Various Norwegian data indicate that women with a higher level of education are more politically active, report less submissiveness, less conflict avoidance, and more gender-egalitarian norms than do women with lower education. Higher education may, however, not be especially conducive to the development of solidarity among women. And higher education alone is not enough for women to gain power.

The analyses in the preceding paragraphs show that the time has come to see the premises on which women work outside the home as more important than such work itself. Work outside the home as a policy must be judged in terms of pressure toward equal wages and working conditions and the avoidance of a female reserve labor force. The question of consequences in terms of solidarity formation on the part of women—and men—is also relevant.

The last point has become very clear in statements from young western European Marxists: if the struggle for equality between men and women is a struggle *between* men and women, then this would lead to a weakening of the solidarity of the working class and must at present be given low priority. Marxist groups offer other reasons as well for taking a conservative stand in the question of married women's work, such as the extra exploitation of women, and the pressure on men's wages in general.[17]

If sex differentiation and sex discrimination are mainly the results of social forces and not deeply of rooted antagonism between men and women, the solidarity between men and women is probably less served by women being isolated housewives than industrial employees. Under certain circumstances, however, men and women will compete for jobs under more equal working conditions, in ways which may decrease their loyality towards each other. The problem is then more to counteract competition among employees who have long-range interests in common, especially since splits in the labor movement are a much more serious and widespread problem than only the hypothesized conflict between male and female workers. More of a danger to a solidary labor movement lies in the tendency of women to go into low paid white-collar work which offers little stimulus for consciousness about equality and political work. This too, however, represents a more general problem than women's participation itself.

If "the premises of work" is one strategic point for changing current sex roles, the "premises of consumption" is another. This contains a wide variety of problems related to sex differentiation, but ultimately it is a question of the direction of production. For example, from the point of view of equality, it is more important to build houses in a new way and on a sufficient scale than to produce a broad range of the commodities which today dominate the consumers and which are necessary for production to be kept up. The housing industry should be nationalized and put in the service of reasonable, more or less collective types of housing, building for flexible families and for the needs of children.

As has been shown by the above summary and elaboration of theoretical descriptions, the breakdown of sex differentiation is not only an economic question. The privatizing and latency of sex roles requires a "consciousness-raising," in small groups as well as in the existing women's organizations. In particular, training in groups with young couples who try to share work in a new way should be attempted. It is on this level of attitude changes that the question of cooperation between women and between men and women has a direct bearing.

The point is of special importance since it is sometimes maintained to be related to the all-important question of women's solidarity towards each other.

Solidarity and identification with one's own and the opposite gender are feelings that obviously are sensitive to social circumstances. The social devaluation and isolation of women has proved dangerous to their solidarity with each other, and their over-identification with man, the stronger, is a problem to any attempt at liberation of women as well as men. Some of these psychological states may be broken down in the individual's work with herself and others, but this will often be a fight against a society.

Individual men may be antagonistic to equality between the genders, but even this is a result of social circumstances. The view that the more or less hopeless and bitter fight between man and woman within the four walls of a home can bring about a revolution in sex roles is denied by all reasonable analyses of the forces of revolution as well as of sex differentiation.

The individual consciousness of the problems of sex differentiation is, however, one of the initiators of change, and this consciousness must be brought to bear on social as well as psychological maintenance of the system. The ambivalence of the situation constitutes a temptation to passivity, for the individual man or woman who attempts to change current sex roles moves in a field of ambivalence, not only socially but also psychologically. The tension between practicing equality, which may be the individual's intention ("the project," to use Sartre's word), on the one hand, and his "embeddedness" in past experiences, emotions, learned norms, and values on the other,[14] is expressed in the institutional setting as well.

REFERENCES

1. W.J. Goode, *World Revolution and Family Patterns* (New York: The Free Press, 1963).
2. E. Bott, *Family and Social Network* (London: Tavistock Publications, 1957).
3. E. Boulding, *The Road to Parliament for Women,* International seminar on the participation of women in public life. Rome 1966, Mimeo.
4. F. Engels, *The Origin of the Family, Private Property and the State* (New York: International Publishing Company, 1942).
5. A. Bebel, *Die Frau und der Sozialismus* (Berlin: Dietz Verlag, 1946).
6. V. Lenin, *Marx-Engels-Marxisme* (Oslo: A/S Norsk Forlag Ny Dag, 1952).
7. S. de Beavoir, *The Second Sex* (London: Bantam Books, 1953).

8. E. Sullerot, *Kvinden og fremtiden* (Demain des femines) (København: Gyldendal, 1969).
9. J. Mitchell, *"Women: The Longest Revolution,"* New Left Review, no. 40, 1966.
10. L. Hem, *Kjønnsdifferensiering og kvinneunderdrykkelse* (Sex Differentiation and Suppression of Women) Kontrast. 1971.
11. A. Montagu, *The Natural Superiority of Women* (New York: MacMillan, 1968).
12. I. Nissen, 'The Role of the Sexual Constellation,' *Acta Sociologica,* no. 1—2, 1971.
13. H. Holter, *Sex Roles and Social Structure* (Oslo: Universitetsforlaget, 1970).
14. L. Hem, *Forsøksgymnaset. En studie av forandring* (The Experimental Gymnasium. A Study of Change). 1977, Oslo: University Press, 1971.
15. J. Henry, *Culture against Man* (London: Tavistock Publications, 1966).
16. E. Dahlstrom, 'Analys av kønsrollsdebatten.' In *Kvinners liv og arbeid* (Stockholm: Studiesällskapet Näringsliv och Samhälle, 1962).
17. K. Ohrlander, *Kvinner som slaver* (Women as slaves) (Stockholm: Bonniers, 1969).

Chapter 36

EQUAL PAY FOR EQUAL WORK*

THE INTERNATIONAL LABOUR OFFICE

562 MILLION WOMEN IN THE WORLD GAINFULLY EMPLOYED

WOMEN make up more than a third of the world's economically active population and 46 out of every 100 women between 15 and 64 years of age are employed.

It is estimated that of the world's 1,637 million persons employed in 1975, about 562 million are women. The female labour force in the more developed regions–some 187 million in 1970–may be expected to increase by some 20 million each decade and to number about 254 million by the year 2000. In the less developed regions, the female labour force has been estimated as reaching over 603 million in the year 2000.

The percentage of women in the total labour force in the major areas of the world varies considerably. The lowest figure is found in Latin America with about 20 percent; Africa, South Asia, and Oceania have about 30 percent, while in Europe and northern North America about 35 percent of all persons in the labour force are women; East Asia has a rather high percentage (about 39), while the U.S.S.R. has the extremely high level of around 51 women for every 100 persons in its labour force.

The available statistics indicate, however, that in certain areas women make up less than 12 percent of the total percentage of persons at work (north Africa, middle America [mainland], tropical South America, Polynesia, and Micronesia), and in others between 12 and 21 percent (southern Africa, the Caribbean, temperate South America, middle South Asia, South East Asia, and southern Europe).

In the United States women made up 38 percent of the total workforce in 1972 as against 30 percent in 1950. In Canada the number of working women rose from 27 percent of the total labour force in 1962 to over 33 percent in 1972. Australia and New Zealand have also both

Reproduced from the UNESCO Courier, March, 1975.

registered considerable increases in women's employment.

In Japan there has been a dramatic rise in women's employment. In 1972 women workers represented 38 percent of the entire labour force and 43 percent of the female population of 15 years of age and over.

In eastern Europe women continue to play a highly important role in economic life. In Hungary women constituted 42 percent of the workforce in 1971 (as against 38 percent in 1963) ; in Czechoslovakia 47 percent in 1969 (as against 43 percent in 1955) ; in Poland 40 percent of the labour force in 1972; and in Bulgaria, at the end of 1971, women in employment comprised 46 percent of the total active population. In Romania and the German Democratic Republic they represent nearly 50 percent.

In the less developed countries the great bulk of the female labour force is still in agriculture, e.g. over 90 percent in some countries in Africa). In most of the industrialized countries the percentage of women in agriculture is low (under 10 percent in many cases and between 1 and 2 percent in the United Kingdom and the United States).

With some exceptions, e.g. Asia, women form a large part of the total labour force in the professional and technical category, in some cases actually outnumbering men (largely because of the predominance of women in educational and health services). They comprise only a small proportion of administrative, executive, and managerial workers. On the other hand, they make up a large part of the clerical workforce in many countries, particularly in the more developed ones, and form a high proportion of the sales force in some countries. In most countries they are only thinly represented in the ranks of craftsmen, production workers, and labourers.

In most countries women continue to be concentrated in a limited number of occupations, in most instances at relatively low levels of skill and responsibility.

In this connexion it should be pointed out that there is a clear correlation between the education and training of women and their participation in economic activity. The general rule appears to be that the higher the levels of education the greater the woman's commitment to work, whether with or without short interruptions for childbearing and rearing. There is no such direct link between the level of education and the economic activity of men.

Another factor which influences women's participation in economic life far more than men's is the number and age of their children. As long as in most countries it continues to be assumed that the mother bears the principal responsibility for the care of young children, and as long as the social infrastructure in respect of child care remains inadequate for the demands made upon it, the presence of preschool and primary-school children will tend to have a limiting effect on the labour force participation of married women.

The increase in the number and proportion of employed married women has been accompanied by an increase in the number and proportion of working mothers.

In the United States, between 1940 and 1972, the number of working mothers increased more than eightfold. It is estimated that in Canada 1 million children have mothers who work. In western Europe and the Nordic countries, the proportion of working mothers with small children is constantly increasing. In the Federal Republic of Germany, more than a quarter of the economically active women have at least 1 child under 15 years of age.

France, in 1968, among mothers aged under 35, 51 percent of those with one child were at work. In Austria the 1969 micro-census showed that 46 percent of mothers with children under 15 were working.

In the U.S.S.R. and eastern Europe a very high proportion of the women in employment have dependent children. In Poland about half of all women workers had children under 16 years of age in 1973.

Part-time employment has also continued to increase. Although part-time employment is not for women only, the bulk of the part-time labour force is made up of women. In some countries the number of women employed on a part-time basis is considerable.

Some economists have advanced a theory on a three-phase life for women: the initial period of work coming before marriage and up to the birth of the first or second child; the second phase comprising withdrawal from employment until the last child has grown up; and the third phase being the return to employment until the normal age of retirement. This theory has been contested on the basis of facts brought out in recent studies of the pattern of women's work and home life in a number of countries.

In some of the more developed Western countries, there is evidence of a trend towards a continuous working career as against the three-phase lifework cycle; this sometimes takes the form of full-time employment (with sometimes some years on a part-time basis) but there is a continuity of work.

There is also evidence that women's commitment to work varies with the level of education. In the socialist countries the educational and social system and policy presuppose an almost continuous working career on the part of the vast majority of women. On the other hand, non-participation after marriage remains a common pattern among married women in some of these countries, at least until the children have grown up.

In many developing countries women—whether by necessity or by choice—tend to remain at work and the cycle of their work life is largely continuous. This may be traced partly to family poverty, partly to the high rate of women's participation in agriculture and partly to other factors, including the tradition of working hard (as in Asia and Africa) and their primary responsibility for family maintenance.

MYTHS THAT DIE HARD

Historical and political factors have proved to be of critical importance in changing the status of women, in particular in countries which have achieved independence or undergone a national revolution or a complete change of political, economic, and social structures. Economic factors are also of basic importance in determining the extent of the employment opportunities available to women.

Experience has shown how difficult it is, at a time of chronic and growing unemployment and underemployment, to ensure women's right to work on a footing of equality with men. In most cases women workers are seen as a threat to men, as intruders in a male domain. And even in many developed countries women's right to work is dependent on the buoyancy of the economy. In periods of economic recession it is easy to see how fragile is their right to equality of opportunity and treatment.

Almost everywhere there remains a clear division of labour by sex with jobs labelled as "men's work" and "women's work." While the line of demarcation may vary with time and place, what is significant is the persistence of distinctions based on sex stereotypes.

As has often been emphasized, job labelling of this kind is both dangerous and discriminatory. It leads to recruitment based on sex rather than on capacity, and it perpetuates unproven beliefs about women's abilities and inabilities as workers. It places unjust barriers in the way of opportunities for advancement.

It creates a situation in which work traditionally done by men commands higher pay and prestige while that traditionally done by women is accorded lower pay and prestige and is consistently undervalued. It has no inherent logic.

The fact that in most countries girls and women are still to be found preparing for typically "feminine" occupations has caused considerable concern in countries which have been trying to overcome the division of the employment market into "women's work" and "men's work."

It is interesting that the budget proposals of the Swedish National Labour Market Board for the financial year 1974/1975 contained two proposals aimed at breaking down sex-linked occupational choice and recruitment practices.

The Board proposed that a training grant of 5 Swedish crowns per hour (approximately $1.00) should be paid for a maximum period of

6 months, to employers who train men for "women's" jobs and vice versa.

This would be for an experimental period of three years. It also proposed that, on a two-year experimental basis, employment subsidies of the same amount for jobs created under regional development schemes should be conditional upon at least 40 percent of the new jobs going to each sex. These proposals have been approved by the Swedish Parliament.

In the United Kingdom, the Trades Union Congress has urged that special grants be made to firms which train girls and women for jobs outside the traditional range of women's work (especially at technician level).

Equal Pay for Equal Work

One of the most blatant forms of discrimination against women continues to be unequal payment for work of equal value. Acceptance of the principle of equal pay means that minimum wages must be the same for men and women, that in the public sector the same salary scale must apply to men and women without discrimination and that in the private sector action towards equal pay, for example by the revision of collective agreements, must be stimulated and supported.

The general picture and the trends are encouraging. But there are still many practical difficulties to be overcome. In many countries employers are reluctant to apply the principle fairly even when they accept it, and reveal a tendency to evade equal pay by a variety of practices and by reference to "economic factors" or the need for "technological innovation."

Why is it that so often when women enter an occupation in any large numbers wages fall or fail to rise? Why is it that wages are traditionally low in so-called women's occupations? It would appear that in male-dominated societies women's work is apt, without reason, to be regarded as of less value than that of men.

However important it may be to achieve equal pay for equal work, this is only one aspect of the broader question of women's wages. Their chief characteristic almost everywhere is their low level as compared with those of men.

While failure to apply the principle of equal pay fully and fairly may be an element in this situation, it is not the only factor: others include the heavy concentration of women in badly paid industries and occupations, their often lower level of education, training and work experience, the handicaps imposed on them by society as a result of their responsibilities, and outright discrimination in employment.

Moreover, women tend to work shorter hours than men and fewer bonus hours, e.g. at night or on Sundays or holidays. And where wages are determined with regard to length of service, women's generally lower seniority may be an additional factor. ILO studies of the position in industrialized countries suggest that women's wages are about 50 to 80 percent of men's for the same work time.

Can differences in women's wages be justified by differences in their work performance? Are women "reliable" workers?

These questions are often asked and all too often left unanswered, leaving the inference that there is little doubt that women are less steady workers than men.

A number of myths about women as workers are crumbling under the pressure of facts.

Women are often accused of excessive absenteeism or of having a high rate of turnover. In the United States, a Public Health Service survey of work time lost due to illness or injury in 1967 showed that women lost on the average 5.6 days as compared to 5.3 days for men. A number of European surveys have come to the same general conclusions.

Analyses indicate that the skill level of the job, the marital status and age of the workers, length of service, and record of job stability provide better clues to differences in job performance than does the fact that the worker is a man or a woman.

For Women Only

In many countries, industrial and social history has left a heritage of protective legislation applying to women only. This legislation, however well intended, has sometimes led to discrimination against them as workers. The prohibition of underground work for women is the most common form of protective legislation applying to women only.

Most countries also specify a series of other occupations from which women are barred on the grounds that the work is dangerous or unhealthy for them. In many cases physical strength was a primary factor in the prohibitions and restrictions; in other cases health protection from the standpoint of women's role as a mother was a leading factor. In still other cases, there appears to have been a notion of protecting women from work regarded as "unpleasant" and "unsuitable for women." The general trend today seems to be to attack the hazards as hazards for all workers and to improve the standards of protection for men as well as women.

On the other hand where women, because of their biological function of reproduction, do incur proven special health risks as new techniques and substances are introduced, they do require and should receive special protection and this should not be regarded as discriminatory or in conflict with the principle of equality of opportunity and treatment. There will always remain a limited sphere in which women will need protection: that of maternity.

Maternity Protection

Maternity protection is a most important matter for working mothers and for society as a whole. Greater responsibility for maternity protection is being assumed by the State, on the grounds that maternity is a clearly recognized social function.

Considerable progress towards maternity protection has been made during the last decade. The ILO standards on this subject have continued to provide the framework for national action. Today, few countries lack some system of maternity protection for women workers.

Nevertheless, even if the essentials of maternity protection are now being extended almost everywhere, women workers still have many practical problems connected with pregnancy, childbirth, and the care of infants.

One of the more interesting recent developments in maternity protection has been the extension of the period of authorized maternity leave beyond the normal statutory or prescribed period, without loss of employment rights.

This extension of leave is now common practice in the socialist countries of Eastern Europe. For example, in Bulgaria a working mother, following obligatory paid leave, may take further leave for between 8 and 12 months at a minimum basic wage and still further unpaid leave with employment rights protected until the child is 3 years old.

In Poland a mother may take leave until her child is 3 years old, with guarantee of re-employment and related benefits. In Hungary, after 5 months' maternity leave with full pay, a working mother may choose to remain at home until her child is 3 years old and during this period, which is counted as a period of employment for retirement purposes, she receives a monthly mother's allowance and the guarantee of returning to her former job. In the German Democratic Republic, a mother may take one year's unpaid leave after paid maternity leave, and during this extra leave her job is reserved and she returns to work without loss of seniority or pension rights.

Certain other European countries have also introduced somewhat similar arrangements. In Spain after the period of paid maternity leave, a working mother may take voluntary unpaid leave for an additional period of at least one year and not more than 3 years; at any time during this period she may apply for reinstatement and the employer is obliged to appoint her to the first vacancy which occurs in the same or a similar category. In Italy a woman may take an optional extra 6 months' maternity leave after the statutory compulsory and extended period.

On January 1, 1974, Sweden became the first country to enact legislation making cash maternity benefits payable also to the father. Under this law either working parent may stay at home to care for a newborn child and collect the cash benefit. The husband instead of the wife may opt for the period of extended leave or the period may be divided between them, with the same safeguards relating to reinstatement in employment, seniority, and pension entitlements.

Several countries provide for a period of birth leave for fathers: in France paid leave of 3 days is reimbursed to the employer by the family allowance fund, while in Sweden the period is 10 days. In Norway it has been proposed that men workers whose wives are in gainful employment should be entitled to from 2 to 4 weeks' child care leave during the first year of the baby's life and that benefits be paid to men workers during such leave.

Child Care

Despite the steady increase in the number of married women workers with young children, the child-care services and facilities have in most countries been slow to respond to new needs. The time is past when society can refuse to provide community child-care services in the hope of dissuading mothers from leaving their children and going to work: this flies in the face of facts.

The trade unions in a great many countries are giving serious and continuing attention to the problem of child care and are putting it forward as a basic right for workers.

Who Works Longer?

International comparative research carried out under the auspices of Unesco has shown that, almost without exception, married women generally work longer hours at home than their husbands because of the traditional division of family chores and concept of sex roles. On the whole, working mothers had less than two-thirds of the free time that their husbands enjoyed. Their total weekly hours of work amounted to between 70 and 80.

Change in the position of women in economic life, the family, and society implies change in the role of men in these spheres. In turn, this implies change in social attitudes, which themselves define and confine men's and women's roles in all walks of life. Problems may be discussed as "women's problems" but they must be considered as problems of men, women, and children, of society as a whole.

Section X

SPECIAL RESOURCES

THIS LAST section has been assembled to provide persons who have serious interests in the area of counseling and career development of women with some basic and vital information.

Rita S. Rapoza has compiled a selected annotated bibliography of bibliographies. Special resources about women are identified and described as well as selected general reference works. In this original bibliography, it is the author's intention to break down the myth that materials about women are not available. This guide gives the interested reader access to a wide array of information about the world of women. It is hoped that the following bibliography of bibliographies will enable the reader to compile an original list of resources on the career development and counseling of women to meet her or his particular needs.

Chapter 37

EXPLORING THE WORLD OF WOMEN: A SELECTED GUIDE TO THE LITERATURE

RITA S. RAPOZA

ONE OF the most durable myths in the area of the development of women is that there is little information to be found. In fact, an enormous amount of informative material is now available, and new contributions to the literature are constantly being added. This chapter is a bibliography of bibliographies; each of the annotated references listed is in itself a guide to more resources about women.

A few examples serve to illustrate the range and the number of resources accessible through this guide. Berkowitz, Mangi, and Williamson (1974), in their *Who's Who and Where in Women's Studies,* describe a clearinghouse with a collection of "syllabi from more than 4600 women's studies courses and more than 100 programs on U. S. college campuses." Maccoby and Jacklin (1974) in *The Psychology of Sex Differences,* cite and annotate approximately 1400 references. Worldwide activities of women are reported by sources such as the *United Nations Documents Index* (1950-date) and *The New York Times Index* (1913-present). For the teacher, researcher, speaker, or librarian wishing to learn of or provide a modest yet comprehensive collection of materials on women, Wheeler (1972) annotates approximately 318 sources for a basic book collection. Materials pertaining to women in medicine and the biological sciences have been gathered by Audrey Davis (1974) in a bibliography of more than 600 references.

This bibliography is divided into a section devoted to specific bibliographies about women and a section of more general reference sources. Current materials (from 1970 to the present) were sought, as well as publications unique in content. This annotated bibliography should be helpful to the reader who wants to consult a variety of sources pertaining to women; it should also make the reader aware that there are many such sources already available.

BIBLIOGRAPHIES ABOUT WOMEN

Astin, H. S., Suniewick, N. and Dweck, S. *Women: A Bibliography on Their Education and Careers.* Washington, D.C.: Human Service Press, Sponsored by University Research Corporation and the Institute of Life Insurance, 1971.

The 352 references are fully annotated though somewhat dated. Authors seem intent on helping the reader save time. The preface as well as the two introductory chapters, "Overview of the Findings" by Helen Astin, and "Beyond the Findings: Some Interpretations and Implications for the Future," by Nancy Suniewick, give the reader a good indication of the line of research cited in this bibliography. The subject headings preceding each annotation let the reader know immediately if further reading would be appropriate. There are seven major categories in this bibliography: Determinants of Career Choice, Marital and Familial Status of Working Women, Women in the World of Work, Developmental Studies, History and Economics of Women at Work, Commentaries and Policy Papers, and Continuing Education of Women. Particularly useful, though not fully comprehensive, is the last selection on Continuing Education of Women. Educational policies, such as nursing emphasis, volunteer and/or paid employment preparation, are described for the various schools. Annotations are clear, lengthy and complete.

Banks, J., Szymanski, C. and Tobin, N. *Bibliographies of Career-Related Materials.* Newton, Massachusetts: Education Development Center, National Institute of Education, 1975.

This Career Education Project was intended to help adults to plan, to prepare, and to find a career. Of particular concern to the project were the needs of persons who spent a majority of their time in the home and consequently away from sources of "career-related information and assistance."

The first half of this publication is a listing of the holdings of the Project's Resource Center. Although these complete bibliographic citations are not annotated, the reader is furnished with information such as: alternative order ing sources (e.g. ERIC, U.S. Government Printing Office, National Technical Information Service), price of item, hard cover items, a special notation system "to indicate that an annotation of that item appears in the accompanying annotated bibliography."

The second half of this work is an annotated bibliography covering seven major topics: (1) Counseling; (2) Career Education; (3) Directories and Other Information on Financial Aid; (4) The Job Search; (5) Occupational Information; (6) Directories of Educational and Training Resources; and (7) Women. A special feature under the last topic (Women) is the annotated "Bibliographies and Information Sources" section.

Berkowitz, T., Mangi, J. and Williamson, J. (Eds.) *Who's Who and Where in Women's Studies.* Old Westbury, New York: Feminist Press, 1974.

Section I lists instructor, department, name of course and when the course was taught. Section II lists similar information catalogued by the specific faculty member's name. Section III lists departments which offer courses on women including the instructor's name. It is of interest to note that eight courses are listed under Guidance, Guidance and Counseling, and Guidance and Student Personnel. Numerous courses under the heading of Psychology are offered and by such leaders in the field as S. Osipow, P. Chesler and A. Anastasi. Women's Studies Programs are also given with symbols for different degree levels such as minors, B.A., A.A., M.A., and Ph.D. There is an explanation of the Clearinghouse on Women's Studies with its "syllabi from more than 4,600 women's studies courses and more than 100 programs on U.S. college campuses." An excellent starting place for those teaching women's studies at the elementary, secondary, and higher education levels.

Catalyst. New York: National Headquarters, 14 East 60th Street.

"A national non-profit organization that helps to expand career opportunities for college-educated women. Catalyst works directly with women, local resource centers (50), educators, and employers and seeks to open new channels of communication among them."

This organization has approximately 41 bibliographies which can be purchased for the price of 50¢ to $3.00. Some of the bibliographies include information on the following topics: Absenteeism and Turnover of Women Workers, Androgyny, Black Professional Women, Child-Care Deductions, Dual-Career Families, Equal Rights Amendment, Job Hunting, Women in Management, Wage Rates, and Earnings of Women.

Davis, A. B. *Bibliography on Women with Special Emphasis on Their Roles in Science and Society*. New York: Science History Publications, 1974.

A highly selective resource for acquainting the reader with basic reference works in locating materials in the field of medicine and the biological sciences. The introduction is excellent in that several key bibliographies are mentioned as the sources from which the references were selected including *The Library of Congress Catalogue; A Cumulative List of Works (1950-1973), Index Medicus, Index Catalogue of the Library of the Surgeon-General's Office.* This bibliography includes some hard to find items absent in bibliographies, for example: special chapters from books, patents, lectures, bibliographies from women's courses, archival and manuscript resources, special periodical issues devoted to women in part or in whole from journals such as *Journal of the American Pharmaceutical Association.* There are suggested subject headings as well as subheadings listed in the introduction. This bibliography is not annotated and contains approximately 600 references.

Davis, L. G. *The Black Woman in American Society: A Selected Annotated Bibliography*. Boston, Massachusetts: G. K. Hall and Company, 1975.

This source represents an attempt to address the relative neglect of the study of black women. There are 1184 citations and listings with the Books section completely annotated, and the Articles section partially annotated. There are listings for (1) General Reference Works; (2) Selected Current Black Periodicals; (3) Reports, Pamphlets, Speeches, and Government Documents. Special features include the identification of the following: (1) United States Libraries with major Black History Collections; (2) National Organizations of Black Women; (3) Black Women Who Are Newspaper Publishers and Editors (alphabetically by state); (4) Black Women Elected Officials (by state with position and address); (5) Statistics of the Number of Black Women in Rural and Urban United States. There is a general index with subjects, authors, joint authors, compilers, and editors.

Friedman, B., Greenstein, G. E., Kofron, E., Pollack, F. and Williamson, J. *Women's Work and Women's Studies/1973-1974*. New York: The Barnard College Women's Center, 1975.

This is the third in a series entitled *Women's Work and Women's Studies.* This volume is a partially annotated bibliography of "books, articles, papers, pamphlets and research about women and feminism." This resource is divided into the following categories: Abortion, Arts and Media, Contemporary Women's Movement, Cultural Studies, Education, Employment, Family Organization, Government and Politics, History, Legal Status, Literary Criticism, Mental and Physical Health, Rape, Religion, Sex Roles and Sex Differences, Sexuality, Bibliographies and Resources. Under the Bibliographies and Resources section added references are given for almost all of the already mentioned categories. The 3,944 works cited have been limited to publications originating in the United States. Newspaper and popular magazine articles have not been included. Special features of the Appendix of Bibliographical Sources include the reference works consulted in compiling this bibliography. There is one author index only.

Harrison, C. E. *Women's Movement Media: A Source Guide.* New York: Bowker, 1975.

This resource guide describes over 550 women's movement organizations and is an attempt to compile information not usually picked up by commonly used indexing services. There are five major sections: Part I — Publishers, Distributors, New Services and Products; Part II — Women's Research Centers and Library Research Collections; Part III — Women's Organizations and Centers; Part IV — Governmental and Quasi-Governmental Organizations and Agencies; Part V — Special Interests.

Part I is particularly helpful for locating specialized book distributors and for locating products by feminists for feminists. Part V has such headings as Women's Studies, Employment-Consultants, Employment-Counseling and Training, and Lesbian Interests. Four special indexes conclude this resource: Geographic Index (active groups by state, especially good for U.S. and Canada, incomplete for all other countries), Media Title Index (books, printed media, pamphlets, leaflets, brochures, flyers), Name Index of Groups, and Subject Index.

Special features of the text include the author's attempt to gather information about Canada as well as the United States. In addition to references to books and periodicals, the author has included citations to tapes, records, and services for women. The Continuing Education section describes different programs at various institutions and also lists Women's Studies Programs.

Jacobs, S. E. *Women in Perspective: A Guide for Cross-Cultural Studies.* Urbana: University of Illinois Press, 1974.

This sourcebook, containing approximately 5,000 references, is "intended for use by students and faculty interested in women's studies in general and in analysis of women in cross-cultural perspectives specifically." Sources are divided into two parts: Part I — Geographical Topics and Part II — Subject Topics. Part I classifies references geographically for Africa, Middle East, Asia, Europe, Oceania, South America and North America. Often introductory texts and general references for a major division are cited before references for a specific country are listed. Part II gives the reader the opportunity to approach the different parts of the world through subject topics such as Socialization, Role Development and Child-Rearing Practices, Psychological Studies, Futurism and Utopianism, Biographies and Autobiographies. The last three sections of Part II are particularly worth noting for the following special features: Bibliographies, Publications of Women's Studies Collectives and Centers, and Publications Useful for Dealing with Sex Discrimination. There is an author index and the references have full bibliographic information but are not annotated.

Krichmar, A. *The Women's Rights Movement in the United States 1848-1970: A Bibliography and Sourcebook.* Metuchen, New Jersey: The Scarecrow Press, 1972.

This partially annotated bibliography is particularly useful in tracking down manuscript sources, state and federal government publications, and women's liberation serial publications (1968 to present as well as retrospective periodicals). Books, articles, pamphlets and/or government documents are cited throughout sections entitled: General, Legal and Political Status, Equal Rights Amendment, Suffrage, Economic Status, Education, Religion, Biography, and Manuscript Sources.

Special Libraries and Groups, Manuscript Sources, Bibliographies and Indexes, and Federal Government Documents are some of the headings under the

Selected References Section. The Biography section is useful for finding articles about famous women, past and present. The Manuscript Sources section is arranged by state and details of the materials are carefully described. Papers, records, correspondence, letters, pamphlets, location, and dates are often given for each entry. There are several indexes included: Manuscript Index, Author Index, Subject Index, and Index to Serials. Finally, there is a Women's Liberal Serial Publications section arranged alphabetically by state with the name and address of the serial publication.

Lynn, N. B., Matasar, A. B. and Rosenberg, M. B. *Research Guide in Women's Studies.* Morristown, New Jersey: General Learning Press, 1974.

This work is based largely on another text called *Research Guide for Undergraduates in Political Science* by Carl Kalvelage, Morley Segal and Peter J. Anderson. The first three chapters are technical "how to," guides to writing a research paper. Examples are taken from publications about women. Basic references as well as social science information concerned with women are the foci for three chapters. The statistics chapter is concise and clearly written and will give the reader of research publications some background to commonly used terms. Section nine lists information about women's centers and organizations. The last chapter lists by social science subjects, names of courses, teachers, institutions and addresses.

Maccoby, E. E. and Jacklin, C. N. *The Psychology of Sex Differences.* Stanford, California: Stanford University Press, 1974.

Almost half the book consists of approximately 1400 annotated references. These annotations are in addition to the 305 references cited throughout the text. The authors systematically perused selected journals, Psychological Abstracts, books and chapters from January 1966 to spring 1973. They also contacted authors "whose published reports indicated that sex had been a variable." Of special note is chapter ten which is a summary and commentary on the outcomes of research on sex differences. There is one general index for specific authors and subjects.

Rosenberg, M. B. and Bergstrom, L. V. (Comps. and Eds.) *Women and Society: A Critical Review of the Literature with a Selected Annotated Bibliography.* Beverly Hills, California: Sage Publications, 1975.

Women in History, Women at Work, and Women in Politics are the themes reviewed in the bibliographic essay which serves as the introduction to this source. Almost 4,000 references are cited and partially annotated for the following topics: Sociology, Political Science (Feminism and Equal Rights are emphasized here), History, Women in Philosophy and Religion, Literature and the Arts, Psychology (few, yet noteworthy, references), Anthropology, and Economics.

The General Reference Works on Women section is quite informative in that 71 Bibliographies, 10 Biographical Dictionaries, 37 Directories of Women's Organizations and Institutes, 28 Women's Periodicals and Newspapers, and 22 Women's Collections and Libraries References are given to the reader. An additional special feature is a short listing of special journal articles on women. These compilers have attempted to annotate many of their sources although sometimes with only a one line description. There are several indexes: Author-Organization Index, Index of Persons not cited as authors, Places, Subjects, and Topics Index.

Tack, M. W. and Ashford, D. T. *Dimensions on Women's Employment in Non-Traditional Female Occupations (A Selected Bibliography January 1970-July 1975).* Olympia, Washington: Commission for Vocational Education. Prepared for: The United States Office of Education, Bureau of Occupational and Adult Education under Contract No. P00750303, September, 1975.

This source was developed for persons seeking information about women successfully employed in occupations other than those related to homemaking, nursing, elementary education, secondary education, and stenography.

An excellent introduction with clear definitions, limitations, and methodology is given. Indexes, specialized bibliographies, Library of Congress and Education Resources Information Center were utilized to compile this listing of references. A systematic approach to different governmental departments, bureaus, and private foundations was employed for this selected, specialized bibliography including personal consultation, telephone conversations, and written communication.

Bibliographic citations to articles, books, brochures, and dissertations are given two descriptors: a reference code number, and an asterisk to denote "emphasis on women in non-traditional occupations." The master reference code lists 18 different categories under which a citation might be classified. The authors usually gave only one code number to each citation, however, some references are assigned two code numbers. Examples of classifications are: Agricultural Occupations, Proprietor or Ownership Occupations, and Transportation and Public Utility Occupations.

Wheeler, H. *Womanhood Media: Current Resources About Women.* Metuchen, New Jersey: The Scarecrow Press, 1972.

Part I contains a 200 item Women's Liberation Awareness Inventory with answer key. Part II provides descriptive information about standard reference works (e.g. government documents, handbooks, directories) to writers, researchers, public speakers, teachers, and students. Part III cites approximately 318 annotated sources that the author recommends for a basic book collection. Special notation is given to sources which are more appropriate in terms of content, style, and reading level for the junior and senior high school student. Part IV covers non-book resources such as pamphlets, Movement periodicals, special journal issues on women, and audiovisual resources. Part V lists women's centers, collections, caucuses, Women's Liberation Organizations, Groups and Centers, and Women's Studies Programs. Coverage for this last section is for Canada as well as the United States.

Women Studies Abstracts. Rush, New Jersey: Rush Publishing Co., 1972-present.

Persons starting women's studies programs should consult this major source. It is the hope of the compilers that this resource will be of use to companies and organizations in their affirmative action plans and to libraries in providing answers on the research and studies on women. Focal themes covered by this abstracting service are: Education and Socialization, Sex Roles, Similarities, Characteristics and Differences, Employment, Sexuality, Family, Society and Government, Mental and Physical Health, Family Planning — Childbirth and Abortion, Media, Interpersonal Relations, Women's Liberation Movement. After each of these sections the reader is provided with an annotated bibliography. Some of the sources described are from journals and from conferences. The "Additional Articles" section is not annotated. There is some attempt to include foreign journals in this abstracting service.

GENERAL REFERENCES

Book Review Digest. New York: H. W. Wilson, 1905-present.

Certain qualifications have to be met before a book is reviewed in this resource: (1) the book must have been published or distributed in the United States; (2) the non-fiction books must have received two or more reviews; (3) the fiction works must have received four or more reviews; (4) reviews must be published within eighteen months following a book's publication; and (5) one of the reviews must have been published in a United States journal. Standard information in the main body of the text consists of the name of the authors listed alphabetically with title of work, pagination, price, year of publication along with review excerpts arranged alphabetically by the name of the review journal. The complete reference to the original review makes it easy to locate the review in full context. Approximately 72 periodicals are indexed and subject and title indexes are available to the reader.

Book Review Index. Detroit: Gale Research, 1965-present.

This comprehensive resource reviews approximately 35,400 different books, lists approximately 76,400 review citations and indexes 230 periodicals. The citations are simply listed under the name of the author; there are no subject entries or excerpts from the reviews. A valuable resource in trying to determine the pros and cons of materials pertaining to women for both purchase in libraries and/or distribution to students.

Chall, L. P. (Ed.) *Sociological Abstracts*. San Diego, California: American Sociological Association, Eastern Sociological Society, International Sociological Association and the Midwest Sociological Society, 1953-date.

The Eastern Sociological Society and the Midwest Sociological Society cosponsor this classified abstract journal. The table of contents reflects the broad range of sociological topics covered with the latest subject area entitled *feminist studies*. Sociological articles in English and in various foreign languages are the primary offering of this source. There are several indexes: subject index, author index, and a periodical index. This publication also records abstracts of papers presented at annual meetings of the different sociological association meetings.

Current Index to Journals in Education (CJIE). New York: CCM Information Services, 1969-date.

"The practicing educator, reference librarian, and educational researcher" are the main populations for whom this resource attempts to provide information. Currently CJIE examines more than 700 publications, primarily periodical literature in education. Each work has a complete bibliographic citation and a description. There is an author index and a subject index. A special feature is the "Journal Contents Index," a listing of the table of contents of a particular journal for a current month. Excellent for keeping aware of the latest publications in a variety of journals in just minutes.

Humanities Index. New York: H. W. Wilson, 1974/75-present.

Formerly part of *Social Sciences and Humanities Index*. Currently the *Humanities Index* is a single resource indexing approximately 260 periodicals. There are reviews of books following the main body of the Index. These are particularly helpful in trying to evaluate material. Subject headings such as Women, Women in Christianity, Women in Literature, Women in Television, Women's Liberation Movement, and Women's Societies and Clubs are listed in this publication.

Jennings, G. (Manager) *Subject Guide to Forthcoming Books*. New York: R. R. Bowker, 1967-present.

Published six times a year, this particular resource is excellent for listing "all books expected to be published in the U.S.A. during the next five months." There are subject categories and special notations for juvenile, young adult, elementary, junior high and senior high school publications. This source is a companion to *Forthcoming Books, Now Including New Books In Print; A Forecast Of Books To Come*.

Koltay, E. I. (Ed.) *Ulrich's International Periodicals Directory: A Classified Guide to Current Periodicals, Foreign and Domestic*, 16th edition. New York: Bowker, 1975-76.

Excellent for the reader who has located a specific journal article and would like to find similar materials published by that particular journal. This comprehensive list has over 300 different indexing and abstracting services cited and covers scientific, technical, and medical journals as well as those in the arts, humanities, social sciences, and business. The very last section of the volume has a *Women's Interests* periodical listing. Standard information for the 57,000 in print periodicals listed include such data as: date of origin of the periodical, the frequency with which it is published, the price, the editor, microfilm availability, and the address of the periodical.

La Beau, D. and Tarbert, G. C. (Eds.) *Biographical Dictionaries Master Index.* Detroit, Michigan: Gale Research, 1975-76.

A simple and expedient way of researching more than fifty *Who's Whos.* This particular listing indexes collective biographies such as *American Men and Women of Science, Current Biographies, Contemporary Authors* and *Foremost Women in Communications.* Many of the biographical sources include both sexes. Over 725,000 persons are listed. After each name there are abbreviation symbols. The reader need only turn to the beginning pages of the volume to decode the abbreviation (s).

National Union Catalog, 1968-1972: A Cumulative Author List Representing Library of Congress Printed Cards and Titles Reported By Other American Libraries. Ann Arbor, Michigan: Edwards Pub. Inc. 1973-present.

The Library of Congress with its various collections and holdings is an indispensable bibliographic work for research. Compilers of bibliographies, as well as teachers, students, and librarians, often start their work by consulting the photocopied catalogue cards of the Library of Congress. Listed here are some of the more commonly-used collections: *Catalog-Motion Pictures and Filmstrips, Current National Bibliographies, New Serial Titles, National Union Catalog of Manuscript Collections.*

The New York Times Index. New York: New York Times Company, 1913-present.

"The Master-Key to the News since 1851. The only service summarizing and classifying news alphabetically by subjects, persons, organizations." For comprehensive newspaper coverage of women in the United States and the world, this is an outstanding resource. It has an excellent classification system and descriptions of many important speeches, reports, and books. Just reading the subject headings and descriptions on the pages devoted to women gives the reader an idea of the state of women's activities and current issues being discussed about women by both females and males. This work is particularly helpful for learning the names of active, outstanding women.

Psychological Abstracts. Lancaster, Pennsylvania: American Psychological Association, 1927-present.

Although non-evaluative in its approach, the thrust of this resource is scientific with "850 journals, technical reports and monographs" abstracted in 30 to 50 words. Specific researchers, writers, leaders in the field can be located through the author index. The subject index has several key words in locating information about women: human females, human sex differences, sex roles, sex-linked developmental differences, housewives, wives, Women's Liberation Movement, daughters, day care (child), female criminals, female delinquents, femininity, lesbianism, mother absence, mother-child relations, and mothers.

Resources in Education. Washington, D.C.: National Institute of Education, 1975-present. Original title was Educational Resources Information Center (ERIC).

Particularly focused to index and to describe "unpublished or fugitive" type of documents, e.g. technical and research reports, conference papers, speeches, program descriptions, teacher and curriculum guides, and statistic compilations.

This work is indexed in three ways: subject, author, and institution. Besides the complete bibliographic citation and abstract, the reader can find the organization where the document originated, as well as locate an alternative for obtaining the document with the price. Resources in Education has its own format style and a reference librarian should be consulted for maximum use, especially in locating the most appropriate headings.

Sheehy, E. P. (Comp.) *Guide to reference books.* 9th ed. Chicago: American Library Association, 1976.

A reference book basic to research and aimed primarily at persons in the field of library science. There are 5 basic divisions: (A) General Reference Works, (B) The Humanities, (C) Social Sciences, (D) History and Area Studies, (E) Pure and Applied Sciences. Although information on reference works about women can be located in several divisions, most of the citations are listed under section CC Sociology where six bibliograpies and two directories are annotated. There is an index which includes author, subject, and most title entries. This 1015 page volume has an annotation for each reference. Bibliographies, indexes, encyclopedias, handbooks, dictionaries, criticisms, and directories are often standard research guides described under the more defined areas such as religion, economics, and biological sciences.

Social Sciences Index. New York: H. W. Wilson 1974/75-present.

Formerly part of *Social Sciences and Humanities Index.* Currently the *Social Sciences Index* is a single resource indexing approximately 263 periodicals. Like the Humanities Index there are reviews of books following the main body of the index. Subject headings such as Women, Women as Executives and Women in Medicine can be found in this index.

United Nations Documents Index. New York: United Nations, 1950-date.

Issued in English, French, Russian, and Spanish, this publication contains information of the major aspects of the participation of Member States in the United Nations. Introductory notes as well as the different indexes (e.g. Subject Index, Country Index, Index to Resolutions) help locate materials easily. Essential in being informed about the activities, decisions, and interests of women throughout the world.

U.S. Superintendent of Documents. *Monthly Catalog of United States Government Publications.* Washington, D.C.: Government Printing Office, 1895-present.

The most comprehensive listing of United States government publications. As the title indicates there are monthly issues with an individual index. For saving time, there is a yearly index which compiles the entries under subject headings such as Women and Women's Bureau. The reader can locate a variety of information compiled by or reported to the different branches of the government with its special reports, longitudinal studies, monographs, and papers. For those who have never used this index before, a reference librarian would be helpful because of the unique two-step system designed for locating materials.

APPENDICES

A CHART of federal laws and regulations concerning sex discrimination in educational institutions has been designed and reported by Bernice Sandler and her colleagues from the Association of American Colleges. This legal information is essential to administrators at all levels of education and to persons participating in social action or policy development involving the employment and education of females.

The Women's Bureau of the Department of Labor, the official guardian of women's rights in the world of work, provides a "do it yourself" manual for employers and other groups interested in increasing opportunities for women in the skilled trades. The suggestions listed in this article could serve as a guide for designing and implementing equal employment policies.

Appendix 1

FEDERAL LAWS[1] AND REGULATIONS CONCERNING SEX DISCRIMINATION IN EDUCATIONAL INSTITUTIONS[2] PROJECT ON THE STATUS & EDUCATION OF WOMEN, ASSOCIATION OF AMERICAN COLLEGES, WASHINGTON, D.C.

	Executive Order 11246 as amended by 11375	**Title VII of the Civil Rights Act of 1964** as amended by the Equal Employment Opportunity Act of 1972
Effective date	Oct. 13, 1968	March 24, 1972 (July 1965 for nonprofessional workers.) (Institutions with 15-24 employees are not covered until March 24, 1973.)
Which institutions are covered	All institutions with federal contracts of over $10,000.[7]	All institutions with 15 or more employees.
What is prohibited[3]	Discrimination in employment (including hiring, upgrading, salaries, fringe benefits, training, and other conditions of employment) on the basis of race, color, religion, national origin or sex. Covers all employees.	Discrimination in employment (including hiring, upgrading, salaries, fringe benefits, training and other conditions of employment) on the basis of race, color, religion, national origin or sex. Covers all employees.
Exemptions from coverage	None.	Religious institutions are exempt with respect to the employment of individuals of a particular *religion* or *religious order* (including those limited to one sex) to perform work for that institution. (Such institutions are not exempt from the prohibition of discrimination based on sex, color and national origin.)

Equal Pay Act of 1963 as amended by the Education Amendments of 1972 (Higher Education Act)	Title IX of the Education Amendments of 1972 (Higher Education Act)[13]	Title VII (Section 799A) & Title VIII (Section 845) of the Public Health Service Act as amended by the Comprehensive Health Manpower Act & the Nurse Training Amendments Act of 1971[18]
July 1, 1972 (June, 1964, for non-professional workers.)	July 1, 1972 (Admissions provisions effective July 1, 1973.)	Nov. 18, 1971
All institutions.	All institutions receiving federal monies by way of a grant, loan, or contract (other than a contract of insurance or guaranty).	All institutions receiving or benefiting from a grant, loan guarantee, or interest subsidy to health personnel training programs or receiving a contract under Title VII or VIII of the Public Health Service Act.[19]
Discrimination in salaries (including almost all fringe benefits) on the basis of sex. Covers all employees.	Discrimination against students or others[14] on the basis of sex.[15]	Discrimination in admission of students on the basis of sex and against some employees.[20]
None.	*Religious institutions* are exempt if the application of the anti-discrimination provisions are not consistent with the religious tenets of such organizations. *Military schools* are exempt if their primary purpose is to train individuals for the military services of the U.S. or the merchant marine. *Discrimination in admissions*[16] is prohibited only in vocational institutions (including vocational high schools), graduate and professional institutions, and public undergraduate coeducational institutions.	None.

FEDERAL LAWS[1] AND REGULATIONS CONCERNING SEX DISCRIMINATION IN EDUCATIONAL INSTITUTIONS[2] PROJECT ON THE STATUS & EDUCATION OF WOMEN, ASSOCIATION OF AMERICAN COLLEGES, WASHINGTON, D.C.

	Executive Order 11246 as amended by 11375	**Title VII of the Civil Rights Act of 1964** as amended by the Equal Employment Opportunity Act of 1972
Who enforces the provisions?	Office of Federal Contract Compliance (OFCC) of the Department of Labor has policy responsibility and oversees federal agency enforcement programs. OFCC has designated HEW as the Compliance Agency responsible for enforcing the Executive Order for all contracts with educational institutions. HEW's Office for Civil Rights (Division of Higher Education) conducts the reviews and investigations.	Equal Employment Opportunity Commission (EEOC).[9]
How is a complaint made?	By letter to OFCC or Secretary of HEW.	By a sworn complaint form, obtainable from EEOC.
Can complaints of a pattern of discrimination be made as well as individual complaints?	Yes. However, individual complaints are referred to EEOC.	Yes.
Who can make a complaint?[4]	Individuals and/or organizations on own behalf or on behalf of aggrieved employee(s) or applicant(s).	Individuals and/or organizations on own behalf or on behalf of aggrieved employee(s) or applicant(s). Members of the commission may also file charges.
Time limit for filing complaints[5]	180 days.	180 days.
Can investigations be made without complaints?	Yes. Government can conduct periodic reviews without a reported violation, as well as in response to complaints. Pre-award reviews are mandatory for contracts over $1,000,000.	No. Government can conduct investigations only if charges have been filed.

Equal Pay Act of 1963 as amended by the Education Amendments of 1972 (Higher Education Act)	**Title IX of the Education Amendments of 1972** (Higher Education Act)[13]	**Title VII (Section 799A) & Title VIII (Section 845) of the Public Health Service Act** as amended by the Comprehensive Health Manpower Act & the Nurse Training Amendments Act of 1971[18]
Wage and Hour Division of the Employment Standards Administration of the Department of Labor.	Federal departments and agencies which are empowered to extend financial aid to educational programs and activities. HEW's Office for Civil Rights (Division of Higher Education) is expected to have primary enforcement powers to conduct the reviews and investigations.[17]	HEW's Office for Civil Rights (Division of Higher Education) conducts the reviews and investigations.
By letter, telephone call, or in person to the nearest Wage and Hour Division office.	Procedure not yet specified. A letter to Secretary of HEW is acceptable.	Procedure not yet specified. A letter to Secretary of HEW is acceptable.
Yes.	Yes.	Yes.
Individuals and/or organizations on own behalf or on behalf of aggrieved employee(s).	Individuals and/or organizations on own behalf or on behalf of aggrieved party.	Individuals and/or organizations on own behalf or on behalf of aggrieved party.
No official limit, but recovery of back wages is limited by statute of limitations to two years for a non-willful violation and three years for a willful violation.	Procedure not yet determined.	Procedure not yet determined.
Yes. Government can conduct periodic reviews without a reported violation as well as in response to complaints.	Yes. Government can conduct periodic reviews without a reported violation as well as in response to complaints.	Yes. Government can conduct periodic reviews without a reported violation, as well as in response to complaints.

FEDERAL LAWS[1] AND REGULATIONS CONCERNING SEX DISCRIMINATION IN EDUCATIONAL INSTITUTIONS[2] PROJECT ON THE STATUS & EDUCATION OF WOMEN, ASSOCIATION OF AMERICAN COLLEGES, WASHINGTON, D.C.

	Executive Order 11246 as amended by 11375	**Title VII of the Civil Rights Act of 1964** as amended by the Equal Employment Opportunity Act of 1972
Can the entire institution be reviewed?	Yes. HEW may investigate part or all of an institution.	Yes. EEOC may investigate part or all of an establishment.
Record keeping requirements and government access to records	Institution must keep and preserve specified records relevant to the determination of whether violations have occurred. Government is empowered to review all relevant records.	Institution must keep and preserve specified records relevant to the determination of whether violations have occurred. Government is empowered to review all relevant records.
Enforcement power and sanctions	Government may delay new contracts, revoke current contracts, and debar institutions from eligibility for future contracts.	If attempts at conciliation fail, EEOC or the U.S. Attorney General may file suit.[10] Aggrieved individuals may also initiate suits. Court may enjoin respondent from engaging in unlawful behavior, order appropriate affirmative action, order reinstatement of employees, and award back pay.
Can back pay be awarded?[6]	Yes. HEW will seek back pay only for employees who were not previously protected by other laws allowing back pay.	Yes. For up to two years prior to filing charges with EEOC.
Affirmative action requirements *(There are no restrictions against action which is non-preferential)*	Affirmative action plans (including numerical goals and timetables) are required of all contractors with contracts of $50,000 or more and 50 or more employees.[8]	Affirmative action is not required unless charges have been filed, in which case it may be included in conciliation agreement or be ordered by the court.

Equal Pay Act of 1963 as amended by the Education Amendments of 1972 (Higher Education Act)	Title IX of the Education Amendments of 1972 (Higher Education Act)[13]	Title VII (Section 799A) & Title VIII (Section 845) of the Public Health Service Act as amended by the Comprehensive Health Manpower Act & the Nurse Training Amendments Act of 1971[18]
Yes. Usually the Wage-Hour Division reviews the entire establishment.	Yes. HEW may investigate those parts of an institution which receive federal assistance (as well as other parts of the institution related to the program, whether or not they receive direct federal assistance). If the institution receives *general institutional aid,* the entire institution may be reviewed.	Yes. HEW may investigate those parts of an institution which receive federal assistance under Title VII and VIII (as well as other parts of the institution related to the program, whether or not they receive assistance under these titles).
Institution must keep and preserve specified records relevant to the determination of whether violations have occurred. Government is empowered to review all relevant records.	Institution must keep and preserve specified records relevant to the determination of whether violations have occurred. Government is empowered to review all relevant records.	Institution must keep and preserve specified records relevant to the determination of whether violations have occurred. Government is empowered to review all relevant records.
If voluntary compliance fails,[11] Secretary of Labor may file suit. Aggrieved individuals may initiate suits when Department of Labor has not done so. Court may enjoin respondent from engaging in unlawful behavior, and order salary raises, back pay and assess interest.	Government may delay new awards, revoke current awards, and debar institution from eligibility for future awards. Department of Justice may also bring suit at HEW's request.	Government may delay new awards, revoke current awards, and debar institution from eligibility for future awards. Department of Justice may also bring suit at HEW's request.
Yes. For up to two years for a nonwillful violation and three years for a willful violation.	Probably, to the extent that employees are covered.	Probably, to the extent that employees are covered.
Affirmative action, other than salary increases and back pay, is not required.	Affirmative action may be required after discrimination is found.	Affirmative action may be required after discrimination is found.

FEDERAL LAWS[1] AND REGULATIONS CONCERNING SEX DISCRIMINATION IN EDUCATIONAL INSTITUTIONS[2] PROJECT ON THE STATUS & EDUCATION OF WOMEN, ASSOCIATION OF AMERICAN COLLEGES, WASHINGTON, D.C.

	Executive Order 11246 as amended by 11375	**Title VII of the Civil Rights Act of 1964** as amended by the Equal Employment Opportunity Act of 1972
Coverage of labor organizations	Any agreement the contractor may have with a labor organization can not be in conflict with the contractor's affirmative action commitment.	Labor organizations are subject to the same requirements and sanctions as employers.
Is harassment prohibited?	Institutions are prohibited from discharging or discriminating against any employee or applicant for employment because he/she has made a complaint, assisted with an investigation or instituted proceedings.	Institutions are prohibited from discharging or discriminating against any employee or applicant for employment because he/she has made a complaint, assisted with an investigation or instituted proceedings.
Notification of complaints	Notification of complaints has been erratic in the past. HEW is proposing notifying institutions of complaints within 10 days. HEW notifies institutions a few weeks prior to investigation.	EEOC notifies institutions of complaints within 10 days.
Confidentiality of names	Individual complainant's name is usually given to the institution. Investigation findings are kept confidential by government, but can be revealed by the institution. Policy concerning government disclosure concerning investigations and complaints has not yet been issued. The aggrieved party and respondent are not bound by the confidentiality requirement.	Individual complainant's name is divulged when an investigation is made. Charges are not made public by EEOC, nor can any of its efforts during the conciliation process be made public by the commission or its employees. If court action becomes necessary, the identity of the parties involved becomes a matter of public record. The aggrieved party and respondent are not bound by the confidentiality requirement.
For further information, contact	Division of Higher Education Office of Civil Rights Department of HEW Washington, D.C. 20201 *or* Office of Federal Contract Compliance Employment Standards Administration Department of Labor Washington, D.C. 20210 *or* Regional HEW or DOL Office	Equal Employment Opportunity Commission 1800 G Street, N.W. Washington, D.C. 20506 *or* Regional EEOC Office

Equal Pay Act of 1963 as amended by the Education Amendments of 1972 (Higher Education Act)	**Title IX of the Education Amendments of 1972** (Higher Education Act)[13]	**Title VII (Section 799A) & Title VIII (Section 845) of the Public Health Service Act** as amended by the Comprehensive Health Manpower Act & the Nurse Training Amendments Act of 1971[18]
Labor organizations are prohibited from causing or attempting to cause an employer to discriminate on the basis of sex. Complaints may be made and suits brought against these organizations.	Procedure not yet clear. Any agreement the institution may have with a labor organization can not be in conflict with the nondiscrimination provisions of the legislation.	Procedure not yet clear. Any agreement the institution may have with a labor organization can not be in conflict with the nondiscrimination provisions of the legislation.
Institutions are prohibited from discharging or discriminating against any employee because he/she has made a complaint, assisted with an investigation or instituted proceedings.	Institutions will be prohibited from discharging or discriminating against any participant or potential participant because he/she has made a complaint, assisted with an investigation or instituted proceedings.	Institutions will be prohibited from discharging or discriminating against any participant or potential participant because he/she has made a complaint, assisted with an investigation or instituted proceedings.
Complaint procedure is very informal. Employer under review may or may not know that a violation has been reported.	Procedure not yet determined.	Procedure not yet determined.
The identity of a complainant, as well as the employer (and union, if involved), is kept in strict confidence.[12] If court action becomes necessary, the identity of the parties involved becomes a matter of public record. The aggrieved party and respondent are not bound by the confidentiality requirement.	Identity of complainant is kept confidential if possible. If court action becomes necessary, the identity of the parties involved becomes a matter of public record. The aggrieved party and respondent are not bound by the confidentiality requirement.	Identity of complainant is kept confidential if possible. If court action becomes necessary, the identity of the parties involved becomes a matter of public record. The aggrieved party and respondent are not bound by the confidentiality requirement.
Wage and Hour Division Employment Standards Administration Department of Labor Washington, D.C. 20210 *or* Field, Area, or Regional Wage and Hour Office	Division of Higher Education Office for Civil Rights Department of HEW Washington, D.C. 20201 *or* Regional HEW Office	Division of Higher Education Office for Civil Rights Department of HEW Washington, D.C. 20201 *or* Regional HEW Office

Footnotes

General

1. State employment and/or human relations laws may also apply to educational institutions. The Equal Rights Amendment to the U.S. Constitution, passed by the Congress and now in the process of ratification would, when ratified, forbid discrimination in publicly supported schools at all levels, including students and faculty.

2. Unless otherwise specified, "institution" includes public and private colleges and universities, elementary and secondary schools, and preschools.

3. A bona fide seniority or merit system is permitted under all legislation, provided the system is not discriminatory on the basis of sex or any other prohibited ground.

4. There are no restrictions against making a complaint under more than one anti-discrimination law at the same time.

5. This time limit refers to the time between an alleged discriminatory act and when a complaint is made. In general, however, the time limit is interpreted liberally when a continuing practice of discrimination is being challenged, rather than a single, isolated discriminatory act.

6. Back pay cannot be awarded prior to the effective date of the legislation.

Executive Order 11246 as amended by 11375

7. The definition of "contract" is very broad and is interpreted to cover all government contracts (even if nominally entitled "grants") which involve a benefit to the federal government.

8. As of January 19, 1973, all covered educational institutions, both public and private, must have *written* affirmative action plans.

Title VII of the Civil Rights Act of 1964 as amended by the Equal Employment Opportunity Act

9. In certain states that have fair employment laws with prohibitions similar to those of Title VII, EEOC automatically defers investigation of charges to the state agency for 60 days. (At the end of this period, EEOC will handle the charges unless the state is actively pursuing the case. About 85 percent of deferred cases return to EEOC for processing after deferral.)

10. Due to an ambiguity in the law as it relates to public institutions, it is not yet clear whether EEOC *or* the Attorney General will file suit in all situations which involve public institutions.

Equal Pay Act of 1963 as amended by the Education Amendments of 1972 (Higher Education Act)

11. Over 95 percent of all Equal Pay Act investigations are resolved through voluntary compliance.

12. Unless court action is necessary, the name of the parties need not be revealed. The identity of a complainant or a person furnishing information is never revealed without that person's knowledge and consent.

Title IX of the Education Amendments of 1972 (Higher Education Act)
(Minority women are also protected from discrimination on the basis of their race or color by Title VI of the Civil Rights Act of 1964.)

13. Final regulations and guidelines for Title IX of the Education Amendments of 1972 have not yet been published. This chart includes information which is explicitly stated in the law, as well as how the law is likely to be interpreted in light of other precedents and developments.

14. The sex discrimination provision of Title IX is patterned after Title VI of the Civil Rights Act of 1964, which forbids discrimination on the basis of race, color and national origin in all federally assisted programs. By specific exemption, the prohibitions of Title VI do not cover employment practices (except where

the primary objective of the federal aid is to provide employment). However, there is no similar exemption for employment in Title IX.

15. Title IX states that: "No person . . . shall, on the basis of sex, be excluded from participation in, be denied the benefits of, or be subjected to discrimination under any education program or activity receiving federal financial assistance. . . ."

16. The following are exempted from the *admissions* provision:

Private undergraduate institutions.

Elementary and secondary schools other than vocational schools.

Single-sex public undergraduate institutions. (If public single-sex undergraduate institutions decide to admit both sexes, they will have 7 years to admit female and male students on a nondiscriminatory basis, provided their plans are approved by the Commissioner of Education.)

Note 1. *These exemptions apply to admissions only.* Such institutions are still subject to all other anti-discrimination provisions of the Act.

Note 2. Single-sex professional, graduate and vocational schools at all levels have until July, 1979, to achieve nondiscriminatory admissions, provided their plans are approved by the Commissioner of Education.

17. Under Title VI of the 1964 Civil Rights Act, which Title IX of the Education Amendments closely parallels, federal agencies which extend aid to educational institutions have delegated their enforcement powers to HEW. A similar delegation of enforcement power is expected under Title IX.

Title VII & Title VIII of the Public Health Service Act as amended by the Comprehensive Health Manpower Act & the Nurse Training Amendments Act of 1971

18. Final regulations and guidelines for Title VII and VIII of the Public Health Service Act have not yet been published. This chart includes information which is explicitly stated in the law, as well as how the law is likely to be interpreted in light of other precedents and developments.

19. Schools of medicine, osteopathy, dentistry, veterinary medicine, optometry, pharmacy, podiatry, public health, allied public health personnel and nursing are specifically mentioned in Titles VII and VIII. Regulations issued June 1, 1972, by the Secretary of HEW specify that *all* entities applying for awards under Titles VII or VIII are subject to the nondiscrimination requirements of the act.

20. HEW regulations state: "Nondiscrimination in admission to a training program includes nondiscrimination in all practices relating to applicants to and students in the program; nondiscrimination in the enjoyment of every right, privilege and opportunity secured by admission to the program; and nondiscrimination in all employment practices relating to employees working directly with applicants to or students in the program."

Appendix 2

STEPS TO OPENING THE SKILLED TRADES TO WOMEN

U.S. DEPARTMENT OF LABOR—JUNE, 1974

MANPOWER projections for the 1970s point to the skilled trades and apprentice-type jobs as an area of rapid employment increase. This area is also one in which women are greatly underrepresented, although many women have the necessary aptitudes and potential skills.

As a route out of the traditional "female" jobs—many of which are dead end and low paying—women are increasingly seeking entry into well-paying craft jobs which provide opportunities for advancement and job satisfaction. Legislation calling for equal employment opportunity and affirmative action to eliminate sex discrimination has opened many doors formerly closed to women workers.

Today, employers are seeking help in recruiting, training, and employing women for the skilled trades. This situation is reminiscent of the World War II production years when, according to a Bureau of the Census survey, 6.7 million women entered the labor force between December 1941 and March 1944. And of this number, 2.9 million were first time entrants in the occupational category of "craftsmen, foremen,[1] operatives, and nonfarm laborers."

Women proved they could perform well in such jobs as welders, machine operators, and shipfitters, and in a myriad of other industrial jobs. Some of the women were pioneers in new fields, while others came in when the initial attitudes and job skill requirements had been well established.

When the war ended, most of the women were gradually phased out of the skilled jobs. And for about a decade and a half after the war, their numbers were too few to be counted, in accordance with the usual Census methods. During the sixties, however, the number of

[1] "Craftsmen, foremen" are now called "craft and kindred workers." The change was made in the modification of sex-stereotyped occupational titles in the Bureau of the Census occupational classification system. U.S. Office of Management and Budget, *Statistical Reporter,* October 1973, pp. 67-68.

women employed as craft workers increased by about 80 percent, rising from 277,140 in 1960 to 494,871 in 1970. Data for 1973 from the Current Population Survey, although not strictly comparable with data from the Decennial Census, suggest that the growth of women workers in skilled occupations has continued. In 1973, 561,000 women were employed as craft workers, and they represented 4 percent of the total.

Another positive trend toward the fuller utilization of women in skilled jobs is reflected in vocational school enrollment data for 1972. In that year the number of women enrolled in technical programs was 33,006, up from 22,890 in 1966-67. The increase was even greater among women enrolled in trade and industrial training courses, rising from 155,808 in 1966-67 to 279,680 in 1972.

What Are the First Steps Employers Must Take to Increase The Employment of Women in the Skilled Trades?

- Know specifically the legal requirements for equal employment opportunity and affirmative action programs. Know what practices are discriminatory in effect, if not in principle.
- Examine your own prejudices—do the facts support them? Acknowledge if they don't.
- Assert and publicize a clear and firm policy statement on equal opportunity, including specific reference to opportunities for women. See that the statement receives continued attention at all management levels, and that it is brought to the attention of all agencies and organizations with which you do business.
- Educate management, supervisory personnel, and all workers toward a realistic appraisal and acceptance of women as workers.
- Modify the recruiting process. See that job postings are accessible to both men and women. Expand help-wanted advertising to include minority news media and women's interest media.
- Make certain that only valid job-related testing procedures are established for all jobs. Give special attention to language limitations of some minority women.
- See that job requirements are job related. Review all job descriptions for discriminatory qualifications.
- Select employees for training programs at all levels on the basis of ability without regard to sex. Analyze promotion procedures for discriminatory practices.
- Enlist the support of employed women, both union and non-union, to provide impetus for change in attitude toward training

and work opportunities for all women. Ask them for suggestions on how to further the company's equal employment opportunity policy.

- Include nondiscrimination clauses in collective bargaining agreements; modify seniority provisions if they perpetuate separate lines of progression for women and men; eliminate sex discrimination in such areas as apprenticeship training and termination, layoff, and recall practices.
- Work with vocational schools to improve and increase related courses and to change attitudes toward training women for skilled trades.
- Take a community leadership role in advocating women for industrial jobs.
- Develop systems to monitor and measure progress regularly. If results are not satisfactory, find out why and make necessary changes.

What Can Employers Do to Better Utilize Women Workers Once They Have Been Hired?

- Give *pre-job training* at the entry level, with the objective of conditioning the new employee mentally and physically.
  - –Give orientation to the world of work: attendance requirements, work clothing needs, remedial education to assist in taking tests and filling out forms, with special attention to language limitations of some women minorities.
  - –Give orientation at job site: expose to noise, shift changes, rest and meal areas, health facilities.
  - –Give instructions in the terminology, use, and care of tools. (Some individuals lack mechanical familiarity but have mechanical ability.)
  - –Give necessary physical training to meet the demands of some jobs.
  - –Sensitize both men and women as to interpersonal relations. Attitudes toward the work situation should be objective rather than personal. This should include deemphasizing personal feelings toward possible offensive language and actions.
  - –Provide safety and health education.
- Modify and emphasize the *training* process for all inexperienced workers.
  - –Train on production, if possible, but prior to pressures of production goals.
  - –Train under conditions which approximate those of employ-

ment, including hazards.

–Be sure that new women employees are not harrassed on the job.

–Use audio-visual aids to supplement written material when lecturing.

–Be sure related instruction courses are pertinent and that individual employees are aware of their importance.

–Give full explanations of work procedures and demonstrate repeatedly.

–Break jobs down to simplest components.

–Limit inexperienced employees to work in which they have been trained until they feel secure. (Apprehension due to insecurity is the biggest cause of fatigue–not the work itself.)

–Build self-assurance. Some women lack confidence in their ability to perform jobs traditionally reserved for men.

- Provide supportive services.

–Have as a model for new women workers, if possible, a senior woman worker with a sense of responsibility toward them.

–Provide a counselor on site to help new workers deal with problems that cause absenteeism and turnover, such as inadequate housing and transportation; unsatisfactory arrangements for care of children; lack of conditioning to meet the physical demands of the job; accumulative fatigue; too heavy load of outside duties; and unhappy working relationships.

–Provide child care facilities on site or advocate them as community services.

–Provide opportunity for group discussions of common problems.

What Can Unions Do to Open the Skilled Trades to Women?

- Encourage women union members to aspire to and prepare for skilled trades jobs and apprenticeship programs as a route out of low-paying clerical, service, and production jobs.
- Insist that affirmative action plans for apprenticeship and other skilled trades training programs include women as well as minorities.
- Include nondiscrimination clauses in collective bargaining agreements. Eliminate sex discrimination in such areas as apprenticeship training and termination, layoff, and recall practices.
- Examine seniority policies to see if they perpetuate patterns of discrimination. The Equal Employment Opportunity Commission can give technical assistance on how seniority policies can be made nondiscriminatory.

- Be sure that new employees are not harrassed on the job.
- See that women are utilized effectively in leadership roles, both as staff and elective officers.

What Can Women Do to Accelerate Their Entry into the Skilled Trades?

- Think skilled trades–include these among your range of job possibilities.
- Be aware of the laws and their enforcement provisions for equal opportunity in employment, education, and training.
- Investigate the personal and financial rewards that accompany employment in a skilled trade.
- Contact employers directly about the kinds of jobs women are holding. Express your interest and be aware of openings that occur. Learn the application procedures.
- Inquire of individual women or organizations engaged in promoting new job opportunities for women–including local State Employment Security offices.
- Indicate your willingness to try a job that uses your mechanical ability as well as your intelligence.
- Once on the work site, realize that you may encounter difficulties in interpersonal relationships as you perform jobs in which few women are employed.
- Don't give up in face of a few hardships if this is the job you want–and you know you can do it.

What Special Programs Are Underway To Help Women Enter the Skilled Trades?

Several different approaches are being used to facilitate the entry of women into nontraditional jobs. Some examples are as follows:

BETTER JOBS FOR WOMEN–DENVER, COLORADO

This unique program was developed by the Bureau of Apprenticeship and Training of the U.S. Department of Labor and is operated by the YWCA of Metropolitan Denver. The project places women into apprenticeship programs or other on-the-job training positions.

Since the program began in March 1971, 109 women have been placed in a variety of occupations such as carpenter, cement mason, electrician, operating engineer, painter, plumber, roofer, steel fabricator; also as business machine repairer, forklift operator, injection molder, mechanic, telephone installer, and tool and die maker.

WOMEN IN APPRENTICESHIP—MADISON, WISCONSIN

The Division of Apprenticeship and Training of the Wisconsin Department of Industry, Labor, and Human Relations and the University of Wisconsin Extension conducted a three-year (July 1970 to June 1973) research and demonstration project on women in apprenticeship. The purpose of the project was to "isolate, analyze, and minimize barriers to the participation of women in the skilled trades." Although resistance to the employment of women in apprenticeship was clearly indicated, women were found employed as lithographer, camera operator, sign painter, television repairer, newspaper printer, meat cutter, second class engineer, and die maker.

One very tangible result of this project was the production of a color film on women in apprenticeable occupations, entitled "Never Underestimate the Power of a Woman." The film was produced by the University of Wisconsin and is available from the Wisconsin Employment Service.

WAGES (WOMEN AND GIRLS' EMPLOYMENT ENABLING SERVICE)—MEMPHIS, TENNESSEE

Sponsored by the Memphis and Shelby County Health and Welfare Planning Council, this pilot project was established in June 1972 to develop new areas of employment for women. The project has developed a skills inventory of women with different kinds of abilities.

As a result of this project, women have received placements in maintenance repair, in the U.S. Postal Service as security guards, and in production work with certain companies which may lead to forklift operator and other skilled jobs.

FEMALE JOB PLACEMENT PROGRAM (FEJOP)—CHATTANOOGA, TENNESSEE

This experimental project was started in the summer of 1971 to increase both the job options and the pay of disadvantaged women who were heads of households in the Model Cities neighborhood.

With the help of FEJOP, women are psychologically motivated and physically conditioned to perform in jobs formerly thought of as men's. Women are earning good wages as forklift operator, spray painter, welder, bench press operator, metal plate polisher, and wood turning lathe operator.

ADVOCATES FOR WOMEN—SAN FRANCISCO, CALIFORNIA

This nonprofit organization is operating the first apprenticeship outreach program for women on the West Coast. The intent of the program is to place women in such apprenticeship jobs as carpenter, electrician, machinist, and dental technician. By the time the contract was effective in December 1973, Advocates already had on file the names of women interested in entering apprentice occupations.

APPRENTICESHIP OUTREACH PROGRAM FOR WOMEN

In April 1974 the Manpower Administration amended three of its apprenticeship outreach contracts to provide new opportunities for women. The Apprenticeship Outreach Program, since its inception in 1964, generally has been directed toward recruiting minority men into apprentice trades. The expanded program places special emphasis on recruiting young women, who will be given the necessary counseling and tutoring to prepare them to enter all apprenticeable occupations.

Three organizations will operate pilot projects in six selected cities. The National Urban League will expand its programs in Atlanta, Chicago, and Los Angeles. The Mexican-American Foundation will conduct a second outreach program in Los Angeles. The Recruitment and Training Program, Inc., formerly the Workers Defense League of the A. Philip Randolph Foundation, will expand its programs in Boston, Cleveland, and New York.

The Women's Bureau and other agencies of the Labor Department, in collaboration with the three organizations, are seeking the cooperation of the National Alliance of Businessmen, the Central Labor Council, building and construction trades councils, employer associations, women's organizations, local Job Corps centers, the mayor of each city, community groups, and local, State, and Federal agencies.

Other Programs

A number of other organizations are also working to increase the number of skilled jobs and to provide training opportunities for girls and women.

- The National Association of Women in Construction (NAWIC) is now offering scholarships to students (girls and boys) who plan to enter a field of study directly related to the construction industry.
- Women in Technical Trades and Professions, Berkeley, California, was formed early in 1970 by feminists concerned with opening blue-collar job opportunities to women.
- Lady Carpenter Institute of Building and Home Improvement, Inc., in New York City, has graduated more than 220 women of all ethnic backgrounds and ages. The Institute serves as a bridge between experience already gained at home and professional job placement in carpentry and cabinetmaking by affording educational opportunities for development of skills and competence.
- Project Repair in San Diego, California, began a pilot program in the summer of 1973 to develop skills competency for young women 14 to 18 years of age in home repair related markets such as appliance and TV repair.
- The American Association of Women Truck Drivers, Charter

Oak, California, was formed about two years ago to assist in or to get training for self-supporting women desiring employment as truck drivers and to eliminate discrimination against them on the basis of sex.

In restating their hiring policies to allow jobs to be filled without regard to sex, companies such as AT&T, Pacific Telephone, General Electric, Chrysler Corporation, Bethlehem Steel, and others are increasing their placements of women into the skilled trades.

For several years women have been accepted into a variety of apprenticeable jobs in the U.S. Armed Services, the National Aeronautics and Space Administration, and a few other federal agencies.

In Conclusion

Employers' and unions' acceptance in attitude and practice of the equal capacity of women to function in the skilled trades and other apprentice-type jobs depends upon knowledge of facts, actual experience, and understanding of equal employment opportunity laws.

Women now have the option to enter such jobs and to resist adverse social pressures and discriminatory practices which have hindered them in the past. Again, knowledge of facts, actual experience, and understanding of equal employment opportunity laws furnish support to their integrated participation in the nation's work force.

INDEX

E

Q

R

T

U

V